GUN DIGEST BOOK OF

SPORTING CLAYS

2nd Edition

Edited by
Harold A. Murtz

THE GUN DIGEST BOOK OF
SPORTING CLAYS, 2nd Edition

STAFF:

Harold A. Murtz, Editor

Ken Ramage, Editor
Firearms and DBI Books

Manuscripts, contributions and inquires, including first class return postage,
should be sent to the DBI Editorial Offices, Krause Publications, 700 E. State Street, Iola, WI
54990-0001. All materials received will receive reasonable care, but we will not be
responsible for their safe return. Material accepted is subject to our requirements for editing
and revisions. Author payment covers all rights and title to the accepted material,
including photos, drawings and other illustrations. Payment is at our current rates.

CAUTION: Technical data presented here, particularly technical data on handloading
and on firearms adjustment and alteration, inevitably reflects individual experience with
particular equipment and components under specific circumstances the reader cannot duplicate
exactly. Such data presentations therefore should be used for guidance only and with caution.
Krause Publications Inc., accepts no responsibility for results obtained using this data.

Published by

kp since 1952

**krause
publications**

700 E. State Street • Iola, WI 54990-0001
Telephone: 715/445-2214

Please call or write for our free catalog.

Our toll-free number to place an order or obtain a free catalog is 800-258-0929 or please use our
regular business telephone 715-445-2214 for editorial comment and further information.

Library of Congress Catalog Number: 91-71896

ISBN: 0-87341-745-3

SPORTING CLAYS
Table of Contents

The Origins of American Sporting Clays

evolution rather than invention

by DICK DIETZ

TRACING THE BEGINNINGS of Sporting Clays raises three questions: Who invented the sport? When? Where? The best answers to these questions, in order, are probably: "No one in particular"; "No specific date"; and "A number of places simultaneously." That may seem a bit vague but, truthfully, so are the exact origins of the sport, at least in its currently recognized form.

Let's begin by defining Sporting Clays. Basically, it is a formalized game of clay target shooting with variable stations and target presentations, having fixed rules for competition and very flexible rules for recreational shooting. It has now become one of three major American clay target sports——the other two being trap and Skeet. One major difference between Sporting Clays and the other two is its far greater variety of sta-

tions, target angles and target release points. Another is the fact that basic Sporting Clays elements themselves are not fixed. They vary from one range to another and, in fact, are often changed within a single range. Trapshooting has just

> From a somewhat cloudy beginning, this game has become a serious—yet fun—sport the whole family can enjoy.

five fixed stations with varying, but limited, target angles at each, all launched from one trap house. Skeet throws one fixed-angle target each from two houses, but creates target variability with eight different shooting stations.

Trapshooting, in its original form of using live birds, was born in England. As far back as 1793, a British publication, titled Sporting Magazine, printed a report on an early form of live bird or pigeon shooting. It occurred at the famous Old Hats Public House near London. There, pigeons were placed beneath a row of top hats, each with a long string attached. When the contestant called "Pull," the string was yanked, turning over the hat and releasing the bird. That's over 200 years ago, and the use of the same call for the target survives today in all of our current clay target sports. It's interesting to note that, even then, a very detailed and extensive set of rules existed governing the conduct of the sport.

During that same, early period, the practice of shooting at inanimate targets in the form of glass balls already existed. But the aerodynamic limitations of glass balls made them a pretty poor substitute for live, feathered flyers and, therefore, limited their use and popularity. That changed dramatically in the late 1870s with the invention of the first saucer-shaped clay targets by an American shooter named George Ligowsky of Cinncinnati, Ohio. As

Author Dick Dietz demonstrates the original "gun down" stance once required at Skeet and still a Sporting Clays regulation. The gun butt can be higher, but must remain below the armpit until the target is thrown.

the story has been reported, Ligowsky got his idea from watching a group of small boys skimming small stones across a body of water. He wasn't interested in how the stones skipped on hitting the water, but in how they carried through the air before they struck the water. Although he wouldn't have understood the term at the time, we know now that what Ligowsky was observing was the gyroscopic effect of a round, spinning object.

He made his first round, concave targets from clay, leading to their permanent and present description as "clay birds." Having also designed a launching device to throw the birds, Ligowsky introduced both at the New York State Game Association Shoot at Coney Island in 1880.

Shortly thereafter, another well-known shooter, Fred Kimball, reportedly improved the performance of these targets by adding fine sand and pitch to the mix. Thus, the future basis for all clay target sports had been created not in England, the origin of wingshooting, but in America. Within a few years, still another American shooter, Adam Bogardus, had formalized the clay target concept into the first trapshooting fields. In the final edition of his remarkable book, *The Gun and its Development*, published in 1910, English firearms historian W.W. Greener, commented on the new American sport of clay bird trapshooting by saying, "In the United States, the sport has many more adherents... It seems probable that the sport will increase in popularity and become world-wide."

From an historical perspective, then, the clay target, and the first formalized clay target sport, trapshooting, originated in the United States. But this was a narrowly-defined, structured sport that didn't really duplicate field hunting, something the British had in mind with their earlier form of live bird trapshooting.

That intent, to simulate field hunting, but with the use of clay birds, surfaced again in England during the 1920s when a form of the variable Sporting Clays layouts we know today was put to use for wing shooting instruction. From that point, the practice grew slowly but steadily, eventually passing from a purely instructional activity to a recognized sport. When Sporting Clays was introduced into the United States in the early 1980s, it was described as a "clay target game designed to simulate field shooting," or "birdshooting without feathers or dogs."

But, let's return to that period of the 1920s for a look at something that was occurring in the United States. A rather interesting parallel was underway. There's no question that our scattergunning brethren in Old England had the right idea with wing shooting instruction, and the use of controlled clay target practice to improve their field gunning. However, they weren't alone in this sensible approach. Some New England Yankees, on the other side of the ocean, had the same idea.

In the early part of the 20th century, there was a dedicated Massachusetts grouse hunter named Charles Davies. Besides his passion for hunting the ruffed rocket, Davies was a perfectionist who hated to miss a shot. Considering the elusiveness of his quarry, however, he did indeed miss with some frequency. Davies also had two young proteges—his son, Henry, and a friend of Henry's named Bill Foster. Frequently, after their mentor had missed a shot in the field, he'd have the two boys set up a small

Good instruction for beginners starts with the basics before actually shooting. Informal Sporting Clays shoots can be loads of fun for veteran and new shooters alike.

Well-known English competitor and instructor, Gary Phillips, delivering shooting tip to protégé, Katy Skahill, a top Sporting Clays shooter herself.

portable trap to practice on clay targets thrown at the same angle as the live bird he'd missed earlier. The boys began taking some similar practice themselves and, gradually, a form of friendly competition evolved. That carried over into the off-season, providing them with an opportunity to shoot when there was no hunting. Ultimately, using a clock as their blueprint, they converted their practice game into a circular field with the trap positioned at 12 o'clock and facing inward toward 6 o'clock. They then made a station at each hour marker to provide a variety of angles to their left and right. Shooting two targets each at each station, plus one directly facing the trap from the middle, added up to 25, or a box of shells. The year was 1915.

The trio called the game "shooting 'round the clock," a fairly descriptive name, considering the layout. But, also considering that it was a form of sport substituting clay birds for live ones, they might just as easily have named it something else, like, for example, "sporting clays." Remember

their original intent. It was to create a "clay target game designed to simulate field shooting." Have we heard that phrase applied elsewhere? The point is this: The concept of Sporting Clays was so eminently sensible and practical, it's no surprise that forms of it developed simultaneously on both sides of the ocean.

Both forms, as we know, developed and grew, but in different directions. Looking back, of course, it's easy to say that the English version, which became Sporting Clays, retained its original purpose, and the American version which became Skeet, did not. Ultimately, American Skeet assumed its present form, was widely and successfully promoted by William Harnden (Bill) Foster. It did away with the field-style "gun down" requirement, and became a structured, competitive sport. Sporting Clays also grew, developed even greater variety, and retained the "gun down" requirement. But, even with its diversity, it has now also become a serious competitive sport.

The history of American-based Sporting Clays reports that it was introduced to this country in the early 1980s. Well, it was, sort of. The truth is, the name Sporting Clays was introduced here at that time, as well as the beginning of serious promotion of it as a clay target game. But similar forms were in active use long before then.

Living on Long Island, New York in the 1950s, I remember hearing of a somewhat exclusive club somewhere out in mid-island that had created an interesting and challenging game.

It consisted of a path winding through the woods with hidden traps located in various spots along the way. Shooters knew when they were near a trap, just as they'd be alerted to the presence of a bird when a dog went on point. But they were never sure exactly where the clay target would come from or the direction it would take. Because the concept of artificial hunting didn't interest me at the time, I never investigated the club.

A few years later, I did find something similar on the grounds of the famous Camp Fire Club of America

A convenient, portable and flexible form of Sporting Clays is "5-Stand," which can be set up on existing Skeet fields with the addition of extra, portable traps.

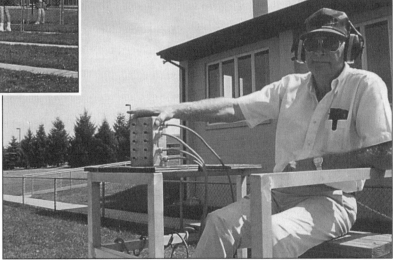

Target puller shows an electronic control box created to choose and release 5-Stand targets from a number of traps. Only one person is needed to run the range.

Clays can serve as an excellent warm-up to sharpen one's hunting senses. Here, author Dietz is shooting Sporting Clays against a wooded background for pre-hunting season practice.

in Chappaqua, New York. The club had two "walk-up" clay target games in which shooters walked toward a trap along a path that had 12 marked points. The puller would release one pair of doubles from one of the points while the shooter was walking, until all 12 points had been covered. In one game, called the "grouse walk," the trap was recessed into a bank below the shooter's level, and threw report doubles at variable angles. In the other, called "bob white," the trap was on the same level and threw simultaneous doubles at fixed angles. The club also had a tower set-up that threw five singles and 10 pairs of simultaneous doubles in a direction toward the shooter but high in the air like duck pass shooting. These games remain in operation at the club today.

When the Remington Arms Company purchased the former, 3000-acre Glen L. Martin estate on Maryland's Eastern Shore in 1956 and renamed it Remington Farms, it inherited another interesting clay target game. This consisted of a single-trap tower, located at the 12 o'clock position of a circle, that threw variable targets out over five stations around the circle. Creating the game's challenge was the location of all stations in the midst of tall, mature trees. To break the targets, the shooter had to pick them out in the gaps between the trees. Remington autoloading shotguns were used and loaded with five shells at each station. The speed of the five consecutive target releases was up to the puller. So, as a shooter progressed from station to station without missing, he got faster and faster targets. After some period of time, the game came to be called "Aw Shucks," which is a toned-down euphemism for the two-word expletive often expressed by shooters when they missed their first target. One wall of the Farms' lodge had a little plaque that listed the names of those who had scored 25 straights on "Aw Shucks." The last time I saw it, in the early 1990s, it had less than a half-dozen names.

Interestingly, one of the first true, English-designed Sporting Clays layouts in the United States was set up at Remington Farms. Like all firearms and/or ammunition manufacturers, Remington was always looking for ways to increase interest and participation in the shooting sports, and viewed inanimate target shooting as the best potential growth area. With some 20 million hunters in the country, but just a small fraction of that total participating in formal trap or Skeet, it was looking for another, less structured game that would be more appealing to hunters.

Many of Remington's executives and employees were active shotgunners who had been exposed somewhere to one or more of the informal, non-typical, clay target games, including their own "Aw Shucks." They were intrigued by the potential of the more completely-developed, British-based "Sporting Clays," that had been frequently written about and praised by Field & Stream

One of Sporting Clays plusses is the favor it has found with lady shooters. Many women shoot Clays to spend more time with their mates.

Sporting Clays also includes events for small-bore shotguns. Here, instructor Gary Greenway watches Outdoor Life shooting editor Jim Carmichel shooting targets over the water with his 28-gauge Remington Model 3200.

shooting editor, Bob Brister. In the mid-1970s, learning that Brister was about to embark on a trip to England to tour some of that country's better-known Sporting Clays layouts, Remington management asked him if he would bring back a detailed report on the sport.

Bob, an ardent supporter of, and participant in, Sporting Clays even to the present, did more than that. He not only provided Remington with an enthusiastic description of the sport's nature and potential, but put Remington in touch with Chris Craddock, one of England's leading experts on range design. The company brought Craddock to its Remington Farms location where he designed and wove into their combination of open fields and woodlots an interesting and challenging Sporting Clays course. It was a unique combination of the British concept of infinitely variable targets and Remington's desire to match these to actual, field-encountered situations that were prevalent in American bird hunting.

Remington viewed Sporting Clays as an excellent vehicle to attract and be beneficial to everyday hunters. However, it realized that the sport needed promotion to gain recognition and popularity in this country, and decided to undertake that task itself. In the early 1980s the company set up a meeting at Remington Farms with Harlan Carter, then executive director, and other officials of the National Rifle Association to discuss means of promoting the sport to American hunters.

Because both the NRA and Remington agreed on the need to attract active hunters to the sport, the decision was made to re-name it Hunter's Clays for the American market. Remington began some promotion activities but realized rather quickly that it was wiser and potentially more effective to have the entire industry behind the promotion rather than one company. It then contacted the National Shooting Sports Foundation which agreed to assume responsibilities for promotional activities. The NSSF produced a booklet describing Hunter's Clays along with information on construction of actual range layouts. But, it didn't have the manpower at the time to travel the country providing promotion and instruction on a first-hand, local basis, and growth was slow.

Meanwhile, back in Bob Brister's home territory of Houston, Texas, a local dentist, Dr. James Moore, began virtually a one-man crusade of promoting the sport. On his own time, Moore traveled extensively, wherever he found interested parties, to make new converts and provide information on building layouts. Moore used the original English name of Sporting Clays which stuck, as the label of Hunter's Clays faded from the picture. He was ultimately instrumental in founding the U.S. Sporting Clays Association in 1985 which set up rules for actual competition and began promoting competitive shoots. The following year, it ran its first national championship tournament. Although he ultimately withdrew from active involvement, Moore may well deserve more credit than any other individual for establishing Sporting Clays in this country.

The sport received another major boost in 1989 with the establishment of the National Sporting Clays Association as a division of the National Skeet Shooting Association in San Antonio, Texas. Extremely well organized and managed, the NSCA has subsequently experienced exceptional growth. It has a full-time executive director, an executive council elected by members, and an advisory council composed of active participants in the sport and industry representatives.

NSCA has established an official set of rules for tournament competition and it sponsors regional and local shoots, state championships, zone championships in seven geographical zones, and an annual national championship with over 1000 competitors. It also publishes an official monthly publication, *Sporting Clays*, keeps official records of all tournaments and shooter averages, and chooses annual Sporting Clays All-American teams in a variety of classifications.

Another name you may come across in relation to *Sporting Clays* is FITASC. This an acronym for the French Sporting Clays organization *Federation Internationale de Tir Aux Armes Sportives de Chasse*. FITASC rules are slightly different and more demanding than those of English Clays. Some tournaments in the United States are conducted under FITASC rules, and NSCA conducts an annual World FITASC Competi-

tion at its home grounds in San Antonio.

Where has this progress, organization and growth led Sporting Clays in this country? Happily, the sport has thrived in two forms. Those who are competition minded can find tournaments virtually throughout the year across the country. Similar to trap and Skeet, competitive Sporting Clays has spawned its own fraternity of friendly camaraderie where matches are not only a test of one's skills, but also a meeting ground for new and old friends.

However, NSCA estimates that there are now some three million Sporting Clays participants in the United States and Canada, and that a high percentage of these use the sport primarily for non-competitive recreation and field practice. Actually, there's a place and need for both competitive and recreational shooters in Sporting Clays. That fact would certainly please the folks responsible for the early promotion of the sport. Besides its competitive form, Sporting Clays has become what they envisioned—the best clay target game available for duplicating and improving field shooting, and an enjoyable off-season substitute for hunting. ●

For many hunters, the original purpose of Sporting Clays remains intact. Here, a duck hunter gets in some pre-season, pass-shooting practice in his waterfowling outfit.

TIPS FOR NEW SHOOTERS

by RICK HINTON

The right attitude and a modicum of equipment are all that's needed to get started in this exciting shooting sport.

Not all Sporting Clays shooters are fancy dressers. A coat with big pockets for toting shells works quite well, thank you.

THE BIGGEST REASON more hunters, or even non-hunters, don't give Sporting Clays a try is simple: "I don't want to be embarrassed," they say. It's an excuse I've heard hundreds of times. And it has validity, despite the curious fact that every person who's ever shot Sporting Clays underwent a similar initiation.

Mine came at the very first Texas State Sporting Clays Championship in Houston in 1986. When I stepped into the first shooting stand, located adjacent to the clubhouse, it seemed as if God and at least a thousand spectators were watching my every move. Between quaking knees and quivering arms, I had plenty of moves, too. I don't know how high pitched my voice sounded when I called "Pull," but I know I sounded neither calm nor cool. The fact that I

hit a couple of the targets only increased my nervousness. Now I'd have to do it again at Station 2, still within view of all those critical eyes, which in reality probably numbered fewer than 20 sets.

It wasn't until I finished my round—still inflicted with a mild case of the shakes—and found myself a spot among the gallery watching the later squads go out that I realized two things: Every shooter stepping into that first station was showing some degree of nervousness; and every spectator, the fellow competitors, was rooting for the shooter, hoping he/she would run the station.

There certainly are less stressful ways to be introduced to Sporting Clays, although after that experience, I can say that participating in a shoot-off in front of a huge crowd is easy.

Embarrassment's bottom line for the newcomer is missing targets, the same ones the rest of the squad is breaking. That will happen almost every time a new shooter shows up alone at the Clays range. He or she will be grouped with one or more veteran shooters and, inevitably, the new shooter will break fewer targets than the regulars. Be prepared for a little pressure, but you can take advantage simply by asking what you're doing wrong. Most shooters are friendly and helpful. In nine cases out of 10, I'll bet their first answer is: "You're stopping your gun." What they mean is you've stopped swinging your gun barrel at the moment you pulled the trigger. Ever hear of follow-through? While the shotgun's barrel slows to a stop, the bird keeps moving, negating your lead and sending the shot string well behind

Rabbit targets, which are rolled edgewise on the ground, challenge new shooters and veterans alike. But it's a fun frustration for most folks until they get their timing and technique polished.

the bird. It's a common malady most hunters don't notice, although occasionally they can get away with it if the quarry is pheasant sized.

The downside of asking for advice can be too many people offering too many fixes. If that happens, one solution is simply to say, "Whoa, that's more than I can absorb at one time. What should I do first?" If you think that sounds ungrateful, think through everything thrown at you, retain what sounds helpful and disregard everything else. If the sensory overload continues, keep applying what seems useful and rejecting what seems less important. Eventually one voice will emerge from the din.

Observation is another very useful tool. Pick out the best shooter in your group and see how he or she sets up for each target presentation. How do they stand? Where do they place their feet? Where do they hold their muzzle? Where are they looking to first

A Skeet shell bag, divided for empties and loaded shells, is a popular and inexpensive way to keep everything handy. Footgear should only be comfortable.

Shooting vests are handy and are a matter of personal preference. Current Clays vests have a full-length pad as on the example at center.

see the target? When they call "Pull" don't turn your attention to the target. Instead, keep watching the shooter. See how they start their swing, how their face makes contact with the comb of the stock, and what their gun is doing when and after they pull the trigger. This may be a form of Zen shooting instruction, but watching what a good shooter does and applying those techniques can prove beneficial when your turn to shoot comes. Ask questions of your newly adopted shooting role model as you walk to the next station. One etiquette tip: While on a station, if your role model is intently studying the target presentations while waiting to shoot next, don't interrupt.

If the Lone Ranger approach doesn't appeal to you, round up a hunting partner, a friend or a neighbor, and go out together. You'll at least know one person you're shoot-

Sporting Clays offers a variety of target sizes and colors, all designed to be challenging—some appear impossible—shots. With the right attitude, each is attainable.

Good hearing protection is a must. Muffs are popular, as are the various ear insert types. Personal preference dictates which will be worn. This shooter should be wearing eye protection!

ing with, and the two of you can share the embarrassment burden. If you're grouped with other shooters, at least one is probably an experienced shooter. Again, by paying attention and asking questions, you'll get some insights into the great Sporting Clays game.

If safety in numbers has more appeal, round up five or six hunting partners and friends and shoot your first Sporting round(s) together. There are advantages and disadvantages to this approach. Among the advantages are fewer chances for embarrassment. If you're shooting with hunting buddies, they no doubt have seen you miss birds, just as you've seen them miss. Being with friends also will make the trip around the course more fun. The disadvantage is you won't learn much because no one in your squad knows any more than you do. Miss a target and ask where you missed and you probably will get two or three conflicting answers, none of which may be right.

The sad reality about most bird hunters is they think they're better shooters than they really are. If a hunter is working a prime field with a good dog, it really doesn't take great shooting skills to bag an opening-day limit of pheasants. And having more loaded shells than empties left over from that first box only makes the experience more heady. A typical Sporting Clays course will throw targets that are far more var-

ied than the typical upland hunter will see all season. That was the observation of the outdoors writer at the local newspaper when I took him out for the first time.

To paraphrase his summation of his round: I could hit the targets I'd seen while grouse or pheasant hunting. But all those other targets—those crossing ones, the incoming and rolling ones—gave me fits. I started out thinking I'd break at least half of them, but I know I didn't.

Intentionally, I didn't take a score sheet along, a practice I strongly recommend for first-time Sporting shooters. Seeing a score of 15 or so breaks after shooting at 50 targets can be a cruel reality check. Often it's more than some hunters' egos can stand.

Here are contrasting ways to deal with such situations, both true stories:

Years ago, a co-worker of my wife's asked if she and I would shoot with him on his first go at Sporting Clays. She'd been hearing tales of his legendary wing shooting abilities for a couple of hunting seasons, so she accepted, thinking him a potential Clays recruit. Unfortunately, I couldn't go on the appointed day, and she took along a score sheet. After the first station, he was frustrated. After the third station, he was flat-out mad. After the fifth station, he packed up his gun and shells and stormed off never to return. He was still angry about those "trick shots and unrealistic shots" the next time

he saw her at work. All he had seen was a going-away target angled slightly down, that same target as a right-to-left crosser, a left-to-right target from a 30-foot tower, a left-to-right quartering-away bird, and an under-the-feet going away bird. Where I saw decoying ducks, mourning doves, flushing bobwhites and wood ducks in flooded timber, he sadly saw nothing but red.

Another fellow showed up at the gun club one day with a newly purchased dove pouch, one of those belts with shell pouches on either side and a game bag in back, a couple of boxes of game loads and a new Remington 1100 12-gauge. He promptly went out and shot eight or nine of 25 targets. He, too, came back to the clubhouse shaking his head, saying he'd shot dove and quail all over West Texas and northern Mexico all his life and couldn't believe he could do so badly at a clay target game. The difference was he kept coming back and shooting the course again and again. Within a year or two, he won the first U.S. Open Sporting Clays championship at Highland Bend Shooting School near Houston. The next year he was runner-up to a British shooter and world champion.

The message isn't difficult to figure out: Be prepared to accept a dose of humiliation, but be constructive and positive in how you handle it.

Regardless of what part of the country in which you live, you'll find

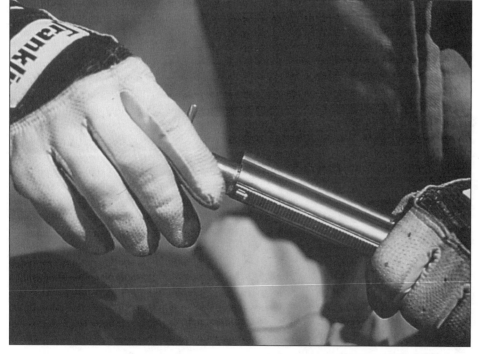

Screw-in choke tubes can prove very helpful for many shooters because target distance varies at each station. However, new shooters can get along very nicely without them for some time.

a variety of Sporting Clays ranges. They can range from a pasture or river bottom equipped with carefully arranged manual, or hand-cocked, traps to upscale clubs with brick or wood clubhouses and trap houses, and a course filled with automatic traps that fire a target with the push of a button. Potentially there is a "gulp" factor at these high-end clubs, starting when you park your well-used hunting rig in a paved parking lot filled with luxury, high-performance cars or sport utility vehicles. It continues when you put on your game vest while the regulars are wearing fancy shooting vests; when you hook your sunglasses around your ears while they are sporting shooting glasses with lenses of various hues; when you stick in your 50-cent foam ear plugs and they are wearing custom-fitted or electronic plugs. While appearances are radically different, generally speaking shooters are shooters. They may talk stock-market investments and you may comment on last night's ball game, but the common ground is: "How the hell did I miss that target?" Breaking birds and having a good time while doing it is everyone's goal.

The cost of a round doesn't always reflect the fanciness of the range either. My local range with one hand-cocked trap per 15 stations costs more than a club my wife and I visited last winter that featured two automatic traps per its 15 stations. On average, expect to pay at least $15 per 50-target round, plus your shells. Tipping the trapper, the person who accompanies you and either cocks and launches targets from manual traps or pushes the button for the automatic traps, often is encouraged.

My gauge for judging the quality of a Sporting Clays range isn't appearance, price of equipment or cost per round (within reason, of course). More simply, it's how often the owner or manager changes the course. Skeet or trap fields from Savannah, Georgia, to Seattle, or from Bangor, Maine, to Barstow, California, throw identical targets. The Sporting Clays club that I most want to shoot will change its target presentations at least every two weeks. Changing the course is a topic of great debate among club regulars. Shooters who want to improve their skills want

frequent change. Shooters who want to improve their scores don't.

If your shotgun is new enough to have interchangeable, screw-in chokes, the best all-round choice is Improved Cylinder (Imp. Cyl.). If your gun has two barrels, the most common choke setup is Skeet in the bottom barrel and Imp. Cyl. in the top. Shooting the bottom barrel first helps suppress muzzle flip because of the weight of the top barrel. If my choke selection sounds too loose for you, remember we're not bird hunting. That's when you want enough choke to anchor your quarry stone-cold dead. In clay target shotgunning games, all you're really striving for is for a visible piece to come off the target. On the score card, that bird is just as dead as one that evaporates in a cloud of smoke. A looser choke offers just a bit more margin for error. Center any target in the shotshell's pattern and you get smoke, or at least a crushed target. Catch a target in the fringe area of a looser choke's pattern and it probably will break. With a tighter choke that

same target is outside the pattern's fringe. That equals a miss.

You often will see shooters changing chokes on almost every station. That's fine. They've no doubt paid big money for a set of aftermarket tubes and they're going to use them. I use aftermarket chokes, too, but my rule for changing them is more basic. If the target is closer than 10 yards, I want the loosest chokes I have—Cyl., Skeet or a diffusion choke. If the target is farther than 40 yards, I want something tighter than Skeet in my two-barrel gun, probably a Light Modified. In a single-barrel gun, I'll either stick with the Imp. Cyl. or replace it with a Light Modified.

Shotshell choice also can be a source of much debate. Most ranges, as well as the national organizations, limit shot size to #7-1/2s, #8s, #8-1/2s and #9s. No. 8 shot is my choice. That size puts more pellets in the pattern than #7-1/2, while maintaining more down-range energy

Manual, or hand-cocked, traps are probably the most common target throwers on Sporting Clays courses, and they work very well. Their portability allows range layouts to be easily changed.

than either #8-1/2 or #9. As with chokes, some shooters will carry quantities of each load: a hot dram equivalent #7-1/2 load for long shots that need more down-range energy capability and a faster muzzle velocity, a normal dram equivalent #8 load for middling distance targets and a light dram equivalent #9 shell for close-in targets. The #9s, being the smallest pellet, put more shot in the pattern, while the slower velocity of "lights" helps reduce first-shot muzzle flip, making the second target easier to acquire.

Shotshells range widely in price, starting at about $4 a box. Those cheaper shells carry names such as "game loads" or "dove and quail loads." Even shotshell manufacturers will agree that you get what you pay for when buying shells. Those shells, called promotional loads, have softer shot that sits atop a wad with either no shot cup or a plastic wrap. Softer shot deforms easier at ignition and during transit through a gun's forcing cone, barrel and choke. Deformed, or out-of-round pellets, are less aerodynamic and tend to veer out of the pattern. The trauma on soft shot is worse when there is no shot cup to protect the pellets during their flight out the barrel.

For $5 or so, you can buy what's commonly referred to as a target load. The extra buck gets you harder shot, a one-piece wad and shot cup, a more desirable hull for reloading and, perhaps, more efficient powder.

A newer trend among cartridge manufacturers is a shell with higher quality shot and wad stuffed inside a cartridge case that's not as desirable for reloading. Names such as Gun Club, Top Gun and Xpert come immediately to mind as brand names offering good components inside a throw-away hull.

As the saying goes, you pays your money and takes your pick. When you miss a bird you shouldn't have, odds are the fault was your mechanics if you're shooting target loads. If you're shooting game loads, that missed "no-miss" target could be faulty mechanics—or your cheap load.

Despite all its comparisons to hunting, Sporting Clays isn't hunting. You will see target presentations that look like a passing mourning dove, flushing pheasant, a busted covey of bobwhite quail,

decoying pintail, running blue quail or a skittish greater Canada. What you don't get is the heart-pounding approach behind the dog on point, the adrenaline surge of the flush, followed by your reflexive, instinctive shouldering of the gun, swinging through the target and slapping the trigger.

In Sporting, you know when the target flushes because you call for it; you know where the target is coming from, where it's going, and you have a good idea how fast it's traveling. Having that information ahead of time gives a shooter plenty of opportunity to over-analyze the

shot. Instead of instinctively swinging, shouldering and shooting the gun, inexperienced shooters are looking at the bird ... the barrel ... and the bird while trying to calculate a lead. Don't. Instead, think about those wonderful shots you made last hunting season when you let your eyes, hands and brain do their jobs, and you only had to slap the trigger and keep the muzzle moving when the brain said "Now!" If you carry that instinctive formula over to Sporting there's no way you'll suffer from embarrassment, real or imagined. And that means the fun has only begun. ●

There are any number of ways to transport gear between stations. This little red wagon is a simple and popular method, but there are many elaborate setups being used. Use what works for you!

Advice for Parents

One of the first rules of introducing a youngster to shotgunning is to get him or her comfortable with the gun while explaining the basics.

The proper gauge for a young shooter is mostly a matter of comfort. This gunner is able to handle the 12-gauge with no problem.

Group sessions usually mean the youngsters are among friends, making them more at ease during the lesson.

Since shooting is as innately American as stars and stripes, everybody knows how to shoot a shotgun, right? Only if we mean putting a shotgun to your shoulder and pulling the trigger.

Properly shooting a shotgun involves so much more. Sadly, such knowledge often is beyond the scope of a well-intentioned parent who is introducing a youngster to shotgunning.

I make no claim to being a shooting instructor, but I've seen enough blunders, well meaning though they may have been, to make me grind my teeth in frustration. So let's throw out some tar and see if any of these common misdeeds stick:

Humans are blessed with five senses, and nothing makes my blood boil more than watching a parent jeopardize two of them due to a lack of eye and ear protection. Foam ear plugs—the cylinders that can be rolled up and inserted—cost about a half-buck a pair and are part of the equation. Used in conjunction with the familiar muff-type hearing protectors, these two items will provide the best protection for the least amount of money. Many times I have used scissors to cut those plugs to get them to fit inside really young ears. The problem is that most kids lose or are going to misplace at least one. So be prepared to have several back-ups on hand. Of course, when a kid loses his ear muffs, the investment is considerably more.

Protective glasses don't have to be the traditional yellow tint found in most gun shops. Other options are available. Otherwise, check out hardware stores that usually offer a selection of clear glasses or goggles for people using string trimmers or other power tools. The total investment to help ensure a lifetime of quality hearing and sight should be about $25 or so. As a parent, make sure you set the example by always using your eye and ear protection.

Humans also are blessed with three-dimensional vision—if both eyes are open. Close one eye, and depth perception vanishes. Too many kids start out closing one eye. Often it's because of a parent's misconception; other times the child is mimicking a movie or TV shooter. Encourage your young shooter to keep both eyes open. Insist on it, even. The benefits over a shooting lifetime will far outweigh any temporary problems while fixing the problem.

A 410-bore as a starter gun is another of my peeves. The bore size/shot mass combination is terribly inefficient. A skilled wingshooter can do all right with a 410, but in the hands of a beginner, its payload deficiencies often prove more painful than the added recoil of a bigger gauge.

Paying attention to a shooter's mechanics is as important as watching the target. This youngster needs to keep both eyes open and his weight off his back foot.

With his NSCA-certified instructor watching closely, a youngster gets a confidence boost with this smoked target. He was all smiles afterward.

One substitute that's proving quite successful for helping train young wingshooters is a BB gun, sans sights. Ammo is extremely reasonable, especially compared to the cost of a box of 410 shells. Perhaps the biggest crusader for the BB-gun school of wingshooting instruction is Leon Measures. He starts kids out shooting stationary 3-pound coffee cans. By the time he's finished with them, they're shooting aspirin tablets and BBs out of the air. He offers a kit that includes a sightless BB gun, an instruction book, an instructional video, two pairs of safety glasses and 1500 BBs. The price is about $165. Contact him at Shoot Where You Look, Dept. GD, 408 Fair, Livingston, Texas, 77351.

Eventually a young shooter will need a shotgun. The 20-gauge is the route most people take, and there's nothing wrong with it. It's the gauge most gun manufacturers use on their lines of youth-model guns. Many of these are pump actions, although semi-automatic and double-barrel youth guns are also available. Pumps have one safety advantage when in the hands of the beginning shooter. Unlike an autoloader or double gun, a pump can't be fired again until the shooter pumps the action. As the novice transforms into a seasoned, young shooter, that pump-gun advantage can turn into a disadvantage, especially on parent-child outings to the local Sporting Clays range. Even veteran pump-gun shooters often have a difficult time cycling their guns quickly enough to break the second target on simultaneous pairs.

One alternative to a pump gun might be starting a youngster on a gas-operated semi-auto that has a full-length plug installed in the magazine. The plug limits the beginning shooter to one shot, but switching to full use of the gun is merely a plug change away. Gas-operated guns also have less recoil, which is a bonus. It doesn't take that many shots from a pump gun or double before a beginning shooter starts feeling the recoil. Regardless of the gun, keep the sessions short. Too much shooting—and accumulated recoil—can turn what's supposed to be a fun experience into a painful ordeal.

Ammunition for a 20-gauge is easily found. It's cheaper than other small gauges, and there's a variety of load choices. Traditionally, 20s pack 7/8-ounce of shot over a 2-1/2-dram equivalent of powder. Avoid anything stouter, like 1-ounce loads, for your beginner. Some ammo makers, Estate and Fiocchi come to mind, make a lighter, 3/4-ounce training load for 20s. For 20-gauge reloaders, there are plenty of recipes for the lighter, 3/4-ounce loads, too.

Far too many people, parents teaching youngsters included, use the wad as a reference point to determine where they are missing a target. Compared even to out-of-round shot, a wad has the aerodynamics of a brick. For the where-the-wad-is-the-shotstring-is theory to work, the wad must be in the center of the pattern all the way to the target. Modern one-piece wads with shotcups that have those split petals are designed fall out of the pattern as quickly as possible. Don't believe me? Hang a 40x40-inch piece of patterning paper with a colored bullseye in the center on a frame, step back 30 to 40 yards, aim at the bullseye and shoot. Walk to the paper and find the spot were the pellet strikes are closest together. Then look for a big tear in paper, where the wad struck—assuming it reached the paper. No big tear means the wad didn't even hit the paper. Do that 10 times. If the wad strike is anywhere near the dense core of the pattern on even half of the targets, I guess I'll have to eat my words. What this lesson will teach you is how far from the shotstring the wad really can be.

Whether youth- or adult-sized, all off-the-rack guns subscribe to the one-gun-fits-all theory. And we all know that doesn't work. If the beginner's trigger-hand thumb is too close to the nose when shooting, you may need to add some length to the pad. If the cheek is well back on the comb, you may need to shorten the stock even more. There are other gun-fitting tweaks that probably are needed, but most are best left in the hands of qualified fitters or shooting instructors.

Hand a shotgun to any first-time shooter and ask them to shoulder it as if they intended to shoot, and more beginners than not will lean backward, putting most of their weight on their rear foot, while having their feet in a front-to-back, almost straight line Your young shooter should be trained to have his or her weight slightly forward. If they are right handed, pretend they are standing on a clock's face and position the left foot at about 12 o'clock and the right foot between 2 o'clock and 3 o'clock. By squaring up their body to the target, their natural shoulder pocket is more accessible to the gunstock's butt, and they have more swing room on crossing targets. Also have your young shooter square up to the spot where they intend to break the target. Most beginners face where they expect to first see the target, and they often run out of swing before they can pull the trigger. Another good habit to develop in a beginning shooter is how to properly shoulder the gun. A better term might be "cheeking the gun" because the accepted method is to bring the gun's stock to the cheek. Many beginners lower their heads, hence cheek, to the gun's comb. Since the eyes are the rear sight on a shotgun, it's best to keep them still and move the gun.

A better way to start off a youngster in shooting is to get some experienced help. A lot of gun clubs offer classes or instructional sessions for kids because, after all, kids are their future. The more knowledgeable, and patient, of the club's members run the kids through various paces, stressing gun safety and proper shooting form. In my part of the country, at least, the Boy Scouts offer shooting programs, including merit badges. The National Rifle Association also offers or helps out with other kids' shooting programs.

The absolute best way to start a youngster is to send her or him to a qualified, certified shooting instructor. If your child wanted to take up golf or tennis, lessons would be an option so they could play the game to its fullest and get the maximum enjoyment. Why not the same with shooting? A good shooting instructor not only starts kids out with the right habits, they can pick out potential pitfalls and work on them before a problem develops. You'd better be careful, though, because when your child quickly starts shooting better than you, you may start thinking seriously about taking some lessons. ●

The Essentials of Sporting Clays

There are certain basic needs to participate in this game, and they can range from plain-Jane equipment to state-of-the-art high-tech gear.

by JOHN TAYLOR

IN ITS PUREST form, Sporting Clays is a representation of game shooting with clay targets substituted for fur and feathers. Begun in Great Britain, Sporting Clays came to these shores decades ago in the form of "Crazy Quail" and other "walks" that threw clay targets as the shooter progressed down a path. About 20-plus years ago, Sporting Clays in its present form took root on these shores. Today, courses across

the United States, in Canada, Mexico and Europe all provide their individual treatment of the game but, fundamentally, Sporting Clays is a substitute for field shooting.

If one takes that approach, he should be able to go to his local course with his favorite shotgun and have a great time. However, as with many things in our society, Sporting Clays has become rarified, highly competitive with the consequence

that as in all the other shooting sports, equipment has evolved in kind and cost and guns have become specialized. Perhaps we can sort it all out in the next few pages.

Before we go any further, let's get one item out of the way. All Sporting Clays facilities require that shooters wear both eye and hearing protection. It simply amazes me that shooters somehow think that these two protective measures are unnec-

A case is necessary if only to legally transport a shotgun to and from home and the Sporting Clays field. For travel by automobile, this soft-style case is fine. However, the shooter who plans to check his shotgun as airline baggage will need a hard, lockable case such as this one from Americase.

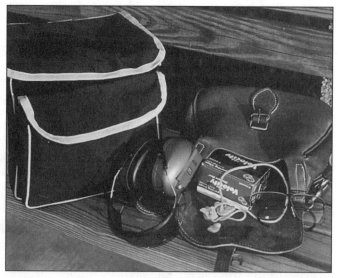

Hearing and eye protection, and a bag to carry the day's ammunition are all part of the necessary things the Sporting Clays shooter needs, at the bare minimum. They add to safety and enjoyment of the sport.

essary. Cigarette filters, cotton balls, and other things are used in the ears, but none of these afford any protection. Only if the ear canal is completely blocked are hearing-protection devices effective. Ear plugs can be those familiar and simple foam cylinders that cost about 50 cents a pair, they can be custom moulded inserts that go for about $25 to $45, or they can be special moulded plugs with high-tech electronic systems costing $600 and more. Whatever the choice, remember that to be successful, a plug must seal the ear canal; nothing else is satisfactory.

The other style of hearing protection is the muff. These are as good if not slightly better than plugs, because they shield the ear and surrounding bone structures from the sharp spike of the report. Their drawbacks are that some are difficult to wear while wearing a hat or cap, really a design flaw in not making the headband a little longer, and they are hot in the summer. These, too, come in different styles. The cheapest are just muffs, but some are fitted with electronic circuitry that allows the user to carry on a conversation while providing complete protection from gunfire sound levels. These units require a certain noise level to actuate the electronics; sound below that is not muffled.

In tests, it has been determined that for the maximum protection of one's hearing, the best practice is to use a combination of both muffs and plugs. The two combined really do attenuate the damaging sounds of gunfire, and should be considered by all shooters.

We only get one pair of eyes, and to have to remind a supposed experienced shooter that he needs protective glasses on the field goes into the realm of stupidity. Few are the really experienced shooters who have not been struck by a ricocheted pellet, a piece of broken target, gas blown back from a failed case, or even been in the fall zone of pellets from another stand. Any one of these instances can result in eye damage and blindness; severe injury at the least. To go onto any firearms range without shooting glasses is folly.

Strictly speaking, shooting glasses for clay target sports ride high on the face to accommodate the position of the eyes when the cheek is properly on the stock. Remember, the eye is really the rear sight of a shotgun. Many simply shoot with their regular eyeglasses, and this is certainly okay. However, it is a good idea to tell your optometrist that you will be shooting with your glasses so that he can supply them with hardened lenses, similar to ones worn by those whose occupation requires safety glasses.

Shooting glasses are available in several styles. Many companies such as Bushnell, Zeiss, and Bausch & Lomb offer shooting-style non-prescription glasses in a wide price range. Outfits like Decot Hy-Wyd Sports Glasses offer complete service in both prescription and non-prescription lenses and in a wide variety of tints.

Lens tints are a discussion in themselves. Suffice to say that if you have 20/20 vision or wear contact lenses, then it is possible to buy various colored lenses relatively inexpensively. For prescription users, the cost is much higher. The best advice is to check out the Sporting Clays clubs in your area, then select the lens color that will best help you see the particular color of targets thrown by them against the most prevalent background. Currently, the best advice seems to be one of the pink- or orange-tinted "blue-blocking" lenses for daytime. By eliminating the blue portion of the spectrum, these lenses tend to make targets stand out against green backgrounds. They are even more helpful if your club throws all-orange targets. As a second pair of lenses, a very pale yellow or clear makes the most sense. These can be worn for nighttime shooting, or when the weather gets bad and you end up shooting in the rain or snow. Regardless of the style, brand and color of glasses, be very sure that

you and all your group have some kind of eye protection when you set foot on any range.

Much of the interest Sporting Clays provides is in how courses are constructed and how they use the topography to show challenging and difficult targets. Because of this feature, shooters must be able to be self-contained as they move from station to station. Skeet and trap shooters often can park their car or truck adjacent to the field, but that's not so with Sporting Clays. Therefore, some kind of bag is needed to carry ammunition, extra choke tubes, extra lenses, sun screen, insect repellent, a water bottle, towel and whatever else the shooter chooses to burden himself with during the day.

Several companies such as 10x and Bob Allen make shooting bags that will accommodate several boxes of shells, with separate pockets for glasses, choke tubes, etc. If the shooter uses different loads for different targets, he then needs to keep his ammo boxed so he can keep it straight. If he doesn't, then one of the British-style leather or canvas cartridge bags will serve him well,

The four styles of shotguns that can be used for Sporting Clays (left to right): over/under, side-by-side, autoloading and the pump-action. Of these, the auto and over/under are the most popular and universally used.

since most of these will hold 200 or more rounds.

When our shooter gets to the shooting station, he then needs some means of taking the required number of shotshells, plus a couple extras for malfunctions, up to the cage for shooting. Although first-timers can be forgiven, nothing slows down a squad more than someone fishing around in his trouser pockets for shells. At a minimum, a pouch worn on a belt is necessary. Some courses provide shelves in each shooting cage where the shooter can place a box of shells. Invariably, these are knocked over at least once, spilling the contents on the ground and usually upsetting the rest of the squad as the hapless gunner picks up his spilled ammo. So, in addition to a way to lug 100 or 200 shells around, the shooter needs a means to take a few to each station.

Most Sporting Clays shooters opt for a shooting vest. These provide two or more pockets for shells, some have a pocket across the back for fired hulls, a breast pocket for glasses, and most have an additional, long narrow pocket for choke tubes. In its truest form, Sporting Clays is shot with the gun dismounted, therefore most Clays vests have a full-length leather or cloth pad running up the gun side of the garment.

When cold weather comes, the shooter has a number of clothing options. Many purchase a winter shooting coat such as made by Bob Allen and others. In really foul weather many will wear a waterfowl hunting coat or one of the oiled cotton coats so popular in Britain. Others choose to don a sweater and/or windbreaker with their regular summer vest over the top. Still other winter shooters simply make do with a regular winter coat and carry their shells in a pouch. Of these, perhaps the made-for-shooting coat or sweater/windbreaker/vest are the best. If shooting the low or dismounted gun, it is advantageous to have the smooth surface of a shooting coat or vest against which to mount the gun.

Gloves are often necessary in winter shooting, although many shooters will temporarily remove their trigger hand glove for a better feel of the trigger. Many wear a glove on the off hand, the one that grips the forend, year 'round. A golf glove is most frequently used; some companies make shooting gloves that are similar to the golf style, but often a bit heavier. Using a glove affords the shooter a firmer grip on the forend without having to clamp down, something that often slows the swing.

Other accessories for the Sporting Clays shooter are toe pads on which he or she can rest their empty and opened shotgun while waiting to shoot. These protect both the shoe and the gun muzzle. Since racks are provided at most stands, this little accessory isn't, perhaps, as useful as in Skeet. Crank-style or even power-driven choke tube wrenches might be of use if changing choke tubes is one's thing. They certainly speed the process, but the slower, manual wrench is generally needed to loosen and tighten tubes.

Transporting a shotgun to and from a club or Sporting Clays layout requires some kind of case. Some states are very strict regarding the

Two lady shooters waiting to shoot a station; one prefers a vest, the other a pouch. Use what works for you.

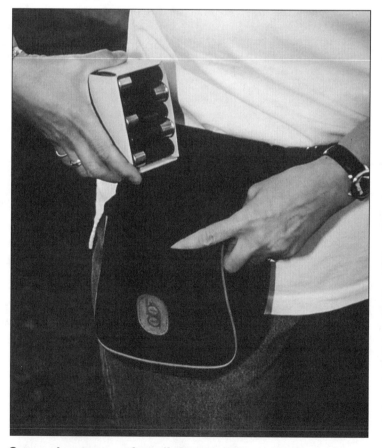

Some shooters prefer a light pouch to carry enough ammunition to the cage for each station, and this one will work quite well.

transportation of firearms and, anyway, most shooters case their gun just to protect it. If one becomes really addicted to Sporting Clays, there may arise the need to fly somewhere to compete. Then you'll need real protection!

For around the county, any number of soft cases will suffice. Companies like Bob Allen, Penguin, Kolpin and others make a whole array, and firearms manufacturers like Browning market well-made soft cases that afford all the protection necessary for local outings and around the course.

Traveling any distance with a good shotgun or flying to another region poses a entirely new set of parameters. One of Hoppe's or Koplin's moulded plastic cases sold at K-Mart for $29.95 may suffice, but I wouldn't bet much on them for heavy-duty use. On a recent trip I saw an aluminum-plastic case peeled open like a banana. The owner's shotguns were miraculously not damaged, but it wasn't a pretty sight.

In my experience, one of the best cases made is by Americase in Texas. These incorporate a solid, machined aluminum frame with a 1/4-inch Duron laminate inserted in the sides to save weight. Duron is a tempered hardboard to which is laminated a layer of fiberglass. Cases are made to fit individual shotguns, rifles and bows, and are virtually indestructible. Briley Manufacturing and Holland & Holland supply Americase products as their case of choice.

At the start of this story, I said that to shoot Sporting Clays in its non-competitive form, one only had to go forth with his favorite field gun and have at it. However, in truth, it isn't all that simple. Any Clays course worth its salt, and five-stand setup for that matter, will throw a quarter or even half of the targets as pairs. In other words, two targets sailing past the firing position at the same time. Taken at face value, this immediately rules out any single-barreled shotgun, be it an Iver Johnson clunker to an Ithaca Sousa-Grade trap gun. It also pretty well eliminates pumps and certainly bolt-action guns from being viable Clays guns. Don't get me wrong; to go out and shoot a round of Sporting Clays to get in shape for hunting with a Winchester Model 12, Remington 870 or Mossberg 500 or 835 is not a crime against nature. In such an informal setting it's easy to ask the trapper to not throw simultaneous pairs, but to make them following or report pairs (following pairs are released as quickly as the trapper can get a second target on the arm and release it following the launch of the first target; in a report pair the second target is released when the shooter shoots at the first target) and no great harm is done. But, like most clay target games, once tempted it's hard not to want to shoot the whole course as it was designed.

Sporting Clays is essentially a 12-gauge game. But that's not to say one can't use a 16- or 20-gauge or even a 28. The 410-bore, unless it's a part of a competition, isn't really a consideration except for the experts bored with the larger guns. Far better for a beginning youngster or lady to use a 28-gauge that has enough shot and patterns it well, than the 410. The 20-gauge makes sense as an alternative to the 12 for those who are recoil sensitive or have a physical problem that prevents them from shooting the 12. However, Sporting Clays is a 12-gauge game for the moment, and the recoil-sensitive shooter should explore the very light target loads currently cataloged by the major ammunition makers before going resorting to the smaller guns.

Because two shots are required and, in fact, allowed to be fired at even single targets on some courses, we can eliminate the single shot and the bolt-action because it is impossibly slow. The pump gets the thumbs down because even if the legendary Herb Parsons—who could throw seven clay targets into the air and break them all with a Model 12 before any hit the ground—were shooting he would find it difficult to shuck quick enough for some targets. We are then left with semi-automatic and twin-tubed shotguns.

Screw-in choke tubes have become common and allow the Sporting Clays shooter to tailor his patterns to each station around the course. However, it is the author's experience that one can negotiate the majority of courses with open tubes such as Skeet and Improved Cylinder, making choke changing unnecessary.

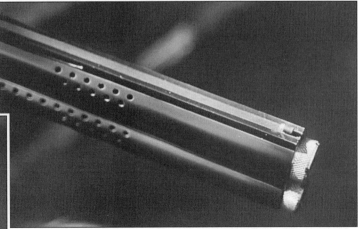

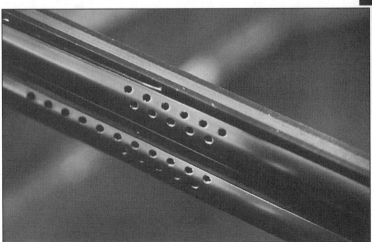

Porting of barrels ensures that there is no muzzle rise or jump when the shot is fired. Porting is one of the most useful barrel modifications since it also lessens recoil felt at the cheek and helps eliminate fatigue.

There are two types of semi-automatic or autoloading shotguns; recoil- and gas-operated. The epitome of the recoil-operated semi-automatic shotgun is the Browning Automatic-5, recently dropped from Browning's inventory just short of its centenary. First sold to sportsmen in 1905, this type of shotgun locks the breech bolt and barrel together, the two recoiling until they strike the rear of the receiver, when they are unlocked and the barrel is pushed forward by a powerful spring that surrounds the magazine tube. As the barrel goes forward the fired shell is stripped from the chamber and at the end of the barrel's travel, the fired hull is ejected. A split second later the bolt is released and allowed to go forward, driven by a spring in the buttstock. The bolt picks up a fresh cartridge from the magazine and the firing cycle is ready to be repeated. The problem with the recoil gun is the "double shuffle" of the barrel going home followed by the bolt, and the fact that,

advertising notwithstanding, recoil is pretty stiff.

Gas-operated semi-automatics came along right after World War Two. This action bleeds off a small amount of the propellent gases through a port or small hole about seven inches from the mouth of the chamber. These quickly expanding gases exert their force against a piston that in turn shoves a heavy inertia piece rearward. The combined push of gas and inertia are sufficient to open the bolt and push it rearward extracting and ejecting the fired shell. At the end of its travel the bolt is thrust forward by a spring in the buttstock, picking up and chambering a fresh round from the magazine. Although recoil is recoil, because of the inner workings of the gas-operated semi-automatic, the sensation of recoil is spread out over several more milliseconds than with the recoil-operated semi-automatic or any of the fixed-breech shotguns, i.e. pump, side-by-side and over/under. For this

sensation of "softened recoil" many shooters prefer the gas-operated semi-auto.

Currently (1998) Remington offers it's incredibly successful 1100 and 11-87 in Sporting Clays versions. Browning offers its semi-auto Gold gun in a Sporting Clays model complete with ported barrels. Certainly the Benelli series of inertia-style autos can be used to advantage on the Clays field, as can the Franchi Variopress. There's no reason that you couldn't use the Mossberg 9200 auto, either.

If we were to be purists about Sporting Clays, we'd probably use side-by-side doubles. The typical British game gun for over a century, the side-by-side was the gun of choice when Sporting Clays came into being. However, that support has eroded and now most everyone shoots the game with an over/under. In many large Sporting Clays competitions there are events for side-by-side guns. Still and all, other than being

These Clays shooters are dressed in various coats, sweaters and vests for cool weather. Clothing should offer warmth yet allow full movement for proper gun mounting and swing.

Lady competitor Becky Bowen is changing her choke tubes prior to shooting. She's dressed for a nippy late fall day in a sweater with a vest worn over it to carry shells and ensure a good gun mount.

able to fire two quick shots, the side-by-side has all but been eliminated from the competitive side of Sporting Clays. Too, quality side-by-sides tend to be more pricey than purpose-made over/unders, so that also figures into the equation.

Today, the over/under is king of Sporting Clays, and there's little evidence that that ranking will change. Because of its handling similarities to rifles that we all seem to grow up shooting, its single sighting plane, interchangeable choke tubes and the fact that firearms manufacturers have specialized the over/under for Sporting Clays, it's the shotgun of choice. Current over/under makers include Beretta, Browning, Ruger, Remington, Weatherby, Fabarm (imported by H&K), Perazzi, Galazan, SKB, Sigarms, Krieghoff, Merkel and Connecticut Valley

Classics. There are probably several others that have slipped from memory. Holland & Holland, the august London gun maker, now offers their "off the rack" Sporting Competition Gun for about $25,000, give or take a few bucks. The American-made Galazan isn't cheap either. On the other hand, the Browning Citori, Ruger Red Label, Remington Peerless, and Weatherby Orion offer excellent quality, and all have about the same features: screw-in chokes, somewhat straighter stocks and some offer factory ported barrels. For more money, the Krieghoff K-80 and any of the Perazzi shotguns will lighten your wallet by several thousands of dollars.

Selecting an over/under is mostly a matter of trying several different makes and settling on the one you like best within your price range. It

is good to keep in mind that in every instance, a shotgun purchased for Sporting Clays is in and of itself an excellent field gun. In most instances, these guns are chambered for 2-3/4-inch shells. Some 12-gauge Clays over/unders are chambered for 3-inch shells, but for the most part, the shorter chambers are used. For a dove and upland gun, they're hard to beat, except for weight. Guns built for clay target shooting tend to be heavier, and there is a two-fold reason. First, heavier guns have more inertia so the tendency is to continue the swing and not stop, which is the surest way to miss a target. Second, heavier guns recoil less. It is harder to push a fire truck backward than a Volkswagen Beetle, so, too, is it harder to start an 8-plus pound shotgun rearward than a 6-pound game gun. Over the long haul of a 100-tar-

Holland & Holland's fully articulated try gun. In the hands of an expert instructor/gun fitter, a stock can be definitively fit to an individual shooter through shooting and adjusting of the try gun. Measurements are then used to alter the shooter's original stock or to build a new one.

No longer the predominate shotgun on Sporting Clays courses, occasionally one sees a shooter using a side-by-side.

Even though it's obviously hot weather, this shooter is using two gloves to ensure a firm grip on his gun.

get shoot, the heavier gun will swing better and be more comfortable to shoot at day's end.

In the 1970s, the trend was towards short 26-inch barrels on over/unders. All they provide is a gun that feels good in the store and shoots badly on the range. Short-barreled over/unders tend to be muzzle light, whippy and very hard to swing smoothly. Today, Sporting Clays-specific shotguns start with 28-inch barrels and go to 30 and even 32 inches. Many champion shooters prefer either the 30- or 32-inch lengths for the smooth swing they impart. At one time, it was argued that longer barrels provided a longer sighting plane. But as any experienced shooter will state, if you're looking at the barrels or the front sight bead, chances are about 100 percent that you'll miss the target. The reason for longer barrels is a matter of dynamics, handling and feel.

Two aspects affecting shotgun selection are interchangeable chokes and barrel alterations. Screw-in choke tubes are nothing new. In recent history, Winchester made the first modern interchangeable choke tube shotgun, the Model 59. Introduced in 1961, it was an ultra-light gun for its day, using a barrel of very thin steel around which was wound fiberglass thread and fitted with Winchester's first WinChoke tubes. Following the demise of the Model 59, screw-in chokes disappeared until the early 1970s, when gunsmiths such as Stan Baker and Jess Briley began installing aftermarket screw-in tubes. Finally, in the late 1980s and early '90s, gun makers began supplying the shotgunning public with factory-installed choke tubes.

As with other gadgets, the beginner has high hopes for its use: He or she eyes a particular station, then selects the "correct" tube for that target or targets, similar to choosing the right golf club for a particular shot. There are shooters like this, one whose valet trots behind his wealthy employer, who in turn commands a certain constriction from a box of several dozen tubes, and the flunky obediently threads the tube in for his master. A bit ridiculous? You bet. In truth, there aren't many courses that can't be negotiated with a pair of Skeet tubes, or perhaps Cylinder and Skeet or Skeet and Improved Cylinder. It's the technique of shooting and concentration on the target that makes the difference. Few are the targets that require anything beyond those chokes; perhaps Modified for a very high tower shot, not forgetting that a 125-foot high tower is 41-1/2 yards. Modern Sporting Clays ammunition, if nothing else, shoots tight, dense patterns and over-choking only gives the advantage to the other shooters. One instance for Full choke use might be a rabbit target thrown going away so that all that is presented is the edge. In this case it's really a hit or miss proposition, and a very dense pattern is needed so that the slim target can't slip through. But if one is to err, it should be on the open side.

Three alterations from industry standards are currently accepted and boasted about in advertising. One is the lengthening of the chamber forcing cone. This area of the bore is the transition from the larger chamber to the cylinder bore. In the days of paper shotshells loaded with card and felt wads, a sharp, short forcing cone was needed to prevent gas leakage around the bore-sized wads. Plastic gas seals and gas-sealing wads have now eliminated gas leakage, and this now unneeded abrupt transition serves no good purpose, and, in fact, contributes only to the deformation of pellets. By lengthening the chamber forcing cone from about 1/2-inch to 1 to 1-1/2 or even 2 inches, shot deformation is eased, and some claim that recoil seems to be lessened.

Following on from the chamber forcing cone, it is no secret that opening or widening the bore from the standard .729-inch to about .740 also helps baby the shot charge, and again, some say further reduces recoil. Called back- or overboring, when combined with long forcing cones, better quality patterns are the result.

Ken Davies, Holland & Holland's senior instructor, checks the stock dimensions of a student's shotgun. Based on these measurements and perhaps dimensions derived from a session with a try gun, coupled with Davies' immense experience, he can recommend changes to an existing stock

In the continuous search for lessened recoil, barrel porting has become an important factor. Originally done as an aftermarket operation by Larry Kelley under the trade name of Mag-Na-Port and Pro-Port, a series of holes are cut into the top of the barrel just behind the muzzle(s). These holes direct the propellant gases up and somewhat to the rear. While I've never felt any real attenuation of rearward recoil, the lack of muzzle rise or jump is dramatic. Unported shotguns jump up against the cheek as the barrels take an upward hop, but with ported barrels, they stay right where they were. Today, most all Sporting Clays-specific guns made by the major domestic or foreign makers come factory ported, most have lengthened forcing cones and some also come with backbored barrels.

One aspect of shotguns that cannot be overemphasized is fit. To be a successful Sporting Clays shooter, his or her shotgun must fit like a $3,000 suit. Shooting with a dismounted gun requires that when it comes to the shoulder the cheek is at the same place on the comb every time, and that the eyes be directly aligned with the rib. One of the best descriptions of a well-fitted gun is one that shoots where you're looking. Because of the nature of Sporting Clays, many shots are taken using the "instinctive" or "swing-through" style of shooting. To be effective, the shooter must concentrate on the target and allow his mind and reflexes to complete the shot. Without a well-fitted shotgun, the odds are against the shooter.

In recent years, shotgun manufacturers have raised the combs of their guns and slightly lengthened the stocks. However, it's still a "Mr. Average" approach, much like offering every suit in a store in medium size.

Gun fitting can be achieved by experimentation or by working with a competent instructor who understands fitting. Normally he will use a try-gun that has a fully articulated stock. The instructor can then adjust the stock, and by watching the shooter and making adjustments, can arrive at the proper dimensions in a short amount of time. On the other hand, the do-it-yourselfer will need to make one change to his stock, then shoot with it, try to evaluate the results, go to another area of the stock and fiddle with it, and so forth. In truth, he may never get it right by himself.

Most often, shooters need a longer stock. In addition, raising or lowering the comb is needed. Lengthening a stock is simply a matter of adding a slip-on recoil pad or placing washers under the buttplate or pad. Shortening a stock is more delicate since material is being removed. Go slow and test at every turn.

Raising the comb of a stock is easy. Successive layers of moleskin can be stuck onto the comb; leather held on with plastic electrical tape can be used for trial fitting, or one of the Velcro-type comb-raising pads can be used. On some semi-auto shotguns such as the Beretta A-390, various shims are available to raise the comb. In addition, the stocks of a few autoloaders can be made higher by inserting shims between the buttstock and back of the receiver. Lowering a comb is simply a matter of taking material off with a rasp or sandpaper, but work slowly here so too much isn't removed.

U.S. shotgun makers do not build their guns with cast-off or cast-on. These are the lateral bending, usually about 1/4 -to 3/8-inch, of the stock to compensate for the thickness of the shooter's cheek. Cast-off is bending the stock to the right, cast-on is for the left-handed shooter and the stock moves to the left. By combining cast-off or -on when making a stock, the comb is normally made slightly higher and then the cast moves the eye over the rib.

Many shooters will modify the stock of their Sporting Clays gun and simply leave the leather and tape in place, just in case more changes are necessary—or to return to the original configuration. Trap and Skeet shooters seem to be constantly changing things around in the hope of getting just a few more birds, and there's no reason why Clays shooters don't think the same. Shooting slumps can happen any time, and it's possible a little change in the stock will cure the ills.

If tape and moleskin aren't satisfactory then there are two routes to be taken. A custom stocker can transfer the fitter's measurements or one's own experimentally-derived dimensions into a new stock. Outfits like Briley Manufacturing can bend an existing stock to all but the most bizarre specifications. Bending a stock requires heat and a special jig, but it is very successful and can be used in all but the most extreme cases. By bending a stock, the original can be used, but often a new one may be more satisfactory in the long run.

In the final analysis, each shooter must evaluate what and how much equipment he needs, what clothing he prefers and what type of shotgun he shoots best. Then it's a simple matter to select those items from the vast selection provided by the many suppliers to this burgeoning trade.●

The most popular Clays guns are the autoloader, like Remington's 11-87 (above) and the over/under like the Weatherby Orion Classic Sporting. Pumps and side-by-sides are used by few shooters.

Shotgunning Techniques:

HOW TO MAKE FOUR BASIC SHOTS

PULLING THE GUN up in the general direction of the target is one way to put your shotgun into action. But just as there are important basic techniques for throwing a football, hitting a baseball, shooting a basketball, putting a golf ball, or the backhand in tennis, the same goes for shotgunning. Some basic techniques are required before anyone can do anything well. Sure, you can step up and take a whack at whatever, but that does not mean you're going to have success, especially consistent success.

With such a philosophy in mind, I've selected four different but common shots that we encounter in the field and on the range, and examined the basic techniques that can help you improve your performance both in the field and on the Clays course. However, I must mention a couple of points before we start. Just reading about these basics isn't enough. You have to go out and purposely practice them, because without actually prac-

The straightaway target exits from Low House Seven. Learn to see the bird's domes, and even see it spin. Try to stare a hole through the bird.

This is the proper stance for making the straightaway shot using the Low House from Skeet Station Seven. Feet are shoulder-width apart, toes slightly out, half-step forward with left foot. The gun is tucked up under the arm pit, muzzle below flight path.

Here's expert advice on how to set up and make the four shots you'll most likely see in the field and on the Clays course.

by NICK SISLEY

ticing these techniques you're never going to get to proverbial first base. The best place to gain this practice is with clay targets, but with each of the four shots Im going to cover here I'll suggest how to set the shot up on or around a Skeet field or Sporting Clays course. This is simply because most all of you will have either or both in reasonable proximity.

Another important factor, if you're to be successful with what I recommend here, is that merely practicing enough that you completely understand the basics I'm trying to get across isn't enough either. Mastering, or at least becoming better at, anything you're trying to do takes added practice—once you are implementing the proper basic techniques. This is true in any other

sporting endeavor, and I assure you it's true with shotgunning. So let's get started.

The Straightaway Shot

Here we're talking the dead straightaway, as well as a shot that's nearly so, perhaps quartering slightly left or right from dead center. Of course, in the field you never know what shot you're going to get. However, by practicing different shots over and over you'll naturally implement the correct techniques for any shot that suddenly presents itself in the field. Again, repetitive practice is required before you can attain this ability to incorporate the correct techniques. I suggest setting up this straightaway shot by standing at

Station 7 on a Skeet field and shooting the Low House target.

Aim your belly 90 degrees to the right of the center stake (the one the target is supposed to fly over). Place your feet side by side and shoulder-width apart, toes spread slightly outward. Take maybe a quarter- to a half-step forward with the left foot, and tuck the end of the shotgun's buttstock up under your arm pit. Keep the muzzle slightly elevated but below the upcoming bird's flight path. All these directions are for a right-handed shooter.

Now, and only now, are you ready to call for the target. But from a "pre-shot" standpoint you have everything set up perfectly, which is very important to success and it makes the shot so much easier! As the bird comes out tell yourself, "Slow down. Slow down." That's because the tendency is to rush; especially the mount, maybe even the shot. Typically, the novice shooter slams the buttstock to his shoulder, no doubt to try and get that part of the equation over with so he can concentrate on the main job at hand, which is getting to and hitting the target. But this is an incorrect basic philosophy. And technique. Instead, first start the muzzle(s) to the bird, but without consciously looking at the muzzle. Concentrate only on the bird. Stare a hole through it. At this station it's easiest to see the individual rings on the dome, and to see the tar-

To set up for a crossing shot, the body should be aimed toward where you want to break the target, buttstock tucked up under the arm pit, and the muzzle should be slightly below the target's flight path.

get spin. After you've started the muzzle to the bird, then you begin blending in the gun mount. Although the whole procedure isn't a slow one, a shooter usually has to tell himself to slow down. In doing so, the result can be a smooth move to the bird. Gone are the herky-jerky movements so typical of the novice, as well as those of a shooter who misses far too often.

About the time the stock hits the shoulder and the comb touches the cheek, the muzzle will be properly to the bird, and it will be time to hit the trigger. The tendency is to poke the barrels too far above this straightaway target. We seem to be especially prone to do this when we move too fast. Hold right on the bird or just below it, then hit the trigger.

Let's backtrack briefly to talk about what bad happens if we mount the shotgun first, before starting the muzzle to the bird. If the initial move is buttstock-to-shoulder, the muzzle necessarily goes down. After that happens you're figuratively fighting City Hall because the muzzle has to come back up. Not only is time lost

while the target is gaining more distance from you, that smoothness you were trying to achieve via proper basics has flown out the window!

One more point before moving on to Shot Number 2. With the initial move of the muzzle toward the bird, that muzzle should also be shoved forward, as should your body and your weight. The forward movement of your body needs only to be minimal. If you have found that your buttstock hangs up and/or gets poorly positioned for a lot of your shots it's because you haven't (1) practiced the proper technique we're advising here, and (2) you're moving the buttstock to the shoulder before you're moving the muzzle toward the bird. Make every effort to blend in the mount, momentarily after starting the muzzle toward the bird. After mastering the basics at Station 7, continue to practice near-straightway shots by moving around the station a bit, as well as farther from it. This is a shot you'll encounter in virtually any upland hunting, especially when using pointing dogs.

The Hard Crosser

Here we're talking about the bird that passes directly in front, fully or near fully a crossing shot. Sometimes we see this shot in pheasant hunting, or with doves, but especially with ducks and geese, though there are other hard crossing shot possibilities, too. Set up this shot by standing at Station 4 on a Skeet field using the same set up as with the straightaway. Aim your belly at where you're going to break the bird. Ditto for your feet. The tendency is set your belly and feet toward the house where the bird is emerging. Do that and you'll tend to run out of swing when it's time to pull the trigger. Set your feet square with your belly and shoulders, then take that quarter- or half-step with the left foot (again right-handed shooters). Tuck that shotgun butt up under your arm pit, muzzle slightly below the flight path of the about-to-be-released clay bird. Now you're ready to call for the target. It can be launched from either the High House or the Low. Your choice. Practice both.

This shooter is prepared for the hard crosser. You'll need to experiment with muzzle position because where you hold can make the bird easy, difficult or impossible to hit.

This shooter prepares for a ground-hugging rabbit target, so he is set up with the muzzle below the target's expected path.

As the bird emerges, it's critical to use the same philosophy you learned with the straightway. Think, "Slow down. Slow down." Also, start the muzzle along the bird's flight path, then blend in the gun mount. This is the basic technique you want to use so the whole effort can look smooth, unhurried, easy! Mount the gun first and it's the same result as covered with the straightaway—a muzzle that first goes down, away from the target's flight path. When that happens you must then get the muzzle back on track, and in doing so you've lost time (so now the target is probably way ahead of the muzzle) and your movement has been anything but smooth. Experiment with several gun-hold positions here. Should you hold either closer into the house, or out farther from it? What I suggest is a muzzle position that allows the emerging target to get slightly ahead of your muzzle initially. Then, you simply pass the muzzle through the bird and pull the trigger. Again, you should never actually look at the muzzle, only the target. Stare that hole through it. Look at the leading

edge. Watch so intently that you can see the bird's domes. Once you do pull the trigger it's important to follow through. While I did not mention follow through with my suggestions for the straightway, it's just as important with that shot, as is maintaining cheek contact with the wood throughout. Again, follow through is simply good basic technique. So is keeping the head tight to the stock throughout the shot process. Thinking about follow through, how could a golfer, a baseball pitcher, a bowler, a tennis champ, perform well without a proper follow through? Therefore, in shotgunning it's simply good basics to keep the muzzle swinging well beyond where the target is broken (or the bird killed), and for the cheek to maintain stock contact throughout.

A significant amount of body turning is involved with the hard crossing shot. Most of us turn only with the upper body. That's okay, though it's better to turn from the ankles up. Do that and you're turning right from your body's foundation. The result looks better, smoother, and eas-

ier. Upper body shotgunners can't turn as far, and if they turn too far they lose their balance. So about the time the shot goes off they might stumble off the station or into the ging weeds. This is particularly true of "leaners." A leaner is a shooter who, with a hard crossing shot in particular, leans the upper body in the direction the bird is traveling. About the time the shot is finished, that person's center of gravity has shifted well right or left, balance is lost, and off he or she stumbles. Even if the target is smoked or the bird grassed such technique looks awful, and the effort certainly does not breed consistency.

As you gain positive experience from Station 4, begin moving back from the station, first being certain that's it's absolutely safe to do so. You may have to check with shoot management before doing this, but safety is always your first requirement—and mandatory. Eventually, as you move back, you may have to switch to a tighter choke, always easy to do with most of today's shotguns that are equipped with screw-ins.

Once you are properly set up, learn to begin swinging the muzzle toward the target first, then blend in the gun mount in a smooth, easy motion. With practice, it will become a more natural movement.

The hard crossing rabbit target can take a lot of practice to master, but that's all part of the fun. Sporting Clays is meant to be challenging!

The High Incomer

This is a shot many shotgunners fear, especially novices, but it can be the nemesis of experienced shooters, as well. Some blokes are so afraid of a high incomer they never take the shot in the field, usually with the plea of, "That one was too high." While I certainly don't advocate shooting at birds that are too far away, a 40- to 45-yard shot is not one that's too high for a 12-gauge shotgun or for a gunner behind it who knows what he (or she) is doing. One typical incorrect basic that is often seen with this one is mounting the gun early, sometimes as early as first sighting the bird, which might still be well out of range. I guess the reason for doing this reverts back to that incorrect philosophy I first spoke of in the straightaway section: "We can't wait to get the gun mounted so that job can be over with and we can concentrate on the main problem of killing the bird or shattering the target."

Instead, try this. When you see that high incomer in the distance, use the time to begin looking extra hard at the bird. Then, when you feel the bird is at the proper distance (don't wait too long), use that swing-first philosophy that I've espoused so far. Start the muzzle on the target's track first (slightly behind), then blend in the mounting of the gun. Concentrate on making the whole process the smoothest feeling and best looking thing you've ever done. Now the muzzle will naturally be coming up behind the bird. Keep your head solidly on the stock, force yourself to keep the muzzle moving while doing so, blot the bird out and pull the trigger. At first your mind might not want to do that. There could be a mental tendency to want to see the target when you pull the trigger. With that high incomer, especially if it's right over head, you won't be able to see the target when you hit the trigger. Just trust yourself (and me). You've done everything correctly up to this point. You won't miss if you just trust yourself when the muzzle passes through the bird, especially if you maintain solid contact with your cheek on the wood. Take a peek (head off the stock) and your chances of missing become nearly certain.

Where do you practice the High Incomer? It can't be done on a Skeet field. You could set it up with a moveable trap positioned on a high hill, the shooter well below. Some Sporting Clays ranges might also have the type of set up you're looking for. Wherever you set up this practice session, safety for the target thrower is imperative. That person must be well protected from any of the shot pellets, whether the shot is properly or improperly directed.

The Running Rabbit

Every Sporting Clays course has a rabbit target. A special trap is utilized to throw a special target. Consequently, it's easy to set up practice for this one. Of course, in real hunting ground-hugging bunnies provide hunters with lots of challenge. This is a shot where, I think, a sustained-type of lead seldom works well. That's because the clay or cottontail is capable of changing direction so quickly, so easily. With a clay it's the up and down movement that can be so frustrating to the shooter. With real cottontails it's both the up and down and side to side movement that can make the shot extra tough.

So let's set up again with our belly and feet aimed at where we want to break the target, feet square, then that quarter- to half-step forward with the left foot, buttstock tucked up under the arm pit. As with the three previous target situations, only now are you ready to call. Remember, only by setting things up properly beforehand are you practicing correct basics. Also, if you don't practice these correct basics in a non-hunting situation, how are you ever going to incorporate them into a real hunting situation? Agreed, it's not always easy to make these necessary set ups when a bird or bunny first presents itself, but if you practice properly setting up often

After you have the crossing rabbit figured out, try a quartering-away rabbit like this, a very common cottontail possibility in the field.

The straightaway rabbit target is tough to break because you're shooting at its edge, which is purposely thick and tough so it won't break while bouncing on the ground.

enough, and for a number of different shots, you're well on your way to making these movements easy and natural, rather than cumbersome and not even remembered.

Set up your muzzle position slightly below the expected clay's ground path, and so the target will get at least slightly ahead before your swing can begin. You may have to experiment over and over until you discover the perfect muzzle position before calling. Again, because of this clay's unexpected up and down movement, you're better off swinging through this one than trying to sustain lead throughout the swing. As the clay comes out, do what you've already practiced. Start the muzzle along the clay's ground path first, then blend in the gun mount. Looking solely at the bird, swing the muzzle through the bottom of this target, then hit the trigger. Don't be afraid to hold slightly under it. Even if the shot pattern hits mainly below the flight path, enough shot will be

above the center to easily break the target. By swinging from behind it will be easier for you to make an adjustment—if the bunny bounces up to any reasonable degree. Such an adjustment can't be made as easily if you try to sustain your lead on this target. The follow through, with the head on the stock, is just as important here as with any other shot.

Try the rabbit targets first as hard crossers. Master that shot, then try some that are quartering away from you, which is a very common cottontail shot. Finally, try some straightaway rabbits, or at least nearly so. You'll have to get on top of a shooting station above the rabbit trap for the perfect straightaways, but a lot of Sporting Clays courses have such situations. The straightaway clay rabbit can be very tough to break because the pellets are only striking the edge, which is made purposely thick so it won't break during its numerous ground bounces. Consequently, you may

have to switch to a tighter choke and/or to bigger, even harder shot, depending upon distances.

As I suggested at the beginning of all this, practice to first imprint these suggestions is especially critical, but then it's just as important—if not more so— to practice, practice, practice after you know how to use these correct shotgunning basics. I've spent a good many words suggesting that you begin the swing on all targets, then blend in the gun mount. The place to get the proper feel of this can be right in your own home. Of course, select a safe place for this, and make triply certain that the gun is empty. Then simply do it over and over, setting up for a straightaway, then a hard crosser, then a high incomer, then a bouncing rabbit, in each scenario starting the swing first, then blending in the gun mount. Pretty soon everything will become automatic and you'll be on your way to bagging more game and making higher scores at this Sporting Clays game. ●

Instructors can be of great help whether you're an experienced shooter in a slump, or a newcomer to the sport. This one works with a student shooting a high incoming shot.

This is a straightaway shot on a Sporting Clays course, but two birds are in the air instead of one.

TEACHING KIDS

The future of the shooting sports depends on bringing new blood into the game, and here's a proven method for getting youngsters off on the right foot.

FOR MOST OF his life, Leon Measures has been following pointing dogs to Texas quail. He knows that developing a gun dog puppy and training a would-be Sporting Clays shooter are really the same drill. Start 'em early. Give them plenty of safe, correct repetition. Make the game easy to enter, but reasonably challenging. Make certain it is fun.

For a puppy, homing pigeons do all of that. Cheap, hardy, and simple to plant in light cover, pigeons give off lots of scent. They make puppy-pumping clatter when they flush,

then return to their loft to be used over and over again. We fly them between training sessions just to watch them careen high spirals overhead.

To Leon Measures, an air rifle is the shotgunner's training pigeon. His "Shoot Where You Look" home study kit and traveling road show use BB gun practice to hone fundamental wingshooting techniques in really young kids.

Key to the training is a Measures-modified, lever-action air rifle with a cross bolt safety. A non-slip, pebbled strip covers the wooden buttstock.

The forend is the broad, "Skeet" style found on some target shotguns.

Most importantly, the barrel of a Shoot Where You Look BB gun is stripped of any sights. Measures teaches instinctive shooting. His guns are designed to be pointed, never aimed.

You've heard about instinctive wingshooting. The method is grounded in our innate ability to accurately point at moving objects with an index finger. Guns properly mounted at what Leon calls "contact points"—hands, shoulder, face—align our

The first exercise with the BB gun has the student shooting at a paper target, and making adjustments until the BBs hit the "looking place." With practice the shots will consistently hit the mark (far right) and the shooter will be on his/her way to shooting aerial targets.

TO SHOOT

by RANDY LAWRENCE

pointing hand with our vision. If, through practice, we learn where to look, where our gun shoots, and just when to pull the trigger, our eyes and hands will instinctively direct the shot stream to intercept a moving target.

Most beginning (and far too many experienced) Clays shooters miss targets for three reasons: (1) They don't know where to look. They

sneak a peek at their gun's barrel, instead of keeping focus on the target; (2) They don't know how to look. They see only a vague orange blur, a bluster of feathers, a fleeing silhouette; (3) They stop swinging the gun at the instant they pull the trigger.

The Shoot Where You Look BB gun course begins with students learning to mount the gun the same way every time. Head erect, eyes lev-

el, the shooter brings the gun to his face. The "looking place" is a defined portion of the target. The gun barrel is a blur in our peripheral vision; never does it come into focus as the looking place.

A wingshooter's stance is balanced at about armpit width apart. The foot on the trigger hand side is a bit back and turned slightly out. The gun barrel side, or "front," foot is

pointed at the target. Weight is slightly forward, keeping the head down on the stock and, later, helping to soak up recoil.

To prepare for flying targets, Measures' students shoot at stationary ones. First is a dime-sized magic marker spot on the front of a cardboard box. Keeping both eyes open, the student picks a part of the dot as his "looking place," then brings the gun to his contact points.

The shot breaks without hesitation, the student noting where the BB hit in relation to his looking place. If the BB entry hole is high and to the left, the student looks low and to the right for the next try. Adjustments are made with each pull of the trigger until the BB consistently strikes the desired spot.

Once the BB gunner learns how to consistently shoot where he looks, a smooth, swing across the colored dot is incorporated. When the hands bring the barrel blur across the dot, the trigger is pulled without slowing the barrel.

When a youngster can hit the dot with the barrel on the move, it's on to empty cans thrown underhanded by an assistant. The schooled move to mount never changes. The student continues focusing on one part of the target, never the entire can.

Success breeds confidence. Aerial targets get smaller. Pennies spin out of the air. Aspirin tablets powder like miniature white clays. Advanced students snipe tossed BBs, one after another. Measures makes his point: the size of the target doesn't matter. The size of the looking place remains the same.

Ten shots, 100, 2000...whatever it takes to master the drill. There is no recoil to tire or intimidate the shooter. No expensive cartridge or target bill. BB gun wingshooting practice can be done in a basement, inside the garage, or against a tarp hung in the back yard. Put that tarp near a pole light, and practice can go on after dark!

When a Shoot Where You Look-trained student misses, he has a good idea of where he shot and can make adjustments. Later, if his shotgun stroke goes sour, he can return to those basic BB gun drills, resetting the touchstones of good technique. Like the pigeons we enjoy in the air when we're not training dogs, the BB gun gets regular play just because it's a kick to plink cans and puff aspirin tablets.

The meticulous text and companion video to Leon Measures' Shoot Where You Look home study course allows any motivated and conscientious adult the chance to mentor a young person into wingshooting. But moving on to the shotgun might be a great time to call in a pro.

Wingshooting publications are full of advertised traveling schools, or weekend programs at established training sites, where young people can get specialized instruction in small group settings. For one-on-one instruction, the National Sporting Clays Association certifies shotgunning teachers at various stages. Level I instructors are trained to work with the beginner/novice. Levels II and III are experienced teachers who have logged considerable instructional time and have demonstrated proficiency behind the shotgun, and over hundreds of students' shoulders.

Many teaching pros keep "school guns" on hand, often with interchangeable, adjustable stocks for a closer match to the student's physique. But for those looking to outfit

Hand-thrown targets like this pop can are great practice for body position as well as developing hand-eye coordination. Eventually, this shooter will be able to consistently hit an aspirin tossed in the air.

a young shooter, the most economical and practical first gun is the gas- or recoil-operated autoloader. Sleek repeaters such as the Browning Gold, the Beretta 390, or Remington 11-87 use the gas generated by cartridge ignition to work the action, thus bleeding off a good deal of recoil's blow. The Benelli Sport, featuring interchangeable barrel ribs and shim-adjustable stocks, ejects hulls and reloads the gun using recoil inertia. These are lightweight, dynamic firearms, fine-tuned to handle shooter-friendly target loads.

One good choice for youngsters is the Remington Light 20 Youth Model. The 20-gauge gets the nod over another great small bore, the hard-hitting 28-gauge, due to the former's lower priced cartridges and reloading components, not to mention its greater versatility in the field. However, a school gun is the perfect excuse to add a nifty 28-bore autoloader to your family's gun cabinet. The Remington Sporting 28 that ushered my wife into wingshooting handles smoothly, is virtually recoilless, and kills clays with a vengeance.

Sporting Clays has sponsored a resurgence of interest in double-barreled shotguns, particularly the over/under. There is plenty to recommend the twin-barrel gun as a teaching tool. With a flip of the top lever, it is easily shown safe. Any question of barrel obstruction, and we simply open the action and peer down the tubes.

If you're thinking of sending your youngster to shooting school with a double, check out the scaled down SKB youth line, or the Micro guns from Browning. Whatever model you choose, make certain you've matched the weight of the gun to the cartridge. Ultra-light, fixed-breech guns with heavy loads are lethal at both ends!

One reasonably priced double gun that could be cut down, then built back up as the shooter matures is the sturdy Ruger Red Label over/under 20-bore with 26-inch barrels. "Mabel," my Ruger school gun, scales around 6-1/2 recoil-sopping pounds, and is choked Skeet and Skeet for broad patterns with #9 shot.

Although Mabel has fixed chokes, most shotguns marketed today fea-

Shooter Lyndon Cox assumes the ready position for a rising, going-away target: gun against the ribs, muzzle in the anticipated flight path and just under where he will first see the target in focus.

Lyndon Cox and his mentor Greg Staats work on the rising incomer from the low Skeet house. This is one of many great novice targets easily practiced on the Skeet range. (Airport Gun Club, Lancaster, Ohio photo.)

ture interchangeable choke tubes. Don't get carried away with the variety. Our emphasis with the novice is correct shooting technique, not tube swapping. Screw in the Cylinder, Skeet, or Improved Cylinder tubes, then forget'em until it's time to clean the gun.

For now, our concern with gun fit is simply a firearm that can be consistently mounted, then fired effectively and comfortably. Until a rookie shooter develops a grooved technique, a more precise fit would be a waste of time. Master stocker Tom Smith of Weston, Ohio, suggests a shooter fire 1000 rounds through a chosen gun before being fitted by a qualified person. By qualified, we mean an individual who is, in large part, a shooting instructor. His job is to shape gun dimensions to an individual's physique, technique, and particular shooting game. If the time comes for your youngster to have a fitting, get references for Sporting Clays-specific stockers with a long list of satisfied junior customers.

As careful as we are with gun selection, we should be even more discriminating in choosing the best hearing and sight protection. Sound is carried to the inner ear via both the auditory canal as well as conduction, that is, vibrations of the skull bones. In younger shooters, skull bones are still forming, and the broader protection of a lightweight, adjustable muff, worn over a fitted pair of in-the-ear plugs, is the best auditory insurance policy against muzzle blast we can buy.

For kids and instructors, wrap-around shield shooting glasses are a secure, comfortable, economical choice. Polycarbonate lenses made by Protective optics are ballistic tested and come in compact sizes that perfectly fit smaller faces.

Baggy T-shirts may be currently fashionable, but they surely can mess up the shouldering of a shotgun. Bob Allen sportswear markets a youth vest with great features like a mesh or solid back, reloader's pouch for empties, knit side inserts, and a slick leather recoil patch set on either the right or left shoulder. Kids are image conscious; outfitting them with a decent vest that fits them affords a feeling of being "dressed for success," that they belong in the wingshooting game.

Many vests marketed for kids and women feature a padded insert that can be slipped into the shoulder pocket area. If we've done a good job matching our gun to sensible loads and if our shooter can manage a secure mount between contact points, the pad isn't necessary. In fact, it may be intrusive. From our BB gun training, we've learned exactly how it feels when the gun is properly set to shoot where we look. We don't want to be thinking about an unfamiliar mount when faced with our first Sporting Clays target: a high, slow, incomer thrown so that, undisturbed, it plops down at the shooter's feet.

We choose this particular target because of its fat, underbelly presentation, perfect for open chokes and small shot. The high incomer reinforces the move-to-mount fundamental of bringing the gun to our face and keeping it to our face as we look up at a particular portion of that target's front edge. Also, a lazy incomer doesn't cause the same rushed feeling in most students as

Gas- or recoil-operated autoloaders are novice-friendly guns because of their reduced recoil impulse. They're also cheaper than over/unders. Left to right are the Remington 11-87 Sporting, Browning Gold, Beretta 390, and Benelli Sport.

does the fleeing straightaway (which is never really straight) that new shooters sometimes get from back-yard clay target traps.

As with any new target presentation, we have the student watch a few releases so he can get his front foot pointed toward the spot where he plans to kill the target. The student calls for the bird, fixes as his looking place the leading edge of the target, and then "shoots" with his forward hand index finger just as the mark looms largest.

The ready position is one that we recall from our BB gun catechism. The stance is relaxed, yet alert, the stock of the gun resting comfortably against our ribs and tucked slightly under our armpit. The forward hand, index finger extended parallel to the barrels, should have the muzzles in the target's anticipated flight path and inserted about halfway between where we first see the target in focus and where we plan to break the shot.

We call for the bird, our hands moving on the target streak. The gun is raised into the contact points, through the looking place, and beyond. As an instructor of mine used to remind his students, the trigger pull is just something that happens along the shotgun's swing. Keep the gun moving!

Other good novice targets are the Skeet Station 7 blowing in from the high house, or Station 1 rising out of the low house. The target's path, fading ever so slightly to the shooter's side, means that though the sense is still of shooting directly at the bird, we are beginning our inventory of crossing target sight pictures. The shooter notes where he first sees the target in focus, decides where he's going to break the shot, and positions his front foot in front of that spot. This opens the hips, keeping the follow through clear.

His hands position the gun barrels halfway between the break point and where he first sees the target in focus. Looking just behind that first focus point, he calls for the bird.

Again, the looking place is a piece of the leading edge, and the shooter's hands bring the gun to that spot as the swing continues. The shot breaks just after the gun is locked into contact points. We don't chase targets with a mounted gun, riding after it to catch up. The sequence others call, "Move, mount, and

shoot" should really be, "Move-mountshoot—and keep moving."

If we're training only one shooter at a time, we build in rest periods between small series of shots. Have the student rest his arms by racking the gun. Understand that concentration windows with junior shooters are relatively small. Numerous short sessions are much more productive than marathon, pile-up-the-hulls affairs. Muscle and visual memory need reflection time to build reflex reaction.

Some Sporting Clays courses feature rabbit target stations that would simulate the same slight an-

gle we got at Skeet Station 7. This is a good target to get the student's weight over the front foot, and offers a more unpredictable target "flight," as rabbits may roll, hop, scoot, or skid on the target's hard edge. The shooter learns that his hands will subconsciously mirror the bird, no matter where it goes, if the looking place is unwavering. Again, target speed is slow to moderate; we want breaks, success in repetition, confidence in good technique.

When the student has a grasp of Station 7 or that incoming rabbit, the shooter and instructor move to

Young Lyndon Cox focusing on the "looking place" for a high incomer shows good form for making the shot—which he did!

increase target angle. Never do we let the target's angle or speed overmatch the student's stage of development. Neither do we continue to grind away, miss after miss, fatiguing the shooter and undermining all the success we've enjoyed so far.

If our youngster hits the wall, we simply move back to the last spot where he had success. We pause, talk through fundamentals, look at a few targets, then enjoy several breaks. Ideally, we stop a session while our student is still eagerly reaching for the next shell.

When we finally chaperone our new wingshooter out on the Sporting Clays course, we choose presentations that he can read and handle. But there's no harm in sprinkling a round with tougher targets, especially for goal setting and reference for future lessons.

Through that exciting first round, never forget that bird dog puppies need feathers to fetch. Young shooters need target dust hanging in the air. It's up to the trainer to offer safe practice in places and in a manner that keep tails a'wag and smiles bright. ●

Shooter Corinne Cox takes a low house incomer from Skeet Station 1. She has over-extended her forward arm, however, and fatigue will set in quickly.

Ashley Cox has a go at BB-gunning a tossed milk jug. Her mistake here is that her weight is too far back, a common one with novices. Shooters must bend at the waist with the weight over the toes of the front foot.

The best defense against hearing loss from shooting is tightly-fitted plug inserts, along with muffs. This shooter shows the correct technique for inserting plugs by reaching over his head, extending his ear, and making sure the plug is secure.

THE WINGSHOOTER'S LIBRARY

Between shooting practice and trips 'round the clays course, good books and videos reinforce the basic drill, make for a more informed shotgunner, and sometimes nudge us back outside for another go. The value of video lies in the fact that most folks are visual learners; seeing others do what we've been trying to do over a hot gun barrel can make more of the puzzle pieces fall into place. Here are five pieces I'd give to any shooter, but particularly those new to the game:

BOOKS

Davies, Ken. *The Better Shot: Step-by-Step Shotgun Technique with Holland and Holland.* Quiller Press. London. 1992. (1-212-752-7755) Sporting Clays and the shooting school concept were born out of stock fittings conducted on the great gunmakers' shooting grounds. This well-ordered, illustrated text comes straight from the cradle.

McIntosh, Michael. *Shotguns and Shooting.* Countrysport Press. Selma, Alabama. 1995. (1-800-367-4177). Readable prose, good advice, and basic background information on shotgunning by a distinguished teacher and America's best gun writer. The section on "Craft" knocks all the chaff from wingshooting instruction's wheat.

VIDEOS

Ash, Gil, and Jerry Meyer. *Optimum Shotgun Performance in Sporting Clays.* (1-800-862-6399). Along with Ash's wife, Vicki, Gil and Jerry are co-founders of the popular OSP traveling shooting school. Mr. and Mrs. Ash and Jerry Meyer are among wingshooting's most articulate teaching pros. This engaging, concise video is perfect for beginner through advanced shooters, with lots of slo-mo, over-the-rib camera sequences.

Measures, Leon. *Shoot Where You Look Exemplary Instruction.* (1-800-201-5535). Included in this package are Leon's book and video, safety glasses, and wingshooting-specific BB gun with 1500 rounds of ammo, plus healthy doses of Measures's dedication to making safe, sure shotgunners out of our children. Not only will shooters using Leon's methods get closer to some of those peskier clays targets, but any adult lucky enough to study *Shoot Where You Look* with a youngster will get a whole lot closer to him or her as well.

Mitchell, Jack, and Michael McIntosh. *Wingshooting: The Art of Shotgun Technique.* (1-800-925-3339) Jack Mitchell hails from what one might refer to as the wingshooting's "home office," the London Shooting School. Jack has nearly a half-century of teaching behind his insights on this tape, and his friend Michael McIntosh makes for a good foil and model student throughout this one-hour presentation.

DO YOU NEED A COACH?

Under the watchful eye of instructor Steve Schultz, a student in a Federal Wing and Clay Shooting School swings on a bird.

Everyone, from the green beginner to the accomplished gunner, needs a coach at some time during their shooting career, whether it's just to get started or to iron out problems.

by JIM CASADA

Veteran instructor Marty Fischer watches intently as a student fires at a target. This beginner will reap good benefits from such instruction if she practices what the coach preaches.

WHEN BROKEN BITS of clay fail to fly the way we desire, frustration can rapidly replace fun. Moreover, no matter what one's level of wingshooting expertise, the desire to perform a bit better is solidly ingrained in our competitive instincts. Practice can contribute to such improvements, as can shrewd observation of skilled shooters or other forms of self-improvement. In the final analysis, however, whether you are an experienced Clays enthusiast suffering from a temporary case of the "missing 'em blues," or a newcomer to the sport anxious to get off on the right foot, there is nothing that can completely substitute for sound coaching.

Indeed, when I posed the question that serves as the title of this article to upward of a dozen individuals—ranging from top-level professional teachers to casual shooters who enjoy a round of Sporting Clays every cou-

ple of weeks—their response was unanimous. It was a resounding "Yes!" The universal feeling in this mini-survey was that everyone could benefit from some instruction, whether it involved nothing more than a tip from a fellow shooter who noticed a problem, or extended schooling with a master teacher.

Perhaps Mike Jordan, a highly experienced shooter who serves as Manager of Public Relations for Winchester, put it best: "Sporting Clays is just like golf," he said. "How much instruction you need depends on the level of competence you want to achieve, but you can benefit from coaching at all levels."

Equipment Basics

It may sound way too simple, but the logical beginning point for any shooter experiencing problems, or setting out on a course of instruction, is to ascertain that their gun is fully functional and suitable for them. A case in point was mentioned to me by a longtime acquaintance who, while not a competitive Sporting Clays shooter, is a top-drawer competitor in pigeon shoots. "I had bought an expensive new gun," he said, "and it was custom-fitted for me. Yet the first two times I hunted doves with it I was missing far more than ordinarily is the case." He then checked the point of impact for the double barrel and discovered the left barrel shot 9 inches to the right and the right barrel 9 inches to the left. In other words, he had a total disparity of a 18 inches. That is why professional instructors customarily check to see if the gun is shooting where it's supposed to at the outset of a teaching session. It is also something experienced shooters need to keep in mind any time they acquire a new shotgun.

My friend also mentioned custom fitting, and gun fit is another consideration that can create immediate problems even though there is nothing wrong with your shooting form. All but the most expensive shotguns are products of mass production, and they are made to fit the "average" person. That means that these guns may come close to properly fitting a shooter, but chances are great that the stock will need some amount of alteration in order for the shooter to perform up to his/her potential. This is not the place for a detailed discussion of gun fit, but suffice it to say that having a shotgun that is ill-suited to your physique can create difficulties no amount of sound coaching can overcome. An instructor may not be able to fit a gun to your needs, but he can recognize the problem.

You will also want to know, if such is not already the case, which is your dominant eye. This is easily checked by pointing a gun barrel (or your finger) at some object, then alternately closing one eye and then the other to see which distorts the sight picture.

Noted instructor Marty Fischer, who holds a National Sporting Clays Association (NSCA) Level III certificate, indicates that as many as 70 percent of women have opposite eye dominance. This situation occurs much less frequently in males. Dale Christie, who heads up the Remington Shooting School, feels that one explanation for the prevalence of the situation in women is that boys are much more likely to use toys or play games that involve hand-eye coordination than girls.

Certainly identifying your dominant eye is of paramount importance, and a common misconception in this regard is the belief that one's strongest eye is dominant. That may be true, but it also may not. If you find the eye opposite the shoulder where you mount a gun is dominant, two choices present themselves. You can start over from scratch by switching shoulders. This will require the creation of some new muscle memory in mounting, gun handling, trigger pull and the like, but most instructors feel it is the ideal solution. For those who feel uncomfortable with starting over, such as someone who has hunted birds for a lifetime, there are various devices that can be used to block out enough of your dominant eye's field of vision to force the other eye to take over.

All of these factors—point of aim, gun fit, and eye dominance— are things a competent instructor will address at the outset before actual teaching even begins. Even for experienced shooters, though, point

of aim and gun fit need to be addressed whenever a new shotgun is being used, and everyone should know which eye is dominant in order to shoot at the maximum level of their ability.

Working With Beginners

Once those preliminaries are out of the way, serious instruction moves to the forefront. Prospective pupils fall into three distinct categories—rank beginners who have done little shooting of any kind; relative newcomers to Sporting Clays who have considerable wingshooting experience of other sorts; and those who have already had quite a bit of exposure to the sport.

For those who truly merit the description tyro, there is little doubt that instruction from the outset is the best approach. That way, in the words of Marty Fischer, "a shooter does not acquire any bad habits, because it is difficult to undo them." For a true beginner, there are a number of lessons, such as gun safety and the basics of gun operation to learn before moving on to the actual mechanics of how to go about breaking targets.

Instilling proper techniques, then using them with consistency, lie at the heart of solid Sporting Clays performance at any level. Proper gun mount is of the utmost importance, and a solid indication of this is the fact that top-drawer shooters practice mounting every day. Several of the most common reasons for miss-

Using a miniature clay bird to make a point, instructor Steve Schultz explains the concept of lead and the importance of picking up the target quickly to a pupil.

ing targets focus on improper gun mounting. For example, there's the frequent failure, as some laughingly put it, "to get wood to wood" (i.e., the stock flush against the cheek). This can come about in one of two ways: failure to lift the gun until it is flush with the cheek; or the all too understandable tendency to raise the head in order to take a peek.

Other frequently encountered problems include closing one eye as if shooting a rifle, stopping gun swing, aiming rather than pointing, poor timing of the shot, poor foot position, and jerking rather than squeezing the trigger. For beginners, these can be avoided from the outset with a good teacher in the "kindergarten of Clays," one of the staunchest arguments for getting meaningful instruc-

tion. If good techniques have been instilled from the outset, it will prove much easier to overcome lapses in form (and they inevitably will happen) resulting in a spate of poor shooting.

The newcomer has several choices when it comes to initiating the learning process. Taking the formal route by attending a school or paying for professional instruction is probably most effective, but can also be quite expensive. An alternative suggested by Mike Jordan is to seek out one of the best shooters at the local club and see if they will offer some basic insights. "You can also learn quite a bit simply by observing a fine shot," Jordan adds, so don't be afraid to hang around the better shooters to see how they do what they do best.

Help for Intermediate Shooters

With Sporting Clays growing by leaps and bounds even as some types of wingshooting (in particular, quail hunting) decline, and with more and more lodges having Sporting Clays ranges on the grounds, lots of sportsmen are being exposed to the Clays experience. Dale Christie describes the typical background for shotgunners who fall into this category. "They are people," he says, "who have handled guns in the field as hunters—maybe a lot. If they are lifelong sportsmen, they began with BB guns, progressed to a 22, then a small shotgun, and finally to a 12-gauge. In all likelihood, except for some hunter safety education and a

Fischer points out to this student where she should first pick up a springing teal target (above), then follows her swing over her shoulder to determine whether she is using the right amount of lead and/or stopping her swing.

minimum coverage of gun handling, they have no other training."

Yours truly falls into this category, and I had shot perhaps a dozen rounds of Sporting Clays with, at best, a modicum of success. Then I had an opportunity to spend three days at a Federal shooting school under the tutelage of Steve Schultz and his daughter, Stephanie, both highly qualified instructors, and it opened my eyes in a major way. Never mind the fact that over the years I had shot thousands of rounds at all sorts of flying critters, I had a whole host of bad habits. Getting rid of them involved the sizable task of converting a shameless sinner to the straight and narrow way of proper technique. With lots of patience on the part of the Schultz duo though, along with plenty of trigger pulls, my progress was nothing short of remarkable. By school's end my performance was quite credible, although I must confess that in short order there was some backsliding on my part because of a lack of ongoing practice.

The message that school sent is quite clear. Chances are that anyone coming from the game field to the Clays course will have their fair share of faults. In many cases, unlearning these deeply entrenched bad habits actually demands more teaching expertise than is required to get a beginner started. The familiar adage about not being able to teach an old dog new tricks is all too applicable.

The Experienced Shooter

Even the finest shooters can and do run into shooting slumps. If these are prolonged, they have the potential to turn from problems of technique, which usually lie at the heart of the matter, to the mental sphere. You start second guessing every shot, making one adjustment after another without rhyme or reason, and first thing you know, the wheels have really run off your shooting cart.

One plausible solution, particularly if you can do this at the beginning of a slump, is to ask a competent friend for some help. Sometimes he will notice some small hitch in your technique and be able to point it out. Another alternative falls in the

Visiting instructors usually prefer small classes of shooters to keep instruction on a more personal level, and allow more time for individual help.

Quite often, fellow shooters can pick up on small problems with your shooting form through close observation. Most shooters are happy to help out in this regard, if they're able.

Steve Shultz teaches pupils that pointing a finger at a target is quite similar to the way they point the gun, so gun mount and shooting should come easily. It's simply a matter of mechanics.

"shooter heal thyself" category. Both Marty Fischer and Dale Christie have some useful thoughts in this regard. They strongly suggest going back to the basics.

Christie draws particular attention to foot position. As he humorously puts it, "Make sure not just your gun but your belly button points where it should." Sometimes faulty foot placement starts a whole series of problems that result in the body being awkwardly contorted at the point where the shot should be taken. Fischer, for his part, says that the worst thing you can do is miss repeatedly and not have a clue as to what you are doing wrong. "When a particular shot gives you trouble," he suggests, "try it slower and closer. Once you are breaking birds with consistency, gradually work back up to the point where you can deal with the situation which had been troubling you."

By the same token, both these experts make a point of saying that watching or listening to others can have their limitations. "After all," comments Christie, "a good coach isn't trying to create clones. Instead he tries to discern strengths and work on weaknesses." In Fischer's view, "It can be informative to watch others, but once you have techniques that work for you, stick to your game."

There are some coaching tips which, if kept constantly in mind, can always be beneficial to you no matter what your level of skill. On the mental side of the equation, concentration and sensible planning should be at the forefront. There is a reason you are shown a target before shooting, and when you see it you should program yourself with some key considerations in mind—where you can see the bird clearly, where you want to position the gun, and where you want to break the target.

As for physical performance, always be aware of your mechanics. Smooth, consistent gun mount with minimal unnecessary movement should be as close to automatic as the human body can be. As Marty Fischer explains it, "Good shooters always look like they are in slow motion. When the gun is fully mounted they are ready to shoot and do so, breaking the bird."

That fluidity of mechanics and efficiency of performance that characterizes top shooters is what every Clays participant seeks. Coaching, whether it comes from a trained professional, a helpful fellow shooter, personal observation, reading, videos or a combination of these, unquestionably can be helpful. After all, in Sporting Clays as in all aspects of life, we study with success in mind. Appropriate guidance in the form of a coach or instructor can make that success more readily obtainable. ●

Proper gun fit, preferably undertaken by a skilled craftsman who really knows his work, should be determined before serious instruction begins.

Marty Fischer (left) performs some makeshift gun fitting to help a student. If such a modification does help, then a more permanent change to the gun can be made. Where would this world be without duct tape?

A good coach needs to get up close and personal to determine what area of technique needs work, then must figure out how to fix what's wrong. Sometimes bad habits must be unlearned.

Accompanying the rapid growth in the popularity of Sporting Clays has been the development of formal shooting schools. The instruction offered by these schools varies appreciably, from short, individualized sessions to programs stretching over two or three days. Most Sporting Clays courses host guest instructors periodically through the year, or you can opt to attend one of the numerous national schools. The teachers are usually individuals who have certification from the National Sporting Clays Association, which certifies instructors at Levels I, II and III (the latter is the highest rating). These schools are especially useful for the person who is relatively new to the sport or for those who have shot some Sporting Clays but have not enjoyed the benefits of formal instruction. The major national schools are listed here and they can all provide detailed guidance in helping you become a smoother and more proficient marksman. Many offer regional schools along with the programs at the headquarters.

**Federal Wing and
  Clay Shooting School**
900 Ehlen Drive
Anoka, MN 55303
800-888.WING

L.L. Bean Shooting School
Casco Street
Freeport, ME 04033
800-341-4341

**Marty Fischer Sport
Shooting Consultants, Ltd.**
P.O. Box 207
Rincon, GA 31326?
912-826-0072

**Northwest Wing & Clay
Shooting School**
4607 NE Cedar Creek Rd.
Woodland, WA 98674
360-225-5000

Orvis Shootng Schools
Historic Route 7A
Manchester, VT 05254
800-235-9763

**Remington
Shooting School**
14 Hoefler Ave.
Ilion, NY 13357
800-742-7053

**Sporting Classics
Wingshooting School**
  (presented by Beretta)
233-A King St.
Charleston, SC 29401
888-636-8654

For those interested in becoming teachers or simply learning more about how to coach fellow shooters, the NSCA offers an instructor's school. Contact them at NSCA, 5931 Roft Rd., San Antonio, TX 78253.

VIDEO INSTRUCTION

Predictably, the upsurge in the popularity of Sporting Clays has given rise to the production of a host of how-to videos. These are available through various retail outlets and mail order catalogs. The tapes that focus specifically on instruction are listed below:

Andy Duffy's Approach to Winning BIG in Sporting Clays—85 minutes.

The Art of Shooting Flying—two tapes, 120 minutes.

The Comfortable Shooter with Henry Baskerville—60 minutes.

Hitting the Hard Shots in Sporting Clays (instruction from Gary Phillips and Katy Skahill)—70 minutes.

Jon Kruger's Secrets to Success in Sporting Clays—60 minutes.

Optimum Shotgun Performance in Sporting Clays (instruction from Gil Ash and Jerry Meyer)—120 minutes.

Sporting Clays—Develop Your Own Style of Shooting with Marty Fischer—80 minutes.

CLAYS FOR HUNTERS

Competition is fine for some shooters, but what about those who simply want practice for game shooting? Here are some excellent points to ponder.

by TERRY WIELAND

Having your own informal Clays range gives you great flexibility in the presentation of the birds, and reactions to unexpected situations.

Using the natural terrain means simulating actual hunting conditions as you might find them while hunting grouse or pheasant.

SOME YEARS AGO, a rather naive young man drove into a local trap club and pulled a gun out of his car. He snapped it together, bought a couple of Skeet tickets, and walked up to the firing line, ready to go.

The group of regulars standing around took one look at his gun and began to exchange strange glances. When he took his place and called "Pull" the first time, they knew they were dealing with an absolute beginner, and one took it upon himself to walk over to the newcomer, firmly grasp his gun from where it rested under his arm, and pull it up to his shoulder.

"There," he said, "You shoot from the shoulder. You don't want the gun down. It costs you birds!" And he walked away.

The newcomer (me, in case you haven't guessed) rather sheepishly left the gun up, shot an abysmal round, and left. My first experiment in training for live birds on inanimate clays ended in total failure.

The gun I had that day was a Browning side-by-side 20-gauge, choked Modified and Full, with 26-inch barrels. Hardly a Skeet gun, and hence the disdainful looks of the serious club shooters. Shooting from the gun down position was even worse. My hesitant attempt to explain that I just wanted to practice with my field gun, and that I did not care about breaking 25 straight, cut no ice whatever. I left, and never went back there.

That incident took place in the days before Sporting Clays had taken North America by storm, and

from what I have seen, it was not an isolated event. Even today, the serious bird shooter who wants to use clay-target shooting primarily as practice for the field is at a disadvantage unless he is a member of a very tolerant club, or owns a farm where he can set up his own traps and call his own shots.

The twin sports of trap and Skeet have come a long way from their beginnings. Trap originated as practice for formal live pigeon shooting, while Skeet was supposed to resemble grouse hunting. Today, both are highly formalized pastimes in which score matters above all else, and runs of hundreds of birds straight are not unusual even at the local club level. Any resemblance that either one bears to live game shooting has long since been lost.

Practice those shots that give the most trouble. Otherwise you're simply breaking clay targets and wasting time.

By joining an informal Sporting Clays club, you should be able to concentrate more on practicing game shots than simply keeping score. Hinton photo.

Sporting Clays came along at about the same time as Skeet and for exactly the same reason. It originated in England around 1925 and the intent was to simulate wingshooting in every respect—from incoming high pheasants, to ground-skimming red grouse, to dipping, diving wood pigeons and going-away partridge. The traps were not all the same, the clays were of different sizes and had varying flight characteristics, and the stations were set up in different terrain. The emphasis was on reacting to the unexpected—just like hunting ruffed grouse in thick cover, or darting doves over a wheat field.

Since Sporting Clays came to North America, the game has both grown enormously in popularity, and also fallen victim to the disease that robbed trap and Skeet of much of their appeal: an obsession with keeping score. This obsession has led to specialized Sporting Clays guns with interchangeable chokes, demands for standardized courses, and even the suggestion that shooting be allowed from the "gun mounted" position. Needless to say, all of this detracts from the game's value for its original purpose, which is practice for live game.

All of this being the case, what is a devoted bird shooter, who wants to practice on clays solely for the purpose of improving his field shooting, supposed to do?

First of all, join a good Sporting Clays club. You may have to visit a couple of them to find one that suits your tastes and needs, but it is time well spent. Look for an informal club, above all. Just like with hunting, it pays to scout the territory ahead of time. You can't beat 'em unless you join 'em.

Second, be prepared to insist on doing it your way, with your gun, and don't even carry a score card. This is easy to say, but a little more difficult to do. People are naturally competitive, and nobody likes to walk off the course with the lowest score in the group. This is something you have to be prepared to accept, however, if you shoot a field gun because you will be dealing with some natural disadvantages. In the end, remember your initial goal: practice for hunting, not competition.

A few years ago, I was shooting Sporting with Dan Carlisle, the Olympic bronze medalist, as my instructor. My gun was a light English side-by-side with double triggers, and I was shooting it unmounted (naturally) and calling the shot with the safety on. When shooting, I always slide the safety off as the gun comes to my shoulder; this is the proper way in game shooting, and is so natural to me after a lifetime that if I don't feel the safety click off as the gun comes up, it throws my concentration.

Dan pointed out that in terms of scoring, I was putting myself at a definite disadvantage. "On average, having the safety on will cost you five birds out of a hundred," he told me, "And likewise for double triggers."

In other words, shooting my game gun in game-gun style, rather than taking advantage of the rules of Sporting Clays, means that the best score I should ever expect is 90 out of 100. Well, tough, thought I. It will pay off on grouse and quail and doves, and that's what really counts, not dusting a few extra clays. Still, it takes some will power to deliberately put yourself at a disadvantage in front of an audience.

Similarly, though, you can make it work to your advantage.

I shot IPSC for a while, using a Smith & Wesson 44 Magnum Mountain Revolver instead of the usual competition 45 Auto. I did training courses with it, and shot the competitions with it. I learned to speed-load that revolver lightning-quick. Why? Because I had had a very close call with an Alaska brown bear and I wanted practice with the gun I carry in bad-bear country.

I never won an IPSC match with the wheelgun, needless to say, but I had my own mental score card. Any time I did not finish dead last, shooting a heavy hunting gun against tuned competition pieces, was a victory. One time, five other competitors finished below me in a field of about 30, and I was the only revolver shooter. That was a triumph for me, and I accomplished what I set out to do, which was become totally confident with the gun that might be called upon to save my life.

Taking the same approach at a Skeet, trap or Sporting Clays range allows you to practice what you want, the way you want to, yet keep a kind of mental tally that shows your progress.

That, however, is only the beginning.

To really use these games as practice for the field, you have to duplicate field conditions in every way possible. That means wearing the clothes you normally hunt in (including a heavy jacket and gloves) and carrying your cartridges in a belt or pocket, not in a convenient pouch. It also means going out deliberately in bad weather and learning to cope with wind and rain. An advantage of that is that the range is likely to be sparsely populated.

I have found that it helps a lot to go with at least one other friend who is doing the same thing I am because it gives moral support, and it also gives you someone to compare notes with.

Something that is both fun and useful to do is occasionally shoot an entire round using the wrong choke.

Put in Modified and Full, or even Full and Extra-Full, when the right choke would be wide open; this is a situation you often encounter in hunting. The results will be educational, and you might even surprise yourself with how well you can do.

For those lucky enough to have access to one, a private range with a good trap is by far the most useful simply because it is versatile and provides the greatest variety of shots.

Practicing on a Formal Clays Range (Skeet or Sporting)

1. Shoot your field gun as you would in the field, and forget about changing chokes during a round.

2. Dress in hunting clothes, including a heavy jacket, orange vest, hat and gloves, and carry your cartridges in a belt or pocket. Get used to manipulating the gun with gloves on.

3. Make a point of occasionally shooting in cold, windy and rainy weather.

4. Go with a friend who is doing the same thing you are. It will give you moral support.

5. Insofar as the range allows it, use the loads you will hunt with, or as close to it as you can get.

6. Within the limits of safety (and the club rules) shoot from a variety of typical field-carry positions, not just the legal gun-down position.

7. Arrange with the trapper to throw several birds in a row on report, to give you practice reloading quickly.

8. Use the safety on your gun exactly the way you would in a hunting situation. Do not flick it off before you call for the clay.

The main shooting position in the Grouse Butt range at West Wycombe simulates those used on the moors. A half-dozen traps combine to send birds at all angles and heights.

This is an area in which we can learn from the English, who regularly use clays as practice for game shooting.

The best English shooting grounds, such as West Wycombe, near London, give shooters a wide variety of clays games including conventional trap and Skeet, multi-station Sporting Clays layouts that can be programmed to different levels of difficulty, high and medium towers, Compact Sporting (similar to our five-stand) in which you shoot from different stations in a line at clays thrown from half a dozen traps beside, behind and in front of you. West Wycombe also has one range set up to simulate driven red grouse, the high-speed, ground-skimming bird that presents the most dangerous

form of wingshooting. There, you shoot from a butt sunk in the ground, or from one part way up a hill, shooting down at the clays.

Shooters go to West Wycombe in advance of the grouse, pheasant and partridge seasons to brush up on specific aspects of shooting, and most of the time there is nary a score card to be seen. What is even more common is to book an instructor for an hour's lesson.

Steve Denny, the director of West Wycombe, insists that "a broken clay is a wasted clay," meaning that breaking bird after bird teaches you nothing. If you want to learn, go to a station where you miss a lot and work on breaking those targets. This means overcoming our natural ten-

dency to spend more time at what we do best, and less at what we need to work on.

At a private range, this can be worked on in a very effective way that is normally not possible at a formal club.

Let's say you have no trouble whatever with birds going away and rising, lower right to upper left. You hardly ever miss, in fact. But you have real trouble with the same bird when you are 40 yards out in front and it is coming at you and flying over your right shoulder.

On your own range, you can have your trapper throw that bird as you move, a yard or even a foot at a time, from the position where you are most comfortable to the one where

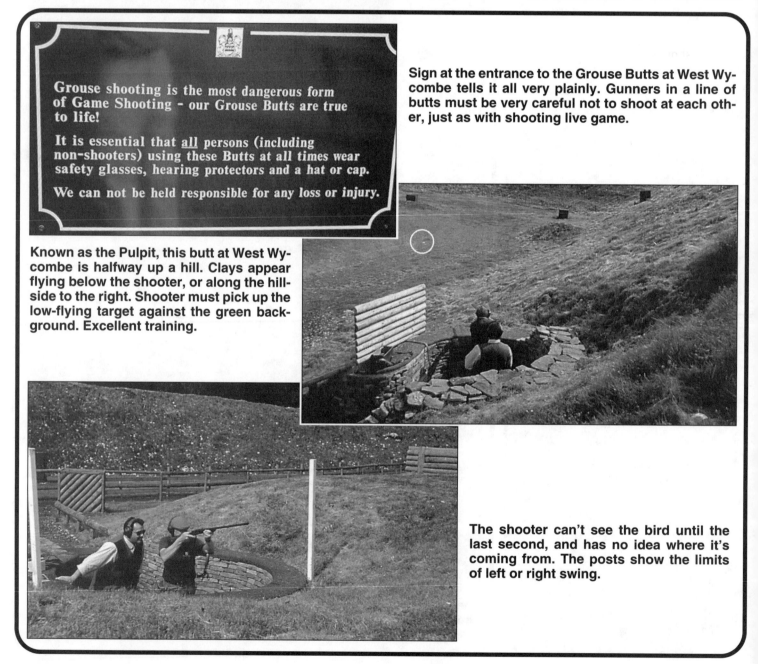

Sign at the entrance to the Grouse Butts at West Wycombe tells it all very plainly. Gunners in a line of butts must be very careful not to shoot at each other, just as with shooting live game.

Grouse shooting is the most dangerous form of Game Shooting - our Grouse Butts are true to life!

It is essential that all persons (including non-shooters) using these Butts at all times wear safety glasses, hearing protectors and a hat or cap.

We can not be held responsible for any loss or injury.

Known as the Pulpit, this butt at West Wycombe is halfway up a hill. Clays appear flying below the shooter, or along the hillside to the right. Shooter must pick up the low-flying target against the green background. Excellent training.

The shooter can't see the bird until the last second, and has no idea where it's coming from. The posts show the limits of left or right swing.

you are least proficient, making small adjustments as you go. If you run into a spot where you simply can't hit anything, retreat to one where you can and pick it up again. If you think that sounds a little like the stations at Skeet, you're right, except that the range of presentations—distances, angles and bird speeds—is almost infinite, unlike Skeet which is a set of predictable stations.

It is also a good idea to mix it up. Spend an hour without calling "Pull." Simply allow your trapper to release the bird when he sees you are reloaded, and surprise you with both timing and presentation. Or mix black clays with orange ones, and declare one a protected species; then throw them in threes or fours, and force the shooter to pick out the proper targets.

You should also use the terrain and the undergrowth to simulate real conditions. Instead of launching birds over a wide open field, stand behind some bushes and shoot at them as they come over, not knowing whether they will be to right or left, in pairs or singles.

If there are two shooters, throw different colored birds and assign each gun a color to shoot at, and none other. Or take adjacent butts 20 yards apart and throw birds in between at varying heights. This will get you used to the idea of not shooting down a line when birds are being driven, as well as picking out which birds are yours and not poaching your neighbor's.

Needless to say, all of the foregoing present more than the usual potential hazards for the shooters and the trapper, so you need to be conscious of safety above all. But that, too, is essential training for the field.

Instead of simply calling "Pull" and waiting for the clay to appear, secure in the knowledge that it is clear shooting down range, you have to be aware at all times of where everyone else is, what they are doing, and what you are shooting at. This requires the utmost in concentration—which, of course, is the key to good shooting whether the target is a whizzing clay, a lofty pheasant, or a ruffed grouse glimpsed through the branches.

And, really, that's what it's all about. ●

The high tower is a staple of English Sporting Clays shooting because of the popularity of driven pheasants. Shooter has only a limited view of birds thrown from the tower.

West Wycombe Compact Sporting layout is similar to North American Five-Stand. There are six positions and six or more traps. It gives the shooter excellent variety for training for game shooting.

TODAY'S CLAYS GUNS

You don't need a special gun for Sporting Clays, but if you get bitten by the bug there are lots to choose from in styles and price to fit nearly everyone.

by RICK HINTON

Over/unders and autoloaders are the preferred types of shotguns for Sporting Clays shooting. The autos are a bit easier on the shoulder.

TODAY'S SPORTING CLAYS gun typically has a barrel length of 24, 26, 28, 30 or 32 inches, or if it's European-made, somewhere in between. Some Sporting guns will have one barrel, others will have two, stacked or side by side, of course. The actions on single-barrel guns typically will be gas- or recoil-operated semi-automatics, or pump actions. The bells and whistles such as porting, overboring, lengthened forcing cones, aftermarket chokes and specialty recoil pads, may or may not be present. In other words, today's Sporting Clays gun is as typical as today's typical Sporting Clays shooter.

Take a group I frequently shot with last spring. One fellow was using a Sporting Clays model over/under that was fitted with a couple hundred dollars worth of Briley replacement chokes. The barrels had been sent off for porting and other work. He hauled his shells, chokes and other accessories around in a pull-cart. Another fellow was using his goose gun, an out-of-production, gas-operated autoloader with a 3-inch chamber. Reliability with 2 3/4-inch target loads, even with 3-dram shells, was iffy, at best. After suffering more gun malfunctions than attempted targets, he moved into a loaner O/U. A third fellow was shooting a basic pump-action 20-gauge. It sported the Modified screw-in choke it came with, and he didn't own any spares. His most-practiced shooting move was to wipe short-shucked hulls out of the ejection port with his trigger hand and still get off a second shot. To carry his shells, he used a fanny pack that was part of his bow-hunting gear. The fourth and fifth shooters were longtime hunting partners. Each owned identical O/U field guns, equipped with the typical Big Three screw-in tubes: Improved Cylinder, Modified and Full. They carried shells and extra chokes in game vests. As for me, I shoot the flavor of the month—whatever gun happens to have landed on my doorstep for testing and evaluation articles in another publication.

If we look closely at our microcosm, we'll see the two faces of Sporting Clays:

The first, and biggest, group includes hunters who are shooting clay targets primarily for recreation. The add-on benefits include improving shooting skills and gaining familiarity with their hunting gun of choice.

The second group numbers year-round shotgunners who are shooting clay targets as practice for upcoming registered events. Whether they're preparing for a league or a competition, their shooting time also sharpens their skills for upland bird hunting.

Now, if we break the "typical" Sporting Clays gun into those two categories, we can make some sense of it.

The majority of Sporting Clays shooters fall into the first category. (I'm guessing here because hard numbers for grass-roots Sporting Clays shooters are as difficult to pinpoint as the next afternoon's active mourning dove field. At my local club, for example, once-a-week regular shooters outnumber registered-target shooters at least six to one. I can't imagine that ratio being radically different elsewhere.) These hunters will show up at the Clays course with their favorite—or, perhaps, only—hunting gun. They'll endure the missed targets due to a short-shucked pump or a jammed autoloader. If they even consider buying a new gun, it will be a hunting gun first. Ironically that's the way Sporting Clays started in his country. In its U.S. infancy in the early to mid-1980s, Sporting's pitch to hunters was, "There's no need to buy a special gun for Sporting Clays. It's a hunter's game, so bring your favorite hunting gun."

While that slogan has been drowned in wave after wave of new "Sporting Clays" model shotguns, shooting the hunting gun is still the popular and practical approach for most recreational Clays shooters.

Many industry observers credit Sporting Clays with revitalizing the gun industry, or at least the smooth-bore end of it. There must be some truth to it, because even now, in the late '90s, long-established gun makers still are introducing new Sporting model guns. And there are plenty of new importers, distributors, and aftermarket companies with these models. The combined offerings are dazzling and bewildering. While over/unders occupy most of the Competition Gun catalog space, semi-autos are increasingly popular.

The line separating field guns and Sporting Clays models is blurry at best and fuzzy at worst. Every gun manufacturer has distinctions for field and Sporting models, and very few are alike. If there was an industry standard for distinguishing the two types, here's a list of the most common tweaks you'd find on a Sporting shotgun:

A barrel with a bore larger than standard 12-gauge, which is .729-inch, give or take a thousandth of an

Shooting doubles is a common practice and is much easier done with an auto or over/under than with a pump gun. Forget using a bolt-action or single shot for these target presentations.

inch or so. Overbored, or backbored, barrels will range from .740 on up. The purpose of the bigger bore is to facilitate the shot's passage through it. Imagine a school's hallway that accommodates five kids abreast. Imagine another that handles eight kids across. If each school has 500 pupils, which school's hallway is better equipped to move kids outside for a practice fire drill? The one with the bigger hall, right? It's the same with shotgun bores. The bigger passageway for the shot payload during its journey from cartridge case to choke constriction means fewer pellets will be damaged. And deformed pellets, which are less aerodynamic, tend to peel out of the pattern or to bump into other pellets in the pattern. The less the stress inside the bore the greater the number of pellets will remain in the pattern, and that downrange efficiency helps break more targets. Another benefit is a reduction in recoil because the shot payload is encountering less resistance.

A lengthened forcing cone. The forcing cone is the transition area between the chamber and the narrower bore. In most hunting

More screw-in choke selection. Most Sporting shotguns will come with more than the customary Improved Cylinder, Modified and Full chokes. Four or five choke tubes are more typical. The selection almost always includes a Skeet tube, which throws a looser pattern than Improved Cylinder. An Improved Modified tube often replaces the Full choke. Its pattern is tighter than Modified, but looser than Full. The fifth choke could be a second Skeet tube or a Full choke tube. Most gun companies offer extra choke tubes as accessories, often in constrictions not included in the Sporting package. There also are plenty of companies that specialize in aftermarket choke tubes. Most offer replacement tubes that are threaded to fit the more popular model shotguns. Most of these outfits also offer custom choke installation which will more closely match their tubes to your gun's inside bore diameter. Inside bore diameters of two guns from the same manufacturer can vary by several thousandths of an inch. That

difference can turn what's supposed to be a Skeet choke into one that's closer to Cylinder, which has no constriction, or Improved Cylinder.

A more efficient recoil pad. While a plastic buttplate or a ventilated recoil pad are fairly standard on hunting guns, Sporting guns often come with solid rubber recoil pads often made of high-tech material to help soak up recoil. Some pads are rounded at the top to help ensure a snag-free gun mount. In the beginning, Sporting Clays rules required a shooter to start with a low gun until the target was visible; rules now allow a shooter to cheek the gun before calling for the target, but Sporting Clays pads still are more accommodating for the low-gun shooter and better equipped to soak up recoil.

A more robust gun. A year-round competition shooter is capable of putting more shells through his or her gun in a year than an average hunter puts through old Betsy in a lifetime. Many Sporting guns are better designed to stand up to that high volume of shells. The more robust design

Browning 802 ES Sporting Clays with extended choke tubes.

guns, the forcing cone is shoulder shaped. In broad terms, the forcing cone resembles that sloped area between a toothpaste container's tube and its spout, with the tube being the chamber and the spout being the barrel. The more pronounced the difference, the more violently the shot is squeezed into the barrel. A lengthened forcing cone replaces the shoulder with a taper, allowing the shot to begin its trip by being gently compressed into the barrel. That gentler start also will help reduce recoil.

Porting means barrels that have little holes (ports) at the muzzle end. The holes bleed off some of the gases that are created during the ignition of the shotgun cartridge. That bleed-off primarily helps reduce muzzle flip. A muzzle that's more under control allows for quicker and easier acquisition of the second target. There may be some recoil reduction benefits, as well, although I won't swear to it.

An old saw about Sporting being a hunter's game meant shooters needed only to bring their hunting gun. Despite so many Sporting Clays model shotguns on the market, many shooters follow that original advice.

may add a few ounces to the gun's weight, but it will help dampen recoil. And a bit of extra weight on a Sporting gun doesn't have the carry factor it might have on a field gun that an upland bird hunter may lug around all day. A pound can make a huge difference here.

Stock dimensions may or may not differ from field guns. Some companies offer adjustable combs that can be changed for drop and cast; others offer extra shims that fit between the rear of the receiver and the stock. Changing the shim alters the stock's drop and cast. But one size fits all pretty well sums up stocks on most Sporting as well as field guns, even with high-grade models.

Other differences may or may not include 2-3/4-inch chambers designed solely for target loads; tapered top ribs, inevitably fitted with a mid-bead, that signature center

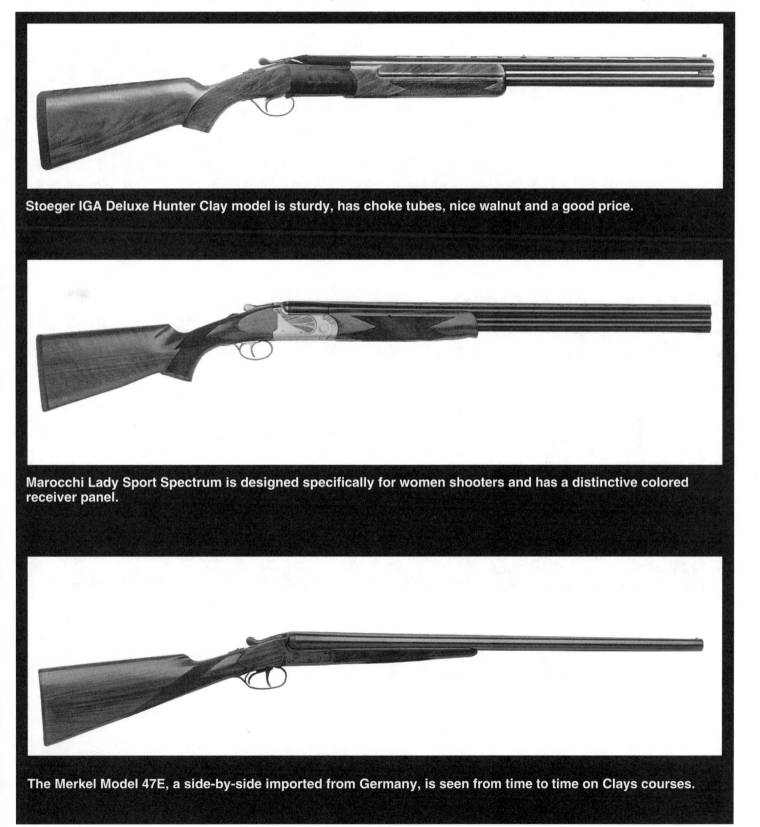

Stoeger IGA Deluxe Hunter Clay model is sturdy, has choke tubes, nice walnut and a good price.

Marocchi Lady Sport Spectrum is designed specifically for women shooters and has a distinctive colored receiver panel.

The Merkel Model 47E, a side-by-side imported from Germany, is seen from time to time on Clays courses.

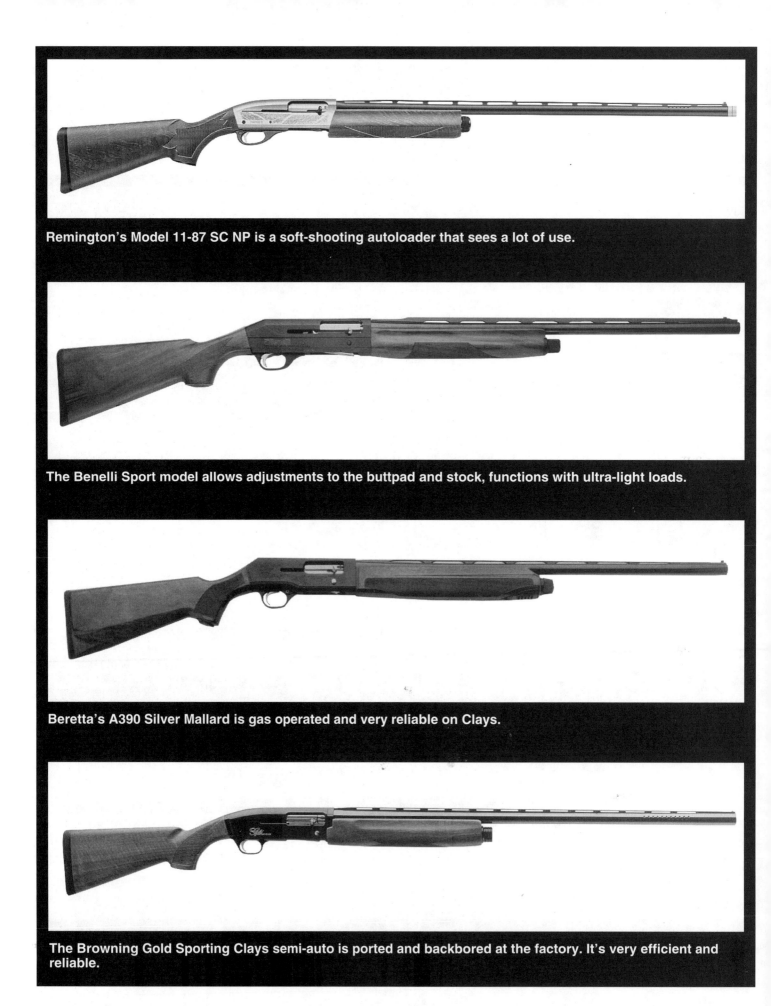

Remington's Model 11-87 SC NP is a soft-shooting autoloader that sees a lot of use.

The Benelli Sport model allows adjustments to the buttpad and stock, functions with ultra-light loads.

Beretta's A390 Silver Mallard is gas operated and very reliable on Clays.

The Browning Gold Sporting Clays semi-auto is ported and backbored at the factory. It's very efficient and reliable.

post that almost every Sporting gun wears; a ventilated mid-rib between the barrels of an O/U to help dissipate heat buildup when shooting.

Money does talk, of course. Gun makers at the higher end of the price ladder will accommodate some degree of customer-specific requests. The more bucks spent, the more customized the gun will be.

If you attend any major Sporting Clays shoot, you'll see gun selection pretty well limited to O/Us or semi-automatics. You may find an occasional side-by-side, but pump-action guns are almost extinct in competitive open Sporting events.

There are advantages and disadvantages to O/Us and autoloaders. The biggest plus for autoloaders—especially gas-operated models—is reduced recoil. Over a long day of shooting, recoil can be fatiguing, and fatigue can cost a shooter targets, especially toward the end of a round. Cost is another plus. A good semi-auto will cost about half what an O/U runs. Reliability, which used to be such a problem, is not much of a factor among the latest model autos. If a modern semi-auto does get balky during a round, there often is a between-station fix, including a quick field-stripping and either wiping down or oiling the innards.

Over/under fans tout the advantage of two chokes, and that is an advantage if a course setter serves up lots of pairs that feature close and far birds. But on most courses such pairs are the exception more than the rule. The O/U also is friendlier to reloaders who can grab and stash hulls every time they break open the gun. Because of that break-open design, the stackbarrel is easier and safer to carry between stations. The underside of the receiver is a natural spot to hold the gun, and it rides comfortably atop a shoulder, too. An over/under is safer, also; breaking it open renders it unshootable, even if it's loaded. But if a superposed gun gets balky during a round, odds favor it being finished for the day.

The average cost of a Sporting model O/U is $1,500, give or take $500. The average cost of a Sporting model semi-auto is $700, give or take. A side-by-side generally will cost more than an over/under.

Those prices are mentioned here for the recreational shooter who gets bitten by Sporting Clays and starts looking for a Clays gun. It does happen, and far more frequently than a non-shooting spouse wants to know about.

So if you are scratching that Sporting Clays itch, here's a brief sampling of what's out there in 12-gauge Sporting model shotguns.

Sporting Model Autoloaders

Beretta's 390 and Browning's Gold are probably the best known. Other brands include Fabarms' Red or Gold Lions (offered through Heckler & Koch, Inc.), Remington's 11-87 and Benelli's short-recoil-operated Sport. At least two aftermarket companies, Ballistic Specialties and Seminole Gun Works, offer Beretta 390 and/or Browning Gold packages that include the gun with most of the features I've already listed. Those companies, as well as Briley Manufacturing, will do custom work on your gun as well, including forcing cones, porting, overboring and matching chokes to bores.

Sporting Model Over/Unders

It's easier to list the gun makers who don't offer a Sporting Clays model than those that do, but I'll refrain from pointing any fingers.

Prices vary widely, starting at under $1,000 and going as high as some home mortgages.

As a rule of thumb, anyway, the higher the price goes, the fancier the wood and engraving get, the easier the on-the-course repairs become and the more customer-specific the features are. Remember that prices among the more basic offerings may vary from suggested retail. If your area has competing gun shops, the better opportunity you have to wheel and deal when buying.

Probably the least expensive Sporting model available is the TR-SC from Tristar Sporting Arms. It's imported from Italy and also is available in a ladies model with a stock designed specifically for a woman. American Arms offers their Spanish-made Silver Sporting which seems to be a good value. Benelli USA recently picked up the Franchi line and will offer the Alcione Sport.

In addition to the Alcione, other middle-priced guns include Beretta's 686s and 687s, plus its 682 Gold competition models. Browning has the popular 425, including a ladies model, the Ultra and the 802 ES. Con-

necticut Valley Classics/Cooper Arms makes upgraded versions of the old Winchester 101. Fabarm, distributed by Heckler & Koch, Inc., numbers a Black Lion Competition gun among its offerings. Marocchi (from Precision Sales) has the Conquista, including left-hand and ladies' models. Remington sells the Model 396 through its custom shop. Sigarms' Sporting models include the SA 3 and SA 5. SKB's Sporting models are the higher-end 785s, the 585s and 505s. Weatherby has a new Orion SSC gun that joins the Athena and Orion lines of Sporting models.

Some of the companies with mid-price offerings do make high-grade guns as well. Importers who handle high-dollar guns include K.B.I. with the extensive Charles Daly line, which has a Sporting model among its offerings, Dynamit Nobel RWS which carries the German-made Rottweil Paragon. Gamba, imported by the The Firing Line in Colorado, makes Daytona and Concorde models. USA Sporting makes competition grade Rottweils, called Rottweil Competitions.

If you want high end, consider Abbiatico & Salvinelli, Italian-made double guns offered through Southwest Shooters Supply in Phoenix, Arizona. Connecticut Shotgun Mfg. Company has a full sidelock O/U, the A. Galazan Grand Royal. Holland and Holland, the famed British game-gun maker, includes an O/U in its line. Kolar Arms' target guns (made in Milwaukee, Wisconsin) include a variety of options and grades. Krieghoff also offers Sporting guns with a number of options and grades. If you like German, consider Merkel. Perazzi USA choices include adjustable stock models and high grades. Rizzini guns (Battista and F.LLI) come in boxlock and sidelock versions, and are handled by New England Arms and W.L. Moore & Co.

Choices, obviously, abound and some models certainly will be easier to find than others. Most of all, remember the basic rule: You don't need a Sporting-model gun to enjoy shooting a round of Sporting Clays. Your favorite hunting gun not only will serve you well on the Sporting course, but by using it you will become a better wing shooter come bird season. As for the Sporting Clays itch? It's more a matter of when you catch it than whether you catch it at all. ●

Accessories for the Well-

by JIM CASADA

A cap or hat provides protection from the sun as well as broken bits of incoming birds and falling shot. Be sure to choose a hat that doesn't limit gun mounting.

TODAY'S SPORTING CLAYS ranges sometimes take on the appearance of outdoor style shows. Indeed, nattily attired and splendidly equipped shooters even evoke comments about "boys and their toys" and "gals and their gadgets." Yet for maximum enjoyment of the sport certain items of equipment are essential, and many other accessories are nice albeit not absolute necessities. Here's a look at gear in both categories and the manner in which it provides safe, pleasant participation in the sport.

"Must-Have" Gear—Protection

Most (though not all) of the accessories that fall into the "must-have" category offer protection of one type or another. First and foremost are ear and eye protection. These are really common sense safety items, and most Sporting Clays ranges require their use. Insurers demand that such requirements be in place, but even if you shoot on a layout where there are no ear and eye regulations enforced, such protection should not be ignored.

Most folks who have handled guns much, be they shotguns, rifles or handguns, have acquaintances who have suffered anywhere from moderate to severe hearing loss because they've failed to use adequate—or any—ear protection. Such problems are easily avoided, and no one wants to risk any diminution in their auditory abilities. Such loss is troublesome under any circumstances,

Dressed Clays Shooter

whether it be in terms of hearing everyday conversation or the ability to detect subtle sounds in the hunting woods (and it should be remembered that many Sporting Clays enthusiasts are keen hunters).

The types of hearing protection vary greatly, from simple and ultra-cheap foam ear plugs or those pink ones on a string, to high-tech electronic devices that enable the wearer to hear normal sounds—such as conversation or the click of a releasing trap—while shutting out gun noise. For all but the most casual of shooters, ear protection deserves considerable attention and a willingness to spend some money.

Reliance on foam ear plugs designed for one-time use is acceptable if your participation involves nothing more than an annual pilgrimage or two to a nearby Clays range or the occasional shoot with friends. One step above the foam plugs are the insert types, usually accompanied by a neck cord that lets them hang free, but tethered, when not in use. These typically feature a series of ridges or baffles designed to create pockets which fracture air waves. They can be used repeatedly and are quite inexpensive.

Even so, you should realize that the level of protection such plugs offer is distinctly inferior. A better choice would be muffs of some type. When shopping for this equipment, you should check the sound attenuation rating of the muffs to ascertain the level of protection, and be sure they will be comfortable in hot and cold weather. Virtually all muffs on the market are equipped with an adjustable frame, and in some instances this frame can be adjusted for various positions according to the shooter's personal preference, ie, over the head or behind. At least one recently introduced product, Remington's Rangemaster, combines padded muffs with shooting glasses that flip up and down with ease. One of the real advantages of this combination of protection is that the goggles fit comfortably over prescription glasses.

The ultimate in ear protection, and it is the choice of most devoted shooters, utilizes battery-operated electronics. Most such systems "clip" or "cut" sounds once they reach a preset level. As a result, the shooter is not exposed to high decibel levels but can hear safe, ordinary sounds. One process, developed by Ridge-Line, takes this protection even further in their Pro Ears. Using a process described as dynamic sound compression, Pro Ears compress sounds so they can be heard, but

---

Some shooters make a fashion show out of this game, but it needn't be that way. Buy and use what works best for you and you'll enjoy the sport even more.

Any shirt will do, of course, but these Safari Cloth shirts from Filson look good and allow full movement for swinging on birds. They're available in short or long sleeve versions.

Filson's Compartment Case has all the good qualities needed in a fine shooting bag, like sturdy handles and zippers, and lots of compartments.

only at a safe level. The result is natural sound with clarity rather than the distortion, interference or shutting off sometimes experienced with other electronic protection.

There are a number of reasons why the serious Clays shooter should use electronic protection. For starters, it offers the safest level of protection. Also, the shooter can carry on ordinary conversations, listen to instruction from a teacher or coach, and hear the telltale and often important sound of a trap throwing a target.

Eyes deserve equal consideration with ears when it comes to protection, and some type of protective glasses should be a part of every shooter's kit. For those who wear corrective eyeglasses, this means prescription lenses, some type of satisfactory flipdowns, or the like. Shooters who wear contacts or enjoy the blessing of 20-20 natural vision, the array of choices is truly impressive. For starters, there are at least a dozen lenses specifically designed for different light conditions. Obviously the beginning shooter is unlikely to acquire a pair of glasses to meet every condition of lighting, but for the dedicated enthusiast this is a significant consideration. Most glasses designed for Sporting Clays feature polarized lenses, which protect the eyes from ultraviolet rays as well as serve normal protective duty.

Other features to keep in mind when it comes to protective glasses are proper fit, custom coating, and weight. According to Bud Decot, the founder of Decot Hy-Wyd Sport Glasses, a leader in the field for a full half-century, the customer also wants to be aware of the potential for fogging and smudging. His Hy-Wyd frame design addresses this by being set behind the lenses, and they also have a self-adjustable bridge to ensure good fit.

While eye and ear protection receive the attention they rightly deserve, there are other matters of personal protection that should be kept in mind. In that regard, a cap or hat is imperative. It affords a screen that not only blocks out sun but can also ward off pieces of broken birds from incoming shots. The most popular chapeau is, of course, the ubiquitous baseball cap, and lots of Clays shooters wear them. There are lots of fun and interesting logos and designs available, so the shooter can nearly tailor his cap to his own tastes. These caps don't cost much, if anything at all (lots of them are given away by manufacturers), and are comfortable for all-day wear. For warm weather shooting, I suggest the mesh-type cap to allow head cooling. In the winter, you can switch to a solid cloth design to keep the wind off that balding pate and afford a little extra warmth. It boils down to the need to wear some sort of head protection, and what works for you is what's important.

Speaking of sun, anyone who is active outdoors, whether enjoying Sporting Clays or some other game,

A shooting vest is a must-have item for Sporting Clays shooters, and they're available in a variety of colors and styles to suit nearly every taste.

needs to be aware of the threat posed by the sun's rays. That is why sun screen should be a part of your kit. In warm weather conditions, you will also want to have insect repellant because you'll be shooting in the bushes, weeds, trees—the boonies.

Finally, when it comes to protection, you will want to safeguard your gun from dings and dents as well as weather. That means a suitable case or cover for transporting the firearm. Though a bit bulky, a hard case is best, even for local trips to the range. These can be bought for under $50 and offer a great deal of protection. For airline travel, your guns need the maximum protection, something just short of a bank vault. A good quality "travel" case can cost upward of several hundred dollars, but it's cheap insurance when you consider what it would cost to replace your gun.

A good gun cleaning kit is an indispensable accessory, although it fits better into the must-have category. Such a kit should include a cleaning or "wipe down" cloth impregnated with silicone, along with the patches, solvents, rods, and brushes needed to keep your prized possession in top operating order. Old-timers used to be fond of saying "oil is the life blood of a machine," and I believe that still holds true. In a similar vein, careful, consistent cleaning is the life of a gun. Dozens of suitable kits are available. One I have found quite useful, perhaps thanks in part to the fact that it is suitable for my hunting rifles as well as shotguns, is the Deluxe Gun Cleaning Kit from Outers. It stores easily and provides everything needed to keep a gun in tip-top condition.

(Right) For shooters who prefer to carry shells and accessories at their waist, a belted shell carrier works well. This Filson model has three compartments to hold most everything needed on station.

(Left) Hunters who also shoot Sporting Clays will find that their game bag, such as this one by Filson, can double as a vest or shell carrier. Empties can go into the rear (game) compartment.

Other Essential Items

Along with protective items, there are a few other "must-haves" to keep in mind. From a practical standpoint, whether one is shooting a 25, 50 or 100-target course, some sort of shell carrier is necessary. This may be a shell apron, a vest with pockets and hull pouches, tote boxes, or what are generally described as tournament bags. We will look at several examples of such gear in fuller detail below, but keep in mind that there are several ways to combine "nice" with "necessary."

Footwear is frequently overlooked in this sport, and Dale Christie, the Director of the Remington Shooting School, feels it belongs in the "essential" category. This can be lightweight hiking or hunting boots, sturdy shoes, or footwear custom-made for Sporting Clays. In every instance though, comfort and durability are preeminent. In many instances the footwear you use for other pursuits will fit the bill quite nicely. For example, Georgia Boot Company's Turkey Trekkers are designed for turkey hunters, but the low-cut version of this boot is lightweight, available in a waterproof version, made for both men and women, and work great for Clays shooters. What you wear needn't be fancy, just functional. When you start winning big-money tournaments you can buy the expensive, custom-made shoes and boots to fit your "elevated station" in life.

Nice But Not Absolutely Necessary

We've already covered footwear and headgear, but there are also items of clothing to cover the shooter from head to toe. Shooting shirts with padded shoulders and perhaps featuring the logo of one's club are functional as well as stylish. Likewise, loose fitting, comfortable pants or shorts enable the shooter to function smoothly when swinging a gun or moving from one station to another. In that regard, the C. C. Filson Company, long recognized for good quality shooting/hunting gear, offers poplin shirts and Shelter shorts and pants ideally suited for Sporting Clays. For colder weather, shooting jackets or sweaters come into play, and in some cases the latter include a padded shoulder which is at once functional and distinctive from a stylistic standpoint.

You will see widely varied attire on any Sporting Clays course, but in all likelihood the majority of the shooters present will be wearing some sort of vest. Typically these have padded shoulders, capacious pockets for hulls, mesh to allow free flow of air, and other features. Columbia's new Smokin' Clays vest, for example, has two large pockets on each side, a roomy pocket in back similar to those found in game vests, sleeves to hold up to six spare choke tubes below the shooter's off shoulder, and adjustable straps for a snug fit at the waist.

For those who find a vest too confining, or want to get meaningful versatility from a garment, a traditional shoulder-strap game bag with full, deep front pockets is one answer. A good example is Filson's Upland Game Bag. Alternatively, there are belted shell aprons and hull pouches that are worn around the waist and hang off the hips.

An all-purpose shooting bag, like a fine vest, is commonplace among today's Sporting Clays enthusiasts. A

Good hearing protection is essential for all shooters. Two of the most popular are the muff types (right) and the electronic inserts that are custom moulded to the ear canal.

good one will have room for shells and/or hulls, hearing and eye protection, choke tubes, and other small items such as choke tube wrenches. Look for a bag with numerous compartments, heavy duty carrying straps, and durable construction. Water-repellant cotton fabric, a strap made from bridle leather fitted with solid brass buckle, and even a nylon-lined pocket to protect hulls for reloading and keep powder from transferring to one's clothing are features of a bag with great utility and style. Most prefer such bags to simple totes that hold anywhere from four to 10 boxes of shells.

Along with accessories that are worn or designed to carry equipment, those for guns should not be overlooked. There are, for example, a number of useful sighting aids that have become available in recent years. All are designed, in one way or another, to afford instant sight acquisition and alignment, help prevent the lifting of the shooter's head to "peek," and promote good shooting basics. Most affix to the gun's rib by use of special adhesive tape or through magnetism. They feature optic light gathering qualities or bright color in order to be highly visible. Most instructors suggest that such sights are a real plus, particularly for beginning shooters who have trouble picking up targets and/or pointing instead or aiming.

Another, more venerable gun "add-on" is a recoil pad. Dedicated Clays shooters may fire hundreds of rounds over the course of just a few days, and even with padded vests or shirts recoil can begin to take a telling toll. No shooter needs a sore shoulder, because that leads to flinching at trigger pull, improper mounting, and other problems. Pads or other recoil reducers are available in a wide variety of styles, and for anyone who shoots a gun where "kick" is a problem, they are money well invested.

Some accessories can only be described as luxuries despite the fact that there is no doubt about their utility. Hand-pulled field carts or gun caddies, along with golf carts that have been customized for Sporting Clays use, fall into this category. The golf carts, in particular, can be gussied up in all sorts of ways, with shooter boxes, gun racks, places to store ammunition and hulls, and the like.

Then there are gun safes, all sorts of reloading equipment, devices that help the shooter judge which choke or shot size will be most effective for a given shot, and, indeed, an incredible array of paraphernalia. As is true of most pastimes, it is possible to spend a lot of money to be outfitted to a "T," but by the same token the casual recreational shooter can get by with minimal expenditure. In the final analysis, accessories are, to an appreciable degree, matters of personal taste and power of the purse. That being duly recognized, there can be no denying the fact that carefully selected gear can add a meaningful measure of pleasure to Sporting Clays. ●

Shooting clothing can be personalized with embroidered designs as desire and pocketbook allow. Both these shooters have electronic hearing protection in two styles—muff and insert styles—according to personal preferences.

AMMO
FOR SPORTING CLAYS

There are some special needs for Clays shooters that are being addressed by the major ammunition makers to make shooting more enjoyable.

by JOHN M. TAYLOR

SPORTING CLAYS HAS been a part of America's shooting scene for at least two decades. During that time this shooting game has gained in momentum and, like any other sport or mass endeavor, has brought on its own trappings.

In the early days of Sporting Clays, common trap and Skeet loads were universally used. And that's not a bad starting place. Although hunting ammunition remains the bread and butter of the major ammo producers, they lavish great care on their target ammo. Trap shooters can often recoup their expenses, and some even make a good living from their sport. Skeet shooters, likewise, can often break even if they win. With those parameters in mind, Federal, Kent (a new player whom we'll talk about later), Remington and Olin/Winchester all load carefully controlled, high-quality loads for competitive Clays shooters.

Sporting Clays derives its interest from the infinite variety of targets a shooter can see on any given course on any given day. Even the five-stand version presents a wide variety of angles and challenges. Because of the complexity of the targets thrown in Sporting Clays, many shooters moved from using moderate target loads to heavy, high-recoil loads. During the mid-1970s, international Skeet also took a similar tack. During that era, the Russians dominated international

Close, going-away targets like these can be shot effectively with very light loads, reducing the important fatigue factor. You don't always need a sledge hammer to swat a fly.

Skeet. In an effort to close the competitive gap, American shooters sought shotguns using the Russian Tula choke, in which the last four or so inches of the barrel was greatly expanded with the choke constriction at the very end of the interior of the barrel. Perazzi, Dynamit Nobel and others copied this choke, and those shooters who could afford these guns snapped them up. So, too, did we emulate the Russians in terms of their international Skeet ammunition. It was discovered that the Russians were using smaller, #10 shot and driving it at higher velocities. Hence, Federal Cartridge Company, at the behest of the military shooting teams, brought out a 4-dram equivalent 1-ounce load using #10 shot. The small shot certainly provided a denser pattern than #9, but the recoil was severe.

Many Sporting Clays shooters use stiff recoiling loads under the assumption that they are quicker and deliver more pellet energy at the target, a very valid view. However, any seasoned competitive shooter will tell you that once certain basics are mastered, shooting games become mental games. The better and longer a competitor can concentrate, the more successful he or she will be and the higher their scores. In clay target shooting, concentration is for a few seconds at a time, and the more the shooter can do to maintain his or her level of concentration, the better he'll shoot. Fatigue is one of the more insidious causes of diminished concentration. In a 50- or 100-target event, the more recoil a shooter is subjected to, the higher the rate of fatigue.

With this in mind, ammunition companies have begun offering not only traditional 3-dram loads, but also lighter loads that provide more comfort in terms of lessened recoil, and hence, less fatigue. Browsing through the catalogs of Federal, Remington and Olin/Winchester, we see the whole spectrum. For example, Federal Cartridge Company lists three 12-gauge loads in their Gold Medal line, a 3-dram equivalent load with a muzzle velocity of 1200 fps loaded with either #7-1/2 or #8 shot. They also show a Special Plastic high velocity load, the catalog stating the dram equivalent to be "special" and giving no muzzle velocity. It seems odd that Federal goes to

the trouble of making this special load, but offers no explanation of its performance. In addition to these hotter loads, Federal offers a Gold Medal Extra-Lite Sporting Clays load. The catalog says "soft recoil" but offers little other information. This, like other 12-gauge Sporting Clays shells, is loaded with 1-1/8 ounces of # 7-1/2 or #8 shot.

As the popularity of Sporting Clays has grown, so too have variations of everything associated with the sport. Encapsulated within many major competitions are sub-events that are limited to side-by-sides or small gauge shotguns, the 28-gauge and 410-bore. The 20-gauge stands alone as an alternative to the larger 12-bore. Women competitors, youngsters and often males with health problems or sensitivity to recoil turn to the 20-gauge as their shotgun of choice. Loaded with 7/8-ounce of good shot at a muzzle velocity of 1200 fps is more than a match for nearly every target thrown, save the thin ultra-hard battue and the occasional long-range target. Federal loads their 20-gauge Sporting round with the choice of #8 or #8-1/2 shot. Number 8-1/2 shot began as a trap and winter Skeet load. The feeling was that for trap it provided nearly the velocity of #8 shot, while giving the shooter a denser pattern for 16-yard trap. For Skeet, it provided nearly

the pattern density of #9 shot, but had better velocity retention when velocities sagged due to cold weather. For Sporting Clays, it does both, giving a little extra vinegar to velocities while sacrificing little in pattern density. In fact, Federal loads only #8-1/2 shot in their 28-gauge and 410-bore Sporting loads.

Turning to Remington, they rely upon their regular line of trap and Skeet loads to fill the bill for the 12-gauge Sporting Clays shooter. In addition to a low recoil load at 1100 fps, they offer a light target load at 1145 fps, a regular target load at 1185 fps and a traditional 3-dram load at 1200 fps. Shot sizes offered are #7-1/2, #8 and #8-1/2. In the small gauges, Remington offers both a 7/8- and 1-ounce 20-gauge in their Premier STS Target loads stuffed with #9 shot. In their Premier STS Sporting Clays loads, they provide the shooter with 20- and 28-gauge loads of #8 shot and the 410-bore with #8-1/2 shot.

Olin/Winchester does not offer specific Sporting Clays loads, but instead directs the shooter to their long-established line of AA target loads. These follow the loading by their competitors with one exception, the Low Recoil/Low Noise load. Many gun clubs are being confronted by neighboring homeowners who object to the noise, so Winchester has put together a neat little load that,

In order for the handloader to produce reloads comparable to factory ammo, he needs to consult and precisely follow known and tested data supplied in the manuals like Hodgdon (shown) or others.

Light loads can break targets as effectively as heavy ones, but with less recoil, which means less punishment to the shooter.

while moving at only 980 fps, is very easy on the shoulder and noticeably lower in decibels. While this load is not universally applicable to Sporting Clays, it certainly could be used for five-stand.

In 1997, a newcomer emerged on the U.S. ammunition market. Kent Cartridge is an established name in Britain, but largely unknown on these shores. Initially, Kent was owned by a group of Canadian hunters/shooters/investors, and was formed to develop and promote an alternative non-toxic shot made of powdered tungsten blended with a polymer. More on this later. In searching for a North American production facility, Kent ultimately purchased the ACTIV ammunition factory in Kearneysville, West Virginia. Both Skeet and trap regulate the velocities and payloads of ammunition. Essentially, 1-1/8 ounces of shot no larger than #7-1/2 traveling at 1200 fps is it for trap. Change the shot to #9 and you have the maximums for Skeet. Sporting Clays however, does not place a velocity restriction on ammunition, but does limit the payload to 1-1/8 ounces of shot between #7-1/2 and 9. The Federation International de Tir Aux Armes Sportives de Chasse, better known as FITASC is far more stringent in their rules that include not allowing competitors to freely change chokes between stands, and other things. FITASC allows loads of no more than 36 grams (1-1/4 ounces) of shot with sizes running from 2.0mm, about our #10, to 2.5mm, or #7, with no velocity restrictions. Kent Sporting ammo provides four 12-gauge choices including a 1-ounce load. The other three are loaded to higher velocities, including one that the company says goes 1300 fps. They also provide one 20-gauge load for Sporting Clays.

The establishment of Kent Cartridge leads to a topic of ever-increasing interest among shooters—non-toxic shot. As we become ever more compressed as a society, and as environmental extremists become more vocal, shooters are becoming more and more aware of the need to

Picking one target and breaking it is the trick here, and one of the light target loads will serve quite well.

Higher targets, like this one flying over a valley, may require a heavier load, but often a slightly tighter choked light load will work just as well.

find a viable alternative to lead shot. For a number of years, the major ammunition manufacturers have offered steel shot—really soft iron—in target loads. Loaded for the 12-gauge with one ounce of #7s, these work under ideal conditions, but are neither a long-range nor a thoroughly dependable load. In shooting a number of steel target loads, it has been my experience that in cold weather there is decidedly incomplete combustion of the powder and that contributes to very uneven performance.

On the plus side, we have seen the introduction of bismuth shot, which very much resembles lead in weight and performance. It is mainly loaded for the hunter, but with a little searching of the Olin/Winchester or Bismuth Cartridge Company's catalogs one can find at least one or two of these non-toxic loads that will work very well for Sporting Clays. In its initial years of production, bismuth shot was produced and loaded only by Bismuth Cartridge Company in Dallas, Texas. However, a few years ago Bismuth and Olin/Winchester formed an alliance and bismuth shot really got moving. This shot was approved by both U.S. and Canadian authorities for waterfowl hunting. Except for the cost, bismuth could be a workable alternative for clay target shooting.

As previously mentioned, Kent Cartridge's tungsten/polymer, and a similar development introduced by Federal, are potentially good choices for non-toxic sporting loads. As this is being written in the early fall of 1998, Kent has just received conditional approval as a non-toxic waterfowl load by the U.S. Fish and Wildlife Service. If history repeats itself, they'll receive full approval in 1999. The key to the effectiveness of tungsten/polymer shot is that tungsten is a very heavy and—like bismuth—an expensive, metal. By varying the amount of tungsten, pellets can be manipulated to provide optimum performance. Currently, in 1998, Kent is manufacturing and loading pellets that are equal in density to nickel-plated lead shot. In shooting a number of ducks and geese in Canada and Uruguay with Kent's tungsten/polymer loads, it is evident to me that it performs very well on game, and should do so on clays, if the need ever arises. Again, cost is a factor.

One of the quirks of both steel and tungsten/polymer is the lack of pellet deformation. Choke was invented, developed if you will, to keep as many soft and easily deformed lead pellets in the pattern as possible. During the first two-thirds of this century, most shotguns were produced with Full-choke barrels.

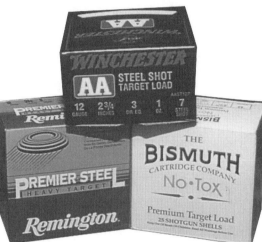

As non-toxic shot becomes more of an issue, shooters may have to turn to ammunition such as these loaded with steel or bismuth shot.

Only die-hard quail and grouse hunters and Skeet shooters opted for open-bored barrels. Otherwise it was pretty much Full choke. And why not? Lead shot, especially before the days of buffering and shot-protecting wrappers, was vulnerable to deformation at least four times before it exited the muzzle. First upon firing, when it is subjected to setback. Simply put, the rearmost pellets begin moving first and are crushed against those in front. Next, the sharp chamber forcing cone, necessitated by the use of card and felt wads that provided little in terms of gas sealing, subjected the unprotected pellets to a squeezing to get them to the cylinder bore. Then, as the shot charge rushed up the bore, the soft pellets were continually scrubbed against the sides of the barrel. Finally, the pellets were again compressed as they went through the choke. By applying Full choke to the shot pattern, more of these deformed pellets could be squeezed back into the pattern.

The introduction of plated shot, shot wrappers and cups and buffering all helped improve downrange lead shot performance. With the introduction of steel, suddenly the shooter was confronted with a very hard shot that simply did not deform, and patterns fired from a Modified choke gave Extra Full performance. Even the light constriction of a Skeet choke yielded tight patterns. In testing, the same seems to hold true with tungsten/polymer. Because this shot has an elasticity to it, probably due to the polymer, it appears to not deform, although, unlike steel, it can be shot in any modern shotgun without worry of damage to barrels. This is not the case with steel.

Handloading

Many, if not most, clay target shooters choose to reload because the saving over factory-loaded ammunition can run as high as 50 percent. However, there are several areas that if recognized can make handloading re-

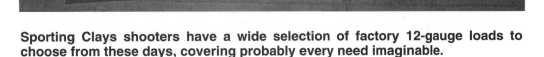

Sporting Clays shooters have a wide selection of factory 12-gauge loads to choose from these days, covering probably every need imaginable.

ally worthwhile and ammunition that can approach commercially produced ammo.

One notion that reloading equipment and component suppliers continually push is that handloads are better than factory ammo. Yes and no. If the handloader carefully follows a proven recipe, uses new or once-fired hulls, is scrupulous about making sure his loader is dropping the exact powder and shot charges specified, operates his press smoothly and consistently to ensure accurate powder drops, and has his press adjusted to provide tight crimps, then his loads will perhaps rival factory ammo. However, even then the odds are against him. The major domestic shotshell ammo companies, Federal, Kent, Remington and Olin/Winchester, all lavish inordinate amounts of time and care on their clay target loads. They seek to provide the very best in consistency, and that is what separates them from handloaders. At least hourly, the ammo companies test randomly selected rounds from each loader. They are checked for both uniformity of pressure and velocity, and to ensure that pressures are within both safe and ballistically balanced parameters. This is something that virtually no handloader can do. If he owns a chronograph, certainly he can check the uniformity of velocity, but unless he is willing to fork over a lot of money, he can only take as fact the pressures stated by the data in a loading manual.

Having said that, handloading is an excellent way to provide the great numbers of shells needed for practice and informal competition. Many Sporting Clays competitors shoot mounds of reloads in practice, but opt for factory ammo at major competitive events.

In choosing a recipe for a reload it must be stressed that only those published in a recognized manual such as Hodgdon's *Shotshell Data Manual* or DBI Books' *Reloading For Shotgunners* should be used; and they should be followed to the letter. Most handloaders first take stock of the components they have on hand, then try to find a load that will use them. While this is common behavior, it is far better to do a little experimenting with several handloads, then settle on one or two and buy

components solely for those. I have three clay target loads that I consistently use. One is a 28-gauge target load using Hodgdon Universal. Another is a 2-3/4-dram equivalent 1-1/8-ounce 12-gauge load using Hodgdon Clays; and the last is a semicopy of the Olin/Winchester Low Recoil/Low Noise 12-gauge load using Hodgdon's Titewad propellant driving 1-1/8 ounces of shot at 1090 fps.

The 28-gauge load is my favorite for Skeet, but my wife prefers the slightly faster 12-gauge load for that game. I like the slower but very mild Titewad load also for Skeet, but shift to the faster load for Sporting Clays, although in tests there seems little reason to do so; the slower load breaks the birds just as well as its faster cousin. Each of these loads uses a different powder, but they all use Olin/Winchester hulls, primers and wads.

In selecting a recipe for a handload it is good to look at the entire concoction, not just the components required. The reason is that while high chamber pressure in a target load is generally best avoided, if the chosen load is to be used in cold and very cold weather, then the shooter is wise to select one that is on the higher side of the pressure scale. Ammunition is generally tested for pressure and velocity at about 70 degrees F. When the temperature rises, so do pressures, and a low-pressure load would be a wise selection for areas such as the south where temperatures are in the high 90s and often into triple digits. Conversely, those who shoot in winter in the northern climes should look at loads that generate higher chamber pressures, because cold weather leads to two specific problems.

The first is that as the temperature drops propellants become harder to ignite, and velocities drop due to incomplete combustion. Higher pressure loads aren't the complete solution, but they tend to help keep velocities up. The second problem is that some of the currently available plastic wads become very brittle in extreme cold, and will, in fact, fracture when fired. If you live in a cold climate, ask around your gun club and I'm sure the knowledgeable shooters will be quick to identify those wads that don't perform well in cold weather.

All in all, handloading shotshells really helps the pocketbook survive Sporting Clays. However, in order to reap the full benefit, handloaders need to recognize that they must assemble their loads using the best components and carefully follow published data to ensure that the loads they create will provide the quality they need.

The Sporting Clays shooter has a wide variety of factory ammunition and handloading data from which to choose. Chosen wisely, he will not only be able to break targets, but also avoid the stress and negative effects of excessive recoil. Using a well-fitted shotgun and good ammo, the shooter's mind is free to concentrate solely on the target, and that is the secret to good wing shooting. ●

Olin/Winchester's Low Recoil Low Noise load does an excellent job of breaking targets despite its 980 fps velocity.

A special spreader load can be used for extremely close targets. This particular one works best through tightly choked barrels.

Small Gauge Sporting: the 28 and 410

by NICK SISLEY

Want to put a little more fun
and challenge into this game?
The small bores can do that and
make shooting easier on the shoulder as a bonus.

When shooting the small bores, use them as you would the 12-gauge and don't do anything different as far as lead or shot placement are concerned. (Barry G. Davis photo.)

THIS CLAY TARGET game, as originally envisioned, was supposed to be a fun thing. While it is still definitely that, Sporting Clays has also become very competitive. The shotguns originally envisioned for the game were supposed to be right out of the hunter's gun cabinet, but today's Clays competition gun has become very, very specialized. If you want to win at Sporting as we prepare to close out this century, you'd better be willing to take advantage of all the features contained in a modern Sporting Clays shotgun, which tend to be only over/unders and gas-operated semi-autos.

But with the importance of competition Sporting Clays, which is essentially a 12-gauge deal, small-gauge events have evolved. At big shoots, the small-gauge events im-mediately precede the major tournament. Let's say 100 12-gauge targets are to be shot on Saturday and 100 more on Sunday; Friday's preliminary games are small-gauge mini-tournaments, or events for pump guns, side by sides, whatever. Some of these mini-tournaments are even held on Saturday and Sunday since it doesn't take all day to shoot 100 12-gauge competition targets. With this rise in popularity of small-gauge competition has come increased awareness and keenness to shoot 410s and 28s. While competitors want to shoot these events so they can win, every-day Sporting Clays gunners are gravitating to shooting these smaller bores because they're so much fun.

So with these thoughts in mind we wanted to cover a number of sub-jects in this arena, like: (1) the 410-bore and 28-gauge guns worthy of consideration for Sporting; (2) the ammo available in both these gauges; (3) data you can use to effectively reload both these small gauges; (4) tips on how you can be more effective shooting the smaller guns with the lighter payloads.

Small Guns

The first one you might consider, especially if you're already accustomed to shooting a gas semi-auto in 12-gauge—hunting or competition—is the Remington 1100 Sporting 28. This is one you'll find feels very good between the hands, handles quick and sure. Frankly, I'd like to see something other than a 25-inch barrel, for I don't think Remington did

Small gauge competitions have evolved at major shoots because the 28 and 410-bores are gaining in popularity. The mini-tournaments are lot of fun. (Skahill photo.)

enough research to find out what barrel lengths intense Sporting Clays shooters are relying upon these days. While their 25-incher might be great for informal Clays and in real hunting situations, the option of a longer barrel(s) would be better for serious clay busters. Of course, the 1100 autoloader has withstood the test of time well. Four Rem chokes are supplied: Skeet, Imp. Cyl., Light Modified and Modified, all good choices. The gun hefts 6-1/2 pounds and its stock dimensions are 14 (too short, most Sporting Clays shooters will say) x1-1/2x2-1/2 inches (quite a bit of drop at the butt, but typical of "hunting" guns for too many decades). I've interjected a couple of negative thoughts on this gun, but overall it's still an excellent small gauge Sporting choice.

One of the easiest 28s to find on sporting goods dealers' shelves will be the Ruger Red Label over/under. As O/Us go, this is not an overly expensive one, but it is an ideal han-dling 28, especially for hunting. The Remington 1100 Sporting 28 is made on the same frame as the 1100 Sporting 20 gauge. However, many years ago Remington went to their 28-gauge frame to market their 20-gauge Lightweight 1100. Eventually, the "standard" weight 20-gauge 1100 was abandoned, no doubt because users liked the Lightweight 20 so much. Ruger came out first with a 20-gauge Red Label in the late 1970s. Some years later their 12-bore Red Label appeared, it on a bigger 12-gauge frame. Both are pretty heavy if you think of them as "game guns." However, Ruger was wise enough to bring the 28-gauge Red Label out on its own, down-sized frame. This was a very important move, and one that makes this gun stand on a higher figurative pedestal than the company's bigger-gauge counterparts.

Interestingly, the 28-gauge Ruger is offered in four configurations, with a regular pistol grip stock and 26- or 28-inch barrels, or with a straight grip and 26- or 28-inch barrels. Weight is nice and light for fast handling, which isn't all that great for serious Sporting—slightly under 6 pounds to very slightly over 6 pounds, depending upon the configuration you select. The Red Labels all come with a stainless steel receiver, are backbored to .563-inch, have longer 1-1/2-inch stainless screw-in chokes, and no between-barrel spacers (ribs). If you think this is a good looking gun, wait until you pick one up. If you have not done so already, you're in for a treat, as they have great feel.

Browning has answered the Sporting Clays shooter's call for specialized and serious shotguns in 12-gauge, and they make both a Grade I and a Golden Clays Model 425 O/U in 20-gauge, but they have yet to offer a 28 or 410 with detailed "Sporting" features. Maybe someday! However, the company does offer both 410 and 28-gauge possibilities in their Citori Hunter model. The one I suggest is the Lightning Hunt-

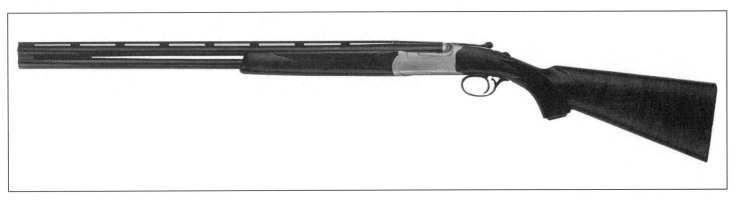

The Ruger 28-gauge Red Label is made on its own frame and is offered in four variations. The receiver is of stainless steel. Great value, great gun.

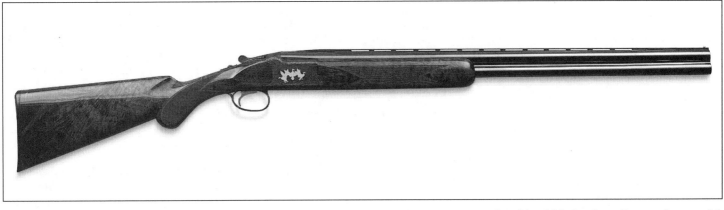

The Browning Citori Grade VI Lightning is an upscale version of the very popular Citori Lightning. Engraving, gold, and beautiful wood.

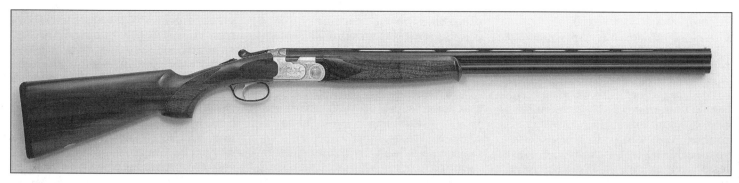

Beretta's 687 is a great handling gun well suited to both upland hunting and Sporting Clays.

er. This model has the semi-pistol grip stock first made famous on the Browning Superposed Lightning. Also, the Lightning model sports a trim, rounded forend of the same appealing dimensions and design. The result is an O/U that looks great, feels great and handles great. In addition, you can select between 26- or 28-inch barrel lengths. The 28-gauge has 2-3/4-inch chambers, the 410 3-inchers. Unfortunately, both these small bores weigh more than the 20-gauge, about 6 pounds, 10 ounces for the 28, nearly 7 pounds for the 410. The extra heft, however, won't hurt you on the Sporting Clays field, though it might be a detriment in certain upland hunting situations, especially those in which you need to be carrying the gun in a constant ready-to-shoot position. With 28-inch barrels the 410 and 28 Citori Lightning Hunters are available only in Grade I. With 26-inch barrels you can select between Grades I, III and VI and Golden Clays. Grade III means a well-engraved receiver in blue or nitride finish. Grade VI adds to the engraving with gold game birds. The Golden Clays model means different engraving, plus gold engraved birds transitioning to a gold clay pigeon. As you move up in grade you also get even better figured walnut. Invector screw-ins are a part of both these small gauge packages.

Like Browning, Beretta offers Sporting Clays specialized shotguns in 12- and 20-gauge, but there are no 28 and 410 offerings designed especially for the game. Not to fret, however, for Beretta does have three excellent choices in 28-bore, each of them wonderfully appealing to the eye, the hand, and in function. All three are more expensive than, say, the 28-gauge Red Label, including

the least expensive Beretta 28-gauge, the 686 Silver Pigeon. But this is a wonderful looking, superb feeling O/U. Because it weighs a mere 5.3 pounds, you know this one is built on its own, individual 28-gauge-size frame—not a bastardization from a 20-gauge frame. Also, 26- and 28-inch barrel lengths are offered, and these are outfitted with screw-in chokes. There's rich scroll engraving, plus game scene stuff, all topped off with an electroless nickel finish that promises to last a great deal longer than standard bluing. There's a thin schnabel forend that puts the hand in extra-close proximity to the barrels. The 686 receiver is one of the best. Like the Red Label, there are no underlocking lugs, so both hands are more in-line, and the forend hand is as close as possible to the barrels, theoretically enhancing the shooter's natural pointing tendencies. In addition to the 28-gauge Silver Pigeon there's also a 20/28 Combo version.

The two other 28-gauge Beretta considerations are the 687 EL Gold Pigeon and the 687 EELL Diamond Pigeon. Both these sport false sideplates, so there's even more room for engraving. The EL Gold Pigeon means gold, engraving, a hunting dog and upland game against a woodland background. There's even more detailed engraving on the EELL, though no gold figures. Both are nearly breathtaking. Same light weight as the Silver Pigeon. Same two barrel-length choices, with screw-in tubes. However, the EL Gold Pigeon is also available in 410, and even it has choke tubes. Finally, a 20/28 combo is available in both models.

Now, what about the "tube route!" Some of you know what I'm talking about, though not everyone, so a

brief explanation is in order. "Tubes" are high strength aircraft aluminum full-length tubes made to fit inside 12-gauge barrels. They are made by two manufacturers in particular, Briley in Houston and Kolar in Racine, Wisconsin, and in 20- and 28-gauge and 410-bore. These are extremely tight fitting tubes. Normally they have to be made so they're individually fit to each barrel. Thus, the tube made for the bottom barrel of an over/under won't fit the top barrel of the same gun. And vice versa. The tubes fit so tight they have to be coaxed into place with a soft mallet. Both companies will still make you 28 or 410 tube sets (one for each barrel of an O/U), but Briley has come up with the technology of "Companion" tubes, small-gauge tubes for 12-bore over/unders that don't have to be individually fit to your barrels. Thus, if barrel lengths are the same, Briley Companion tubes fit any 12-gauge over/under you have—within reason.

Whether you go the Companion route or the standard Briley or Kolar small-gauge tubes, what are the advantages? Cost for one. A set of tubes will cost less than a new gun—$300 bucks for a Companion set in one gauge, for example. There's also the added 10 to 14 ounces of weight to your current over/under. This is bad for a hunting gun since you just can't heft it for very long, particularly in a ready-to-shoot carry. But a heavy gun can be good in a clay target situation, particularly after you become accustomed to the extra heft, which may take several hundred rounds or more. Added weight helps smooth out one's swing. Light weight can cause the barrel(s) to bob around, not what you want to smoke a clay that always flies in a straight line, or nearly so. Added weight also helps keep the swing moving at trigger-pulling time and shortly thereafter. Lightweight shotguns are more prone to stopping, not what you want in the game field or on the range. Added weight also sucks up recoil. Of course, recoil is near non-existent in a 28, and that's one reason for shooting them. Still, a tube set means a 28-gauge recoils even less. Of course, a 410 has so little recoil there's no concern whatever. The

tube set route is an excellent road to take for small gauge Sporting. One of the best.

Small Ammo

What about factory ammo for the small guns? Most manufacturers make 28-gauge and 410 fodder. Winchester has their AA target loads in both gauges, at 1200 fps, 3/4- and 1/2-ounce of shot respectively, size

#9. The same shells are available from Remington and Federal, as well. Additionally, Federal also has both 410 and 28-gauge Sporting Clays loads. These are both a little faster at 1230 fps, and use the same amount of extra-hard #8-1/2 shot. Remington has 410 and 28 Sporting loads at 1200 fps, size #8s for the 28, #8-1/2s for the 410. Winchester has a 1-ounce Game Load in 28 with a full 1 ounce of #6, #7-1/2 and #8 at 1125

The "tube" route is one possibility for shooting small gauge Sporting, and is cheaper than buying another gun (though not as enjoyable, maybe). Kolar and Briley make these full-length aluminum inserts in 20- and 28-gauge, and 410-bore that fit 12-gauge over/unders.

fps, plus both a 3-inch and a 2-1/2-inch 410—the 3-incher with 11/16-ounce of shot at 1135 fps, the 2-1/2-incher with 1/2-ounce at 1225 fps, both offered in #4, #6, and #7-1/2. Winchester also makes shotshells for Bismuth Cartridge. Their 28-gauge has 5/8-ounce of shot at 1250 fps—#4, #6 and #7 sizes, the 3-inch 410 with 9/16-ounce of #4, #6 or #7, the 2-1/2-inch 410 with 7/16-ounce of #7s only.

Remington offers Express Long Range 28s and 410s, the 28s with 3/4-ounce of #6 or #7-1/2 at 1295 fps, the 3-inch 410s with 11/16-ounce of #4, #6 or #7-1/2 at 1135 fps, and their 2-1/2-inch 410s with 1/2-ounce of #4, #6 or #7-1/2 at 1200 fps. One other Remington 410 load is in their Lead Game line, a 2 1/2-inch shell with 1/2-ounce of #6 at 1200 fps. In Federal Classic Lead there are no more 28-gauge shells, but there are 410s—3-inchers with 11/16-ounce of #4, #5, #6, #7-1/2 and #8s at 1135 fps, and 2-1/2-inchers with 1/2-ounce of #6 or #7-1/2 at 1200 fps. Also from Federal are Hi-Power American Eagle 410s,

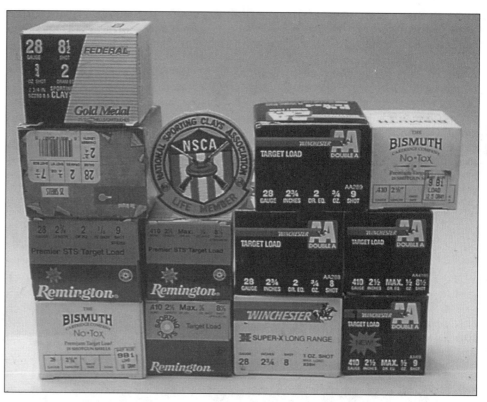

There is a good selection of small gauge ammunition available from hunting loads to target types, and in lead as well as non-toxic Bismuth.

With a set of insert tubes, shooters can compete with four gauges and use the same familiar gun. The weight penalty can be beneficial for Clays shooters, though.

3-inchers with 11/16-ounce of #4, #6, or #7-1/2 at 1135 fps, and 2-1/2-inch 1/2-ounce of #6 at 1200 fps. A few other manufacturers offer 28 and 410 shells, but you can see there are plenty of small-gauge factory loads from which to select.

What about reloading the smaller gauges? You can do it, though the 410, for sure, isn't as easy as re-stuffing 12-gauge hulls. One of the problems is shell tipping as the shell plate is indexed, which is much easier to experience with a "thin" shell (i.e. a 410) compared to a "thick" shell (a 12-gauge). A single-stage reloading press isn't a bad idea for these smaller gauges, especially if you're not going to shoot a great many shells. However, a single-stage is necessarily slow, and you are going to discover that small-gauge Sporting is so much fun that you might want to do more and more of it. If that is true, a progressive 28 and/or 410 press will be highly recommended.

My favorite 28-gauge load used Winchester 540 powder, but that powder has been discontinued. If you still have some 540 powder well stored, try 17.0 to a maximum of 17.5 grains with either the Winchester AA or the new Remington STS case, a Remington or Winchester 209 primer (depending upon which case you are using), AA or Remington wad for the 28, again depending upon which hull you're using, and 3/4 -ounce of hard #8s or #9s. Since 540 is gone, I now load 28s with Hodgdon's Clays Universal, the same AA or STS cases, with wads and primers to match the hulls, 3/4 -ounce of hard #8s or #9s, and 13.2 grains of that Clays Universal.

I only load 2-1/2-inch 410s. Again, I prefer Remington cases, especially the new smooth STS hulls, or Winchester red AAs. These I load with either Winchester 296 or Clays 110 powder using just under 15 grains. With the Remington hulls use Remington or Claybuster wads. With the AA case, the Claybuster wads also work great. Use Winchester 209 primers for the AA cases, Remington 209 with the STS hulls. Shot load is 1/2-ounce of Magnum #8s, #8-1/2s or #9s.

Small-Gauge Techniques

What about actually shooting Sporting Clays with these small loads, small gauges? Don't do anything different. Don't try to be more precise. In fact, maybe do just the opposite. Shoot with more abandon than ever. As I've said before, recoil, or rather the lack of it, is a big, big bonus of the small gauges. Don't try to make extra-long shots, like 45 yards away or more, and don't expect to smoke edge-on targets that are at a distance. Those edge-on birds are the hardest to break, even with a big 12-gauge and 1-1/8 ounces of #7-1/2s, though hard, bigger shot and a more dense pattern are certainly helpful in this situation. What might really surprise you is how the small guns, especially the 28-gauge, hammer the targets so hard. For close-in Clays, a choke of .002- to .005-inch in 28-gauge is about right. Go tighter in constriction if you're going to be shooting at farther birds, say 28 yards and more. Most 410s perform better with a bit more choke, even for the closer 25 yards-and-in targets. Try a minimum choke of .004-inch, but your gun might do even better with .008-inch. Again, twist in tighter chokes when you come upon stations that present longer targets.

Nearby, you'll find a run down on the shotguns we've suggested here for small-gauge Sporting, plus factory ammo for the little guns. You won't be sorry if you give this aspect of the sport a try, because it promises to offer more fun than you expect. Small gauges are also an ideal way to introduce youngsters, and spouses/significant others to shotgunning, but for this I use the 28 rather than the 410. The little guy is just too tough for inexperienced shooters to hit with. Of course, another facet about introducing a new, younger/smaller shooter to Sporting with one of the smaller gauges or even a big 12-bore, is the critical importance of gun fit. Too many people first try Clays with a gun that is ill fit to them. New shooters want and expect success. If they don't find it quickly, they probably won't come back. They'll just move on to some other recreational endeavor where success can be had. While gun fit is so important, that subject requires a full length feature to cover it well. In short, that's another story. ●

If the small gauge shooter keeps the range within reason there's no need to worry about the hitting ability of these pipsqueaks. Tower shots are attainable as with any bore size. (Rick Hinton photo.)

28 & 410 SPORTING CLAYS SHOTGUNS

Remington 1100 Sporting

Gauge/Bore	Chamber (ins.)	Barrel (ins.)	Weight (lbs.)	Stock (ins.)
28	2-3/4	25	6-1/2	14x1-1/2x2-1/2

Ruger Red Label Sporting

Gauge/Bore	Chamber (ins.)	Barrel (ins.)	Weight (lbs.)	Stock (ins.)
28	2-3/4	26, 28	6	14-1/8x1-1/2x2-1/2

Note: Straight or pistol grip

Browning Citori Lightning Field

Gauge/Bore	Chamber (ins.)	Barrel (ins.)	Weight (lbs.)	Stock (ins.)
28	2-3/4	26, 28	6-3/4	14-1/4x1-1/2x2-3/8
410	3	26, 28	7	14-1/4x1-1/2x2-3/8

Note: 28-inch available in Grade I only; 26-inch, 28-gauge and 410 available in Grades I, II, VI, and Golden Clays.

Beretta Silver Pigeon

Gauge/Bore	Chamber (ins.)	Barrel (ins.)	Weight (lbs.)	Stock (ins.)
28	2-3/4	26, 28	5.3	14.5x1.4x2.2

Beretta 687 EL

Gauge/Bore	Chamber (ins.)	Barrel (ins.)	Weight (lbs.)	Stock (ins.)
28	2-3/4	26, 28	5.3	14.5x1.4x2.2
410		2-1/2	26	5.314.5x1.4x2.2

Beretta 687 EELL

Gauge/Bore	Chamber (ins.)	Barrel (ins.)	Weight (lbs.)	Stock (ins.)
28	2-3/4	26, 28	5.3	14.5x1.4x2.2

Note: All three of the above Berettas also available as 20/28 combo, i.e. two sets of barrels.

SMALL GAUGE FACTORY AMMO

Federal Gold Medal

Gauge/Bore	Shell Length	MV(fps)	Charge wgt. (oz)	Shot Size
28	2 3/4	1200	3/4	9
410	2 1/2	1200	1/2	9
28	2 3/4	1230	3/4	8 1/2
410	2 1/2	1230	1/2	8 1/2

Federal Classic Lead

Gauge/Bore	Shell Length	MV(fps)	Charge wgt. (oz)	Shot Size
410	3	1135	11/16	4, 5, 6, 7 1/2, 8
410	2 1/2	1200	1/2	6, 7 1/2

Federal American Eagle

Gauge/Bore	Shell Length	MV(fps)	Charge wgt. (oz)	Shot Size
410	3	1135	11/16	4, 6, 7 1/2
410	2 1/2	1200	1/2	6

Remington STS Target

Gauge/Bore	Shell Length	MV(fps)	Charge wgt. (oz)	Shot Size
28	2 3/4	1200	3/4	9
410	2 1/2	1200	1/2	9

Remington STS Sporting Clays

Gauge/Bore	Shell Length	MV(fps)	Charge wgt. (oz)	Shot Size
28	2 3/4	1200	3/4	8
410	2 1/2	1200	1/2	8 1/2

Remington Express Long Range

Gauge/Bore	Shell Length	MV(fps)	Charge wgt. (oz)	Shot Size
28	2 3/4	1295	3/4	6, 7 1/2
410	3	1135	11/16	4, 6, 7 1/2
410	2 1/2	1200	1/2	4, 6, 7 1/2

Remington Game Loads

Gauge/Bore	Shell Length	MV(fps)	Charge wgt. (oz)	Shot Size
410	2 1/2	1200	1/2	6

Winchester AA Target

Gauge/Bore	Shell Length	MV(fps)	Charge wgt. (oz)	Shot Size
28	2 3/4	1200	3/4	9
410	2 1/2	1200	1/2	9

Winchester Super X High Brass

Gauge/Bore	Shell Length	MV(fps)	Charge wgt. (oz)	Shot Size
28	2 3/4	1125	1	6, 7 1/2, 8
410	3	1135	11/16	4, 6, 7 1/2
410	2 1/2	1200	1/2	4, 6, 7 1/2

Bismuth Cartridge

Gauge/Bore	Shell Length	MV(fps)	Charge wgt. (oz)	Shot Size
28	2 3/4	1250	5/8	4, 6, 7
410	3	1175	9/16	4, 6, 7
410	2 1/2	1075	7/16	7

Spred-R

Gauge/Bore	Shell Length	MV(fps)	Charge wgt. (oz)	Shot Size
28	2 3/4	1200	3/4	7 1/2

Kent Cartridge Ultimate

Gauge/Bore	Shell Length	MV(fps)	Charge wgt. (oz)	Shot Size
28	2 1/2	1180	3/4	6, 7 1/2, 8

Reloading for Sporting Clays

by LES GREEVY

CAN YOU INCREASE LOAD SELECTION?
CAN YOU IMPROVE PERFORMANCE?
CAN YOU SAVE MONEY?

Author Greevy finds he can improve performance and save money by reloading for his 410-bore Remington 1100.

WHY DO PEOPLE reload? Several reasons, I suppose. One would be to increase load selection, to create something that cannot be found otherwise on the market. Whether the unique load is to meet a real or perceived need or just to be different, it really doesn't matter.

Another would be to adjust, change or improve performance, perhaps to reduce recoil or to use different components to widen patterns or extend range. It could be considered an attempt to gain an advantage over the other competitors, what race car driver Dan Gurney called "the unfair advantage."

An additional reason would be to save money. By reusing cases and providing the labor, a reloader should be able to save on the cost of factory ammunition. These reasons apply whether one is reloading centerfire rifle or pistol or shotgun, for either target shooting or hunting.

What can Sporting Clays shooters gain from reloading? With the 12-gauge it would be very difficult to ob-

jectively demonstrate that a shooter could either increase load selection, improve performance or substantially reduce the cost by reloading. However, when reloading the subgauges —the 20-, the 28-gauge, and the 410-bore—real cost reductions are achieved and performance as well as load perimeters can be expanded.

It is a major job to identify the variety of target grade ammunition available for the modern Sporting Clays competitor. Only a few years ago the choices were few. The standard, 1-1/8-ounce target load could be had only in the 2-3/4-dram (1145 fps) or 3-dram (1200 fps) loadings and while quality was excellent, choice was limited.

Now, and somewhat as a result of British influence, a wide variety of 12-gauge target ammunition is being marketed, different loads for different uses with performance tailored and individualized by varying the shot charge and velocity, wads and cases, and with new and cleaner burning powders. Where the imports

lead the domestic producers had to follow.

Lightweight factory loads are now available from 7/8-ounce at 1145 fps (Hull CT12L) and 1200 fps (Fiocchi 12780Z) to the international target load of 7/8-ounce at 1325–1350 fps offered by most makers. Another light, low velocity load is Winchester's AA12FL with 15/16-ounce (26 gram) at 980 fps. This load not only produces low recoil, it is also subsonic, so noise is also reduced.

Once rare, 1-ounce 12-gauge loads are also made by most of the companies in 2-3/4-dram equivalents (1180 fps), 3 dram (1200–1235 fps), as well as faster loads including the Fiocchi 12TX at 1250 fps and the 12CRSR and 12CPTR at 1300 fps.

The traditional 1-1/8-ounce target loadings have also been expanded and now begin at 2-1/2-dram equivalents of powder and 1100 fps (Remington STS12LR) and include the standard 2-3/4-dram (1145 fps) load offered by all, and a new 2-7/8-ounce dram version at 1165 fps (Fiocchi 12

From left: Winchester AA loads in 12-, 20-, 28-gauge, and 410-bore. The 12-gauge is hard to beat in factory form for cost and performance,

Factory 20-gauge loads like these are tough to beat, but the reloader can reduce recoil by careful selection of components and reducing the shot charge a bit.

LITE). On the high velocity side, there's the 3-dram handicap standard at 1200 fps, a new 3-1/4-dram loading at 1250 fps (Fiocchi 12WRNO), and Kent's high speed Super Sporting at 1330 fps (K122SSC32). And if you like to split hairs and eighths, several British companies load 1-1/16-ounce, 3-1/4-dram shells at between 1250 and 1270 fps (Hull HSG12L and Kent K122TR30).

Those who shoot FITASC and enjoy recoil have the Winchester Super Pigeon (AA12SP) load at 3-1/4 drams, 1-1/4 ounces with copper-plated shot again available.

As you can see, the factories have pretty much covered the spectrum of loads and velocities suitable for 12-gauge target use, and there are few blank spaces for the reloader to fill.

Can you increase performance by reloading the 12-gauge? I really don't think so, even though the loading manuals indicate that you can pretty closely duplicate velocities. Over the past eight years, I have shot, chronographed, patterned, cut open, inspected, weighed and mea-sured most every load, domestic and imported, currently in use for Sporting Clays. I have also used and tested most every reloading component available on the market today. I've talked to knowledgeable people in the industry and many discriminating shooters, and while there are many new and improved components including cases, wads and powder, shot is the key to superior target performance. The fact is that the reloader can't buy shot as good as that used by the manufacturers in their best grade target ammunition.

Lightweight 12-gauge loads are being increasingly offered by the factories to reduce both recoil and noise without sacrificing target-busting performance.

A few of the author's favorite components for the smaller bore sizes include Hodgdon's Lil' Gun, Winchester 296 and Alliant Unique powders. He always uses premium-grade hard shot for best performance.

This may be a result of the difficulty and expense of transporting relatively small quantities of lead shot for individual purchase or, possibly because of the reluctance of most reloaders, who tend to be cost conscious, to pay premium prices for best quality shot. Or, it could be because the companies are not putting their best shot in bags for sale to reloaders but are keeping that for themselves. At any rate, the reloader does not have the ability or the facilities or the time or expertise to blend powders and to test for velocity, pressure and pattern the way the manufacturers do, and as a result cannot monitor quality with the same accuracy.

Can you save money by reloading? Even buying components at good prices, it costs about $3.00 per box to reload 12-gauge target ammunition. Bought in quantity, a box of quality target grade ammunition goes for about $4.50. Promotional loads cost less, down to about the $3.50 range. It is very hard to justify the time and effort involved in reloading for those meager savings. Have you ever counted the number of times you actually handle a case that is going to be reloaded? It is handled seven times. Seven times more than a factory shell. It goes something like this: First it is removed from the gun or picked up from the ground and placed in a shell bag; second it is transferred from the shell bag to the container in your car; third, it goes from the car container to the home storage area; fourth, it gets sorted; fifth, it's placed in the press; sixth, it is removed from the press and boxed; seventh, the box is placed in a flat or case, and stored. When comparing the labor expended to the savings, few of us would work for those wages. I wouldn't.

That's for the 12-gauge. For the subgauges, it's a different story. In the 20-gauge there are three loads: the 7/8-ounce standard at 1200 fps; the 1-ounce Skeet load (illegal in Sporting unless shot in the 12-gauge event); and the new 3/4 -ounce promotional load at 1350 fps. The 28-gauge is available in only one load, 3/4-ounce at 1200 fps. There is a British 9/16-ounce shell, but it is not in wide distribution and is intended as a game load. In addition, it is not generally found in target shot sizes.

The 410 2-1/2-inch shell is also made in only one target load and that is 1/2-ounce of shot (typically #9) at 1200 fps. However, Winchester, Remington and Federal do list size #8 and Fiocchi has a 410 dove load in #8 (410GT).

In all three of the subgauges, factory target ammunition is loaded to the same velocity of 1200 fps. This loading was developed for and by Skeet shooters, and for at least the last 30 years they have shot the subgauges with tubed over/unders or gas-operated autoloaders. Both of those guns tend to absorb and reduce recoil. And while tubed O/Us and gas guns are used by Clays shooters, with more and more frequency the well-made gauge-specific over/under Sporting Clays gun is being seen. Some are in the hands of women and some in the hands of young shooters, but all of them are light in weight and shot with 1200 fps ammunition they kick with a sharp, quick rap that can be very disconcerting. We know recoil increases fatigue and decreases scores, and that's a good reason to look for more varied load selection and the ability to change performance by reloading.

Cost is another reason to reload subgauges. The 20-gauge shells cost about the same as 12-gauge, but about $2.50 per box to reload. Perhaps that's not enough to make a difference, but the big savings are in the 28-gauge and the 410. Both cost

Ruger's 28-gauge Sporting Clays over/under is not only deadly on targets, but fun to shoot, too. Greevy has found the balance and handling to be superb.

about $6.00 per box even when bought in quantity, but run about $2.25 and $1.75 respectively to reload. That's a significant savings. In addition, the 28s and 410s tend to be not as well distributed as the larger sizes and the ability to reload assures an adequate supply.

Loading for the 20-gauge is pretty much the same as for the 12. The easiest way to reduce recoil is to reduce velocity, and the easiest way to reduce velocity is to use less powder. Green Dot, International Clays and Universal Clays all are good moderate burn rate powders for the 20-gauge. Using standard wads and subtracting a grain or two of the above powders from the listed 1200 fps load will put you in the 1100 fps bracket, which will be entirely adequate to break targets.

In a 6-pound 20-gauge gun, reducing velocity in a 7/8-ounce load from 1200 fps to 1100 fps reduces recoil by 2.7 foot-pounds of energy (16.3 to 13.6) giving about a 17 percent reduction.

Another way to reduce recoil in the 20-gauge is to cut the shot charge. The 28-gauge does very well on clay targets with 3/4-ounce of shot, and the 20-gauge will do just as well. By proper selection of powder and wads, 3/4-ounce loads can be tailored to achieve a proper crimp without having to resort to the use of card fillers in the shot cup or over the powder. When attempting to reduce recoil by reducing ejecta, there is no point in adding card wads to occupy space when the wad itself increases recoil and does not contribute to the ability of the shell to break the target. Ballistics Products Inc. makes a special long wad (BPSG20L) for use in reduced-charge loads. Also, the Federal 20S1 will usually measure out right with 3/4-ounce loads in both Winchester AA and Remington STS cases.

In the same 6-pound gun referred to earlier, a 3/4-ounce load at 1100 fps will have only 10.5 foot-pounds of recoil energy, a savings of 5.8 foot-pounds, or 35 percent from the standard target load.

The 28-gauge guns tend to be lighter yet and the standard 1200 fps target load can have a rather snappy and uncomfortable kick. Again, as with the 20-gauge, a reduction in velocity to 1100 fps will substantially reduce recoil and yet not degrade target-breaking performance. Unique is probably the best all-round powder for the 28. It burns cool and noticeably extends case life, and is flexible enough to work well through a wide range of velocities and shot weights.

As with the 20-gauge, reducing shot weight is an effective way to reduce recoil. Dropping to an 11/16-ounce payload generally can be made with standard 3/4-ounce wads, but you may have to try a couple of different combinations, such as a Federal wad in the AA case to get a good crimp. Excellent 5/8-ounce loads are made with Remington cases and the Ballistic Products SG28 wad.

My personal favorite is the 9/16-ounce load of #9s using the same BPSG28 wad in Winchester AA cases and Unique powder. This wad has a

Author Greevy can be found in his basement loading room on many evenings while trying to keep his small-gauge guns supplied with ammo. To his right are three other loading machines.

large crush section and is very adaptable. The shot protector cup does not cover the full shot charge and has only two slits. On patterning, you see a dense center from the protected shot but still an adequate fringe from the unprotected pellets. An excellent long-range 28-gauge load uses the BPSG28 wad in a larger case, a Remington or Fiocchi, with 5/8-ounce of shot and Herco or Blue Dot powder for approximately 1400 fps velocity. Hard #7-1/2s and a buffer complete the package which will break targets at almost unbelievable ranges.

Reloading for the 410 is frugal. When you get 800 shells per bag of shot you know you're saving money. The limiting factors with the 410 are the powders and wads. There are only a couple of powders that will work and all are slow burning. I like the ball powders, W296 or H110, but others such Alliant 2400 and IMR4227 also are adaptable.

While it may be odd to say the 410 guns kick, they can be very light and light guns do kick. I recently attended the Vintage Cup World Side By Side Championship and saw guys there shooting British 410 doubles typically weighing less than 5 pounds. Standard 1200 fps loads in these skinny guns were definitely unkind to face and shoulder. Reducing the powder charge a few grains to get velocity down around 1100 fps helps greatly. Cutting back the shot charge is not much of an option in the 410, as the standard 1/2 -ounce load contains not quite 300 #9s and you pretty much need that many to get the job done.

Remember what I said earlier about the ammunition companies loading different shot than what was available to the reloaders. A year ago while testing and patterning 410 reloads against factory ammunition, I could not correlate why the factory

ammunition was typically putting 20 more pellets in the 30-inch circle than my very high quality reloads that were intended to duplicate factory performance with factory components and high quality high-antimony shot. Finally I counted the pellets in my reloads and found the 1/2 -ouncecharge contained approximately 283. When counting the pellets in the factory ammunition, I found an average of 303. That's 20 more pellets or about 7 percent extra. I then weighed and measured the factory pellets and compared them to my weighed and measured bag shot. Surprise. The factory shot was smaller—it was technically not #9 but #9-1/2, thereby allowing 20 more pellets per load and still staying within the weight restriction. Unfair advantage? I called the company involved and asked if I could buy some of that special undersized #9 shot. The answer was no.

The 410-bore can benefit from custom loading and different components should be tested. These three wad designs produced different results that improved the author's scores.

Winchester offers AA target loads in both the 28-gauge and 410-bore, the latter with a half-ounce of #8-1/2 shot.

The 410s, especially the older ones, are generally choked on the tight side. Standard 410 wads have full shot protector cups but no crush section. By use of different wads, patterns can be opened somewhat and there will be some reduction in felt recoil. I use the BPMG410 wad with a short crush section and a shot protector cup that only covers about half of the shot. Everything fits well in the AA case and patterns are noticeably wider. Ballistic Products also makes a 410 wad that is a gas seal only. Without any shot protector cup this BW410 wad has a little longer crush section and requires some compression to get everything in the AA case. However, because the shot is unprotected it will get the benefit of barrel scrub and patterns will be more open yet. This style of ammunition more closely approximates that for which the older guns were originally choked.

And speaking of shot, when loading for the 410 or 28, one should only use the best quality, high-antimony shot. You're not throwing very many pellets at the target and every one must do its duty.

Another thing you will notice with these small bores is that the loading manuals list pressures that are higher than those generally shown for 12- and 20-gauge loads. Because of the higher pressures, and because relatively slight changes in components can have significant changes in pressure, one must be very careful not to exceed recommended loads, and to select powders that are more flexible and produce lower pressures. A good manual is Krause Publications' *Reloading For Shotgunners*, which lists loads for the various Ballistic Products wads and reduced shot charges.

Generally speaking, lower pressure powders produce less recoil, as do softer primers. And while these

reductions are small and hard to identify in the 12-gauge guns they become more significant in the small subgauges.

Another thing you can do when reloading for Sporting Clays is to treat your wads to reduce wad plastic build-up in your gun's bore and choke. I treat wads by spraying them with molybdenum disulfide. By placing wads in a plastic bag and spraying and then shaking, a hundred or so can be treated in less than a minute. This process eliminates plastic fouling.

Unless you really enjoy reloading you are probably not using your time wisely by rolling your own 12-gauge shells for Sporting Clays. You are probably not going to improve the breed or save much money. But for the 28-gauge and 410 you can save and custom load ammunition to suit your needs and, ultimately, improve your scores. It doesn't get much better than that. ●

The 410-bore does kick in the lighter guns. By using different wads, patterns can be opened a bit and some reduction in felt recoil can be achieved.

English Sporting
or FITASC

by KATY SKAHILL

Which One for You?

Same game, different rules,
and each one is challenging in its own way.

Terrain plays an important role in Sporting Clays shooting. This parcour at the 1996 World FITASC Championship in England shows how the course designers take advantage of it.

BY MOST ACCOUNTS, Sporting Clays arrived on the scene in the United States sometime in the 1970s, although there are numerous friendly disputes as to exactly when and where it first appeared. The game was imported here from England, and is now shot all over the world. The version most Americans are familiar with is called English Sporting, for obvious reasons, although the game has undergone various and significant rule changes in the past five years. Originally developed to warm up for high pheasants and rough shooting in England, as well as being employed by the better gun houses in London to assist with gun fit, Sporting Clays also developed in America as a method to prepare oneself for hunting. Thought to be much more realistic as a game substitute than either trap or Skeet, the governing bodies' rule books in England and

America specified that the gun must start in a "down" position.

As Sporting became more popular in the U.S., inevitably, competitions in both countries were attended by shooters from both countries, and the game on both sides of the Atlantic began to be influenced by the other. Aside from rule differences, which I will address shortly, the main differences in English Sporting between the two countries are target presentations. Typically, English targets fly faster, longer, and are more straightforward. American targets are often presented in the woods, with more curl and drop and often at closer range. Interestingly, although top shooters from each of the representative countries have difficulty adapting to the other's style of targets, it can be successfully argued that the English shooters do better in American competitions

than vice versa. This is beginning to change, but it is a slow process.

During the period of development in the U.S., the English association, known as the Clay Pigeon Shooting Association, or CPSA, suddenly changed the gun position rule, allowing shooters to pre-mount the shotgun before calling for the target. At the same time, the most prominent association in the States, the National Sporting Clays Association, or NSCA, changed some of the rules surrounding the scoring of report and following pairs, calling for a complete re-shoot of the pair if either was a "no-bird." The CPSA rule was to "establish" the first bird in either of the following or report pair in the event of a "no-bird" on the second. As you might imagine, this made refereeing during joint championships very difficult, and it was eventually agreed that all parties would adhere

Squad being shown targets at the 1995 West Coast FITASC Championship in California. Each shooter has the permanent line on his vest described in text. The menu board is in front of them.

to the rules of the host country while shooting competitions there. The NSCA did make one major concession, though, by adopting the "free gun mount" rule, after much soul searching, which although certainly not in the spirit of the original game, is much easier to referee. As a practical matter, most good shots rarely, if ever, pre-mount the gun, as it provides little real advantage. It does, however, make it easier for new shooters to participate, who may not be comfortable starting the gun in the down position.

The other version of Sporting Clays is called FITASC, which is an acronym for the ruling body of international Sporting, the *Federation de Tir aux Armes Sportives de Chasse*, based in Paris. There is a certain mystique about FITASC Sporting.

What you've heard about it may intrigue you, or it may scare you. Many times you will hear a particularly long or nasty target referred to as a "Fitasc-type" target. As a result, FITASC (pronounced FEE-task) has become synonymous with 70-yard crossers. There is nothing whatsoever in the FITASC rules requiring targets to be longer or harder, though they often are. There are several possible reasons for this. The simplest is because more than half of the targets shot at are singles at which you are allowed two shots.

The other reason is more complicated. To understand, let's go back to 1992. English Sporting, which is the game played here in the United States most of the time, was and is also the most popular version of the game in England. But the rest of the

world shoots FITASC. So if you were an aspiring British shooter who wanted to add a world title to your resume, you would have to shoot against competitors from other countries. And most other countries, like France, Germany, Spain, Belgium, South Africa, etc., shoot FITASC as their only form of Sporting. So, world championships for many years had been conducted only in the FITASC format. Since there was ample opportunity to shoot English Sporting in England, only a small group of perhaps 10 percent of English shooters pursued the FITASC format. These shooters were looking for either a world title, or a significant challenge, thus by definition were more advanced shooters, and influenced the target presentations toward the difficult end of the spectrum.

The hill country of Spain was the site of the 1995 World FITASC shoot. The shooter is standing in a Hula-Hoop-size circle, as rules specify.

FITASC course designers use natural terrain as much as possible when laying out a course, this one at River Road in California. Again, hidden traps are identified by signs.

John Bidwell, three-time World FITASC Champion shooting at the 1996 World competitions in England. Note the menu in front of him, and the white signs showing locations of hidden traps.

Although it was not their traditional discipline, British shooters quickly rose to the top of the FITASC game, and have remained there ever since. Being a member of the Great Britain team became the highest honor one could earn in the sport, and through a kind of osmosis, FITASC gained popularity among weekend club shooters too.

In 1994, a new world championship event was launched by the CPSA and NSCA based on the English format, and for the first time, shooters now have the option of competing for world titles in both FITASC and English Sporting disciplines. But regardless of your preference, both disciplines have experienced tremendous growth. In FITASC, the growth was so substantial that a "new style" of FITASC had to be introduced to accommodate the 720 shooters who attended the World Championship in France in 1990.

Currently, both old and new styles of FITASC are enjoyed in the United States, with the new style generally saved for events when more than 250 entries are expected. In both styles, 25-bird rounds are shot on layouts called parcours. In old style, a parcour will consist of three shooting stands and four or five traps. The angle and direction of targets will change from the shooter's perspective as he moves from one stand to another.

A squad of six competitors will shoot in rotation on each stand, starting with single targets on stand one. Two shots are allowed at each single target. After the entire squad has shot the singles, the shooters will rotate, and the person who was second in the singles will now start the doubles. In this way, each competitor has to shoot first exactly one time in singles and once in doubles in each round of 25 targets. When the squad moves to stand two, competitor number three will start the singles, and so on.

There are usually four singles and two doubles on each stand in old style, and an extra single will be thrown in somewhere to bring the total for the layout to 25 birds. Only one squad can shoot a layout at a time. The squad is using the same four or five traps at each stand, and the position of the shooting stands changes radically to present the biggest varia-

tion in target presentations possible from one location to the next. In some situations, it can present a safety problem if another squad even waits at stand one, while your squad is finishing on stand three. For this reason, it is quite common to see staging areas where the next squad must wait until it is their turn to shoot. This also adds to the excitement and difficulty level, since previewing targets is thus impossible.

The most obvious disadvantages to old-style FITASC are the limitations on the number of squads that can shoot in a day, and the sometimes complicated scheduling required to keep everything moving smoothly. For this reason, FITASC has always maintained strict rules on punctuality, and very few excuses are considered worthy to allow make-ups.

When new-style FITASC was first introduced in Europe, critics described it as nothing more than squadded English Sporting. In this new style, each stand on a particular layout is totally separate with its own traps dedicated to that stand only, as in English Sporting. As soon as one squad has shot and moved on to the next stand, the next squad of six immediately takes their place. In this way, every stand is always occupied, and more shooters can be put through the course. New-style FITASC requires at least four times the traps, space and referees to be staged properly, and is therefore only cost effective at large shoots.

So now that you can imagine what a FITASC course looks like, what can you expect when you walk on to the first stand of your first FITASC layout? If you are the first shooter on your squad, the referee will ask you to get into the shooting position (usually a Hula Hoop-type circle on the ground, not the wood cages you are used to in English Sporting) and he or she will show you the four or five single targets. Pay close attention even if you are not the first shooter. The referee is not allowed to show the targets again after that first person has been shown. This is one of the many differences between English and FITASC Sporting. Another difference is you must keep your gun below a line on your vest—measured from the middle of your shoulder straight down, it must be at

25 cm, or 9.85 inches—and you may not move the gun at all until the target is visible. That means if you move the gun an inch after you hear the trap go off, you will, at a minimum, have to re-shoot the bird and receive a warning, and a maximum penalty would be a lost target. This is similar to an umpire calling a balk against a major league baseball pitcher for moving inappropriately.

Another difference is in the scoring of report pairs. If the second bird of a pair is irregular, you will "establish" whatever your score was on the first bird. So if you miss the first one, and the second one comes out broken, you will re-shoot the pair, but you can only score "lost and dead" on the pair, even if you hit them both on the re-shot double.

After you have seen the targets, you will call for the first single. If you look down in front of you, there should be a menu that will give you the order of targets to be thrown. It may read, for example: "D single midi, A rabbit, C standard, and B battue." While you were viewing the targets, you may have also noticed that the field is marked with signs that indicate the approximate locations of the traps and/or targets where they first become visible to you. Both the menu and the signs can be of help to a shooter who is nervous or may have difficulty remembering which target is coming next. The referee cannot legally show you the targets again no matter how much you complain once the targets have been demonstrated. You may ask to see a target again during the demonstration if you didn't get a good look at it, but once the demonstration is over, you must rely on the menus and signs—and your memory. Sometimes, the referee will point to the vicinity of the target's appearance and simulate its flight with his finger.

So now you are ready to call for the target. The gun hold position in FITASC is very specific, and the referees are trained very carefully to watch for violations. Usually one warning will be given per layout, then targets will be taken away for further infractions. In addition to keeping the gun below the line, the butt of the gun must be touching the body, on or below that line. The rules recommend rather strongly that the line be permanently affixed to the shooting vest or coat (embroidery is the most common method), be no more than two centimeters wide, and that the measurement be taken from the top of the line or tape.

The line is there not so much, I think, to make mounting the gun more difficult because it's lower, although it does indeed make it tougher if you are not used to it. The line is there to assist the referee in preventing the shooter from raising the gun before the target is visible. It also prevents a shooter from dry swinging and firing the gun while in the shooting stand, which has become quite common among shooters' pre-call rituals. Some referees won't even let you practice mounting your gun in the waiting area! So the drill goes like this: Step in, make sure you know where the target is coming from; set up your feet, load the gun, close it, and point the muzzle where you intend to start your gun moving—all without raising the butt of the gun above that line on your vest.

Make sure you load two shells, even for the singles. You get two shots at it. But make equally sure when you finish your singles that you unload the extra shell if you didn't use it, before you leave the shooting circle or turn around and face your squad. It's important to pay attention during the singles, because you will usually see most of them again in the doubles as report or following pairs. (Simultaneous pairs are very rare in FITASC.)

Although many shooters feel that the gun mount rule is the most significant variation between English Sporting and FITASC, I think the biggest difference is that because you get two shots at each single target, it probably seems fair to the course designer to make it a somewhat more challenging target than if you had only one shot. Resist the temptation to rush your first shot. You will most likely miss and then you won't have learned how to shoot it in the pair. Try as much as possible to take one good shot at the target, and reserve the extra shell for the "Hail Mary."

FITASC is also different in the sense that you will never be able to "groove" a station and build up a good score by repeating the same pair four or five times. In FITASC, you will encounter targets with angles and speeds that will constantly test your ability to read clays, test your handling of the gun, and prove your footwork. But you will only get

FITASC shoots can be more open than English Sporting courses, as seen here in England. Either way, the birds can be very challenging.

that one chance. Then it's on to the next target. For people who do like to "groove" a course, shooting a little FITASC now and again will help you learn to read birds better. Conversely, if you are someone who can hit the first three pairs in English Sporting, then inexplicably miss the last pair, you may be getting bored and losing your focus. In FITASC, you can never let your guard down. But the game is so fascinating you won't want to.

After your entire squad has shot the singles, you will rotate one person, and shoot the doubles. If the menu lists report pairs, the referee will not be showing you any targets. The theory here is that report pairs are nothing more than two singles and you've already seen them. Also, it saves time, a valuable commodity in FITASC. The only thing for you to do here is figure out your gun and foot position.

A little trick I've learned along the way is to pay more attention to setting up for the second target than the first. Also, just like in English Sporting, you may elect to fire twice at the first target if you miss it with the first shot. This can sometimes be a strategically smart move, especially if you missed the second target with two shots in the singles.

If following or simultaneous pairs are listed on the menu, the referee must show them to the shooter first up for doubles, since these are new target presentations. They are considered new because the timing will be different, causing the shooter to look for and possibly shoot the targets in an entirely different place.

The rules concerning scoring should be reviewed before competing in a major competition, of course, and can be obtained by contacting NSCA headquarters in San Antonio, Texas.

Some shooters may feel FITASC seems like more trouble than it is worth. It's definitely not for everyone. Each year, there are more and more places to shoot FITASC in the United States, although is has not and probably never will eclipse the popularity of English Sporting. Plan on shooting a few targets below your average the first few times you try it. Since it's a completely different game, there will be a lot of distractions that keep you from performing your best. But when you get the hang of it you'll enjoy the rituals and rules. And it will make you a better shot. That's what Sporting is all about. ●

Opening ceremonies of the 1996 World FITASC Championships in England. Most of the world shoots the FITASC discipline, and the British seem to dominate it.

CLAYS-RELATED

by MARTY

THERE IS NO doubt that the arrival of Sporting Clays on the North American continent in the mid-1980s has done more for the shotgun shooting sports than any other factor since Skeet was developed almost 80 years ago. The major reason for this resurgence in shotgun shooting has been the numerous ancillary games that have been developed using Sporting Clays-type presentations and rules as a basis of existence.

Some of these games did, in fact, already exist before Sporting came on shore, but in many cases their popularity has blossomed as a result of Sporting Clays and the influx of new shooters the game has attracted. An explanation of what these games are, how they are played and the rules associated with them will provide a better understanding of the importance of Sporting Clays in America.

Crazy Quail

One of the earliest games that enticed shotgunners to burn more powder was Crazy Quail. This fun-filled game was developed to simulate flushing quail. Because of this, it has become very popular with hunting preserves, and today the game serves as a stand-alone fun shooting experience as well as a good warm-up for a day of hunting.

The game consists of a single trap usually positioned below ground in a pit 16 to 27 yards in front of the shooter. The trap is mounted on a swivel base to allow targets to be thrown up to 360 degrees. Since the trap is out of sight of the shooter, he has no idea where the bird will be when he calls for it. It may fly directly over the shooter's head or at any other angle to the left, right and away from the shooter.

Crazy Quail at Winchester's Nilo Farms is a real challenge. The trap is positioned well below ground level, and quick target acquisition is a key to higher scores.

5-Stand Sporting was designed to overlay onto a Skeet field, so any facility with a high house and low house have the makings of a 5-Stand layout.

GAMES

FISCHER

Sporting Clays has given shotgunning and the outdoors a shot in the arm, and other games have spun off from it. Other, older clay target games are still being enjoyed.

Most Crazy Quail setups use a manual machine manned by a trapper. The trap swivels on its base and the trapper will throw either singles, report pairs or true pairs of presentations. A round of Crazy Quail consists of 10 to 25 targets.

Since the majority of Crazy Quail layouts utilize manual equipment, it is critical to ensure the safety of the trapper. This is best accomplished by making sure that the depth of the pit housing the machine is deep enough to completely cover the trapper as he sits on the trap stand.

Some facilities do this by using tapered berms or some type of shot-proof screening to provide proper protection. It's a good idea to have some type of orange or red flag for the trapper to display when it isn't safe to shoot.

5-Stand Sporting is a great spectator game and, as a result, it serves as a focal point for many conservation, charity and celebrity shoots around the country.

Not all 5-Stands are the same. At the Vail Rod and Gun Club, for instance, there is no Skeet field. Instead, the traps are positioned on the ground and in the tower behind the shooters.

Crazy Quail is usually played using only standard size targets thrown at medium speed and at an elevation of 50 to 60 degrees. Using these presentation parameters helps insure that the birds are visible to the shooter and are therefore breakable.

5-Stand Sporting

Once the Sporting Clays juggernaut got rolling in the U.S., demand for the game spread like wildfire. Unfortunately many of the shooting facilities around the country had already utilized most of their available property for trap, Skeet and other shooting disciplines, so finding room for a walk-around Clays course was difficult. At the same time, those facilities that were able to put in Sporting Clays found themselves in serious need of a warm-up game for Sporting.

The answer to their prayers came in the form of 5-Stand Sporting, the brainchild of Raymond Foreman, a Scotsman now living in Canada. There is no question that 5-Stand has become the most popular of all Sporting Clays-related shooting games, as a large percentage of facilities now offer some form of the game. Let's take a look at how this fabulous game is played.

5-Stand Sporting is designed to overlay onto a regulation Skeet field, so it can be played in a relatively small area. The game calls for either six or eight automatic traps and some type of trap controller to present the targets. In its original design, 5-Stand utilized the high and low house traps on a Skeet field, a long incoming target to replicate an incoming bird, a short tower shot from behind the shooter, a springing teal, and a rabbit.

There are five shooting boxes or stands placed in a line from Stations 3 to 5 on the Skeet field. The stands are placed 12 to 15 feet apart, which provides a different shooting angle for each of the targets presented. As the shooters move to the stand to their right after five targets, they face completely different angles and speeds in each of the five boxes.

A round of 5-Stand consists of 25 targets, and there are a number of ways to go about shooting those birds. Foreman's original game called for the target sequence to be unknown to the shooter. In a round,

shooters would receive two true pairs and one single in each shooting stand. The origin of the targets would be unknown, but a siren or buzzer would sound when the true pairs were presented.

Most 5-Stand layouts today give the shooter a menu of shots to go by. The menu will prescribe which shots each shooter gets and when. This format was put into place by the National Sporting Clays Association, and today, 5-Stand targets can be shot for registered competition scores.

Controllers for the game range from direct wire units that throw only the traps that are selected by the operator, to state-of-the-art computerized, wireless controllers capable of throwing a variety of games that can be played on a 5-Stand layout. Of course, the more sophisticated a controller is, the more the initial financial cost will be, so this high-tech arrangement won't be seen with a lot of regularity.

Shooters who achieve good scores at 5-Stand Sporting usually have a few tricks up their sleeve on how to approach the game. The targets presented in the game closely resemble many of the birds one would encounter during a round of Sporting Clays at a course where automatic traps are used. There will be a number of targets going in opposite directions to each other. Getting a read on what the birds are doing and deciding which one to shoot first really helps the shooter plan his strategy for each target presentation.

On most 5-Stands, all of the targets converge to the center of the layout, so the shooter can set his plan to find targets crossing there at some point in their flight. This is an advantage if the sequence of birds is unknown. It helps establish the break point on birds when they are spelled out on a menu of shots, too.

When shooting pairs, the shooter must figure out which bird to take first. This determination is made by deciding which bird, if shot first, will make the second one easier to break. In almost every case, shooters will take the lower of the two in order to give time to locate each bird, and get the muzzle of the gun in place to take the shot.

With targets often going in opposing directions, good muzzle management is a key to higher scores. So

where possible, the shooter should temper his enthusiasm to break the first bird too quickly. In many cases, it would be better to take the first bird at a point that eases the transition of the muzzle to the second bird.

Two Man Flush

The vast majority of shooting games are played for an individual score, but the Two Man Flush was developed for team participation and competition. This one really became popular through the many fun shoot programs held annually for various conservation and charitable groups. Their purpose at was to encourage as much shooting as possible to enhance fund raising, but over time range owners found that it was very popular.

Most of the time Two Man Flush consists of 25 to 30 targets thrown in a time frame of 30 to 45 seconds. Shooters are often limited to the number of shells that can be put into their gun at any given time during the sequence, and they are usually allowed to load only two shells to start. It's common to allow the team to have one shell for each target that will be thrown, i.e. 15 shells are allowed for each shooter in a 30-bird event.

The game may be played on virtually any type of shooting area. The most popular applications, however, are shot on trap or Skeet layouts, utilizing the existing traps, or one or more traps placed strategically for the game itself. As a result, the sequence and presentation variety of the targets are limited only by the imagination of the range manager or person in charge. Often the game is played using an international wobble trap machine capable of throwing high-speed clays at a variety of angles.

The most successful two-man teams formulate a plan of attack prior to calling for the target sequence to begin. Usually, one shooter takes birds until his gun is empty, and then his partner takes over. As long as their timing remains intact, their scores should be pretty good.

On Two Man Flush games with multiple traps, shooters might choose to take only the targets emerging from certain traps. That way each shooter is responsible for designated birds, and his attention can be channeled in only that direction.

Trap House Sporting

In the early '90s, Trap House Sporting was developed in order to place a Sporting layout over an area as small as the width of a regulation Skeet field. The game utilizes a two- to three-tiered portable structure on wheels, and up to 15 traps capable of throwing virtually every target and presentation type found in Sporting.

Up to 13 shooting stations separated by safety screens may be employed on each side of the structure, which gives shooters the opportunity to shoot 50- or 100-shot rounds. The beauty of the game is that the shooter takes more than four shots per station, so the game can be played in less time, and in a much smaller space than needed for a walk-around Sporting Clays course.

Because of its portability, Trap House Sporting can be pulled behind a vehicle and set up in wooded areas or in open fields that have no gun club connection to them at all. As a result, the game may be shot in virtually any approved location where the down range shot fall zones allow for safe shooting.

Quail Walk

Another shooting affair that can be found in both gun club and hunting preserve locations is the Quail Walk. This game is designed to replicate upland bird shooting as the shooter moves slowly along a designated path, more or less in a straight line. As the shooter ambles along, targets

The upper levels of the Trap House Sporting structure provide some interesting tower-like birds. The unit is available in two- and three-level configurations.

Trap House Sporting is actually a portable Sporting Clays course. It can be set up in open fields as well as in wooded areas to make things challenging.

that simulate the flight of game birds or rabbits are flushed or otherwise presented in front of the gun. The game can be set up in both wooded and open field areas, and the traps may be either manual or automatic.

When shooting a Quail Walk, the gunner will achieve better scores if he positions his muzzle straight ahead of himself as he moves along the walk. This gives him a chance to quickly react to targets presented from either the left or the right. Additionally, he should not hold the muzzle too high, since it is more difficult to come down on a target than it is to come up to it.

Supersport

This game was popularized in Europe, and in many ways replicates a day of rough shooting in the field. Supersport utilizes 15 to 30 automatic traps electronically connected to a series of sensors which serve to trigger target releases. Further demonstration of the complexity of the automation required to play Supersport is evidenced by the transmitter worn by the shooter which communicates with the receiving sensor for a corresponding trap.

This game can be the ultimate simulation for live bird shooting, since the entire walking course taken by the shooter is run by computer. Settings for target presentation, when the birds are thrown, as well as for target difficulty can be established in advance of the shooter beginning his round.

There aren't many of these layouts in America. This is primarily due to the somewhat limited number of shooters a layout can accommodate in a day, and the fact that the costs associated with such a layout can be significant.

Dove Tower

Shooters who enjoy shooting birds seem to really like tower shots, since they tend to closely replicate doves, ducks and other driven game birds that might be encountered in the field. As a result of this love for the high bird, many ranges offer high tower shooting.

There is actually no specified tower height to play this game, so shooters could encounter targets presented from structures upward of 160 feet. It's not uncommon for manual traps to be used on towers less than 40 feet high, but for safety reasons automatic machines are typically found on higher structures.

The game usually consists of singles and report pairs presented in rounds of 25 targets. Depending on the game layout, shooters fire at all of the birds from either a single station or from multiple stations. The trap configuration will be stationary or in a wobble mode.

Modern Skeet, Modern Sporting, Modern Trap

These games are played on traditional trap and Skeet fields, and utilize special trap bases for their unique presentations. Developed by Ken Gagnon of Quack Sporting Clays, Inc., these modern games were designed to put a bit of uncertainty into the target presentations of otherwise very structured shooting disciplines.

Modern Skeet is played on a Skeet field with the traps fitted with a special vertically-oscillating base. Since the traps oscillate, the flight line of the birds is unknown to the shooter. This is the main difference between traditional Skeet and the modern version. But there are other differences as well.

In Modern Skeet, shooters get no single targets. Instead, they get a report pair and true double on stations 1, 2, 6 and 7. They get report pairs only on stations 3, 4 and 5, a single

Dove Tower shots provide a great deal of fun for the shooter. Tower heights range from 15 feet to over 150 feet.

on high 8 and a true pair on low 8. While this might sound a bit confusing, it really isn't. What it is, however, is a great deal of fun.

Modern Sporting is played the same way, except the stations on 3, 4 and 5 are eight yards farther back.

Modern Trap is played like regular American trap, except there is a special base for the trap that causes the target to curl instead of flying straight.

There is no doubt that the Modern versions of trap and Skeet provide a unique twist to these games. But shooting is supposed to be fun, and the uncertainty of the target presentation assures a few surprises and lots of shooting fun.

Scrap/Chinese Trap

This game is played on a combination trap/Skeet field. Here, shooters shoot trap targets from the Skeet stations. In most cases, the game is played from the low gun position, and two shots are allowed at single targets.

Follow the Leader

This one is can be played on a trap, Skeet or 5-Stand field, or a combination of two of them. Shooters draw to determine the order they shoot. The first shooter calls for a presentation he wishes to shoot, and if he's successful, the other shooters have to "follow the leader" in shooting the same presentation. Shooters who fail to break the presentation are eliminated and the last shooter standing wins the game.

Rabbit Run

Played on a trap field, Rabbit Run utilizes standard clays and not rabbit clays. The trap is set to throw the targets just above the ground. Shooters stand either on the trap house or just behind it, and shoot a round of 25 targets. The sequence of birds can be either all singles or singles and report pairs.

Annie Oakley

A very popular game played on a trap field and shot from the 27-yard line. For this contest, shooters draw lots to determine the shooting order. Shooting takes place in quantities of three shooters at a time. The first player calls for the bird and shoots at it. If he misses, the second shooter takes a shot. Should he miss, the third person in line shoots. The successful shooter eliminates the preceeding gun from the game and takes his place in the rotation. Should all three miss, no one is eliminated.

As people are eliminated, participants in the order of draw move up to the third position. They are then in the game until eliminated. The last shooter standing is declared the winner.

Make-a-Break

One of the first made-for-TV shooting games, Make-a-Break is rapidly gaining popularity with both competitive and non-competitive shooters alike. It is played by two shooters at a time. Shooting is from a single station, and competition is head to head. Eight traps are used, with two of them placed relatively close to the shooters to throw going away targets. One of these birds is shot first to initiate a shooting sequence. The other six traps on the layout are deployed to present a series of challenging shots. Those traps are numbered two through seven based on the difficulty level of the target. Number two would be considered the easiest of the birds, and number seven would be the most difficult.

Shooters shoot 10 report pairs of birds commencing with a number one bird followed by the other targets in sequence for the first round of shooting. The number one target is always shot first and counts one point if broken. Other targets in the sequence count their designated point value if broken.

After the first round of targets, the drama and suspense of the game begin. Shooters in the four pair bonus round may call for the target of their choice to be combined with the number one target. If a competitor is behind, he can elect to shoot the higher scoring birds. He must hit them, however, or risk losing ground to his competitor very quickly.

A front-running shooter must protect his lead or extend it. This can be done by shooting a fairly high-scoring target that he is comfortable shooting time and time again. The top score at the end of the two rounds is the winner.

As you can see, there are many shooting games to choose from, and new ones are constantly being developed. With all these fun-filled opportunities available for today's shotgunners, it's a safe bet that the shooting sports are in good shape for the future. ●

Games like Annie Oakley provide a real challenger to the shooter. Targets are often broken well in excess of 50 yards. That's good shooting!

CLAYS CLUBS WEST

Here are a dozen top-notch facilities out West.

Ben Avery definitely has a desert feel, and is a friendly place to be.

IN THE 15 years that I've been shooting, I've traveled to many shooting ranges around the country simply for recreational pursuits as well as serious competition. Some I've enjoyed immensely and others were lacking in one way or another, leaving me with the impression that they were just another place at which to shoot. However, over those years and many thousands of shotshells and clay targets, I have discovered that shooting ranges are like people because they have different personalities. It's not just the personality of the management staff, but the atmosphere and environment—the overall feel—of the entire facility that makes such a difference in how comfortable you are at one of these places. Like Ben Avery Clay Target Center, for instance.

Ben Avery Clay Target Center
Carefree, Arizona

37016 N. Archery Dr.
Tel: 602-587-1706
Fax: 602-587-1696

SHOOTING FEES

Membership: $50.00 per year

Member: $13.00/50 targets

Non-member: $18.00/50 targets

When I first started shooting back in the early 1980s, Ben Avery was where I learned about the sport. Back then, it wasn't a very nice facility. You never knew if there were going to be trappers available and the

So many places, so little time! That's the lament of many shooters who want to see the world of Sporting Clays.

by SHARI LeGATE

traps themselves were in terrible condition. Broken targets were a part of the game. The clubhouse was dark and dingy and overall the place was pretty dismal. Then a few years ago, the McGaffee family bought it and Dave McGaffee now runs it. A lot of effort and money went into re-vamping the facility and now it's one of my favorite places to shoot. Not only because Phoenix offers over 300 sunshine-filled days per year, but because of Ben Avery's personality.

When you drive in, the first thing you notice is how clean and mani-cured the grounds are. Walking into the clubhouse, the friendly atmo-sphere and the immediate greeting by the staff projects the professional-ism that the McGaffees bring to the sport. The Sporting Clays course has a rock-lined granite pathway and the course itself is in the midst of the Sonoran Desert. Step into the cage and the target flies out from behind a 100-year-old Sonora cactus. The course is changed on a regular basis to give the beginner as well as the

advanced shooter a diversity of tar-get presentations. The clubhouse is now open and airy with a southwest-ern décor, and has a pro shop and snack bar. This is a great place to bring a first-time shooter.

Rio Grand Valley Shooting Center
Rio Hondo, Texas

P.O. Box 465
Rio Hondo, TX 78583
Tel: 800-409-2489
Fax: 956-748-4212

SHOOTING FEES

Membership: $250.00 per year

Member: $17.00/50 targets

Non-member: $24.00/50 targets

This is a full-service shooting fa-cility and a place to experience an outdoor adventure. Opened two years ago by Mike and Mary Jo Jan-ovsky, the Center is more than just a shooting facility. It also has a wild-

life sanctuary with deer, javelina and feral hogs, along with coyotes, bobcats, and rats, rabbits, rattle-snakes and other varmints. Mike and Mary Jo are deeply involved in fish and wildlife conservation and they bring that same passion to Sporting Clays. When building the facility, located on 400 acres of na-tive brush, they brought in World Champion shotgunners Scott Rob-ertson and Dan Carlisle to design the 36-station course.

The Center strongly believes in Southern hospitality and everyone who comes to shoot is part of the family. The clubhouse is a full 6000 square feet and is home to the Re-loader Cafe, where daily specials are home-cooked meals, not fast food, frozen microwave dinners. There is also a cozy country fire to gather around during the rare cold days.

In addition to Sporting, 5-Stand is available and you can also try your hand at trap, Skeet, archery, rifle, pistol, fishing and hiking through the desert on the many marked trails.

Rio Grand Valley is a full-service shooting facility for shotgunners, riflemen, handgunners and archery buffs.

The Cody Complex has five courses in a variety of terrains. (Buffalo Bill Historical Center photo.)

A multitude of target presentations keep things interesting at Lanai Pine Sporting Clays.

The Cody Shooting Complex
Cody, Wyoming

61 Country Rd 7WC
Cody, WY 82414
Tel: 307-587-5236.
Fax: Not available

SHOOTING FEES

Membership: $35.00 per year
Member: $10.00/50 targets
Non-member: $12.00/50 targets

One of the best-kept secrets in the west is this wonderful shooting facility and internationally acclaimed firearm museum. The Cody Shooting Complex boasts five different courses that encompass a variety of terrains. Challenging, but fair, the courses are set on hillsides, in deep ravines and pine-tree-covered areas that introduce the shooter to a diversity of target presentations, with optical illusion being the mainstay. In the winter, when the ground is covered by snow, the courses present even more challenging and fun shots as the different colored targets sharply contrast with the white background to bring out the playfulness in all shooters. There is no pro shop or restaurant, but the town of Cody is just minutes away and has several well-equipped sporting goods stores. One of them has an in-house gunsmith and one of the best Mexican restaurants that I've ever enjoyed.

After a morning of shooting, any avid shooter should visit the Cody Firearms Museum at The Buffalo Bill Historical Center. In 1976, the Winchester Collection, an outstanding assemblage of 4500 firearms created by major American manufacturers, was put on display here. Today, the museum houses the worlds largest and most important collection of American arms, as well as European arms dating back to the 16th century. It's a perfect way to end a satisfying day of shooting.

Lanai Pine Sporting Clays
Lanai, Hawaii

P.O. Box 310
Lanai City, HI 96763
Tel: 808-563-4600
Fax: 808-565-3868

SHOOTING FEES

Membership: None available

$65.00/50 targets

$125.00/100 targets

When vacationing in Hawaii, thoughts of white beaches, suntanned bodies and snorkeling come to mind, not Sporting Clays. But nestled on the north side of the island of Lanai on the plains of Mahana, Lanai Pine Sporting Clays offers four clay target shooting disciplines amidst spectacular views of Molokai and Maui across the Auau Channel. This shooting facility and resort is not for those light of pocket money. The Lodge at Koele is a gracious upcountry resort and reflects the atmosphere of a gentlemen's hunting lodge with high ceilings and huge stone fireplaces.

This Sporting Clays course is designed to appeal to both skilled and new shooters alike. It features 14 stations that are situated within a 200-acre pine wooded valley overlooking Molokai. Target presentation includes standard, mini, rabbit, battue, and midi, and mimic traditional game such as flushed pheasants and chukar, high-flying ducks and rabbits. The pro shop is located at the course and is complete with Sporting accessories and a snack shop. The amenities at this facility are absolutely top drawer, but it's the Clays course itself that makes it worthwhile to stop here and shoot. It's an unforgettable experience.

Lanai Pine Sporting Clays offers spectacular vistas with four clay target disciplines.

Pachmayr International Shooting Park El Monte, California

831 N. Rosemead Blvd., S.
El Monte, CA 91733
Tel: 626-579-5201
Fax: 626-579-5201

SHOOTING FEES

Membership: $95.00 per year

Member: $18.00/50 targets

Non-member: $25.00/100 targets

When driving through the gate to Pachmayr International Shooting Park, you can't help but notice how well appointed the facility is. Pachmayr has that L.A./Hollywood personality. It's a little aloof when you first arrive, but once they get to know you, you're brought into the fold. The home shooting ground for two Olympic champions and a number of celebrities, Pachmayr is located 15 minutes east of Los Angeles and 9 miles south of Pasadena. This sprawling facility boasts every shotgun game imaginable. The 16-station Sporting Clays course offers every specialty target, standard targets and many extras that aren't normally seen, including one of the most challenging duck towers on the West Coast.

A secret about Pachmayr I'll let out is their on-site restaurant. It serves one of the best pastrami sandwiches outside of New York! Sitting outside on the covered patio, relaxing and watching the 5-Stand, you sometimes forget that you're in the heart of metropolitan southern California.

Sage Hill Clay Sports Reno, Nevada

11500 Mira Loma Road
Reno, NV 89511
Tel: 702-851-1123
Fax: 702-851-7786
E-mail: shcs@aol.com

SHOOTING FEES

Membership: $150.00 per year

Member: $15.00/50 targets

Non-member: $17.50/50 targets

On your next visit to Reno or Lake Tahoe, take a day to stop at Sage Hill. Home to the U.S. Winter Championships, the Sporting Clays course has been expanded to a total of 25 stations. The setting is high desert, meaning no trees, with severe definition to the landscape, meaning hills. On a daily basis, only 10 stations are open at a time, but walking through the shooting trail, through the hills, is a great time in and of itself. And, the different targets offered at each station are a joy to shoot at. One particular station overlooks a ravine and the target flies outward from underneath the station into the sage-covered hill as another target crosses from right to left. Between the background and the ravine, the targets appear much more difficult than they actually are. This is a fun course for a beginner shooter and a deceiving one for the experienced gunner.

The clubhouse encompasses 7500 square feet and has a full-service bar and snack shop. A beautiful stone fireplace separates the bar from the rest of the clubhouse seating area, and the 5-Stand can be watched from huge bay windows that make up one side of the building. Sage Hill also offers great family activities in addition to shooting. Twenty-four hour gaming, great dining, hotel/casino lodging are fun, and there's always Lake Tahoe and its own beauty and recreation only 30 minutes away. For the history buffs, Virginia City is only 20 minutes away down the road.

Dallas Gun Club course is shot through the trees and over water, and has a challenging duck tower.

The Clubhouse at Dallas Gun Club offers all the amenities for a comfortable day of shooting.

Dallas Gun Club
Lewisville, Texas

3601 I-35 South
Lewisville, TX 75067
Tel: 972-462-7180
Fax: 972-462-0716
E-mail: www.dallasgunclub.com

SHOOTING FEES

Membership: $1,500.00 per year

Member: $24.00/100 targets

Non-member: $32.00/100 targets

I first walked into the Dallas Gun Club in the late 1980s and was impressed with how well run and maintained it was, from the perfectly designed landscape to the stone Skeet houses. I was also impressed by how expensive it was to shoot there. This was not a club at which the average or beginner shooter might want to begin their shooting sports journey. But that was then and this is now.

The club has become much more shooter-friendly since then. Clinics are held on a regular basis, memberships are offered more openly, and strangers welcomed onto the range. Founded in 1946, Dallas Gun Club is located on 690 wooded acres south of Lewisville. It is designed to appeal to both skilled and novice shooters, and the 12-station Sporting Clays course offers a variety of target presentations. Redesigned every two weeks to ensure diversity, the course is shot through trees and over water. In addition, a challenging duck tower over the tree line provides a fun-filled day of shooting. The 5000-square-foot-plus clubhouse is professionally staffed and maintains a full-service pro shop, dining room, bar and lounge.

Big Sky Sporting Clays
Polson, Montana

3100 Irvine Flats Rd.
Polson, MT 59860
Tel: 406-833-2000
Fax: 406-833-6106
Email: clays@cyberport.net

SHOOTING FEES

Membership: $100.00 per year

Member: $28.00/100 targets

Non-member: $30.00/100 targets

Rick Vancoast has taken the personality of Montana and created a premiere shooting facility among a majestic setting and breathtaking views. This is a place where you will want to linger a few days and return again and again. Big Sky Sporting Clays is Montana. Located in the beautiful Mission Valley of western Montana, the club is surrounded by the Mission Mountains and it's wilderness on the west, Flathead Lake on the north and the Mission Valley on the south.

The Clays course is one of the best I've ever shot, because the incredible scenery is a part of each station and each shot. The two 12-station courses are built along a breathtaking gorge overlooking the Flathead River. Follow the well-groomed verdant paths and you can't help but be impressed by the effort to conceal the

Challenging shooting situations and impeccable facilities make Big Sky a great place to shoot.

traps and provide comfort and convenience to the shooter. The imagination expended in providing the challenging shooting situations adds to the spectacular setting. Rabid Badger charges you from in front and below a bridge, initiated from a concealed trap in the creek bottom. The Goose Pit is only missing the frost of a fall morning. The 3000 square foot clubhouse has a small pro shop that can provide any accessories needed.

Midway Farms is a popular facility that offers two 50-target courses, a hunting preserve and cozy clubhouse.

Midway Farms, Inc.
Rayette, Missouri

700 Country Road 404
Rayette, MO 65248
Tel: 660-248-3838

SHOOTING FEES

Membership: None available

$15.00/50 targets

$28.00/100 targets

Acclaimed as one of the most scenic and aesthetically pleasing courses in the country, Midway Farms provides diversified targets in a most pleasant setting. I've not shot there, but I included it in this profile because of the many comments I've received from other shooters who have been there. I don't always get to all the facilities that I would like and I would hate to not include one because of my busy schedule. The many other shooters who shot there rave about the club and it's course.

This retreat center and hunt preserve offers two 50-target courses. Forty traps offer a wide variety of left, right, high, low and overhead shots that are challenging for experienced shooters and exciting for the novice. Trees and water make the shooting trail pleasantly appealing when walking from station to station. The clubhouse is covers about 2700 square feet, and doesn't have a pro shop, but loaner guns and ammunition are available.

Coyote Valley Sporting Clays
Morgan Hill, California

1000 San Bruno Ave.
Morgan Hill, CA 95037
Tel: 408-778-3600
Fax: Not available

SHOOTING FEES

Membership: $89.00 per year

Member: $29.00/100 targets

Non-member: $36.00/100 targets

Outside of San Jose, California, nestled up against the mountains, is challenging Sporting Clays facility owned and operated by Tom and Nancy Ebert. Shooting here, one is pleasantly surprised to enjoy the wide-open ranch land and oak-studded hillsides just minutes away from the city. What struck me the most was how Coyote Valley offers a complete shooting experience marked by helpful and courteous personnel who are really interested in serving the customer. Regardless of your prior shooting experience, you'll feel comfortable during your visit from the time you arrive.

The club has a full range of clay target shooting opportunities. There are two courses available, the automated 10-station Main Course and the 12-station Mountain course. The Main Course offers targets that are challenging and breakable, allowing newcomers good success. More advanced shooters enjoy shooting from alternate shooting positions, or may opt for the Mountain Course, which has a more demanding presentation of mostly true pairs and specialty targets. The full service clubhouse is well stocked with clothing and accessories and everything needed for enjoyment of the sport, and gun rental is available. And if you're traveling from out of town, your gun rental is on the house.

Woods and Water, Inc.
Catoosa, Oklahoma

Rt.1, Box 319
Catoosa, OK 74015
Tel: 918-266-5551

SHOOTING FEES

Membership: $1,425.00 per year (includes unlimited Sporting Clays)

Non-member: $15.00/50 targets

$25.00/100 targets

Coyote Valley Sporting Clays has a country feel, yet is just minutes from the city.

Woods and Water has 50- and 100-target courses. The lodge is a B&B with gourmet restaurant.

What makes Woods and Water so enticing is that when you go to its two courses, you are literally walking into the woods. The 50-target, nine-station course, and 100-target, 13-station course are set into the woods, not clear-cut land. The 50-target course is set up primarily for the novice shooter, and is a great introduction for a beginner. It could also serve as a refresher for the more experienced shooter. However, the 100-bird course challenges the intermediate and advanced shooters. While you're on the grounds, you're apt to come across deer and other wildlife sharing the trails with you. The 1200-square-foot clubhouse offers a complete pro shop and a deli-style restaurant.

Owned originally by William Skelley of Skelley Oil in the '20s and '30s, Woods and Water is surrounded by history. The beautifully restored bed and breakfast lodge also houses a gourmet restaurant. This is a superb shooting facility that lets you experience and enjoy the outdoors as well as, perhaps, a romantic weekend.

Claythorne Lodge
Columbus, Kansas

1329 NW 100th
Columbus, KS 66725
Tel: 316-597-2568
Fax: 316-597-255-

SHOOTING FEES

Membership: $700.00 per year

Member: $16.00/50 targets

Non-member: $23.00/50 targets

Kansas is one of my favorite places, mainly because of all the pheasant hunting I've done there, but also because it has a personality all its own. I firmly believe that Dorothy was mistaken when she commented in the Wizard of Oz: "We're not in Kansas anymore, Toto." All my experiences there have confirmed that it certainly could be in the land of Oz. And Claythorne Lodge is part of that Oz magic.

Just 35 minutes from the Joplin, Missouri, airport, Claythorne boasts some of the most beautiful courses in the country. There are five unique courses that consist of over 100 stations. The four 10-station courses and one 5-station course are set on 280 acres of trees, hills and fish-stocked ponds. The courses are changed every few weeks to offer diverse target presentations to entertain the novice and challenge the most skilled Clays enthusiast. The pro shop has all the necessary accessories and outdoor gear for clay target shooting.

But what makes Claythorne Lodge so special is the staff. They are truly dedicated to providing a shooting experience that you will enjoy and remember. For instance, there is no restaurant or snack shop, but if you notify them ahead that you would like food, they are happy to accommodate with home-style cooking. The Lancasters, who own the Claythorne, are shooters themselves, of course, and know what guests appreciate. As a result, this facility offers a gorgeous setting and great targets.

These, then, are some of my favorite shooting clubs west of the Mississippi, my cream of the crop. It is the wonderful facilities such as these that make Sporting Clays—and trap and Skeet, for that matter—so enjoyable, because there seem to be relatively few sports that can be enjoyed in such beautiful settings with great companionship and friendly competition like these.

If you find yourself near any one of these clubs, drop in for a round of Clays or even a cup of coffee and see just how comfortable you'll be. You owe it to yourself once in a while. ●

The pro shop at Claythorne has all the necessities for clay target shooting should you forget something at home.

Claythorne Lodge has a variety of courses set in hills, trees and over stocked ponds, and offer great targets in splendid countryside.

CLAYS IN THE EAST

12 WORTH THE TRIP

BACK ABOUT 15 years ago, when Sporting Clays crossed the big pond from England and made its debut in the United States, it didn't take a rocket scientist or fortune teller to realize it was inherently blessed with all of the elements necessary to become the biggest thing since sliced bread for recreational shotgun shooters on this side of the Atlantic. From that first planted seed, the game spread like crabgrass in an unattended suburban lawn.

Since that first flush of excitement when, like brand-new Wal-Marts opening all around the country, it seemed as if each week brought a spate of new clubs, the expansion has leveled off considerably. Shoestring operations by the score faded away as quickly as they appeared as shooters became more discriminating about target quality and the caliber of experience they expected for their money. The Sporting Clays grounds that made it over the hump, even prospered, during this transition period are now among the best in the country, and the region east of the Mississippi, just as it had been when the whole thing started, can lay claim to many of them.

One caveat here: It's impractical and, frankly, unfair to think one person could select the definitive top 12 Sporting Clays grounds in the East. Personal preferences and prejudices are different, and what I might consider necessary and a major plus, you may not. In a way, it's like going to Baskin-Robbins, and, after looking at the long list of the ice cream flavors available, asking a total stranger to select the handful you should buy for your own special party. So, to maintain perspective, keep in mind that what we have here is a list of clubs that, frankly, could be much longer.

Some are like a fancy, four-star restaurant with all of the trappings, while others more resemble a small town cafe serving up country cooking. However, the single factor that links them together is top quality Sporting targets. Most have other shooting games for you to play. And they all have a special character that will leave a permanent stamp on your memory. So, grab your gear, and let's get on with it.

It's not easy to pick a dozen of the best Sporting Clays facilities east of the Mississippi, but author Davis narrowed his list to these fine clubs.

by BARRY G. DAVIS

Knowledge, equipment, terrain, and experience enable Addieville East Farm to successfully host a half-dozen significant Sporting competitions a year.

Shooters take a break between fields at one of the permanent gazebos on the backside of the Sporting course.

Addieville East Fam
Mapleville, Rhode Island

200 Pheasant Dr.
Tel: 401-568-3185
Fax: 401-568-3009

SHOOTING FEES

Membership: $50.00 per year

Member: $15.00/50 targets

Non-member: $20.00/50 targets

Rhode Island, the smallest state in the Union, is home to two of the best Sporting Clays grounds in the country. Geoff and Paula Gaebe's Addieville East Farm in Mapleville, only 20 minutes northwest of Providence, is a 900-acre hunting preserve that stepped into Sporting Clays in the mid-'80s. Geoff became a committed student of the game, and the Sporting course is now spread across 75 rolling acres of woods and open fields.

During spring and summer, 38 separate shooting fields, with multiple traps at each, are available on an everyday basis to provide a vast array of target presentations. Add in four practice towers for "tall" targets and a special flurry sequence reminiscent of what game shooters practice on in England, and a shooter can spend days just trying to do it all. Addieville East is also known as a competition ground, putting on six blue-chip tournaments a year, including the unique Vintage Cup/World Side-by-Side Championship in late September. Throw in onsite, full-time instruction and a comfortable clubhouse that includes overnight capabilities, and you have a totally self-contained ground suitable for shooters of any level.

Peace Dale Sporting Clays
Peace Dale, Rhode Island

411 Rose Hill Rd.
Tel: 401-789-3730
Fax: 401-783-0896

SHOOTING FEES

Membership: None available

Member: $15.00/50 targets

Only minutes from Interstate 95, historic Newport, and scenic Narragansett, the Frisella family's Peace Dale Sporting Clays has carved out a thoroughly earned reputation as "the home of tough targets." Variety is key at Peace Dale, and course setter Richie Frisella, Jr., out of sheer necessity, has become a diabolical genius at coming up with innovative target presentations. With three 50-target courses of eight or nine stands each going at all times, and one course dismantled and a new one built every week, year round, the club's league and coterie of regular shooters get to see more different targets in a single year than most shooters see in a decade. In addition,

the 210-acre ground also has at least one FITASC layout and a 5-Stand available. And every six weeks they put on a "clock shot," a Peace Dale exclusive that offers up 50 of the most challenging targets you'll ever see.

Peace Dale is a "blue collar" ground, costs are shooter friendly, and the clubhouse atmosphere has the comfortable informality of a good buddy's living room. With motels, bed & breakfasts, seafood restaurants, and some of the most beautiful beaches in New England only a stone's throw away, it's not hard to see why many consider it one of the top pure shooter's grounds in the country.

Orvis Sandanona
Millbrook, New York

P. O. Box 450
Tel: 914-677-9701
Fax: 914-677-0092

SHOOTING FEES

Membership: $100.00 per year

Member: $45.00/100 targets

Non-member: $65.00/100 targets

In rural Dutchess County, an hour north of the Big Apple, Orvis Sandanona Shooting Grounds sits on 400 of the most beautiful acres you can imagine. The original Sandanona was one of the first major Sporting grounds in the country, but it fell on hard times a few years back. Resurrected by Orvis, a company known worldwide for quality, the meticulously manicured ground has returned to a rightful place of pre-eminence.

Good terrain helps to make good targets, and Orvis Sandanona is blessed with wonderful terrain—rolling hills, ridges and natural open flats surrounded by stands of hardwoods. Twenty shooting fields, with multiple traps at each, are designed to accommodate Sporting shooters of all levels, from expert to novice. The multiple level design is critical because the ground does a substantial amount of corporate entertainment and shooting instruction, in addition to upland hunts and Continental-style bird releases during the fall season. To put a final layer of icing on the cake, there's also a full ZZ Bird layout, a simulated live pigeon game

Shooters begin Peace Dale's unique Clock Shot sequence that's lots of fun.

This shooter is about to take a target emerging from behind the tree at Peace Dale.

that's as addictive as the real thing. As befitting the Orvis status, shooting costs are at the upper end of the scale, and reservations are a must. However, you only live once, and just setting foot on a ground as gorgeous as Sandanona (especially in early fall when the leaves are in full color) let alone shooting targets you may never have experienced if you come from flat land, is worth the extra premium.

M&M Hunting Preserve and Sporting Clays Pennsville, New Jersey

2 Winslow Rd.
Tel: 609-935-1230
Fax: 609-935-9356

SHOOTING FEES

Membership: None available
$15.00/50 targets

Situated on historic Salem Creek in rural Pennsville, only minutes from the southern terminus of the New Jersey Turnpike, the Matarese family's 2200-acre M&M Preserve and Sporting Clays is, at first glance, almost an anachronism in the Union's most populated state. The Sporting Clays portion of the ground opened in 1992, and has quickly evolved to encompass roughly 100 acres of fields, scrub, and pine woods.

Following a 5-Stand warm-up layout, 20 separate shooting fields, with two or three traps and two or three stations per field, give a bare minimum of 60 different "looks" of target presentations, many of which are of pure tournament quality. The variety and quality have obviously paid dividends because 14-year-old Anthony Matarese, Jr., is the current NSCA Sub-Junior national champi-

on and an SCA and NSCA All-American, while younger brother Mike, also an All-American, is knocking on the door.

Besides recreational Sporting, the ground, with its spacious clubhouse and expansive outdoor pavilion, plays host to one of the top competitions in the country, the Masters Cup. Take note, though, that M&M is closed during the summer because it also happens to be one of the largest commercial game bird hatcheries in the country. In excess of 20,000 pheasants and 170,000 mallard ducks are raised, both for their own preserve program, and to be shipped as far away as Mississippi. On the plus side, however, there are few facilities anywhere capable of matching M&M for a multi-day combination Sporting Clays and bird hunt during the fall and winter season.

The ever-growing shell pile at Orvis Sandanona. (Orvis Sandanona photo.)

An instructor watches over the shoulder of a shooter as she practices on one of the ground's towers. (Orvis Sandanona photo.)

The manicured clubhouse/office/lodge area of the Orvis shooting ground. (Orvis Sandanona photo.)

Multiple traps at the numerous shooting fields provide a rich combination of target presentations.

This shooter attempts a crossing target from the low tower at one of the pond shooting fields.

At Hopkins Game Farm, the shooting fields are designed to optimize the terrain.

Hopkins Game Farm
Kennedyville, Maryland

Box 218
Tel: 410-348-5287
Fax: 410-348-5141

SHOOTING FEES

Membership: None available
$18.00/50 targets

When the topic of competitions comes up, one of the names sure to be at the top of the list is Hopkins Game Farm on Maryland's northern Eastern Shore. George and Patty Hopkins' 600-acre working farm has hosted, at one time or another, just about every big traveling shoot in the country since it incorporated Sporting in 1989. Unlike most of the Eastern Shore, the 90 acres of fields, hedgerows, and strips of woods the Hopkins have dedicated to clays has enough terrain variations, like valleys, deep cuts, wide slopes, and small ponds, to add an extra helping of spice to the already wide assortment of target presentations.

Because of its reputation as a tournament facility, don't be misled into believing the ground is not suitable for plain, old recreational Sporting shooters, too. With 30 separate shooting fields, each with at least two stations per field, Linda, the vastly experienced chief trapper, can organize various sequences of targets to fit every conceivable level of difficulty and challenge. A permanent 5-Stand is only a few steps away from the back door of the all-purpose clubhouse, and if you get a little recoil weary from shooting, you can whack a bucket of balls on the golf driving range just across the parking lot. If you're really worn out, accommodations are available in the ground's country-style lodge next door.

The Homestead
Hot Springs, Virginia

Box 2000
Tel: 540-839-7787
Fax: 540-839-7544

SHOOTING FEES

Membership: $120.00 per year

Member: $25.00/100 targets

Non-member: $55.00/100 targets

Nestled in the heart of the Appalachian Mountains in western Virginia, The Homestead, established in 1766, is one of America's premier getaway resorts. The complex's massive hotel is the command center for multi-season activities that range from fishing, biking, golf, and tennis in the summer to skiing in the winter. Of more immediate interest to Sporting shooters, however, is the Homestead's two superbly designed Sporting Clays courses. With more than two dozen different shooting stands and multiple traps, perfect advantage is taken of the one thing the ground has in spades: terrain. The up and down nature of the mountains lends itself perfectly to an incredible variety of target presentations. Picture downhill quartering targets thrown well below foot level at one stand to sky high driven clays from the top of a ridge at another, and you'll get the picture. Club manager David Judah has been around the game long enough to know the difference between silly targets and good ones, and puts the emphasis on the latter. In addition to the Sporting courses, 5-Stand, trap, and Skeet are also available.

The Homestead experience isn't inexpensive. However, everyone deserves to indulge themselves with something unique and special now and then, and package plans offered by the ground can help to lighten the load.

The Homestead also has nicely manicured Skeet fields. (The Homestead photo.)

Hermitage Farm Shooting Sports Camden, South Carolina

P.O. Box 1258
Tel: 803-432-0210
Fax: 803-425-7348
E-mail: hfss@infoave.net

SHOOTING FEES

Membership: $100.00 per year

Member: $24.00/100 targets

Non-member: $32.00/100 targets

Mountainous terrain of The Homestead enables targets to be thrown from high above your head to way below your feet. (The Homestead photo.)

If getting away from it all was a Sporting shooter's intent, then Hermitage Farm Shooting Sports in Camden, South Carolina would be one place to hide. Located only minutes off of Interstate 20 in the heart of the state, the ground's two Sporting courses, with nearly 30 stations between them, are distinctly different. For example, set in a curving stand of hardwoods adjacent to the clubhouse, the "woods" course optimizes generous windows cut in the trees and makes smart use of changes in terrain. The "open" course, on the other hand, plays best into the hands of more experienced shooters because, being more technical, it requires both a greater degree of patience, and the ability to read the subtle lines of deceptive targets.

For sheer shooter enjoyment, however, the permanent FITASC layout set in a patch of bottomland next to one of the ground's ponds is the real highlight. The target variety from the multiple shooting pegs, especially those thrown over the water, give it a "feel" that, though hard to define, is something special nonetheless. With a Skeet field and 5-Stand for both building confidence and warming up, the ground covers all of the realistic bases. Hermitage Farm is home to world class Junior shooter Jaybie Cantey, so, if you think about it, the ground's target formula obviously works.

**The Meadows
Smarr, Georgia**

P.O. Box 377
Tel: 912-994-9910
Fax: 912-994-2472

SHOOTING FEES

Membership: $100.00 per year

Member: $25.00/100 targets

Non-member: $35.00/100 targets

Long a hotbed of American Sporting Clays, Georgia boasts more than two dozen clubs within its borders. Smack in the middle, geographically,

The club's 5-Stand layout is over one of the ponds on the property. (Hermitage Farms Shooting Sports photo.)

The cozy clubhouse at the Hermitage Farm ground. (Hermitage Farm Shooting Sports photo.)

and just a couple hundred yards off I-75, is The Meadows National Gun Club in Smarr. Managed by the British instructor duo of Peter and Wendy Crabtree, the 400-acre club, as the host for the 1998 U.S. Open Championship, expanded its scope with numerous additions and improvements.

The "everyday" Sporting course is 16 stations, balanced between woods and open fields, and, unlike the overwhelming majority of grounds that have no link to what's the norm across the big pond, shooters can get a real taste of true English-style Sporting targets mixed in with the more familiar American stuff. Add in a Wobble Trap field, a 5-Stand, and a tower capable of throwing a 100-foot-high target, along with a really neat log clubhouse and pro shop nestled in a wooded alcove, and The Meadows is the ideal central location for a tour of Georgia.

White Oak Plantation
Tuskegee, Alabama

5215 County Rd. 10
Tel: 334-727-9258
Fax: 334-727-3411

SHOOTING FEES

Membership: $100.00 per year

Member: $25.00/100 targets

Non-member: $38.00/100 targets

The Pitman family's 15,000-acre White Oak Plantation in Tuskegee, Alabama, is a complete shooting and hunting facility that follows a single credo: do it right, or don't do it at all. Laid out in a broad circle around the ground's newly remodeled guest lodges, dining hall, pro shop and main office, is an all automatic Sporting Clays course whose stations run the gamut from pine woods to open fields to stands set over a lake fully-stocked with bass and bream. Besides the Sporting course, there's a Wobble field, an eight-machine, point-scoring format "Challenge" that matches shooters one on one, and an enclosed 5-Stand that can be shot in all but the worst of

The Meadows' rustic log clubhouse and pro shop flies both the American and British flags. (The Meadows photo.)

Both open fields (here) and woods stations characterize The Meadows excellent facilities. (The Meadows photo.)

weather. Recently added is an International/FITASC layout, which, if you haven't tried it, is the most enjoyable form of Sporting going.

As one of the founding grounds of the The Triple Crown Championship and the host for the 1998 SCI International Championship, White Oak has gained a world class reputation. Add in pure Southern hospitality at its best and special overnight, all-inclusive shooting packages at reasonable rates, and it's a "must" on any traveling shooter's itinerary.

Grinders Switch Club
Nashville, Tennessee

1608 Chickering Rd.
Tel: 931-729-9732
Fax: Not available

SHOOTING FEES

Membership: $1000.00 per year

Member: $25.00/100 targets

Non-member: $48.50/100 targets

For Sporting shooters, there's more to Nashville than just country music. Located about an hour west of the city, on a thousand-plus acres of Tennessee hill country, with terrain that ranges from open flats to steep sided ridges, is Grinders Switch. Though primarily a membership club, the ground is happy to entertain visitors if they call ahead. And it's definitely worth the call. With five separate Sporting courses, each capable of being shot at three different levels of difficulty, it's possible to

White Oak's covered 5-Stand can be shot in nearly any kind of weather.

Several of White Oak's Sporting stations are sited on the fully stocked lake.

spend several days never shooting the same clays twice.

At the top of the course list, however, is the legendary Little Switzerland layout. It's set on the steep sideslopes of a deep, narrow ravine, and served by three remote-release automatic traps that are also remotely adjustable to a dozen separate positions each. This modified international Sporting layout is simply one of the most awesome in the world. No one ever gets the best of it, yet no one ever walks away feeling as if they'd had enough. The same goes for nearby Music City where a night on the town is equally memorable in its own right.

Twin SS Sporting Clays and Gun club East Greenville, Pennsylvania

9173 Jane's Ln.
Tel: 215-679-6633
Fax: 215-679-6635

SHOOTING FEES

Membership: $250.00 per year

Member: $22.00/100 targets

Non-member: $28.00/100 targets

The gently rolling terrain of rural eastern Pennsylvania is almost a carbon copy of western England, and a half-hour north of Philadelphia, just off the Northeast Extension of the Pennsylvania Turnpike, Twin SS Sporting Clays is very much like one of its English shooting school counterparts. The course is logically laid out, and there's a remodeled, 4000-square-foot, early 1800s "barn" clubhouse. And it should resemble one of the schools because Dan Carlisle, a former Olympic medalist, world champion, and one of the top shooting instructors in America is the general manager and club pro.

The 110-acre ground's 16-station primary, all-automatic Sporting course employs two traps per stand, and is set up with the flexibility typical of a teaching ground. With a third of the stations set along perimeter strips of hardwoods and the remainder in open fields, it's designed to fully optimize many of the presentations, especially those out of the daunting 90-foot tower, from a variety of positions. Anyone who shoots Sporting more than casually knows it's often the smallest bits of expert advice that can make the difference between misses and steady target breaks, and having that advice come from someone who's "been there, done that" is a major plus.

The opportunity to shoot the legendary Little Switzerland at Grinders Switch is alone worth the trip.

The daunting 90-foot tower at Twin SS can throw some awesome targets.

The historic clubhouse at Twin SS Sporting Clays is nearly completed.

house. Unassuming is probably the best way to describe Hidden Haven. It's a ground where you can shoot yourself silly, and feel totally at home from the first target to the last.

There you have it, a dozen Sporting Clays grounds east of the Mississippi that are definitely worth the trip. Unfortunately, there's a problem. Too many excellent grounds had to be left out; clubs like Hunters Creek in Michigan, Whaleback Farm in New York, Grassy Lake Lodge in Kentucky, J&P in Maryland, Catawba in North Carolina, and at least a half-dozen others, including the superb new T&M Ranch in Orlando, Florida. So, maybe, down the road a bit the opportunity will arise to add them to the profile list. Until then, get out your map, pick up the phone, make some calls, and experience some of the best clay shooting America has to offer. ●

Hidden Haven
Sugar Grove, Ohio

9257 Buckeye Rd.
Tel: 740-746-8568
Fax: 740-746-8605

SHOOTING FEES

Membership: $50.00 per year

Member: $12.00/50 targets

Non-member: $14.00/50 targets

With trap machines and shooting stands too numerous to count spread around its 90 acres, Hidden Haven, about an hour southeast of Columbus, Ohio, is another of those unique "shooter's" grounds whose forte is offering a mind-boggling variety of target presentations. In fact, by design, it's possible to shoot 10 50-target courses that range in difficulty from novice grade "cupcake" clays all the way up to gut-wrenching expert level targets capable of stretching the ability of the best of shooters.

Varied terrain obviously makes a difference, and Hidden Haven's blend of interweaving slopes and hollows and steep rocky outcroppings provide an ideal natural framework for imaginative target setting. Beyond the multitude of Sporting targets, there's also a FITASC layout, which can be shot from three different sets of pegs, and a 5-Stand immediately behind the unassuming farmhouse-tyle club-

Lady shooters on one of the too-numerous-to-count stands. Target presentations can range from "cupcake" to extremely difficult at your option.

Are Registered Targets for You?

— by RICK HINTON

Not all shooters want to get involved with registered competition, but it does have its advantages.

For most recreational Sporting Clays shooters, registered ... gulp ... targets are the scariest part of the game. Registered targets equal competition, and competition elevates a fun pastime to a higher, more pressure-filled intensity notch

That's a common perception among many customers at Sporting Clays ranges. They enjoy coming out and shooting; if they get real daring, they may shoot in a league. But joining a national organization, shooting in sanctioned competitions and having their scores sent off for comparison with other shooters isn't for them. That's really all registered targets are: a means of grouping shooters with others of comparable abilities. A classification system's goal is to level the shooting field, so to speak, by grouping the 90 percent shooters in one class, the 80 percent shooters in another, and on down to the 50 percent and below shooters.

At the clubs I shoot most frequently, there are five or six league shooters for every registered shooter. Competition is the reason cited for most of those league shooters shunning registered targets. Its a rationale I don't understand. For me,

In registered shoots, target presentations often are unusual, limited only by safety considerations, the terrain, and the resources of the host club.

anyway, a 10-week league packs far more pressure than a Sunday afternoon registered shoot.

In league, my teammates and I (and everyone else) are studying the weekly scores, seeing what our team members must shoot to either move ahead of another team or to stay in front of an up-and-coming team. So for 10 weeks, everyone goes out to shoot knowing what kind of score they'd better turn in. Some folks thrive on that kind of pressure, but missing an easy target or two can ruin your day and your team's standing in the league.

In a registered shoot, I go out and shoot to the best of my ability, turn in my score card and see how all the scores shake out. It's clean, quick and done. If someone beats me by a couple of targets, I regretfully can recall all the targets I shouldn't have missed. But it's over, and the slate is clean for the next registered shoot I enter.

Registered targets have one other great appeal for me—the possibility of new target presentations. For registered shoots, tournaments, competitions—whatever you want to call them—astute range owners will change the course, usually making it a bit more difficult. Sometimes the changes will be subtle: tweaks in target speed, angle or elevation, or maybe an added bit of curl here and there. The truly enterprising range owner will open new stations and close some regular ones for the registered shoot. That gives the course a new look.

Whatever approach they take, the change is designed to challenge all the shooters. Remember, there aren't a whole lot of first-time shooters in registered events. The change also reduces the potential of home-course advantage, which gives out-of-town shooters a better chance. Lets face it, anyone who shoots the same course once or twice a week for four months should have an enormous advantage over a visitor of comparable shooting skills seeing the course for the first time. So changes should help the visiting shooter. As a visiting shooter I love to hear the scorekeeper approach a station and wonder what the range owner has done to it. Unfortunately it doesn't always work that way. A few times, I've traveled to a shoot and heard the scorekeeper/field judge marvel about the targets being just like he shot in last week's league. There's no point in getting mad, but I can get even by avoiding that club as much as possible in the future.

Of course, I pay for the privilege of shooting registered targets. Annually, one membership check goes to the National Sporting Clays Association in San Antonio, Texas, and another goes to Sporting Clays of America in Sugar Grove, Ohio. I also pay a fee for registering my targets. The NSCA gets 2 cents a target and SCA gets 3 cents. That fee is either added on to, or included, in entry fees for registered shoots.

Registered shoot entry fees generally will cost more than a comparable number of rounds. Say a club charges $15 per 50 targets, thus $30 for 100 targets. If the club puts on a shoot, logic would say a 100-target registered shoot should cost $30, plus the $2 or $3 target fee. But the

This competitor has just fired at a high bird over his head, hoping to record another hit for record. This station appears to be in the boonies.

club that sticks to that pricing is a rare and wonderful find. And I can understand a bit more overhead for running a shoot. Among the possible added costs might be trophies, additional hired help, pre-shoot coffee and doughnuts, mailing fliers, the paperwork involved in sending scores (plus the target fees) to the national organization, and other things I can't imagine.

So what's a 100-target registered shoot going to cost you? The going rate in my part of the country (the Dakotas) is about $35. A lot of registered shooters in other parts of the country are gasping right now. They probably are paying between $50 and $100 for the same 100-target registered shoot.

Another reason registered shoots may cost more is purse money. You pay $5 or more in anticipation of finishing high enough in your class to win back some money. Some clubs will build that money into their entry fee; other clubs give shooters the option of shooting for money. Another money game is Lewis class, which disregards shooters' classifications and bases classes on scores only. Lewis class is a bit like a raffle. Say 80 shooters enter a Lewis class event with four classes. After everyone has finished shooting, the scores are ranked in order from highest to lowest. The top shooter, naturally, wins Class A (and there may or may not be runner-up awards in each class, depending on any number of factors); Class B starts with the 21st best score; C with the 41st and D with the 61st. A complicated set of tie-breakers may move some scores up or down, but that's more than we need to deal with here. Because of the raffle-like way Lewis events are scored, many see them as an attraction for new shooters, who may hit a C or D class. Others see Lewis as rewarding luck more than skill, while true cynics mutter, "I shot just badly enough to hit a Lewis class." There are plenty of other money options offered, often regional in nature, but its best to have club management explain what they are.

Before you decide if registered shoots are for you, lets hit some of the high points about the National Sporting Clays Association and Sporting Clays of America, the two national organizations. Descriptions are based on each organization's current rule books, so bear in mind there may be changes in subsequent editions.

You can contact the NSCA at 5931 Roft Road, San Antonio, TX, 78253-0007; telephone 210/688-3371. The SCA can be reached by writing to 9257 Buckeye Road, Sugar Grove, OH 43155-9632; call them at 740/746-8334.

The annual dues for the NSCA is $40 and it includes a 12-month sub-

A club doesn't need sophisticated equipment or layouts to host a registered shoot, just good organization and personnel to keep things running smoothly.

This fancy club has station-specific birds at each stand to signify what the targets are supposed to signify. It's a nice facility with comfortable amenities.

Shooting registered targets often means you have company, like a score-keeper or field judge at each station, or walking with you on the round.

scription to Sporting Clays magazine. The SCA charges $35 per year and includes a quarterly newsletter.

Classification System

Perhaps the biggest difference between the organizations, and probably the most talked about aspect of either group is the way shooters are classified.

NSCA—There are seven classes, plus five concurrents. Starting from the top, the classes are Masters, AA, A, B, C, D and E. Every member has one of those class designations. Some members, because of gender or age, also are eligible for a concurrent class: Lady, Senior, Veteran, Sub Junior and Junior.

A shooter's classification is best described as based on a floating average, using performance within a class. During the year, January 1 to December 31, a shooter may move up by winning his or her class in a "major shoot." In smaller shoots, class winners may be given punches on their class card. Any shooter who accumulates four punches is moved up a class. Punches are carried over to the next year. In small shoots, depending on the number of shooters attending and the number of shooters in class, a class winner may receive no punches. The NSCA also recommends small shoots use Lewis class, and no punches are given to Lewis class winners.

SCA—Class is based on percentages after 300 targets: AA is 80 percent and over; A is 70 to 79.9; B is in the 60s, C in the 50s and D is 49.9 percent and below. Concurrents are Lady, Senior, Veteran, Sub Junior and Junior. Every additional 100 targets are calculated into the cumulative average, and shooters may move up based on their new average. At the end of the shooting year, December 31, averages are calculated and shooters are classed for the next year, based on their averages.

There are provisions in each organization for a shooter to move down in class, but such a move requires a check-off from the national organization.

New Shooters

NSCA—Shooters new to clay target sports automatically go into C class. After 300 targets, they are reviewed and may be reclassed, either up or down. Shooters classified by another Sporting Clays organization will continue in that class. Shooters with registered trap or Skeet backgrounds will be classified one class lower than that highest class attained in those disciplines.

SCA—Shooters need 300 targets to earn a classification. New shooters with fewer targets may be as-signed a class or may be temporarily classed by blind draw. A blind draw identifies certain stations, and the shooters average on those stations determines the temporary class. It's called "blind" because the shooter doesn't know which stations count for that temporary average.

Each organization also has a "known ability" rule. If a shooter's known ability is well above, or in some cases below, the assigned class, the shooter may be moved to a more appropriate class.

Concurrent Classes

NSCA—Rules permit one person to win their class and their concurrent, thus a Lady shooter could win her class as well as the Ladies event.

Shooters often get an idea about a station's target presentation by checking out—and heeding—the description of the presumed quarry.

Trees and foliage can sometimes hamper fast target acquisition, but seasoned competitors have trained themselves to react for the best possible scores.

Registered shoots can offer opportunities to visit posh gun clubs that often have steep initiation fees and membership dues. It's a treat to shoot at these places if you're not accustomed to it.

SCA—If eligible for class and concurrent awards, rules state a shooter will declare one title after completion of the tournament.

Gun Mount

Both organizations use a free mount rule, meaning a shooter may have the gun shouldered or use some form of low gun hold before calling for the target. Both organizations originally had a "low gun" rule, which required the shotgun stock to be below the arm pit and not be mounted until the target was visible.

The free mount rule makes it easier for many beginning shooters, and the original rule was a devil to enforce.

Rule Books

NSCA—Issued annually with class card and previous year's shooting history. New rules or changes are noted in italics. It gets an A for frequency, but a C-minus for clarity when there is a rules problem.

SCA—Issued periodically (the most current I have is from 1996). Rule changes also are noted in italics. It gets a D for frequency, but a B+ for clarity because it includes "approved rulings" paragraphs, which list examples of specific questions or problems and cites the proper decision.

Backgrounds

SCA—If you count its previous lives as the United States Sporting Clays Association, the SCA is the oldest organization, founded in 1985 in Houston. Houston generally is regarded as the birthplace of Sporting Clays in the United States, so the association is natural. The leadership, name and headquarters all changed in the early '90s. The USSCA became Sporting Clays of America, with a new president and a new headquarters in Norwalk, Conn. When then-president Fred Collings retired, the SCA took the novel step of moving its headquarters to the home state of its new president, Ron Blosser, instead of moving Blosser to Connecticut. The name change to SCA also marked a change in philosophy, which will be touched upon later.

Whether shooting for the sheer fun or it or in serious competition, a chipped target is just as dead as this thoroughly

Shooting stands need not be elaborate. This wooden pallet serves to position the shooter at this registered shoot recently.

NSCA—Founded as a separate entity in 1989 by the National Skeet Shooting Association as a rival to the USSCA. It shares a headquarters building and some staff with the NSSA at the National Gun Club complex in San Antonio, Texas. The executive director of both organizations is Mike Hampton. Lois Lessing is the NSCA assistant director. The sprawling and beautiful gun club is the site of the national championship each September, plus other events.

Philosophies

NSCA—Although member gun clubs may follow different philosophies, its major shoots are big and involve substantial money, some of which is built into the entry fees. Corporate sponsorship helps supplement those purses. These big shoots will attract almost all of the best shooters in the U.S., plus many top competitors from overseas. Entry fees and payouts will be the same whether a shooter is in Master Class or Class E.

It's the bigger organization with more members and member clubs. It has clubs in all 50 states, plus more in Australia, Canada, the Dominican Republic, Jamaica, Mexico, and Puerto Rico-Virgin Islands. Club and individual membership continues to grow, numbers show. It offers a rewards program for individuals and clubs that sign up new members.

SCA—The new name also ushered in a new philosophy for the SCA. It has turned into more of a grass-roots organization, emphasizing lower cost shoots with purse money strictly as an option. The no-purse, lower cost entry fee certainly could be an attraction for the non-gambling shooter who wants to shoot quality targets at a national event. Although strongest in the Northeast and Midwest, Blosser says individual and club membership is growing.

SCA also will register targets that members shoot in tournaments sanctioned by the NSCA or some international Sporting Clays organizations. SCA has several rewards programs, based on signing up members or registering targets. Members who register 1500 targets, including NSCA and even league targets, earn a free membership for the following year. The registered target fee is $3 per hundred, though.

Consolidation or merger talks between the two rival organizations have been on and off, rumored and hinted at since the beginning. Personally, I think the philosophical differences will keep the organizations independent for now. If the shooters en masse begin endorsing one philosophy over the other, one organization may have to rethink its position. And that will take years.

Other Choices

Some clubs will offer a separate hunters' class event for their registered shoots. It's separate from the regular event and open only to shooters who do not belong to either national organization. Lewis class is the usual method of assigning classes.

Clubs keep looking at more and different ways to attract all their league shooters who normally shun registered shoots. One successful method is to hold a tournament within the tournament for league shooters; each participant's final score is based on that day's score, plus their league handicap.

So are registered targets for you? It all depends on where you're coming from and where you want to go. For me, at least, I like the security of a classification system, despite real and perceived flaws. Being classified means I can participate in a registered shoot anywhere in the country and stand a reasonable chance of competing against my peers. In an out-of-state hunter's class, I'd never know how many top-gun-caliber shooters might be lurking there. So I pay my money and take my chances in my class.

It works for me.　　●

Some shooters, because of gender or age, can compete in regular as well as concurrent classes and earn different rankings in each classification.

Where Manners Matter

"Where are we to learn grace, or doesn't it matter any more?"
—Vance Bourjaily in the Unnatural Enemy

by RANDY LAWRENCE

"**MANNERS MAKETH THE** man," the old saying goes. I would amend that to, "Manners maketh or breaketh a day shooting Sporting Clays."

Manners, as they pertain to shotgunning, begin and end with safety. They shape how we enjoy ourselves. Manners determine whether or not we are good company to others. Proper range etiquette may even enable us to shoot well.

What it boils down to is being thoughtful. Thoughtfulness and consideration for others begin with mental and physical preparation for a day at the range.

Come ready to shoot under a variety of conditions. Don't be the man or woman who shows up at the gun club without ear and eye protection, without a shooting vest or shell bag, bug dope or sunscreen. Such folks end up inconveniencing others, ei-

ther by mooching equipment or making companions wait while what should have been packed ahead of time has to be scrounged or purchased at the club pro shop.

Many Clays facilities have several course options, rated by degree of difficulty. If you are new to Sporting Clays, or are in the company of novice shooters, be honest about that and ask club personnel about stands set up for beginners.

First thing when you arrive, decide whether you're going to go for just one round of 50 birds at a time, or maybe shoot another course on the way back to the clubhouse. Shotgun shells are heavy, and you don't want to tote around a lot of extra ammo that you'll never need. By the same token, you'd rather not leave your squad mates out on the course, twiddling their choke tubes, while you hike back to the clubhouse to get more shells.

We tote additional shells for clays that need to be reshot because of gun, target, or shooter "malfunctions." Do not take extra ammo for the sole purpose of coaxing the trapper into throwing "just one more pair" once your sequence at a particular stand is over. Those "one more pair" pulls add up; a young trapper, eager to please, may acquiesce but, in effect, you and he are stealing.

If you want to shoot extra birds, and your companions don't mind waiting while you do, keep scrupulous track in the margins of the scorecard, and count on paying for those birds when you've finished. It's only right that you do so.

And speaking of the scorecard, you may call it heresy, but the best shotgun coach of my acquaintance says that most recreational Clays shooters would perform better if they did not keep score. I know, I

Shooters waiting their turn should have their vests stocked with shells, proper choke tube in place, and an idea of how they want to set up for the target.

know. Americans are all about "scoreboard." As Chevy Chase says in the movie Caddy Shack, if we don't keep score, how are we to measure ourselves against other men?

If you find yourself paying more attention to your score than shooting well or having fun, leave that measuring business to the tournament shooters. Don't bring a pencil. Don't keep track in your head. Use the scorecard merely to check the target menu at each station.

Keeping score in and of itself is not a bad thing. Obviously, it's one way of marking improvement from station to station, from round to round. It's what we do with our tally that's a problem.

For example, when the score's the thing, sometimes there's a question about whether or not anyone but the shooter saw the required "discernible piece" that determines a target break. Nothing sours a round of Sporting more quickly than someone who's either unsafe or always begging for targets.

Keep your priorities in order. Whenever possible, shoot with like-minded people. If you want to grow up to be a tournament shooter, seek those folks out and train with them. Is muzzleloading your game? There are shooters who would love to join you. My friends in the Vintagers shooting club, based in New England, meet once a month, dressed in Edwardian shooting kit, to wave classic hammer side-by-side shotguns at Sporting Clays. They have a lot of fun doing it their way.

In my circle of regular Sporting Clays companions, the only shots that matter come in the duck marsh, out of a dove blind, over the point of a good bird dog. Sporting Clays is simply a game we love to play (that's play, not suffer through), fun practice that can help us better hold up our part of the bargain during the bird season.

Two of us are former high school football coaches. We are all competitive in one arena or another. In fact, we won our club's summer Sporting Clays league this past year and were darned proud of that.

But we're probably not good company for the hard-core target sharks. Those who need golf green quiet on the firing line or psychiatric help during a mini-slump wouldn't enjoy our giggling in the background. We hoot

Shooter at far left holds an empty gun with action open. Ideally, she should have the muzzle in her hand with the stock up over her shoulder, or the muzzle pointing skyward, like the pump gunner waiting her turn.

Golf carts are handy but can be a distraction if used carelessly. Cart courtesy means not driving through when a shooter is on stand. Stop and kill the motor.

at each other's silly misses, hooray a great break. We shoot at a lot of targets, stay safe, and try not to impose the way we play the game on others.

Steve, our team captain, has made a courageous comeback from a nearly fatal car wreck. For him to shoot several rounds of Clays means using a golf cart to get around the course. No problem. We bought him a set of fuzzy dice to hang from the roof brace, loaded our stuff in the back, and piled in.

We quickly learned that there's an etiquette to golf cart use, too. Users must take time to secure their guns in padded racks. When we can, we offer the trapper a seat. From our own, pre-wheels annoyance with Crazed Cart Cruisers, we've promised not to tool by while others are trying to shoot. Manners dictate turning the motor off and waiting until there's a break in the action.

When we get to the first station, we decide on an order in which we want to shoot, then rotate the line-up from station to station. That way nobody has to be the first fish in the barrel at every stand.

The initial shooter at a stand is generally afforded a "show bird" or sample target sequence. If the trap-per is throwing pairs and they are radically different from single targets in trajectory or speed, he should give the first shooter a sample of those, too.

We wait until everyone in our squad is ready, then ask the trapper if he'll pull that show bird on our call. The first shooter should be standing in the box with an empty gun, watching intently. Only one set of demo birds should be permitted per squad.

If we arrive at a station while another group is shooting, we'll watch three or four people shoot the target sequence, then pass on a show bird. When it's our turn, we need only to climb into the box, get set, and call Pull!

Everyone has more fun and certainly shoots with more energy and concentration if the squad keeps moving. When we arrive at a station, we check the scorecard to see how many targets are to be thrown then put that many shells, and several extras, in a vest pocket or cartridge belt bag. If the show bird demands a choke tube change, we take care of that as quickly as possible. Whatever we do, we try to be ready to step into the box when our name is called.

Woe to squads saddled with a chronic sufferer of Screwinis Outis-itis. Such obsessive-compulsives are convinced that not shooting technique, but rather a few thousands of choke constriction either way makes the critical difference between lost and dead. The squad waits...and waits...and waits...while this wretch frantically tries to read the color code, number of notches, or numerals on a rack of choke tubes that look like pipes for the Winchester Cathedral organ.

"Gotta ditch this Improved Cylinder Briley," he mumbles, as his name is called for the third time. "Where did I put that Seminole Light Modified one?"

Choke and load combinations can make a difference. But if you're the guy or gal everyone else is always waiting on to change choke tubes (and you've noticed your scores lagging behind as well), you might want to take another look at your approach to the game.

As a Sporting Clays shooter, you need to be flexible about target presentations. The National Sporting Clays Association rule book states that a "no bird" (what we called in my childhood a "do-over") can be

The Dan'l Boone pose is picturesque but breaks the rule of never having the gun muzzle pointed at any part of your, or anyone else's, body.

Accidents are the height of bad manners and sloppy gun handling. Both shooters have gun muzzles in a safe attitude, and actions open, but the one in front must be careful not to hit the man behind him with the buttstock.

claimed if the mark is "launched in an obviously different trajectory" from previous presentations.

In a recreational round, my friends and I don't expect each bird to come out precisely the same way. By the same token, we've paid to shoot Sporting Clays. If we can't see the bird or don't have a reasonable chance of shooting, we'll ask for the target to be thrown again. If wind, bright sun, or foliage, make a particular presentation unshootable, we'll politely ask the trapper if we can make those targets up at another station or return to this spot later in the round.

Occasionally, someone setting targets has a radically different idea about what constitutes an interesting or "fair" target. My friends have grown comfortable with their own agenda. If a target doesn't even remotely simulate a game bird scenario, they may politely "pass" on a station and, with the trapper's permission, use those shells on a later mark that's more representative of the kind of shooting we do.

Most often, though, if a safe target flies, we try to make it die. We once held an informal league of dog trainers, hunting guides, woods bums, and a smattering of unsuspecting normal people. The league rules were simple: (1) no choke tube changes after the round started; (2) no scores would ever be posted; (3) no do-overs except out of safety concerns; and (4) if the trapper asked if a shooter wanted a show bird, the only honorable response was, "Hellnojustpullit!" And he would. This was a lot of fun and everyone enjoyed the relaxed atmosphere and attitudes. It also opened some eyes for those folks who had previously taken things too seriously.

But sometimes targets break before we have a chance to "justpullit." NSCA rules note that "in the event of a 'no bird' on any report, simultaneous, or following pair, nothing can be established. Two good targets must be presented to record the score." That's why we bring along a dozen or so additional cartridges to shoot a round of 50.

There can be a multitude or reasons to use those extras, too: occasionally, guns malfunction; reloads don't go "bang"; a shooter forgets to push the safety off, or short shucks a pump gun, or isn't even looking in

the right place for the bird. Formal Sporting Clays rules mandate that on the fourth gun malfunction, the bird is counted as "lost." In tournament shooting, they count as "lost" any bird that goes by unshot because of "shooter malfunctions." In a recreational round, be generous with each other, but conservative with the range owner's clays.

In any case, it's always safety first. If the trigger is pulled and the gun doesn't bark, the shooter must keep the muzzles pointed downrange and assess the situation. We always err on the side of extreme caution when addressing a gun glitch.

You'll read elsewhere in this book about shotgun actions being always kept open and guns unloaded when

Constant choke tube changes may not only hold up a shooting squad, but also can be a detriment to good, basic marksmanship. Keep changes to a minimum.

Leaving hull litter is a discourtesy to other shooters. It's easy to use a convenient shell bucket like this one if you don't want the empties. A cleaner range is also safer.

Don't offer shooting advice unless asked. Here, NSCA instructor Kevin Townsend works with another coach, Wendy Williamson, at Seven Lakes Lodge in Meeker, Colorado.

This pump gunner has the action racked open and facing out for others to see. The muzzle is secure as well. This shows good manners and respect.

Shooters should wait quietly and unobtrusively for their turn. Note the gentleman crowding the shooting cage, pantomiming the shot. This can be very distracting for the shooter.

shooters are not in the shooting box. But shotgun etiquette should apply even to obviously empty, open firearms on the Clays course.

The best rule is never to cover any part of your body—or anyone else's—with the muzzle of the gun. If you are standing there in a picturesque Dan'l Boone pose, hands over the muzzle of an open gun, that's sloppy. If you have a double gun broken over your shoulder with the barrels swinging in the face of the person behind you, that's annoying. If you have the same gun broken with the stock over your shoulder, turn suddenly, and crack a person in the face who is standing near you, that's inexcusable.

Don't crowd a shooter in the box. Likewise, don't ever stand behind the shooting cage, practicing your move-to-mount with an empty gun. This tends to make everyone nervous. It would be exactly the same if you were practicing your swing on the tee while another player was trying his best to drive that little golf ball straight down the fairway. It's just plain inconsiderate behavior.

And please, please, please don't offer coaching unless it's solicited. If it is, don't volunteer advice unless you know what you're talking about.

Don't show your ignorance by telling shooters, "You were behind that one," or "Lead this next one about 17 inches" from a position 10 yards behind and to one side. Women and kids, even those who are experienced and proficient, are most often abused by the self-appointed Clays guru.

Blessed are the great tournament shooters or accomplished Clays coaches who, when out for a round of Sporting, have the grace to wait until they're asked before informally trouble shooting someone else's shotgun stroke.

If you have the privilege of shooting a round with a teaching pro, treat him or her the way you should any other professional. Don't try to get free consultation in the course of your round. Wait until you're finished, then ask that person if he or she would mind discussing your shooting goals with the idea of perhaps booking a lesson. If the two of you hit it off, make an appointment.

If a particular Clays course has a policy of claiming all hulls that hit the ground, let 'em go. If you're permitted to pick up your empties, please do, even if you don't reload. It keeps the range neater and reduces the owner's costs in the long run.

Double guns with ejectors are easy to manage. On opening the action, cushion the empty's throw with the palm of the off hand, then stow hulls in a belt or vest pouch or maybe in a nearby trash bucket. Once again, that's just being considerate.

Autoloaders and pumps are a bit less convenient because of the way they eject the empties. Don't hold up the rest of the squad while you crawl around scrounging every last hull. Wait until everyone has shot, pick up what you can, then move on to the next station.

And finally, good Sporting Clays manners should extend to your trapper, too. Usually, those who pull our targets are high school kids working a part-time job. Most get a nominal day fee, then count on tips beyond that.

In our region, $3 per shooter, per 50-bird round, is considered the minimum tip. Most of us take into account the weather, the number of shooters in our party, the length of time we're out on the course, and the trapper's hustle. When in doubt about what to give, ask the range owner.

Note that shooters who take care of their trappers tend to get especially attentive service on return visits. We want a trapper ready to show us a bird when the squad is in place. We want correctly placed targets in the right sequence. A sulking, indolent trapper can be like dragging a ball and chain around the course. That doesn't mean you have to buy him a new Bimmer, but be courteous and tip appropriately. If the trapper is a real problem, notify the range owner about the situation.

Sullen or sunny, keep that trapper safe at all times. If, for any reason, you feel his position is unsafe from the vantage of your shooting stand, don't shoot that station. Politely express your concern to the range owner at the end of the round.

In consideration for safety, use of "adult" language, and overall courtesy, remember that your trapper is someone else's son or daughter. He or she is also a potential future shooter, of which we can never have enough. Take responsibility for that potential, treating each youngster the way you hope someone would treat you, or a child of your own. After all, where are they to learn grace? Perhaps you would agree that it matters more now than ever. ●

In a Five-Stand shooting set up like this one, each gunner must be ready in turn to shoot (note shooter at left). The vintage garb and exposed-hammer double add to the fun for this specialty shooter.

Competition Shooting and a Look at the Governing Bodies

Shooting in actual competition can be exhilarating, frustrating, depressing and gratifying—all at the same meet. If shooters keep the proper perspective it can be a lot of fun. (Randy Lawrence photo.)

ONE OF THE joys of being involved in a sport that you start as a hobby, and participate in for the sheer sake of loving it, is to move on to the next level. Competition shooting. Entering the competition world of the shooting sports can be exciting, exhilarating, intimidating and frustrating. As with all competitive sports, the competition is intense, emotional, and the politics played only add to the sense of futility that be a part of competitive events.

Competition does get the headlines, but it's the recreational shooters who support the sport. In 1996, there were over 1 million people who shot Sporting Clays 20 or more times per year. A conservative guess is that more than 4 million people participate in the sport at more than 1000 Sporting Clays ranges throughout

the country. Of the million-plus people that frequent Sporting Clays, only about two percent (about 20,000) are competitive shooters. The remainder is the core base of the sport—the weekend recreational shooter who is involved because of their love of shooting, whether it's hunting or target shooting. The friendly banter and camaraderie among shooters exists at this level and will let you enjoy the sport for years.

If you plan on entering the competition world of Sporting Clays, be prepared for some interesting times. To begin, one must join the association that legally governs the sport in the United States.

The National Sporting Clays Association, located in San Antonio, Texas, is a non-profit organization that has as its purpose to promote and

govern this sport throughout the United States and other countries, in a way that is beneficial to all who enjoy and participate in the game. The NSCA has the responsibility for the formulation, regulation and enforcement of official policies and rules, the shooting of registered targets, the conduct of the shooters and the duties of shoot management. It is the national governing body of Sporting Clays in the United States and is recognized by the world as the governing body for FITASC in this country.

It is a membership-driven organization and memberships are available to individuals and clubs. Current enrollment is about 13,500 individual members and 640 NSCA member clubs, with NSCA representation in all 50 states in the U.S. and 10 foreign countries. Membership is represented by an Executive Council, which employs an Executive Director to manage NSCA affairs.

The organizational structure of the NSCA can be somewhat complicated. Within the NSCA is the Advisory Council that is made up of shooters, industry people and range owners. The Advisory Council has the responsibility of recommending procedures of conduct, rules and general operating methods to help the sport function and grow. There are 45 available positions divided equally between representatives of Industry, Range Owners and Shooters. The primary function of the Advisory Council is to promote and guide the Association. Elections are held annually to keep the perspective fresh and up to date. From the Advisory Council is an Executive Council that is elected from, and comprised of, six members of the Advisory Council, two representing Industry, two representing Range Owners and two representing Shooters, each serving a two-year term. The primary function of the Executive Council is to promote and guide the Advisory Council and act on behalf of the Advisory Council on matters needing immediate attention. Representation of the individual states comes from the elected NSCA Delegate. This person is elected by the members of that state and serves a two-year term. The primary function of the NSCA Delegate, in the absence of the State Association, is to work with the State representative and members and clubs in the state to approve registered shoot dates, to promote the NSCA within the state, and to help organize and support a state association. In addition to the Delegate is the State Representative. One NSCA member, who resides in that state, is appointed by the NSCA Delegate and/or State Representative Committee to serve that state. The primary function is to work with the NSCA Delegate to finalize shoot dates and promote the

organization. In each state, there is also a State Association, recognized by the NSCA, comprised of the members and clubs within that state. The State Association works with the Delegate and State Representative to support the clubs and members within the rules and parameters of the NSCA.

The structure of the NSCA can be a bit cumbersome, but necessary for an organization as large as this one. However, there are some benefits of belonging to it. The NSCA hosts the Sporting Clays National Championships at their home ground, The National Shooting Complex, which no other organization of its type can boast. The event brings in about 1200 competitors each year and also provides a venue for the industry to present the latest in guns, ammo, clothing and equipment.

The NSCA also annually recognizes up to three All-American teams in each of the six categories, depending upon the number of members who qualify. A certain number of registered targets must be shot within a certain time period, plus there must be attendance in designated shooting competitions. An All-State Team for each state is selected by the organization in an effort to recognize more shooters for their shooting ability. Again, certain criteria must be met to qualify for this recognition.

Another benefit that the organization offers is the Instructor Certification course that offers three levels of certification. Along the lines of the Professional Golf Association, the purpose of the instructor certification course is to offer consistent, widespread and proper instruction on how to participate in the shooting sports. The registration fee for each course varies, and the levels available must be taken in sequence: Level I is teaching beginner to novice; Level II teaches intermediates; and Level III is for the advanced instructors. It takes a minimum of four years and over 600 hours of instruction to complete the certification program.

A program that has been very successful in the past years is the NSCA League & Sweepstakes that begins April 1st each year and runs through October 1st. This program works with clubs and is diversified enough so that a club may host as many 10-week leagues during this time period as desired. The prizes are given away by a random drawing so new shooters can compete with experienced shooters on an equal basis.

> Shooting registered targets may not be for everyone, but it can be a lot of fun. Here's a look at what it takes to form a working organization that holds the shooters together.

by SHARI LeGATE

The National Sporting Clays Association governs and promotes the sport with a number of good programs like offering scholarships (in conjunction with Buick Motor Division) and the League & Sweepstakes that works with clubs.

A scholarship program is available to eligible high school seniors from NSCA in conjunction with Buick Motor Division. Each year, $5,000 is awarded to a student who has excelled at their performance in school. Awarded strictly on academic scores, the student must be an active competitive shooter and a member of NSCA.

The official magazine of the National Sporting Clays Association is Sporting Clays Magazine. This monthly publication has feature articles and photos of clubs, number of courses, tournament and registered shoot schedules with results along with highlights of the events. The magazine is complimentary with membership.

The NSCA also supports an All-American Team. The team consists of the top shooters from the previous year. Men's, women's, seniors, junior and sub-junior teams are chosen each year.

A classification system that was created by the NSCA is computerized by score/best shooter rather than by averages to create a fair and equitable chance for all. Essentially, this is a shoot record of each member who has "registered" their competition targets with the organization. A shooter's classification carries over from one shooting year to the next. All new shooters will be assigned a class. A classification card is provided to all shooters every year. To maintain the integrity of the classification system, all NSCA members shooting at the time of an NSCA Registered Event must register their targets. A shooter's classification will be reviewed at the end of the year. On the basis of performance in class, a shooter may be moved in class on a yearly basis. A shooter is responsible for entering his/her scores with the date and the score shot on the back of their classification card, and to assure that all placements are properly recorded on their classification card.

There has been an enormous amount of controversy over this classification system. Upon entering the competition arena, the term "sandbagger" will be heard quite frequently. A sandbagger is a competitor who intentionally misleads the association about their level of shooting ability. Many times, the association will have "classed" a competitor in a lower class because the history of scores reported had determined that placement. Or that particular shooter intentionally shot lower scores so that the score reported places the shooter in the lower class. The advantage to that? There really isn't one. Perhaps that shooter would like

You meet the nicest folks at Sporting Clays events, and many form life-long friendships. Camaraderie is one of the wonderful by-products of shooting. These fellas competed in the Buffalo Bill Celebrity Shootout. (Buffalo Bill Historical Center photo.)

to win the money or prizes that are designated for that class. Eventually, the true shooting ability shows and that competitor is moved to the proper class. However, usually the respect level from other competitors is lowered. Nevertheless, the official governing body has no real way of knowing if all that occurred. They will class every shooter where their scores indicate.

All of these benefits and the right to compete are offered for a nominal membership fee of $40 per year, which includes a one-year subscription to Sporting Clays Magazine. Competitive shooters pay an additional $2 per 100 targets to the NSCA to register their targets, keep individual shooter records, and tournament placement. Fees to the individual state organization may add some additional cost. For more information on the National Sporting Clays Association, call 800-877-5338 or write to The NSCA, 5931 Roft Rd., San Antonio, TX 78253-9261.

Another group that is growing, and has about 1500 members as this is written, is the Sporting Clays of America (SCA), Inc. This is a young organization that was taken over by the current administration two years ago and moved to Ohio. Unlike the NSCA, the SCA is not responsible for governing the sport in the United States or to represent it to the international Sporting community. The thrust of the SCA is to promote the shooting sports as a fun, family-oriented activity. It encourages open shooting and doesn't require membership if you don't shoot for the prize money. The structure of the SCA is not nearly as complex or confusing as the NSCA. Membership is $35 for one year; family memberships are $65. The benefits of belonging to the SCA are almost the same as the NSCA: registration of scores at clubs affiliated with the SCA; a schedule of shooting tournaments; and the opportunity to compete for prizes and awards. They also host a National Championship and the SCI Championships, which is their version of FITASC.

Where the NSCA is more structured and rigid, the SCA is more relaxed. Like the NSCA, there is an Advisory Board that is comprised of Industry, Range Owners and Shooters. However, the major difference between the two boards is that the

SCA's Advisory Board is to design programs that are member and club driven. One of the most successful programs instituted last year by the board is the All-Star program. It is open to all members and clubs and encourages members to record with SCA all targets shot in practice, club events, fun shoots, SCA tournaments or any other organization tournaments. They have instituted a shooter-friendly recreational program, which awards free membership to anyone who records 1500 targets with the organization, no matter where they've shot. In addition, each of these members' names will be entered in a drawing for additional prizes at the end of the year. Shooters who record 2000 targets and main-

tain their average or move up in class, will receive an All-Star patch or certificate, and for every 500 targets recorded above the required 1500, points will be awarded to go toward additional prizes. According to Ron Blosser, president of the SCA, the organization has experienced a 15-20 percent growth purely as a result of the All-Star program.

The All-American program is a two-step, strictly competitive process that enables shooters of all classes to qualify for an opportunity at All-American status in their class. Step one is to qualify by placing in the top five of your letter class, or top three in the subclass at any of the scheduled All-American Series Qualifier events. For step

Male, female, young or old—anyone can shoot in competition in a large variety of classes to suit their skill level. You don't have to be an expert.

two, to attain final All-American recognition, you must place in the top five of your letter class or subclass at the SCA National Championships. When final score is compiled at the National Championships, five shooters in each letter and subclass will have achieved All-American status in their respective classes and be recognized for their competitive achievement.

Even though the SCA is a relatively new organization, they are working toward providing good quality targets at a lower entry fee. Another focus is to remove the money aspect from the competition and bring it back to a sporting event, one that encourages open shooting and to better the sport. The Sporting Clays of America, Inc. is located at 9257 Buckeye Rd, Sugar Grove, OH 43155-9632; telephone: 740/746-8334

There are many benefits to joining the ranks of the competition shooter. One is the experience of competitive sports, but more important are the many friendships that will develop over the years. Some will last a lifetime. The opportunity to travel throughout the United States and the world during a shooting career is unlimited. As the sport grows, and it will, despite the controversies that sometimes surround it, it will continue to draw participants from all walks of life. Neither the sport, nor the governing bodies are much more than 10 years old, and it will take many years of evolution and growth before both will reach their full potential. ●

One of the joys of shooting Sporting Clays is the chance to travel to other clubs to shoot in their registered contests. This is the Lana'i Pine club in Hawaii.

Sporting Clays, like other clay target games, can test one's powers of concentration. This shooter just finished a not-so-good station, but will try to do better next time she shoots. (Rick Hinton photo.)

Home Improvements

There aren't too many projects that can be tackled by the do-it-yourselfer, but here are a few that can be handled in the home workshop.

by PATRICK SWEENEY

WHAT CAN YOU do to improve the performance of your Sporting Clays shotgun? The obvious and expensive solution is buy a better gun that has all of the bells and whistles you want or need. Since not every shooter has the need, wherewithal or desire to plunk down multiple thousands of dollars to improve their score a few birds, we will not go there.

Instead, we will look into improving the basic gun, whether it is a plain Remington 870 or a somewhat more upscale Browning.

Any modifications you plan to make will require at least a modest investment. Some changes will require more investment than a new gun would cost, and I will not suggest you do those, but point you toward the professional gunsmith who specializes in shotgun work to guide you on your journey to that elusive perfect score.

You must remember, though, the gun is not always to blame when scores are not what you think

they should be. It could very possibly be your technique or mechanics while shooting, and little or nothing you do to the gun will improve on that. Before you go messing with the gun, please be sure you are doing everything right before altering the tool in your hands. If you're convinced a few modifications to the gun can help you break a few extra birds, here are a couple of projects you should be able to perform without undue difficulty if

you are at all handy with tools.

The first thing to look at are sights. Or rather, beads. A standard single bead on the end of the barrel has served shooters for many years, even decades. But is it enough? Not if it's a plain brass or aluminum bead. To catch and keep your eye, you can replace that metal blob with a white or orange one. Some shooters do well with the white, while others just lose that color in the background clutter or the sky. I much prefer orange.

The white or orange bead is the style known as a Bradley bead. Instead of the bead being one piece that's screwed into the barrel, the Bradley bead has a

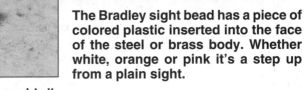

The Bradley sight bead has a piece of colored plastic inserted into the face of the steel or brass body. Whether white, orange or pink it's a step up from a plain sight.

Left to right—Carlson orange bead, aluminum front bead, aluminum mid-rib bead, and a Bradley bead. The mid-rib unit is much smaller than the front bead.

Pliers will damage a standard bead, so you'll need a bead vise to install one (here in the right-hand vise). The Bradley requires smooth-faced pliers to turn it in completely and without damage (right).

tombstone-shaped body, with the bead inset into the face toward the shooter. The body is usually a durable alloy, while the bead can be a bright, if fragile plastic. A variation of the Bradley bead is the Raybar. Here, the plastic goes through the post, instead of being assembled by placing the plastic bead on the front of the post. Light striking the front of the plastic bead travels through it to the rear of the bead, making it appear to glow.

Changing a bead is easy, most of the time. You'll need smooth-faced pliers or a bead vise, a tap of the correct size, a small half-round file and a padded vise. Look up the thread size of your shotgun, and get a new bead with the same thread. For most

shotguns this will be a 6-48 thread. With the pliers, unscrew the old bead. Use the tap to either clean up the threads or cut new ones. If the old shank size was smaller than the new one, you will have to drill the hole out with a #31 drill.

If you have to drill the hole out, look in the bore to see if the old hole goes all the way through. Remove the choke tube if your shotgun has one. If the old hole does not go through, be sure not to drill the new hole into the bore. If the old one does, then drill yours through as this will make tapping much easier.

If you are installing a plain bead, lock it in the Brownells bead wrench if you have it. Trying to install a bead

with pliers is simply asking to damage the bead. Screw the new bead into the freshly tapped hole. If it does not easily screw all the way down, check the threads for burrs on the bore side. If you have not drilled through into the bore you may have to file the shank of the bead a bit shorter.

Bradley beads can be installed with smooth-faced pliers, but work carefully. These beads must turn all the way down to the rib or barrel to squarely face the shooter. Sometimes burrs on the edge of the hole will keep it from seating properly. In this case, use a larger drill than the #31 to deburr just the edge of the hole.

Once you have the bead smoothly screwing down into the barrel, re-

When the orange Marble Arms Sunspot up front isn't enough, Sweeney clips the Hi-Viz sight onto the rib. It has stayed in place for thousands of shots, and never come loose.

move it and degrease the bead and hole. Apply Loctite and then screw the bead back in. Stand the barrel on its muzzle for a couple of hours until the Loctite has had a chance to harden. If you don't, you might find Loctite that has wicked down into the threads of your screw-in choke and hardened.

If you have drilled through into the bore, once the Loctite has hardened, use a small half-round file to dress the base of the bead shank flush with the bore. A temporary approach to a brighter bead is to use one of the new fiber optic sights. I use the Hi-Viz, a type that clamps to the rib with magnets. Each sight comes with five colors that can be changed between stands if you need to. I keep the sight in my pocket, and if I find myself in a dark stand or on a shot with a clut-tered background where I need to see the bead better, I slip it on.

A mid-rib (center) bead can improve your hit percentage by helping to ensure your eye is located in the same spot over the stock when you aim. The mid-rib bead differs from the front one in several respects. It is much smaller. Where a standard front bead is .175-inch in diameter, mid-rib beads are only .068-inch. The mid-rib bead also uses a smaller shank. Instead of a #31 drill and a 6-48 tap, the mid-rib bead requires a #45 drill and a 3-56 tap. It does not come as a Bradley bead, only as a plain brass or aluminum round-head. You can only install it on a barrel with a rib because the barrel tapers down from the receiver and you won't be able to see it. Most importantly, you must not drill through into the bore with this one. Filing the base of the bead at the muzzle is a snap. Trying to file or polish the base of the bead when it is 12 inches down the bore would be a real headache.

To install the mid-rib bead, find the rib post closest to the middle of the barrel. Measure the center of the rib. Brownells makes a gadget for this, and it is so handy it is worth it for even one job. Centerpunch the spot, and drill the rib with a #45 drill. Only drill to the bottom of the rib post, and not into the barrel wall. Tap the hole with the 3-56 tap, screw in the bead and you're ready to go.

Fear of recoil can really disrupt your shooting cadence and cause scores to reach new lows. Shooters can become recoil shy gradually over time until they flinch badly each time they pull the trigger. Though it's not

After the forcing cone reamer is well oiled, insert it into the bore until it stops. Turn it clockwise two or three revolutions, using moderate pressure to take small cuts on the cone.

After making a few cuts, pull the reamer straight out of the bore. Turning it backwards will dull the cutters. Brush the flutes clean and re-oil before making the next pass.

The Kick-Eez Sorbothane® cheek pad can save your face from recoil. Combined with a good recoil pad it can improve your scores and fun.

possible to eliminate recoil, there are four approaches that can lessen its effects: forcing cone reaming; padding the cheekpiece; barrel porting; and installing or upgrading the recoil pad.

Reaming the forcing cone to a gentler angle not only decreases felt recoil but it can improve patterns as well. This is a simple operation that you can do at home, provided you have the reamer. A reamer costs about $60 dollars, not quite twice what a gunsmith would charge to do the job for you. If you have a double you want reamed, then the expenditure makes sense. By working over more than two barrels, you are saving money.

If you have chrome-lined bores you will have to invest in a reamer with carbide cutting edges. This one costs

about $150, and should not be used on a bore that does not have a chrome lining, so determine exactly what you have before shelling out your hardearned cash.

To ream the bore, you need a padded vise to securely hold the barrel, a large tap handle, the reamer and high-sulfur cutting oil. Clamp the barrel in the padded vise muzzle down with a can under the muzzle to catch the oil that will run out. With the reamer in the tap handle, dip the edges in the cutting oil and then gently slide it into the bore. Turn the reamer two or three revolutions clockwise, then pull it straight out. Do not turn the reamer backward. Brush the chips off, re-oil the flutes, and repeat. After a dozen turns, swab the bore out and

look inside with a strong light. You should see the cut forming at the front of the old forcing cone. Repeat the cutting and inspection until the rear edge of the newly-reamed forcing cone no longer has a dark shoulder.

Brush the reamer clean and store it back in its plastic sleeve. Filter the oil out of the collection can back into its original can. Thoroughly clean the bore and you are done.

The recoil you feel has two components, the rearward thrust against your shoulder, and the upward pivot of the stock against your cheek. A simple way to dampen the upward jolt is to pad the stock. Kick-Eez makes adhesive-backed pads you can put on the stock comb to lessen the sting. Their pads are made of Sorbothane® and

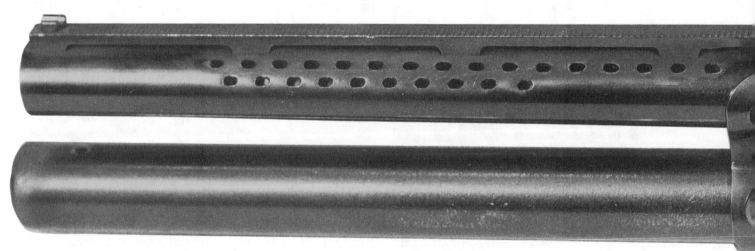

Barrel porting is an effective way to reduce muzzle flip. This barrel, ported by Mag-Na-Port, has the standard treatment plus Pigeon Porting which adds up to a lot of holes.

come in several thicknesses. Be aware that adding thickness to the stock will elevate your pattern/point of impact. The thickest pad can raise the pattern about eight inches at 40 yards. If the pad solves your recoil problem, then you can adjust the pattern. However, once you've licked the recoil problem you can easily remove the pad and your pattern goes back to where it should be. Taking the pad off is easy. Use your fingertips or thumbnail to lift an edge of it, and then place a few drops of oil or mineral spirits there. The oil or solvent will lift the adhesive, and you can gradually peel the pad off.

I found that the middle of the pad thickness range was very comfortable for me, and my pattern had only moved four inches at 40 yards. This was not a problem, so I have left my cheekpad on. It has survived four seasons of vigorous use and shows no signs of giving up.

Barrel porting is one of those things that looks simple, but it can't be done at home. The solution is to ship the barrel(s) off to Mag-Na-port. The crew there will cut the ports according to your instructions and send it right back to you. I favor more holes rather than less, and ask for Pigeon Porting. On my heavy-recoiling competition guns, I had them burn two and even three sets of ports. It costs more, but

the muzzle does not come up at all. (There are other outfits that do barrel porting, of course, and I mention Mag-Na-Port simply because I've used them with good success.) Do not let your buddy the home gunsmith convince you he can drill holes that will work "just as good." The best you can hope for is an unobtrusive and ineffective "porting" job. At worst he can perform an ugly job that quickly clogs with plastic from the wads, and has also destroyed your patterns.

Installing a recoil pad is not something you can do with a few simple home tools. At a minimum you will need a large disk sander. A better choice would be a belt sander. You will also like to have a separate room to sand in, as the rubber dust and particles will get all over everything. When I was installing recoil pads on a weekly basis, I found it best to do them all on a single day, so I could consolidate the cleanup that took a shopvac, extensive brooming, and even combing the rubber out of my hair. This job makes quite a mess of a shop.

My advice: Leave this to the professional, unless you like the taste of ground rubber.

The softest pads I have used are the Pachmayr Decelerator® and the Kick-Eez Sorbothane®. Both are soft on the shoulder, but Pachmayr has

gone one better. They offer a Sporting Clays pad that has a horseshoe of harder plastic at the top. This hard insert will slide over your shirt and be less likely to catch on anything. It goes over the curve of your shoulder, and won't bang against you on recoil.

Of course, if you are shooting a beautiful London double with a checkered buttplate, or checkered bare wood, it would be a sacrilege to cut that stock and install a chunk of rubber. You'll just have to shoot in a padded vest, or wear a pad under your shirt.

These few jobs are about all you'll want to tackle at home unless you are pretty well experienced at gun work, and have a good inventory of gunsmithing tools. In addition, there really isn't much else you'll need to do to your gun to make it an efficient clay target burner.

If you're tempted to tear into the innards of a side by side or over/under to do a little "tuning" or a trigger job, be advised that you are asking for trouble if you're not thoroughly familiar with these mechanisms. What might seem like a simple tune up can quickly turn into a nightmare when you can't get it back together.

Leave the big projects to the experts. Other shooters, your wallet, and your ego will all appreciate it. ●

A soft, thick recoil pad is a blessing to the active shooter, but isn't a do-it-yourself job for the average hobbyist. Left to right—Pachmayr Decelerator®, Sorbothane®, and ventilated rubber.

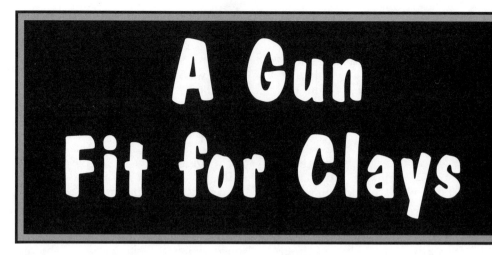

A Gun Fit for Clays

YOU COULD MAKE a mini-career out of listing all the reasons why Sporting Clays has been good for American shotgunning, and follow it up with a mini-retirement hobby of trying to decide which benefits have been most useful to the greatest number of shooters.

If you asked me (and as Gene Hill used to say to me, you probably wanted to, but it just slipped your mind), I'd pick two things that have made an enormous difference to clay and game shooters alike. One is the rediscovery of how smoothly and sweetly a gun with long barrels can swing, and the other, even more important, is a growing appreciation for guns that truly fit.

Time was—and not so long ago—that American shooters generally dismissed gun fit as just some overrated hocus-pocus of interest to no one but the British, and available only in made-to-order guns that cost more than a college degree. Sporting Clays was the catalyst in proving both notions wrong.

It's not that we didn't come by our former attitude honestly. American makers didn't really invent the standardized, factory-built gun, but we certainly perfected it, to the point that anyone with a few dollars to spare could own a well-made, reason-

ably good-handling gun capable of delivering several lifetimes of reliable service. But this meant we all had guns with stock dimensions made for the "average" man—which is to say, for nobody in particular.

Because there is no American tradition of fitting guns to shooters, American shooters have long had to fit themselves to guns. And being physically adaptable creatures, we did it pretty well, all things considered. We even revised our target games to compensate for the shortcomings of off-the-rack factory guns: What's pre-mounting in trap and Skeet if not an opportunity for shooters to fit themselves to their guns be-

fore they call for a target? The premount rules grew out of a quest for higher scores, true, but the main reason why scores weren't higher in the low-gun days is that nobody can consistently shoot at his best with a gun that doesn't fit properly. Sporting Clays changed all that.

Sporting Clays is a low-gun game, as every target game should be and as game shooting has to be. (I'm aware that NSCA has caved in to pressure from those to whom score is everything and now allows premounted guns, but this is not the time for me to get started on what I think of that piece of nonsense.) Shooting low-gun means handling a

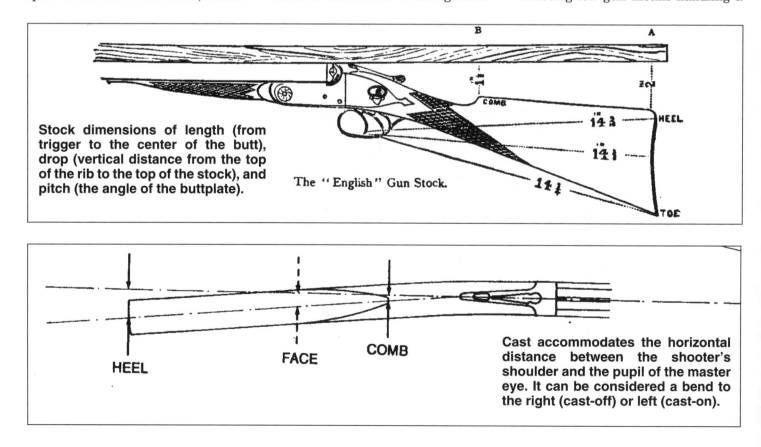

Stock dimensions of length (from trigger to the center of the butt), drop (vertical distance from the top of the rib to the top of the stock), and pitch (the angle of the buttplate).

The "English" Gun Stock.

Cast accommodates the horizontal distance between the shooter's shoulder and the pupil of the master eye. It can be considered a bend to the right (cast-off) or left (cast-on).

"A fitted gun is one that points exactly where your eyes are looking when all you do is raise it to your cheek without moving your head."

by MICHAEL MC INTOSH

shotgun as it was meant to be handled, and this, in turn, has led shooters to realize that gun fit isn't just frippery—indeed, it is the key to being the best shot you can be.

The concept is very simple: A fitted gun is one that points exactly where your eyes are looking when all you do is raise it to your cheek without moving your head.

That's the end result. Getting there is somewhat more complicated, of course, but even so, gun fit is not the arcane voodoo that some would have you believe it is. It's a matter of having a stock that suits your height, weight and build, the length of your arms and neck, the shape of your shoulders and chest and the bone structure of your face. I know this adds up to a lot of factors, but the good side is that they can all be accommodated by relatively few actual dimensions on the gun itself.

But before I describe them, I must offer a cautionary note: Gun fit is of real value only after you've developed a sound, consistent shooting technique. If you can't swing and mount a gun exactly the same way almost every time, fit is next to meaningless. A fitted gun is not a panacea for sloppy shooting. On the contrary, it's the last refinement that will help you cross the line between competency and expertise, and its value is predicated entirely upon first achieving a level of skill measurable by consistency. If your technique is shaky, if you handle a gun like a weekend golfer swings a sand wedge, then you need a good shooting school a lot more than you need a gun fitting. In shooting as in every physical skill, First Things First applies. Technique precedes everything.

That said, here are the dimensions of a gun stock in which fit resides.

Length I begin with length because it's the dimension that everybody seems to get most cranked up about, even though it's one of the least important. There are no prescriptions for the proper length of a gun stock. It needs to be short enough that the butt doesn't snag on your clothes or your body as you mount it, but long enough to keep the base of your trigger-hand thumb comfortably separated from the end of your nose—else shooting becomes a self-contact sport, which is both disconcerting and painful.

A stock also needs to be long enough that you don't have to roll your shoulder forward very far to make contact with the butt. A little shoulder roll is necessary to integrate the gun with your body and to maintain your physical focus on the target; too much leaves you hunched over, cramped, and unable to swing the gun freely.

The difference between enough and too much is very little. The traditional American preference tends toward stocks that are too short; that's mainly because the writers and pundits who shaped the American view almost invariably made their mark in mounted-gun target shooting—so just remember that they were accustomed to fitting themselves to the gun rather than the other way around, and take their advice with a large dosage of salt.

To put this into practical perspective, let's say the typical factory stock, from 14 to 14-1/2 inches long, is fine if you stand 5 feet 6 to 5 feet 8 inches. If you're taller, up to about 6 feet 1, you'll shoot a lot better with 15 inches length of pull, and the minimum useful length increases exponentially from there. I'm 6 feet tall, wear a 33-inch shirtsleeve, and all my guns measure from 15 to 15-1/4. I can handle one that's a half-inch longer, but make it a half-inch shorter and my shooting suffers.

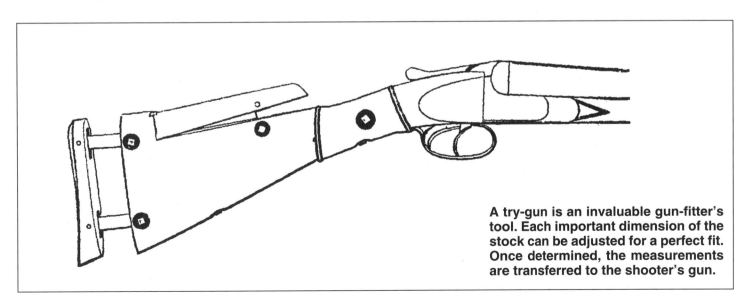

A try-gun is an invaluable gun-fitter's tool. Each important dimension of the stock can be adjusted for a perfect fit. Once determined, the measurements are transferred to the shooter's gun.

Drop The English call this "bend." It refers to the vertical distance from the top of the rib, the plane along which your master eye should look, to the top of the stock, which at the front end needs to be nestled right into the little shelf under your cheekbone and which at the rear should be level with the top of your shoulder. Drop, therefore, accommodates the distance from the pupil of your eye to both your cheekbone and shoulder.

Traditionally, drop is measured at the tip of the comb and at the heel of the stock, with perhaps a third measurement taken at the "face," where your cheek actually contacts the stock, about three inches back from the tip of the comb.

Cast Cast is the horizontal equivalent of drop, the distance from the centerline of the rib to the centerline of the butt. Cast accommodates the distance from the pupil of your master eye to the spot where the butt rests against your shoulder. Right-handed shooters need their stocks offset to the right; this is called cast-off.

Lefties need them bent the other way, referred to as cast-on.

Pitch is the angle of the butt in relation to the horizontal plane of the rib, and it accommodates the shape of a shooter's shoulder and upper chest. The objective is to have the entire surface of the butt in uniform contact with your body. If only the heel touches your shoulder, the gun is apt to shoot low and kick down off your shoulder as it recoils; if only the toe is in contact, you'll have a high-shooting gun that jabs painfully into your pectoral muscle every time you pull the trigger.

As with length, there is no prescription for any of these dimensions that will suit everyone. Drop is influenced by the slope of your shoulders, the length of your neck, and the height of your cheekbones. Women, with their lovely high cheekbones and longer necks, usually need higher stocks than men. Cast depends on the width of your face and the shape of your shoulders, because those characters determine where the stock

is in relation to your eye and where the butt comes to rest against your shoulder. The contour of your upper chest dictates pitch. Not surprisingly, women typically require less pitch than men do.

Although a session with a competent gun fitter is the best way to learn what stock dimensions suit you best, there's a simple, reliable way of learning how well your gun fits and how it can be altered to fit you better, a method attributed to English gunmaker and shooting instructor Robert Churchill.

All you need is a patterning board, a measuring tape, and a box of cartridges. Some sheets of paper at least three feet square will do, though an old bedsheet suspended on a wire is better, and a steel plate covered with fresh white paint is best of all.

First, measure off exactly 16 yards from the plate. Measure, don't pace it; it's important to have precisely 48 feet between your eyes and the target. Then paint a black dot, an inch or two in diameter, on the plate. Stand on the

Gun fitter working in an English gun shop. Once the proper dimensions are close, further adjustments will be made at the range after firing a hundred or so shells at clay targets and analyzing the results.

Stock fitter Bryan Bilinski using Robert Churchill's 16-yard fitting method. Shooters can use the same procedure by themselves to determine how well, or poorly, their guns fit. The results can be surprising.

With eyes focused only on the target, the shooter simply raises the gun and fires. The object is not to rush but, above all, not to aim. Actual measurement of the 16-yard firing distance is critical.

Stock Fitters

Although stock fitting requires neither a crystal ball nor a mojo, it does require skill and experience, and the fact is, not everybody who hangs out a shingle to the effect actually is capable of accomplishing a proper fit. Sticking some sort of flashlight gizmo into your barrels is a start, but a truly complete fitting involves a try-gun—a shotgun with a specially made stock that's adjustable in all of the critical dimensions—and a few hours' shooting, first at a pattern plate and then at flying targets. There are no shortcuts, no quick fixes, and certainly no substitute for doing it right.

Getting a good fitting is relatively easy in England; just consult any reputable gun maker or shooting school. Finding the same level of expertise in the United States is more difficult but by no means impossible. The following list is not meant to condemn anyone by exclusion, but it does include fitters whom I know from first-hand experience to be truly good at what they do.

Bryan Bilinski
Fieldsport Ltd.
3313 W. South Airport Rd.
Traverse City, MI 49684
616-933-0767

Jon Hollinger
Aspen Outfitting Co.
9 Dean St.
Aspen, CO 81611
970-925-3406

Pat LaBoone
Clear Creek Outdoors
2550 Hwy. 23
Wrenshall, MN 55797
218-384-3670

Keith Lupton
Pawling Mountain Club
P.O. Box 573
Pawling, NY 12564
914-855-3825

Jack Mitchell
c/o Geoff Gaebe
Addieville East Farm
200 Pheasant Dr.
Mapleville, RI 02839
401-568-3185

16-yard line, assume a proper ready position with the gun butt just tucked under your arm, your weight on your leading foot, and your upper body and head in such position that all you have to do is lift the gun to your cheek. Focus your eyes on the black dot, and in one motion raise the gun and fire it.

Don't rush, don't dawdle, and above all, don't look at the gun. Look at the dot and shoot at it as if it was a straightaway target. Do this four or five times.

If you've mounted and fired just by pointing the gun rather than aiming, and if your mount is consistent, your patterns will strike in essentially the same place. Odd shots—flyers, rifle shooters call them—will be obvious. Ignore those. Find the center of the majority of your patterns and measure the distance between there and the center of the black dot. This value in inches tells you how well or poorly your stock fits in increments of 1/16-inch.

Let's say your patterns consistently center four inches below the center of the dot and two inches left. This means that in order for this gun to shoot right where you look, the stock needs to be a quarter-inch (4/16) higher and cast an eighth-inch (2/16) to the right. At 16 yards, every inch the pattern center deviates from dead-on translates as a sixteenth-inch on the stock—up, down, or sideways.

As to which way adjustments need to be made, it's useful to remember that a shotgun stock works the same way as a rifle sight. To zero in a rifle, you move the rear sight in the direction you want the bullet to move on the target; the same applies to a gun stock.

What you're looking for are patterns that consistently print about 60 percent above the dot, 40 percent below, and spread equally from side to side. When you have that, you have a gun that shoots where you look.

You can make temporary adjustments to the stock by adding layers of moleskin to the comb or shaving down the top and side with a plane or a wood rasp, adding length with a slip-on pad or making it shorter by swapping the buttpad for a thinner plate. When you get it where it needs to be, take it to a stockmaker and have the stock bent, lengthened, shortened, built up, cut down or, best of all, treat yourself to a custom stock.

Develop a consistent technique, shoot a gun that truly fits, and you'll be surprised at what a good shot you really are. ●

The distance in inches between the center of the patterns and the center of the target point translates to stock measurements in 1/16-inch increments. That may seem to be splitting hairs to some, but it can make a big difference in shooting qualities.

The Shotgun Barrel:

Forcing Cones, Back-Boring, Porting & Chokes

*It's much more than just
a tube to hold the sight bead!
The barrel design affects
how your gun shoots and recoils.*

by LARRY S. STERETT

IN GRANDAD'S DAY, about the only thing he was concerned with so far as his shotgun went, was if a dime would slip into the muzzle of his 12-bore to be sure the choke was "correct," and that it shot nearly every time he pulled the trigger. The fact that it kicked like a mule probably meant that it shot "hard," and that was considered good. Today,

there are a number of things that can be done with a shotgun barrel to make the felt recoil seem less, and to improve our chances of hitting those whirling disks of black, white, orange or green. My intention here is to give the reader a better understanding of the shotgun barrel, and what can be done to make the gun perform better than ever.

Back in the mid-1800s when breech-loading shotguns were developed, the gauges had already been pretty much standardized. The number of spherical lead balls of a specific diameter that would weigh 1 pound determined the gauge. Hence, if four such balls weighed a pound, it was a 4-gauge, and if it took 16 balls of a particular diameter to weigh one pound, it was designated a 16-gauge. The exception is the 410, developed earlier in this century. It is not a gauge, but the designation of the bore diameter of the barrel, thus it's correct label should be 410-bore. Even so, any number of shotgun makers mislabel their guns as 410-gauge. This is done in spite of the fact that it requires approximately 67-1/2 balls of .410-inch diameter to weigh 1 pound, making, in truth, a 67-1/2-gauge shotgun.

While the most popular gauge in Europe for many years was the 16, it has now been mainly replaced by the 12, which was and continues to be the most popular in the U.K., Canada and the United States. Thus, for our purposes, most of the references will be to the 12-gauge, or 12-bore as it is often called in the U.K. The standard bore diameter of the 16-gauge is accepted as 0.662-inch, while that of the 12 is 0.729-inch. However, due to varying manufacturing tolerances and non-standard-

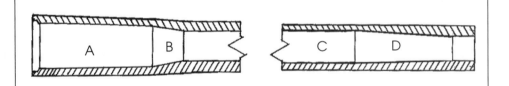

The shotgun barrel's four basic sections are: chamber (A); forcing cone (B); barrel bore (C); and choke (D).

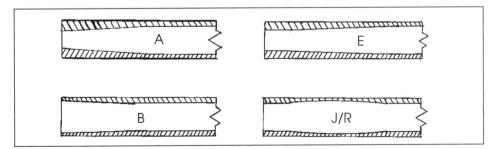

The four most common choke types are: (A) American, used with many screw-in choke tubes; (B) Bell, used mainly in Skeet guns to open patterns; (E) English, used in the U.K. and U.S.; (J/R) Jug or recess, used mostly to put some choke back in a damaged barrel.

ization between countries, bore diameters for all shotguns marked 12-gauge will not measure the same. In the U.S., for example, if the bore goes between 0.7250- and 0.745-inch, it is considered a 12-gauge. Yet, I have measured the bores of many European and Japanese-made shotguns and found them as small as 0.720-inch. Others have been as large as 0.731- to 0.735-inch, but not considered back-bored, a topic we will discuss later.

The interior of the shotgun barrel is divided into four basic sections. Starting from the breech, these include the chamber, forcing cone, bore proper, and choke. The chamber dimensions in the U.S. are based on SAAMI specifications, while those in the U.K. are according to the British Proof Law, revised. Other countries generally follow the standards adopted by those countries having proof houses. Thus, 12-gauge shotshells made in Greece or India will chamber properly in guns manufactured on the other side of the globe.

Near the front end of the shotgun chamber the bore dimension should measure 0.797/.798-inch. To make the transition to bore diameter smooth, a taper or truncated conical section called a forcing cone is located forward of the chamber. If the forcing cone is too abrupt or short, compression of the wad column and shot charge produces additional recoil. In the old days a steep angle was fine for the then-current thicker paper hulls in which the wad column consisted of a hard card over-powder wad and wool or felt filler wads. To prevent gas leakage or seepage past the wads it was necessary to get the wads into the bore and seal it as quickly as possibly. A short forcing cone could do this.

Short forcing cones can create some problems, including increased pressure and felt recoil. If the chamber is shorter than the overall fired shell length, part or all of the crimp portion of the shell may extend into the forcing cone area creating an obstruction. Since no two objects can occupy the same location at the same time, something has to give. Often the crimp portion of the case is ripped off and passes down the barrel with the shot charge and wad column. This creates higher pressure at the point of obstruction and increased felt recoil. In some thin-barrel shotguns, barrels have reportedly burst at this point when a modern 2-3/4 inch shell has been fired in a gun with shorter chamber, such as 2-1/2 inches. Over the years, 12-gauge shotshells have been made in lengths ranging from 2 inches to 4 inches. The old 2-, 2-1/2-, and 2-5/8-inch shells are only sometimes used as specialty loads, and you certainly won't see them on any Sporting Clays course.

Another forcing cone problem occurred when thin metal hulls were used, and later the modern plastic

Left: Bore diameter of this single barrel measures 0.731-inch, slightly larger than the standard 12-gauge's 0.729-inch. **Right:** This foreign over/under with choke tubes measures 0.720-inch, well under the norm.

shells. The thin metal hulls required the use of a larger diameter wad or one that was more flexible. The hard card over-powder wads did not compress easily around the circumference. Winchester solved the problem of the hard wad by using a thin folded C-wad over the powder. As the wad unfolded it would reach a diameter nearly equal to the bore diameter of a 5-gauge shotgun, thereby effectively sealing any 12-gauge bore against blowby or gas-leakage. It worked well when introduced and it is still being used today.

To provide a smoother transition from the chamber to the barrel bore, a number of gunsmiths took to lengthening the forcing cone, reducing the amount of taper and extending the cone for a greater or longer distance. Thus, in place of a forcing cone 3/8- to 5/8-inch in length it was extended out to 1-1/2 inches, or more. A few cones have reportedly been as long as 5 inches, and possibly more. This reduces both felt recoil and internal pressure, and can improve patterns since there is less abrupt shot crowding within the column.

If a lengthened forcing cone can reduce felt recoil and possibly improve patterns, why not extend it all the way to the choke area, you might ask. It has been tried, but it's time consuming and expensive. An easier solution is back-boring, sometimes called over-bore. In place of the regular 0.729-inch bore diameter, the barrel is bored to a larger diameter, such as 0.740-inch, which is approaching 11-gauge dimensions. Currently, several U.S. shotgun manufacturers are back-boring many of their shotguns, opening them to 0.735- or 0.745-inch, in addition to lengthening the forcing cones. However, there is an increasing number of gunsmiths specializing in shotguns who will back-bore a gun to any reasonable bore diameter. There are a couple of specialists providing new oversize barrels, like Washington-based Stan Baker who introduced his Big Bore in the mid-1980s. Moneymaker Guncraft in Nebraska has their "Custom .780 Barrel." Both are actually 10-gauge barrels with 12-gauge chambers. Having used the Baker on a Perazzi receiver and the Custom .780 on a

Remington 11-87, I can vouch for the reduced recoil and improved patterns, depending on the load being used. The larger bore reduces the length of the shot string, which tends to improve patterns, but it requires a wad column with a good elastic gas seal flange to prevent gas leakage and blown patterns. Hard wads will sometimes tip in the oversize bore, disrupting the smooth movement down the barrel.

Exactly what pattern percentages a choke will deliver depends on many variables, but the basics are the accepted figures I give here. A barrel without any choke is a Cylinder bore, without any constriction, and should measure 0.729-inch at the muzzle. It's strictly for short range use. Riot guns of yesteryear had such barrels, and some rabbit hunters prefer them for hunting in brush. Skeet shooting is done at short range, and most Skeet shooters opt for Skeet or Improved Cylinder chokes, which contain from two to a dozen points of constriction, a bore reduction of from 0.002- to .012-inch. This amounts to a reduction of

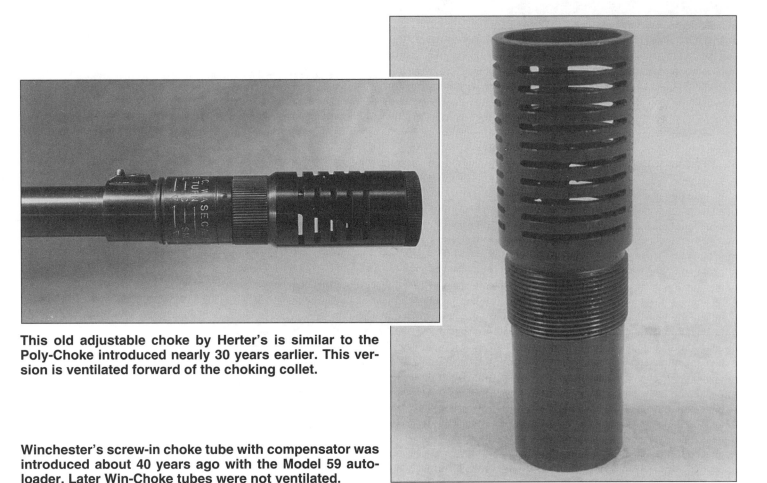

This old adjustable choke by Herter's is similar to the Poly-Choke introduced nearly 30 years earlier. This version is ventilated forward of the choking collet.

Winchester's screw-in choke tube with compensator was introduced about 40 years ago with the Model 59 autoloader. Later Win-Choke tubes were not ventilated.

about one to three percent in bore diameter.

Trap shooters prefer their guns to have Improved Modified or Full chokes, depending on their handicap, since the target starts out at a minimum of 16 yards from the firing point. Sporting Clays and similar clay target games fall somewhere in between as to choke requirements. The targets may be crossing from either direction, high or low outgoing or incoming, or even rolling, bouncing along the ground. Most shooters will do better on Sporting Clays with a more open choke, based on what I have observed. At a shoot in Canada, one competitor used an over/under with Improved Cylinder choke tubes. He was only two targets off the high shooter. The rest of us used autoloaders with Modified tubes and didn't score so well. The Improved Cylinder choke is intended to place 35 to 45 percent of the shot charge within a 30-inch circle at 40 yards, with higher percentages at less than 40 yards.

Modified choke has 16 to 24 points of constriction in the bore diameter, and is supposed to produce patterns averaging 60 percent at 40 yards. Depending on the load used, a Modified choke may produce patterns that average higher or lower than the norm. For most Sporting Clays layouts a shooter with an autoloader having an Improved Cylinder or Modified choke should do pretty well at most every station. At a celebrity shoot in Chester, England, a few years ago I watched Prince Andrew, Captain Phillips, Sean Connery and other well-known shooters using Purdey, Boss and Holland & Holland side by sides choked Improved Cylinder/Modified shoot very well. The gamekeepers won the event, but the Royals were only a couple of birds behind.

Chokes for shotguns have been around for more than 130 years,

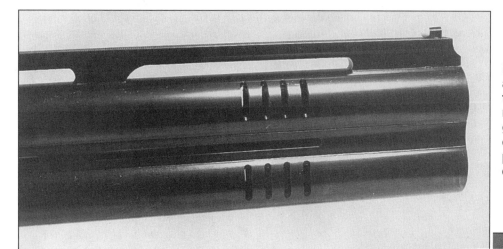

Barrel porting can take various forms as seen here on a trio of over/unders, top to bottom: four ports in each barrel to the rear of the choke; a Czech gun with 10 slots forward of the fixed chokes; a series of small holes in parallel rows. Ports in the Rhino choke tube are angled to the rear.

with the first patented design being a rather narrow ring threaded onto the outside of the barrel muzzle. It had a slight amount of constriction on the inside but whether it actually tightened the patterns to any extent is unknown. According to Sylvester Roper, the inventor, "Said detachable muzzle is slightly contracted at its forward end, and, when attached to the gun, will have the effect of causing it to throw the shot more compactly than when it is removed."

The majority of the early chokes, as developed by Greener, Kimble, Johnson, and others, and which did work were integral with the barrel.

Machined or swaged so the interior of the barrel muzzle was smaller than the bore diameter, the chokes were divided into five basic designations, with the first being Cylinder, or no choke, just regular bore diameter. Second came the Improved Cylinder, or as the British call it the Quarter Choke. This choke, with minimum constriction, should produce patterns averaging in the 40 to 50 percent range, depending on the load and gun. The next step up is the Modified or Half-Choke, which should produce 60 percent patterns at 40 yards. Increasing the muzzle constriction a few more points produced the Im-

proved Modified choke, capable of producing patterns in the 65 percent range. Last is the Full choke which is designed to produce patterns of at least 70 percent. This generally consists of 35 to 40 points of constriction, although it can be and has been less.

The fixed or integral chokes generally fall into six categories: American; English; swaged; bell; jug; and Tula. The choke area of most shotguns begins within about 2-1/2 to 3 inches of the muzzle, regardless of whether it's a fixed choke or screw-in. Exceptions are the adjustable chokes and screw-on tubes attached to the exterior of the barrel. In addition, some fixed chokes begin farther back from the muzzle than 3 inches.

The American-style choke consists of a taper from the beginning of the choke area to the muzzle. The English-style choke is similar except it has a short parallel section following the choke taper. This parallel section can be as long as an inch, but is generally a half-inch or less.

Swaged chokes tend to be found on low-priced single-barrel shotguns, and would probably never be seen on guns at a Sporting Clays course. A plain gun barrel with no rib, choke or sight bead is rammed into a hardened, conical female die with enough force to squeeze the muzzle to a smaller diameter. The amount of swaging determines the degree of choke.

The Bell choke is similar to the American choke in reverse. Instead of the muzzle being smaller in diameter than the bore, it is opened so the diameter is larger. It can go from 0.729-inch to 0.740-inch to open up an overly tight pattern.

The Jug or recessed choke was done by gunsmiths to provide some degree of constriction to barrels which had been cut off due to some damage. It consisted of removing a few thousandths of an inch of metal to the rear of the muzzle leaving a short parallel section at the muzzle. The shot charge then expanded slightly in the jug or enlarged area and then "choked" back to bore diameter. Screw-in chokes have for the most part done away with the need for jug chokes, provided the barrel walls are thick enough to be threaded internally for the tubes.

The Tula choke is named after the Russian arsenal where it was appar-

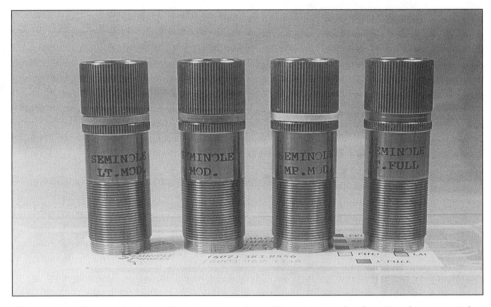

These Seminole choke tubes have colored bands to designate the constriction. They extend beyond the muzzle and are serrated for a positive grip.

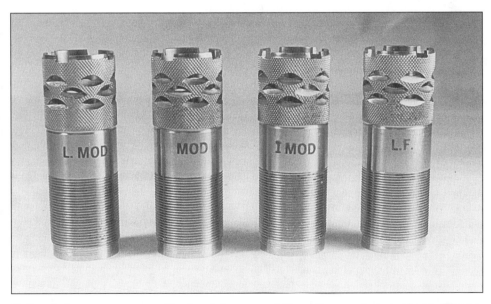

Briley tubes are among the best known of the aftermarket designs. These particular tubes have an unusual port shape.

These tubes, an Accu-Choke by Mossberg (top barrel), and a Winchoke from Winchester, represent two styles from the 1980s. Both extend well beyond the muzzle and can be removed by hand or wrench.

Winchester was one of the first U.S. gun makers to have choke tubes as standard equipment. This is an early set of tubes with the original wood-handled wrench.

ently developed. It is interesting, but is seldom seen these days.

Six decades after the first choke was patented one of the most famous of a new crop of shotgun chokes came into being. Designed by E. F. White, the new design consisted of an adjustable collet that attached to the outside of the barrel muzzle. Called the Poly-Choke, it permitted a range of choke constrictions from Cylinder to Full simply by hand tightening the collet. A twist of the wrist could change the choke in a second. Although the Poly-Choke is not frequently seen today, it could be ideal for shooters using an autoloader or pump-action shotgun for Sporting Clays. Just change the choke for the shots expected at a given station: open for close incoming or rabbits and tighter for the outgoing high flyers.

In an attempt to reduce recoil even further, barrel porting or ventilating has blossomed in recent years. Porting is not really new, but appeared in the 1920s and possibly even prior to that. One of first applications of this was introduced more than 60 years ago as the Cutts Compensator, designed by Richard Cutts. It consists of a ventilated cage-like cylinder that attached to the muzzle of a shotgun barrel, from which all choke had been removed, and featured a series of screw-in choke tubes that extended beyond the cage. Later, there was even an adjustable choke for the unit. Some few years later, Pachmayr came out with the PowerPac which was similar, except the bulk of the screw-in choke tube extended back into the ventilated cage rather projecting forward. Even later, the Poly-Choke was ventilated, but the ventilated portion was forward of the choke, not preceding it.

From the late 1940s into the 1960s, choke devices of a variety of designs appeared with amazing frequency. Some worked rather well, others didn't. Then Winchester introduced their Model 59 autoloader with the glass-wound barrel and a screw-in Win-Lite Win-Choke. There was no bulge on the muzzle, and it had a ventilated muzzle section with the choke contained completely within the barrel.

The race was on. Removable, replaceable choke tubes were now being installed inside the barrel, so why not just ventilate the barrel proper? Some bolt-action shotguns with adjustable

chokes had slots machined in the barrel to reduce recoil and it worked, at least to a degree. It should work equally well on pumps, autoloaders, over/unders and even side by sides. Mag-na-Port, later Pro-Port, was one of the leaders in using electrical discharge machining to produce true precision venting of the barrel preceding the choke area, whether using fixed or screw-in choke tubes. The shape of the ports vary according to the manufacturer's or gunsmith's concept. They may be circular, trapezoidal, oval, slots, or even drop-shaped, and perpendicular to the barrel bore or slanted to the rear.

Barrel porting does work. It reduces muzzle jump significantly, in

addition to felt recoil. Back-boring can also make a difference in felt recoil and can give more uniform patterns at the same time.

The lengthened forcing cone, back-bored barrel, porting, and replaceable screw-in choke tubes have long been aftermarket features, and many now come as standard on a number of shotguns. All are worthwhile features for dedicated Sporting Clays shooters that combine to make an enjoyable sport even moreso. If you are serious about your sport, by all means look into having your barrel(s) modified by a qualified gunsmith or company that specializes in this type of work. You won't be sorry. ●

Many of the second wave of choke tubes fit flush with the muzzle and had notches in the end to facilitate removal with a wrench.

This is a screw-in choke tube used by Greener in England 40 years ago. In the U.S., Ljutic used a similar design for several years.

The Engraver's Art

MAN HAS LONG had an affinity for decorating things. Many thousands of years ago, he beautified his abode by painting pictures and symbols on the cave walls. Later, when he got around to inventing stone clubs and axes, they were also decorated by hanging feathers, fur, shells and other adornments on them. If he didn't have objects to decorate, he often embellished his own body to make him distinctive or fearsome looking. Colors were obtained from various vines, roots, barks, berries and other sources. These pigments were then rubbed into "artistic" gashes cut into the recipient's hide. Assuming that he didn't die of blood poisoning, which, I might add, was common, this pride of Cavetown was permanently beautified for all to see and admire. Perhaps such enhancements made him sexier

to the local lasses. These were probably the first tattoos.

When the iron age rolled around, suits of armor and edged weaponry crafted of metal replaced the bear skin robes and stone clubs that were in use. Obviously, these new technological advances were quickly decorated in various ways. Finally, when a young Chinese lad mixed a concoction of sulfur and saltpeter together and discovered that it went bang when exposed to an open flame, the age of the firearm was upon us. It didn't take long for one's firearm to become the primary recipient of its owner's lust for aggrandizement. It has remained so ever since.

Until the past few decades or so, there have been precious few American born-engravers. Those who practiced their art in this country had

names like Nimschke, Gustave Young (really the Americanized version of the German name Jung), Helfricht, Fugger, Kornbrath or Griebel. It doesn't take a brain surgeon to recognize that these family names are not exactly home born and bred. Most were originally from either Germany or Austria.

Recently however, folks with names like Churchill, McKenzie, Rabeno, Evans, Welch, Wallace, Smith, Tomlin and many others, some as American as apple pie, have taken up the art of engraving. Some floundered for a while, but these days take a back seat to no one. A few, like Winston Churchill and Lynton McKenzie (born in Australia but an American citizen for many years), are exceedingly well known. I know them both and have been familiar

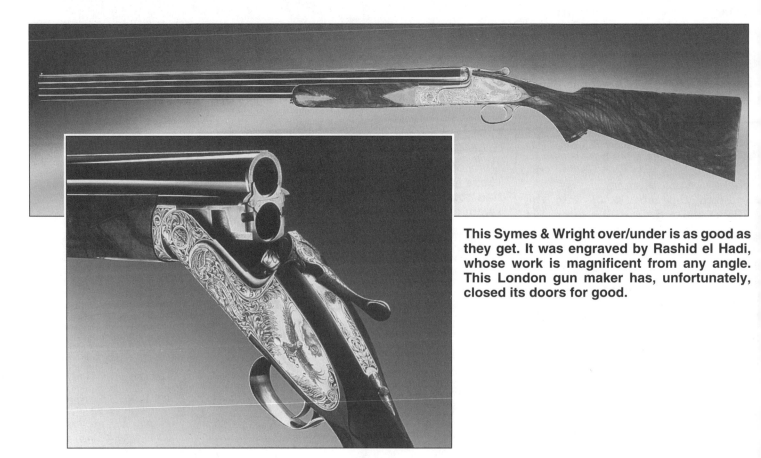

This Symes & Wright over/under is as good as they get. It was engraved by Rashid el Hadi, whose work is magnificent from any angle. This London gun maker has, unfortunately, closed its doors for good.

Good gun engraving can certainly enhance the value of your shotgun, but a lot of thought should go into selecting patterns and engravers.

by TOM TURPIN

with their work for many years. Others have managed to stay relatively unknown except to a few. I suspect their principal clients didn't want to share them with anyone else. To insure this, they kept the engravers so fully occupied with their own work that they just couldn't get the publicity they really deserved. In addition, many worked for larger companies and all their work was credited to the company, not to the artisan.

I try to stay informed when it comes to the gunmaking industry in all it's aspects, including engraving and engravers. A few years ago, during the annual Custom Gunmakers and Engravers Exhibition in Reno, one of my tasks was to participate as one of the judges to select an award-winning piece of work. The champion project was engraved by Ron Smith, a Texan I had never heard of before. His work was superb; I've seen none better, and even though I

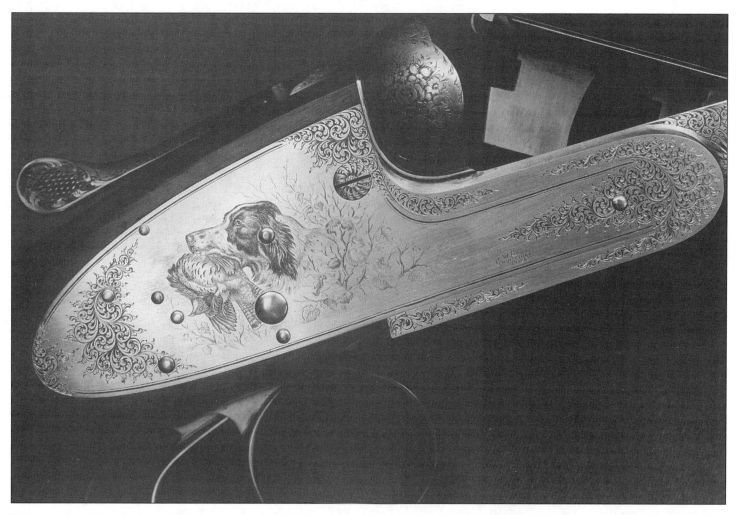

This fine Purdey double gun was engraved by one of America's finest artisans, Winston Churchill. He used a combination of English scroll and a magnificent bulino scene of dog and grouse. This is extremely tasteful engraving.

think I'm current on who's who in the business, he was a total unknown to me. I must have been under one big Arizona rock for a long time!

The point of all this is that American aficionados desiring top quality engraving for their smoke-pole, have a choice of engraving talent that has never been better. The talents of the new people coming into the field boggle the mind. They are not all guys, either. One lady, Lisa Tomlin, can inlay an elephant on a floorplate that is so good that you want to run from its charge. Her work is delicately done, almost like it is painted on, and is truly magnificent. Her artistry will be with us for a long time to come, too. I have socks older than she is.

Marty Rabeno has been turning out excellent work for a long time. However, in my opinion at least, his recent work is so good it is awe-inspiring. His bulino scenes are particularly extraordinary.

Numerous others have improved in quantum leaps in recent years. Although many American engravers were woefully lacking when stacked up against their European competition just a few decades ago, the same cannot be said today. Our best are, at a minimum, on a par with the best of the European masters, and some would say most of them are even better. I won't go that far—yet—but at the rate of improvement I have seen in the past five years, it surely won't be all that long until I can safely make that statement.

Many shotgun shooters have found Skeet and trap to be a bit ho-hum for their tastes, but I have yet to find one bored with Sporting Clays shooting. If they are, all they need to do is go to another field. Each course has similarities, but each is also different. While some are much less challenging to shoot than others, none that I have visited are boring.

Naturally, as the sport became more popular, and courses started springing up around the country, it was only natural that the shooters began having their favorite scatter-guns scratched on by many of our engravers with the appropriate designs. Of course, there was no reason not to. A finely engraved shotgun is every bit as at home on a Sporting Clays field

This Perazzi Special Sporting gun got the royal treatment by American engraver Mike Dubber. Not content with just gold gold for the inlays, Dubber also used green gold and white gold on this spectacular gun.

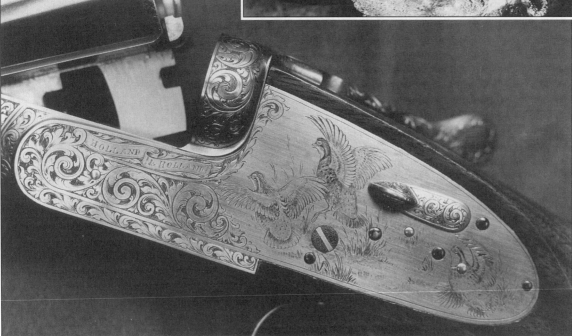

Lynton McKenzie did the beautiful work on this Holland & Holland gun. The job consists of medium-size scroll and bulino quail scenes.

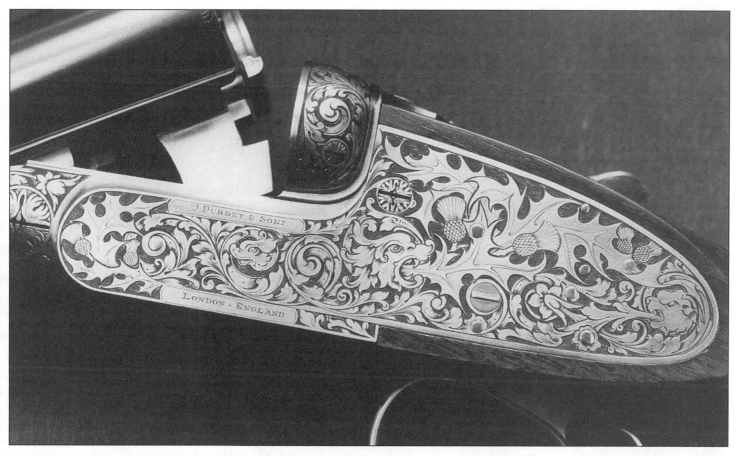

This Purdey sidelock double was engraved by England's best known engraver, Ken Hunt. The design is very bold and quite unusual for the normally very conservative British. The fire-breathing animals blend quite well with the scrolls.

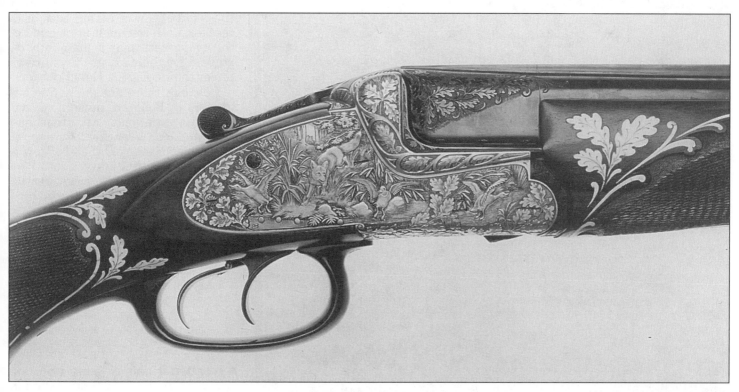

This Heym over/under is an excellent example of how ornate Germanic engraving often gets. Not only are the locks and frame relief engraved and inlaid, but the stock has also been inlaid with ivory and silver wire. Not for everyone, of course, but this is typical Germanic work at its best. All work by the late Erich Boessler.

as it is in the Scottish grouse butts, perhaps even more so.

Some shooters have their scatterguns adorned with scenes befitting their real purpose—with inlaid clay targets, shooting stations and such. Most, however, resort to traditional-style engraving with scrollwork and if there is inlay work involved, it usually depicts upland hunting scenes.

The different styles of engraving are usually categorized by the country where the style supposedly originated. There are English scroll, Italian scroll, German scroll and American scrolls. Frankly, these so-called styles relate more to size of the scrollwork than it does to a particular design. American scroll is generally thought of as large and somewhat coarse, German scroll is medium size and bold, English scroll much smaller and delicate, and Italian scroll downright tiny and dainty. In general, those descriptions are fairly accurate; at least they were. Anymore though, American engravers are quite adept at expertly achieving any of the styles of scrollwork.

The same is true when it comes to executing game scenes, either cut into the steel itself or inlaid with gold or other precious metals. The Germans and Austrians have the reputation of rendering bold, deep-relief game scenes, whereas the English and Italians do mostly delicate bank note or bulino-type vignettes. The best of the Italian engravers are able to achieve bulino scenes so refined that a magnifying glass is necessary to fully appreciate the quality of the work. Some of the work is so delicate that if the light comes from the wrong angle, it can hardly be seen at all. Two of the Italian masters that made exquisite bulino panoramas synonymous with Italian engraving are Angelo Galeazzi and Firmo Fracassi. Many others have followed in their footsteps.

The Germanic style of engraving is perhaps best known to American aficionados. After all, most of the early "American" engravers worked mostly in this style and were graduates of Teutonic apprenticeship programs. Germany and Austria have many excellent artisans, including Claus Willig, Rolf Peter, Gerd Rausch, and many others. Alas, one of the best, and my close friend of many years, Herr Erich Boessler, is now engraving for Sporting fans in heaven. He passed away much too soon at age 69 in 1997. Although Erich was a true master engraver by any definition of the word, he was at his best as a teacher. Both Herren Rausch and Peter, along with many, many others, studied for their Master Certificates under the tutelage of Herr Boessler.

Though there are many fine engravers in Belgium, none have captured international attention like the late Louis Vrancken. He was responsible for many of the FN Browning patterns that have become so well known. He was a very versatile engraver and could do Germanic-, English- or Italian-style engraving with equal artistic excellence.

The same is true of English engravers. When one thinks of English engraving, Ken Hunt springs to

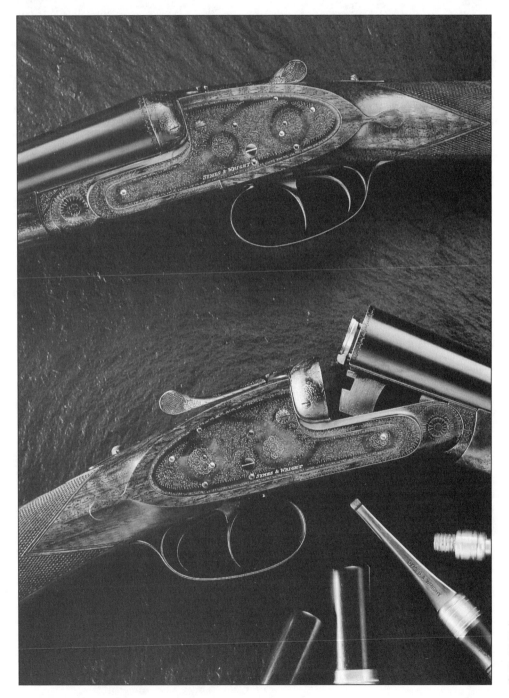

A wonderful pair of guns from the now-closed Symes & Wright shop in London. These guns exemplify the graceful and delicate English scroll engraving style.

mind. There are others, but none so well known as Mr. Hunt. Another fantastic engraver living in England, or last I heard he did, is Rashid el Hadi. Obviously, with that name, he is not originally from England. He did some awesome work for the now sadly defunct London firm of Symes & Wright. Where he is and what he is doing these days, I can't say, but he is so talented that I'm sure that he is engraving for someone.

Selecting an engraver to scratch a design on one's favorite scattergun is no easy chore. A number of factors influence that decision, or should. First is the engraver's style. Each has one and with many it is distinctive enough that a knowledgeable viewer can recognize the artist immediately. Even casual viewers of art can usually recognize the work of Van Gogh, Picasso, or Chagall. Studied viewers

can recognize Monet, Rembrandt, Degas and the others. So it is with engraving and engravers. I can usually spot the work of McKenzie, Swartley, Churchill, Rabeno and several others about as far as I can see it. I am learning the work of several others, like Smith, Evans, Welch and Wallace. Others, I have not seen often enough to quickly recognize.

A second major deciding factor is cost, of course. Some engravers have a minimum-cost job that they will accept. That cost is generally quite high, pretty much eliminating a client of average income. Others are more affordable, but in such demand that their delivery times are often measured in years. The task of finding an engraver that is affordable, with reasonably short delivery times, and whose style of engraving matches the client's taste, is indeed a tough one. The end result is well worth the struggle, though.

Some engravers will only do certain types of engraving and others will do most anything. Both Galeazzi and Fracassi, for example, have developed such renown for their bulino renditions that they do nothing else today. Other engravers execute all the accompanying engraving on a piece. On the other hand, the late Erich Boessler did everything from typical Germanic engraving to tiny English scrolls, to copying Parker A1 Special patterns and nearly everything in between. He did magnificent stock carving, scrimshaw work on ivory, and even made dies to make decorative pewter plates! In this latter work, everything had to be done in reverse. I watched him check his

work one day as he used modeling clay pressed into the design that he had just cut into the steel. He was truly a multi-faceted engraver.

Most engravers do work that falls somewhere between these two extremes. Few are as versatile as Boessler, but most are more flexible than Galeazzi and Fracassi. One thing for sure, there is an engraver out there for practically all tastes. It is just a matter of finding the right one. The best place to start would be with the Firearms Engravers Guild of America. For sure, not all engravers are members of the Guild, but many are. Bob Evans is the Secretary of the Guild and can be reached at 332 Vine Street, Oregon City, OR 97045 for more information.

How does one decide on precisely the right pattern for his pet scattergun? Danged if I know. Perhaps best is to collect brochures from various engravers to provide a basis for thought. Another way is to either buy books that showcase engraving or visit the library. If they don't have them on hand, perhaps they can get them on inter-library loan. I have a book coming out on the subject (from Krause Publications) that will provide many photographic examples of various styles of engraving and the work of many different engravers. Author R.L. Wilson has a book called *Steel Canvas* that provides many examples of fine engraving. There are one or two Italian books out on engraving and I am told that they are excellent. James Meek's excellent *The Art of Engraving* is still available from Brownells and is a terrific reference. Both Prudhomme's and

Left and bottom views of a Garbi double as engraved by German Master Engraver Claus Willig. His scrolls are beautifully executed, animal figures masterfully designed, and everything is in perfect balance.

Wisconsin - based engraver Ron Lutz has developed this high-relief style with excellent scroll work. Gold wire border inlays accent the panels tastefully. Lutz does most of his work on Kolar shotguns.

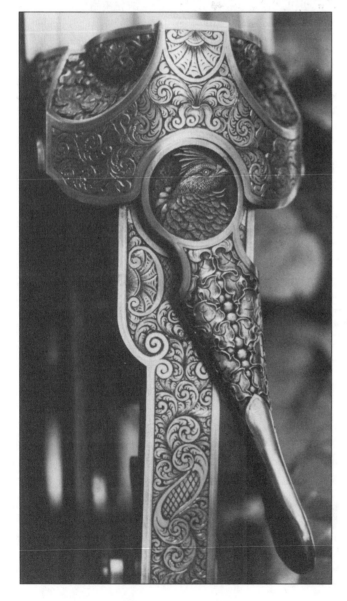

Bleile's books on engraving are out of print, but, here again, the library might have one or be able to get one to review. Both are somewhat dated but still provide a valuable reference of styles.

Deciding on a style for a pattern is often accomplished by selecting a particular engraver. Many really execute only one basic styling but with minor variations. If that engraver's work is particularly admired, then he can often be given his head to proceed and the client will surely be pleased with the result. On the other hand, one can select a particular pattern from some source and then try to find an engraver to pretty much duplicate it, with individual nuances, of course. It has been my experience that the former method works a bit better than the latter. Most engravers work better in a style they are comfortable with and the resulting engraving generally reflects their contentment. Sometimes, an engraver will accept a commission to do a pattern that they really don't care for, and the resulting work will show that attitude. I like to establish broad guidelines for a pattern, such as animals or birds to be inlaid, scroll size, etc., and leave the rest to the engraver. I have yet to be disappointed. Perhaps one day I will, but it hasn't occurred yet. I was once mildly disappointed in a job that I had been overly specific on. The engraver carried out my instructions explicitly and I had no quarrel with his execution of my in-structions. It was my speci-fied styling that was faulty. It sounded better than it looked. I should have given the artisan great-er flexibility. I haven't made that mistake since.

Finally, taste in engrav-ing is like taste in cars, women and spirits. Each individual is blessed with a personal taste (or lack thereof) that fits him. No one else may agree with it, but so be it. I have a sidekick whose choice of engraving runs to the ornate in extreme. He likes very deep relief work with lots of gold. His guns are exquisitely crafted, but a bit too flamboyant for my taste. I get nightmares thinking about them. I prefer engraving that is more sedate. My buddy calls my engraving preferences boring. Still, we are both pleased with the engraving that has been done for us. He wouldn't be caught dead using my guns and I would have to cover his up with a bit of Mossy Oak or Realtree camouflage before I'd be seen with them. That's the beauty of engraving though: each can get what he wants if he has the time and money to do so. My pal is happy with his guns and I am pleased with mine. That's all that is necessary.

Not only does the addition of well-done and tasteful engraving generally add value to one's scattergun, it personalizes it. The shooter can take pride in the fact that it is his gun, it is unique, and there is not another precisely like it. It has been converted from merely a tool to a work of art. And that's what engraving is all about. ●

This Parker left the factory as a VHE grade, but was upgraded to this outstanding A1 Special by Erich Boessler. The engraving is a copy of the early Parker pattern.

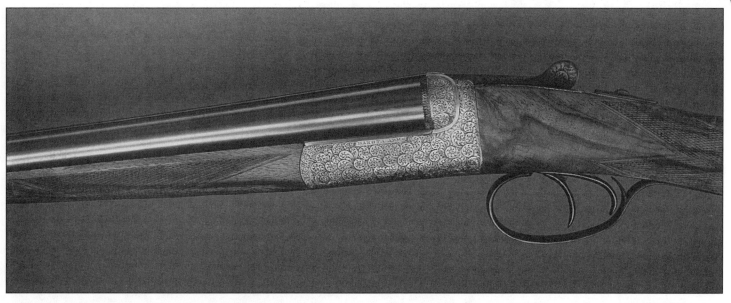

Primarily known as a rifle builder, Dakota Arms also builds a top quality shotgun. This top-of-the-line model is the Dakota Legend and sports full-coverage scroll work on the frame. The "factory" engraving was done by Englishman Ron Collings, now in California.

It doesn't take much to keep
your Sporting Clays shotgun
running smoothly and looking like new.
It'll pay big dividends in the long run.

by PATRICK SWEENEY

YOU'VE TAKEN THE plunge. You find you like it so much you've bought a shotgun just for Sporting Clays. Rather than haul around your battered old duck gun, you splurged and went for something really nice. Now,

how do you keep it looking nice and working like that proverbial Swiss watch? (Remember when watches needed oil?) Or maybe you haven't made the jump even though you've wanted to, but just the same you want

to keep your faithful old Remington 870 looking good. After all, Sporting Clays is not always fair weather shooting. At least, not here in Michigan.

Unlike with your duck gun, you are not going to be faced with the

A good hard case offers vastly more protection than the flimsy cloth types. Protection is what you want, not ease of handling and storage.

emergency option of having to use your brand-new Browning, Beretta or—God forbid, Krieghoff—as an oar. But you will be out in the rain, snow, wind and cold if you are at all serious about the game. Swinging after a hard-thrown bird, you may bang the barrels against the limit posts. Scrambling along the trail, you may scratch the stock on branches, or even slip and inadvertently use the gun to break your fall.

And you will be shooting many rounds through it, so you need to know how to keep it looking as good in the future as it does now. Even though this sounds like pretty basic stuff, read along because you'll probably pick up a tip or two you hadn't thought of before.

The maintenance of your shotgun starts from the moment you purchase it. There are three categories of maintenance and three areas to maintain. The categories are transit, environment and cleaning. The three areas are the exterior metal, the stock, and the bores and action.

To protect your shotgun in transit, do yourself and your gun a favor by investing in a good hard case. While you do not have to invest in a heavy-duty, welded aluminum case, cloth sleeves do not offer enough protection for your new prize. I have seen forends broken and barrels dented on shotguns transported in soft cases. A quick stop, a sudden swerve, and the cargo in your trunk can shift. If something hard falls on the soft case, your gun will suffer. The cheapest hard case can be bought for under $20, and is worth many times that.

The environment of the range, of course, depends on the weather. On a sunny day you may not have to go to any extra lengths to protect the gun. Go out and shoot, and have fun. But, inclement weather means additional effort. The old standby of paste wax still works. If the weather forecast calls for rain or snow, then a liberal application of paste wax to the exterior surfaces will protect your shotgun. Don't forget to remove the forend and apply wax to the barrels underneath and the inside of the forearm. Oil will also work to protect the metal, but will make holding on tough. You may want a slick-handling shotgun, but you don't want one slick to handle!

You can't be too careful in protecting the exterior metal. The bluing protects your barrels, but needs protection itself. If the pretty over/under has a grayed receiver, it must be protected or it will darken. Always—and I mean always—wipe the barrels and action down before you put them away. Not just on a rainy day, but even on a sunny bluebird day. On that sunny day you may have dripped perspiration on your barrels. I learned about sweat the hard way many years ago. I had been shooting a 45 auto pistol on a hot summer day, and hadn't noticed a

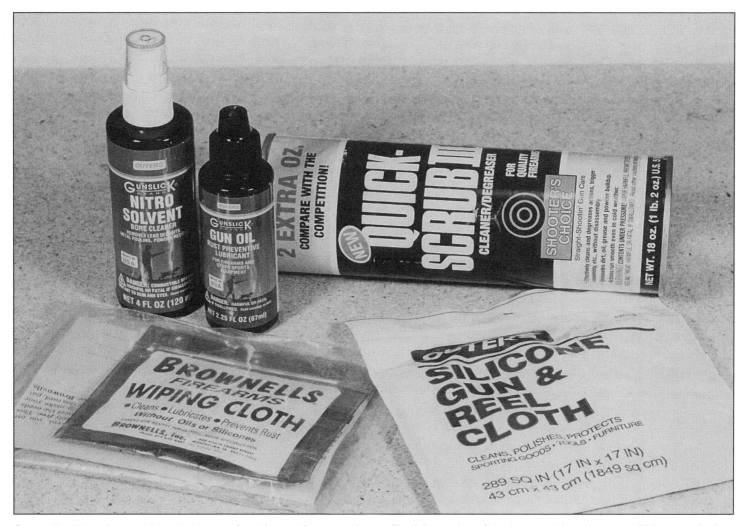

Once the bore is scrubbed clean, wipe the entire gun down (inside and out) before putting it away. Silicone cloths as well as gun oil go a long way in preventing damage.

drop of sweat that fell on it. The next time I took it out to shoot, there was a big rust spot on the slide. That spot acted as a reminder for years. Don't let the same happen to you. Even if you haven't dripped onto your shotgun, your sweaty hands (remember, sweat contains salts) have touched the barrels repeatedly. Some folks are cursed with such high concentrations of salt/acid in their perspiration that they can leave rusty fingerprints on a barrel literally within minutes. So, wipe the barrels first with a clean dry cloth to remove perspiration and other moisture, then wipe them with either a silicone cloth or an oily cloth. A piece of sheepskin doused with gun oil or Break-Free works very well. You don't need to slather the oil on, just a light coat will do to eradicate the fingerprints and moisture. Only then is it safe to put the gun away.

On a cold day, after coming home from the range, keep the gun in its case and let it warm up to room temperature before you wipe it off and put it away. This allows gradual warming and helps prevent condensation from forming on the metal. If the gun is cold enough when you uncase it in the house, frost may form everywhere, inside and out. So, leave it in the case for an hour or two. If you do wipe it down too soon, condensation will form again after you have wiped it off and your efforts will have been in vain.

If the gun gets wet, get it out of the case as soon as possible and plan to spend some time wiping it down repeatedly to take care of the rain/snow as well as condensation that may form on the cold metal. This is all part of the game and really isn't a chore if you truly like shotguns and shooting Sporting Clays.

The cost of not wiping down the barrels can be steep. I have had customers bring in shotguns stored damp in the case after a day's hunt or competition. Sometimes they forgot about the wet conditions, other times they were just plain lazy. The bluing on the barrels was often lifted, and sometimes even rusted, where the cloth or foam touched the steel. On one memorable instance, the foam from the case was stuck to the rusted steel, and when we pulled the foam away chunks of it were left sticking to the rusted spots. That was a very ugly scene, believe me.

Despite your best efforts at careful handling, the bluing will show some wear. The edges will turn bright, and the occasional nick or scratch you don't remember happening will appear. The procedure to touch these spots up is to clean, degrease, blue and oil. Take a small ball of OOOO steel wool. Place a few drops of oil on the scratched or worn area, and scrub lightly with the steel wool. This will clean oxidation off of the bare steel, and the oil floats the particles so they won't scratch. Use rubbing alcohol or an aerosol cleaner like Gun Scrubber or Brownells TCE Cleaner-Degreaser to remove all oily residue from the area. Apply a touch-up bluing agent such as the Outers touch-up pen or Brownells Oxpho-blue to the bare spot.

After it has worked on the steel for a minute, wipe it off and re-apply. Do this several times. Let the last application dry, and then place a few drops of oil on the area. Rub the oil with a clean patch, then buff lightly with a new ball of OOOO steel wool with oil in it.

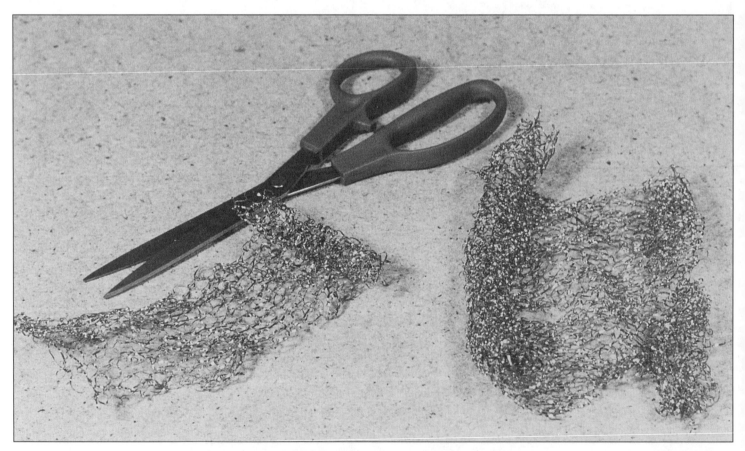

The best thing for scrubbing plastic and lead fouling from a barrel is the copper scouring pads sold at the grocery store. Simply cut a piece to wrap around a bore swab and have at it.

Wood is less forgiving than steel. An impact against a branch or post that will not harm steel may leave your stock or forend dented. Rubbing against branches can scratch the finish. Shooters who wear class rings or wedding rings can find the wood scratched, gouged and dented by them, and belt buckles can cause their share of damage. What to do? First, take the rings off, change buckles, and be careful when walking through the woods.

Light scratches usually can be rubbed out. If your stock has a synthetic finish and the scratch does not go through it into the wood, then an ultra-fine rubbing compound can lessen the scratch. Use the finest rubbing compound you can get. Remember, your intention is to rub down the finish. If you work too long you will hit wood. A severely scratched finish requires careful sanding, re-spraying the finish and blending the edges of the new application. Check with the manufacturer/importer to get a list of compatible synthetic sprays.

Reactions between the old finish and the new spray can sometimes yellow the original finish, or cause it to chip and peel.

Varnish or lacquer finishes are simpler to work with. With these, a light scratch can be rubbed out, but the heavier scratches will require sanding. If you decide to deal with the scratches yourself, the sandpaper must be ultra-fine, 600 grit or finer. If you want to repair the scratch and overspray the sanded area, call the shotgun manufacturer/importer and ask for the name brands of compatible finishes. When you spray, use a light touch and mask the checkering with tape and paper. Try to avoid spraying near the checkering because it will only clog it up. Let the new finish cure a day longer than the manufacturer's suggested time, then use rubbing compound to blend the old and new areas of finish.

Oil finishes are a cinch. Again, find out which oils will be safe to use. Use ultra-fine sandpaper to remove the scratch and then re-apply the correct oil finish.

Be sure to work slowly here, and sand with a light touch only in the direction of the grain. You don't want to introduce cross scratches, and to avoid low spots it best to use some sort of backer for the sandpaper to keep the surface level.

The third aspect of your maintenance is cleaning. Cleaning the bore of a shotgun is an area often neglected. Many shooters feel that if they have taken a few passes with a bore brush and some patches the job is done, which can be an expensive mistake. Spending a weekend shooting multiple rounds, especially on a hot day, can heavily foul a bore. While the powder residue wipes out easily, the plastic from wads does not. Back in the old days, lead was a nuisance. With one-piece wads and light payloads, the only thing to touch the bore is plastic. But what a mess it can make.

Plastic does not attract moisture, but it does nothing to protect your bore, and if there's enough of a build-up it can disrupt patterns. How to clean it out? The traditional method is to use bore solvent, a brush and patches, but there is an easier way. Go to the grocery store and buy copper scouring wrap, which is copper sheet shredded into coarse filaments, and looks like magnified steel wool. Unwrap a sheet of it and cut a piece that will wrap around your bore swab. Run the copper swab back and forth through the bore. Every few passes, pull the swab out to inspect the bore and clean the plastic off the "brush." With just a dozen passes you will have scrubbed all the plastic out of the bore. Save the swab, as it can be used repeatedly. I developed this trick to clean the bores of my bowling pin shotguns. Bowling pins require buckshot to consistently knock them down, and the combination of plastic and lead left in the bores was difficult to scrub clean. While harder than the plastic and lead, the copper is much softer than your barrel steel and will not scratch.

This copper scouring approach works even easier on the plastic left behind by target loads than it does on the lead from buckshot.

You will also find plastic builds up in your chokes. To clean barrels with a fixed choke, push the rod just to the muzzle and then rotate the rod. If you push the swab out of the muzzle you can't pull it back, and will have to unscrew the swab and start over.

Don't neglect your choke tubes if your gun is so equipped. Letting the tubes get gummed up with gunk is inviting a stuck tube, or a cross-threaded choke. Wipe and brush the threads clean and give them a light film of oil.

Choke tubes and barrel threads need attention, too. Clean each of these with a good brush and lubricate lightly. You don't want to cross-thread one of these!

If you have one, a thread cleaner makes cleaning the barrel threads a snap. If you don't, then get in there with a regular cleaning brush and rotate it around the threads. Brush the loosened residue out of the bore, then spray the threads with aerosol cleaner and oil them. It's probably a good idea to treat the threads with an anti-seize compound such as the Birchwood-Casey Choke Tube Lube. This could prevent a surprise down the road when it's time to change tubes and you can't get it out.

With the plastic and powder gone, a lightly oiled patch down the bore finishes the job. Don't be tempted to neglect your bores just because they are chrome-lined. Steel will rust even when protected by hard chrome. Given time and the proper (that is, neglected) environment, your bores will shed their chrome and cause you headaches. Which means it could be time to buy new barrels, and on an over/under that can be very costly. They may even become unsafe.

The last point is the action. If you are shooting with your trusty old pump or auto, then it is easy enough to remove the trigger assembly and bolt from the receiver to scrub or flush out the powder granules and accumulated grunge. Don't be afraid to get in there with a patch on your finger lightly moistened with Break Free or FP-10 and give everything a light coat to keep things working smoothly and prevent rust. Just don't be of the mind that if a little oil is good, a lot is better. A lot of lube can only gum up the works and cause malfunctions, especially in cold weather. So go easy with the oil here.

If you are using a double barrel, I do not recommend taking the action apart. The working parts are enclosed by the receiver, and powder residue does not get in easily. There are no cross pins to press out to allow easy removal of the trigger mechanism, as with the Remington shotguns. Depending on which double you have, you may be faced with one or two, or five or six screws. Unless you know the removal order, you could damage the shotgun. Even if you get lucky and remove them in the right order, when you are done you'll be faced with a three-dimensional jigsaw puzzle. If you slip up and remove one wrong screw or pin, you could be faced with compressing a strong spring while reassembling the action. Without the right tool, you can't get that spring back in place even with an extra pair of hands. Once a year or so, it's a good practice to take your shotgun to a professional gunsmith, one who is familiar with your brand and model shotgun. He has the tools, the books and the experience to strip and clean your action, and give it a tune-up.

With the right attitude, you could be like the fellow I shot with the last time I was out in the snow shooting Clays. He was using a London Best 12-gauge with moderate engraving. I didn't want to pry as to the value, but I had seen similar guns at Jaqua's going for half the price of a nice house. When we were done, he let this beauty warm up in the clubhouse, then inspected it and wiped it down. After a silicone cloth rubbing it went back into its felt-lined case for the trip home. He loved that shotgun, and took good care of it. It took care of him, as he and that gun beat my score that day. ●

Double barrel shotguns are tricky to disassemble. To prevent handing your gunsmith a pile of parts to put back together, leave this job to the pros. Besides, they don't get very dirty inside.

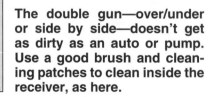

The double gun—over/under or side by side—doesn't get as dirty as an auto or pump. Use a good brush and cleaning patches to clean inside the receiver, as here.

This shotgun wasn't wiped down after a day in the rain, and the moisture lifted the bluing. Drip marks near the forend show where water dripped out when the case was moved. Don't let this happen to you.

SPORTING CLAYS
Catalog & Reference

Shotgunning Catalog

Directory of the Arms Trade

Benelli Sport

BENELLI LEGACY AUTO SHOTGUN

Gauge: 12, 3" chamber. **Barrel:** 26", 28" (Full, Mod., Imp. Cyl., Imp. Mod., Skeet choke tubes). Mid-bead sight. **Weight:** 7.1 to 7.6 lbs. **Length:** 49-5/8" overall (26" barrel). **Stock:** European walnut with high-gloss finish. Special competition stock comes with drop adjustment kit. **Features:** Uses the Montefeltro rotating bolt inertia recoil operating system with a two-piece steel/aluminum etched receiver (bright on lower, blue upper). Drop adjustment kit allows the stock to be custom fitted without modifying the stock. Black lower receiver finish, blued upper. Introduced 1998. Imported from Italy by Benelli U.S.A.
Price: **$1,320.00**

Benelli Sport Shotgun

Similar to the Legacy model except has matte blue receiver, two carbon fiber interchangeable ventilated ribs, adjustable buttpad, adjustable buttstock, and functions with ultra-light target loads. Walnut stock with satin finish. Introduced 1997. Imported from Italy by Benelli U.S.A.
Price: **$1,315.00**

BERETTA AL390 SILVER MALLARD AUTO SHOTGUN

Gauge: 12, 20, 3" chamber. **Barrel:** 24", 26", 28", 30", Mobilchoke choke tubes. **Weight:** 6.4 to 7.2 lbs. **Stock:** Select walnut or matte black synthetic. Adjustable drop and cast. **Features:** Gas-operated action with self-compensating valve allows shooting all loads without adjustment. Alloy receiver, reversible safety; chrome-plated bore; floating vent. rib. Matte-finish models for turkey/waterfowl and Deluxe with gold, engraving; camo models have Advantage finish. Youth models in 20-gauge and slug model available. Introduced 1992. Imported from Italy by Beretta U.S.A.
Price: Walnut or synthetic **$860.00**
Price: Gold Mallard, 12 and 20 . . . . **$1,025.00**
Price: 20-gauge, 20-gauge Youth **$860.00**
Price: Camouflage model. **$904.00**

SHOTGUNS — AUTOLOADERS

Beretta AL390 Sport Trap/Skeet/Sporting Shotgun

Beretta AL390 Sport Trap/Skeet/Sporting Shotguns

Similar to the AL390 Silver Mallard except has lower-contour, rounded receiver. Available with ported barrel. Trap has 30", 32" barrel (Full, Imp. Mod., Mod. choke tubes); Skeet has 26", 28" barrel (fixed Skeet); Sporting has 28", 30" (Full, Mod., Imp. Cyl., Skeet tubes). Introduced 1995. Imported from Italy by Beretta U.S.A.

Price: AL390 Sport Trap **$900.00**
Price: As above, fixed Full choke. **$890.00**
Price: AL390 Sport Skeet. **$890.00**
Price: AL390 Sport Sporting **$900.00**

BROWNING GOLD HUNTER AUTO SHOTGUN

Gauge: 12, 20, 3" chamber. **Barrel:** 12-ga.—26", 28", 30", Invector Plus choke tubes; 20-ga.—26", 30", Invector choke tubes. **Weight:** 7 lbs., 9 oz. (12-ga.), 6 lbs., 12 oz. (20-ga.). **Length:** 46-1/4" overall (20-ga., 26" barrel). **Stock:** 14"x1-1/2"x2-1/3"; select walnut with gloss finish; palm swell grip. **Features:** Self-regulating, self-cleaning gas system shoots all loads; lightweight receiver with special non-glare deep black finish; large reversible safety button; large rounded trigger guard, gold trigger. The 20-gauge has slightly smaller dimensions; 12-gauge have back-bored barrels, Invector Plus tube system. Introduced 1994. Imported by Browning.

Price: 12- or 20-gauge **$734.95**
Price: Extra barrels **$272.95**

Browing Gold Sporting Clays Auto

Browning Gold Sporting Clays Auto

Similar to the Gold Hunter except 12-gauge only with 28" or 30" barrel; front and center beads on tapered ventilated rib; ported and back-bored Invector Plus barrel; 2-3/4" chamber; satin-finished stock with solid, radiused recoil pad with hard heel insert; non-glare black alloy receiver has "Sporting Clays" inscribed in gold. Introduced 1996. Imported from Japan by Browning.

Price: **$759.95**

Remington Model 11-87 Premier

REMINGTON MODEL 11-87 PREMIER SPORTING CLAYS

Gauge: 12, 2-3/4" chamber. **Barrel:** 26", 28", vent. rib, Rem Choke (Skeet, Imp. Cyl., Mod., Full); Light Contour barrel. Medium height rib. **Weight:** 7.5 lbs. **Length:** 46.5" overall (26" barrel). **Stock:** 14-3/16"x1-1/2"x2-1/4". Walnut, with cut checkering; sporting clays butt pad. **Features:** Top of receiver, barrel and rib have matte finish; shortened magazine tube and forend; lengthened forcing cone; ivory bead front sight; competition trigger. Special no-wrench choke tubes marked on the outside. Comes in two-barrel fitted hard case. Introduced 1992.
Price: **$779.00**

Remington Model 11-87 SC NP

Remington Model 11-87 SC NP Shotgun

Similar to the Model 11-87 Sporting Clays except has low-luster nickel-plated receiver with fine-line engraving, and ported 28" or 30" Rem choke barrel with matte finish. Tournament-grade American walnut stock measures 14-3/16" x 2-1/4" x 1-1/2". Sporting Clays choke tubes have knurled extensions. Introduced 1997. Made in U.S. by Remington.
Price: **$827.00**

SHOTGUNS — AUTOLOADERS

Remington Model 1100 LT-20 Premier

REMINGTON MODEL 1100 LT-20 AUTO

Gauge: 20. **Barrel:** 25" (Full, Mod.), 26", 28" with Rem Chokes. **Weight:** 7-1/2 lbs. **Stock:** 14"x1-1/2"x2-1/2". American walnut, checkered pistol grip and forend. **Features:** Quickly interchangeable barrels. Matted receiver top with scroll work on both sides of receiver. Cross-bolt safety.
Price: With Rem Chokes, 20-ga. about $659.00
Price: Youth Gun LT-20 (21" Rem Choke) $659.00
Price: 20-ga., 3" magnum $659.00
Price: Skeet, 26", cut checkering, Rem. Choke $781.00

Remington 1100 Sporting 20

Remington Model 1100 Sporting 20 Shotgun

Similar to the Model 1100 LT-20 except has tournament-grade American walnut stock with gloss finish and sporting-style recoil pad, 28" Rem Choke barrel for Skeet, Imp. Cyl., Light Modified and Modified. Introduced 1998.
Price: $781.00

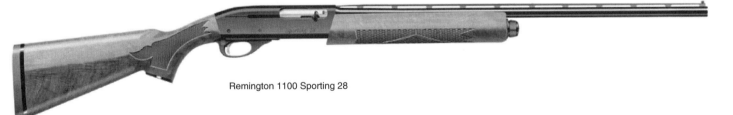

Remington 1100 Sporting 28

Remington Model 1100 Sporting 28

Similar to the 1100 LT-20 except in 28-gauge with 25" barrel; comes with Skeet, Imp. Cyl., Light Mod., Mod. Rem Choke tubes. Fancy walnut with gloss finish, Sporting rubber buttpad. Made in U.S. by Remington. Introduced 1996.
Price: $781.00

Beretta 686 Onyx Sporting O/U Shotgun

BERETTA 686 ONYX SPORTING O/U SHOTGUN

Gauge: 12, 3" chambers. **Barrel:** 28", 30" (Mobilchoke tubes). **Weight:** 7.7 lbs. **Stock:** Checkered American walnut. **Features:** Intended for the beginning Sporting Clays shooter. Has wide, vented 12.5mm target rib, radiused recoil pad. Matte black finish on receiver and barrels. Introduced 1993. Imported from Italy by Beretta U.S.A.
Price: $1,470.00

Beretta Model SO5 Shotgun

BERETTA MODEL SO5, SO6, SO9 SHOTGUNS

Gauge: 12, 2-3/4" chambers. **Barrel:** To customer specs. **Stock:** To customer specs. **Features:** SO5—Trap, Skeet and Sporting Clays models; SO6, SO6 EELL, and SO9 are field models. SO6 has a case-hardened or silvered receiver with contour hand engraving. SO6 EELL has hand-engraved receiver in a fine floral or "fine English" pattern or game scene, with bas-relief chisel work and gold inlays. SO6 and SO6 EELL are available with sidelocks removable by hand. Imported from Italy by Beretta U.S.A.
Price: SO5 Trap, Skeet, Sporting. $13,000.00
Price: SO6 Trap, Skeet, Sporting. $17,500.00
Price: SO6 EELL Field, custom specs. $28,000.00
Price: SO9 (12, 20, 28, 410, 26", 28", 30", any choke) $31,000.00

Beretta 682 Gold Sporting

BERETTA SPORTING CLAYS SHOTGUNS

Gauge: 12 and 20, 2-3/4" and 3" chambers. **Barrel:** 28", 30", 32" Mobilchoke. **Stock:** Close-grained walnut. **Features:** Equipped with Beretta Mobilchoke flush-mounted screw-in choke tube system. Dual-purpose O/U for hunting and Sporting Clays.12- or 20-gauge, 28", 30" Mobilchoke tubes (four, Skeet, Imp. Cyl., Mod., Full). Wide 12.5mm top rib with 2.5mm center groove; 686 Silver Pigeon has silver receiver with scroll engraving; 687 Silver Pigeon Sporting has silver receiver, highly figured walnut; 687 EL Gold Pigeon Sporting has game scene engraving with gold inlaid animals on full sideplate. Introduced 1994. Imported from Italy by Beretta U.S.A.

Price: 682 Gold Sporting, 28", 30", 31" (with case) **$2,910.00**
Price: 682 Gold Sporting, 28", 30", ported, adj. l.o.p. **$3,035.00**
Price: 686 Silver Pigeon Sporting **$1,795.00**
Price: 686 Silver Pigeon Sporting (20-gauge) **$1,795.00**
Price: 687 Silver Pigeon Sporting **$2,575.00**
Price: 687 Silver Pigeon Sporting (20 gauge) **$2,575.00**
Price: 687 EELL Diamond Pigeon Sporter (hand engraved sideplates, deluxe wood) **$5,310.00**
Price: ASE Gold Sporting Clay **$12,145.00**

Beretta 687EL Gold Pigeon Sporting O/U

Similar to the 687 Silver Pigeon Sporting except has sideplates with gold inlay game scene, vent. side and top ribs, bright orange front sight. Stock and forend are of high grade walnut with fine-line checkering. Available in 12-gauge only with 28" or 30" barrels and Mobilchoke tubes. Weight is 6 lbs., 13 oz. Introduced 1993. Imported from Italy by Beretta U.S.A.
Price: **$4,015.00**

Browning Citori White Lightnin

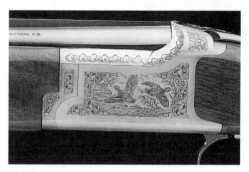

Citori Grade III

BROWNING CITORI O/U SHOTGUN

Gauge: 12, 20, 28 and 410. **Barrel:** 26", 28" in 28 and 410. Offered with Invector choke tubes. All 12- and 20-gauge models have back-bored barrels and Invector Plus choke system. **Weight:** 6 lbs., 8 oz. (26" 410) to 7 lbs., 13 oz. (30" 12-ga.). **Length:** 43" overall (26" bbl.). **Stock:** Dense walnut, hand checkered, full pistol grip, beavertail forend. Field-type recoil pad on 12-ga. field guns and trap and Skeet models. **Sights:** Medium raised beads, German nickel silver. **Features:** Barrel selector integral with safety, automatic ejectors, three-piece takedown. Imported from Japan by Browning. Contact Browning for complete list of models and prices.

Price: Grade I, Hunting, Invector, 12 and 20 . . . . $1,334.00
Price: Grade I, Lightning, 28 and 410, Invector $1,418.00
Price: Grade III, Lightning, 28 and 410, Invector $2,242.00
Price: Grade VI, 28 and 410 Lightning, Invector $3,145.00
Price: Grade I, Lightning, Invector Plus, 12, 20 . . . . $1,376.00
Price: Grade I, Hunting, 28", 30" only, 3-1/2", Invector Plus $1,418.00
Price: Grade III, Lightning, Invector, 12, 20 . . . . $2,006.00
Price: Grade VI, Lightning, Invector, 12, 20 . . . . $2,919.00
Price: Gran Lightning, 26", 28", Invector, 12 ,20 . . . . $1,869.00
Price: Gran Lightning, 28, 410 . . . . $1,969.00
Price: White Lightning (silver nitride receiver with
engraved scroll and rosette, 12-ga., 26", 28") $1,421.00

Browning Citori Sporting Hunter

Browning Citori Sporting Hunter

Similar to the Citori Hunting I except has Sporting Clays stock dimensions, a Superposed-style forend, and Sporting Clays butt pad. Available in 12-gauge with 3" chambers, 26", 28", all with Invector Plus choke tube system. Introduced 1998. Imported from Japan by Browning.
Price: 12-gauge, 3-1/2" $1,519.00
Price: 12-, 20-gauge, 3" $1,435.00

Browning Citori Ultra Sporter

Similar to the Citori Hunting except has slightly grooved, semi-beavertail forend, satin-finish stock, radiused rubber buttpad. Has three interchangeable trigger shoes, trigger has three length of pull adjustments. Ventilated rib tapers from 13mm to 10mm; 28" or 30" barrels (ported or non-ported) with Invector Plus choke tubes. Ventilated side ribs. Introduced 1989.
Price: With ported barrels, gray or blue receiver $1,722.00
Price: Golden Clays $3,203.00

Browning Special

Browning Special
Sporting Clays

Similar to the Citori Ultra Sporter except has full pistol grip stock with palm swell, gloss finish, 28", 30" or 32" barrels with back-bored Invector Plus chokes (ported or non-ported); high post tapered rib. Also available as 28" and 30" two-barrel set. Introduced 1989.

Golden Clays

Price: With ported barrels $1,565.00
Price: As above, adjustable comb $1,775.00
Price: Golden Clays $3,203.00
Price: With adjustable comb stock $3,413.00

Browning Micro Citori Lightning

Similar to the standard Citori 20-ga. Lightning except scaled down for smaller shooter. Comes with 24" Invector Plus back-bored barrels, 13-3/4" length of pull. Weighs about 6 lbs., 3 oz. Introduced 1991.
Price: Grade I $1,428.00

Browning Lightning Sporting Clays

Browning Lightning Sporting Clays

Similar to the Citori Lightning with rounded pistol grip and classic forend. Has high post tapered rib or lower hunting-style rib with 30" back-bored Invector Plus barrels, ported or non-ported, 3" chambers. Gloss stock finish, radiused recoil pad. Has "Lightning Sporting Clays Edition" engraved and gold filled on receiver. Introduced 1989.

Price: Low-rib, ported. $1,496.00
Price: High-rib, ported $1,565.00
Price: Golden Clays, low rib, ported. $3,092.00
Price: Golden Clays, high rib, ported $3,203.00
Price: Adjustable comb stock, all models, add. $210.00

Browning 802 ES

BROWNING LIGHT SPORTING 802 ES O/U

Gauge: 12, 2-3/4" chambers. **Barrel:** 28", back-bored Invector Plus. Comes with flush-mounted Imp. Cyl. and Skeet; 2" extended Imp. Cyl. and Mod.; and 4" extended Imp. Cyl. and Mod. tubes. **Weight:** 7 lbs., 5 oz. **Length:** 45" overall. **Stock:** 14-3/8" 1/8"x1-9/16"x1-3/4. Select walnut with radiused solid recoil pad, schnabel-type forend. **Features:** Trigger adjustable for length of pull; narrow 6.2mm ventilated rib; ventilated barrel side rib; blued receiver. Introduced 1996. Imported from Japan from Browning.
Price: $1,880.00

Browning 425 Sporting Clays

BROWNING 425 SPORTING CLAYS

Gauge: 12, 20, 2-3/4" chambers. **Barrel:** 12-ga.—28", 30", 32" (Invector Plus tubes), back-bored; 20-ga.—28", 30" (Invector Plus tubes). **Weight:** 7 lbs., 13 oz. (12-ga., 28"). **Stock:** 14-13/16" (1/8")x1-7/16"x2-3/16"(12-ga.). Select walnut with gloss finish, cut checkering, schnabel forend. **Features:** Grayed receiver with engraving, blued barrels. Barrels are ported on 12-gauge guns. Has low 10mm wide vent rib. Comes with three interchangeable trigger shoes to adjust length of pull. Introduced in U.S. 1993. Imported by Browning.
Price: Grade I, 12-, 20-ga., Invector Plus. $1,775.00
Price: Golden Clays, 12-, 20-ga., Invector Plus. $3,308.00
Price: Adjustable comb stock, add. $210.00

Browning 425 WSSF Shotgun

Browning 425 WSSF Shotgun

Similar to the 425 Sporting Clays except in 12-gauge only, 28" barrels, has stock dimensions specifically tailored to women shooters (14-1/4"x1-1/2"x1-1/2"); top lever and takedown lever are easier to operate. Stock and forend have teal-colored finish or natural walnut with Women's Shooting Sports Foundation logo. Weighs 7 lbs., 4 oz. Introduced 1995. Imported by Browning.
Price: $1,775.00

Charles Daly Field Hunter AE

CHARLES DALY FIELD HUNTER OVER/UNDER SHOTGUN

Gauge: 12, 20, 28 and 410 bore (3" chambers, 28 ga. has 2-3/4"). **Barrel:** 28" Mod & Full, 26 " Imp. Cyl. & Mod (410 is Full & Full). **Weight:** About 7 lbs. **Length:** NA. **Stock:** Checkered walnut pistol grip and forend. **Features:** Blued engraved receiver, chrome moly steel barrels; gold single selective trigger; automatic safety; extractors; gold bead front sight. Introduced 1997. Imported from Italy by K.B.I., Inc.

Price: 12 or 20 ga. **$699.00**
Price: 28 ga. **$779.00**
Price: 410 bore. **$819.00**

Charles Daly Superior Sporting

Charles Daly Superior Sporting O/U

Similar to the Field Hunter except 28" or 30" barrels; silvered, engraved receiver; five choke tubes; ported barrels; red bead front sight. Introduced 1997. Imported from Italy by K.B.I., Inc.

Price: **$1,099.00**

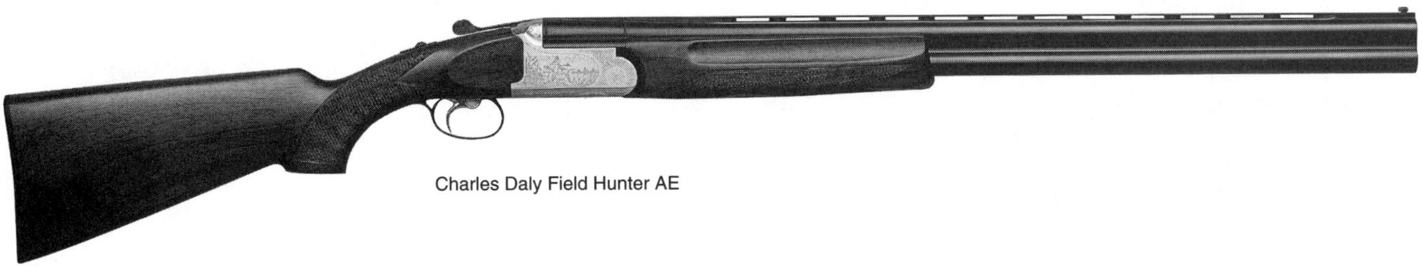

Charles Daly Field Hunter AE

CHARLES DALY EMPIRE DL HUNTER O/U

Gauge: 12, 20, 410, 3" chambers, 28-ga., 2-3/4". **Barrel:** 26", 28" (12, 20, choke tubes), 26" (Imp. Cyl. & Mod., 28-ga.), 26" (Full & Full, 410). **Weight:** About 7 lbs. **Stock:** Checkered walnut pistol grip buttstock, semi-beavertail forend; recoil pad. **Features:** Silvered, engraved receiver; chrome moly barrels; gold single selective trigger; automatic safety; automatic ejectors; red bead front sight, metal bead middle sight. Introduced 1997. Imported from Italy by K.B.I., Inc.

Price: 12 or 20 . . . . $1,159.00
Price: 28 . . . . $1,224.00
Price: 410 . . . . $1,269.00
Price: Empire EDL (dummy sideplates) 12 or 20 . . . . $1,319.00
Price: Empire EDL, 28 . . . . $1,384.00
Price: Empire EDL, 410 . . . . $1,424.00

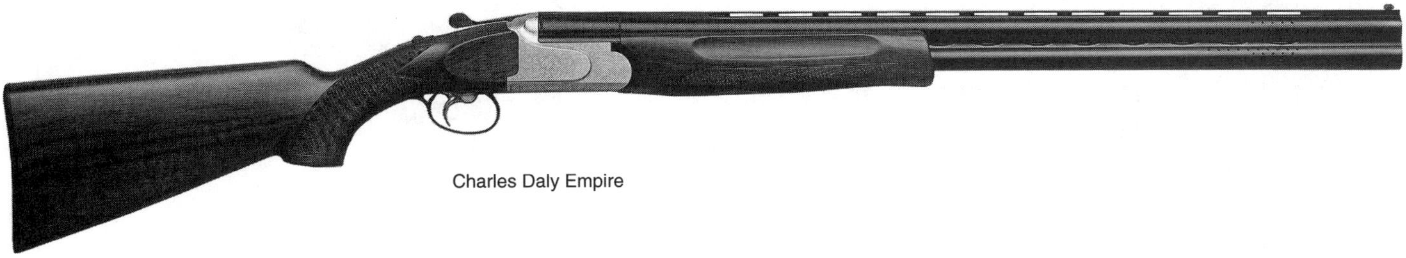

Charles Daly Empire

Charles Daly Empire Sporting O/U

Similar to the Empire DL Hunter except 12- or 20-gauge only, 28", 30" barrels with choke tubes; ported barrels; special stock dimensions. Introduced 1997. Imported from Italy by K.B.I., Inc.

Price: $1,299.00

CHARLES DALY DIAMOND GTX SPORTING O/U SHOTGUN

Gauge: 12, 20, 3" chambers. **Barrel:** 28", 30" with choke tubes. **Weight:** About 8.5 lbs. **Stock:** Checkered deluxe walnut; Sporting Clays dimensions. Pistol grip; semi-beavertail forend; hand rubbed oil finish. **Features:** Chromed, hand-engraved receiver; chrome moly steel barrels; GTX detachable single selective trigger system with coil springs, automatic safety; automatic ejectors; red bead front sight; ported barrels. Introduced 1997. Imported from Italy by K.B.I., Inc.

Price: $5,455.00

Franchi Alcione Sporting SL12

FRANCHI ALCIONE SPORTING SL12 O/U

Gauge: 12, 2-3/4" chambers. **Barrel:** 30", three extended choke tumes. **Weight:** 7.7 lbs. **Length:** 47" overall. **Stock:** Select walnut. Left-hand stock available. **Features:** Interchangeable sideplates; full interchangeability of barrels with adjustable forend; 10mm ventilated rib; barrel parting. Introduced 1998. Imported from Italy by Benelli USA.
Price: . . . . **NA**

Kolar Sporting O/U

KOLAR SPORTING OVER/UNDER

Gauge: 12, 2-3/4" chambers. **Barrel:** 28", 30", 32"; five extended screw-in chokes (ten constrictions available). Carrier barrel with tubes optionally available. **Weight:** NA. **Stock:** 1-3/8"x1-7/8"x2-1/2"x14-5/8"; French walnut with matte finish, schnabel forend. **Features:** Single selective, detachable, mechanical trigger adjustable for length. Barrels have a flat tramline rib; regulated to shoot a 50/50 point of impact. Over-bored barrels with long forcing cones. Custom stock dimensions available. Comes with aluminum airline case. Made in U.S. by Kolar.
Price: $7,295.00
Price: Elite Gold $10,795.00

Krieghoff K-80 O/U

KRIEGHOFF K-80
SPORTING CLAYS O/U

Gauge: 12. **Barrel:** 28", 30" or 32" with choke tubes. **Weight:** About 8 lbs. **Stock:** #3 Sporting stock designed for gun-down shooting. **Features:** Choice of standard or lightweight receiver with satin nickel finish and classic scroll engraving. Selective mechanical trigger adjustable for position. Choice of tapered flat or 8mm parallel flat barrel rib. Free-floating barrels. Aluminum case. Imported from Germany by Krieghoff International, Inc.

Price: Standard grade with five choke tubes, from **$8,150.00**

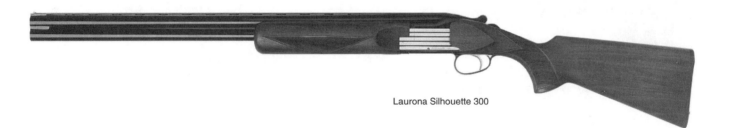

Laurona Silhouette 300

LAURONA SILHOUETTE 300 SPORTING CLAYS

Gauge: 12, 2-3/4" or 3" chambers. **Barrel:** 28", 29" (Multichoke tubes, flush-type or knurled). **Weight:** 7 lbs., 12 oz. **Stock:** 14-3/8"x1-3/8"x2-1/2". European walnut with full pistol grip, beavertail forend. Rubber buttpad. **Features:** Selective single trigger, automatic selective ejectors. Introduced 1988. Imported from Spain by Galaxy Imports.

Price: **$1,250.00**
Price: Silhouette Ultra-Magnum, 3-1/2" chambers. **$1,365.00**

Marocchi Classic Doubles Model 92

MAROCCHI CLASSIC DOUBLES MODEL 92 SPORTING CLAYS O/U SHOTGUN

Gauge: 12, 3" chambers. **Barrel:** 30"; backbored, ported (ContreChoke Plus tubes); 10 mm concave ventilated top rib, ventilated middle rib. **Weight:** 8 lbs. 2 oz. **Stock:** 14-1/4"-14-5/8"x 2-1/8"x1-3/8"; American walnut with checkered grip and forend; Sporting Clays buttpad. **Features:** Low profile frame; fast lock time; automatic selective ejectors; blued receiver and barrels. Comes with three choke tubes. Ergonomically shaped trgger adjustable for pull length without tools. Barrels are backbored and ported. Introduced 1996. Imported from Italy by Precision Sales International.
Price: **$1,598.00**

Marocchi Conquista

MAROCCHI CONQUISTA SPORTING CLAYS O/U SHOTGUNS

Gauge: 12, 2-3/4" chambers. **Barrel:** 28", 30", 32" (Contrechoke tubes); 10mm concave vent. rib. **Weight:** About 8 lbs. **Stock:** 14-1/2"-14-7/8"x2-3/16"x1-7/16"; American walnut with checkered grip and forend; Sporting Clays butt pad. **Sights:** 16mm luminescent front. **Features:** Has lower monoblock and frame profile. Fast lock time. Ergonomically-shaped trigger is adjustable for pull length. Automatic selective ejectors. Coin-finished receiver, blued barrels. Comes with five choke tubes, hard case. Also available as true left-hand model—opening lever operates from left to right; stock has left-hand cast. Introduced 1994. Imported from Italy by Precision Sales International.
Price: Grade I, right-hand. **$1,995.00**
Price: Grade I, left-hand. **$2,120.00**
Price: Grade II, right-hand **$2,330.00**
Price: Grade II, left-hand **$2,685.00**
Price: Grade III, right-hand, from **$3,599.00**
Price: Grade III, left-hand, from **$3,995.00**

Marocchi Lady Sport Spectrum

Marocchi Lady Sport O/U Shotgun

Ergonomically designed specifically for women shooters. Similar to the Conquista Sporting Clays model except has 28" or 30" barrels with five Contrechoke tubes, stock dimensions of 13-7/8"-14-1/4"x1-11/32"x2-9/32"; weighs about 7-1/2 lbs. Also available as left-hand model—opening lever operates from left to right; stock has left-hand cast. Also available with colored graphics finish on frame and opening lever. Introduced 1995. Imported from Italy by Precision Sales International.

Price: Grade I, right-hand. **$2,120.00**
Price: Left-hand, add (all grades). **$101.00**
Price: Lady Sport Spectrum (colored receiver panel) **$2,199.00**
Price: Lady Sport Spectrum, left-hand. **$2,300.00**

Perazzi MX8 Special

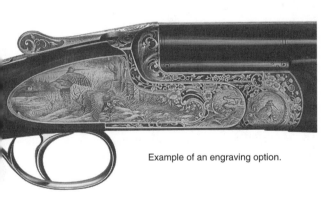

Example of an engraving option.

PERAZZI MX8
SPECIAL SPORTING O/U

Gauge: 12, 2-3/4" chambers. **Barrel:** 28-3/8" (Imp. Mod. & Extra Full), 29-1/2" (choke tubes). **Weight:** 7 lbs., 12 oz. **Stock:** Special specifications. **Features:** Has single selective trigger; flat 7/16"x5/16" vent. rib. Many options available. Imported from Italy by Perazzi U.S.A., Inc.

Price: **$10,730.00**

Perazzi Sporting Classic

Perazzi Sporting Classic O/U

Same as the MX8 Special Sporting except is deluxe version with select wood and engraving, Available with flush mount choke tubes, 29.5" barrels. Introduced 1993.
Price: From. **$10,730.00**

Remington Peerless

REMINGTON PEERLESS OVER/UNDER SHOTGUN

Gauge: 12, 3" chambers. **Barrel:** 26", 28", 30" (Imp. Cyl., Mod., Full Rem Chokes). **Weight:** 7-1/4 lbs. (26" barrels). **Length:** 43" overall (26" barrels). **Stock:** 14-3/16"x1-1/2"x2-1/4". American walnut with Imron gloss finish, cut-checkered grip and forend. Black, ventilated recoil pad. **Features:** Boxlock action with removable sideplates. Gold-plated, single selective trigger, automatic safety, automatic ejectors. Fast lock time. Mid-rib bead, Bradley-type front. Polished blue finish with light scrollwork on sideplates, Remington logo on bottom of receiver. Introduced 1993.
Price: **$1,172.00**

Remington 396 Sporting

REMINGTON 396 SPORTING OVER/UNDER

Gauge: 12,2-3/4" chambers. **Barrel:** 28", 30"; Skeet, Imp. Skeet, Imp. Cyl., Mod. Rem Choke tubes. **Weight:** 7-1/2 lbs. **Stock:** 14-3/16"x1-1/2"x2-1/4". Satin-finished American walnut. **Features:** Ported chrome-moly barrels with 10mm non-stepped rib; lengthened forcing cones; Sporting Clays recoil pad; palm swell pistol grip; engraved, silvered receiver. Introduced 1996. Made in U.S. by Remington.
Price: **$2,126.00**

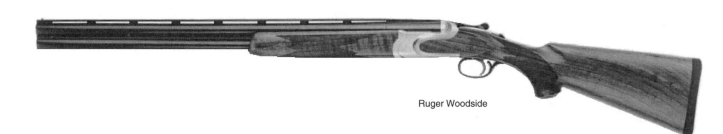

Rizzini Sporting EL

RIZZINI S790 SPORTING EL OVER/UNDER

Gauge: 12, 2-3/4" chambers. **Barrel:** 28", 29.5", Imp. Mod., Mod., Full choke tubes. **Weight:** 8.1 lbs. **Stock:** 14"x1-1/2"x2". Extra-fancy select walnut. **Features:** Boxlock action; automatic ejectors; single selective trigger; 10mm top rib. Comes with case. Introduced 1996. Imported from Italy by Wm. Larkin Moore & Co.

Price: **$6,000.00**

Ruger Woodside

RUGER WOODSIDE OVER/UNDER SHOTGUN

Gauge: 12, 3" chambers. **Barrel:** 26", 28" (Full, Mod., Imp. Cyl. and two Skeet tubes), 30" (Mod., Imp. Cyl. and two Skeet tubes). **Weight:** 7-1/2 to 8 lbs. **Stock:** 14-1/8"x1-1/2"x2-1/2". Select Circassian walnut; pistol grip or straight English grip. **Features:** Has a newly patented Ruger cocking mechanism for easier, smoother opening. Buttstock extends forward into action as two side panels. Single selective mechanical trigger, selective automatic ejectors; serrated free-floating rib; back-bored barrels with stainless steel choke tubes. Blued barrels, stainless steel receiver. Engraved action available. Introduced 1995. Made in U.S. by Sturm, Ruger & Co.

Price: **$1,675.00**
Price: Woodside Sporting Clays (30" barrels) **$1,675.00**

SHOTGUNS — OVER / UNDERS

Ruger Red Label

RUGER RED LABEL O/U SHOTGUN

Gauge: 12, 20, 3" chambers; 28 2-3/4" chambers. **Barrel:** 26", 28" (Skeet, Imp. Cyl., Full, Mod. screw-in choke tubes). Proved for steel shot. **Weight:** About 7 lbs. (20-ga.); 7-1/2 lbs. (12-ga.). **Length:** 43" overall (26" barrels). **Stock:** 14"x1-1/2"x2-1/2". Straight grain American walnut. Checkered pistol grip and forend, rubber butt pad. **Features:** Choice of blue or stainless receiver. Single selective mechanical trigger, selective automatic ejectors; serrated free-floating vent. rib. Comes with two Skeet, one Imp. Cyl., one Mod., one Full choke tube and wrench. Made in U.S. by Sturm, Ruger & Co.

Price: Red Label with pistol grip stock **$1,215.00**
Price: English Field with straight-grip stock **$1,215.00**

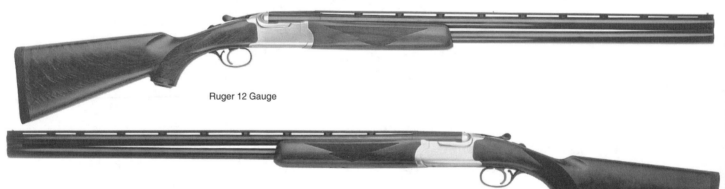

Ruger 12 Gauge

Ruger 20 Gauge

Ruger Sporting Clays O/U Shotgun

Similar to the Red Label except 30" back-bored barrels, stainless steel choke tubes. Weighs 7.75 lbs., overall length 47". Stock dimensions of 14-1/8"x1-1/2"x2-1/2". Free-floating serrated vent rib with brass front and mid-rib beads. No barrel side spacers. Comes with two Skeet, one Imp. Cyl., one Mod. choke tubes. Full and Extra-Full available at extra cost. 12 ga. introduced 1992, 20 ga. introduced 1994.

Price: 12 or 20 . . . . **$1,349.00**

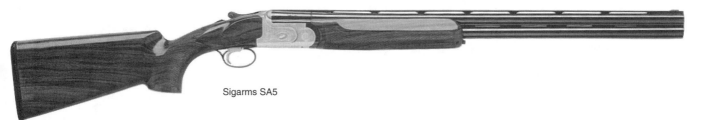

Sigarms SA3

SIGARMS SA3 OVER/UNDER SHOTGUN

Gauge: 12, 20, 3" chambers. **Barrel:** 26", 27" (Full, Mod, Imp. Cyl. choke tubes). **Weight:** 7 lbs. **Stock:** Select grade walnut; checkered grip and forend. **Features:** Chrome-lined bores; single selective trigger, automatic ejectors; satin nickel receiver finish, rest blued. Introduced 1997. Imported by Sigarms, Inc.
Price: Field, 12-gauge **$1,335.00**
Price: Sporting Clays **$1,675.00**
Price: Field, 20-gauge **$1,335.00**

Sigarms SA5

SIGARMS SA5 OVER/UNDER SHOTGUN

Gauge: 12, 20, 3" chamber. **Barrel:** 26-1/2", 27" (Full, Imp. Mod., Mod., Imp. Cyl., Cyl. choke tubes). **Weight:** 6.9 lbs. (12-gauge), 5.9 lbs. (20-gauge). **Stock:** 14-1/2" x 1-1/2" x 2-1/2". Select grade walnut; checkered 20 l.p.i. at grip and forend. **Features:** Single selective trigger, automatic ejectors; hand-engraved detachable sideplated; matte nickel receiver, rest blued; tapered bolt lock-up. Introduced 1997. Imported by Sigarms, inc.
Price: Field, 12-gauge **$2,670.00**
Price: Sporting Clays **$3,185.00**
Price: Field 20-gauge. **$2,670.00**

SKB Model 585

SKB MODEL 585 OVER/UNDER SHOTGUN

Gauge: 12 or 20, 3"; 28, 2-3/4"; 410, 3". **Barrel:** 12-ga.—26", 28", 30", 32", 34" (Inter-Choke tube); 20-ga.—26", 28" (Inter-Choke tube); 28—26", 28" (Inter-Choke tube); 410—26", 28" (Imp. Cyl. & Mod., Mod. & Full). Ventilated side ribs. **Weight:** 6.6 to 8.5 lbs. **Length:** 43" to 51-3/8" overall. **Stock:** 14-1/8"x1-1/2"x2-3/16". Hand checkered walnut with high-gloss finish. Target stocks available in standard and Monte Carlo. **Sights:** Metal bead front (field), target style on Skeet, trap, Sporting Clays. **Features:** Boxlock action; silver nitride finish with Field or Target pattern engraving; manual safety, automatic ejectors, single selective trigger. All 12-gauge barrels are back-bored, have lengthened forcing cones and longer choke tube system. Sporting Clays models in 12-gauge with 28" or 30" barrels available with optional 3/8" step-up target-style rib, matte finish, nickel center bead, white front bead. Introduced 1992. Imported from Japan by G.U., Inc.

Price: Field **$1,329.00**
Price: Two-barrel Field Set, 12 & 20 . . . . **$2,129.00**
Price: Two-barrel Field Set, 20 & 28 or 28 & 410) **$2,179.00**
Price: Trap, Skeet **$1,429.00**
Price: Two-barrel trap combo. **$2,129.00**
Price: Sporting Clays model. **$1,149.00** to **$1,529.00**
Price: Skeet Set (20, 28, 410) **$3,329.00**

SKB Model 505

SKB Model 505 Shotguns

Similar to the Model 585 except blued receiver, standard bore diameter, standard Inter-Choke system on 12, 20, 28, diffrent receiver engraving. Imported from Japan by G.U. Inc.

Price: Field, 12 (26", 28"), 20 (26" only). **$1,049.00**
Price: Sporting Clays, 12 (28", 30") **$1,149.00**

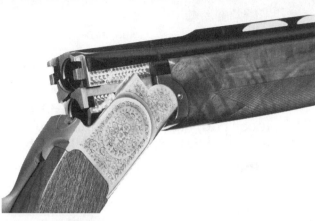

SKB Model 785

SKB MODEL 785
OVER/UNDER SHOTGUN

Gauge: 12, 20, 3"; 28, 2-3/4"; 410, 3".
Barrel: 26", 28", 30", 32" (Inter-Choke tubes). **Weight:** 6 lbs., 10 oz. to 8 lbs.
Stock: 14-1/8"x1-1/2"x2-3/16" (Field). Hand-checkered American black walnut with high-gloss finish; semi-beavertail forend. Target stocks available in standard or Monte Carlo styles. **Sights:** Metal bead front (Field), target style on Skeet, trap, Sporting Clays models. **Features:** Boxlock action with Greener-style cross bolt; single selective chrome-plated trigger, chrome-plated selective ejectors; manual safety. Chrome-plated, over-size, back-bored barrels with lengthened forcing cones. Introduced 1995. Imported from Japan by G.U. Inc.
Price: Field, 12 or 20 . . . . **$1,949.00**
Price: Field, 28 or 410 . . . . **$2,029.00**
Price: Field set, 12 and 20 . . . . **$2,829.00**
Price: Field set, 20 and 28 or 28 and 410 . . . . **$2,929.00**
Price: Sporting Clays, 12 or 20 . . . . **$2,099.00**
Price: Sporting Clays, 28 . . . . **$2,169.00**
Price: Sporting Clays set, 12 and 20 . . . . **$2,999.00**
Price: Skeet, 12 or 20 . . . . **$2,029.00**
Price: Skeet, 28 or 410 . . . . **$2,069.00**
Price: Skeet, three-barrel set, 20, 28, 410 . . . . **$4,089.00**
Price: Trap, standard or Monte Carlo. **$2,029.00**
Price: Trap combo, standard or Monte Carlo. **$2,829.00**

STOEGER/IGA CONDOR I OVER/UNDER SHOTGUN

Gauge: 12, 20, 3" chambers. **Barrel:** 26" (Imp. Cyl. & Mod. choke tubes), 28" (Mod. & Full choke tubes). **Weight:** 6-3/4 to 7 lbs. **Stock:** 14-1/2"x1-1/2"x2-1/2". Oil-finished hardwood with checkered pistol grip and forend. **Features:** Manual safety, single trigger, extractors only, ventilated top rib. Introduced 1983. Imported from Brazil by Stoeger Industries.
Price: With choke tubes. **$559.00**
Price: Condor Supreme (same as Condor I with single trigger,
choke tubes, but with auto. ejectors), 12- or 20-ga., 26", 28". **$629.00**

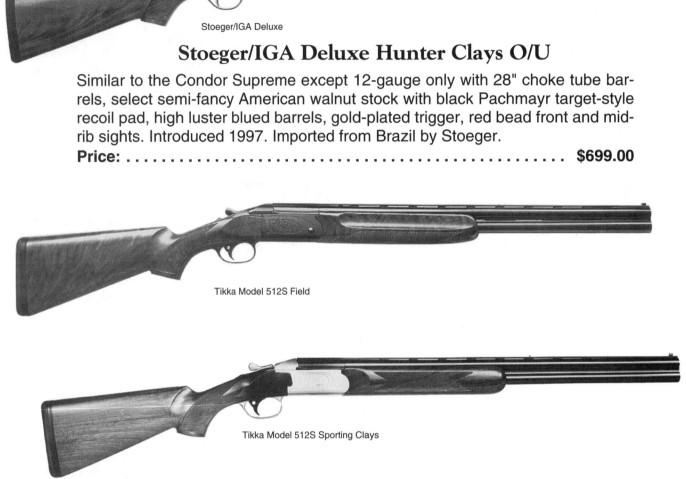

Stoeger/IGA Deluxe

Stoeger/IGA Deluxe Hunter Clays O/U

Similar to the Condor Supreme except 12-gauge only with 28" choke tube barrels, select semi-fancy American walnut stock with black Pachmayr target-style recoil pad, high luster blued barrels, gold-plated trigger, red bead front and mid-rib sights. Introduced 1997. Imported from Brazil by Stoeger.

Price: **$699.00**

Tikka Model 512S Field

Tikka Model 512S Sporting Clays

TIKKA MODEL 512S FIELD GRADE OVER/UNDER

Gauge: 12, 20, 3" chambers. **Barrel:** 26", 28", with stainless steel screw-in chokes (Imp. Cyl, Mod., Imp. Mod., Full); 20-ga., 28" only. **Weight:** About 7-1/4 lbs. **Stock:** American walnut. Standard dimensions—13-9/10"x1-1/2"x2-2/5". Checkered pistol grip and forend. **Features:** Free interchangeability of barrels, stocks and forends into double rifle model, combination gun, etc. Barrel selector in trigger; auto. top tang safety; barrel cocking indicators. Introduced 1980. Imported from Italy by Stoeger.

Price: Model 512S (ejectors), Field Grade. **$1,325.00**
Price: Model 512S Sporting Clays, 12-ga., 28", choke tubes **$1,360.00**

Tristar Model 333SCL

TRISTAR MODEL 333 OVER/UNDER

Gauge: 12, 20, 3" chambers. **Barrel:** 12 ga.—26", 28", 30"; 20 ga.—26", 28"; five choke tubes. **Weight:** 7-1/2-7-3/4 lbs. **Length:** 45" overall. **Stock:** Hand-checkered fancy grade Turkish walnut; full pistol grip, semi-beavertail forend; black recoil pad. **Features:** Boxlock action with silvered, hand-engraved receiver; automatic selective ejectors, mechanical single selective trigger; stainless steel firing pins; auto safety; hard chrome bores. Introduced 1995. Imported from Turkey by Tristar Sporting Arms, Ltd.

Price: **$799.95**

Tristar Model 333SC Over/Under

Same as the Model 333 except has 11mm rib with target sight beads, elongated forcing cones, ported barrels, stainless extended Sporting choke tubes (Skeet, Imp. Cyl., Imp. Cyl., Mod.), Sporting Clays recoil pad. Introduced 1996. Imported from Turkey by Tristar Sporting Arms, Ltd.

Price: **$899.95**

Tristar Model 333SCL Over/Under

Same as the Model 333SC except has special stock dimensions for female shooters: 13-1/2x1-1/2"x3"x1/4". Introduced 1996. Imported from Turkey by Tristar Sporting Arms, Ltd.

Price: **$899.95**

Tristar TR SC

TRISTAR TR SC "EMILLIO RIZZINI" OVER/UNDER

Gauge: 12, 2-3/4" chambers. **Barrel:** 28", 30" (Imp. Cyl., Mod., Full choke tubes). **Weight:** 7-1/2-8 lbs. **Length:** 46" overall (28" barrel). **Stock:** 1-1/2" x 2-3/8" x 14-3/8". Semi-fancy walnut; pistol grip with palm swell; semi-beavertail forend; black Sporting Clays recoil pad. **Features:** Silvered boxlock action with Four Locks locking system, auto ejectors, single selective (inertia) trigger, auto safety. Hard chrome bores. Vent. 10mm rib with target-style front and mid-rib beads, vent. spacer rib. Introduced 1998. Imported from Italy by Tristar Sporting Arms, Ltd.
Price: **$869.00**

Tristar TR L

Tristar TR L "Emillio Rizzinni" Over/Under

Similar to the TR SC model except 12- or 20-ga., 2-3/4" chambers, and has stock dimensions designed for female shooters (1-1/2" x 3" x 13-1/2"). Standard grade walnut. Introduced 1998. Imported from Italy by Tristar Sporting Arms, Ltd.
Price: **$869.00**

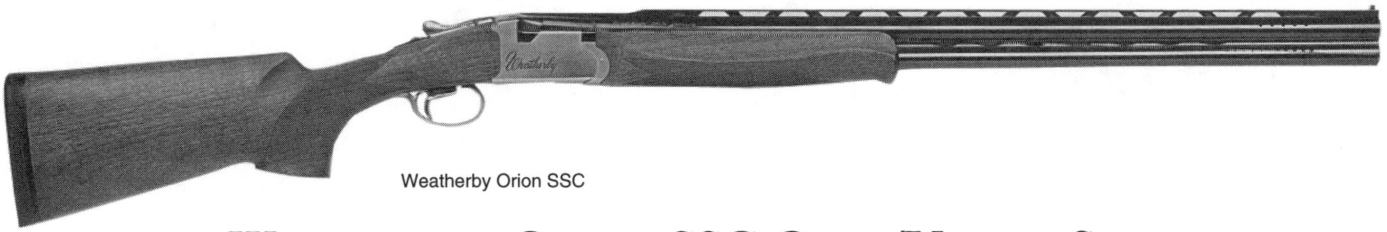

Weatherby Orion SSC

WEATHERBY ORION SSC OVER/UNDER SHOTGUN

Gauge: 12, 3" chambers. **Barrel:** 28", 30", 32" (Skeet, SC1, Imp. Cyl., SC2, Mod. IMC choke tubes). **Weight:** About 8 lbs. **Stock:** 14-3/4"x2-1/4"x1-1/2". Claro walnut with satin oil finish; schnabel forend tip; Sporter-style pistol grip; Pachmayr Decelerator recoil pad. **Features:** Designed for Sporting Clays competition. Has lengthened forcing cones and backboring; ported barrels with 12mm grooved rib with mid-bead sight; mechanical trigger is adjustable for length of pull. Introduced 1998. Imported from Japan by Weatherby.
Price: **$1,749.00**

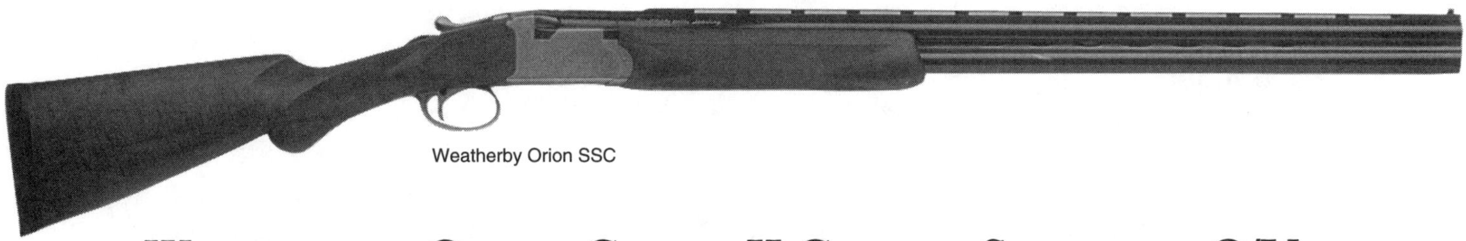

Weatherby Orion SSC

WEATHERBY ORION GRADE II CLASSIC SPORTING O/U

Gauge: 12, 3" chambers. **Barrel:** 28", 30"; five choke tubes. **Weight:** 7-1/2 to 8 lbs. **Stock:** 14-1/4"x2-1/4"x1-1/2". High gloss finish on Claro walnut; rounded pistol grip; slender forend. **Features:** Broadway-style stepped competition vent rib, vent middle rib; radius heel Sporting Clays recoil pad; silver/gray nitride receiver with hand-engraved scroll and clay pigeon monogram in gold-plate overlay. Introduced 1993. Imported by Weatherby.
Price: **$1,499.00**

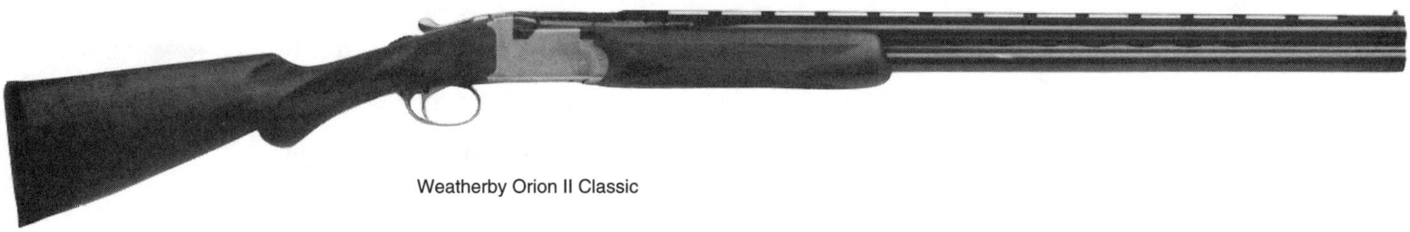

Weatherby Orion II Classic

Weatherby Orion Grade II Sporting Clays

Similar to the Orion II Classic Sporting except has traditional pistol grip with diamond inlay, and standard full-size forend. Available in 12-gauge only, 28", 30" barrels with Skeet, Imp. Cyl., SC2, Mod. Has lengthened forcing cones, backboring, stepped competition rib, radius heel recoil pad, hand-engraved, silver/nitride receiver. Introduced 1992. Imported by Weatherby.
Price: **$1,499.00**

American Arms Brittany

AMERICAN ARMS BRITTANY SHOTGUN

Gauge: 12, 20, 3" chambers. **Barrel:** 12-ga.—27"; 20-ga.—25" (Imp. Cyl., Mod., Full choke tubes). **Weight:** 6 lbs., 7 oz. (20-ga.). **Stock:** 14-1/8"x1-3/8"x2-3/8". Hand-checkered walnut with oil finish, straight English-style with semi-beavertail forend. **Features:** Boxlock action with case-color finish, engraving; single selective trigger, automatic selective ejectors; rubber recoil pad. Introduced 1989. Imported from Spain by American Arms, Inc.
Price: **$885.00**

BERETTA MODEL 452 SIDELOCK SHOTGUN

Gauge: 12, 2-3/4" or 3" chambers. **Barrel:** 26", 28", 30", choked to customer specs. **Weight:** 6 lbs., 13 oz. **Stock:** Dimensions to customer specs. Highly figured walnut; Model 452 EELL has walnut briar. **Features:** Full sidelock action with English-type double bolting; automatic selective ejectors, manual safety; double triggers, single or single non-selective trigger on request. Essentially custom made to specifications. Model 452 is coin finished without engraving; 452 EELL is fully engraved. Imported from Italy by Beretta U.S.A.
Price: 452. . . . . **$31,500.00**
Price: 452 EELL. **$43,500.00**

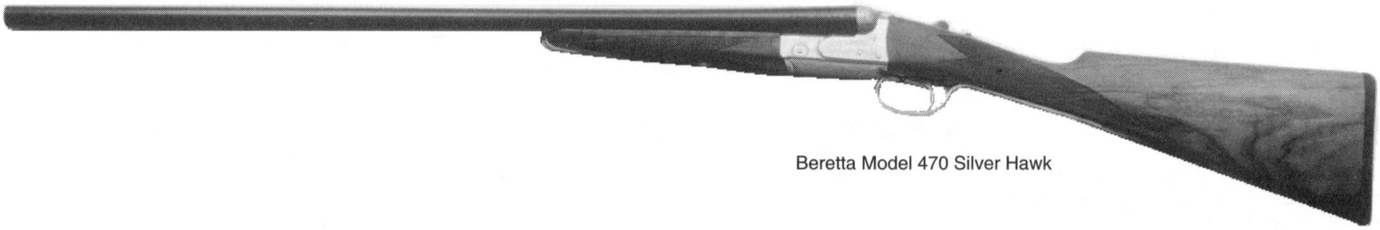

Beretta Model 470 Silver Hawk

BERETTA MODEL 470 SILVER HAWK SHOTGUN

Gauge: 12, 20, 3" chambers. **Barrel:** 26" (Imp. Cyl. & Imp. Mod.), 28" (Mod. & Full). **Weight:** 5.9 lbs. (20-gauge). **Stock:** Select European walnut, straight English grip. **Features:** Boxlock action with single selective trigger; selector provides automatic ejection or extraction; silver-chrome action and forend iron with fine engraving; top lever highlighted with gold inlaid hawk's head. Comes with ABS case. Introduced 1997. Imported from Italy by Beretta U.S.A.
Price: **$3,210.00**

Charles Daly Field Hunter

CHARLES DALY FIELD HUNTER DOUBLE SHOTGUN

Gauge: 10, 12, 20, 28, 410 (3" chambers; 28 has 2-3/4"). **Barrel:** 32" (Mod. & Mod.), 28, 30" (Mod. & Full), 26" (Imp. Cyl. & Mod.) 410 (Full & Full). **Weight:** 6 lbs. to 11.4 lbs. **Stock:** Checkered walnut pistol grip and forend. **Features:** Silvered, engraved receiver; gold single selective trigger in 10-, 12-, and 20-ga.; double triggers in 28 and 410; automatic safety; extractors; gold bead front sight. Introduced 1997. Imported from Spain by K.B.I., Inc.

Price: 10-ga. **$919.00**
Price: 12- or 20-ga. **$749.00**
Price: 28-ga. **$799.00**
Price: 410-bore **$799.00**
Price: Field Hunter AE-MC (choke tubes, 10 ga.) **$1,019.00**
Price: As above, 12 or 20. . . . . **$879.00**

Charles Daly Diamond DL

CHARLES DALY DIAMOND DL DOUBLE SHOTGUN

Gauge: 12, 20, 410, 3" chambers, 28, 2-3/4" chambers. **Barrel:** 28" (Mod. & Full), 26" (Imp. Cyl. & Mod.), 26" (Full & Full, 410). **Weight:** About 5-7 lbs. **Stock:** Select fancy European walnut, English-style butt, beavertail forend; hand-checkered, hand-rubbed oil finish. **Features:** Drop-forged action with gas escape valves; demiblock barrels with concave rib; selective automatic ejectors; hand-detachable double safety sidelocks with hand-engraved rose and scrollwork. Hinged front trigger. Color case-hardened receiver. Introduced 1997. Imported from Spain by K.B.I., Inc.

Price: 12 or 20 . . . . **$5,599.00**
Price: 28. . . . . **$6,079.00**
Price: 410. . . . . **$6,079.00**

CHARLES DALY DIAMOND REGENT DL DOUBLE SHOTGUN

Gauge: 12, 20, 410, 3" chambers, 28, 2-3/4" chambers. **Barrel:** 28" (Mod. & Full), 26" (Imp. Cyl. & Mod.), 26" (Full & Full, 410). **Weight:** About 5-7 lbs. **Stock:** Special select fancy European walnut, English-style butt, splinter forend; hand-checkered; hand-rubbed oil finish. **Features:** Drop-forged action with gas escape valves; demiblock barrels of chrome-nickel steel with concave rib; selective automatic-ejectors; hand-detachable, double-safety H&H sidelocks with demi-relief hand engraving; H&H pattern easy-opening feature; hinged trigger; coin finished action. Introduced 1997. Imported from Spain by K.B.I., Inc.

Price: 12 or 20 . . . . **$19,999.00**
Price: 28. . . . . **$20,499.00**
Price: 410. . . . . **$20,499.00**

Fabarm Classic Lion

FABARM CLASSIC LION DOUBLE SHOTGUN

Gauge: 12, 3" chambers. **Barrel:** 26" (Cyl., Imp. Cyl., Mod., Imp. Mod., Full choke tubes). **Weight:** 7.2 lbs. **Length:** 47.6" overall. **Stock:** Oil-finished European walnut. **Features:** Boxlock action with single selective trigger, automatic ejectors, automatic safety. Introduced 1998. Imported from Italy by Heckler & Koch, Inc.

Price: Grade I. **$1,488.00**
Price: Grade II (sidelock action). **$2,110.00**

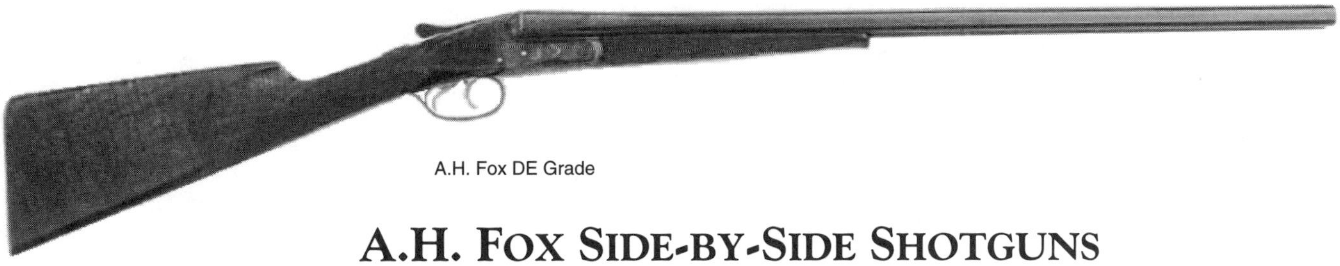

A.H. Fox DE Grade

A.H. FOX SIDE-BY-SIDE SHOTGUNS

Gauge: 16, 20, 28, 410. **Barrel:** Length and chokes to customer specifications. Rust-blued Chromox or Krupp steel. **Weight:** 5-1/2 to 6-3/4 lbs. **Stock:** Dimensions to customer specifications. Hand-checkered Turkish Circassian walnut with hand-rubbed oil finish. Straight, semi- or full pistol grip; splinter, schnabel or beavertail forend; traditional pad, hard rubber buttplate or skeleton butt. **Features:** Boxlock action with automatic ejectors; double or Fox single selective trigger. Scalloped, rebated and color case-hardened receiver; hand finished and hand-engraved. Grades differ in engraving, inlays, grade of wood, amount of hand finishing. Add $1,000 for 28 or 410-bore. Introduced 1993. Made in U.S. by Connecticut Shotgun Mfg.

Price: CE Grade **$9,500.00**
Price: XE Grade **$11,000.00**
Price: DE Grade **$13,500.00**
Price: FE Grade **$18,500.00**
Price: Exhibition Grade **$26,000.000**
Price: 28/410 CE Grade **$8,200.00**
Price: 28/410 XE Grade **$9,700.00**
Price: 28/410 DE Grade **$13,800.00**
Price: 28/410 FE Grade **$14,700.00**
Price: 28/410 Exhibition Grade **$26,000.00**

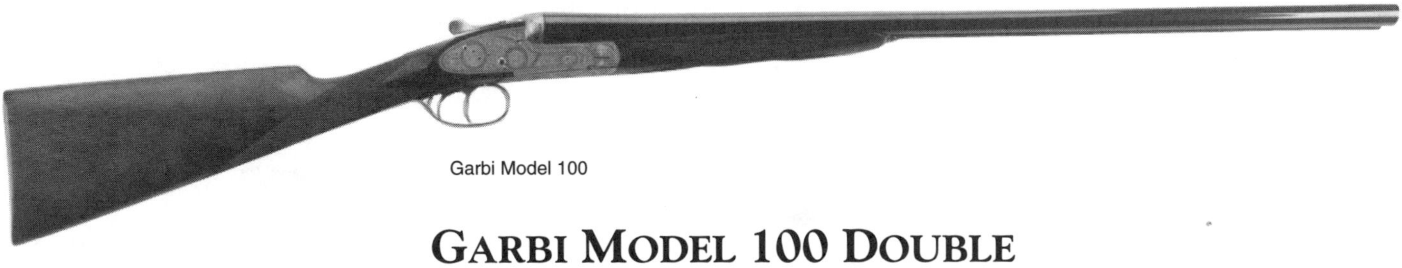

Garbi Model 100

GARBI MODEL 100 DOUBLE

Gauge: 12, 16, 20, 28. **Barrel:** 26", 28", choked to customer specs. **Weight:** 5-1/2 to 7-1/2 lbs. **Stock:** 14-1/2"x2-1/4"x1-1/2". European walnut. Straight grip, checkered butt, classic forend. **Features:** Sidelock action, automatic ejectors, double triggers standard. Color case-hardened action, coin finish optional. Single trigger; beavertail forend, etc. optional. Five other models are available. Imported from Spain by Wm. Larkin Moore.

Price: From **$4,300.00**

Garbi Model 101

Garbi Model 101 Side-by-Side

Similar to the Garbi Model 100 except is hand engraved with scroll engraving, select walnut stock. Better overall quality than the Model 100. Imported from Spain by Wm. Larkin Moore.
Price: From **$5,550.00**

Garbi Model 103A

Garbi Model 103A, B Side-by-Side

Similar to the Garbi Model 100 except has Purdey-type fine scroll and rosette engraving. Better overall quality than the Model 101. Model 103B has nickel-chrome steel barrels, H&H-type easy opening mechanism; other mechanical details remain the same. Imported from Spain by Wm. Larkin Moore.
Price: Model 103A, from **$6,850.00**
Price: Model 103B, from **$9,750.00**

Garbi Model 200 Side-by-Side

Similar to the Garbi Model 100 except has heavy-duty locks, magnum proofed. Very fine Continental-style floral and scroll engraving, well figured walnut stock. Other mechanical features remain the same. Imported from Spain by Wm. Larkin Moore.
Price: **$9,350.00**

Bill Hanus Birdgun

BILL HANUS BIRDGUN

Gauge: 16, 20, 28. **Barrel:** 27", 20- and 28-ga.; 28", 16-ga. (Skeet 1 & Skeet 2). **Weight:** 5 lbs., 4 oz. to 6 lbs., 4 oz. **Stock:** 14-3/8"x1-1/2"x2-3/8", with 1/4" cast-off. Select walnut. **Features:** Boxlock action with ejectors; splinter forend, straight English grip; checkered butt; English leather-covered handguard included. Made by AYA. Introduced 1998. Imported from Spain by Bill Hanus Birdguns.
Price: **$1,895.00**

Merkel Model 47E

MERKEL MODEL 47E SIDE-BY-SIDE SHOTGUNS

Gauge: 12, 3" chambers, 16, 2-3/4" chambers, 20, 3" chambers. **Barrel:** 12-, 16-ga.—28"; 20-ga.—26-3/4" (Imp. Cyl. & Mod., Mod. & Full). **Weight:** About 6-3/4 lbs. (12-ga.). **Stock:** Oil-finished walnut; straight English or pistol grip. **Features:** Anson & Deeley-type boxlock action with single selective or double triggers, automatic safety, cocking indicators. Color case-hardened receiver with standard Arabesque engraving. Imported from Germany by GSI.
Price: Model 47E (H&H ejectors) $2,695.00
Price: Model 147 (extractors, silver-grayed receiver with hunting scenes) $2,995.00
Price: Model 147E (as above with ejectors) $3,195.00
Price: Model 122 (as above with false sideplates, fine engraving)
. . . . $4,995.00

Merkel Model 47SL, 147SL Side-by-Sides

Similar to the Model 122 except with Holland & Holland-style sidelock action with cocking indicators, ejectors. Silver-grayed receiver and sideplates have Arabesque engraving, engraved border and screws (Model 47SL), or fine hunting scene engraving (Model 147SL). Imported from Germany by GSI.
Price: Model 47SL $5,295.00
Price: Model 147SL $6,695.00
Price: Model 247SL (English-style engraving, large scrolls) $6,995.00
Price: Model 447SL (English-style engraving, small scrolls) $8,995.00

SHOTGUNS — SIDE BY SIDES

PARKER REPRODUCTIONS SIDE-BY-SIDE SHOTGUN

Gauge: 12, 16/20 combo, 20, 28, 2-3/4" and 3" chambers. **Barrel:** 26" (Skeet 1 & 2, Imp. Cyl. & Mod.), 28" (Mod. & Full, 2-3/4" and 3", 12, 20, 28; Skeet 1 & 2, Imp. Cyl. & Mod., Mod. & Full 16-ga. only). **Weight:** 6-3/4 lbs. (12-ga.) **Stock:** Checkered (26 lpi) AAA fancy California English or Claro walnut, skeleton steel and checkered butt. Straight or pistol grip, splinter or beavertail forend. **Features:** Exact reproduction of the original Parker—parts interchange. Double or single selective trigger, selective ejectors, hard-chromed bores, designed for steel shot. One, two or three (16-20, 20) barrel sets available. Hand-engraved snap caps included. Introduced 1984. Made by Winchester. Imported from Japan by Parker Division, Reagent Chemical.

Price: D Grade, one-barrel set $3,370.00
Price: Two-barrel set, same gauge $4,200.00
Price: Two-barrel set, 16/20 . . . . $4,870.00
Price: Three-barrel set, 16/20/20 . . . . $5,630.00
Price: A-1 Special two-barrel set $11,200.00
Price: A-1 Special three-barrel set $13,200.00

Piotti King No. 1

PIOTTI KING NO. 1 SIDE-BY-SIDE

Gauge: 12, 16, 20, 28, 410. **Barrel:** 25" to 30" (12-ga.), 25" to 28" (16, 20, 28, 410). To customer specs. Chokes as specified. **Weight:** 6-1/2 lbs. to 8 lbs. (12-ga. to customer specs.). **Stock:** Dimensions to customer specs. Finely figured walnut; straight grip with checkered butt with classic splinter forend and hand-rubbed oil finish standard. Pistol grip, beavertail forend, satin luster finish optional. **Features:** Holland & Holland pattern sidelock action, automatic ejectors. Double trigger with front trigger hinged standard; non-selective single trigger optional. Coin finish standard; color case-hardened optional. Top rib; level, file-cut standard; concave, ventilated optional. Very fine, full coverage scroll engraving with small floral bouquets, gold crown in top lever, name in gold, and gold crest in forend. Imported from Italy by Wm. Larkin Moore.

Price: From $22,500.00

Piotti King Extra Side-by-Side

Similar to the Piotti King No. 1 except highest quality wood and metal work. Choice of either bulino game scene engraving or game scene engraving with gold inlays. Engraved and signed by a master engraver. Exhibition grade wood. Other mechanical specifications remain the same. Imported from Italy by Wm. Larkin Moore.

Price: From $28,200.00

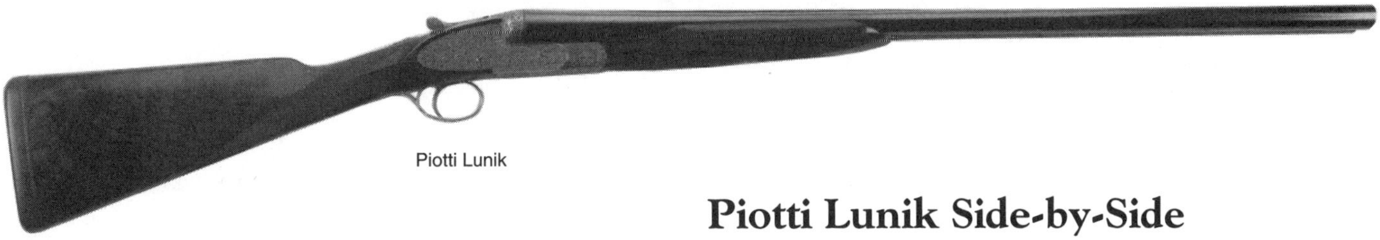

Piotti Lunik

Piotti Lunik Side-by-Side

Similar to the Piotti King No. 1 except better overall quality. Has Renaissance-style large scroll engraving in relief, gold crown in top lever, gold name and gold crest in forend. Best quality Holland & Holland-pattern sidelock ejector double with chopper lump (demi-bloc) barrels. Other mechanical specifications remain the same. Imported from Italy by Wm. Larkin Moore.
Price: From **$24,400.00**

PIOTTI PIUMA SIDE-BY-SIDE

Gauge: 12, 16, 20, 28, 410. **Barrel:** 25" to 30" (12-ga.), 25" to 28" (16, 20, 28, 410). **Weight:** 5-1/2 to 6-1/4 lbs. (20-ga.). **Stock:** Dimensions to customer specs. Straight grip stock with walnut checkered butt, classic splinter forend, hand-rubbed oil finish are standard; pistol grip, beavertail forend, satin luster finish optional. **Features:** Anson & Deeley boxlock ejector double with chopper lump barrels. Level, file-cut rib, light scroll and rosette engraving, scalloped frame. Double triggers with hinged front standard, single non-selective optional. Coin finish standard, color case-hardened optional. Imported from Italy by Wm. Larkin Moore.
Price: From **$12,900.00**

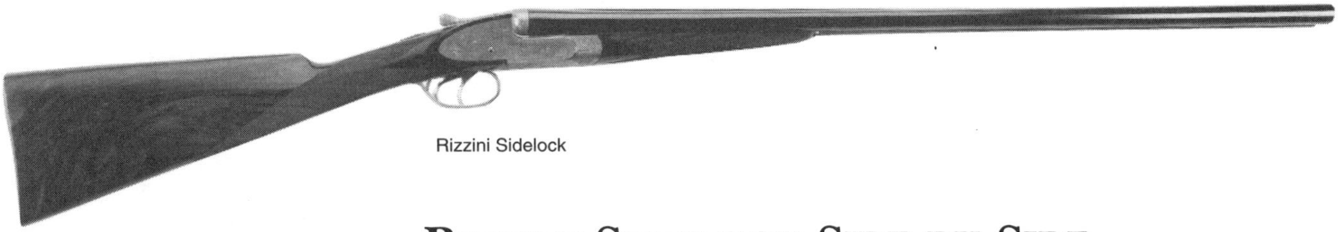

Rizzini Sidelock

RIZZINI SIDELOCK SIDE-BY-SIDE

Gauge: 12, 16, 20, 28, 410. **Barrel:** 25" to 30" (12-, 16-, 20-ga.), 25" to 28" (28, 410). To customer specs. Chokes as specified. **Weight:** 6-1/2 lbs. to 8 lbs. (12-ga. to customer specs). **Stock:** Dimensions to customer specs. Finely figured walnut; straight grip with checkered butt with classic splinter forend and hand-rubbed oil finish standard. Pistol grip, beavertail forend, satin luster finish optional. **Features:** Holland & Holland pattern sidelock action, auto ejectors. Double triggers with front trigger hinged optional; non-selective single trigger standard. Coin finish standard. Top rib level, file cut standard; concave optional. Imported from Italy by Wm. Larkin Moore.
Price: 12-, 20-ga., from **$45,000.00**
Price: 28, 410 bore, from **$50,000.00**

SKB Model 385 Side-by-Side

SKB MODEL 385 SIDE-BY-SIDE

Gauge: 12, 20, 3" chambers; 28, 2-3/4" chambers. **Barrel:** 26" (Imp. Cyl., Mod., Skeet choke tubes). **Weight:** 6-3/4 lbs. **Length:** 42-1/2" overall. **Stock:** 14-1/8"x1-1/2"x2-1/2". American walnut with straight or pistol grip stock, semi-beavertail forend. **Features:** Boxlock action. Silver nitrided receiver with engraving; solid barrel rib; single selective trigger, selective automatic ejectors, automatic safety. Introduced 1996. Imported from Japan by G.U. Inc.
Price: **$1,769.00**
Price: Field Set, 20-, 28-ga., 26", English or pistol grip **$2,499.00**

SKB Model 385

SKB Model 385 Sporting Clays

Similar to the Field Model 385 except 12-gauge only; 28" barrel with choke tubes; raised ventilated rib with metal middle bead and white front. Stock dimensions 14-1/4"x1-7/16"x1-7/8". Introduced 1998. Imported from Japan by G.U. Inc.
Price: **$1,899.00**

SKB Model 485 Side-by-Side

Similar to the Model 385 except has dummy sideplates, extensive upland game scene engraving, semi-fancy American walnut English or pistol grip stock. Imported from Japan by G.U. Inc.
Price: **$2,369.00**

Stoeger/IGA
Deluxe Uplander

STOEGER/IGA UPLANDER SIDE-BY-SIDE SHOTGUN

Gauge: 12, 20, 28, 2-3/4" chambers; 410, 3" chambers. **Barrel:** 26" (Full & Full, 410 only, Imp. Cyl. & Mod.), 28" (Mod. & Full). **Weight:** 6-3/4 to 7 lbs. **Stock:** 14-1/2"x1-1/2"x2-1/2". Oil-finished hardwood. Checkered pistol grip and forend. **Features:** Automatic safety, extractors only, solid matted barrel rib. Double triggers only. Introduced 1983. Imported from Brazil by Stoeger Industries.
Price: **$424.00**
Price: With choke tubes **$464.00**

Stoeger/IGA Deluxe Uplander Shotgun

Similar to the Uplander except with semi-fancy American walnut with thin black Pachmayr rubber recoil pad, matte lacquer finish. Choke tubes and 3" chambers standard 12- and 20-gauge; 28-gauge has 26", 3" chokes, fixed Mod. & Full. Double gold plated triggers; extractors. Introduced 1997. Imported from Brazil by Stoeger.
Price: 12, 20. . . . . **$559.00**
Price: 28, 410. . . . . **$519.00**

Stoeger/IGA Ladies Side-by-Side

Stoeger/IGA Ladies Side-by-Side

Similar to the Uplander except in 20-ga. only with 24" barrels (Imp. Cyl. & Mod. choke tubes), 13" length of pull, ventilated rubber recoil pad. Has extractors, double triggers, automatic safety. Introduced 1996. Imported from Brazil by Stoeger.
Price: **$478.00**

SHOTSHELL RELOADING PRESSES

DILLON SL 900

Press Type: Progressive
Avg. Rounds Per Hour: 700-900
Weight: 51 lbs.

Features: 12-ga. only; factory adjusted to load AA hulls; extra large 25-pound capacity shot hopper; fully-adjustable case-activated shot system; hardened steel starter crimp die; dual-action final crimp and taper die; tilt-out wad guide; auto prime; auto index; strong mount machine stand. From Dillon Precision Products.
Price: **$799.95**

HOLLYWOOD Automatic Shotshell Press

Press Type: Progressive
Avg. Rounds Per Hour: 1,800
Weight: 100 lbs.

Features: Ductile iron frame; fully automated press with shell pickup and ejector; comes completely set up for one gauge; one starter crimp; one finish crimp; wad guide for plastic wads; decap and powder dispenser unit; one wrench for inside die lock screw; one medium and one large spanner wrench for spanner nuts; one shellholder; powder and shot measures. Available for 10, 12, 20, 28 or 410. From Hollywood Engineering.
Price: **$3,600.00**

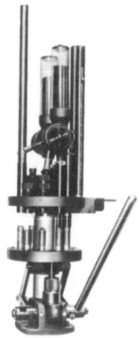

HOLLYWOOD Progressive Press

Press Type: Progressive
Avg. Rounds Per Hour: 400
Weight: 100 lbs.

Features: Made of ductile iron; comes completely equipped to reload one gauge; one starter crimp; one finish crimp; wad guide for plastic wads; decap and powder dispenser unit; one wrench for inside die lock screw; one medium and one large spanner wrench for spanner nuts; one shellholder; powder and shot measures. Available for 10, 12, 16, 20, 28 or 410. From Hollywood Engineering.
Price: **$2,800.00**

SHOTSHELL RELOADING PRESSES

HOLLYWOOD Senior Turret Press

Press Type: Turret
Avg. Rounds Per Hour: 200
Weight: 50 lbs.

Features: Multi-stage press constructed of ductile iron comes completely equipped to reload one gauge; one starter crimp; one finish crimp; wad guide for plastic wads; decap and powder dispenser unit; one wrench for inside die lock screw; one medium and one large spanner wrench for spanner nuts; one shellholder; powder and shot measures. Available for 10, 12, 16, 20, 28 or 410. From Hollywood Engineering.

Price: Press with die set $785.00
Price: Press only $600.00
Price: Senior Single-Stage Press $500.00

HOLLYWOOD Shotshell Die Sets

Complete 1-1/2 die set for one gauge to include: starter crimp; finish crimp; wad guide for plastic wads; decap and powder dispenser unit; wrench for inside die lock screw; medium and large spanner wrench for spanner nuts; shellholder. Available for 10, 12, 16, 20, 28 and 410. From Hollywood Engineering.

Price: $195.00

HORNADY 366 Auto

Press Type: Progressive
Avg. Rounds Per Hour: NA
Weight: 25 lbs.

Features: Heavy-duty die cast and machined steel body and components; auto primer feed system; large capacity shot and powder tubes; adjustable for right- or left-hand use; automatic charge bar with shut-off; swing-out wad guide; primer catcher at base of press; interchangeable shot and powder bushings; life-time warranty. Available for 12, 20, 28 2-3/4 and 410 2-1/2. From Hornady Mfg. Co.

Price: $390.00
Price: Die set, 12, 20, 28 . . . . $96.50
Price: Magnum conversion dies, 12, 20 . . . . $21.20

SHOTSHELL RELOADING PRESSES

HORNADY
Apex 3.1 Gas-Assist Auto

Press Type: Auto
Avg. Rounds Per Hour: NA
Weight: 15 lbs.

Features: Features shell retainer system; full-length collet size die to automatically size the full length of brass; shell-actuated auto primer feed; shell-actuated automatic powder/shot drop with shell detect; cam-activated dual-action crimp/taper die; auto index converts single stage shellplate to progressive. Includes a gas-assist indexing assembly which rotates the shellplate smoothly regardless of handle speed. Available for 12, 20, 28 gauges or 410 bore. From Hornady Mfg. Co.

Price: 12, 20 . . . . **$399.95**
Price: 28, 410 . . . . **$399.95**

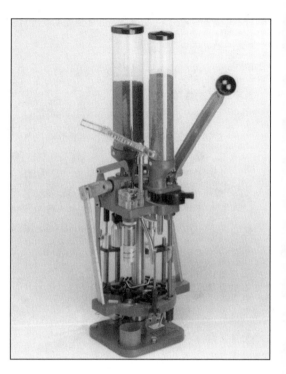

LEE Load-All II

Press Type: Single stage
Avg. Rounds Per Hour: 100
Weight: 3 lbs., 3 oz.

Features: Loads steel or lead shot; built-in primer catcher at base with door in front for emptying; recesses at each station for shell positioning; optional primer feed. Comes with safety charge bar with 24 shot and powder bushings. Available for 12-, 16- or 20-gauge. From Lee Precision, Inc.

Price: **$49.98**

MEC 600 Jr. Mark V

Press Type: Single stage
Avg. Rounds Per Hour: 200
Weight: 10 lbs.

Features: Spindex crimp starter for shell alignment during crimping; a cam-action crimp die; Pro-Check to keep charge bar properly positioned; adjustable for three shells. Available in 10, 12, 16, 20, 28 gauges and 410 bore. Die set not included. From Mayville Engineering Company, Inc.

Price: **$167.50**
Price: Die set. **$59.38**

MEC 650

Press Type: Progressive

Avg. Rounds Per Hour: 400

Weight: NA

Features: Six-station press; does not resize except as separate operation; auto primer feed standard; three crimping stations for starting, closing and tapering crimp. Die sets not available. Available in 12, 16, 20, 28 and 410. From Mayville Engineering Company, Inc.

Price: $329.39

MEC 8567 Grabber

Press Type: Progressive

Avg. Rounds Per Hour: 400

Weight: 15 lbs.

Features: Ten-station press; auto primer feed; auto-cycle charging; three-stage crimp; power ring resizer returns base to factory specs; resizes high and low base shells; optional kits to reload three shells and steel shot. Available in 12, 16, 20, 28 gauge and 410 bore. From Mayville Engineering Company, Inc.

Price:. **$472.54**
Price: 3" kit, 12-ga. **$39.19**
Price: 3" kit, 20-ga. **$24.00**
Price: Steel shot kit **$23.22**

MEC 9000G

Press Type: Progressive

Avg. Rounds Per Hour: 400

Weight: 18 lbs.

Features: All same features as the MEC Grabber, but with auto-indexing and auto-eject. Finished shells automatically ejected from shell carrier to drop chute for boxing. Available in 12, 16, 20, 28 and 410. From Mayville Engineering Company, Inc.

Price: $573.73
Price: 3" kit, 12-ga. $39.19
Price: 3" kit, 20-ga. $24.00
Price: Steel shot kit $23.22

SHOTSHELL RELOADING PRESSES

MEC 9000H

Press Type: Progressive

Avg. Rounds Per Hour: 400

Weight: 23 lbs.

Features: Same features as 9000G with addition of foot pedal-operated hydraulic system for complete automation. Operates on standard 110V household current. Comes with bushing-type charge bar and three bushings. Available in 12, 16, 20, 28 gauge and 410 bore. From Mayville Engineering Company, Inc.

Price:. **$1,386.09**
Price: Steel shot kit **$23.22**

MEC Sizemaster

Press Type: Single stage

Avg. Rounds Per Hour: 150

Weight: 13 lbs.

Features: Power ring eight-fingered collet resizer returns base to factory specs; handles brass or steel, high or low base heads; auto primer feed; adjustable for three shells. Available in 10, 12, 16, 20, 28 gauges and 410 bore. From Mayville Engineering Company, Inc.

Price: $252.39
Price: Die set, 12, 16, 20, 28, 410 . . . . $88.67
Price: Die set, 10-ga. $104.06
Price: Steel shot kit $14.34
Price: Steel shot kit, 12-ga. 31/2 . . . . $70.27

MEC Steelmaster

Press Type: Single stage

Avg. Rounds Per Hour: 150

Weight: 13 lbs.

Features: Same features as Sizemaster except can load steel shot. Press is available for 3-1/2 10-ga. and 12-ga. 2-3/4 ,3 or 3-1/2. For loading lead shot, die sets available in 10, 12, 16, 20, 28 and 410. From Mayville Engineering Company, Inc.

Price:. $262.65
Price: 10 ga. 3-1/2 ". $289.08

Du-O-Matic 375C

PONSNESS/WARREN Du-O-Matic 375C

Press Type: Progressive
Avg. Rounds Per Hour: NA
Weight: 31 lbs.

Features: Steel or lead shot reloader; large shot and powder reservoirs; bushing access plug for dropping in shot buffer or buckshot; positive lock charging ring to prevent accidental flow of powder; double-post construction for greater leverage; removable spent primer box; spring-loaded ball check for centering size die at each station; tip-out wad guide; two-gauge capacity tool head. Available in 10 (extra charge), 12, 16, 20, 28 and 410 with case lengths of 2-1/2, 2-3/4, 3 and 3-1/2 inches. From Ponsness/ Warren.

Price: $269.00
Price: 12-ga. 3-1/2 ; 3 12, 20, 410 . . . .$285.00
Price: 12, 20 2-3/4. . . . .$358.95
Price: 10-ga. press $295.00

PONSNESS/WARREN
Hydro-Multispeed

Hydraulic system developed for the Ponsness/Warren L/S-1000. Also usable for the 950, 900 and 800 series presses. Three reloading speed settings operated with variable foot pedal control. Features stop/reverse at any station; automatic shutdown with pedal control release; fully adjustable hydraulic cylinder rod to prevent racking or bending of machine; quick disconnect hoses for ease of installation. Comes preassembled with step-by-step instructions. From Ponsness/Warren.

Price: $849.00
Price: Cylinder kit $379.95

PONSNESS/WARREN
L/S-1000

Frame: Die cast aluminum
Avg. Rounds Per Hour: NA
Weight: 55 lbs.

Features: Fully progressive press to reload steel, bismuth or lead shot. Equipped with new Uni-Drop shot measuring and dispensing system which allows the use of all makes of shot in any size. Shells automatically resized and deprimed with new Auto-Size and De-Primer system. Loaded rounds drop out of shellholders when completed. Each shell pre-crimped and final crimped with Tru-Crimp system. Available in 10-gauge 3-1/2 or 12-gauge 2-3/4 and 3 . 12-gauge 3-1/2 conversion kit also available. 20-gauge 2-3/4 and 3 special order onlyFrom Ponsness/Warren.

Price: 12 ga.. . . . . $755.00
Price: 10 ga.. . . . . $799.00
Price: Conversion kit $44.95

SHOTSHELL RELOADING PRESSES

PONSNESS/WARREN Size-O-Matic 900 Elite

Press Type: Progressive

Avg. Rounds Per Hour: 500-800

Weight: 49 lbs.

Features: Progressive eight-station press; frame of die cast aluminum; center post design index system ensures positive indexing; timing factory set, drilled and pinned. Automatic features include index, deprime, reprime, powder and shot drop, crimp start, tapered final crimp, finished shell ejection. Available in 12, 20, 28 and 410. 16-ga. special order. Conversion kit converts the 900 press to the new 950 Elite. Kit includes the new shellholders, seating port, resize/primer knockout assembly and new crimp assembly. From Ponsness/Warren.

Price:. **$679.00**
Price: Tooling, 12, 20, 28, 410. . . . .**$177.00**

NEW! Platinum 2000 Series

PONSNESS/WARREN Platinum 2000

Press Type: Progressive

Avg. Rounds Per Hour: 500-800

Weight: 52 lbs.

Features: Progressive eight-station press is similar to the 900 and 950 except has die removal system that allows removal of any die component during the reloading cycle. Comes standard with 25-lb. shot tube, 19" powder tube, brass adjustable priming feed allows adjustment of primer seating depth. From Ponsness/Warren.

Price . . . .**Contact manufacturer**

PONSNESS/WARREN 950 Elite

Press Type: Progressive

Avg. Rounds Per Hour: 500-800

Weight: 55 lbs.

Features: Same as the 900 Elite, but comes with the L/S 1000 shellholder and resizing system which automatically seats shells into new shellholders and resizes them in primer knockout station. Conversion kit allows converting 900 Elite to 950. Handles both high and low brass with no alteration. Available in 12, 20 and 28 gauges. From Ponsness/Warren.

950 Elite

Price:. **$679.00**
Price: Tooling 12 ga. **$195.00**
Price: Conversion kit **$169.00**

THE SHOTGUNNER'S LIBRARY

FOR COLLECTOR ◆ HUNTER ◆ SHOOTER ◆ OUTDOORSMAN

IMPORTANT NOTICE TO BOOK BUYERS

Books listed here may be bought from Ray Riling Arms Books Co., 6844 Gorsten St., P.O. Box 18925, Philadelphia, PA 19119, phone 215/438-2456; FAX: 215-438-5395. Joe Riling is the researcher and compiler of "The Arms Library" and a seller of gun books for over 30 years.

The Riling stock includes books classic and modern, many hard-to-find items, and many not obtainable elsewhere. These pages list a portion of the current stock. They offer prompt, complete service, with delayed shipments occurring only on out-of-print or out-of-stock books.

NOTICE FOR ALL CUSTOMERS: Remittance in U.S. funds must accompany all orders. For U.S. add $2.00 per book for postage and insurance. Minimum order $10.00. For UPS add 50% to mailing costs.

All foreign countries add $5.00 per book. All foreign orders are shipped at the buyer's risk unless an additional $5 for insurance is included.

Payments in excess of order or for "Backorders" are credited or fully refunded at request. Books "As-Ordered" are not returnable except by permission and a handling charge on these of $2.00 per book is deducted from refund or credit. Only Pennsylvania customers must include current sales tax.

A full variety of arms books also available from Rutgers Book Center, 127 Raritan Ave., Highland Park, NJ 08904/908-545-4344; FAX: 908-545-6686 or I.D.S.A. Books, 1324 Stratford Drive, Piqua, OH 45356/937-773-4203; FAX: 937-778-1922.

BALLISTICS and HANDLOADING

ABC's of Reloading, 6th Edition, by C. Rodney James and the editors of *Handloader's Digest*, DBI Books, a division of Krause Publications, Iola, WI, 1997. 288 pp., illus. Paper covers. $21.95.
The definitive guide to every facet of cartridge and shotshell reloading.

The Complete Handloader for Rifles, Handguns and Shotguns, by John Wootters, Stackpole Books, Harrisburg, PA, 1988. 214 pp., $29.95.
Loading-bench know-how.

Complete Reloading Guide, by robert & John Traister, Stoeger Publishing Co., Wayne, NJ, 1997. 608 pp., illus. Paper covers. $34.95
Perhaps the finest, most comprehensive work ever published on the subject of reloading.

Handloader's Digest, 18th Edition, edited by Bob Bell, DBI Books, a division of Krause Publications, Inc., Iola, WI, 1998. 480 pp., illus. Paper covers. $27.95.
Top Writers in the field contribute helpful information on techniques and components. Greatly expanded and fully indexed catalog of all currently available tools, accessories and components for metallic, blackpowder cartridge, shotshell reloading and swaging.

Handloader's Guide, by Stanley W. Trzoniec, Stoeger Publishing Co., So. Hackensack, NJ, 1985. 256 pp., illus. Paper covers. $14.95.
The complete step-by-step fully illustrated guide to handloading ammunition.

Handloading, by Bill Davis, Jr., NRA Books, Wash., D.C., 1980. 400 pp., illus. Paper covers. $15.95.
A complete update and expansion of the NRA Handloader's Guide.

Handloading for Hunters, by Don Zutz, Winchester Press, Piscataway, NJ, 1977. 288 pp., illus. $30.00.
Precise mixes and loads for different types of game and for various hunting situations with rifle and shotgun.

Hatcher's Notebook, by S. Julian Hatcher, Stackpole Books, Harrisburg, PA, 1992. 488 pp., illus. $39.95.
A reference work for shooters, gunsmiths, ballisticians, historians, hunters and collectors.

Hodgdon Data Manual No. 26, Hodgdon Powder Co., Shawnee Mission, KS, 1993. 797 pp. $22.95.
Includes Hercules, Winchester and Dupont powders; data on cartridge cases; loads; silhouette; shotshell; pyrodex and blackpowder; conversion factors; weight equivalents, etc.

Hornady Handbook of Cartridge Reloading, 4th Edition, Vol. I and II, Hornady Mfg. Co., Grand Island, NE, 1991. 1200 pp., illus. $28.50.
New edition of this famous reloading handbook. Latest loads, ballistic information, etc.

Lyman Shotshell Handbook, 4th Edition, edited by Edward A. Matunas, Lyman Products Co., Middlefield, CT, 1996. 330 pp., illus. Paper covers. $24.95.
Has 9000 loads, including slugs and buckshot, plus feature articles and a full color I.D. section.

Modern Handloading, by Maj. Geo. C. Nonte, Winchester Press, Piscataway, NJ, 1972. 416 pp., illus. $15.00.
Covers all aspects of metallic and shotshell ammunition loading, plus more loads than any book in print.

Modern Reloading, by Richard Lee, Inland Press, 1996. 510 pp., illus. $24.98.
The how-tos of rifle, pistol amd shotgun reloading plus load data for rifle and pistol calibers.

Reloading for Shotgunners, 4th Edition, by Kurt D. Fackler and M.L. McPherson, DBI Books, a division of Krause Publications, Inc., Iola, WI, 1997. 320 pp., illus. Paper covers. $19.95.
Expanded reloading tables with over 11,000 loads. Bushing charts for every major press and component maker. All new presentation on all aspects of shotshell reloading by two of the top experts in the field.

COLLECTORS

Birmingham Gunmakers, by Douglas Tate, Safari Press, Inc., Huntington Beach, CA, 1997. 300 pp., illus. $50.00.
An invaluable work for anybody interested in the fine sporting arms crafted in this famous British gunmakers' city.

European Gun Makers, by Hans Pfingsten & Robert Jones, Armory Publications, Inc., Coeur d'Alene, ID. 300 pp., illus. $63.00
A study of the double-barrel shotguns and rifles, three-barrel guns (drilling) and four-barrel guns (vierling) made by German and Austrian gun makers.

Game Guns & Rifles: Percussion to Hammerless Ejector in Britain, by Richard Akehurst, Trafalgar Square, N. Pomfret, VT, 1993. 192 pp., illus. $39.95.
Long considered a classic this important reprint covers the period of British gunmaking between 1830-1900.

The Golden Age of Remington, by Robert W.D. Ball, Krause publications, Iola, WI, 1995. 194 pp., illus. $29.95.
For Remington collectors or firearms historians, this book provides a pictorial history of Remington through World War I. Includes value guide.

Gun Collecting, by Geoffrey Boothroyd, Sportsman's Press, London, 1989. 208 pp., illus. $29.95.
The most comprehensive list of 19th century British gunmakers and gunsmiths ever published.

Gunmakers of Illinois, 1683-1900, Vol. 1, by Curtis L. Johnson, George Shumway Publisher, York, PA, 1997. 200 pp., illus. $50.00.
This first volume covering the alphabet from A to F of a projected three-volume series, records the available names, dates, biographical details, and illustrates the work undertaken, by almost 1600 Illinois gunsmiths and gunmakers.

Gunmakers of London 1350-1850, by Howard L. Blackmore, George Shumway Publisher, York, PA, 1986. 222 pp., illus. $35.00.
A listing of all the known workmen of gun making in the first 500 years, plus a history of the guilds, cutlers, armourers, founders, blacksmiths, etc. 260 gunmarks are illustrated.

Gunsmiths of Illinois, by Curtis L. Johnson, George Shumway Publishers, York, PA, 1995. 160 pp., illus. $50.00.
Genealogical information is provided for nearly one thousand gunsmiths. Contains hundreds of illustrations of rifles and other guns, of handmade origin, from Illinois.

The Gunsmiths of Manhattan, 1625-1900: A Checklist of Tradesmen, by Michael H. Lewis, Museum Restoration Service, Bloomfield, Ont., Canada, 1991. 40 pp., illus. Paper covers. $4.95.
This listing of more than 700 men in the arms trade in New York City prior to about the end of the 19th century will provide a guide for identification and further research.

History of Winchester Repeating Arms Company, by Herbert G. Houze, Krause Publications, Iola, WI, 1994. 800 pp., illus. $50.00.
The complete Winchester history from 1856-1981.

How to Buy and Sell Used Guns, by John Traister, Stoeger Publishing Co., So. Hackensack, NJ, 1984. 192 pp., illus. Paper covers. $10.95.
A new guide to buying and selling guns.

Maine Made Guns and Their Makers, by Dwight B. Demeritt, Friends of the Maine State Museum, Augusta, ME, 1997. 438 pp., illus. $55.00.
An enlarged and updated edition of the definitive work on Maine made guns and their makers.

Marlin Firearms: A History of the Guns and the Company That Made Them, by Lt. Col. William S. Brophy, USAR, Ret., Stackpole Books, Harrisburg, PA, 1989. 672 pp., illus. $75.00.
The definitive book on the Marlin Firearms Co. and their products.

Matt Eastman's Guide to Browning Belgium Firearms 1903-1994, by Matt Eastman, Matt Eastman Publications, Fitzgerald, GA, 1995. 150 pp. Paper covers. $14.95.
Covers all Belgium models through 1994. Manufacturing production figures on the Auto-5 and Safari rifles.

Modern Gun Values, The Gun Digest Book of, 10th Edition, by the Editors of Gun Digest, DBI Books, a division of Krause Publications, Inc., Iola, WI., 1996. 560 pp. illus. Paper covers. $21.95.
Greatly updated and expanded edition describing and valuing over 7,000 firearms manufactured from 1900 to 1996. The standard for valuing modern firearms.

Modern Guns Identification & Value Guide, Eleventh Edition, by Russell and Steve Quartermous, Collector Books, Paducah, KY, 1996. 504 pp., illus. Paper covers. $12.95.
A popular guidebook featuring 2500 models of rifle, handgun and shotgun from 1900 to the present with detailed descriptions and prices.

Mossberg: More Gun for the Money, by V. and C. Havlin, Investment Rarities, Inc., Minneapolis, MN, 1995. 304 pp., illus. Paper covers. $24.95.
The history of O. F. Mossberg and Sons, Inc.

Official Guide to Gunmarks, 3rd edition, by Robert H. Balderson, House of collectibles, New York, NY, 1996. 367 pp., illus. Paper covers. $15.00.
Identifies manufacturers' marks that appear on American and foreign pistols, rifles and shotguns.

Official Price Guide to Antique and Modern Firearms, by Robert H. Balderson, House of Collectibles, New York, NY, 1996. 300 pp., illus. Paper covers. $17.00.
More than 30,000 updated prices for firearms manufactured from the 1600's to the present.

Sporting Collectibles, by Jim and Vivian Karsnitz, Schiffer Publishing Ltd., West Chester, PA, 1992. 160 pp., illus. Paper covers. $29.95.
The fascinating world of hunting related collectibles presented in an informative text.

Winchester: An American Legend, by R.L. Wilson, Random House, New York, NY, 1991. 403 pp., illus. $65.00.
The official history of Winchester firearms from 1849 to the present.

The Winchester Book, by George Madis, David Madis Gun Book Distributor, Dallas, TX, 1986. 650 pp., illus. $49.50.
A new, revised 25th anniversary edition of this classic book on Winchester firearms. Complete serial ranges have been added.

Winchester Dates of Manufacture 1849-1984, by George Madis, Art & Reference House, Brownsboro, TX, 1984. 59 pp. $5.95.
A most useful work, compiled from records of the Winchester factory.

Winchester Engraving, by R.L. Wilson, Beinfeld Books, Springs, CA, 1989. 500 pp., illus. $125.00.
A classic reference work, of value to all arms collectors.

The Winchester Handbook, by George Madis, Art & Reference House, Lancaster, TX, 1982. 287 pp., illus. $19.95.
The complete line of Winchester guns, with dates of manufacture, serial numbers, etc.

Winchester Shotguns and Shotshells, by Ronald W. Stadt, Krause Publications, Iola, WI, 1995. 256 pp., illus. $34.95.
The definitive book on collectible Winchester shotguns and shotshells manufactured through 1961.

GENERAL

Cartridges of the World, 8th Edition, by Frank Barnes, edited by M. L. McPherson, DBI Books, a division of Krause Publications, Inc., Iola, WI, 1997. 480 pp., illus. Paper covers. $24.95.
Completely revised edition of the general purpose reference work for which collectors, police, scientists and laymen reach first for answers to cartridge identification questions.

Complete Guide to Guns & Shooting, by John Malloy, DBI Books, a division of Krause Publications, Inc., Iola, WI, 1995. 256 pp., illus. Paper covers. $18.95.
What every shooter and gun owner should know about firearms, ammunition, shooting techniques, safety, collecting and much more.

Exploded Long Gun Drawings, The Gun Digest Book of, edited by Harold A. Murtz, DBI Books, a division of Krause Publications, Inc., Iola, WI, 512 pp., illus. Paper covers. $20.95.
Containing almost 500 rifle and shotgun exploded drawings.

Gun Digest 1999, 53rd Edition, edited by Ken Warner, DBI Books, a division of Krause Publications, Inc., Iola, WI, 1998. 544 pp., illus. Paper covers. $24.95
An all-new edition of the most read and respected gun book in the world for the last half century.

Gunfitting: The Quest for Perfection, by Michael Yardley, Safari Press, Huntington Beach, CA, 1995. 128 pp., illus. $24.95.
The author, a very experienced shooting instructor, examines gun stocks and gunfitting in depth.

Gun Talk, edited by Dave Moreton, Winchester Press, Piscataway, NJ, 1973. 256 pp., illus. $9.95.
A treasury of original writing by the top gun writers and editors in America. Practical advice about every aspect of the shooting sports.

Gun Trader's Guide, 21st Edition, published by the Stoeger Publishing Co., Wayne, NJ, 1998. 592 pp., illus. Paper covers. $23.95.
Complete specifications and curretn prices for used guns. Prices of over 5,000 handguns, rifles and shotguns both domestic and foreign.

Guns & Shooting: A Selected Bibliography, by Ray Riling, Ray Riling Arms Books Co., Phila., PA, 1982. 434 pp., illus. Limited, numbered edition. $75.
A limited edition of this superb bibliographical work, the only modern listing of books devoted to guns and shooting.

Guns Illustrated 1999, 31st Edition, edited by Harold A. Murtz, DBI Books, a division of Krause Publications, Inc., Iola, WI, 1998. 352 pp., illus. Paper covers. $22.95
The journal for gun buffs. Timely, top-of-the-line writing packed with highly informative, technical articles on a wide range of shooting topics covered by some the top writers in the industry.

Modern Custom Guns, Walnut, Steel, and Uncommon Artistry, by Tom Turpin, Krause Publications, Iola, WI, 1997. 206 pp., illus. $49.95.
From exquisite engraving to breathtaking exotic woods, the mystique of today's custom guns is expertly detailed in word and awe-inspiring color photos of rifles, shotguns and handguns.

Modern Gun Values, 10th Edition, The Gun Digest Book of by the editors of Gun Digest, DBI Books, a division of Krause Publications, Inc., Iola, WI, 1996. 560 pp., illus. paper covers. $21.95.
Greatly updated and expanded edition describing and valuing over 7,000 firearms manufactured between 1900 and 1995. The standard reference for valuing modern firearms.

Modern Sporting Guns, by Christopher Austyn, Safari Press, Huntington Beach, CA, 1994. 128 pp., illus. $40.00.
A discussion of the "best" English guns; round action, over-and-under, boxlocks, hammer guns, bolt action and double rifles as well as accessories.

E.C. Prudhomme, Master Gun Engraver, A Retrospective Exhibition: 1946-1973, intro. by John T. Amber, The R. W. Norton Art Gallery, Shreveport, LA, 1973. 32 pp., illus. Paper covers. $9.95.
Examples of master gun engravings by Jack Prudhomme.

The Shooter's Bible 1999, No. 90, edited by William S. Jarrett, Stoeger Publishing co. Wayne, NJ, 1998. 576 pp., illus. Paper covers. $23.95.
Over 3,000 firearms currently offered by major American and foreign gunmakers. Represented are handguns, rifles, shotguns and black powder arms with complete specifications and retail prices.

Sporting Collectibles, by Dr. Stephen R. Irwin, Stoeger Publishing Co., Wayne, NJ, 1997. 256 pp., illus. Paper covers. $19.95.
A must book for serious collectors nad admirers of sporting collectibles.

The Winchester Era, by David Madis, Art & Reference House, Brownsville, TX, 1984. 100 pp., illus. $14.95.
Story of the Winchester company, management, employees, etc.

Winchester Repeating Arms Company by Herbert Houze, Krause Publications, Inc., Iola, WI. 512 pp., illus. $50.00.

GUNSMITHING

The Art of Engraving, by James B. Meek, F. Brownell & Son, Montezuma, IA, 1973. 196 pp., illus. $33.95.
A complete, authoritative, imaginative and detailed study in training for gun engraving. The first book of its kind—and a great one.

Artistry in Arms, The R. W. Norton Gallery, Shreveport, LA, 1970. 42 pp., illus. Paper covers. $9.95.
The art of gunsmithing and engraving.

Checkering and Carving of Gun Stocks, by Monte Kennedy, Stackpole Books, Harrisburg, PA, 1962. 175 pp., illus. $39.95.
Revised, enlarged cloth-bound edition of a much sought-after, dependable work.

Custom Gunstock Carving, by Philip Eck, Stackpole Books, Mechanicsburg, PA, 1995. 232 pp., illus. $34.95.
Featuring a gallery of more than 100 full-size patterns for buttstocks, grips, accents and borders that carvers can use for their own projects.

Exploded Long Gun Drawings, The Gun Digest Book of, edited by Harold A. Murtz, DBI Books, a division of Krause Publications, Inc., Iola, WI. 512 pp., illus. Paper covers. $20.95.
Containing almost 500 rifle and shotgun exploded drawings. An invaluable aid to both professionals and hobbyists.

The Finishing of Gun Stocks, by Harold Hoffman, H&P Publishers, San Angelo, TX, 1994. 98 pp., illus. Paper covers. $17.95.
Covers different types of finishing methods and finishes.

Firearms Assembly/Disassembly, Part V: Shotguns, Revised Edition, The Gun Digest Book of, by J.B. Wood, DBI Books, a division of Krause Publications, Inc., Iola, WI, 1992. 480 pp., illus. Paper covers. $19.95.
Covers 46 popular shotguns plus over 250 variants with step-by-step instructions on how to dismantle and reassemble each. The most comprehensive and professional presentation available to either hobbyist or gunsmith.

Firearms Assembly 3: The NRA Guide to Rifle and Shotguns, NRA Books, Wash., DC, 1980. 264 pp., illus. Paper covers. $13.95.
Text and illustrations explaining the takedown of 125 rifles and shotguns, domestic and foreign.

Firearms Bluing and Browning, By R.H. Angier, Stackpole Books, Harrisburg, PA. 151 pp., illus. $18.95.
A world master gunsmith reveals his secrets of building, repairing and renewing a gun, quite literally, lock, stock and barrel. A useful, concise text on chemical coloring methods for the gunsmith and mechanic.

Firearms Disassembly—With Exploded Views, by John A. Karns & John E. Traister, Stoeger Publishing Co., S. Hackensack, NJ, 1995. 320 pp., illus. Paper covers. $19.95.
Provides the do's and don'ts of firearms disassembly. Enables owners and gunsmiths to disassemble firearms in a professional manner.

Gunsmith Kinks, by F.R. (Bob) Brownell, F. Brownell & Son, Montezuma, IA, 1st ed., 1969. 496 pp., well illus. $18.95.
A widely useful accumulation of shop kinks, short cuts, techniques and pertinent comments by practicing gunsmiths from all over the world.

Gunsmith Kinks 2, by Bob Brownell, F. Brownell & Son, Publishers, Montezuma, IA, 1983. 496 pp., illus. $18.95.
A collection of gunsmithing knowledge, shop kinks, new and old techniques, shortcuts and general know-how straight from those who do them best—the gunsmiths.

Gunsmith Kinks 3, edited by Frank Brownell, Brownells Inc., Montezuma, IA, 1993. 504 pp., illus. $19.95.
Tricks, knacks and "kinks" by professional gunsmiths and gun tinkerers. Hundreds of valuable ideas are given in this volume.

Gunsmithing, by Roy F. Dunlap, Stackpole Books, Harrisburg, PA, 1990. 742 pp., illus. $34.95.
A manual of firearm design, construction, alteration and remodeling. For amateur and professional gunsmiths and users of modern firearms.

Gunsmithing at Home: Lock, Stock and Barrel, by John Traister, Stoeger Publishing Co., Wayne, NJ, 1997. 320 pp., illus. Paper covers. $19.95.
A Complete step-by-step fully illustrated guide to the art of gunsmithing.

The Gunsmith's Manual, by J.P. Stelle and Wm. B. Harrison, The Gun Room Press, Highland Park, NJ, 1982. 376 pp., illus. $19.95.
For the gunsmith in all branches of the trade.

Handbook of Hard-to Find Guns Parts Drawings, by LeeRoy Wisner, Brownells, Inc., Montezuma, IA, 1997. Unpaginated. Deluxe edition. $54.95.
Over 2901 dimensioned drawings covering 147 guns from 36 manufacturers. The most valuable tool you'll ever buy for your shop.

The NRA Gunsmithing Guide—Updated, by Ken Raynor and Brad Fenton, National Rifle Association, Wash., DC, 1984. 336 pp., illus. Paper covers. $19.95.

Material includes chapters and articles on all facets of the gunsmithing art.

Practical Gunsmithing, by the editors of American Gunsmith, DBI Books, a division of Krause Publications, Inc., Iola, WI, 1996. 256 pp., illus. Paper covers. $19.95.

A book intended primarily for home gunsmithing, but one that will be extremely helpful to professionals as well.

Shotgun Gunsmithing, The Gun Digest Book of, by Ralph Walker, DBI Books, a division of Krause Publications, Inc., Iola, WI, 1983. 256 pp., illus. Paper covers. $16.95.

The principles and practices of repairing, individualizing and accurizing modern shotguns by one of the world's premier shotgun gunsmiths.

HUNTING

NORTH AMERICA

Advanced Wild Turkey Hunting & World Records, by Dave Harbour, Winchester Press, Piscataway, NJ, 1983. 264 pp., illus. $19.95.

The definitive book, written by an authority who has studied turkeys and turkey calling for over 40 years.

After the Hunt With Lovett Williams,by Lovett Williams, Krause Publications, Iola, WI, 1996. 256 pp., illus. Paper covers. $15.95.

The author carefully instructs you on how to prepare your trophy turkey for a trip to the taxidermist. Plus help on planning a grand slam hunt.

Autumn Passages, Compiled by the editors of Ducks Unlimited Magazine, Willow Creek Press, Minocqua, WI, 1997. 320 pp. $27.50.

An exceptional collection of duck hunting stories.

Bare November Days, by George Bird Evans et al, Countrysport Press, Traverse City, MI, 1992. 136 pp., illus. $39.50.

A new, original anthology, a tribute to ruffed grouse, king of upland birds.

The Best of Babcock, by Havilah Babcock, selected and with an introduction by Hugh Grey, The Gunnerman Press, Auburn Hills, MI, 1985. 262 pp., illus. $19.95.

A treasury of memorable pieces, 21of which have never before appeared in book form.

The Best of Field & Stream, edited by J.I. Merritt, with Margaret G. Nichols and the editor of *Field & Stream,* Lyons & Burford, New York, NY, 1995. 352 pp., illus. $25.00.

100 years of great writing from America's premier sporting magazine.

The Best of Nash Buckingham, by Nash Buckingham, selected, edited and annotated by George Bird Evans, Winchester Press, Piscataway, NJ, 1973. 320 pp., illus. $35.00.

Thirty pieces that represent the very cream of Nash's output on his whole range of outdoor interests—upland shooting, duck hunting, even fishing.

Better on a Rising Tide, by Tom Kelly, Lyons & Burford Publishers, New York, NY, 1995. 184 pp. $22.95.

Tales of wild turkeys, turkey hunting and Southern folk.

Big December Canvasbacks, by Worth Mathewson, Sand Lake Press, Amity, OR, 1997. 171 pp., illus. By David Hagenbaumer. Limited, signed and numbered edition. $29.95.

Duck hunting stories.

Big Woods, by William Faulkner, wilderness adventures, Gallatin Gateway, MT, 1998. 208 pp., illus. Slipcased. $60.00.

A colleciton of Faulkner's best hunting stories that belongs in the library of every sportsman.

Birdhunter, by Richard s. Grozik, Safari Press, Huntington Beach, CA, 1998. 180 pp., illus. Limited, numbered and signed edition. Slipcased. $60.00.

An entertaining salute to the closeness between man and his dog, man and his gun, and man and the great outdoors.

Birds on the Horizon, by Stuart Williams, Countrysport Press, Traverse City, MI, 1993. 288 pp., illus. $49.50.

Wingshooting adventures around the world.

Call of the Quail: A Tribute to the Gentleman Game Bird, by Michael McIntosh, et al., Countrysport Press, Traverse City, MI, 1990. 175 pp., illus. $39.50.

A new anthology on quail hunting.

Come October, by Gene Hill et al, Countrysport Press, Inc., Traverse City, MI, 1991. 176 pp., illus. $39.50.

A new and all-original anthology on the woodcock and woodcock hunting.

The Complete Guide to Bird Dog Training, by John R. Falk, Lyons & Burford, New York, NY, 1994. 288 pp., illus. $22.95.

The latest on live-game field training techniques using released quail and recall pens. A new chapter on the services available for entering field trials and other bird dog competitions.

The Complete Guide to Game Care & Cookery, 3rd Edition, by Sam Fadala, DBI Books, a division of Krause Publications, Inc., Iola, WI, 1994. 320 pp., illus. Paper covers. $18.95.

Over 500 photos illustrating the care of wild game in the field and at home with a separate recipe section providing over 400 tested recipes.

The Complete Smoothbore Hunter, by Brook Elliot, Winchester Press, Piscataway, NJ, 1986. 240 pp., illus. $16.95.

Advice and information on guns and gunning for all varieties of game.

Covey Rises and Other Pleasures, by David H. Henderson, Amwell Press, Clinton, NJ, 1983. 155 pp., illus. $17.50.

A collection of essays and stories concerned with field sports.

Coveys and Singles: The Handbook of Quail Hunting, by Robert Gooch, A.S. Barnes, San Diego, CA, 1981. 196 pp., illus. $11.95.

The story of the quail in North America.

Dabblers & Divers: A Duck Hunter's Book, compiled by the editors of Ducks Unlimited Magazine, Willow Creek Press, Minocqua, WI, 1997. 160 pp., illus. $39.95.

A word-and-photographic portrayal of waterfowl hunter's singular intimacy with, and passion for, watery haunts and wildfowl.

Dancers in the Sunset Sky, by Robert F. Jones, The Lyons Press, New York, NY, 1997. 192 pp., illus. $22.95.

The musings of a bird hunter.

Doves and Dove Shooting, by Byron W. Dalrymple, New Win Publishing, Inc., Hampton, NJ, 1992. 256 pp., illus. $17.95.

The author reveals in this classic book his penchant for observing, hunting, and photographing this elegantly fashioned bird.

Dove Hunting, by Charley Dickey, Galahad Books, NY, 1976. 112 pp., illus. $10.00.

This indispensable guide for hunters deals with equipment, techniques, types of dove shooting, hunting dogs, etc.

Drummer in the Woods, by Burton L. Spiller, Stackpole Books, Harrisburg, PA, 1990. 240 pp., illus. Soft covers. $16.95.

Twenty-one wonderful stories on grouse shooting by "the Poet Laureate of Grouse."

Duck Decoys and How to Rig Them, by Ralf Coykendall, revised by Ralf Coykendall, Jr., Nick Lyons Books, New York, NY, 1990. 137 pp., illus. Paper covers. $14.95.

Sage and practical advice on the art of decoying ducks and geese.

The Duck Hunter's Handbook, by Bob Hinman, revised, expanded, updated edition, Winchester Press, Piscataway, NJ, 1985. 288 pp., illus. $15.95.

The duck hunting book that has it all.

Eastern Upland Shooting, by Dr. Charles C. Norris, Countrysport Press, Traverse City, MI, 1990. 424 pp., illus. $29.50.

A new printing of this 1946 classic with a new, original Foreword by the author's friend and hunting companion, renowned author George Bird Evans.

A Fall of Woodcock, by Tom Huggler, Countrysport Press, Selman, AL, 1997. 256 pp., illus. $39.00.

A book devoted to the woodcock and to those who await his return to their favorite converts each autumn.

A Gallery of Waterfowl and Upland Birds, by Gene Hill, with illustrations by David Maass, Petersen Prints, Los Angeles, CA, 1978. 132 pp., illus. $44.95.

Gene Hill at his best. Liberally illustrated with 51 full-color reproductions of David Maass' finest paintings.

Getting the Most Out of Modern Waterfowling, by John O. Cartier, St. Martin's Press, NY, 1974. 396 pp., illus. $22.50.

The most comprehensive, up-to-date book on waterfowling imaginable.

Gordon MacQuarrie Trilogy: Stories of the Old Duck Hunters, by Gordon MacQuarrie, Willow Creek Press, Minocqua, WI, 1994. $49.00.

A slip-cased three volume set of masterpieces by one of America's finest outdoor writers.

The Grand Passage: A Chronicle of North American Waterfowling, by Gene Hill, et al., Countrysport Press, Traverse City, MI, 1990. 175 pp., illus. $39.50.

A new original anthology by renowned sporting authors on our world of waterfowling.

Grouse and Woodcock, A Gunner's Guide, by Don Johnson, Krause Publications, Iola, WI, 1995. 256 pp., illus. Paper covers. $14.95.

Find out what you need in guns, ammo, equipment, dogs and terrain.

Grouse of North America, by Tom Huggler, NorthWord Press, Inc., Minocqua, WI, 1990. 160 pp., illus. $29.95.

A cross-continental hunting guide.

Grouse Hunter's Guide, by Dennis Walrod, Stackpole Books, Harrisburg, PA, 1985. 192 pp., illus. $18.95.

Solid facts, observations, and insights on how to hunt the ruffed grouse.

Gunning for Sea Ducks, by George Howard Gillelan, Tidewater Publishers, Centreville, MD, 1988. 144 pp., illus. $14.95.

A book that introduces you to a practically untouched arena of waterfowling.

Hill Country, by Gene Hill, Countrysport Press, Traverse City, MI, 1996. 180 pp., illus. $25.00.

Stories about hunting, fishing, dogs and guns.

How to Hunt, by Dave Bowring, Winchester Press, Piscataway, NJ, 1982. 208 pp., illus. Paper covers. $10.95; cloth, $15.00.

A basic guide to hunting big game, small game, upland birds, and waterfowl.

A Hunter's Fireside Book, by Gene Hill, Winchester Press, Piscataway, NJ, 1972. 192 pp., illus. $16.95.

An outdoor book that will appeal to every person who spends time in the field—or who wishes he could.

A Hunter's Road, by Jim Fergus, Henry Holt & Co., NY, 1992. 290 pp. $22.50

A journey with gun and dog across the American uplands.

The Hunter's Shooting Guide, by Jack O'Connor, Outdoor Life Books, New York, NY, 1982. 176 pp., illus. Paper covers. $5.95.

A classic covering rifles, cartridges, shooting techniques for shotguns/rifles/handguns.

The Hunter's World, by Charles F. Waterman, Winchester Press, Piscataway, NJ, 1983. 250 pp., illus. $29.95.

A classic. One of the most beautiful hunting books that has ever been produced.

Hunting Adventure of Me and Joe, by Walt Prothero, Safari Press, Huntington Beach, CA, 1995. 220 pp., illus. $22.50.

A collection of the author's best and favorite stories.

Hunting America's Game Animals and Birds, by Robert Elman and George Peper, Winchester Press, Piscataway, NJ, 1975. 368 pp., illus. $16.95.

A how-to, where-to, when-to guide—by 40 top experts—covering the continent's big, small, upland game and waterfowl.

Hunting Ducks and Geese, by Steven Smith, Stackpole Books, Harrisburg, PA, 1984. 160 pp., illus. $19.95.

Hard facts, good bets, and serious advice from a duck hunter you can trust.

Hunting the American Wild Turkey, by Dave Harbour, Stackpole Books, Harrisburg, PA, 1975. 256 pp., illus. $24.95.

The techniques and tactics of hunting North America's largest, and most popular, woodland game bird.

Hunting Wild Turkeys in the West, by John Higley, Stoneydale Press, Stevensville, MT, 1992. 154 pp., illus. Paper covers. $12.95.

Covers the basics of calling, locating and hunting turkeys in the western states.

I Don't Want to Shoot an Elephant, by Havilah Babcock, The Gunnerman Press, Auburn Hills, MI, 1985. 184 pp., illus. $19.95.

Eighteen delightful stories that will enthrall the upland gunner for many pleasurable hours.

In Search of the Wild Turkey, by Bob Gooch, Greatlakes Living Press, Ltd., Waukegan, IL, 1978. 182 pp., illus. $9.95.

A state-by-state guide to wild turkey hot spots, with tips on gear and methods for bagging your bird.

Jaybirds Go to Hell on Friday, by Havilah Babcock, The Gunnerman Press, Auburn Hills, MI, 1985. 149 pp., illus. $19.95.

Sixteen jewels that reestablish the lost art of good old-fashioned yarn telling.

A Listening Walk...and Other Stories, by Gene Hill, Winchester Press, Piscataway, NJ, 1985. 208 pp., illus. $15.95.

Vintage Hill. Over 60 stories.

Mixed Bag, by Jim Rikhoff, National Rifle Association of America, Wash., DC, 1981. 284 pp., illus. Paper covers. $9.95.

Reminiscences of a master raconteur.

Modern Pheasant Hunting, by Steve Grooms, Stackpole Books, Harrisburg, PA, 1982. 224 pp., illus. Paper covers. $10.95.

New look at pheasants and hunters from an experienced hunter who respects this splendid gamebird.

Modern Waterfowl Guns and Gunning, by Don Zutz, Stoeger Publishing Co., So. Hackensack, NJ, 1985. 224 pp., illus. Paper covers. $11.95.

Up-to-date information on the fast-changing world of waterfowl guns and loads.

More and Better Pheasant Hunting, by Steve Smith, Winchester Press, Piscataway, NJ, 1986. 192 pp., illus. $15.95.

Complete, fully illustrated, expert coverage of the bird itself, the dogs, the hunt, the guns, and the best places to hunt.

More Grouse Feathers, by Burton L. Spiller, Crown Publ., NY, 1972. 238 pp., illus. $25.00.

Facsimile of the original Derrydale Press issue of 1938. Guns and dogs, the habits and shooting of grouse, woodcock, ducks, etc. Illus. by Lynn Bogue Hunt.

Mostly Tailfeathers, by Gene Hill, Winchester Press, Piscataway, NJ, 1975. 192 pp., illus. $15.95.

An interesting, general book about bird hunting.

My Health is Better in November, by Havilah Babcock, University of S. Carolina Press, Columbia, SC, 1985. 284 pp., illus. $19.95.
Adventures in the field set in the plantation country and backwater streams of SC.

The North American Waterfowler, by Paul S. Bernsen, Superior Publ. Co., Seattle, WA, 1972. 206 pp. Paper covers. $9.95.
The complete inside and outside story of duck and goose shooting. Big and colorful, illustrations by Les Kouba.

Old Wildfowling Tales, Volume 2, edited by Worth Mathewson, Sand Lake Press, Amity, OR, 1996. 240 pp. $21.95.
A collection of duck and geese hunting stories based around accounts from the past.

Pheasant Days, by Chris Dorsey, Voyageur Press, Stillwater, MN, 1992. 233 pp., illus. $24.95.
The definitive resource on ringnecks. Includes everything from basic hunting techniques to the life cycle of the bird.

Pheasant Hunter's Harvest, by Steve Grooms, Lyons & Burford Publishers, New York, NY, 1990. 180 pp. $22.95.
A celebration of pheasant, pheasant dogs and pheasant hunting. Practical advice from a passionate hunter.

*Pheasant Tales, by Gene Hill et al, Countrysport Press, Traverse City, MI, 1996. 202 pp., illus. $39.00.
Charley Waterman, Michael McIntosh and Phil Bourjaily join the author to tell some of the stories that illustrate why the pheasant is America's favorite game bird.

Pheasants of the Mind, by Datus Proper, Wilderness Adventures Press, Bozeman, MT, 1994. 154 pp., illus. $25.00.
No single title sums up the life of the solitary pheasant hunter like this masterful work.

Quail Hunting in America, by Tom Huggler, Stackpole Books, Harrisburg, PA, 1987. 288 pp., illus. $19.95.
Tactics for finding and taking bobwhite, valleys, Gambel's Mountain, scaled-blue, and Mearn's quail by season and habitat.

Ringneck! Pheasants & Pheasant Hunting, by Ted Janes, Crown Publ., NY, 1975. 120 pp., illus. $15.95.
A thorough study of one of our more popular game birds.

Ruffed Grouse, edited by Sally Atwater and Judith Schnell, Stackpole Books, Harrisburg, PA, 1989. 370 pp., illus. $59.95.
Everything you ever wanted to know about the ruffed grouse. More than 25 wildlife professionals provided in-depth information on every aspect of this popular game bird's life. Lavishly illustrated with over 300 full-color photos.

The Season, by Tom Kelly, Lyons & Burford, New York, NY, 1997. 160 pp., illus. $22.95.
The delight and challenges of a turkey hunter's Spring season.

Shorebirds: The Birds, The Hunters, The Decoys, by John M. Levinson & Somers G. Headley, Tidewater Publishers, Centreville, MD, 1991. 160 pp., illus. $49.95.
A thorough study of shorebirds and the decoys used to hunt them. Photographs of more than 200 of the decoys created by prominent carvers are shown.

Spring Gobbler Fever, by Michael Hanback, Krause Publications, Iola, WI, 1996. 256 pp., illus. Paper covers. $15.95.
Your complete guide to spring turkey hunting.

Successful Goose Hunting, by Charles L. Cadieux, Stone Wall Press, Inc., Washington, DC, 1986. 223 pp., illus. $24.95.
Here is a complete book on modern goose hunting by a lifetime waterfowler and professional wildlifer.

Taking More Birds, by Dan Carlisle and Dolph Adams, Lyons & Burford Publishers, New York, NY, 1993. 160 pp., illus. Paper covers. $15.95.
A practical handbook for success at Sporting Clays and wing shooting.

Tales of Quails 'n Such, by Havilah Babcock, University of S. Carolina Press, Columbia, SC, 1985. 237 pp. $19.95.
A group of hunting stories, told in informal style, on field experiences in the South in quest of small game.

*Tears and Laughter, by Gene Hill, Countrysport Press, Traverse City, MI, 1996. 176 pp., illus. $25.00.
In twenty-six stories, Gene Hill explores the ancient and honored bond between man and dog.

Timberdoodle, by Frank Woolner, Nick Lyons Books, N. Y., NY, 1987. 168 pp., illus. $18.95.
The classic guide to woodcock and woodcock hunting.

*Timberdoodle Tales, by T. Waters, Safari Press, Inc., Huntington Beach, CA, 1997. 220 pp., illus. $30.00.
A fresh appreciation of this captivating bird and the ethics of its hunt.

Timberdoodle Tales: Adventures of a Minnesota Woodcock Hunter, Safari Press, Huntington Beach, CA, 1997. 220 pp., illus. $35.00.
The life history and hunt of the American woodcock by the author.

The Trickiest Thing in Feathers, by Corey Ford; compiled and edited by Laurie Morrow and illustrated by Christopher Smith , Wilderness Adventures, Gallatin Gateway, MT, 1998. 208 pp., illus. $29.95.
Here is a collection of Corey Ford's best wing-shooting stories, many of them previously unpublished.

The Turkey Hunter's Book, by John M. McDaniel, Amwell Press, Clinton, NJ, 1980. 147 pp., illus. Paper covers. $11.95.
One of the most original turkey hunting books to be published in many years.

Turkey Hunter's Digest, Revised Edition, by Dwain Bland, DBI Books, a division of Krause Publications, Inc., Iola, WI, 1994. 256 pp., illus. Paper covers. $17.95.
A no-nonsense approach to hunting all five sub-species of the North American wild turkey that make up the Royal Grand Slam.

Turkey Hunting with Gerry Blair, by Gerry Blair, Krause Publications, Iola, WI, 1993. 280 pp., illus. $19.95.
Novice and veteran turkey hunters alike will enjoy this complete examination of the varied wild turkey subspecies, their environments, equipment needed to pursue them and the tactics to outwit them.

The Upland Equation: A Modern Bird-Hunter's Code, by Charles Fergus, Lyons & Burford Publishers, New York, NY, 1996. 86 pp. $18.00
A book that deserves space in every sportsman's library. Observations based on first-hand experience.

The Upland Gunner's Book, edited by George Bird Evans, The Amwell Press, Clinton, NJ, 1985. 263 pp., illus. In slipcase. $27.50.
An anthology of the finest stories ever written on the sport of upland game hunting.

Upland Tales, by Worth Mathewson (Ed.), Sand Lake Press, Amity, OR, 1996. 271 pp., illus. $21.95.
A collection of articles on grouse, snipe and quail.

Waterfowling Horizons: Shooting Ducks and Geese in the 21st Century, by Chris and Jason Smith, Wilderness Adventures, Gallatin Gateway, MT, 1998. 320 pp., illus. $49.95.
A compendium of the very latest in everything for the duck and goose hunter today.

Whispering Wings of Autumn, by Gene Hill and Steve Smith, Wilderness Adventures Press, Bozeman, MT, 1994. 150 pp., illus. $29.00.
Hill and Smith, masters of hunting literature, treat the reader to the best stories of grouse and woodcock hunting.

Wildfowlers Season, by Chris Dorsey, Lyons & Burford Publishers, New York, NY, 1998. 224 pp., illus. $37.95.

Modern methods for a classic sport.

The Wild Turkey Book, edited and with special commentary by J. Wayne Fears, Amwell Press, Clinton, NJ, 1982. 303 pp., illus. $22.50.
An anthology of the finest stories on wild turkey ever assembled under one cover.

Wings for the Heart, by Jerry A. Lewis, West River Press, Corvallis, MT, 1991. 324 pp., illus. Paper covers. $14.95.
A delightful book on hunting Montana's upland birds and waterfowl.

Wisconsin Hunting, by Brian Lovett, Krause Publications, Iola, WI, 1997. 208 pp., illus. Paper covers. $16.95.
A comprehensive guide to Wisconsin's public hunting lands.

Woodcock Shooting, by Steve Smith, Stackpole Books, Inc., Harrisburg, PA, 1988. 142 pp., illus. $16.95.
A definitive book on woodcock hunting and the characteristics of a good woodcock dog.

World Record Whitetail: The Hanson Buck Story, by Milo Hanson with Ian McMurchy, Krause Publications, Iola, WI, 1995. 144 pp., illus. Paper covers. $9.95.
How do you top a deer hunting record that stood for 80 years? Milo Hanson shares in his firsthand account of bagging the largest whitetail ever scored in the history of B&C measurements.

SHOTGUNS

Advanced Combat Shotgun: The Stress Fire Concept, by Massad Ayoob, Police Bookshelf, Concord, NH, 1993. 197 pp., illus. Paper covers. $9.95.
Advanced combat shotgun fighting for police.

The American Shotgun, by Charles Askins, Wolfe Publishing Co., Prescott, AZ, 1988. 321 pp., illus. $39.00.
A limited edition reprint. Askins covers shotguns and patterning extremely well.

The American Shotgun, by David F. Butler, edited by C. Kenneth Ramage, Lyman Publications, Middlefield, CT, 1973. 243 pp., illus. Paper covers. $14.95.
A comprehensive history of the American smoothbore's evolution from Colonial times to the present day.

American Shotgun Design and Performance, by L.R. Wallack, Winchester Press, Piscataway, NJ, 1977. 184 pp., illus. $16.95.
An expert lucidly recounts the history and development of American shotguns.

Best Guns, by Michael McIntosh, Countrysport, Inc., Traverse City, MI, 1989. 288 pp., illus. $39.50.
Devoted to the best shotguns ever made in the United States and the best presently being made in the world.

The Better Shot, by Ken Davies, Quiller Press, London, England, 1992. 136 pp., illus. $39.95.
Step-by-step shotgun technique with Holland and Holland.

Black Powder Hobby Gunsmithing, by Sam Fadala and Dale Storey, DBI Books, a division of Krause Publications, Inc., Iola, WI, 1994. 256 pp., illus. Paper covers. $18.95
A how-to-guide for gunsmithing blackpowder pistols, rifles and shotguns from two men at the top of their respective fields.

The British Shotgun, Volume 1, 1850-1870, by I.M. Crudington and D.J. Baker, Barrie & Jenkins, London, England, 1979. 256 pp., illus. $59.95.
An attempt to trace, as accurately as is now possible, the evolution of the shotgun during its formative years in Great Britain.

*Boothroyd on British Shotguns, by Geoffrey Boothroyd, Sand Lake Press, Amity, OR, 1996. 221 pp., illus. plus a 32 page reproduction of the 1914 Webley & Scott catalog. A limited, numbered edition. $34.95.
Based on articles by the author that appeared in the British Publication *Shooting Times & Country Magazine*.

*The British Over-and-Under Shotgun, by Geoffrey and Susan Boothroyd, Sand Lake Press, Amity, OR, 1996. 137 pp., illus. $34.95.
Historical outline of the development of the O/U shotgun with individual chapters devoted to the twenty-two British makers.

Boss & Co. Builders of Best Guns Only, by Donald Dallas, Safari Press, Huntington Beach, CA, 1996. 336 pp., illus. $75.00
The Browning Superposed: John M. Browning's Last Legacy, by Ned Schwing, Krause Publications, Iola, WI, 1996. 496 pp., illus. $49.95.
An exclusive story of the man, the company and the best-selling over-and-under shotgun in North America.

Clay Pigeon Shooting for Beginners and Enthusiasts, by John King, The Sportsman's Press, London, England, 1991. 94 pp., illus. $24.95.
John King has devised this splendid guide to clay pigeon shooting in the same direct style in which he teaches at his popular Barbury Shooting School near Swindon.

Clay Shooting, by Peter Croft, Ward Lock, London, England, 1990. 160 pp., illus, $29.95.
A complete guide to Skeet, trap and sporting shooting.

Clay Target Handbook, by Jerry Meyer, Lyons & Buford, Publisher, New York, NY, 1993. 182 pp., illus. $22.95.
Contains in-depth, how-to-do-it information on trap, skeet, sporting clays, international trap, international skeet and clay target games played around the country.

Clay Target Shooting, by Paul Bentley, A&C Black, London, England, 1987. 144 pp., illus. $25.00.
Practical book on clay target shooting written by a very successful international competitor, providing valuable professional advice and instruction for shooters of all disciplines.

A Collector's Guide to United States Combat Shotguns, by Bruce N. Canfield, Andrew Mowbray Inc., Publishers, Lincoln, RI, 1993. 184 pp., illus. Paper covers. $24.00.
Full coverage of the combat shotgun, from the earliest examples to the Gulf War and beyond.

The Complete Clay Shot, by Mike Barnes, Trafalgar Square, N. Pomfret, VT, 1993. 192 pp., illus. $39.95.
The latest compendium on the clay sports by Mike Barnes, a well-known figure in shotgunning in the U.S. and England.

Cradock on Shotguns, by Chris Cradock, Banford Press, London, England, 1989. 200 pp., illus. $45.00.
A definitive work on the shotgun by a British expert on shotguns.

The Defensive Shotgun, by Louis Awerbuck, S.W.A.T. Publications, Cornville, AZ, 1989. 77 pp., illus. Soft covers. $12.95.
Cuts through the myths concerning the shotgun and its attendant ballistic effects.

The Double Shotgun, by Don Zutz, Winchester Press, Piscataway, NJ, 1985. 304 pp., illus. $20.95.
Revised, updated, expanded edition of the history and development of the world's classic sporting firearms.

Ed Scherer on Sporting Clays, by Ed Scherer, Ed Scherer, Elk Grove, WI, 1993. 200 pp., illus. Paper covers. $29.95.
Covers footwork, gun fit, master eye checks, recoil reduction, noise abatement, eye and ear protection, league shooting, shot sizes and chokes.

Exploded Long Gun Drawings, The Gun Digest Book of, edited by Harold A. Murtz, DBI Books, a division of Krause Publications, Inc., Iola, WI. 512 pp., illus. Paper covers. $20.95.

Containing almost 500 rifle and shotgun exploded drawings. An invaluable aid to both professionals and hobbyists.

Field, Cover and Trap Shooting, by Adam H. Bogardus, Wolfe Publishing Co., Prescott, AZ, 1988. 446 pp., illus. $45.00.
A limited edition reprint. Hints for skilled marksmen as well as young sportsmen. Includes haunts and habits of game birds and waterfowl.

Finding the Extra Target, by Coach John R. Linn & Stephen A. Blumenthal, Shotgun Sports, Inc., Auburn, CA, 1989. 126 pp., illus. Paper covers. $14.95.
The ultimate training guide for all the clay target sports.

Firearms Assembly/Disassembly, Part V: Shotguns, Revised Edition, The Gun Digest Book of, by J.B. Wood, DBI Books, a division of Krause Publications, Inc., Iola, WI, 1992. 480 pp., illus. Paper covers. $19.95.
Covers 46 popular shotguns plus over 250 variants. The most comprehensive and professional presentation available to either hobbyist or gunsmith.

A.H. Fox "The Finest Gun in the World", revised and enlarged edition, by Michael McIntosh, Countrysport, Inc., New Albany, OH, 1995. 408 pp., illus. $49.00.
The first detailed history of one of America's finest shotguns.

Game Gun, by Richard Grozik, country Sport Press, Traverse City, MI, 1997. 203 pp., illus. $39.00.
A revision of a classic on the craftsmanship and function of double guns.

Game Shooting, by Robert Churchill, Countrysport Press, Selma, AL, 1998. 258 pp., illus. $34.95.
The basis for every shotgun instructional technique devised and the foundation for all wingshooting and the game of sporting clays.

The Golden Age of Shotgunning, by Bob Hinman, Wolfe Publishing Co., Inc., Prescott, AZ, 1982. $22.50.
A valuable history of the late 1800s detailing that fabulous period of development in shotguns, shotshells and shotgunning.

Grand Old Shotguns, by Don Zutz, Shotgun Sports Magazine, Auburn, CA, 1995. 136 pp., illus. Paper covers. $19.95
A study of the great smoothbores, their history and how and why they were discontinued. Find out the most sought-after and which were the best shooters.

Hartman on Skeet, By Barney Hartman, Stackpole Books, Harrisburg, PA, 1973. 143 pp., illus. $19.95.
A definitive book on Skeet shooting by a pro.

The Italian Gun, by Steve Smith & Laurie Morrow, wilderness Adventures, Gallatin Gateway, MT, 1997. 325 pp., illus. $49.95.
The first book ever written entirely in English for American enthusiasts who own, aspire to own, or simply admire Italian guns.

The Ithaca Featherlight Repeater; the Best Gun Going, by Walter C. Snyder, Southern Pines, NC, 1998. 300 pp., illus. $89.95.
Describes the complete history of each model of the legendary Ithaca Model 37 and Model 87 Repeaters from their conception in 1930 throught 1997.

L.C. Smith Shotguns, by Lt. Col. William S. Brophy, The Gun Room Press, Highland Park, NJ, 1979. 244 pp., illus. $35.00.
The first work on this very important American gun and manufacturing company.

The Little Trapshooting Book, by Frank Little, Shotgun Sports Magazine, Auburn, CA, 1994. 168 pp., illus. Paper covers. $19.95.
Packed with know-how from one of the greatest trapshooters of all time.

Lock, Stock, and Barrel, by C. Adams & R. Braden, Safari Press, Huntington Beach, CA, 1996. 254 pp., illus. $24.95.
The process of making a best grade English gun from a lump of steel and a walnut tree trunk to the ultimate product plus practical advise on consistent field shooting with a double gun.

A Manual of Clayshooting, by Chris Cradock, Hippocrene Books, Inc., New York, NY, 1983. 192 pp., illus. $39.95.
Covers everything from building a range to buying a shotgun, with lots of illus. & dia.

*__Mental Training for the Shotgun Sports,__ by Michael J. Keyes, Shotgun Sports, Auburn, CA, 1996. 160 pp., illus. Paper covers. $24.95.
The most comprehensive book ever published on what it takes to shoot winning scores at trap, Skeet and Sporting Clays.

The Model 12, 1912-1964,by Dave Riffle, Dave Riffle, Ft. Meyers, FL, 1995. 274 pp., illus. $49.95.
The story of the greatest hammerless repeating shotgun ever built.

The Mysteries of Shotgun Patterns, by George G. Oberfell and Charles E. Thompson, Oklahoma State University Press, Stillwater, OK, 1982. 164 pp., illus. Paper covers. $25.00.
Shotgun ballistics for the hunter in non-technical language.

The Orvis Wing-Shooting Handbook, by Bruce Bowlen, Nick Lyons Books, New York, NY, 1985. 83 pp., illus. Paper covers. $10.95.
Proven techniques for better shotgunning.

*__Parker Guns "The Old Reliable",__ by Ed Muderiak, Safari Press, Inc., Huntington Beach, CA, 1997. 325 pp., illus. $40.00.
A look at the small beginnings, the golden years, and the ultimate decline of the most famous of all American shotgun manufacturers.

Positive Shooting, by Michael Yardley, Safari Press, Huntington Beach, CA, 1995. 160 pp., illus. $30.00.
This book will provide the shooter with a sound foundation from which to develop an effective, personal technique that can dramatically improve shooting performance.

Purdey's, the Guns and the Family, by Richard Beaumont, David and Charles, Pomfert, VT, 1984. 248 pp., illus. $39.95.
Records the history of the Purdey family from 1814 to today, how the guns were and are built and daily functioning of the factory.

*__Reloading for Shotgunners, 4th Edition,__ by Kurt D. Fackler and M.L. McPherson, DBI Books, a division of Krause Publications, Inc., Iola, WI, 1997. 320 pp., illus. Paper covers. $19.95.
Expanded reloading tables with over 11,000 loads. Bushing charts for every major press and component maker. All new presentation on all aspects of shotshell reloading by two of the top experts in the field. (Available October 1997.)

Remington Double Shotguns, by Charles G. Semer, Denver, CO, 1997. 617 pp., illus. $60.00.
This book deals with the entire production and all grades of double shotguns made by Remington during the period of their production 1873-1910.

75 Years with the Shotgun, by C.T. (Buck) Buckman, Valley, Publ., Fresno, CA, 1974. 141 pp., illus. $10.00.
An expert hunter and trapshooter shares experiences of a lifetime.

The Shooting Field with Holland & Holland, by Peter King, Quiller Press, London, England, new & enlarged edition, 1990. 184 pp., illus. $49.95.
The story of a company which has produced excellence in all aspects of gunmaking.

The Shotgun in Combat, by Tony Lesce, Desert Publications, Cornville, AZ, 1979. 148 pp., illus. Paper covers. $10.00.
A history of the shotgun and its use in combat.

Shotgun Digest, 4th Edition, edited by Jack Lewis, DBI Books, a division of Krause Publications, Inc., Iola, WI, 1993. 256 pp., illus. Paper covers. $17.95.
A look at what's happening with shotguns and shotgunning today.

Shotgun Gunsmithing, The Gun Digest Book of, by Ralph Walker, DBI Books, a division of Krause Publications, Inc., Iola, WI, 1983. 256 pp., illus. Paper covers. $16.95.
The principles and practices of repairing, individualizing and accurizing modern shotguns by one of the world's premier shotgun gunsmiths.

The Shotgun: History and Development, by Geoffrey Boothroyd, Safari Press, Huntington Beach, CA, 1995. 240 pp., illus. $35.00.
The first volume in a series that traces the development of the British shotgun from the 17th century onward.

Shotgun Stuff, by Don Zutz, Shotgun Sports, Inc., Auburn, CA, 1991. 172 pp., illus. Paper covers. $19.95.
This book gives shotgunners all the "stuff" they need to achieve better performance and get more enjoyment from their favorite smoothbore.

Shotgunner's Notebook: The Advice and Reflections of a Wingshooter, by Gene Hill, Countrysport Press, Traverse City, MI, 1990. 192 pp., illus. $24.50.
Covers the shooting, the guns and the miscellany of the sport.

Shotgunning: The Art and the Science, by Bob Brister, Winchester Press, Piscataway, NJ, 1976. 321 pp., illus. $18.95.
Hundreds of specific tips and truly novel techniques to improve the field and target shooting of every shotgunner.

Shotgunning Trends in Transition, by Don Zutz, Wolfe Publishing Co., Prescott, AZ, 1990. 314 pp., illus. $29.50.
This book updates American shotgunning from post WWII to present.

Shotguns and Cartridges for Game and Clays, by Gough Thomas, edited by Nigel Brown, A & C Black, Ltd., Cambs, England, 1989. 256 pp., illus. Soft covers. $24.95.
Gough Thomas' well-known and respected book for game and clay pigeon shooters in a thoroughly up-dated edition.

Shotguns and Gunsmiths: The Vintage Years, by Geoffrey Boothroyd, Safari Press, Huntington Beach, CA, 1995. 240 pp., illus. $35.00.
A fascinating insight into the lives and skilled work of gunsmiths who helped develop the British shotgun during the Victorian and Edwardian eras.

Shotguns and Shooting, by Michael McIntosh, Countrysport Press, New Albany, OH, 1995. 258 pp., illus. $30.00.
The art of guns and gunmaking, this book is a celebration no lover of fine doubles should miss.

Side by Sides of the World, by Charles E. Carder, Avil Onze Publications, Delphos, OH, 1997. 181 pp., illus. Paper covers. $24.95.
Double barrel shotguns from the early 1800's to the present. 1,295 different names found on side by sides.

Sidelocks & Boxlocks, by Geoffrey Boothroyd, Sand Lake Press, Amity, OR, 1991. 271 pp., illus. $35.00.
The story of the classic British shotgun.

Spanish Best: The Fine Shotguns of Spain, by Terry Wieland, Countrysport, Inc., Traverse City, MI, 1994. 264 pp., illus. $49.50.
A practical source of information for owners of Spanish shotguns and a guide for those considering buying a used shotgun.

The Sporting Clay Handbook, by Jerry Meyer, Lyons and Burford Publishers, New York, NY, 1990. 140 pp., illus. Soft covers. $17.95.
Introduction to the fastest growing, and most exciting, gun game in America.

Sporting Clays, The Gun Digest Book of, by Jack Lewis and Steve Comus, DBI Books, a division of Krause Publications, Inc., Iola, WI, 1991. 256 pp., illus. Paper covers. $18.95.
A superb introduction to the fastest growing gun game in America.

Sporting Clays, by Michael Pearce, Stackpole Books, Harrisburg, PA, 1991. 192 pp., illus. $18.95.
Expert techniques for every kind of clays course.

Successful Clay Pigeon Shooting, compiled by T. Hoare, Trafalgar Square, N. Pomfret, VT, 1993. 176 pp., illus. $39.95.
This comprehensive guide has been written by ten leading personalities for all aspiring clay pigeon shooters.

*__The Tactical Shotgun,__ by Gabriel Suzrez, Paladin Press, Boulde, CO, 1996. 232 pp., illus. Paper covers. $25.00.
The best techniques and tactics for employing the shotgun in personal combat.

Taking More Birds, by Dan Carlisle & Dolph Adams, Lyons & Burford, New York, NY, 1993. 120 pp., illus. $19.95.
A practical guide to greater success at sporting clays and wing shooting.

Trap & Skeet Shooting, 3rd Edition, by Chris Christian, DBI Books, a division of Krause Publications, Inc., Iola, WI, 1994. 288 pp., illus. Paper covers. $17.95.
A detailed look at the contemporary world of trap, Skeet and Sporting Clays.

*__Trapshooting is a Game of Opposites,__ by Dick Bennett, Shotgun Sports, Inc., Auburn, CA, 1996. 129 pp., illus. Paper covers. $19.95.
Discover everything you need to know about shooting trap like the pros.

Turkey Hunter's Digest, Revised Edition, by Dwain Bland, DBI Books, a division of Krause Publications, Inc., Iola, WI, 1994. 256 pp., illus. Paper covers. $17.95.
Presents no-nonsense approach to hunting all five sub-species of the North American wild turkey.

U.S. Shotguns, All Types, reprint of TM9-285, Desert Publications, Cornville, AZ, 1987. 257 pp., illus. Paper covers. $9.95.
Covers operation, assembly and disassembly of nine shotguns used by the U.S. armed forces.

U.S. Winchester Trench and Riot Guns and Other U.S. Military Combat Shotguns, by Joe Poyer, North Cape Publications, Tustin, CA, 1992. 124 pp., illus. Paper covers. $15.95.
A detailed history of the use of military shotguns, and the acquisition procedures used by the U.S. Army's Ordnance Department in both World Wars.

The Winchester Model Twelve, by George Madis, David Madis, Dallas, TX, 1984. 176 pp., illus. $19.95.
A definitive work on this famous American shotgun.

The Winchester Model 42, by Ned Schwing, Krause Pub., Iola, WI, 1990. 160 pp., illus. $34.95.
Behind-the-scenes story of the model 42's invention and its early development. Production totals and manufacturing dates; reference work.

Winchester Shotguns and Shotshells, by Ron Stadt, Krause Pub., Iola, WI. 288 pp., illus. $34.95.
Must-have for Winchester collectors of shotguns manufactured through 1961.

Winchester's Finest, the Model 21, by Ned Schwing, Krause Publicatons, Inc., Iola, WI, 1990. 360 pp., illus. $49.95.
The classic beauty and the interesting history of the Model 21 Winchester shotgun.

The World's Fighting Shotguns, by Thomas F. Swearengen, T.B.N. Enterprises, Alexandria, VA, 1979. 500 pp., illus. $34.95.
The complete military and police reference work from the shotgun's inception to date, with up-to-date developments.

AMMUNITION, COMMERCIAL

ACTIV Industries, Inc.
American Ammunition
Arizona Ammunition, Inc.
Arms Corporation of the Philippines
A-Square Co., Inc.
Atlantic Rose, Inc.
Bergman & Williams
Big Bear Arms & Sporting Goods, Inc.
Black Hills Ammunition, Inc.
Blammo Ammo
Blount, Inc., Sporting Equipment Div.
Brenneke KG, Wilhelm
Brown Dog Ent.
Buffalo Bullet Co., Inc.
BulletMakers Workshop, The
Bull-X, Inc.
California Magnum
Casull Arms Corp.
CBC
Clean Shot Technologies Inc.
Colorado Sutlers Arsenal
Cor-Bon Bullet & Ammo Co.
Cubic Shot Shell Co. Inc.
Cumberland States Arsenal
Dead Eye's Sport Center
Delta Frangible Ammunition, LLC
Denver Bullets, Inc.
Diana
Dynamit Nobel-RWS, Inc.
Effebi SNC, Dr. Franco Beretta
Eldorado Cartridge Corp.
Eley Ltd.
Elite Ammunition
Estate Cartridge, Inc.
Executive Protection Institue
Federal Cartridge Co.
Fiocchi of America, Inc.
4W Ammunition
Hunters Supply
Garrett Cartridges, Inc.
Garthwaite Pistolsmith, Jim
Gibbs Rifle Co., Inc.
Glaser Safety slug Inc.
Goldcoast Reloaders, Inc.
Groenewold, John
Gun City Inc
Hansen & Co.
Hansen Cartridge Co.
Hart & Son, Inc., Robert W.
Hirtenberger Aktiengesellschaft
Hornady Mfg. Co.
ICI-America

IMI
Ion Industries Inc.
Israel Military Industries Ltd.
Jones, J.D.
Keng's Firearms Specialty, Inc.
Kent Cartridge Mfg. Co. Ltd.
Lapua Ltd.
Lightfield Ammunition Corp.
Lock's Philadelphia Gun Exchange
M&D Munitions Ltd.
MagSafe Ammo Co.
Maionchi-L.M.I.
Markell, Inc.
Mathews & Son, Inc., George E.
McBros Rifle Co.
Men—Metallwerk Elisenhuette, GmbH
Mullins Ammunition
NECO
New England Ammunition Co.
Oklahoma Ammunition Co.
Parker & Sons Gunsmithing
Omark Industries
Outdoor Sports Hdqtr
Pacific Cartridge, Inc.
Paragon Sales & Serv
PMC/Eldorado Cartridge Corp.
Polywad, Inc.
Pony Express Reloaders
Precision Delta Corp.
Pro Load Ammunition, Inc.
R.E.I.
Remington Arms Co., Inc.
Rucker Dist. Inc.
RWS
Slug Group, Inc.
Spence, George W.
Talon Mfg. Co., Inc.
TCCI
Thompson Bullet Lube Co.
3-D Ammunition & Bullets
3-Ten Corp.
USAC
Valor Corp.
Victory USA
Vihtavuori Oy/Kaltron-Pettibone
Voere-KGH m.b.H.
Vom Hoffe
Weatherby, Inc.
Westley Richards & Co.
Widener's Reloading & Shooting
  Supply, Inc.
Winchester Div., Olin Corp.
Zero Ammunition Co., Inc.

AMMUNITION, FOREIGN

AFSCO Ammunition
Armscorp USA, Inc.
A-Square Co., Inc.
Atlantic Rose, Inc.
Beeman Precision Airguns
BulletMakers Workshop, The
B-West Imports, Inc.
CBC
Cheddite France, S.A.
Cubic Shot Shell Co., Inc.
Dead Eye's Sport Center
Diana
DKT, Inc.
Dynamit Nobel-RWS, Inc.
E Arthur Brown Co
Fiocchi of America, Inc.
First, Inc., Jack
Fisher Enterprises, Inc.
Fisher, R. Kermit
FN Herstal
Forgett Jr., Valmore J.
Gibbs Rifle Co., Inc.
GOEX, Inc.
Groenewold, John
Hansen & Co.
Hansen Cartridge Co.
Heidenstrom Bullets
Hirtenberger Aktiengesellschaft
Hornady Mfg. Co.
IMI
IMI Services USA, Inc.
Israel Military Industries Ltd.

JägerSport, Ltd.
K.B.I., Ltd.
Keng's Firearms Specialty, Inc.
Magnum Research, Inc.
MagSafe Ammo Co.
MagTech Recreational Products, Inc.
Maionchi-L.M.I.
MAST Technology
Merkuria Ltd.
Mullins Ammunition
Naval Ordnance Works
Oklahoma Ammunition Co.
Old Western Scrounger, Inc.
Paragon Sales & Serv
Paul Company Inc.
Petro-Explo, Inc.
Precision Delta Corp.
R.E.T. Enterprises
RWS
Sentinel Arms
Southern Ammunition Co., Inc.
Spence, George W.
Stratco, Inc.
SwaroSports, Inc.
T.F.C. S.p.A.
USA Sporting Inc.
Vom Hoffe
Vihtavuori Oy/Kaltron-Pettibone
Yukon Arms Classic Ammunition

AMMUNITION COMPONENTS—BULLETS, POWDER, PRIMERS, CASES

Acadian Ballistic Specialties
Accuracy Unlimited (Littleton, CO)
Accurate Arms Co., Inc.
Accurate Bullet Co.
Action Bullets, Inc.
ACTIV Industries, Inc.
Alaska Bullet Works, Inc.
Alliant Techsystems
Allred Bullet Co.
Alpha LaFranck Enterprises
American Products Inc.
Arco Powder
Armfield Custom Bullets
A-Square Co., Inc.
Atlantic Rose, Inc.
Baer's Hollows
Ballard Built
Ballistic Products, Inc.
Barnes Bullets, Inc.
Beartooth Bullets
Beeline Custom Bullets Limited
Bell Reloading, Inc.
Belt MTN Arms
Berger Bullets, Ltd.
Bergman & Williams
Berry's Mfg., Inc.
Bertram Bullet Co.
Big Bore Bullets of Alaska
Big Bore Express
Bitterroot Bullet Co.
Black Belt Bullets
Black Hills Shooters Supply
Black Powder Products
Blount, Inc., Sporting Equipment Div.
Brenneke KG, Wilhelm
Briese Bullet Co., Inc.
Brown Co., E. Arthur
Brown Dog Ent.
BRP, Inc.
Bruno Shooters Supply
Buck Stix—SOS Products Co.
Buckeye Custom Bullets
Buckskin Bullet Co.
Buffalo Arms Co.
Buffalo Rock Shooters Supply
Bullet, Inc.
Bullseye Bullets
Bull-X, Inc.
Butler Enterprises
Buzztail Brass
Calhoon Varmint Bullets, James
Canyon Cartridge Corp.
Carnahan Bullets
Cascade Bullet Co., Inc.
Casull Arms Corp.
Cast Performance Bullet Company
CCI
Champion's Choice, Inc.
Cheddite France, S.A.
CheVron Bullets
C.J. Ballistics, Inc.
Colorado Sutlers Arsenal
Competitor Corp., Inc.
Cook Engineering Service
Cor-Bon Bullet & Ammo Co.
Cumberland States Arsenal
Cummings Bullets
Curtis Cast Bullets
Curtis Gun Shop
Custom Bullets by Hoffman
D&J Bullet Co. & Custom Gun Shop,
  Inc.
Dakota Arms, Inc.
Dixie Gun Works, Inc.
DKT, Inc.
Dohring Bullets
Double A Ltd.
Eichelberger Bullets, Wm.
Eldorado Cartridge Corp.
Elkhorn Bullets
Epps, Ellwood
Federal Cartridge Co.
Fiocchi of America, Inc.
Forkin, Ben
4W Ammunition
Fowler, Bob
Fowler Bullets
Foy Custom Bullets
Freedom Arms, Inc.

Fusilier Bullets
G&C Bullet Co., Inc.
Gander Mountain, Inc.
Gehmann, Walter
GOEX, Inc.
Golden Bear Bullets
Gonic Bullet Works
Gotz Bullets
"Gramps" Antique Cartridges
Granite Custom Bullets
Grayback Wildcats
Green Mountain Rifle Barrel Co., Inc.
Grier's Hard Cast Bullets
Group Tight Bullets
Gun City
Hammets VLD Bullets
Hardin Specialty Dist.
Harris Enterprises
Harrison Bullets
Hart & Son, Inc., Robert W.
Hawk, Inc.
Hawk Laboratories, Inc.
Haydon Shooters' Supply, Russ
Heidenstrom Bullets
Hercules, Inc.
Hi-Performance Ammunition
  Company
Hirtenberger Aktiengesellschaft
Hobson Precision Mfg. Co.
Hodgdon Powder Co.
Hornady Mfg. Co.
HT Bullets
Huntington Die Specialties
Hunters Supply
IMI Services USA, Inc.
Imperial Magnum Corp.
IMR Powder Co.
J-4, Inc.
J&D Components
J&L Superior Bullets
Jensen Bullets
Jensen's Firearms Academy
Jericho Tool & Die Co. Inc.
Jester Bullets
JLK Bullets
JRP Custom Bullets
Ka Pu Kapili
Kasmarsik Bullets
Kaswer Custom, Inc.
Keith's Bullets
Ken's Kustom Kartridge
Keng's Firearms Specialty, Inc.
Kent Cartridge Mfg. Co. Ltd.
KJM Fabritek, Inc.
KLA Enterprises
Knight Rifles
Lage Uniwad
Lapua Ltd.
Lawrence Brand Shot
Legend Products Corp.
Liberty Shooting Supplies
Lightfield Ammunition Corp.
Slug Group, Inc.
Lightning Performance Innovations,
  Inc.
Lindsley Arms Cartridge Co.
Littleton, J.F.
Loweth, Richard H.R.
Lomont Precision Bullets
M&D Munitions Ltd.
Magnus Bullets
Maine Custom Bullets
Maionchi-L.M.I.
Marchmon Bullets
Markesbery Muzzle Loaders, Inc.
MarMik, Inc.
Marple & Associates, Dick
MAST Technology
Mathews & Son, Inc., George E.
McMurdo, Lynn
Meister Bullets
Men—Metallwerk Elisenhuette, GmbH
Merkuria Ltd.
Michael's Antiques
Mitchell Bullets, R.F.
MI-TE Bullets
Modern Muzzleloading, Inc.
MoLoc Bullets
Montana Armory, Inc.

Montana Precision Swaging
Mountain State Muzzleloading
  Supplies, Inc.
Mt. Baldy Bullet Co.
Mulhern, Rick
Murmur Corp.
Mushroom Express Bullet Co.
Nagel's Bullets
National Bullet Co.
Naval Ordnance Works
Navy Arms Co.
Necromancer Industries, Inc.
Norma
North American Shooting Systems
North Devon Firearms Services
Northern Precision Custom Swaged
  Bullets
Nosler, Inc.
Oklahoma Ammunition Co.
Old Wagon Bullets
Old Western Scrounger, Inc.
Ordnance Works, The
Oregon Trail Bullet Company
Pacific Cartridge, Inc.
Pacific Rifle Co.
Page Custom Bullets
Patrick Bullets
Pease Accuracy, Bob
Petro-Explo, Inc.
Phillippi Custom Bullets, Justin
Pinetree Bullets
PMC/Eldorado Cartridge Corp.
Polywad, Inc.
Pomeroy, Robert
Precision Components
Precision Components and Guns
Precision Delta Corp.
Precision Munitions, Inc.
Prescott Projectile Co.
Price Bullets, Patrick W.
PRL Bullets
Professional Hunter Supplies
Rainier Ballistics Corp.
Ranger Products
Red Cedar Precision Mfg.
Redwood Bullet Works
Reloading Specialties, Inc.
Remington Arms Co., Inc.
Rhino
Rifle Works & Armory
R.I.S. Co., Inc.
R.M. Precision, Inc.
Robinson H.V. Bullets
Rolston, Inc., Fred W.
Rubright Bullets
SAECO
Scharch Mfg., Inc.
Schmidtman Custom Ammunition

Schneider Bullets
Schroeder Bullets
Scot Powder
Seebeck Assoc., R.E.
Shappy Bullets
Shilen, Inc.
Sharps Arms Co. Inc., C.
Sierra Bullets
SOS Products Co.
Specialty Gunsmithing
Speer Products
Spencer's Custom Guns
Stanley Bullets
Star Ammunition, Inc.
Star Custom Services
Stark's Bullet Mfg.
Starke Bullet Company
Stewart's Gunsmithing
Swift Bullet Co.
Talon Mfg. Co., Inc.
Taracorp Industries
TCCI
TCSR
T.F.C. S.p.A.
Thompson Precision
3-D Ammunition & Bullets
TMI Products
Traditions, Inc.
Trico Plastics
Trophy Bonded Bullets, Inc.
True Flight Bullet Co.
Tucson Mold, Inc.
Unmussig Bullets, D.L.
USAC
Vann Custom Bullets
Vihtavuori Oy/Kaltron-Pettibone
Vincent's Shop
Viper Bullet and Brass Works
Vom Hoffe
Warren Muzzleloading Co., Inc.
Watson Trophy Match Bullets
Weatherby, Inc.
Western Nevada West Coast Bullets
Widener's Reloading & Shooting
  Supply
Williams Bullet Co., J.R.
Winchester Div., Olin Corp.
Windjammer Tournament Wads, Inc.
Winkle Bullets
Woodleigh
Worthy Products, Inc.
Wosenitz VHP, Inc.
Wyant Bullets
Wyoming Bonded Bullets
Wyoming Custom Bullets
Yukon Arms Classic Ammunition
Zero Ammunition Co., Inc.

BOOKS (Publishers and Dealers)

Accurate Arms Co. Inc.
American Handgunner Magazine
Armory Publications, Inc.
Arms & Armour Press
Ballistic Products, Inc.
Barnes Bullets, Inc.
Beeman Precision Airguns
Blackhawk West
Blacksmith Corp.
Blacktail Mountain Books
Blue Book Publications, Inc.
Blue Ridge Machinery & Tools, Inc.
Boone's Custom Ivory Grips
Brown Co., E. Arthur
Brownell Checkering Tools, W.E.
Brownell's, Inc.
Bullet'n Press
Calibre Press, Inc.
Cape Outfitters
Clearview Products
Colonial Repair
Colorado Sutlers Arsenal
Corbin Mfg. & Supply, Inc.
Cumberland States Arsenal
DBI Books
Dixon Muzzleloading Shop Inc.
Flores Publications, Inc., J.
Forgett Jr., Valmore J.
Golden Age Arms Co.
Groenewold, John
Gun City
Gun Hunter Books
Gun Hunter Trading Co.

Gun List
Gun Parts Corp., The
Gun Room Press, The
Gun Works, The
Guncraft Books
Guncraft Sports, Inc.
Gunnerman Books
GUNS Magazine
H&P Publishing
Handgun Press
Harris Publications
Hawk Laboratories, Inc.
Hawk, Inc.
Heritage/VSP Gun Books
High North Products Inc.
Hodgdon Powder Co., Inc.
Home Shop Machinist, The
Hornady Mfg. Co.
Hungry Horse Books
I.D.S.A. Books
Info-Arm
Ironside International Publishers, Inc.
Koval Knives
Krause Publications, Inc.
Lapua Ltd.
Lethal Force Institute
Lyman Products Corp.
Madis Books
Magma Enginerring Co.
Marmik Inc.
Martin Bookseller, J.
McKee Publications
Montana Armory, Inc.

Mountain South
Mulberry House Publishing
New Win Publishing, Inc.
NgraveR Co., The
OK Weber, Inc.
Outdoor Sports Hdqtr
Outdoorsman's Bookstore, The
Paintball Games International
  Magazine (Aceville Publications)
Petersen Publishing Co.
Pettinger Books, Gerald
Police Bookshelf
Precision Shooting, Inc.
PWL Gunleather
Remington Double Shotguns
R.G.-G., Inc.
Riling Arms Books Co., Ray
Rocky Mountain Wildlife Products
Rutgers Book Center
S&S Firearms
Safari Press, Inc.
Saunders Gun & Machine Shop
Semmer, Charles

Sharps Arms Co. Inc., C.
Shootin' Accessories, Ltd.
Sierra Bullets
SPG, Inc.
Stackpole Books
Stewart Game Calls, Inc., Johnny
Stoeger Industries
Stoeger Publishing Co.
"Su-Press-On" Inc.
Thomas, Charles C.
Track of the Wolf, Inc.
Trafalgar Square
Trotman, Ken
Tru-Balance Knife Co.
Vintage Industries, Inc.
VSP Publishers
WAMCO—New Mexico
Wells Creek Knife & Gun Work
Wilderness Sound Products Ltd.
Williams Gun Sight Co.
Winchester Press
Wolfe Publishing Co.
Wolf's Western Traders

CHOKE DEVICES, RECOIL ABSORBERS AND RECOIL PADS

Accuright
Action Products, Inc.
Allen Co., Bob
Allen Sportswear, Bob
Answer Products Co.
Arms Ingenuity Co.
Baer Custom, Inc., Les
Baker, Stan
Bansner's Gunsmithing Specialties
Bartlett Engineering
Briley Mfg., Inc.
Brooks Tactical Systems
Brownells Inc.
B-Square Co., Inc.
Buffer Technologies
Bull Mountain Rifle Co.
C&H Research
Cape Outfitters
Cation
Chuck's Gun Shop
Clearview Products
Colonial Arms, Inc.
Connecticut Shotgun Mfg. Co.
CRR, Inc./Marble's Inc.
Danuser Machine Co.
Dayson Arms Ltd.
Dever Co., Jack
Dina Arms Corporation
Elsen, Inc., Pete
Galazan
Gentry Custom Gunmaker, David
Graybill's Gun Shop
Guns
ings Barrels
Holland's
I.N.C., Inc.

Jackalope Gun Shop
Jaeger, Inc., Paul/Dunn's
J.P. Enterprises, Inc.
Kick Eez
Lawson Co., Harry
London Guns Ltd.
Lyman Products Corp.
Mag-Na-Port International, Inc.
Marble Arms
Mathews & Son, Inc., George E.
Meadow Industries
Menck, Gunsmith Inc., T.W.
Michaels of Oregon Co.
Middlebrooks Custom Shop
Morrow, Bud
Nelson/Weather-rite, Inc.
Nu-Line Guns Inc.
One Of A Kind
Original Box, Inc.
Palsa Outdoor Products
PAST Sporting Goods, Inc.
Pro-Port Ltd.
Protektor Model
Que Industries
R.M. Precision, Inc.
Shell Shack
Shotguns Unlimited
Simmons Gun Repair, Inc.
Spencer's Custom Guns
Stone Enterprises Ltd.
3-Ten Corp.
Trulock Tool
Uncle Mike's
Vortek Products Inc.
Wise Guns, Dale

CLEANING AND REFINISHING SUPPLIES

AC Dyna-tite Corp.
Acculube II, Inc.
Accupro Gun Care
American Gas & Chemical Co., Ltd.
Answer Products Co.
Armite Laboratories
Armsport, Inc.
Atlantic Mills, Inc.
Atsko/Sno-Seal, Inc.
Barnes Bullets, Inc.
Beeman Precision Airguns
Bill's Gun Repair
Birchwood Casey
Blackhawk East
Blount, Inc., Sporting Equipment Div.
Blue and Gray Products, Inc.
Break-Free, Inc.
Bridgers Best
Brown Co., E. Arthur
Brownells Inc.
Camp-Cap Products Division
Cape Outfitters
Chem-Pak, Inc.
CONKKO
Connecticut Shotgun Mfg. Co
Crane & Crane Ltd.
Creedmoor Sports, Inc.
CRR, Inc./Marble's Inc.
Custom Products
D&H Prods. Co., Inc.

Dara-Nes, Inc.
Decker Shooting Products
Deepeeka Exports Pvt. Ltd.
Desert Mountain Mfg.
Dewey Mfg. Co., Inc., J.
Du-Lite Corp.
Dutchman's Firearms, Inc., The
Dykstra, Doug
E&L Mfg., Inc.
Eezox, Inc.
Ekol Leather Care
Faith Associates, Inc.
Flashette Co.
Flitz International Ltd.
Fluoramics, Inc.
Frontier Products Co.
G96 Products Co., Inc.
Goddard, Allen
Golden Age Arms Co.
Gozon Corp., U.S.A.
Great Lakes Airguns
Groenewold, John
Guardsman Products
Gunsmithing Inc
Heatbath Corp.
Hoppe's Div.
Hornady Mfg. Co.
Hydrosorbent Products
Iosso Products
Jedediah Starr Trading Co.

Johnston Bros.
K&M Service
Kellogg's Professional Products
Kent Cartridge Mfg. Co. Ltd.
Kesselring Gun Shop
Kleen-Bore, Inc.
Laurel Mountain Forge
Lee Supplies, Mark
LEM Gun Specialties, Inc.
Lewis Lead Remover, The
List Precision Engineering
Lone Star Rifle Co., Inc.
LPS Laboratories, Inc.
Marble Arms
Markesberry Bros.
Micro Sight Co.
Minute Man High Tech Industries
Mountain View Sports, Inc.
MTM Molded Products Co., Inc.
Muscle Products Corp.
Nesci Enterprises, Inc.
Northern Precision Custom Swaged Bullets
Now Products, Inc.
October Country
Old World Oil Products
Omark Industries
Original Mink Oil, Inc.
Outers Laboratories, Div. of Blount
Ox-Yoke Originals, Inc.
P&M Sales and Service
PanaVise Products, Inc.
Parker & Sons Gunsmithing
Parker Gun Finishes
Paul Company Inc.
Pendleton Royal
Penguin Industries, Inc.
Precision Reloading, Inc.

ProlixÆ Lubricants
Pro-Shot Products, Inc.
R&S Industries Corp.
Radiator Specialty Co.
Rickard, Inc., Pete
RIG Products Co.
Rooster Laboratories
Rusteprufe Laboratories
Rusty Duck Premium Gun Care Products
Saunders Gun & Machine Shop
Shiloh Creek
Shooter's Choice
Shootin' Accessories, Ltd.
Silencio/Safety Direct
Sinclair International
Sno-Seal, Inc.
Southern Bloomer Mfg Co.
Spencer's Custom Guns
Stoney Point Products, Inc.
Svon Corp.
Tag Distributors
TDP Industries, Inc.
Tetra Gun Lubricants
Texas Platers Supply Co.
T.F.C. S.p.A.
Thompson Bullet Lube Co.
Thompson/Center Arms
Track of the Wolf, Inc.
United States Products Co.
Venco Industries, Inc.
Warren Muzzleloading Co., Inc.
WD-40 Co.
Wick, David E.
Willow Bend
Wolf's Western Traders
Young Country Arms
Z-Coat Industrial Coatings, Inc.

ENGRAVERS, ENGRAVING TOOLS

Ackerman & Co.
Adair Custom Shop, Bill
Adams, John J. & Son Engravers
Adams Jr., John J.
Ahlman Guns
Alfano, Sam
Allard, Gary
Allen Firearm Engraving
Altamont Co.
American Pioneer Video
Anthony and George Ltd.
Baron Technology
Barraclough, John K.
Bates Engraving, Billy
Bell, Sid
Blair Engraving, J.R.
Bleile, C. Roger
Boessler, Erich
Bone Engraving, Ralph
Bratcher, Dan
Brgoch, Frank
Brooker, Dennis
Brownell Checkering Tools, W.E.
Burgess, Byron
CAM Enterprises
Churchill, Winston
Clark Firearms Engraving
Collings, Ronald
Creek Side Metal & Woodcrafters
Cullity Restoration, Daniel
Cupp, Custom Engraver, Alana
Custom Gun Engraving
Davidson, Jere
Dayton Traister
Delorge, Ed
Desquesnes, Gerald
Dolbare, Elizabeth
Drain, Mark
Dubber, Michael W.
Engraving Artistry
Evans Engraving, Robert
Eversull Co., Inc., K.
Eyster Heritage Gunsmiths, Inc., Ken
Firearms Engraver's Guild of America
Flannery Engraving Co., Jeff W.
Forty Five Ranch Enterprises
Fountain Products
Francotte & Cie S.A., Auguste
Frank E. Hendricks Master En
Frank Knives
French, Artistic Engraving, J.R.
Gene's Custom Guns
George, Tim
Glimm, Jerome C.

Golden Age Arms Co.
Gournet, Geoffroy
Grant, Howard V.
Griffin & Howe, Inc.
Gun Room, The
Guns
Gurney, F.R.
Gwinnell, Bryson J.
Hale/Engraver, Peter
Hamilton, Jim
Hands Engraving, Barry Lee
Harris Gunworks
Harris Hand Engraving, Paul A.
Harwood, Jack O.
Hawken Shop, The
Hendricks, Frank E.
Heritage Wildlife Carvings
Hiptmayer, Armurier
Hiptmayer, Heidemarie
Horst, Alan K.
Ingle, Engraver, Ralph W.
Jaeger, Inc., Paul/Dunn's
Jantz Supply
Johns Master Engraver, Bill
Kamyk Engraving Co., Steve
Kane, Edward
Kehr, Roger
Kelly, Lance
Klingler Woodcarving
Koevenig's Engraving Service
Kudlas, John M.
LeFever Arms Co., Inc.
Leibowitz, Leonard
Lindsay, Steve
Little Trees Ramble
Lutz Engraving, Ron
Lyons Gunworks, Larry
Master Engravers, Inc.
McCombs, Leo
McDonald, Dennis
McKenzie, Lynton
Mele, Frank
Metals Hand Engraver
Mittermeier, Inc., Frank
Montgomery Community College
Mountain States Engraving
Nelson, Gary K.
New England Custom Gun Service
New Orleans Jewelers Supply Co.
NgraveR Co., The
Oker's Engraving
P&S Gun Service
Pedersen, C.R.
Pedersen, Rex C.

Pilgrim Pewter, Inc.
Pilkington, Scott
Piquette, Paul R.
Potts, Wayne E.
Rabeno, Martin
Reed, Dave
Reno, Wayne
Riggs, Jim
Roberts, J.J.
Rohner, Hans
Rohner, John
Rosser, Bob
Rundell's Gun Shop
Runge, Robert P.
Sampson, Roger
Scott Pilkington Little Tree
Schiffman, Mike
Sherwood, George
Singletary, Kent
Smith, Mark A.
Smith, Ron

Smokey Valley Rifles
Theis, Terry
Thiewes, George W.
Thirion Gun Engraving, Denise
Thompson/Center Arms
Valade Engraving, Robert
Vest, John
Viramontez, Ray
Vorhes, David
Wagoner, Vernon G.
Wallace, Terry
Warenski, Julie
Warren, Kenneth W.
Weber & Markin Custom Gunsmiths
Welch, Sam
Wells, Rachel
Wessinger Custom Guns & Engraving
Wood, Mel
Yee, Mike
Ziegel Engineering

GAME CALLSGUNS, FOREIGN—IMPORTERS (Manufacturers)

●Accuracy International (Anschutz GmbH target rifles)
●AcuSport Corporation (Anschutz GmbH)
●Air Rifle Specialists (airguns)
●American Arms, Inc. (Fausti Cav. Stefano & Figlie snc; Franchi S.p.A.; Grulla Armes; Uberti, Aldo; Zabala Hermanos S.A.; blackpowder arms)
American Frontier Firearms Mfg. Inc. (single-action revolvers)
●Amtec 2000, Inc. (Erma Werke GmbH)
●Armsport, Inc. (Bernadelli S.p.A., Vincenzo)
●Auto-Ordnance Corp. (Techno Arms)
●●Beauchamp & Son, Inc. (Pedersoli and Co., Davide)
●Bell's Legendary Country Wear (Miroku, B.C./Daly, Charles)
Benelli USA Corp.
●Beretta U.S.A. Corp. (Beretta S.p.A., Pietro)
Big Bear Arms & Sporting Goods, Inc. (Russian/Big Bear Arms)
●Bohemia Arms Co. (BRNO)
British Sporting Arms
●Browning Arms Co. (Browning Arms Co.)
B-West Imports, Inc.
●Cabela's (Pedersoli and Co., Davide; Uberti, Aldo; blackpowder arms)
●Cape Outfitters (Armi Sport; Pedersoli and Co., Davide; San Marco; Societa Armi Bresciane Srl.; blackpowder arms)
●Century International Arms, Inc. (FEG)
●Champion Shooters' Supply (Anschutz GmbH)
●Champion's Choice (Anschutz GmbH; Walther GmbH, Carl; target rifles)
●Chapuis USA (Chapuis Armes)
●Champlin Firearms, Inc. (Chapuis Armes; M.Thys)
Christopher Firearms Co., Inc., E.
●Cimarron Arms (Uberti, Aldo; Armi San Marco; Pedersoli)
●CVA (blackpowder arms)
●CZ USA
●Dixie Gun Works, Inc. (Pedersoli and Co., Davide; Uberti, Aldo; blackpowder arms)
●Dynamit Nobel-RWS, Inc. (Brenneke KG, Wilhelm; Diana; Gamo; Norma Precision AB; RWS)
●E.A.A. Corp. (Astra-Sport, S.A.; Sabatti S.r.l.; Tanfoglio Fratelli S.r.l.; Weihrauch KG, Hermann; Star Bonifacio Echeverria S.A.)
Eagle Imports, Inc. (Bersa S.A.)
●Ellett Bros. (Churchill)
●EMF Co., Inc. (Dakota; Hartford; Pedersoli and Co., Davide; San Marco; Uberti, Aldo; blackpowder arms)
●Euroarms of America, Inc. (blackpowder arms)
Eversull Co., Inc., K.

●Fiocchi of America, Inc. (Fiocchi Munizioni S.p.A.)
●Forgett Jr., Valmore J. (Navy Arms Co.; Uberti, Aldo)
Franzen International, Inc. (Peters Stahl GmbH)
●Galaxy Imports Ltd., Inc. (Hanus Birdguns, Bill; Ignacio Ugartechea S.A.; Laurona Armas Eibar, S.A.D.)
●Gamba, USA (Societa Armi Bresciane Srl.)
●Gamo USA, Inc. (Gamo airguns)
Giacomo Sporting, Inc.
●Glock, Inc. (Glock GmbH)
●Great Lakes Airguns (air pistols & rifles)
●Griffin & Howe, Inc. (Arrieta, S.L.)
●GSI, Inc. (Mauser Werke Oberndorf; Merkel Freres; Steyr- Mannlicher AG)
G.U., Inc. (New SKB Arms Co.; SKB Arms Co.)
●Gun Shop, The (Ugartechea S.A., Ignacio)
Gunsite Custom Shop (Accuracy International Precision Rifles)
Gunsite Training Center (Accuracy International Precision Rifles)
●Gunsmithing, Inc. (Anschutz GmbH)
●Hammerli USA (Hammerli USA)
●Hanus Birdguns, Bill (Ugartechea S.A., Ignacio)
●Heckler & Koch, Inc. (Benelli Armi S.p.A.; Heckler & Koch, GmbH)
●IAR, Inc. (Uberti, Kimar, Armi San Marco, S.I.A.C.E.)
Imperial Magnum Corp. (Imperial Magnum Corp.)
●Import Sports Inc. (Llama Gabilondo Y Cia)
●Interarms (Helwan; Howa Machinery Ltd.; Interarms; Korth; Norinco; Rossi S.A., Amadeo; Star Bonifacio Echeverria S.A.; Walther GmbH, Carl)
●Israel Arms International, Inc. (KSN Industries, Ltd.)
Ithaca Gun Co., LLC (Fabarm S.p.A.)
I.S.S.
●JägerSport, Ltd. (Voere-KGH m.b.H.)
J.R. Distributing (Wolf competition guns)
●K.B.I., Inc. (FEG; Miroku, B.C./ Daly, Charles)
Kemen American (Armas Kemen S.A.)
●Keng's Firearms Specialty, Inc. (Lapua Ltd.; Ultralux)
Kongsberg America L.L.C. (Kongsberg)
●Krieghoff International, Inc (Krieghoff Gun Co., H.)
K-Sports Imports, Inc.
●Labanu, Inc. (Rutten; air rifles)
●Lion Country Supply (Ugartechea S.A., Ignacio)
London Guns Ltd. (London Guns Ltd.)
●Magnum Research, Inc.
MagTech Recreational Products, Inc. (MagTech)
●Mandall Shooting Supplies, Inc. (Arizaga; Atamec-Bretton; Cabanas; Crucelegui, Hermanos; Erma Werke

GmbH; Firearms Co. Ltd./Alpine; Hammerli Ltd.; Korth; Krico Jagd-und Sportwaffen GmbH; Morini; SIG; Tanner; Zanoletti, Pietro; blackpowder arms)
Marx, Harry (FERLIB)
MCS, Inc. (Pardini)
•MEC-Gar U.S.A., Inc. (MEC-Gar S.R.L.)
•Moore & Co., Wm. Larkin (Garbi; Piotti; Rizzini, Battista; Rizzini F.lli)
•Nationwide Sports Distributors, Inc. (Daewoo Precision Industries Ltd.)
•Navy Arms Co. (Navy Arms Co.; Pedersoli and Co., Davide; Pietta; Uberti, Aldo; blackpowder and cartridge arms)
•New England Arms Co. (Arrieta, S.L.; Bertuzzi; Bosis; Cosmi Americo & Figlio s.n.c.; Dumoulin, Ernest; Lebeau-Courally; Rizzini, Battista; Rizzini F.lli)
•New England Custom Gun Service (AYA; EAW)
•Nygord Precision Products (FAS; Morini; Pardini Armi Srl; Steyr-Mannlicher AG; TOZ; Unique/M.A.P.F.)
OK Weber, Inc. (target rifles)
•Orvis Co., Inc., The (Arrieta, S.L.)
•Para-Ordnance, Inc. (Para- Ordnance Mfg., Inc.)
•Paul Co., The (Norma Precision AB; Sauer)
Pelaire Products (Whiscombe air rifle)
•Perazzi USA, Inc. (Armi Perazzi S.p.A.)
•Powell Agency, William, The (William Powell & Son [Gunmakers] Ltd.)
•Precision Sales International, Inc. (BSA Guns Ltd.; Marocchi o/u shotguns)
P.S.M.G. Gun Co. (Astra Sport, S.A.; Interarms; Star Bonifacio Echeverria S.A.; Walther GmbH, Carl)

•Quality Arms, Inc. (Arrieta, S.L.)
Sarco, Inc.
•Savage Arms, Inc. (Lakefield Arms Ltd.; Savage Arms [Canada], Inc.)
Schuetzen Pistol Works (Peters Stahl GmbH)
Scott Fine Guns Inc., Thad
•Sigarms, Inc. (Hammerli Ltd.; Sauer rifles; SIG-Sauer)
•SKB Shotguns (SKB Arms Co.)
Specialty Shooters Supply, Inc. (JSL Ltd.)
Sphinx USA Inc. (Sphinx Engineering SA)
•Springfield, Inc. (Springfield, Inc.)
•Stoeger Industries (IGA; Sako Ltd.; Tikka; target pistols)
Stone Enterprises Ltd. (airguns)
•Swarovski Optik North America Ltd.
•Taurus Firearms, Inc. (Taurus International Firearms)
•Taylor's & Co., Inc. (Armi San Marco; Armi Sport; I.A.B.; Pedersoli and Co., Davide; Pietta; Uberti, Aldo)
•Track of the Wolf, Inc. (Pedersoli and Co., Davide)
Tradewinds, Inc. (blackpowder arms)
Tristar Sporting Arms, Ltd. (Turkish, German, Italian and Spanish made firearms)
Trooper Walsh
Turkish Firearms Corp. (Turkish Firearms Corp.)
•Uberti USA, Inc. (Uberti, Aldo; blackpowder arms)
USA Sporting Inc. (Armas Kemen S.A.)
Vintage Arms, Inc.
•Weatherby, Inc. (Weatherby, Inc.)
•Westley Richards Agency USA (Westley Richards)
•Whitestone Lumber Corp. (Heckler & Koch; Bennelli Armi S.p.A.)
•Wingshooting Adventures (Arrieta, S.L.)
•World Class Airguns (Air Arms)

GUNS, FOREIGN—MANUFACTURERS (Importers)

•Accuracy International Precision Rifles (Gunsite Custom Shop; Gunsite Training Center)
•Air Arms (World Class Airguns)
Armas Kemen S.A. (Kemen America; USA Sporting Inc.)
•Armi Perazzi S.p.A. (Perazzi USA, Inc.)
Armi San Marco (Taylor's & Co., Inc.; Cimarron Arms; IAR, Inc.)
•Armi Sport (Cape Outfitters; Taylor's & Co., Inc.)
Arms Corporation of the Philippines Armscorp USA Inc.
•Arrieta, S.L. (Griffin & Howe, Inc. New England Arms Co.; The Orvis Co., Inc.; Quality Arms, Inc.; Wingshooting Adventures)
•Astra Sport, S.A. (E.A.A. Corp.; P.S.M.G. Gun Co.)
•Atamec-Bretton (Mandall Shooting Supplies, Inc.)
•AYA (New England Custom Gun Service)
BEC Scopes (BEC, Inc.)
•Benelli Armi S.p.A. (Heckler & Koch, Inc.; Whitestone Lumber Co.)
•Beretta S.p.A., Pietro (Beretta U.S.A. Corp.)
•Bernardelli S.p.A., Vincenzo (Armsport, Inc.)
Bersa S.A. (Eagle Imports, Inc.)
•Bertuzzi (New England Arms Co.)
•Blaser Jagdwaffen GmbH (Bondini Paolo (blackpowder arms)
Borovnik KG, Ludwig
•Bosis (New England Arms Co.)
•Brenneke KG, Wilhelm (Dynamit Nobel-RWS, Inc.)
•BRNO (Bohemia Arms Co.)
Brocock Ltd.
Brolin Industries Inc. (Mauser)
•Browning Arms Co. (Browning Arms Co.)
•BSA Guns Ltd. (Groenewold, John; Precision Sales International, Inc.)
•Cabanas (Mandall Shooting Supplies, Inc.)

•CBC
•Chapuis Armes (Champlin Firearms, Inc.; Chapuis USA)
•Churchill (Ellett Bros.)
•Cosmi Americo & Figlio s.n.c. (New England Arms Co.)
•Crucelegui, Hermanos (Mandall Shooting Supplies, Inc.)
Cryo-Accurizing
•Daewoo Precision Industries Ltd. (Nationwide Sports Distributors, Inc.)
•Dakota (EMF Co., Inc.)
•Diana (Dynamit Nobel-RWS, Inc.)
•Dumoulin, Ernest (New England Arms Co.)
•EAW (New England Custom Gun Service)
•Effebi SNC-Dr. Franco Beretta (Erma Werke GmbH (Amtec 2000, Inc.; Mandall Shooting Supplies, Inc.)
•Fabarm S.p.A. (Ithaca Gun Co., LLC) Ed's Gun House
Euro-Imports
F.A.I.R. Techni-Mec s.n.c.
Fanzoj GmbH
•FAS (Nygord Precision Products)
•Fausti Cav. Stefano & Figlie snc (American Arms, Inc.)
•FEG (Century International Arms, Inc.; K.B.I., Inc.)
Felk Inc.
FERLIB (Marx, Harry)
•Fiocchi Munizioni S.p.A. (Fiocchi of America, Inc.)
•Firearms Co. Ltd./Alpine (Mandall Shooting Supplies, Inc.)
Firearems International
FN Herstal
•Franchi S.p.A (American Arms, Inc.)
•FWB (Beeman Precision Airguns)
Galaxy Imports LTD Inc.
•Gamba S.p.A.-Societa Armi Bresciane Srl., Renato (Gamba, USA)
•Gamo (Daisy Mfg. Co.; Dynamit Nobel-RWS, Inc.; Gamo USA, Inc.)
•Garbi, Armas Urki (Moore & Co., Wm. Larkin)

Gaucher Armes S.A.
•Glock GmbH (Glock, Inc.)
Goergen's gun Shop Inc.
•Grulla Armes (American Arms, Inc.)
Gunsmithing Inc
•Hammerli Ltd. (Hammerli USA; Mandall Shooting Supplies, Inc.; Sigarms, Inc.)
•Hartford (EMF Co., Inc.)
Hartmann & Weiss GmbH
•Heckler & Koch, GmbH (Heckler & Koch, Inc.)
Hege Jagd-u. Sporthandels, GmbH
•Helwan (Interarms)
Holland & Holland Ltd.
•Howa Machinery Ltd. (Interarms)
I.A.B. (Taylor's & Co., Inc.)
•IGA (Stoeger Industries)
IMI
Imperial Magnum Corp. (Imperial Magnum Corp.)
Inter Ordnance of America
•Interarms (Interarms; P.S.M.G. Gun Co.)
JSL Ltd. (Specialty Shooters Supply, Inc.)
Kimar (IAR, Inc.)
Kongsberg (Kongsberg America L.L.C.)
•Korth (Interarms; Mandall Shooting Supplies, Inc.)
•Krico Jagd-und Sportwaffen GmbH (Mandall Shooting Supplies, Inc.)
•Krieghoff Gun Co., H. (Krieghoff International, Inc.)
•KSN Industries, Ltd. (Israel Arms International, Inc.)
•Lakefield Arms Ltd. (Savage Arms, Inc.)
Lakelander U.S.A. Inc.
Lanber Armas, S.A.
•Lapua Ltd. (Keng's Firearms Specialty, Inc.)
•Laurona Armas Eibar S.A.D. (Galaxy Imports Ltd., Inc.)
•Lebeau-Courally (New England Arms Co.)
•Llama Gabilondo Y Cia (Import Sports Inc.)
London Guns Ltd. (London Guns Ltd.)
Madis, George
Mandell Shooting Supply
MagTech (MagTech Recreational Products, Inc.)
•Marocchi F.lli S.p.A. (Precision Sales International, Inc.)
•Mauser Werke Oberndorf (GSI, Inc.)
•MEC-Gar S.R.L. (MEC-Gar U.S.A., Inc.)
•Merkel Freres (GSI, Inc.)
•Miroku, B.C./Daly, Charles (Bell's Legendary Country Wear; K.B.I., Inc.)
Miltex Inc.
•Morini (Mandall Shooting Supplies; Nygord Precision Products)
M.Thys (Champlin Firearms, Inc.)
•Navy Arms Co. (Forgett Jr., Valmore J.; Navy Arms Co.)
•New SKB Arms Co. (G.U., Inc.)
Norica, Avnda Otaola
•Norinco (Century International Arms, Inc.; Interarms)
•Norma Precision AB (Dynamit Nobel-RWS Inc.; The Paul Co., Inc.)
•Para-Ordnance Mfg., Inc. (Para-Ordnance, Inc.)
•Pardini Armi Srl. (Nygord Precision Products; MCS, Inc.)
•Pedersoli and Co., Davide (Beauchamp & Son, Inc.; Cabela's; Cape Outfitters; Cimarron Arms; Dixie Gun Works, Inc.; EMF Co., Inc.; Navy Arms Co.; Track of the Wolf, Inc.)

Pease International
Perugini-Visini & Co. s.rl.
Peters Stahl GmbH (Franzen International, Inc.)
•Pietta (Navy Arms Co.; Taylor's & Co., Inc.)
•Piotti (Moore & Co., Wm. Larkin)
•Powell & Son Ltd., William (Powell Agency, The, William)
•Rigby & Co., John
•Rizzini, Battista (Moore & Co., Wm. Larkin; New England Arms Co.)
•Rizzini F.lli (Moore & Co., Wm. Larkin; New England Arms Co.)
•Rossi S.A., Amadeo (Interarms)
Rutten (Labanu, Inc.)
•RWS (Dynamit Nobel-RWS, Inc.)
•Sabatti S.R.L. (E.A.A. Corp.)
•Sako Ltd. (Stoeger Industries)
•San Marco (Cape Outfitters; EMF Co., Inc.)
S.A.R.L. G. Granger
•Sauer (Paul Co., The; Sigarms, Inc.)
•Savage Arms (Canada), Inc. (Savage Arms, Inc.)
•S.I.A.C.E. (IAR, Inc.)
•SIG (Mandall Shooting Supplies, Inc.)
•SIG-Sauer (Sigarms, Inc.)
Scott Pilkington Little Tree
•Societa Armi Bresciane Srl. (Cape Outfitters; Gamba, USA)
Sphinx Engineering SA (Sphinx USA Inc.)
•Springfield, Inc. (Springfield, Inc.)
•Star Bonifacio Echeverria S.A. (E.A.A. Corp.; Interarms; P.S.M.G. Gun Co.)
•Steyr-Mannlicher AG (GSI, Inc.; Nygord Precision Products)
•Tanfoglio Fratelli S.r.l. (E.A.A. Corp.)
•Tanner (Mandall Shooting Supplies, Inc.)
•Taurus International Firearms (Taurus Firearms, Inc.)
Taurus S.A., Forjas
Techno Arms (Auto-Ordnance Corp.)
T.F.C. S.p.A.
•Tikka (Stoeger Industries)
•TOZ (Nygord Precision Products)
Turkish Firearms Corp. (Turkish Firearms Corp.)
•Uberti, Aldo (American Arms, Inc.; Cabela's; Cimarron Arms; Dixie Gun Works, Inc.; EMF Co., Inc.; Forgett Jr., Valmore J.; IAR, Inc.; Navy Arms Co.; Taylor's & Co., Inc.; Uberti USA, Inc.)
•Ugartechea S.A., Ignacio (Aspen Ou t fitting Co.; Gun Shop, The; Hanus Birdguns, Bill; Lion Country Supply)
•Ultralux (Keng's Firearms Specialty, Inc.)
•Unique/M.A.P.F. (Nygord Precision Products)
Valtro USA Inc.
•Voere-KGH m.b.H. (JägerSport, Ltd.)
•Walther GmbH, Carl (Champion's Choice; Interarms; P.S.M.G. Gun Co.)
•Weatherby, Inc. (Weatherby, Inc.)
•Webley & Scott Ltd. (Beeman Precision Airguns; Groenewold, John)
•Weihrauch KG, Hermann (Beeman Precision Airguns; E.A.A. Corp.)
•Westley Richards & Co. (Westley Richards Agency USA)
Whiscombe (Pelaire Products)
•Wolf (J.R. Distributing)
•Zabala, Hermanos S.A. (American Arms, Inc.)
•Zanoletti, Pietro (Mandall Shooting Supplies, Inc.)
Zoli, Antonio

GUNS, U.S.-MADE

A.A. Arms, Inc.
•Accu-Tek
Acra-Bond Laminates
•Airrow
Allred Bullet Co.
•American Arms, Inc.

•American Derringer Corp.
American Frontier Firearms Co.
A.M.T.
Angel Arms Inc.
•ArmaLite, Inc.
Armscorp USA Inc.

A-Square Co., Inc.
Austin & Halleck
●Auto-Ordnance Corp.
●Baer Custom, Inc., Les
●Barrett Firearms Mfg., Inc.
Bar-Sto Precision Machine
●Beretta S.p.A., Pietro
●Beretta U.S.A. Corp.
Big Bear Arms & Sporting Goods, Inc.
●Bond Arms, Inc.
●Braverman Corp., R.J.
Brockman's Custom Gunsmithin
●Brolin Industries Inc.
●Brown Co., E. Arthur
Brown Products, Inc., Ed
●Browning Arms Co. (Parts & Service)
●Bushmaster Firearms
Calhoon Varmint Bullets, James
●Calico Light Weapon Systems
●Cape Outfitters
Casull Arms Corp.
●Century Gun Dist., Inc.
●Champlin Firearms, Inc.
●Colt's Mfg. Co., Inc.
●Competitor Corp., Inc.
Conetrol Scope Mounts
●Connecticut Shotgun Mfg. Co.
●Connecticut Valley Classics
Coonan Arms
Cooper Arms
Crossfire LLC
Cryo-Accurizing
●Cumberland Arms
Cumberland Mountain Arms
●CVA
●CVC
Daisy manufacturing
●Dakota Arms, Inc.
Dangler, Homer L.
●Davis Industries
●Dayton Traister
●Dixie Gun Works, Inc.
Downsizer Corp.
●Eagle Arms, Inc.
●Emerging Technologies, Inc.
●Essex Arms
E Arthur Brown Co
Ed's Gun House
Enterprise Arms Inc.
FN Herstal
●Forgett Jr., Valmore J.
Fort Worth Firearms
Frank Custom Classic Arms, Ron
●Freedom Arms, Inc.
Fulton Armory
Galazan
Genecco Gun Works, K.
Gentry Custom Gunmaker, David
●Gibbs Rifle Co., Inc.
●Gilbert Equipment Co., Inc.
●Gonic Arms, Inc.
Gunsite Custom Shop
Gunsite Gunsmithy
●H&R 1871, Inc.
●Harris Gunworks
Harrington & Richardson
●Hawken Shop, The
Heritage Firearms
Heritage Manufacturing, Inc.
Hesco-Meprolight
Hi-Point Firearms
●HJS Arms, Inc.
Hoenig, George
Holston Ent. Inc.
H-S Precision, Inc.
Hutton Rifle Ranch
IAR Inc.
Imperial Russian Armory
●Intratec
Ithaca Gun Co., LLC
Jones, J.D.
J.P. Enterprises, Inc.
J.P. Gunstocks Inc.
JS Worldwide DBA
●Kahr Arms

Kelbly, Inc.
●Kel-Tec CNC Industries, Inc.
●Kimber of America, Inc.
K.K. Arms Co.
●Knight's Mfg. Co.
LaFrance Specialties
●Lakefield Arms Ltd.
⋆L A R Mfg., Inc.
●Laseraim, Inc.
Lever Arms Service Ltd.
Ljutic Industries, Inc.
Lock's Philadelphia Gun Exchange
●Lorcin Engineering Co., Inc.
Madis, George
Mag-Na-Port International, Inc.
●Magnum Research, Inc.
Mandell Shooting Supply
●Marlin Firearms Co.
●Maverick Arms, Inc.
●McBros Rifle Co.
Miller Arms, Inc.
●MKS Supply, Inc.
M.O.A. Corp.
Montana Armory, Inc.
●Mossberg & Sons, Inc., O.F.
Mountain Rifles Inc.
MPI Stocks
New England Firearms
NCP Products, Inc.
●North American Arms, Inc.
North Star West
Nowlin Mfg. Co.
Nowling Gun Shop
October Country
Olympic Arms, Inc.
Oregon Arms, Inc.
Parker & Sons Gunsmithing
Phillips & Rogers, Inc.
●Phoenix Arms
Professional Ordnance, Inc.
Proware Inc.
●Quality Parts Co.
Raptor Arms Co., Inc.
●Remington Arms Co., Inc.
Republic Arms, Inc.
Rifle Works & Armory
●Rocky Mountain Arms, Inc.
Rogue Rifle Co., Inc.
Rogue River Rifleworks
RPM
Ruger
●Savage Arms (Canada), Inc.
Scattergun Technologies, Inc.
●Seecamp Co., Inc., L.W.
Sharps Arms Co., Inc., C.
Shepherd & Turpin Dist. Company
●Shiloh Rifle Mfg.
Small Arms Specialties
●Smith & Wesson
●Sporting Arms Mfg., Inc.
Springfield, Inc.
STI International
●Stoeger Industries
Sturm, Ruger & Co., Inc.
Sundance Industries, Inc.
Sunny Hill Enterprizes, Inc.
●Swivel Machine Works, Inc.
●Tar-Hunt Custom Rifles, Inc.
●Texas Armory
●Taurus Firearms, Inc.
●Thompson/Center Arms
Time Precision, Inc.
Tristar Sporting Arms, Ltd.
●Ultra Light Arms, Inc.
UFA, Inc.
U.S. Repeating Arms Co.
Wallace, Terry
●Weatherby, Inc.
Wescombe, Bill
Wesson Firearms Co., Inc.
Wesson Firearms, Dan
Whildin & Sons Ltd., E.H.
●Wildey, Inc.
●Wilkinson Arms
Z-M Weapons

HEARING PROTECTORS

Aero Peltor
Ajax Custom Grips, Inc.
Autauga Arms, Inc.
Brown Co., E. Arthur
Brown Products, Inc., Ed

Browning Arms Co.
Clark Co., Inc., David
E-A-R, Inc.
Electronic Shooters Protection, Inc.
Faith Associates, Inc.

Flents Products Co., Inc.
Gentex Corp.
Hoppe's Div.
Kesselring Gun Shop
North Specialty Products
Paterson Gunsmithing

Peltor, Inc.
Penguin Industries, Inc.
R.E.T. Enterprises
Rucker Dist. Inc.
Silencio/Safety Direct
Willson Safety Prods. Div.

STOCKS (Commercial and Custom)

Accuracy Unlimited (Glendale, AZ)
Ackerman & Co.
Acra-Bond Laminates
Ahlman Guns
Amrine's Gun Shop
Arms Ingenuity Co.
Arundel Arms & Ammunition, Inc., A.
Baelder, Harry
Bain & Davis, Inc.
Balickie, Joe
Bansner's Gunsmithing Specialties
Barnes Bullets, Inc.
Beitzinger, George
Belding's Custom Gun Shop
Bell & Carlson, Inc.
Benchmark Guns
Biesen, Al
Biesen, Roger
Billeb, Stephen L.
Billings Gunsmiths, Inc.
Black Powder Specialties
Bohemia Arms Co.
Blount, Inc., Sporting Equipment Div.
Boltin, John M.
Borden's Accuracy
Bowerly, Kent
Boyds' Gunstock Industries, Inc.
Brace, Larry D.
Brgoch, Frank
Briganti, A.J.
Broad Creek Rifle Works
Brockman's Custom Gunsmithin
Brown Co., E. Arthur
Brown Precision, Inc.
Buckhorn Gun Works
Bull Mountain Rifle Co.
Bullberry Barrel Works, Ltd.
Burkhart Gunsmithing, Don
Butler Creek Corp.
Calico Hardwoods, Inc.
Cape Outfitters
Camilli, Lou
Campbell, Dick
Carter's Gun Shop
Caywood, Shane J.
Chambers Flintlocks Ltd., Jim
Chicasaw Gun Works
Christman Jr., Gunmaker, David
Churchill, Winston
Claro Walnut Gunstock Co.
Clifton Arms, Inc.
Cloward's Gun Shop
Cochran, Oliver
Coffin, Charles H.
Coffin, Jim
Colonial Repair
Colorado Gunsmithing Academy
Colorado School of Trades
Conrad, C.A.
Creedmoor Sports, Inc.
Curly Maple Stock Blanks
Custom Checkering Service
Custom Gun Products
Custom Gun Stocks
Custom Riflestocks, Inc.
D&D Gunsmiths, Ltd.
D&G Presicion Duplicators
D&J Bullet Co. & Custom Gun Shop, Inc.
Dakota Arms Inc.
Dangler, Homer L.
D.D. Custom Stocks
de Treville & Co., Stan
Dever Co., Jack
Devereaux, R.H. "Dick"
DGR Custom Rifles
DGS, Inc.
Dillon, Ed
Dowtin Gunworks
Dressel Jr., Paul G.
Duane Custom Stocks, Randy
Duane's Gun Repair
Duncan's Gunworks, Inc.
Echols & Co., D'Arcy
Eggleston, Jere D.
Erhardt, Dennis

Eversull Co., Inc., K.
Fajen, Inc., Reinhart
Farmer-Dressel, Sharon
Fibron Products, Inc.
Fisher, Jerry A.
Flaig's
Folks, Donald E.
Forster, Kathy
Forster, Larry L.
Forthofer's Gunsmithing & Knifemaking
Francotte & Cie S.A., Auguste
Frank Custom Classic Arms, Ron
Game Haven Gunstocks
Gene's Custom Guns
Gervais, Mike
Gillmann, Edwin
Giron, Robert E.
Glaser Safety Slug Inc.
Goens, Dale W.
Golden Age Arms Co.
Gordie's Gun Shop
Goudy Classic Stocks, Gary
Grace, Charles E.
Great American Gun Co.
Green, Roger M.
Greene, M.L.
Greene Precision Duplicators
Greenwood Precision
Griffin & Howe, Inc.
Gun Shop, The
Guns
Gunsmithing Ltd.
Hallberg Gunsmith, Fritz
Halstead, Rick
Hamilton, Jim
Hanson's Gun Center, Dick
Harper's Custom Stocks
Harris Gunworks
Hart & Son, Inc., Robert W.
Harwood, Jack O.
Hastings Barrels
Hecht, Hubert J.
Heilmann, Stephen
Hensley Gunmaker, Darwin
Heppler, Keith M.
Heydenberk, Warren R.
High Tech Specialties, Inc.
Hillmer Custom Gunstocks, Paul D.
Hines Co., S.C.
Hiptmayer, Armurier
Hiptmayer, Klaus
Hoelscher, Virgil
Hoenig & Rodman
H-S Precision, Inc.
Huebner, Corey O.
Hughes, Steven Dodd
Ide, Kenneth G.
Island Pond Gun Shop
Ivanoff, Thomas G.
Jackalope Gun Shop
Jaeger, Inc., Paul/Dunn's
Jamison's Forge Works
Jarrett Rifles, Inc.
Johnson Wood Products
J.P. Gunstocks, Inc.
KDF, Inc.
Keith's Custom Gunstocks
Kelbly, Inc.
Ken's Rifle Blanks
Kilham & Co.
Kimber
Klein Custom Guns, Don
Klingler Woodcarving
Knippel, Richard
Kokolus, Michael M.
Lawson Co., Harry
Lind Custom Guns, Al
Lynn's Custom Gunstocks
Lyons Gunworks, Larry
Mac's .45 Shop
Marple & Associates, Dick
Masen Co., Inc., John
Mazur Restoration, Pete
McBros Rifle Co.
McCann's Muzzle-Gun Works

McCament, Jay
McCullough, Ken
McDonald, Dennis
McFarland, Stan
McGowen Rifle Barrels
McGuire, Bill
McKinney, R.P.
McMillan Fiberglass Stocks, Inc.
Mercer Custom Stocks, R.M.
Michaels of Oregon Co.
Mid-America Recreation, Inc.
Miller Arms, Inc.
Morrison Custom Rifles, J.W.
MPI Fiberglass Stocks
MWG Co.
NCP Products, Inc.
Nelson, Stephen
Nettestad Gun Works
New England Arms Co.
New England Custom Gun Service
Newman Gunshop
Nickels, Paul R.
Norman Custom Gunstocks, Jim
Oakland Custom Arms, Inc.
Oil Rod and Gun Shop
OK Weber, Inc.
Old World Gunsmithing
One Of A Kind
Or-ön
Orvis Co., The
Ottmar, Maurice
P&S Gun Service
Pacific Research Laboratories, Inc.
Pagel Gun Works, Inc.
Paragon Sales & Serv
Paulsen Gunstocks
Pecatonica River Longrifle
PEM's Mfg. Co.
Perazone, Brian
Perazzi USA, Inc.
Pohl, Henry A.
Powell & Son (Gunmakers) Ltd.,
    William
R&J Gun Shop
Ram-Line Blount, Inc.
Rampart International
Reagent Chemical and Research, Inc.
Reiswig, Wallace E.
Richards Micro-Fit Stocks
Rimrock Rifle Stocks
RMS Custom Gunsmithing
Robinson, Don
Robinson Firearms Mfg. Ltd.
Rogers Gunsmithing, Bob
Roto Carve
Royal Arms Gunstocks
Ryan, Chad L.
Sanders Custom Gun Service
Saville Iron Co.

Schiffman, Curt
Schiffman, Mike
Schiffman, Norman
Schumakers Gun Shop
Schwartz Custom Guns, David W.
Schwartz Custom Guns, Wayne E.
Score High Gunsmithing
Shell Shack
Sile Distributors, Inc.
Simmons Gun Repair, Inc.
Six Enterprises
Skeoch, Brian R.
Smith, Sharmon
Speiser, Fred D.
Stiles Custom Guns
Storey, Dale A.
Stott's Creek Armory, Inc.
Strawbridge, Victor W.
Sturgeon Valley Sporters
Swan, D.J.
Swift River Gunworks
Szweda, Robert
Talmage, William G.
Taylor & Robbins
Tecnolegno S.p.A.
T.F.C. S.p.A.
Thompson/Center Arms
Tiger-Hunt
Tirelli
Tom's Gun Repair
Track of the Wolf, Inc.
Trevallion Gunstocks
Tucker, James C.
Turkish Firearms Corp.
Tuttle, Dale
Vest, John
Vic's Gun Refinishing
Vintage Industries, Inc.
Volquartsen Custom Ltd.
Von Minden Gunsmithing Services
Walker Arms Co., Inc.
Walnut Factory, The
Weber & Markin Custom Gunsmiths
Weems, Cecil
Wells Custom Gunsmith, R.A.
Wells, Fred F.
Wenig Custom Gunstocks, Inc.
Werth, T.W.
Wessinger Custom Guns & Engraving
Western Gunstock Mfg. Co.
Williams Gun Sight Co.
Williamson Precision Gunsmithing
Windish, Jim
Winter, Robert M.
Working Guns
Wright's Hardwood Gunstock Blanks
Yee, Mike
Zeeryp, Russ

TARGETS, BULLET AND CLAYBIRD TRAPS

Action Target, Inc.
American Target
American Whitetail Target Systems
A-Tech Corp.
Autauga Arms, Inc.
Beomat of America Inc.
Birchwood Casey
Blount, Inc., Sporting Equipment Div.
Blue and Gray Products, Inc.
Brown Manufacturing
Bull-X, Inc.
Caswell International Corp.
Champion Target Co.
Dapkus Co., Inc., J.G.
Datumtech Corp.
Dayson Arms Ltd.
D.C.C. Enterprises
Detroit-Armor Corp.
Diamond Mfg. Co.
Estate Cartridge, Inc.
Federal Champion Target Co.
Freeman Animal Targets
G.H. Enterprises Ltd.
Gozan Corp.
Hiti-Schuch, Atelier Wilma
H-S Precision, Inc.
Hunterjohn
Innovision Enterprises
Kennebec Journal
Kleen-Bore, Inc.
Lakefield Arms Ltd.
Littler Sales Co.
Lyman Instant Targets, Inc.

Lyman Products Corp.
M&D Munitions Ltd.
Mendez, John A.
MSR Targets
National Target Co.
N.B.B., Inc.
North American Shooting Systems
Nu-Teck
Outers Laboratories, Div. of Blount
Ox-Yoke Originals, Inc.
Passive Bullet Traps, Inc.
PlumFire Press, Inc.
Quack Decoy & Sporting Clays
Redfield, Inc.
Remington Arms Co., Inc.
Rockwood Corp., Speedwell Div.
Rocky Mountain Target Co.
Savage Arms (Canada), Inc.
Savage Range Systems, Inc.
Schaefer Shooting Sports
Seligman Shooting Products
Shooters Supply
Shoot-N-C Targets
Thompson Target Technology
Trius Products, Inc.
White Flyer Targets
World of Targets
X-Spand Target Systems
Z's Metal Targets & Frames
Zriny's Metal Targets

TRAP AND SKEET SHOOTER'S EQUIPMENT

Allen Co., Bob
Allen Sportswear, Bob
Bagmaster Mfg., Inc.
Baker, Stan
Beomat of America Inc.
Beretta S.p.A., Pietro
Cape Outfitters
Clymer Manufacturing Co., Inc.
Crane & Crane Ltd.
Dayson Arms Ltd.
Estate Cartridge, Inc.
F&A Inc.
Fiocchi of America, Inc.
Game Winner Inc,
G.H. Enterprises Ltd.
Hastings Barrels
Hillmer Custom Gunstocks, Paul D.
Hoppe's Div.
Hunter Co., Inc.
Jenkins Recoil Pads Inc
K&T Co.
Kalispel Case Line
Lakewood Products, LLC
Lynn's Custom Gunstocks
Mag-Na-Port International, Inc.
Maionchi-L.M.I.
Meadow Industries
MEC Inc.
Moneymaker Guncraft Corp.
MTM Molded Products Co., Inc.
NCP Products, Inc.
Noble Co., Jim
Pachmayr LTD
PAST Sporting Goods, Inc.
Penguin Industries, Inc.
Perazzi USA, Inc.
Pro-Port Ltd.
Protektor Model
Quack Decoy & Sporting Clays
Remington Arms Co., Inc.
Rhodeside, Inc.
Shootin' Accessories, Ltd.
Shooting Specialties
ShurKatch Corporation
Titus, Daniel
Trius Products, Inc.
Warne Manufacturing
X-Spand Target Systems

A

A&B Industries, Inc. (See Top-Line USA, Inc.)

A&J Products, Inc., 5791 Hall Rd., Muskegon, MI 49442-1964

A&M Waterfowl, Inc., P.O. Box 102, Ripley, TN 38063/901-635-4003; FAX: 901-635-2320

A&W Repair, 2930 Schneider Dr., Arnold, MO 63010/314-287-3725

A.A. Arms, Inc., 4811 Persimmont Ct., Monroe, NC 28110/704-289-5356, 800-935-1119; FAX: 704-289-5859

A.B.S. III, 9238 St. Morritz Dr., Fern Creek, KY 40291

AC Dyna-tite Corp., 155 Kelly St., P.O. Box 0984, Elk Grove Village, IL 60007/847-593-5566; FAX: 847-593-1304

Acadian Ballistic Specialties, P.O. Box 61, Covington, LA 70434

Acculube II, Inc., 4366 Shackleford Rd., Norcross, GA 30093-2912

Accupro Gun Care, 15512-109 Ave., Surrey, BC U3R 7E8, CANADA/604-583-7807

Accuracy Den, The, 25 Bitterbrush Rd., Reno, NV 89523/702-345-0225

Accuracy Innovations, Inc., P.O. Box 376, New Paris, PA 15554/814-839-4517; FAX: 814-839-2601

Accuracy International, 9115 Trooper Trail, P.O. Box 2019, Bozeman, MT 59715/406-587-7922; FAX: 406-585-9434

Accuracy International Precision Rifles (See U.S. importer—Gunsite Custom Shop; Gunsite Training Center)

Accuracy Unlimited, 7479 S. DePew St., Littleton, CO 80123

Accuracy Unlimited, 16036 N. 49 Ave., Glendale, AZ 85306/602-978-9089; FAX: 602-978-9089

Accura-Site (See All's, The Jim Tembelis Co., Inc.)

Accurate Arms Co., Inc., 5891 Hwy. 230 West, McEwen, TN 37101/931-729-4207, 800-416-3006; FAX 931-729-4211

Accurate Bullet Co., 159 Creek Road, Glen Mills, PA 19342/610-399-6584

Accuright, RR 2 Box 397, Sebeka, MN 56477/218-472-3383

Accu-Tek, 4510 Carter Ct., Chino, CA 91710/909-627-2404; FAX: 909-627-7817

Ace Custom 45's, Inc., 18801/2 Upper Turtle Creek Rd., Kerrville, TX 78028/210-257-4290; FAX: 210-257-5724

Ace Sportswear, Inc., 700 Quality Rd., Fayetteville, NC 28306/919-323-1223; FAX: 919-323-5392

Ackerman & Co., 16 Cortez St., Westfield, MA 01085/413-568-8008

Ackerman, Bill (See Optical Services Co.)

Acra-Bond Laminates, 134 Zimmerman Rd, Kalispell, MT 59901/406-257-9003; FAX 406-257-9003

Action Bullets, Inc., RR 1, P.O. Box 189, Quinter, KS 67752/913-754-3609; FAX: 913-754-3629

Action Direct, Inc., P.O. Box 830760, Miami, FL 33283/305-559-4652; FAX: 305-559-4652

Action Products, Inc., 22 N. Mulberry St., Hagerstown, MD 21740/301-797-1414; FAX: 301-733-2073

Action Target, Inc., P.O. Box 636, Provo, UT 84603/801-377-8033; FAX: 801-377-8096

Actions by "T," Teddy Jacobson, 16315 Redwood Forest Ct., Sugar Land, TX 77478/281-277-4008; WEB www.actionsbyt.com

ACTIV Industries, Inc., 1000 Zigor Rd., P.O. Box 339, Kearneysville, WV 25430/304-725-0451; FAX: 304-725-2080

AcuSport Corporation, 1 Hunter Place, Bellefontaine, OH 43311-3001/513-593-7010; FAX: 513-592-5625

Ad Hominem, 3130 Gun Club Lane, RR Orillia, Ont. L3V 6H3, CANADA/705-689-5303; FAX: 705-689-5303

Adair Custom Shop, Bill, 2886 Westridge, Carrollton, TX 75006

Adams & Son Engravers, John J., 87 Acorn Rd., Dennis, MA 02638/508-385-7971

Adams Jr., John J., 87 Acorn Rd., Dennis, MA 02638/508-385-7971

ADCO Sales Inc., 10 Cedar St., Unit 17, Woburn, MA 01801/617-935-1799; FAX: 617-935-1011

Adkins, Luther, 1292 E. McKay Rd., Shelbyville, IN 46176-9353/317-392-3795

Advance Car Mover Co., Rowell Div., P.O. Box 1, 240 N. Depot St., Juneau, WI 53039/414-386-4464; FAX: 414-386-4416

Adventure 16, 4620 Alvarado Canyon Rd., San Diego, CA 92120/619-283-6314

Adventure Game Calls, R.D. 1, Leonard Rd., Spencer, NY 14883/607-589-4611

Adventurer's Outpost, P.O. Box 70, Cottonwood, AZ 86326/800-762-7471; FAX: 602-634-8781

Aero Peltor, 90 Mechanic St., Southbridge, MA 01550/508-764-5500; FAX: 508-764-0188

African Import Co., 20 Braunecker Rd., Plymouth, MA 02360/508-746-8552

AFSCO Ammunition, 731 W. Third St., P.O. Box L, Owen, WI 54460/715-229-2516

Ahlman Guns, 9525 W. 230th St., Morristown, MN 55052/507-685-4243; FAX: 507-685-4280

Ahrends, Kim, Custom Firearms, Inc., Box 203, Clarion, IA 50525/515-532-3449; FAX: 515-532-3926

Aimpoint U.S.A, 420 W. Main St., Geneseo, IL 61254/309-944-1702

Aimtech Mount Systems, P.O. Box 223, 101 Inwood Acres, Thomasville, GA 31799/912-226-4313; FAX: 912-227-0222

Air Arms, Hailsham Industrial Park, Diplocks Way, Hailsham, E. Sussex, BN27 3JF ENGLAND/011-0323-845853 (U.S. importers—World Class Airguns)

Air Rifle Specialists, P.O. Box 138, 130 Holden Rd., Pine City, NY 14871-0138/607-734-7340; FAX: 607-733-3261

Air Venture Airguns, 9752 E. Flower St., Bellflower, CA 90706/562-867-6355

Airgun Repair Centre, 3227 Garden Meadows, Lawrenceburg, IN 47025/812-637-1463; FAX: 812-637-1463

Airrow (See Swivel Machine Works, Inc.)

Aitor-Cuchilleria Del Norte, S.A., Izelaieta, 17, 48260 Ermua (Vizcaya), SPAIN/43-17-08-50; FAX: 43-17-00-01

Ajax Custom Grips, Inc., 9130 Viscount Row, Dallas, TX 75247/214-630-8893; FAX: 214-630-4942; WEB: http://www.ajaxgrips.com

A.K.'s Gun Shop, 3221 2nd Ave. N., Great Falls, MT 59401/406-454-1831

Aker International, Inc., 2248 Main St., Suite 6, Chula Vista, CA 91911/619-423-5182; FAX: 619-423-1363

Alaska Bullet Works, Inc., 9978 Crazy Horse Drive, Juneau, AK 99801/907-789-3834; FAX: 907-789-3433

Alcas Cutlery Corp. (See Cutco Cutlery)

Alco Carrying Cases, 601 W. 26th St., New York, NY 10001/212-675-5820; FAX: 212-691-5935

Aldis Gunsmithing & Shooting Supply, 502 S. Montezuma St., Prescott, AZ 86303/602-445-6723; FAX: 602-445-6763

Alessi Holsters, Inc., 2465 Niagara Falls Blvd., Amherst, NY 14228-3527/716-691-5615

Alex, Inc., Box 3034, Bozeman, MT 59772/406-282-7396; FAX: 406-282-7396

Alfano, Sam, 36180 Henry Gaines Rd., Pearl River, LA 70452/504-863-3364; FAX: 504-863-7715

All American Lead Shot Corp., P.O. Box 224566, Dallas, TX 75062

All Rite Products, Inc., 5752 N. Silverstone Circle, Mountain Green, UT 84050/801-876-3330; 801-876-2216

All's, The Jim J. Tembelis Co., Inc., P.O. Box 108, Winnebago, WI 54985-0108/414-725-5251; FAX: 414-725-5251

Allard, Gary, Creek Side Metal & Woodcrafters, Fishers Hill, VA 22626/703-465-3903

Allen Co., Bob, 214 SW Jackson, P.O. Box 477, Des Moines, IA 50315/515-283-2191; 800-685-7020; FAX: 515-283-0779

Allen Co., Inc., 525 Burbank St., Broomfield, CO 80020/303-469-1857, 800-876-8600; FAX: 303-466-7437

Allen Firearm Engraving, 339 Grove Ave., Prescott, AZ 86301/520-778-1237

Allen Mfg., 6449 Hodgson Rd., Circle Pines, MN 55014/612-429-8231

Allen Sportswear, Bob (See Allen Co., Bob)

Alley Supply Co., P.O. Box 848, Gardnerville, NV 89410/702-782-3800

Alliant Techsystems, Smokeless Powder Group, 200 Valley Rd., Suite 305, Mt. Arlington, NJ 07856/800-276-9337; FAX: 201-770-2528

Allred Bullet Co., 932 Evergreen Drive, Logan, UT 84321/801-752-6983; FAX: 801-752-6983

Alpec Team, Inc., 201 Ricken Backer Cir., Livermore, CA 94550/510-606-8245; FAX: 510-606-4279

Alpha 1 Drop Zone, 2121 N. Tyler, Wichita, KS 67212/316-729-0800

Alpha Gunsmith Division, 1629 Via Monserate, Fallbrook, CA 92028/619-723-9279, 619-728-2663

Alpha LaFranck Enterprises, P.O. Box 81072, Lincoln, NE 68501/402-466-3193

Alpha Precision, Inc., 2765-B Preston Rd. NE, Good Hope, GA 30641/770-267-6163

Alpine's Precision Gunsmithing & Indoor Shooting Range, 2401 Government Way, Coeur d'Alene, ID 83814/208-765-3559; FAX: 208-765-3559

Altamont Co., 901 N. Church St., P.O. Box 309, Thomasboro, IL 61878/217-643-3125, 800-626-5774; FAX: 217-643-7973

Alumna Sport by Dee Zee, 1572 NE 58th Ave., P.O. Box 3090, Des Moines, IA 50316/800-798-9899

AmBr Software Group Ltd., P.O. Box 301, Reistertown, MD 21136-0301/800-888-1917; FAX: 410-526-7212

American Ammunition, 3545 NW 71st St., Miami, FL 33147/305-835-7400; FAX: 305-694-0037

American Arms, Inc., 715 Armour Rd., N. Kansas City, MO 64116/816-474-3161; FAX: 816-474-1225

American Derringer Corp., 127 N. Lacy Dr., Waco, TX 76705/800-642-7817, 817-799-9111; FAX: 817-799-7935

American Display Co., 55 Cromwell St., Providence, RI 02907/401-331-2464; FAX: 401-421-1264

American Frontier Firearms Mfg. Inc., P.O. 744, Aguanga, CA 92536/909-763-0014; FAX: 909-763-0014

American Gas & Chemical Co., Ltd., 220 Pegasus Ave., Northvale, NJ 07647/201-767-7300

American Gripcraft, 3230 S. Dodge 2, Tucson, AZ 85713/602-790-1222

American Gunsmithing Institute, 1325 Imola Ave., #504, Napa, CA 94559/707-253-0462; FAX: 707-253-7149

American Handgunner Magazine, 591 Camino de la Reina, Suite 200, San Diego, CA 92108/619-297-5350; FAX: 619-297-5353

American Pioneer Video, P.O. Box 50049, Bowling Green, KY 42102-2649/800-743-4675

American Products Inc., 14729 Spring Valley Road, Morrison, IL 61270/815-772-3336; FAX: 815-772-8046

American Safe Arms, Inc., 1240 Riverview Dr., Garland, UT 84312/801-257-7472; FAX: 801-785-8156

American Sales & Mfg Co., P.O. Box 677, Laredo, TX 78042/210-723-6893; FAX: 210-725-0672

American Security Products Co., 11925 Pacific Ave., Fontana, CA 92337/909-685-9680, 800-421-6142; FAX: 909-685-9685

American Small Arms Academy, P.O. Box 12111, Prescott, AZ 86304/602-778-5623

American Target, 1328 S. Jason St., Denver, CO 80223/303-733-0433; FAX: 303-777-0311

American Target Knives, 1030 Brownwood NW, Grand Rapids, MI 49504/616-453-1998

American Whitetail Target Systems, P.O. Box 41, 106 S. Church St., Tennyson, IN 47637/812-567-4527

Americase, P.O. Box 271, 1610 E. Main, Waxahachie, TX 75165/800-880-3629; FAX: 214-937-8373

Ames Metal Products, 4323 S. Western Blvd., Chicago, IL 60609/773-523-3230; FAX: 773-523-3854

Amherst Arms, P.O. Box 1457, Englewood, FL 34295/941-475-2020; FAX: 941-473-1212

Amrine's Gun Shop, 937 La Luna, Ojai, CA 93023/805-646-2376

Amsec, 11925 Pacific Ave., Fontana, CA 92337

A.M.T., 6226 Santos Diaz St., Irwindale, CA 91702/818-334-6629; FAX: 818-969-5247

Amtec 2000, Inc., 84 Industrial Rowe, Gardner, MA 01440/508-632-9608; FAX: 508-632-2300

Analog Devices, Box 9106, Norwood, MA 02062

Andela Tool & Machine, Inc., RD3, Box 246, Richfield Springs, NY 13439

Andres & Dworsky, Bergstrasse 18, A-3822 Karlstein, Thaya, Austria, EUROPE, 0 28 44-285

Angel Arms, Inc., 1825 Addison Way, Haywood, CA 94545/510-783-7122

Angelo & Little Custom Gun Stock Blanks, P.O. Box 240046, Dell, MT 59724-0046

Anschutz GmbH, Postfach 1128, D-89001 Ulm, Donau, GERMANY (U.S. importers—Accuracy International; AcuSport Corporation; Champion Shooters' Supply; Champion's Choice; Gunsmithing, Inc.)

Ansen Enterprises, Inc., 1506 W. 228th St., Torrance, CA 90501-5105/310-534-1837; FAX: 310-534-3162

Answer Products Co., 1519 Westbury Drive, Davison, MI 48423/810-653-2911

Anthony and George Ltd., Rt. 1, P.O. Box 45, Evington, VA 24550/804-821-8117

Antique American Firearms (See Carlson, Douglas R.)

Antique Arms Co., 1110 Cleveland Ave., Monett, MO 65708/417-235-6501

AO Safety Products, Div. of American Optical Corp. (See E-A-R, Inc., Div. of Cabot Safety Corp.

Apel GmbH, Ernst, Am Kirschberg 3, D-97218 Gerbrunn, GERMANY/0 (931) 707192

Aplan Antiques & Art, James O., HC 80, Box 793-25, Piedmont, SD 57769/605-347-5016

Arcadia Machine & Tool, Inc. (See AMT)

Arco Powder, HC-Rt. 1, P.O. Box 102, County Rd. 357, Mayo, FL 32066/904-294-3882; FAX: 904-294-1498

Aristocrat Knives, 1701 W. Wernsing Ave., Effingham, IL 62401/800-953-3436; FAX: 217-347-3083

Arizaga (See U.S. importer—Mandall Shooting Supplies, Inc.)

Arizona Ammunition, Inc., 21421 No. 14th Ave., Suite E, Phoenix, AZ 85727/602-516-9004; FAX: 602-516-9012

Arkansas Mallard Duck Calls, Rt. Box 182, England, AR 72046/501-842-3597

Arkfeld Mfg. & Dist. Co., Inc., 1230 Monroe Ave., Norfolk, NE 68702-0054/402-371-9430; 800-533-0676

ArmaLite, Inc., P.O. Box 299, Geneseo, IL 61254/309-944-6939; FAX: 309-944-6949

Armament Gunsmithing Co., Inc., 525 Rt. 22, Hillside, NJ 07205/908-686-0960

Armas Kemen S.A. (See U.S. importers—Kemen America; USA Sporting)

Armfield Custom Bullets, 4775 Caroline Drive, San Diego, CA 92115/619-582-7188; FAX: 619-287-3238

Armi Perazzi S.p.A., Via Fontanelle 1/3, 1-25080 Botticino Mattina, ITALY/030-2692591; FAX: 030 2692594 (U.S. importer—Perazzi USA, Inc.)

Armi San Marco (See U.S. importers—Taylor's & Co., Inc.; Cimarron Arms; IAR, Inc.)

Armi San Paolo, via Europa 172-A, I-25062 Concesio, 030-2751725 (BS) ITALY

Armi Sport (See U.S. importers—Cape Outfitters; Taylor's & Co., Inc.)

Armite Laboratories, 1845 Randolph St., Los Angeles, CA 90001/213-587-7768; FAX: 213-587-5075

Armoloy Co. of Ft. Worth, 204 E. Daggett St., Fort Worth, TX 76104/817-332-5604; FAX: 817-335-6517

Armor (See Buck Stop Lure Co., Inc.)

Armor Metal Products, P.O. Box 4609, Helena, MT 59604/406-442-5560; FAX: 406-442-5650

Armory Publications, Inc., 2615 N. 4th St., No. 620, Coeur d'Alene, ID 83814-3781/208-664-5061; FAX: 208-664-9906

Armoury, Inc., The, Rt. 202, Box 2340, New Preston, CT 06777/860-868-0001; FAX: 860-868-2919

A.R.M.S., Inc., 230 W. Center St., West Bridgewater, MA 02379-1620/508-584-7816; FAX: 508-588-8045

Arms & Armour Press, Wellington House, 125 Strand, London WC2R 0BB ENGLAND/0171-420-5555; FAX: 0171-240-7265

Arms Corporation of the Philippines, Bo. Parang Marikina, Metro Manila, PHILIPPINES/632-941-6243, 632-941-6244; FAX: 632-942-0682

Arms Craft Gunsmithing, 1106 Linda Dr., Arroyo Grande, CA 93420/805-481-2830

Arms Ingenuity Co., P.O. Box 1, 51 Canal St., Weatogue, CT 06089/203-658-5624

Arms, Programming Solutions (See Arms Software)

Arms Software, 4851 SW Madrona St., Lake Oswego, OR 97035/800-366-5559; FAX: 503-697-3337

Armscorp USA, Inc., 4424 John Ave., Baltimore, MD 21227/410-247-6200; FAX: 410-247-6205

Armsport, Inc., 3950 NW 49th St., Miami, FL 33142/305-635-7850; FAX: 305-633-2877

Arnold Arms Co., Inc., P.O. Box 1011, Arlington, WA 98223/800-371-1011, 360-435-1011; FAX: 360-435-7304

Aro-Tek, Ltd., 206 Frontage Rd. North, Suite C, Pacific, WA 98047/206-351-2984; FAX: 206-833-4483

Arratoonian, Andy (See Horseshoe Leather Products)

Arrieta, S.L., Morkaiko, 5, 20870 Elgoibar, SPAIN/34-43-743150; FAX: 34-43-743154 (U.S. importers—Griffin & Howe; Jansma, Jack J.; New England Arms Co.; The Orvis Co., Inc.; Quality Arms, Inc.; Wingshooting Adventures)

Art Jewel Enterprises Ltd., Eagle Business Ctr., 460 Randy Rd., Carol Stream, IL 60188/708-260-0400

Art's Gun & Sport Shop, Inc., 6008 Hwy. Y, Hillsboro, MO 63050

Artistry in Leather (See Stuart, V. Pat)

Arundel Arms & Ammunition, Inc., A., 24A Defense St., Annapolis, MD 21401/410-224-8683

Ashby Turkey Calls, P.O. Box 1466, Ava, MO 65608-1466/417-967-3787

A-Square Co., Inc., One Industrial Park, Bedford, KY 40006-9667/502-255-7456; FAX: 502-255-7657

Astra Sport, S.A., Apartado 3, 48300 Guernica, Espagne, SPAIN/34-4-6250100; FAX: 34-4-6255186 (U.S. importer—E.A.A. Corp.; P.S.M.G. Gun Co.)

Atamec-Bretton, 19, rue Victor Grignard, F-42026 St.-Etienne (Cedex 1) FRANCE/77-93-54-69; FAX: 33-77-93-57-98 (U.S. importer—Mandall Shooting Supplies, Inc.)

A-Tech Corp., P.O. Box 1281, Cottage Grove, OR 97424

Atlanta Cutlery Corp., 2143 Gees Mill Rd., Box 839 CIS, Conyers, GA 30207/800-883-0300; FAX: 404-388-0246

Atlantic Mills, Inc., 1295 Towbin Ave., Lakewood, NJ 08701-5934/800-242-7374

Atlantic Research Marketing Systems (See A.R.M.S., Inc.)

Atlantic Rose, Inc., P.O. Box 1305, Union, NJ 07083

Atsko/Sno-Seal, Inc., 2530 Russell SE, Orangeburg, SC 29115/803-531-1820; FAX: 803-531-2139

Audette, Creighton, 19 Highland Circle, Springfield, VT 05156/802-885-2331

Austin & Halleck, 1099 Welt, Weston, MO 64098/816-386-2176; FAX: 816-386-2177

Austin's Calls, Bill, Box 284, Kaycee, WY 82639/307-738-2552

Autauga Arms, Inc., Pratt Plaza Mall No. 13, Prattville, AL 36067/800-262-9563; FAX: 334-361-2961

Auto Arms, 738 Clearview, San Antonio, TX 78228/512-434-5450

Automatic Equipment Sales, 627 E. Railroad Ave., Salesburg, MD 21801

Auto-Ordnance Corp., Williams Lane, West Hurley, NY 12491/914-679-4190

Autumn Sales, Inc. (Blaser), 1320 Lake St., Fort Worth, TX 76102/817-335-1634; FAX: 817-338-0119

AWC Systems Technology, P.O. Box 41938, Phoenix, AZ 85080-1938/602-780-1050

AYA (See U.S. importer—New England Custom Gun Service)

A Zone Bullets, 2039 Walter Rd., Billings, MT 59105/800-252-3111; 406-248-1961

Aztec International Ltd., P.O. Box 2616, Clarkesville, GA 30523/706-754-8282; FAX: 706-754-6889

B

B&D Trading Co., Inc., 3935 Fair Hill Rd., Fair Oaks, CA 95628/800-334-3790, 916-967-9366; FAX: 916-967-4873

B&G Bullets (See Northside Gun Shop)

Badger Shooters Supply, Inc., P.O. Box 397, Owen, WI 54460/800-424-9069; FAX: 715-229-2332

Baekgaard Ltd., 1855 Janke Dr., Northbrook, IL 60062/708-498-3040; FAX: 708-493-3106

Baelder, Harry, Alte Goennebeker Strasse 5, 24635 Rickling, GERMANY/04328-722732; FAX: 04328-722733

Baer Custom, Les, Inc., 29601 34th Ave., Hillsdale, IL 61257/309-658-2716; FAX: 309-658-2610

Baer's Hollows, P.O. Box 284, Eads, CO 81036/719-438-5718

Bagmaster Mfg., Inc., 2731 Sutton Ave., St. Louis, MO 63143/314-781-8002; FAX: 314-781-3363; WEB: http://www.bagmaster.com

Bain & Davis, Inc., 307 E. Valley Blvd., San Gabriel, CA 91776-3522/818-573-4241, 213-283-7449

Baker, Stan, 10,000 Lake City Way, Seattle, WA 98125/206-522-4575

Baker's Leather Goods, Roy, P.O. Box 893, Magnolia, AR 71753/501-234-0344

Balaance Co., 340-39 Ave. S.E. Box 505, Calgary, AB, T2G 1X6 CANADA

Bald Eagle Precision Machine Co., 101-A Allison St., Lock Haven, PA 17745/717-748-6772; FAX: 717-748-4443

Balickie, Joe, 408 Trelawney Lane, Apex, NC 27502/919-362-5185

Balland Rifle & Cartridge Co. LLC, 113 W Yellowstone Ave., Cody WY 82414/307-587-4914; FAX: 307-527-6097

Ballard Built, P.O. Box 1443, Kingsville, TX 78364/512-592-0853

Ballard Industries, 10271 Lockwood Dr., Suite B, Cupertino, CA 95014/408-996-0957; FAX: 408-257-6828

Ballistic Engineering & Software, Inc., 185 N. Park Blvd., Suite 330, Lake Orion, MI 48362/313-391-1074

Ballistic Products, Inc., 20015 75th Ave. North, Corcoran, MN 55340-9456/612-494-9237; FAX: 612-494-9236

Ballistic Program Co., Inc., The, 2417 N. Patterson St., Thomasville, GA 31792/912-228-5739, 800-368-0835

Ballistic Research, 1108 W. May Ave., McHenry, IL 60050/815-385-0037

Bandcor Industries, Div. of Man-Sew Corp., 6108 Sherwin Dr., Port Richey, FL 34668/813-848-0432

Bang-Bang Boutique (See Holster Shop, The)

Banks, Ed, 2762 Hwy. 41 N., Ft. Valley, GA 31030/912-987-4665

Bansner's Gunsmithing Specialties, 261 East Main St. Box VH, Adamstown, PA 19501/800-368-2379; FAX: 717-484-0523

Barami Corp., 6689 Orchard Lake Rd. No. 148, West Bloomfield, MI 48322/248-738-0462; FAX: 248-738-2542

Barbour, Inc., 55 Meadowbrook Dr., Milford, NH 03055/603-673-1313; FAX: 603-673-6510

Barnes Bullets, Inc., P.O. Box 215, American Fork, UT 84003/801-756-4222, 800-574-9200; FAX: 801-756-2465; WEB: http://www.itsnet.com/home/bbullets

Baron Technology, 62 Spring Hill Rd., Trumbull, CT 06611/203-452-0515; FAX: 203-452-0663

Barraclough, John K., 55 Merit Park Dr., Gardena, CA 90247/310-324-2574

Barramundi Corp., P.O. Drawer 4259, Homosassa Springs, FL 32687/904-628-0200

Barrett Firearms Manufacturer, Inc., P.O. Box 1077, Murfreesboro, TN 37133/615-896-2938; FAX: 615-896-7313

Barsotti, Bruce (See River Road Sporting Clays)

Bar-Sto Precision Machine, 73377 Sullivan Rd., P.O. Box 1838, Twentynine Palms, CA 92277/619-367-2747; FAX: 619-367-2407

Barta's Gunsmithing, 10231 US Hwy. 10, Cato, WI 54206/414-732-4472

Barteaux Machete, 1916 SE 50th Ave., Portland, OR 97215-3238/503-233-5880

Bartlett Engineering, 40 South 200 East, Smithfield, UT 84335-1645/801-563-5910

Basics Information Systems, Inc., 1141 Georgia Ave., Suite 515, Wheaton, MD 20902/301-949-1070; FAX: 301-949-5326

Bates Engraving, Billy, 2302 Winthrop Dr., Decatur, AL 35603/256-355-3690

Bauer, Eddie, 15010 NE 36th St., Redmond, WA 98052

Baumgartner Bullets, 3011 S. Alane St., W. Valley City, UT 84120

Bausch & Lomb Sports Optics Div. (See Bushnell Sports Optics Worldwide)

Bauska Barrels, 105 9th Ave. W., Kalispell, MT 59901/406-752-7706

Bear Archery, RR 4, 4600 Southwest 41st Blvd., Gainesville, FL 32601/904-376-2327

Bear Arms, 121 Rhodes St., Jackson, SC 29831/803-471-9859

Bear Hug Grips, Inc., P.O. Box 16649, Colorado Springs, CO 80935-6649/800-232-7710

Bear Mountain Gun & Tool, 120 N. Plymouth, New Plymouth, ID 83655/208-278-5221; FAX: 208-278-5221

Beartooth Bullets, P.O. Box 491, Dept. HLD, Dover, ID 83825-0491/208-448-1865

Beauchamp & Son, Inc., 160 Rossiter Rd., P.O. Box 181, Richmond, MA 01254/413-698-3822; FAX: 413-698-3866

Beaver Lodge (See Fellowes, Ted)

Beaver Park Products, Inc., 840 J St., Penrose, CO 81240/719-372-6744

BEC, Inc., 1227 W. Valley Blvd., Suite 204, Alhambra, CA 91803/818-281-5751; FAX:818-293-7073

Beeline Custom Bullets Limited, P.O. Box 85, Yarmouth, Nova Scotia CANADA B5A 4B1/902-648-3494; FAX: 902-648-0253

Beeman Precision Airguns, 5454 Argosy Dr., Huntington Beach, CA 92649/714-890-4800; FAX: 714-890-4808

Behlert Precision, Inc., P.O. Box 288, 7067 Easton Rd., Pipersville, PA 18947/215-766-8681, 215-766-7301; FAX: 215-766-8681

Beitzinger, George, 116-20 Atlantic Ave., Richmond Hill, NY 11419/718-847-7661

Belding's Custom Gun Shop, 10691 Sayers Rd., Munith, MI 49259/517-596-2388

Bell & Carlson, Inc., Dodge City Industrial Park/101 Allen Rd., Dodge City, KS 67801/800-634-8586, 316-225-6688; FAX: 316-225-9095

Bell Alaskan Silversmith, Sid (See Heritage Wildlife Carvings)

Bell Reloading, Inc., 1725 Harlin Lane Rd., Villa Rica, GA 30180

Bell's Gun & Sport Shop, 3309-19 Mannheim Rd, Franklin Park, IL 60131

Bell's Legendary Country Wear, 22 Circle Dr., Bellmore, NY 11710/516-679-1158

Bellm Contenders, P.O. Box 459, Cleveland, UT 84518/801-653-2530

Belltown, Ltd., 11 Camps Rd., Kent, CT 06757/860-354-5750

Belt MTN Arms, 107 10th Ave. SW, White Sulphur Springs, MT 59645/406-586-4495

Ben's Machines, 1151 S. Cedar Ridge, Duncanville, TX 75137/214-780-1807; FAX: 214-780-0316

Benchmark Guns, 12593 S. Ave. 5 East, Yuma, AZ 85365

Benchmark Knives (See Gerber Legendary Blades)

Benelli Armi, S.p.A., Via della Stazione, 61029 Urbino, ITALY/39-722-307-1; FAX: 39-722-327427 (U.S. importers—Heckler & Koch, Inc.; Whitestone Lumber Co.)

Benelli USA Corp., 17603 Indian Head Hwy., Ascokeek, MD 20607/301-283-6981; FAX: 301-283-6988

Bengtson Arms Co., L., 6345-B E. Akron St., Mesa, AZ 85205/602-981-6375

Benjamin/Sheridan Co., Crossman, Rts. 5 and 20, E. Bloomfield, NY 14443/716-657-6161; FAX: 716-657-5405

Bentley, John, 128-D Watson Dr., Turtle Creek, PA 15145

Beomat of America Inc., 300 Railway Ave., Campbell, CA 95008/408-379-4829

Beretta S.p.A., Pietro, Via Beretta, 18-25063 Gardone V.T. (BS) ITALY/XX39/30-8341.1; FAX: XX39/30-8341.421 (U.S. importer—Beretta U.S.A. Corp.)

Beretta U.S.A. Corp., 17601 Beretta Drive, Accokeek, MD 20607/301-283-2191; FAX: 301-283-0435

Berger Bullets, Ltd., 5342 W. Camelback Rd., Suite 200, Glendale, AZ 85301/602-842-4001; FAX: 602-934-9083

Bergman & Williams, 2450 Losee Rd., Suite F, Las Vegas, NV 89030/702-642-1901; FAX: 702-642-1540

Bernardelli S.p.A., Vincenzo, 125 Via Matteotti, P.O. Box 74, Gardone V.T., Brescia ITALY, 25063/39-30-8912851-2-3; FAX: 39-30-8910249 (U.S. importer—Armsport, Inc.)

Berry's Bullets (See Berry's Mfg., Inc.)

Berry's Mfg., Inc., 401 North 3050 East St., St. George, UT 84770/801-634-1682; FAX: 801-634-1683

Bersa S.A., Gonzales Castillo 312, 1704 Ramos Mejia, ARGENTINA/541-656-2377; FAX: 541-656-2093 (U.S. importer—Eagle Imports, Inc.)

Bertram Bullet Co., P.O. Box 313, Seymour, Victoria 3660, AUSTRALIA/61-57-922912; FAX: 61-57-991650

Bertuzzi (See U.S. importer—New England Arms Co.)

Better Concepts Co., 663 New Castle Rd., Butler, PA 16001/412-285-9000

Beverly, Mary, 3201 Horseshoe Trail, Tallahassee, FL 32312

Bianchi International, Inc., 100 Calle Cortez, Temecula, CA 92590/909-676-5621; FAX: 909-676-6777

Biesen, Al, 5021 Rosewood, Spokane, WA 99208/509-328-9340

Biesen, Roger, 5021 W. Rosewood, Spokane, WA 99208/509-328-9340

Big Beam Emergency Systems, Inc., 290 E. Prairie St., Crystal Lake, IL 60039

Big Bear Arms & Sporting Goods, Inc., 1112 Milam Way, Carrollton, TX 75006/972-416-8051, 800-400-BEAR; FAX: 972-416-0771

Big Bore Bullets of Alaska, P.O. Box 872785, Wasilla, AK 99687/907-373-2673; FAX: 907-373-2673

Big Bore Express, 7154 W. State St., Boise, ID 83703/800-376-4010; FAX:208-376-4020

Big Sky Racks, Inc., P.O. Box 729, Bozeman, MT 59771-0729/406-586-9393; FAX: 406-585-7378

Big Spring Enterprises "Bore Stores", P.O. Box 1115, Big Spring, Rd./Yellville, AR 72687/870-449-5297; FAX: 870-449-4446; E-MAIL: BIGSPRNG@mtnhome.com

Bilal, Mustafa, 908 NW 50th St., Seattle, WA 98107-3634/206-782-4164

Bill's Custom Cases, P.O. Box 2, Dunsmuir, CA 96025/916-235-0177; FAX: 916-235-4959

Bill's Gun Repair, 1007 Burlington St., Mendota, IL 61342/815-539-5786

Billeb, Stephen L., 1101 N. 7th St., Burlington, IA 52601/319-753-2110

Billings Gunsmiths, Inc., 1841 Grand Ave., Billings, MT 59102/406-256-8390

Billingsley & Brownell, P.O. Box 25, Dayton, WY 82836/307-655-9344

Birchwood Casey, 7900 Fuller Rd., Eden Prairie, MN 55344/800-328-6156, 612-937-7933; FAX: 612-937-7979

Birdsong & Assoc., W.E., 1435 Monterey Rd., Florence, MS 39073-9748/601-366-8270

Bismuth Cartridge Co., 3500 Maple Ave., Suite 1650, Dallas, TX 75219/800-759-3333, 214-521-5880; FAX: 214-521-9035

Bison Studios, 1409 South Commerce St., Las Vegas, NV 89102/702-388-2891; FAX: 702-383-9967

Bitterroot Bullet Co., Box 412, Lewiston, ID 83501-0412/208-743-5635

Black Belt Bullets (See Big Bore Express)

Black Hills Ammunition, Inc., P.O. Box 3090, Rapid City, SD 57709-3090/605-348-5150; FAX: 605-348-9827

Black Hills Shooters Supply, P.O. Box 4220, Rapid City, SD 57709/800-289-2506

Black Powder Products, 67 Township Rd. 1411, Chesapeake, OH 45619/614-867-8047

Black Sheep Brand, 3220 W. Gentry Parkway, Tyler, TX 75702/903-592-3853; FAX: 903-592-0527

Blackhawk East, Box 2274, Loves Park, IL 61131

Blackhawk West, Box 285, Hiawatha, KS 66434

Blackinton & Co., Inc., V.H., 221 John L. Dietsch, Attleboro Falls, MA 02763-0300/508-699-4436; FAX: 508-695-5349

Blackjack Knives, Ltd., 1307 W. Wabash, Effingham, IL 62401/217-347-7700; FAX: 217-347-7737

Blacksmith Corp., 830 N. Road No. 1 E., P.O. Box 1752, Chino Valley, AZ 86323/520-636-4456; FAX: 520-636-4457

BlackStar AccuMax Barrels, 11501 Brittmoore Park Drive, Houston, TX 77041/281-721-6040; FAX: 281-721-6041

BlackStar Barrel Accurizing (See BlackStar AccuMax Barrels)

Blacktail Mountain Books, 42 First Ave. W., Kalispell, MT 59901/406-257-5573

Blair Engraving, J.R., P.O. Box 64, Glenrock, WY 82637/307-436-8115

Blammo Ammo, P.O. Box 1677, Seneca, SC 29679/803-882-1768

Blaser Jagdwaffen GmbH, D-88316 Isny Im Allgau, GERMANY (U.S. importer—Autumn Sales, Inc.)

Bleile, C. Roger, 5040 Ralph Ave., Cincinnati, OH 45238/513-251-0249

Blocker Holsters, Inc., Ted., Clackamas Business Park Bld. A, 14787 S.E. 82nd, Dr./Clackamas, OR 97015/503-557-7757; FAX: 503-557-3771

Blount, Inc., Sporting Equipment Div., 2299 Snake River Ave., P.O. Box 856, Lewiston, ID 83501/800-627-3640, 208-746-2351; FAX: 208-799-3904

Blue and Gray Products, Inc. (See Ox-Yoke Originals, Inc.)

Blue Book Publications, Inc., One Appletree Square, 8009 34th Ave. S., Suite, 175/Minneapolis, MN 55425/800-877-4867, 612-854-5229; FAX: 612-853-1486

Blue Mountain Bullets, HCR 77, P.O. Box 231, John Day, OR 97845/541-820-4594

Blue Ridge Machinery & Tools, Inc., P.O. Box 536-GD, Hurricane, WV 25526/800-872-6500; FAX: 304-562-5311

BMC Supply, Inc., 26051 - 179th Ave. S.E., Kent, WA 98042

B.M.F. Activator, Inc., 803 Mill Creek Run, Plantersville, TX 77363/409-894-2005, 800-527-2881

Bob's Gun Shop, P.O. Box 200, Royal, AR 71968/501-767-1970; FAX 501-767-1970

Bob's Tactical Indoor Shooting Range & Gun Shop, 122 Lafayette Rd., Salisbury, MA 01952/508-465-5561

Boessler, Erich, Am Vogeltal 3, 97702 Munnerstadt, GERMANY/9733-9443

Bohemia Arms Co., 17101 Los Modelos St., Fountain Valley, CA 92708/619-442-7005; FAX: 619-442-7005

Boker USA, Inc., 1550 Balsam Street, Lakewood, CO 80215/303-462-0662; FAX: 303-462-0668

Boltin, John M., P.O. Box 644, Estill, SC 29918/803-625-2185

Bo-Mar Tool & Mfg. Co., Rt. 8, Box 405, Longview, TX 75604/903-759-4784; FAX: 903-759-9141

Bonanza (See Forster Products)

Bond Arms, Inc., P.O. Box 1296, Granbury, TX 76048/817-573-5733; FAX: 817-573-5636

Bond Custom Firearms, 8954 N. Lewis Ln., Bloomington, IN 47408/812-332-4519

Bondini Paolo, Via Sorrento, 345, San Carlo di Cesena, ITALY I-47020/0547 663 240; FAX: 0547 663 780 (U.S. importer—blackpowder arms)

Bone Engraving, Ralph, 718 N. Atlanta, Owasso, OK 74055/918-272-9745

Boone Trading Co., Inc., P.O. Box BB, Brinnan, WA 98320

Boone's Custom Ivory Grips, Inc., 562 Coyote Rd., Brinnon, WA 98320/206-796-4330

Boonie Packer Products, P.O. Box 12204, Salem, OR 97309/800-477-3244, 503-581-3244; FAX: 503-581-3191

Borden's Accuracy, RD 1, Box 250BC, Springville, PA 18844/717-965-2505; FAX: 717-965-2328

Border Barrels Ltd., Riccarton Farm, Newcastleton SCOTLAND U.K. TD9 0SN

Borovnik KG, Ludwig, 9170 Ferlach, Bahnhofstrasse 7, AUSTRIA/042 27 24 42; FAX: 042 26 43 49

Bosis (See U.S. importer—New England Arms Co.)

Boss Manufacturing Co., 221 W. First St., Kewanee, IL 61443/309-852-2131, 800-447-4581; FAX: 309-852-0848

Bostick Wildlife Calls, Inc., P.O. Box 728, Estill, SC 29918/803-625-2210, 803-625-4512

Bowen Classic Arms Corp., P.O. Box 67, Louisville, TN 37777/423-984-3583

Bowen Knife Co., Inc., P.O. Box 590, Blackshear, GA 31516/912-449-4794

Bowerly, Kent, 26247 Metolius Meadows Dr., Camp Sherman, OR 97730/541-595-6028

Boyds' Gunstock Industries, Inc., 3rd & Main, P.O. Box 305, Geddes, SD 57342/605-337-2125; FAX: 605-337-3363

Boyt, 509 Hamilton, P.O. Drawer 668, Iowa Falls, IA 50126/515-648-4626; FAX: 515-648-2385

Brace, Larry D., 771 Blackfoot Ave., Eugene, OR 97404/541-688-1278; FAX 541-607-5833

Bradley Gunsight Co., P.O. Box 340, Plymouth, VT 05056/860-589-0531; FAX: 860-582-6294

Brass and Bullet Alloys, P.O. Box 1238, Sierra Vista, AZ 85636/602-458-5321; FAX: 602-458-9125

Brass Eagle, Inc., 7050A Bramalea Rd., Unit 19, Mississauga, Ont. L4Z 1C7, CANADA/416-848-4844

Bratcher, Dan, 311 Belle Air Pl., Carthage, MO 64836/417-358-1518

Brauer Bros. Mfg. Co., 2020 Delman Blvd., St. Louis, MO 63103/314-231-2864; FAX: 314-249-4952

Braverman Corp., R.J., 88 Parade Rd., Meridith, NH 03293/800-736-4867

Break-Free, Inc., P.O. Box 25020, Santa Ana, CA 92799/714-953-1900; FAX: 714-953-0402

Brenneke KG, Wilhelm, Ilmenauweg 2, 30851 Langenhagen, GERMANY/0511/97262-0; FAX: 0511/97262-62 (U.S. importer—Dynamit Nobel-RWS, Inc.)

Bretton (See Atamec-Bretton)

Bridgers Best, P.O. Box 1410, Berthoud, CO 80513

Briese Bullet Co., Inc., RR1, Box 108, Tappen, ND 58487/701-327-4578; FAX: 701-327-4579

Brigade Quartermasters, 1025 Cobb International Blvd., Dept. VH, Kennesaw, GA 30144-4300/404-428-1248, 800-241-3125; FAX: 404-426-7726

Briganti, A.J., 512 Rt. 32, Highland Mills, NY 10930/914-928-9573

Briley Mfg., Inc., 1230 Lumpkin, Houston, TX 77043/800-331-5718; Web: www.briley.com

British Antiques, P.O. Box 7, Latham, NY 12110/518-783-0773

British Sporting Arms, RR1, Box 130, Millbrook, NY 12545/914-677-8303

BRNO (See U.S. importers—Bohemia Arms Co.)

Broad Creek Rifle Works, 120 Horsey Ave., Laurel, DE 19956/302-875-5446; FAX 302-875-1448

Brockman's Custom Gunsmithing, P.O. Box 357, Gooding, ID 83330/208-934-5050

Brocock Ltd., 43 River Street, Digbeth, Birmingham, B5 5SA ENGLAND/011-021-773-1200

Broken Gun Ranch, 10739 126 Rd., Spearville, KS 67876/316-385-2587; FAX: 316-385-2597

Brolin Industries Inc., 2755 Thompson Creek Rd., Pomona, CA 91767/909-392-7822; FAX: 909-392-7824

Brooker, Dennis, Rt. 1, Box 12A, Derby, IA 50068/515-533-2103

Brooks Tactical Systems, 279-C Shorewood Ct., Fox Island, WA 98333-9725/253-549-2866; FAX: 253-549-2703

Brown Co., E. Arthur, 3404 Pawnee Dr., Alexandria, MN 56308/320-762-8847

Brown, H.R. (See Silhouette Leathers)

Brown Dog Ent., 2200 Calle Camelia, 1000 Oaks, CA 91360/805-497-2318; FAX: 805-497-1618

Brown Manufacturing, P.O. Box 9219, Akron, OH 44305/800-837-GUNS

Brown Precision, Inc., 7786 Molinos Ave., Los Molinos, CA 96055/916-384-2506; FAX: 916-384-1638

Brown Products, Inc., Ed, 43825 Muldrow Trail, Perry, MO 63462/573-565-3261; FAX: 573-565-2791

Brownell Checkering, W.E., 9390 Twin Mountain Circle, San Diego, CA 92126/619-695-2479; FAX: 619-695-2479

Brownells, Inc., 200 S. Front St., Montezuma, IA 50171/515-623-5401; FAX: 515-623-3896

Browning Arms Co., One Browning Place, Morgan, UT 84050/801-876-2711; FAX: 801-876-3331

Browning Arms Co. (Parts & Service), 3005 Arnold Tenbrook Rd., Arnold, MO 63010-9406/314-287-6800; FAX: 314-287-9751

BRP, Inc., High Performance Cast Bullets, 1210 Alexander Rd., Colorado Springs, CO 80909-3932/719-633-0658

Bruno Shooters Supply, 111 N. Wyoming St., Hazleton, PA 18201/717-455-2281; FAX: 717-455-2211

Brunton U.S.A., 620 E. Monroe Ave., Riverton, WY 82501/307-856-6559; FAX: 307-856-1840

Brynin, Milton, P.O. Box 383, Yonkers, NY 10710/914-779-4333

BSA Guns Ltd., Armoury Rd. Small Heath, Birmingham, ENGLAND B11 2PX/011-021-772-8543; FAX: 011-021-773-0845 (U.S. importers—Groenewold, John; Precision Sales International, Inc.)

BSA Optics, 3911 SW 47th Ave., #914, Ft. Lauderdale, FL 33314/954-581-2144; FAX: 954-581-3165

B-Square Company, Inc., P.O. Box 11281, 2708 St. Louis Ave., Ft. Worth, TX 76110/817-923-0964, 800-433-2909; FAX: 817-926-7012

Bucheimer, J.M., Jumbo Sports Products, 721 N. 20th St., St. Louis, MO 63103/314-241-1020

Buck Knives, Inc., 1900 Weld Blvd., P.O. Box 1267, El Cajon, CA 92020/619-449-1100, 800-326-2825; FAX: 619-562-5774, 800-729-2825

Buck Stix—SOS Products Co., Box 3, Neenah, WI 54956

Buck Stop Lure Co., Inc., 3600 Grow Rd. NW, P.O. Box 636, Stanton, MI 48888/517-762-5091; FAX: 517-762-5124

Buckeye Custom Bullets, 6490 Stewart Rd., Elida, OH 45807/419-641-4463

Buckhorn Gun Works, 8109 Woodland Dr., Black Hawk, SD 57718/605-787-6472

Buckskin Bullet Co., P.O. Box 1893, Cedar City, UT 84721/801-586-3286

Buckskin Machine Works, A. Hunkeler, 3235 S. 358th St., Auburn, WA 98001/206-927-5412

Budin, Dave, Main St., Margaretville, NY 12455/914-568-4103; FAX: 914-586-4105

Buenger Enterprises/Goldenrod Dehumidifier, 3600 S. Harbor Blvd., Oxnard, CA 93035/800-451-6797; FAX: 805-985-1534

Buffalo Arms Co., 3355 Upper Gold Creek Rd., Samuels, ID 83864/208-263-6953; FAX: 208-265-2096

Buffalo Bullet Co., Inc., 12637 Los Nietos Rd., Unit A, Santa Fe Springs, CA 90670/310-944-0322; FAX: 310-944-5054

Buffalo Rock Shooters Supply, R.R. 1, Ottawa, IL 61350/815-433-2471

Buffer Technologies, P.O. Box 104930, Jefferson City, MO 65110/573-634-8529; FAX: 573-634-8522

Bull Mountain Rifle Co., 6327 Golden West Terrace, Billings, MT 59106/406-656-0778

Bullberry Barrel Works, Ltd., 2430 W. Bullberry Ln. 67-5, Hurricane, UT 84737/801-635-9866; FAX: 801-635-0348

Bullet, Inc., 3745 Hiram Alworth Rd., Dallas, GA 30132

Bullet'n Press, 19 Key St., Eastport, Maine 04631/207-853-4116

Bullet Swaging Supply, Inc., P.O. Box 1056, 303 McMillan Rd, West Monroe, LA 71291/318-387-3266; FAX: 318-387-7779

BulletMakers Workshop, The, RFD 1 Box 1755, Brooks, ME 04921

Bullseye Bullets, 1610 State Road 60, No. 12, Valrico, FL 33594/813-654-6563

Bull-X, Inc., 520 N. Main, Farmer City, IL 61842/309-928-2574; FAX: 309-928-2130

Burgess, Byron, P.O. Box 6853, Los Osos, CA 93412/805-528-1005

Burkhart Gunsmithing, Don, P.O. Box 852, Rawlins, WY 82301/307-324-6007

Burnham Bros., P.O. Box 1148, Menard, TX 78659/915-396-4572; FAX: 915-396-4574

Burris Co., Inc., P.O. Box 1747, 331 E. 8th St., Greeley, CO 80631/970-356-1670; FAX: 970-356-8702

Bushmann Hunters & Safaris, P.O. Box 293088, Lewisville, TX 75029/214-317-0768

Bushmaster Firearms (See Quality Parts Co./Bushmaster Firearms)

Bushmaster Hunting & Fishing, 451 Alliance Ave., Toronto, Ont. M6N 2J1 CANADA/416-763-4040; FAX: 416-763-0623

Bushnell Sports Optics Worldwide, 9200 Cody, Overland Park, KS 66214/913-752-3400, 800-423-3537; FAX: 913-752-3550

Bushwacker Backpack & Supply Co. (See Counter Assault)

Bustani, Leo, 8195 No. Mil Tr., Suite A Box 13, W. Palm Beach, FL 33410/305-622-2710

Buster's Custom Knives, P.O. Box 214, Richfield, UT 84701/801-896-5319

Butler Creek Corp., 290 Arden Dr., Belgrade, MT 59714/800-423-8327, 406-388-1356; FAX: 406-388-7204

Butler Enterprises, 834 Oberting Rd., Lawrenceburg, IN 47025/812-537-3584

Butterfield & Butterfield, 220 San Bruno Ave., San Francisco, CA 94103/415-861-7500

Buzztail Brass (See Grayback Wildcats)

B-West Imports, Inc., 2425 N. Huachuca Dr., Tucson, AZ 85745-1201/602-628-1990; FAX: 602-628-3602

C

C3 Systems, 678 Killingly St., Johnston, RI 02919

C&D Special Products (See Claybuster Wads & Harvester Bullets)

C&H Research, 115 Sunnyside Dr., Box 351, Lewis, KS 67552/316-324-5445

C&J Enterprises, Inc., 7101 Jurupa Ave., No. 12, Riverside, CA 92504/909-689-7758; FAX 909-689-7791

C&T Corp. TA Johnson Brothers, 1023 Wappoo Road, Charleston, SC 29407-5960

Cabanas (See U.S. importer—Mandall Shooting Supplies, Inc.)

Cabela's, 812-13th Ave., Sidney, NE 69160/308-254-6644, 800-237-4444; FAX: 308-254-6745

Cabinet Mtn. Outfitters Scents & Lures, P.O. Box 766, Plains, MT 59859/406-826-3970

Cache La Poudre Rifleworks, 140 N. College, Ft. Collins, CO 80524/303-482-6913

Cadre Supply (See Parts & Surplus)

Calhoon Varmint Bullets, James, Shambo Rt., 304, Havre, MT 59501/406-395-4079

Calibre Press, Inc., 666 Dundee Rd., Suite 1607, Northbrook, IL 60062-2760/800-323-0037; FAX: 708-498-6869

Cali'co Hardwoods, Inc., 3580 Westwind Blvd., Santa Rosa, CA 95403/707-546-4045; FAX: 707-546-4027

Calico Light Weapon Systems, 405 E. 19th St., Bakersfield, CA 93305/805-835-9605; FAX: 805-835-9605

California Magnum, 20746 Dearborn St., Chatsworth, CA 91313/818-341-7302; FAX: 818-341-7304

California Sights (See Fautheree, Andy)

Camdex, Inc., 2330 Alger, Troy, MI 48083/810-528-2300; FAX: 810-528-0989

Cameron's, 16690 W. 11th Ave., Golden, CO 80401/303-279-7365; FAX: 303-628-5413

Camilli, Lou, 600 Sandtree Dr., Suite 212, Lake Park, FL 33403-1538

Camillus Cutlery Co., 54 Main St., Camillus, NY 13031/315-672-8111; FAX: 315-672-8832

Campbell, Dick, 20,000 Silver Ranch Rd., Conifer, CO 80433/303-697-0150; FAX 303-697-0150

Camp-Cap Products, P.O. Box 173, Chesterfield, MO 63006/314-532-4340; FAX: 314-532-4340

Canjar Co., M.H., 500 E. 45th Ave., Denver, CO 80216/303-295-2638; FAX: 303-295-2638

Cannon's, Andy Cannon, Box 1026, 320 Main St., Polson, MT 59860/406-887-2048

Cannon Safe, Inc., 9358 Stephens St., Pico Rivera, CA 90660/310-692-0636, 800-242-1055; FAX: 310-692-7252

Canons Delcour, Rue J.B. Cools, B-4040 Herstal, BELGIUM 32.(0)42.40.61.40; FAX: 32(0)42.40.22.88

Canyon Cartridge Corp., P.O. Box 152, Albertson, NY 11507/FAX: 516-294-8946

Cape Outfitters, 599 County Rd. 206, Cape Girardeau, MO 63701/314-335-4103; FAX: 314-335-1555

Caraville Manufacturing, P.O. Box 4545, Thousand Oaks, CA 91359/805-499-1234

Carbide Checkering Tools (See J&R Engineering)

Carbide Die & Mfg. Co., Inc., 15615 E. Arrow Hwy., Irwindale, CA 91706/818-337-2518

Carhartt, Inc., P.O. Box 600, 3 Parklane Blvd., Dearborn, MI 48121/800-358-3825, 313-271-8460; FAX: 313-271-3455

Custom Gun Engraving, D-97422 Schweinfurt, Siedlerweg 17, GERMANY/01149-9721-41446; FAX: 01149-9721-44413

Carlson, Douglas R., Antique American Firearms, P.O. Box 71035, Dept. GD, Des Moines, IA 50325/515-224-6552

Carnahan Bullets, 17645 110th Ave. SE, Renton, WA 98055

Carolina Precision Rifles, 1200 Old Jackson Hwy., Jackson, SC 29831/803-827-2069

Carrell's Precision Firearms, 643 Clark Ave., Billings, MT 59101-1614/406-962-3593

Carroll Bullets (See Precision Reloading, Inc.)

Carry-Lite, Inc., 5203 W. Clinton Ave., Milwaukee, WI 53223/414-355-3520; FAX: 414-355-4775

Carter's Gun Shop, 225 G St., Penrose, CO 81240/719-372-6240

Cartridge Transfer Group, Pete de Coux, 235 Oak St., Butler, PA 16001/412-282-3426

Cascade Bullet Co., Inc., 2355 South 6th St., Klamath Falls, OR 97601/503-884-9316

Cascade Shooters, 2155 N.W. 12th St., Redwood, OR 97756

Case & Sons Cutlery Co., W.R., Owens Way, Bradford, PA 16701/814-368-4123, 800-523-6350; FAX: 814-768-5369

Case Sorting System, 12695 Cobblestone Creek Rd., Poway, CA 92064/619-486-9340

Cash Mfg. Co., Inc., P.O. Box 130, 201 S. Klein Dr., Waunakee, WI 53597-0130/608-849-5664; FAX: 608-849-5664

Caspian Arms Ltd., 14 North Main St., Hardwick, VT 05843/802-472-6454; FAX: 802-472-6709

Cast Performance Bullet Company, 12441 U.S. Hwy. 26, Riverton, WY 82501/307-856-4347

Casull Arms Corp., P.O. Box 1629, Afton, WY 83110/307-886-0200

Caswell International Corp., 1221 Marshall St. NE, Minneapolis, MN 55413-1055/612-379-2000; FAX: 612-379-2367

CATCO, 316 California Ave., #341N, Reno, NV 89509/707-253-8338; FAX: 707-253-7149

Catco-Ambush, Inc., P.O.Box 300, Corte Madera, CA 94926

Cathey Enterprises, Inc., P.O. Box 2202, Brownwood, TX 76804/915-643-2553; FAX: 915-643-3653

Cation, 2341 Alger St., Troy, MI 48083/810-689-0658; FAX: 810-689-7558

Catoctin Cutlery, P.O. Box 188, 17 S. Main St., Smithsburg, MD 21783/301-824-7416; FAX: 301-824-6138

Caywood, Shane J., P.O. Box 321, Minocqua, WI 54548/715-277-3866 evenings

CBC, Avenida Humberto de Campos, 3220, 09400-000 Ribeirao Pires-SP-BRAZIL/55-11-742-7500; FAX: 55-11-459-7385

CCG Enterprises, 5217 E. Belknap St., Halton City, TX 76117/800-819-7464

CCI, Div. of Blount, Inc., Sporting Equipment Div., 2299 Snake River Ave.,, P.O. Box 856/Lewiston, ID 83501 800-627-3640, 208-746-2351; FAX: 208-746-2915

Cedar Hill Game Calls, L.L.C., Rt. 2 Box 236, Downsville, LA 71234/318-982-5632; FAX: 318-368-2245

Celestron International, P.O. Box 3578, 2835 Columbia St., Torrance, CA 90503/310-328-9560; FAX: 310-212-5835

Centaur Systems, Inc., 1602 Foothill Rd., Kalispell, MT 59901/406-755-8609; FAX: 406-755-8609

Center Lock Scope Rings, 9901 France Ct., Lakeville, MN 55044/612-461-2114

CenterMark, P.O. Box 4066, Parnassus Station, New Kensington, PA 15068/412-335-1319

Central Specialties Ltd. (See Trigger Lock Division/Central Specialties Ltd.)

Century Gun Dist., Inc., 1467 Jason Rd., Greenfield, IN 46140/317-462-4524

Century International Arms, Inc., P.O. Box 714, St. Albans, VT 05478-0714/802-527-1252, 800-527-1252; FAX: 802-527-0470; WEB: www.centuryarms.com

CFVentures, 509 Harvey Dr., Bloomington, IN 47403-1715

C-H Tool & Die Corp. (See 4-D Custom Die Co.)

Chace Leather Products, 507 Alden St., Fall River, MA 02722/508-678-7556; FAX: 508-675-9666

Chadick's Ltd., P.O. Box 100, Terrell, TX 75160/214-563-7577

Chambers Flintlocks Ltd., Jim, Rt. 1, Box 513-A, Candler, NC 28715/704-667-8361

Champion Shooters' Supply, P.O. Box 303, New Albany, OH 43054/614-855-1603; FAX: 614-855-1209

Champion Target Co., 232 Industrial Parkway, Richmond, IN 47374/800-441-4971

Champion's Choice, Inc., 201 International Blvd., LaVergne, TN 37086/615-793-4066; FAX: 615-793-4070

Champlin Firearms, Inc., P.O. Box 3191, Woodring Airport, Enid, OK 73701/580-237-7388; FAX: 580-242-6922

Chapman Academy of Practical Shooting, 4350 Academy Rd., Hallsville, MO 65255/573-696-5544, 573-696-2266

Chapman Manufacturing Co., 471 New Haven Rd., P.O. Box 250, Durham, CT 06422/203-349-9228; FAX: 203-349-0084

Chapuis Armes, 21 La Gravoux, BP15, 42380 St. Bonnet-le-Chateau, FRANCE/ (33)77.50.06.96 (U.S. importer—Champlin Firearms, Inc.; Chapuis USA)

Chapuis USA, 416 Business Park, Bedford, KY 40006

Checkmate Refinishing, 370 Champion Dr., Brooksville, FL 34601/904-799-5774

Cheddite France, S.A., 99, Route de Lyon, F-26501 Bourg-les-Valence, FRANCE/33-75-56-4545; FAX: 33-75-56-3587

Chelsea Gun Club of New York City, Inc., 237 Ovington Ave., Apt. D53, Brooklyn, NY 11209/718-836-9422, 718-833-2704

Chem-Pak, Inc., 11 Oates Ave., P.O. Box 1685, Winchester, VA 22604/800-336-9828, 703-667-1341; FAX: 703-722-3993

Cherry's Fine Guns, P.O. Box 5307, Greensboro, NC 27435-0307/919-854-4182

Chesapeake Importing & Distributing Co. (See CIDCO)

CheVron Bullets, RR1, Ottawa, IL 61350/815-433-2471

CheVron Case Master (See CheVron Bullets)

Chicago Cutlery Co., 1536 Beech St., Terre Haute, IN 47804/800-457-2665

Chicasaw Gun Works, 4 Mi. Mkr., Pluto Rd., Box 868, Shady Spring, WV 25918-0868/304-763-2848; FAX: 304-763-2848

Chipmunk (See Oregon Arms, Inc.)

Chippewa Shoe Co., P.O. Box 2521, Ft. Worth, TX 76113/817-332-4385

Choate Machine & Tool Co., Inc., P.O. Box 218, 116 Lovers Ln., Bald Knob, AR 72010/501-724-6193, 800-972-6390; FAX: 501-724-5873

Chopie Mfg., Inc., 700 Copeland Ave., LaCrosse, WI 54603/608-784-0926

Christensen Arms, 385 North 3050 East, St. George, UT 84790/435-624-9535; FAX: 435-674-9293

Christie's East, 219 E. 67th St., New York, NY 10021/212-606-0400

Christman Jr., David, Gunmaker, 937 Lee Hedrick Rd., Colville, WA 99114/509-684-1438

Christopher Firearms Co., Inc., E., Route 128 & Ferry St., Miamitown, OH 45041/513-353-1321

Chu Tani Ind., Inc., P.O. Box 2064, Cody, WY 82414-2064

Chuck's Gun Shop, P.O. Box 597, Waldo, FL 32694/904-468-2264

Churchill (See U.S. importer—Ellett Bros.)

Churchill, Winston, Twenty Mile Stream Rd., RFD P.O. Box 29B, Proctorsville, VT 05153/802-226-7772

Churchill Glove Co., James, P.O. Box 298, Centralia, WA 98531

CIDCO, 21480 Pacific Blvd., Sterling, VA 22170/703-444-5353

Ciener, Inc., Jonathan Arthur, 8700 Commerce St., Cape Canaveral, FL 32920/407-868-2200; FAX: 407-868-2201

Cimarron Arms, P.O. Box 906, Fredericksburg, TX 78624-0906/210-997-9090; FAX: 210-997-0802

Cincinnati Swaging, 2605 Marlington Ave., Cincinnati, OH 45208

Citadel Mfg., Inc., 5220 Gabbert Rd., Moorpark, CA 93021/805-529-7294; FAX: 805-529-7297

C.J. Ballistics, Inc., P.O. Box 132, Acme, WA 98220/206-595-5001

Clark Co., Inc., David, P.O. Box 15054, Worcester, MA 01615-0054/508-756-6216; FAX: 508-753-5827

Clark Custom Guns, Inc., 336 Shootout Lane, Princeton, LA 71067/318-949-9884; FAX: 318-949-9829

Clark Firearms Engraving, P.O. Box 80746, San Marino, CA 91118/818-287-1652

Clarkfield Enterprises, Inc., 1032 10th Ave., Clarkfield, MN 56223/612-669-7140

Claro Walnut Gunstock Co., 1235 Stanley Ave., Chico, CA 95928/530-342-5188; FAX 530-342-5199

Classic Arms Corp., P.O. Box 106, Dunsmuir, CA 96025-0106/916-235-2000

Classic Guns, Inc., Frank S. Wood, 3230 Medlock Bridge Rd., Suite 110, Norcross, GA 30092/404-242-7944

Claybuster Wads & Harvester Bullets, 309 Sequoya Dr., Hopkinsville, KY 42240/800-922-6287, 800-284-1746, 502-885-8088; FAX: 502-885-1951

Clean Shot Technologies, Inc., 21218 St. Andrews Blvd., #504, Boca Raton, FL 33433/888-866-2532; FAX: 561-479-7039

Clearview Mfg. Co., Inc., 413 S. Oakley St., Fordyce, AR 71742/501-352-8557; FAX: 501-352-7120

Clearview Products, 3021 N. Portland, Oklahoma City, OK 73107

Cleland's Outdoor World, Inc., 10306 Airport Hwy., Swanton, OH 43558/419-865-4713; FAX 419-865-5865

Clements' Custom Leathercraft, Chas, 1741 Dallas St., Aurora, CO 80010-2018/ 303-364-0403; FAX:303-739-9824

Clenzoil Corp., P.O. Box 80226, Sta. C, Canton, OH 44708-0226/330-833-9758; FAX: 330-833-4724

Clerke Co., J.A., P.O. Box 627, Pearblossom, CA 93553-0627/805-945-0713

Clift Mfg., L.R., 3821 Hammonton Rd., Marysville, CA 95901/916-755-3390; FAX: 916-755-3393

Clift Welding Supply & Cases, 1332-A Colusa Hwy., Yuba City, CA 95993/916-755-3390; FAX: 916-755-3393

Cloward's Gun Shop, 4023 Aurora Ave. N, Seattle, WA 98103/206-632-2072

Clymer Manufacturing Co., Inc., 1645 W. Hamlin Rd., Rochester Hills, MI 48309-1530/810-853-5555, 810-853-5627; FAX: 810-853-1530

C-More Systems, P.O. Box 1750, 7553 Gary Rd., Manassas, VA 22110/703-361-2663; FAX: 703-361-5881

Cobalt Mfg., Inc., 1020 Shady Oak Dr., Denton, TX 76205/800-690-9923; FAX: 940-383-4281

Cobra Sport S.r.l., Via Caduti Nei Lager No. 1, 56020 San Romano, Montopoli v/Arno (Pi), ITALY/0039-571-450490; FAX: 0039-571-450492

Coffin, Charles H., 3719 Scarlet Ave., Odessa, TX 79762/915-366-4729

Coffin, Jim (See Working Guns)

Cogar's Gunsmithing, P.O. Box 755, Houghton Lake, MI 48629/517-422-4591

Coghlan's Ltd., 121 Irene St., Winnipeg, Man., CANADA R3T 4C7/204-284-9550; FAX: 204-475-4127

Cold Steel, Inc., 2128-D Knoll Dr., Ventura, CA 93003/800-255-4716, 800-624-2363 (in CA); FAX: 805-642-9727

Cole's Gun Works, Old Bank Building, Rt. 4, Box 250, Moyock, NC 27958/919-435-2345

Cole-Grip, 16135 Cohasset St., Van Nuys, CA 91406/818-782-4424

Coleman Co., Inc., 250 N. St. Francis, Wichita, KS 67201

Coleman's Custom Repair, 4035 N. 20th Rd., Arlington, VA 22207/703-528-4486

Collings, Ronald, 1006 Cielta Linda, Vista, CA 92083

Colonial Arms, Inc., P.O. Box 636, Selma, AL 36702-0636/334-872-9455; FAX: 334-872-9540

Colonial Knife Co., Inc., P.O. Box 3327, Providence, RI 02909/401-421-1600; FAX: 401-421-2047

Colonial Repair, P.O. Box 372, Hyde Park, MA 02136-9998/617-469-4951

Colorado Gunsmithing Academy, 27533 Highway 287 South, Lamar, CO 81052/719-336-4099, 800-754-2046; FAX: 719-336-9642

Colorado School of Trades, 1575 Hoyt St., Lakewood, CO 80215/800-234-4594; FAX: 303-233-4723

Colorado Shooter's Supply, 1163 W. Paradise Way, Fruita, CO 81521/303-858-9191

Colorado Sutlers Arsenal (See Cumberland States Arsenal)

Colt Blackpowder Arms Co., 110 8th Street, Brooklyn, NY 11215/212-925-2159; FAX: 212-966-4986

Colt's Mfg. Co., Inc., P.O. Box 1868, Hartford, CT 06144-1868/800-962-COLT, 860-236-6311; FAX: 860-244-1449

Combat Military Ordnance Ltd., 3900 Hopkins St., Savannah, GA 31405/912-238-1900; FAX: 912-236-7570

Companhia Brasileira de Cartuchos (See CBC)

Compass Industries, Inc., 104 East 25th St., New York, NY 10010/212-473-2614, 800-221-9904; FAX: 212-353-0826

Compasseco, Ltd., 151 Atkinson Hill Ave., Bardtown, KY 40004/502-349-0910

Competition Electronics, Inc., 3469 Precision Dr., Rockford, IL 61109/815-874-8001; FAX: 815-874-8181

Competitive Pistol Shop, The, 5233 Palmer Dr., Ft. Worth, TX 76117-2433/817-834-8479

Competitor Corp., Inc., Appleton Business Center, 30 Tricnit Road, Unit 16, New Ipswich, NH 03071-0508/603-878-3891; FAX: 603-878-3950

Component Concepts, Inc., 10240 SW Nimbus Ave., Suite L-8, Portland, OR 97223/503-684-9262; FAX: 503-620-4285

Concept Development Corp., 14715 N. 78th Way, Suite 300, Scottsdale, AZ 85260/800-472-4405; FAX: 602-948-7560

Condon, Inc., David, 109 E. Washington St., Middleburg, VA 22117/703-687-5642

Conetrol Scope Mounts, 10225 Hwy. 123 S., Seguin, TX 78155/210-379-3030, 800-CONETROL; FAX: 210-379-3030

CONKKO, P.O. Box 40, Broomall, PA 19008/215-356-0711

Connecticut Shotgun Mfg. Co., P.O. Box 1692, 35 Woodland St., New Britain, CT 06051-1692/860-225-6581; FAX: 860-832-8707

Connecticut Valley Classics (See CVC)

Conrad, C.A., 3964 Ebert St., Winston-Salem, NC 27127/919-788-5469

Continental Kite & Key (See CONKKO)

Cook Engineering Service, 891 Highbury Rd., Vermont VICT 3133 AUSTRALIA

Coonan Arms (JS Worldwide DBA), 1745 Hwy. 36 E., Maplewood, MN 55109/612-777-3156; FAX: 612-777-3683

Cooper Arms, P.O. Box 114, Stevensville, MT 59870/406-777-5534; FAX: 406-777-5228

Cooper-Woodward, 3800 Pelican Rd., Helena, MT 59602/406-458-3800

Corbin Mfg. & Supply, Inc., 600 Industrial Circle, P.O. Box 2659, White City, OR 97503/541-826-5211; FAX: 541-826-8669

Cor-Bon Bullet & Ammo Co., 1311 Industry Rd., Sturgis, SD 57785/800-626-7266; FAX: 800-923-2666

Corkys Gun Clinic, 4401 Hot Springs Dr., Greeley, CO 80634-9226/970-330-0516

Corry, John, 861 Princeton Ct., Neshanic Station, NJ 08853/908-369-8019

Cosmi Americo & Figlio s.n.c., Via Flaminia 307, Ancona, ITALY I-60020/071-888208; FAX: 39-071-887008 (U.S. importer—New England Arms Co.)

Costa, David (See Island Pond Gun Shop)

Coulston Products, Inc., P.O. Box 30, 201 Ferry St., Suite 212, Easton, PA 18044-0030/215-253-0167, 800-445-9927; FAX: 215-252-1511

Counter Assault, Box 4721, Missoula, MT 59806/406-728-6241; FAX: 406-728-8800

Country Armourer, The, P.O. Box .308, Ashby, MA 01431-0308/508-827-6797; FAX: 508-827-4845

Cousin Bob's Mountain Products, 7119 Ohio River Blvd., Ben Avon, PA 15202/412-766-5114; FAX: 412-766-5114

Cox, Ed C., RD 2, Box 192, Prosperity, PA 15329/412-228-4984

CQB Training, P.O. Box 1739, Manchester, MO 63011

Craftguard, 3624 Logan Ave., Waterloo, IA 50703/319-232-2959; FAX: 319-234-0804

Craig Custom Ltd., Research & Development, 629 E. 10th, Hutchinson, KS 67501/316-669-0601

Crandall Tool & Machine Co., 19163 21 Mile Rd., Tustin, MI 49688/616-829-4430

Crane & Crane Ltd., 105 N. Edison Way 6, Reno, NV 89502-2355/702-856-1516; FAX: 702-856-1616

Creative Concepts USA, Inc., P.O. Box 1705, Dickson, TN 37056/615-446-8346, 800-874-6965; FAX: 615-446-0646

Creative Craftsman, Inc., The, 95 Highway 29 North, P.O. Box 331, Lawrenceville, GA 30246/404-963-2112; FAX: 404-513-9488

Creedmoor Sports, Inc., P.O. Box 1040, Oceanside, CA 92051/619-757-5529

Creek Side Metal & Woodcrafters (See Allard, Gary)

Creekside Gun Shop, Inc., Main St., Holcomb, NY 14469/716-657-6338; FAX: 716-657-7900

Crimson Trace, 1433 N.W. Quimby, Portland, OR 97209/503-295-2406; 503-295-2225

Crit'R Call (See Rocky Mountain Wildlife Products)

Crosman Airguns, Rts. 5 and 20, E. Bloomfield, NY 14443/716-657-6161; FAX: 716-657-5405

Crosman Blades (See Coleman Co., Inc.)

Crosman Products of Canada Ltd., 1173 N. Service Rd. West, Oakville, Ontario, L6M 2V9 CANADA/905-827-1822

Crossfire LLC, 2169 Greenville Rd., La Grange, GA 30241/706-882-8070; FAX: 706-882-9050

Crouse's Country Cover, P.O. Box 160, Storrs, CT 06268/860-423-8736

CRR, Inc./Marble's Inc., 420 Industrial Park, P.O. Box 111, Gladstone, MI 49837/906-428-3710; FAX: 906-428-3711

Crucelegui, Hermanos (See U.S. importer—Mandall Shooting Supplies, Inc.)

Cryo-Accurizing, 2101 East Olive, Decatur, IL 62526/217-423-3070; FAX: 217-423-3075

Cubic Shot Shell Co., Inc., 98 Fatima Dr., Campbell, OH 44405/330-755-0349

Cullity Restoration, Daniel, 209 Old County Rd., East Sandwich, MA 02537/508-888-1147

Cumberland Arms, 514 Shafer Road, Manchester, TN 37355/800-797-8414

Cumberland Knife & Gun Works, 5661 Bragg Blvd., Fayetteville, NC 28303/919-867-0009

Cumberland Mountain Arms, P.O. Box 710, Winchester, TN 37398/615-967-8414; FAX: 615-967-9199

Cumberland States Arsenal, 1124 Palmyra Road, Clarksville, TN 37040

Cummings Bullets, 1417 Esperanza Way, Escondido, CA 92027

Cupp, Alana, Custom Engraver, P.O. Box 207, Annabella, UT 84711/801-896-4834

Curly Maple Stock Blanks (See Tiger-Hunt)

Curtis Custom Shop, RR1, Box 193A, Wallingford, KY 41093/703-659-4265

Curtis Cast Bullets, 527 W Babcock St., Bozeman, MT 59715/406-587-8117; FAX: 406-587-8117

Curtis Gun Shop (See Curtis Cast Bullets)

Custom Barreling & Stocks, 937 Lee Hedrick Rd., Colville, WA 99114/509-684-5686 (days), 509-684-3314 (evenings)

Custom Bullets by Hoffman, 2604 Peconic Ave., Seaford, NY 11783

Custom Calls, 607 N. 5th St., Burlington, IA 52601/319-752-4465

Custom Checkering Service, Kathy Forster, 2124 SE Yamhill St., Portland, OR 97214/503-236-5874

Custom Chronograph, Inc., 5305 Reese Hill Rd., Sumas, WA 98295/360-988-7801

Custom Firearms (See Ahrends, Kim)

Custom Gun Products, 5021 W. Rosewood, Spokane, WA 99208/509-328-9340

Custom Gun Stocks, Rt. 6, P.O. Box 177, McMinnville, TN 37110/615-668-3912

Custom Gunsmiths, 4303 Friar Lane, Colorado Springs, CO 80907/719-599-3366

Custom Hunting Ammo & Arms (See CHAA, Ltd.)

Custom Products (See Jones Custom Products, Neil A.)

Custom Quality Products, Inc., 345 W. Girard Ave., P.O. Box 71129, Madison Heights, MI 48071/810-585-1616; FAX: 810-585-0644

Custom Riflestocks, Inc., Michael M. Kokolus, 7005 Herber Rd., New Tripoli, PA 18066/610-298-3013

Custom Shop, The, 890 Cochrane Crescent, Peterborough, Ont. K9H 5N3 CANADA/705-742-6693

Custom Tackle and Ammo, P.O. Box 1886, Farmington, NM 87499/505-632-3539

Cutco Cutlery, P.O. Box 810, Olean, NY 14760/716-372-3111

Cutlery Shoppe, 5461 Kendall St., Boise, ID 83706-1248/800-231-1272

CVA, 5988 Peachtree Corners East, Norcross, GA 30071/800-251-9412; FAX: 404-242-8546

CVC, 48 Commercial Street, Holyoke, MA 01040/413-552-3184; FAX: 413-552-3276

Cylinder & Slide, Inc., William R. Laughridge, 245 E. 4th St., Fremont, NE 68025/402-721-4277; FAX: 402-721-0263

CZ USA, 40356 Oak Park Way, Suite W, Oakhurst, CA 93664

D

D&D Gunsmiths, Ltd., 363 E. Elmwood, Troy, MI 48083/810-583-1512; FAX: 810-583-1524

D&G Precision Duplicators (See Greene Precision Duplicators)

D&H Precision Tooling, 7522 Barnard Mill Rd., Ringwood, IL 60072/815-653-4011

D&H Prods. Co., Inc., 465 Denny Rd., Valencia, PA 16059/412-898-2840, 800-776-0281; FAX: 412-898-2013

D&J Bullet Co. & Custom Gun Shop, Inc., 426 Ferry St., Russell, KY 41169/606-836-2663; FAX: 606-836-2663

D&L Industries (See D.J. Marketing)

D&L Sports, P.O. Box 651, Gillette, WY 82717/307-686-4008

D&R Distributing, 308 S.E. Valley St., Myrtle Creek, OR 97457/503-863-6850

Dade Screw Machine Products, 2319 NW 7th Ave., Miami, FL 33150/305-573-5050

Daewoo Precision Industries Ltd., 34-3 Yeoeuido-Dong, Yeongdeungoo-GU, 15th, Fl./Seoul, KOREA (U.S. importer—Nationwide Sports Distributors, Inc.)

Daisy Mfg. Co., P.O. Box 220, Rogers, AR 72757/501-621-4210; FAX: 501-636-0573

Dakota (See U.S. importer—EMF Co., Inc.)

Dakota Arms, Inc., HC 55, Box 326, Sturgis, SD 57785/605-347-4686; FAX: 605-347-4459

Dakota Corp., 77 Wales St., P.O. Box 543, Rutland, VT 05701/802-775-6062, 800-451-4167; FAX: 802-773-3919

Daly, Charles (See B.C. Miroku/Charles Daly)

DAMASCUS-U.S.A., 149 Deans Farm Rd., Tyner, NC 27980/252-221-2010; FAX: 252-221-2009

Dan's Whetstone Co., Inc., 130 Timbs Place, Hot Springs, AR 71913/501-767-1616; FAX: 501-767-9598

Dangler, Homer L., Box 254, Addison, MI 49220/517-547-6745

Danner Shoe Mfg. Co., 12722 NE Airport Way, Portland, OR 97230/503-251-1100, 800-345-0430; FAX: 503-251-1119

Danuser Machine Co., 550 E. Third St., P.O. Box 368, Fulton, MO 65251/573-642-2246; FAX: 573-642-2240

Dapkus Co., Inc., J.G., Commerce Circle, P.O. Box 293, Durham, CT 06422

Dara-Nes, Inc. (See Nesci Enterprises, Inc.)

Darlington Gun Works, Inc., P.O. Box 698, 516 S. 52 Bypass, Darlington, SC 29532/803-393-3931

Data Tech Software Systems, 19312 East Eldorado Drive, Aurora, CO 80013

Datumtech Corp., 2275 Wehrle Dr., Buffalo, NY 14221

Dave's Gun Shop, 555 Wood Street, Powell, Wyoming 82435/307-754-9724

Davidson, Jere, Rt. 1, Box 132, Rustburg, VA 24588/804-821-3637

Davis, Don, 1619 Heights, Katy, TX 77493/713-391-3090

Davis Co., R.E., 3450 Pleasantville NE, Pleasantville, OH 43148/614-654-9990

Davis Industries, 15150 Sierra Bonita Ln., Chino, CA 91710/909-597-4726; FAX: 909-393-9771

Davis Leather Co., Gordon Wm., P.O. Box 2270, Walnut, CA 91788/909-598-5620

Davis Products, Mike, 643 Loop Dr., Moses Lake, WA 98837/509-765-6178, 509-766-7281 orders only

Davis Service Center, Bill, 7221 Florin Mall Dr., Sacramento, CA 95823/916-393-4867

Day & Sons, Inc., Leonard, P.O. Box 122, Flagg Hill Rd., Heath, MA 01346/413-337-8369

Dayson Arms Ltd., P.O. Box 532, Vincennes, IN 47591/812-882-8680; FAX: 812-882-8680

Daystate Ltd., Birch House Lanee, Cotes Heath, Staffs, ST15.022 ENGLAND/ 01782-791755; FAX: 01782-791617

Dayton Traister, 4778 N. Monkey Hill Rd., P.O. Box 593, Oak Harbor, WA 98277/360-679-4657; FAX:360-675-1114

DBASE Consultants (See Arms, Peripheral Data Systems)

DBI Books, Division of Krause Publications, (Editorial office) 700 E. State St., Iola, WI 54990/715-445-2214: FAX: 715-445-4087: Orders: 800-258-0929

D-Boone Ent., Inc., 5900 Colwyn Dr., Harrisburg, PA 17109

D.C.C. Enterprises, 259 Wynburn Ave., Athens, GA 30601

D.D. Custom Stocks, R.H. "Dick" Devereaux, 5240 Mule Deer Dr., Colorado Springs, CO 80919/719-548-8468

de Coux, Pete (See Cartridge Transfer Group)

de Treville & Co., Stan, 4129 Normal St., San Diego, CA 92103/619-298-3393

Dead Eye's Sport Center, RD 1, Box 147B, Shickshinny, PA 18655/717-256-7432

Decker Shooting Products, 1729 Laguna Ave., Schofield, WI 54476/715-359-5873

DeckSlider of Florida, 27641-2 Reahard Ct., Bonita Springs, FL 33923/800-782-1474

Deepeeka Exports Pvt. Ltd., D-78, Saket, Meerut-250-006, INDIA/011-91-121-512889, 011-91-121-545363; FAX: 011-91-121-542988, 011-91-121-511599

Deer Me Products Co., Box 34, 1208 Park St., Anoka, MN 55303/612-421-8971; FAX: 612-422-0526

Defense Training International, Inc., 749 S. Lemay, Ste. A3-337, Ft. Collins, CO 80524/303-482-2520; FAX: 303-482-0548

Degen Inc. (See Aristocrat Knives)

deHaas Barrels, RR 3, Box 77, Ridgeway, MO 64481/816-872-6308

Del Rey Products, P.O. Box 91561, Los Angeles, CA 90009/213-823-0494

Delhi Gun House, 1374 Kashmere Gate, Delhi, INDIA 110 006/(011)2940974 2940814; FAX: 91-11-2917344

Delorge, Ed, 2231 Hwy. 308, Thibodaux, LA 70301/504-447-1633

Del-Sports, Inc., Box 685, Main St., Margaretville, NY 12455/914-586-4103; FAX: 914-586-4105

Delta Arms Ltd., P.O. Box 1000, Delta, VT 84624-1000

Delta Enterprises, 284 Hagemann Drive, Livermore, CA 94550

Delta Frangible Ammunition, LLC, P.O. Box 2350, Stafford, VA 22555-2350/540-720-5778, 800-339-1933; FAX: 540-720-5667

Dem-Bart Checkering Tools, Inc., 6807 Bickford Ave., Old Hwy. 2, Snohomish, WA 98290/360-568-7356; FAX: 360-568-1798

Denver Bullets, Inc., 1811 W. 13th Ave., Denver, CO 80204/303-893-3146; FAX: 303-893-9161

Denver Instrument Co., 6542 Fig St., Arvada, CO 80004/800-321-1135, 303-431-7255; FAX: 303-423-4831

DeSantis Holster & Leather Goods, Inc., P.O. Box 2039, 149 Denton Ave., New Hyde Park, NY 11040-0701/516-354-8000; FAX: 516-354-7501

Desert Mountain Mfg., P.O. Box 130184, Coram, MT 59913/800-477-0762, 406-387-5361; FAX 406-387-5361

Detroit-Armor Corp., 720 Industrial Dr. No. 112, Cary, IL 60013/708-639-7666; FAX: 708-639-7694

Dever Co., Jack, 8590 NW 90, Oklahoma City, OK 73132/405-721-6393

Devereaux, R.H. "Dick" (See D.D. Custom Stocks)

Dewey Mfg. Co., Inc., J., P.O. Box 2014, Southbury, CT 06488/203-264-3064; FAX: 203-262-6907

DGR Custom Rifles, RR1, Box 8A, Tappen, ND 58487/701-327-8135

DGS, Inc., Dale A. Storey, 1117 E. 12th, Casper, WY 82601/307-237-2414; FAX 307-237-2414

DHB Products, P.O. Box 3092, Alexandria, VA 22302/703-836-2648

Diamond Machining Techonology (See DMT—Diamond Machining Technology)

Diamond Mfg. Co., P.O. Box 174, Wyoming, PA 18644/800-233-9601

Diana (See U.S. importer—Dynamit Nobel-RWS, Inc.)

Dibble, Derek A., 555 John Downey Dr., New Britain, CT 06051/203-224-2630

Dietz Gun Shop & Range, Inc., 421 Range Rd., New Braunfels, TX 78132/210-885-4662

Dilliott Gunsmithing, Inc., 657 Scarlett Rd., Dandridge, TN 37725/423-397-9204

Dillon, Ed, 1035 War Eagle Dr. N., Colorado Springs, CO 80919/719-598-4929; FAX: 719-598-4929

Dillon Precision Products, Inc., 8009 East Dillon's Way, Scottsdale, AZ 85260/602-948-8009, 800-762-3845; FAX: 602-998-2786

Dina Arms Corporation, P.O. Box 46, Royersford, PA 19468/610-287-0266; FAX: 610-287-0266

Division Lead Co., 7742 W. 61st Pl., Summit, IL 60502

Dixie Gun Works, Inc., Hwy. 51 South, Union City, TN 38261/901-885-0561, order 800-238-6785; FAX: 901-885-0440

Dixon Muzzleloading Shop, Inc., 9952 Kunkels Mill Rd., Kempton, PA 19529/610-756-6271

D.J. Marketing, 10602 Horton Ave., Downey, CA 90241/310-806-0891; FAX: 310-806-6231

DKT, Inc., 14623 Vera Drive, Union, MI 49130-9744/616-641-7120, 800-741-7083 orders only; FAX: 616-641-2015

DLO Mfg., 10807 SE Foster Ave., Arcadia, FL 33821-7304

DMT—Diamond Machining Technology, Inc., 85 Hayes Memorial Dr., Marlborough, MA 01752/508-481-5944; FAX: 508-485-3924

Dogtown Varmint Supplies, 1048 Irvine Ave. No. 333, Newport Beach, CA 92660/714-642-3997

Dohring Bullets, 100 W. 8 Mile Rd., Ferndale, MI 48220

Dolbare, Elizabeth, P.O. Box 222, Sunburst, MT 59482-0222

Donnelly, C.P., 405 Kubli Rd., Grants Pass, OR 97527/541-846-6604

Doskocil Mfg. Co., Inc., P.O. Box 1246, 4209 Barnett, Arlington, TX 76017/817-467-5116; FAX: 817-472-9810

Double A Ltd., P.O. Box 11306, Minneapolis, MN 55411/612-522-0306

Douglas Barrels, Inc., 5504 Big Tyler Rd., Charleston, WV 25313-1398/304-776-1341; FAX: 304-776-8560

Downsizer Corp., P.O. Box 710316, Santee, CA 92072-0316/619/448-5510; FAX: 619-448-5780

Dowtin Gunworks, Rt. 4, Box 930A, Flagstaff, AZ 86001/602-779-1898

Dr. O's Products Ltd., P.O. Box 111, Niverville, NY 12130/518-784-3333; FAX: 518-784-2800

Drain, Mark, SE 3211 Kamilche Point Rd., Shelton, WA 98584/206-426-5452

Dremel Mfg. Co., 4915-21st St., Racine, WI 53406

Dressel Jr., Paul G., 209 N. 92nd Ave., Yakima, WA 98908/509-966-9233; FAX: 509-966-3365

Dri-Slide, Inc., 411 N. Darling, Fremont, MI 49412/616-924-3950

Dropkick, 1460 Washington Blvd., Williamsport, PA 17701/717-326-6561; FAX: 717-326-4950

DTM International, Inc., 40 Joslyn Rd., P.O. Box 5, Lake Orion, MI 48362/313-693-6670

Duane Custom Stocks, Randy, 110 W. North Ave., Winchester, VA 22601/703-667-9461; FAX: 703-722-3993

Duane's Gun Repair (See DGR Custom Rifles)

Dubber, Michael W., P.O. Box 312, Evansville, IN 47702/812-424-9000; FAX: 812-424-6551

Duck Call Specialists, P.O. Box 124, Jerseyville, IL 62052/618-498-9855

Duffy (See Guns Antique & Modern DBA/Charles E. Duffy)

Du-Lite Corp., Charles E., 171 River Rd., Middletown, CT 06457/203-347-2505; FAX: 203-347-9404

Dumoulin, Ernest, Rue Florent Boclinville 8-10, 13-4041 Votten, BELGIUM/41 27 78 92 (U.S. importer—New England Arms Co.)

Duncan's Gun Works, Inc., 1619 Grand Ave., San Marcos, CA 92069/619-727-0515

Dunham Co., P.O. Box 813, Brattleboro, VT 05301/802-254-2316

Dunphy, Ted, W. 5100 Winch Rd., Rathdrum, ID 83858/208-687-1399; FAX: 208-687-1399

Duofold, Inc., RD 3 Rt. 309, Valley Square Mall, Tamaqua, PA 18252/717-386-2666; FAX: 717-386-3652

DuPont (See IMR Powder Co.)

Dutchman's Firearms, Inc., The, 4143 Taylor Blvd., Louisville, KY 40215/502-366-0555

Dybala Gun Shop, P.O. Box 1024, FM 3156, Bay City, TX 77414/409-245-0866

Dykstra, Doug, 411 N. Darling, Fremont, MI 49412/616-924-3950

Dynalite Products, Inc., 215 S. Washington St., Greenfield, OH 45123/513-981-2124

Dynamit Nobel-RWS, Inc., 81 Ruckman Rd., Closter, NJ 07624/201-767-7971; FAX: 201-767-1589

Dyson & Son Ltd., Peter, 3 Cuckoo Lane, Honley, Huddersfield, Yorkshire HD7 2BR, ENGLAND/44-1484-661062; FAX: 44-1484-663709

E

E&L Mfg., Inc., 4177 Riddle by Pass Rd., Riddle, OR 97469/541-874-2137; FAX: 541-874-3107

E.A.A. Corp., P.O. Box 1299, Sharpes, FL 32959/407-639-4842, 800-536-4442; FAX: 407-639-7006

Eagan, Donald V., P.O. Box 196, Benton, PA 17814/717-925-6134

Eagle Arms (See ArmaLite, Inc.)

Eagle Grips, Eagle Business Center, 460 Randy Rd., Carol Stream, IL 60188/800-323-6144, 708-260-0400; FAX: 708-260-0486

Eagle Imports, Inc., 1750 Brielle Ave., Unit B1, Wanamassa, NJ 07712/908-493-0333; FAX: 908-493-0301

Eagle International Sporting Goods, Inc., P.O. Box 67, Zap, ND 58580/888-932-4536; FAX: 701-948-2282

E-A-R, Inc., Div. of Cabot Safety Corp., 5457 W. 79th St., Indianapolis, IN 46268/800-327-3431; FAX: 800-488-8007

Eastman Products, R.T., P.O. Box 1531, Jackson, WY 83001/307-733-3217, 800-624-4311

EAW (See U.S. importer—New England Custom Gun Service)

Echols & Co., D'Arcy, 164 W. 580 S., Providence, UT 84332/801-753-2367

Eclectic Technologies, Inc., 45 Grandview Dr., Suite A, Farmington, CT 06034

Eckelman Gunsmithing, 3125 133rd St. SW, Fort Ripley, MN 56449/218-829-3176

Ed's Gun House, P.O. Box 62, Minnesota City, MN 55959/507-689-2925

Edenpine, Inc. c/o Six Enterprises, Inc., 320 D Turtle Creek Ct., San Jose, CA 95125/408-999-0201; FAX: 408-999-0216

EdgeCraft Corp./Sam Weiner, 825 Southwood Road, Avondale, PA 19311-9765/610-268-0500, 800-342-3255; FAX: 610-268-3545

Edmisten Co., P.O. Box 1293, Boone, NC 28607

Edmund Scientific Co., 101 E. Gloucester Pike, Barrington, NJ 08033/609-543-6250

Ednar, Inc., 2-4-8 Kayabacho, Nihonbashi, Chuo-ku, Tokyo, JAPAN 103/81(Japan)-3-3667-1651; FAX: 81-3-3661-8113

Eezox, Inc., P.O. Box 772, Waterford, CT 06385-0772/860-447-8282, 800-462-3331; FAX: 860-447-3484

Effebi SNC-Dr. Franco Beretta, via Rossa, 4, 25062 Concesio, Italy/030-2751955; FAX: 030-2180414 (U.S. importer—Nevada Cartridge Co.

Efficient Machinery Co., 12878 N.E. 15th Pl., Bellevue, WA 98005

Eggleston, Jere D., 400 Saluda Ave., Columbia, SC 29205/803-799-3402

EGW Evolution Gun Works, 4050 B-8 Skyron Dr., Doylestown, PA 18901/215-348-9892; FAX: 215-348-1056

Eichelberger Bullets, Wm., 158 Crossfield Rd., King of Prussia, PA 19406

EK Knife Co., c/o Blackjack Knives, Ltd., 1307 Wabash Ave., Effingham, IL 62401

Ekol Leather Care, P.O. Box 2652, West Lafayette, IN 47906/317-463-2250; FAX: 317-463-7004

El Dorado Leather (c/o Dill), P.O. Box 566, Benson, AZ 85602/520-586-4791; FAX: 520-586-4791

El Paso Saddlery Co., P.O. Box 27194, El Paso, TX 79926/915-544-2233; FAX: 915-544-2535

Eldorado Cartridge Corp. (See PMC/Eldorado Cartridge Corp.)

Electro Prismatic Collimators, Inc., 1441 Manatt St., Lincoln, NE 68521

Electronic Shooters Protection, Inc., 11997 West 85th Place, Arvada, CO 80005/303-456-8964; 800-797-7791; FAX: 303-456-7179

Electronic Trigger Systems, Inc., P.O. Box 13, 230 Main St. S., Hector, MN 55342/320-848-2760; FAX: 320-848-2760

Eley Ltd., P.O. Box 705, Witton, Birmingham, B6 7UT, ENGLAND/021-356-8899; FAX: 021-331-4173

Elite Ammunition, P.O. Box 3251, Oakbrook, IL 60522/708-366-9006

Elk River, Inc., 1225 Paonia St., Colorado Springs, CO 80915/719-574-4407

Elkhorn Bullets, P.O. Box 5293, Central Point, OR 97502/541-826-7440

Ellett Bros., 267 Columbia Ave., P.O. Box 128, Chapin, SC 29036/803-345-3751, 800-845-3711; FAX: 803-345-1820

Ellicott Arms, Inc./Woods Pistolsmithing, 3840 Dahlgren Ct., Ellicott City, MD 21042/410-465-7979

Elliott Inc., G.W., 514 Burnside Ave., East Hartford, CT 06108/203-289-5741; FAX: 203-289-3137

Elsen, Inc., Pete, 1529 S. 113th St., West Allis, WI 53214

Emerging Technologies, Inc. (See Laseraim Technologies, Inc.)

EMF Co., Inc., 1900 E. Warner Ave. Suite 1-D, Santa Ana, CA 92705/714-261-6611; FAX: 714-756-0133

Empire Cutlery Corp., 12 Kruger Ct., Clifton, NJ 07013/201-472-5155; FAX: 201-779-0759

Engineered Accessories, 1307 W. Wabash Ave., Effingham, IL 62401/217-347-7700; FAX: 217-347-7737

English, Inc., A.G., 708 S. 12th St., Broken Arrow, OK 74012/918-251-3399

Englishtown Sporting Goods Co., Inc., David J. Maxham, 38 Main St., Englishtown, NJ 07726/201-446-7717

Engraving Artistry, 36 Alto Rd., RFD 2, Burlington, CT 06013/203-673-6837

Enguix Import-Export, Alpujarras 58, Alzira, Valencia, SPAIN 46600/(96) 241 43 95; FAX: (96) (241 43 95) 240 21 53

Enhanced Presentations, Inc., 5929 Market St., Wilmington, NC 28405/910-799-1622; FAX: 910-799-5004

Enlow, Charles, 895 Box, Beaver, OK 73932/405-625-4487

Ensign-Bickford Co., The, 660 Hopmeadow St., Simsbury, CT 06070

Entre`prise Arms Inc., 15861 Business Center Dr., Irwindale, CA 91706

EPC, 1441 Manatt St., Lincoln, NE 68521/402-476-3946

Epps, Ellwood (See "Gramps" Antique Cartridges)

Erhardt, Dennis, 3280 Green Meadow Dr., Helena, MT 59601/406-442-4533

Erickson's Mfg., Inc., C.W., 530 Garrison Ave. N.E., P.O. Box 522, Buffalo, MN 55313/612-682-3665; FAX: 612-682-4328

Erma Werke GmbH, Johan Ziegler St., 13/15/FeldiglSt., D-8060 Dachau, GERMANY (U.S. importers—Amtec 2000, Inc.; Mandall Shooting Supplies, Inc.)

Eskridge Rifles, Steven Eskridge, 218 N. Emerson, Mart, TX 76664/817-876-3544

Essex Arms, P.O. Box 345, Island Pond, VT 05846/802-723-4313

Essex Metals, 1000 Brighton St., Union, NJ 07083/800-282-8369

Estate Cartridge, Inc., 12161 FM 830, Willis, TX 77378/409-856-7277; FAX: 409-856-5486

Euber Bullets, No. Orwell Rd., Orwell, VT 05760/802-948-2621

Euro-Imports, 614 Millar Ave., El Cajon, CA 92020/619-442-7005; FAX: 619-442-7005

Euroarms of America, Inc., P.O. Box 3277, Winchester, VA 22604/540-662-1863; FAX: 540-662-4464

European American Armory Corp. (See E.A.A. Corp.)

Europtik Ltd., PO Box 319, Dunmore PA 18512/717-347-6049;717-969-4330

Eutaw Co., Inc., The, P.O. Box 608, U.S. Hwy. 176 West, Holly Hill, SC 29059/803-496-3341

Evans, Andrew, 2325 NW Squire St., Albany, OR 97321/541-928-3190; FAX: 541-928-4128

Evans Engraving, Robert, 332 Vine St., Oregon City, OR 97045/503-656-5693

Evans Gunsmithing (See Evans, Andrew)

Eversull Co., Inc., K., 1 Tracemont, Boyce, LA 71409/318-793-8728; FAX: 318-793-5483

Excalibur Enterprises, P.O. Box 400, Fogelsville, PA 18051-0400/610-391-9105; FAX: 610-391-9220

Exe, Inc., 18830 Partridge Circle, Eden Prairie, MN 55346/612-944-7662

Executive Protection Institute, Rt. 2, Box 3645, Berryville, VA 22611/540-955-1128

C. Eyears, Roland, 576 Binns Blvd., Columbus, OH 43204-2441

Eyster Heritage Gunsmiths, Inc., Ken, 6441 Bishop Rd., Centerburg, OH 43011/614-625-6131

Eze-Lap Diamond Prods., P.O. Box 2229, 15164 Weststate St., Westminster, CA 92683/714-847-1555; FAX: 714-897-0280

E-Z-Way Systems, P.O. Box 4310, Newark, OH 43058-4310/614-345-6645, 800-848-2072; FAX: 614-345-6600

F

F&A Inc. (See ShurKatch Corporation)

Fabarm S.p.A., Via Averolda 31, 25039 Travagliato, Brescia, ITALY/030-6863629; FAX: 030-6863684 (U.S. importer—Ithaca Gun Co., LLC)

Fagan & Co., William, 22952 15 Mile Rd., Clinton Township, MI 48035/810-465-4637; FAX: 810-792-6996

Fair Game International, P.O. Box 77234-34053, Houston, TX 77234/713-941-6269

F.A.I.R. Techni-Mec s.n.c. di Isidoro Rizzini & C., Via Gitti, 41 Zona I, dustriale/25060 Marcheno (Brescia), ITALY 030/861162-8610344; FAX: 030/8610179

Faith Associates, Inc., 1139 S. Greenville Hwy., Hendersonville, NC 28792/828-692-1916; FAX: 828-697-6827

Famas (See U.S. importer—Century International Arms, Inc.)

Fanzoj GmbH, Griesgasse 1, 9170 Ferlach, AUSTRIA 9170/(43) 04227-2283; FAX: (43) 04227-2867; email: jfanzoj@netway.at

Far North Outfitters, Box 1252, Bethel, AK 99559

Farm Form Decoys, Inc., 1602 Biovu, P.O. Box 748, Galveston, TX 77553/409-744-0762, 409-765-6361; FAX: 409-765-8513

Farmer-Dressel, Sharon, 209 N. 92nd Ave., Yakima, WA 98908/509-966-9233; FAX: 509-966-3365

Farr Studio, Inc., 1231 Robinhood Rd., Greeneville, TN 37743/615-638-8825

Farrar Tool Co., Inc., 12150 Bloomfield Ave., Suite E, Santa Fe Springs, CA 90670/310-863-4367; FAX: 310-863-5123

FAS, Via E. Fermi, 8, 20019 Settimo Milanese, Milano, ITALY/02-3285844; FAX: 02-33500196 (U.S. importer—Nygord Precision Products)

Faulhaber Wildlocker, Dipl.-Ing. Norbert Wittasek, Seilergasse 2, A-1010 Wien, AUSTRIA/OM-43-1-5137001; FAX: OM-43-1-5137001

Faulk's Game Call Co., Inc., 616 18th St., Lake Charles, LA 70601/318-436-9726

Faust, Inc., T.G., 544 Minor St., Reading, PA 19602/610-375-8549; FAX: 610-375-4488

Fausti Cav. Stefano & Figlie snc, Via Martiri Dell Indipendenza, 70, Marcheno, ITALY 25060 (U.S. importer—American Arms, Inc.)

Fautheree, Andy, Black Powder Specialties, P.O. Box 4607, Pagosa Springs, CO 81157/970-731-5003; FAX 970-731-5009

Feather, Flex Decoys, 1655 Swan Lake Rd., Bossier City, LA 71111/318-746-8596; FAX: 318-742-4815

Federal Arms Corp. of America, 7928 University Ave., Fridley, MN 55432/612-780-8780; FAX: 612-780-8780

Federal Cartridge Co., 900 Ehlen Dr., Anoka, MN 55303/612-323-2300; FAX: 612-323-2506

Federal Champion Target Co., 232 Industrial Parkway, Richmond, IN 47374/800-441-4971; FAX: 317-966-7747

Federated-Fry (See Fry Metals)

FEG, Budapest, Soroksariut 158, H-1095 HUNGARY (U.S. importers—Century International Arms, Inc.; K.B.I., Inc.)

Feinwerkbau Westinger & Altenburger GmbH (See FWB)

Feken, Dennis, Rt. 2 Box 124, Perry, OK 73077/405-336-5611

Felk Inc., 2121 Castlebridge Rd., Midlothian, VA 23113/804-794-3744

Fellowes, Ted, Beaver Lodge, 9245 16th Ave. SW, Seattle, WA 98106/206-763-1698

Feminine Protection, Inc., 10514 Shady Trail, Dallas, TX 75220/214-351-4500; FAX: 214-352-4686

Ferguson, Bill, P.O. Box 1238, Sierra Vista, AZ 85636/520-458-5321; FAX: 520-458-9125

FERLIB, Via Costa 46, 25063 Gardone V.T. (Brescia) ITALY/30-89-12-586; FAX: 30-89-12-586 (U.S. importer—Harry Marx)

Ferris Firearms, 7110 F.M. 1863, Bulverde, TX 78163/210-980-4424

Fibron Products, Inc., P.O. Box 430, Buffalo, NY 14209-0430/716-886-2378; FAX: 716-886-2394

Fiocchi Munizioni S.p.A. (See U.S. importer—Fiocchi of America, Inc.)

Fiocchi of America, Inc., 5030 Fremont Rd., Ozark, MO 65721/417-725-4118, 800-721-2666; FAX: 417-725-1039

Firearm Training Center, The, 9555 Blandville Rd., West Paducah, KY 42086/502-554-5886

Firearms Co. Ltd./Alpine (See U.S. importer—Mandall Shooting Supplies, Inc.)

Firearms Engraver's Guild of America, 332 Vine St., Oregon City, OR 97045/503-656-5693

Firearms International, 5709 Hartsdale, Houston, TX 77036/713-460-2447

First, Inc., Jack, 1201 Turbine Dr., Rapid City, SD 57701/605-343-9544; FAX: 605-343-9420

Fish Mfg. Gunsmith Sptg. Co., Marshall F., Rd. Box 2439, Rt. 22 North, Westport, NY 12993/518-962-4897

Fisher, Jerry A., 553 Crane Mt. Rd., Big Fork, MT 59911/406-837-2722

Fisher Custom Firearms, 2199 S. Kittredge Way, Aurora, CO 80013/303-755-3710

Fisher Enterprises, Inc., 1071 4th Ave. S., Suite 303, Edmonds, WA 98020-4143/206-771-5382

Fisher, R. Kermit (See Fisher Enterprises, Inc.)

Fitz Pistol Grip Co., P.O. Box 610, Douglas City, CA 96024/916-778-0240

Flaig's, 2200 Evergreen Rd., Millvale, PA 15209/412-821-1717

Flambeau Products Corp., 15981 Valplast Rd., Middlefield, OH 44062/216-632-1631; FAX: 216-632-1581

Flannery Engraving Co., Jeff W., 11034 Riddles Run Rd., Union, KY 41091/606-384-3127

Flashette Co., 15620 Oak Park Ave., Oak Forest, IL 60452/708-532-9193; FAX: 708-532-9624

Flayderman & Co., Inc., N., P.O. Box 2446, Ft. Lauderdale, FL 33303/305-761-8855

Fleming Firearms, 7720 E 126th St. N, Collinsville, OK 74021-7016/918-665-3624

Flents Products Co., Inc., P.O. Box 2109, Norwalk, CT 06852/203-866-2581; FAX: 203-854-9322

Flintlocks, Etc. (See Beauchamp & Son, Inc.)

Flitz International Ltd., 821 Mohr Ave., Waterford, WI 53185/414-534-5898; FAX: 414-534-2991

Flores Publications, Inc., J. (See Action Direct, Inc.)

Flow-Rite of Tennessee, Inc., 107 Allen St., P.O. Box 196, Bruceton, TN 38317/901-586-2271; FAX: 901-586-2300

Fluoramics, Inc., 18 Industrial Ave., Mahwah, NJ 07430/800-922-0075, 201-825-7035

Flynn's Custom Guns, P.O. Box 7461, Alexandria, LA 71306/318-455-7130

FN Herstal, Voie de Liege 33, Herstal 4040, BELGIUM/(32)41.40.82.83; FAX: (32)41.40.86.79

Fobus International Ltd., P.O. Box 64, Kfar Hess, ISRAEL/40692 972-9-7964170; FAX: 972-9-7964169

Folks, Donald E., 205 W. Lincoln St., Pontiac, IL 61764/815-844-7901

Foothills Video Productions, Inc., P.O. Box 651, Spartanburg, SC 29304/803-573-7023, 800-782-5358

Foredom Electric Co., Rt. 6, 16 Stony Hill Rd., Bethel, CT 06801/203-792-8622

Forgett Jr., Valmore J., 689 Bergen Blvd., Ridgefield, NJ 07657/201-945-2500; FAX: 201-945-6859; E-MAIL: ValForgett@msn.com

Forgreens Tool Mfg., Inc., P.O. Box 990, 723 Austin St., Robert Lee, TX 76945/915-453-2800; FAX: 915-453-2460

Forkin, Ben (See Belt MTN Arms)

Forrest, Inc., Tom, P.O. Box 326, Lakeside, CA 92040/619-561-5800; FAX: 619-561-0227

Forrest Tool Co., P.O. Box 768, 44380 Gordon Lane, Mendocino, CA 95460/707-937-2141; FAX: 717-937-1817

Forster, Kathy (See Custom Checkering Service)

Forster, Larry L., P.O. Box 212, 220 First St. NE, Gwinner, ND 58040-0212/701-678-2475

Forster Products, 82 E. Lanark Ave., Lanark, IL 61046/815-493-6360; FAX: 815-493-2371

Fort Hill Gunstocks, 12807 Fort Hill Rd., Hillsboro, OH 45133/513-466-2763

Fort Knox Security Products, 1051 N. Industrial Park Rd., Orem, UT 84057/801-224-7233, 800-821-5216; FAX: 801-226-5493

Fort Worth Firearms, 2006-B Martin Luther King Fwy., Ft. Worth, TX 76104-6303/817-536-0718; FAX: 817-535-0290

Forthofer's Gunsmithing & Knifemaking, 5535 U.S. Hwy 93S, Whitefish, MT 59937-8411/406-862-2674

Fortune Products, Inc., HC04, Box 303, Marble Falls, TX 78654/830-693-6111; FAX: 830-693-6394

Forty Five Ranch Enterprises, Box 1080, Miami, OK 74355-1080/918-542-5875

Fotar Optics, 1756 E. Colorado Blvd., Pasadena, CA 91106/818-579-3919; FAX: 818-579-7209

Fouling Shot, The, 6465 Parfet St., Arvada, CO 80004

Fountain Products, 492 Prospect Ave., West Springfield, MA 01089/413-781-4651; FAX: 413-733-8217

4-D Custom Die Co., 711 N. Sandusky St., P.O. Box 889, Mt. Vernon, OH 43050-0889/614-397-7214; FAX: 614-397-6600

Fowler, Bob (see Black Powder Products)

4W Ammunition (See Hunters Supply)

Fowler Bullets, 806 Dogwood Dr., Gastonia, NC 28054/704-867-3259

Fox River Mills, Inc., P.O. Box 298, 227 Poplar St., Osage, IA 50461/515-732-3798; FAX: 515-732-5128

Foy Custom Bullets, 104 Wells Ave., Daleville, AL 36322

Francesca, Inc., 3115 Old Ranch Rd., San Antonio, TX 78217/512-826-2584; FAX: 512-826-8211

Franchi S.p.A., Via del Serpente, 12, 25131 Brescia, ITALY/030-3581833; FAX: 030-3581554 (U.S. importer—American Arms, Inc.)

Francotte & Cie S.A., Auguste, rue du Trois Juin 109, 4400 Herstal-Liege, BELGIUM/32-4-248-13-18; FAX: 32-4-948-11-79

Frank Custom Classic Arms, Ron, 7131 Richland Rd., Ft. Worth, TX 76118/817-284-9300; FAX: 817-284-9300

Frank Knives, 13868 NW Keleka Pl., Seal Rock, OR 97376/541-563-3041; FAX: 541-563-3041

Frankonia Jagd, Hofmann & Co., D-97064 Wurzburg, GERMANY/09302-200; FAX: 09302-20200

Franzen International, Inc. (U.S. importer for Peters Stahl GmbH)

Freedom Arms, Inc., P.O. Box 1776, Freedom, WY 83120/307-883-2468, 800-833-4432 (orders only); FAX: 307-883-2005

Freeman Animal Targets, 5519 East County Road, 100 South, Plainsfield, IN 46168/317-272-2663; FAX: 317-272-2674; E-MAIL: Signs@indy.net; WEB: http://www.freemansighs.com

Fremont Tool Works, 1214 Prairie, Ford, KS 67842/316-369-2327

French, J.R., Artistic Engraving, 1712 Creek Ridge Ct., Irving, TX 75060/214-254-2654

Frielich Police Equipment, 211 East 21st St., New York, NY 10010/212-254-3045

Europtik Ltd., P.O. Box 319,, Dunmore, PA 18512/717-347-6049; FAX: 717-969-4330

Front Sight Firearms Training Institute, P.O. Box 2619, Aptos, CA 95001/800-987-7719; FAX: 408-684-2137

Frontier, 2910 San Bernardo, Laredo, TX 78040/956-723-5409; FAX: 956-723-1774

Frontier Arms Co., Inc., 401 W. Rio Santa Cruz, Green Valley, AZ 85614-3932

Frontier Products Co., 164 E. Longview Ave., Columbus, OH 43202/614-262-9357

Frontier Safe Co., 3201 S. Clinton St., Fort Wayne, IN 46806/219-744-7233; FAX: 219-744-6678

Frost Cutlery Co., P.O. Box 22636, Chattanooga, TN 37422/615-894-6079; FAX: 615-894-9576

Fry Metals, 4100 6th Ave., Altoona, PA 16602/814-946-1611

FTI, Inc., 72 Eagle Rock Ave., Box 366, East Hanover, NJ 07936-3104

Fujinon, Inc., 10 High Point Dr., Wayne, NJ 07470/201-633-5600; FAX: 201-633-5216

Fullmer, Geo. M., 2499 Mavis St., Oakland, CA 94601/510-533-4193

Fulmer's Antique Firearms, Chet, P.O. Box 792, Rt. 2 Buffalo Lake, Detroit Lakes, MN 56501/218-847-7712

Fulton Armory, 8725 Bollman Place No. 1, Savage, MD 20763/301-490-9485; FAX: 301-490-9547

Furr Arms, 91 N. 970 W., Orem, UT 84057/801-226-3877; FAX: 801-226-3877

Fusilier Bullets, 10010 N. 6000 W., Highland, UT 84003/801-756-6813

FWB, Neckarstrasse 43, 78727 Oberndorf a. N., GERMANY/07423-814-0; FAX: 07423-814-89 (U.S. importer—Beeman Precision Airguns)

G

G96 Products Co., Inc., River St. Station, P.O. Box 1684, Paterson, NJ 07544/201-684-4050; FAX: 201-684-3848

G&C Bullet Co., Inc., 8835 Thornton Rd., Stockton, CA 95209/209-477-6479; FAX: 209-477-2813

G&H Decoys, Inc., P.O. Box 1208, Hwy. 75 North, Henryetta, OK 74437/918-652-3314; FAX: 918-652-3400

Gage Manufacturing, 663 W. 7th St., A, San Pedro, CA 90731/310-832-3546

Gaillard Barrels, P.O. Box 21, Pathlow, Sask., S0K 3B0 CANADA/306-752-3769; FAX: 306-752-5969

Galati International, P.O. Box 326, Catawissa, MO 63015/314-257-4837; FAX: 314-257-2268

Galaxy Imports Ltd., Inc., P.O. Box 3361, Victoria, TX 77903/512-573-4867; FAX: 512-576-9622

GALCO International Ltd., 2019 W. Quail Ave., Phoenix, AZ 85027/602-258-8295, 800-874-2526; FAX: 602-582-6854

Gamba S.p.A.-Societa Armi Bresciane Srl., Renato, Via Artigiani, 93, 25063 Gardone Val Trompia (BS), ITALY/30-8911640; FAX: 30-8911648 (U.S. importer—Gamba, USA)

Gamba, USA, P.O. Box 60452, Colorado Springs, CO 80960/719-578-1145; FAX: 719-444-0731

Gamco, 1316 67th Street, Emeryville, CA 94608/510-527-5578

Game Haven Gunstocks, 13750 Shire Rd., Wolverine, MI 49799/616-525-8257

Game Winner, Inc., 2625 Cumberland Parkway, Suite 220, Atlanta, GA 30339/770-434-9210; FAX: 770-434-9215

Gamo (See U.S. importers—Arms United Corp.; Daisy Mfg. Co.; Dynamit Nobel-RWS, Inc.; Gamo USA, Inc.)

Gamo USA, Inc., 3911 SW 47th Ave., Ft. Lauderdale, FL 33314/954-581-5822; FAX: 954-581-3165

Gander Mountain, Inc., P.O. Box 128, Hwy. W,, Wilmot, WI 53192/414-862-2331,Ext. 6425

GAR, 590 McBride Avenue, West Paterson, NJ 07424/201-754-1114; FAX: 201-754-1114

Garbi, Armas Urki, 12-14, 20.600 Eibar (Guipuzcoa) SPAIN/43-11 38 73 (U.S. importer—Moore & Co., Wm. Larkin)

Garcia National Gun Traders, Inc., 225 SW 22nd Ave., Miami, FL 33135/305-642-2355

Garrett Cartridges, Inc., P.O. Box 178, Chehalis, WA 98532/360-736-0702

Garthwaite, Pistolsmith, Inc., Jim, Rt. 2, Box 310, Watsontown, PA 17777/717-538-1566; FAX: 717-538-2965

Gator Guns & Repair, 6255 Spur Hwy., Kenai, AK 99611/907-283-7947

Gaucher Armes, S.A., 46, rue Desjoyaux, 42000 Saint-Etienne, FRANCE/04-77-33-38-92; FAX: 04-77-61-95-72

G.C.C.T., 4455 Torrance Blvd., Ste. 453, Torrance, CA 90509-2806

GDL Enterprises, 409 Le Gardeur, Slidell, LA 70460/504-649-0693

Gehmann, Walter (See Huntington Die Specialties)

Genco, P.O. Box 5704, Asheville, NC 28803

Genecco Gun Works, K., 10512 Lower Sacramento Rd., Stockton, CA 95210/209-951-0706

General Lead, Inc., 1022 Grand Ave., Phoenix, AZ 85007

Gene's Custom Guns, P.O. Box 10534, White Bear Lake, MN 55110/612-429-5105

Gentex Corp., 5 Tinkham Ave., Derry, NH 03038/603-434-0311; FAX: 603-434-3002

Gentner Bullets, 109 Woodlawn Ave., Upper Darby, PA 19082/610-352-9396

Gentry Custom Gunmaker, David, 314 N. Hoffman, Belgrade, MT 59714/406-388-GUNS

George & Roy's, 2950 NW 29th, Portland, OR 97210/503-228-5424, 800-553-3022; FAX: 503-225-9409

George, Tim, Rt. 1, P.O. Box 45, Evington, VA 24550/804-821-8117

Gerber Legendary Blades, 14200 SW 72nd Ave., Portland, OR 97223/503-639-6161, 800-950-6161; FAX: 503-684-7008

Gervais, Mike, 3804 S. Cruise Dr., Salt Lake City, UT 84109/801-277-7729

Getz Barrel Co., P.O. Box 88, Beavertown, PA 17813/717-658-7263

G.G. & G., 3602 E. 42nd Stravenue, Tucson, AZ 85713/520-748-7167; FAX: 520-748-7583

G.H. Enterprises Ltd., Bag 10, Okotoks, Alberta T0L 1T0 CANADA/403-938-6070

Giacomo Sporting USA, 6234 Stokes Lee Center Rd., Lee Center, NY 13363

Gibbs Rifle Co., Inc., Cannon Hill Industrial Park, Rt. 2, Box 214 Hoffman, Rd./Martinsburg, WV 25401 304-274-0458; FAX: 304-274-0078

Gilbert Equipment Co., Inc., 960 Downtowner Rd., Mobile, AL 36609/205-344-3322

Gilkes, Anthony W., 5950 Sheridan Blvd., Arvada, CO 80003/303-657-1873; FAX: 303-657-1885

Gillmann, Edwin, 33 Valley View Dr., Hanover, PA 17331/717-632-1662

Gilman-Mayfield, Inc., 3279 E. Shields, Fresno, CA 93703/209-221-9415; FAX: 209-221-9419

Gilmore Sports Concepts, 5949 S. Garnett, Tulsa, OK 74146/918-250-4867; FAX: 918-250-3845

Giron, Robert E., 1328 Pocono St., Pittsburgh, PA 15218/412-731-6041

Glacier Glove, 4890 Aircenter Circle, Suite 210, Reno, NV 89502/702-825-8225; FAX: 702-825-6544

Glaser Safety Slug, Inc., P.O. Box 8223, Foster City, CA 94404/800-221-3489; FAX: 510-785-6685

Glass, Herb, P.O. Box 25, Bullville, NY 10915/914-361-3021

Glimm's Custom Gun Engraving, 19 S. Maryland, Conrad, MT 59425/406-278-3574

Glock GmbH, P.O. Box 50, A-2232 Deutsch Wagram, AUSTRIA (U.S. importer—Glock, Inc.)

Glock, Inc., P.O. Box 369, Smyrna, GA 30081/770-432-1202; FAX: 770-433-8719

GML Products, Inc., 394 Laredo Dr., Birmingham, AL 35226/205-979-4867

Gner's Hard Cast Bullets, 1107 11th St., LaGrande, OR 97850/503-963-8796

Goddard, Allen, 716 Medford Ave., Hayward, CA 94541/510-276-6830

Goens, Dale W., P.O. Box 224, Cedar Crest, NM 87008/505-281-5419

Goergen's Gun Shop, Inc., Rt. 2, Box 182BB, Austin, MN 55912/507-433-9280

Goldcoast Reloaders, Inc., 4260 NE 12th Terrace, Pompano Beach, FL 33064/954-783-4849; FAX: 954-942-3452

Golden Age Arms Co., 115 E. High St., Ashley, OH 43003/614-747-2488

Golden Bear Bullets, 3065 Fairfax Ave., San Jose, CA 95148/408-238-9515

Gonic Arms, Inc., 134 Flagg Rd., Gonic, NH 03839/603-332-8456, 603-332-8457

Gonic Bullet Works, P.O. Box 7365, Gonic, NH 03839

Gonzalez Guns, Ramon B., P.O. Box 370, 93 St. Joseph's Hill Road, Monticello, NY 12701/914-794-4515

Goodling's Gunsmithing, R.D. 1, Box 1097, Spring Grove, PA 17362/717-225-3350

Goodwin, Fred, Silver Ridge Gun Shop, Sherman Mills, ME 04776/207-365-4451

Gordie's Gun Shop, 1401 Fulton St., Streator, IL 61364/815-672-7202

Gotz Bullets, 7313 Rogers St., Rockford, IL 61111

Goudy Classic Stocks, Gary, 263 Hedge Rd., Menlo Park, CA 94025-1711/415-322-1338

Gould & Goodrich, 709 E. McNeil St., Lillington, NC 27546/910-893-2071; FAX: 910-893-4742

Gournet, Geoffroy, 820 Paxinosa Ave., Easton, PA 18042/610-559-0710

Gozon Corp., U.S.A., P.O. Box 6278, Folson, CA 95763/916-983-2026; FAX: 916-983-9500

Grace, Charles E., 1305 Arizona Ave., Trinidad, CO 81082/719-846-9435

Grace Metal Products, Inc., P.O. Box 67, Elk Rapids, MI 49629/616-264-8133

Graf & Sons, Route 3 Highway 54 So., Mexico, MO 65265/573-581-2266; FAX: 573-581-2875

"Gramps" Antique Cartridges, Box 341, Washago, Ont. L0K 2B0 CANADA/705-689-5348

Granite Custom Bullets, Box 190, Philipsburg, MT 59858/406-859-3245

Grant, Howard V., Hiawatha 15, Woodruff, WI 54568/715-356-7146

Graphics Direct, P.O. Box 372421, Reseda, CA 91337-2421/818-344-9002

Graves Co., 1800 Andrews Ave., Pompano Beach, FL 33069/800-327-9103; FAX: 305-960-0301

Grayback Wildcats, 5306 Bryant Ave., Klamath Falls, OR 97603/541-884-1072

Graybill's Gun Shop, 1035 Ironville Pike, Columbia, PA 17512/717-684-2739

Great American Gunstock Co., 3420 Industrial Drive, Yuba City, CA 95993/916-671-4570; FAX: 916-671-3906

Great Lakes Airguns, 6175 S. Park Ave., Hamburg, NY 14075/716-648-6666; FAX: 716-648-5279

Green, Arthur S., 485 S. Robertson Blvd., Beverly Hills, CA 90211/310-274-1283

Green Genie, Box 114, Cusseta, GA 31805

Green Head Game Call Co., RR 1, Box 33, Lacon, IL 61540/309-246-2155

Green Mountain Rifle Barrel Co., Inc., P.O. Box 2670, 153 West Main St., Conway, NH 03818/603-447-1095; FAX: 603-447-1099

Green, Roger M., P.O. Box 984, 435 E. Birch, Glenrock, WY 82637/307-436-9804

Greene Precision Duplicators, M.L. Greene Engineering Services, P.O. Box, 1150, Golden, CO 80402-1150/303-279-2383

Greenwood Precision, P.O. Box 468, Nixa, MO 65714-0468/417-725-2330

Greg Gunsmithing Repair, 3732 26th Ave. North, Robbinsdale, MN 55422/612-529-8103

Greg's Superior Products, P.O. Box 46219, Seattle, WA 98146

Greider Precision, 431 Santa Marina Ct., Escondido, CA 92029/619-480-8892; FAX: 619-480-9800; E-MAIL: Greider@msn.com

Gremmel Enterprises, 2111 Carriage Drive, Eugene, OR 97408-7537/541-302-3000

GrÈ-Tan Rifles, 29742 W.C.R. 50, Kersey, CO 80644/970-353-6176; FAX: 970-356-9133

Grier's Hard Cast Bullets, 1107 11th St., LaGrande, OR 97850/503-963-8796

Griffin & Howe, Inc., 33 Claremont Rd., Bernardsville, NJ 07924/908-766-2287; FAX: 908-766-1068

Griffin & Howe, Inc., 36 W. 44th St., Suite 1011, New York, NY 10036/212-921-0980

Grifon, Inc., 58 Guinam St., Waltham, MS 02154

Groenewold, John, P.O. Box 830, Mundelein, IL 60060/847-566-2365

Group Tight Bullets, 482 Comerwood Court, San Francisco, CA 94080/650-583-1550

GRS Corp., Glendo, P.O. Box 1153, 900 Overlander St., Emporia, KS 66801/316-343-1084, 800-835-3519

Grulla Armes, Apartado 453, Avda Otaloa, 12, Eiber, SPAIN (U.S. importer—American Arms, Inc.)

GSI, Inc., 108 Morrow Ave., P.O. Box 129, Trussville, AL 35173/205-655-8299; FAX: 205-655-7078

G.U., Inc. (U.S. importer for New SKB Arms Co.; SKB Arms Co.)

Guardsman Products, 411 N. Darling, Fremont, MI 49412/616-924-3950

Gun Accessories (See Glaser Safety Slug, Inc.)

Gun-Alert, 1010 N. Maclay Ave., San Fernando, CA 91340/818-365-0864; FAX: 818-365-1308

Gun City, 212 W. Main Ave., Bismarck, ND 58501/701-223-2304

Gun Doctor, The, 435 East Maple, Roselle, IL 60172/708-894-0668

Gun Doctor, The, P.O. Box 39242, Downey, CA 90242/310-862-3158

Gun-Ho Sports Cases, 110 E. 10th St., St. Paul, MN 55101/612-224-9491

Gun Hunter Books (See Gun Hunter Trading Co.)

Gun Hunter Trading Co., 5075 Heisig St., Beaumont, TX 77705/409-835-3006

Gun Leather Limited, 116 Lipscomb, Ft. Worth, TX 76104/817-334-0225; 800-247-0609

Gun List (See Krause Publications, Inc.)

Gun Locker, Div. of Airmold, W.R. Grace & Co.-Conn., Becker Farms Ind. Park,, P.O. Box 610/Roanoke Rapids, NC 27870 800-344-5716; FAX: 919-536-2201

Gun Parts Corp., The, 226 Williams Lane, West Hurley, NY 12491/914-679-2417; FAX: 914-679-5849

Gun Room, The, 1121 Burlington, Muncie, IN 47302/317-282-9073; FAX: 317-282-5270

Gun Room Press, The, 127 Raritan Ave., Highland Park, NJ 08904/908-545-4344; FAX: 908-545-6686

Gun Shop, The, 5550 S. 900 East, Salt Lake City, UT 84117/801-263-3633

Gun Shop, The, 62778 Spring Creek Rd., Montrose, CO 81401

Gun Shop, The, 716-A South Rogers Road, Olathe, KS 66062

Gun South, Inc. (See GSI, Inc.)

Gun-Tec, P.O. Box 8125, W. Palm Beach, FL 33407

Gun Works, The, 247 S. 2nd, Springfield, OR 97477/541-741-4118; FAX: 541-988-1097

Guncraft Books (See Guncraft Sports, Inc.)

Guncraft Sports, Inc., 10737 Dutchtown Rd., Knoxville, TN 37932/423-966-4545; FAX: 423-966-4500

Gunfitters, The, P.O. 426, Cambridge, WI 53523-0426/608-764-8128

Gunline Tools, 2950 Saturn St., "O", Brea, CA 92821/714-993-5100; FAX: 714-572-4128

Gunnerman Books, P.O. Box 217, Owosso, MI 48867/517-729-7018; FAX: 517-725-9391

Guns, 81 E. Streetsboro St., Hudson, OH 44236/330-650-4563

Guns Antique & Modern DBA/Charles E. Duffy, Williams Lane, West Hurley, NY 12491/914-679-2997

Guns, Div. of D.C. Engineering, Inc., 8633 Southfield Fwy., Detroit, MI 48228/313-271-7111, 800-886-7623 (orders only); FAX: 313-271-7112

GUNS Magazine, 591 Camino de la Reina, Suite 200, San Diego, CA 92108/619-297-5350; FAX: 619-297-5353

Gunsight, The, 1712 North Placentia Ave., Fullerton, CA 92631

Gunsite Custom Shop, P.O. Box 451, Paulden, AZ 86334/520-636-4104; FAX: 520-636-1236

Gunsite Gunsmithy (See Gunsite Custom Shop)

Gunsite Training Center, P.O. Box 700, Paulden, AZ 86334/520-636-4565; FAX: 520-636-1236

Gunsmith in Elk River, The, 14021 Victoria Lane, Elk River, MN 55330/612-441-7761

Gunsmithing, Inc., 208 West Buchanan St., Colorado Springs, CO 80907/719-632-3795; FAX: 719-632-3493

Gunsmithing Ltd., 57 Unquowa Rd., Fairfield, CT 06430/203-254-0436; FAX: 203-254-1535

Gurney, F.R., Box 13, Sooke, BC V0S 1N0 CANADA/604-642-5282: FAX: 604-642-7859

Gusdorf Corp., 11440 Lackland Rd., St. Louis, MO 63146/314-567-5249

Gusty Winds Corp., 2950 Bear St., Suite 120, Costa Mesa, CA 92626/714-536-3587

Gwinnell, Bryson J., P.O. Box 248C, Maple Hill Rd., Rochester, VT 05767/802-767-3664

H

H&B Forge Co., Rt. 2 Geisinger Rd., Shiloh, OH 44878/419-895-1856

H&P Publishing, 7174 Hoffman Rd., San Angelo, TX 76905/915-655-5953

H&R 1871, Inc., 60 Industrial Rowe, Gardner, MA 01440/508-632-9393; FAX: 508-632-2300

H&S Liner Service, 515 E. 8th, Odessa, TX 79761/915-332-1021

Hafner Creations, Inc., P.O. Box 1987, Lake City, FL 32055/904-755-6481; FAX: 904-755-6595

Hagn Rifles & Actions, Martin, P.O. Box 444, Cranbrook, B.C. VIC 4H9, CANADA/604-489-4861

Hakko Co. Ltd., Daini-Tsunemi Bldg., 1-13-12, Narimasu, Itabashiku Tokyo 175, JAPAN/03-5997-7870/2; FAX: 81-3-5997-7840

Hale, Engraver, Peter, 800 E. Canyon Rd., Spanish Fork, UT 84660/801-798-8215

Half Moon Rifle Shop, 490 Halfmoon Rd., Columbia Falls, MT 59912/406-892-4409

Hall Manufacturing, 142 CR 406, Clanton, AL 35045/205-755-4094

Hall Plastics, Inc., John, P.O. Box 1526, Alvin, TX 77512/713-489-8709

Hallberg Gunsmith, Fritz, 532 E. Idaho Ave., Ontario, OR 97914/541-889-3135; FAX: 541-889-2633

Hallowell & Co., 340 W. Putnam Ave., Greenwich, CT 06830/203-869-2190; FAX: 203-869-0692

Hally Caller, 443 Wells Rd., Doylestown, PA 18901/215-345-6354

Halstead, Rick, RR4, Box 272, Miami, OK 74354/918-540-0933

Hamilton, Alex B. (See Ten-Ring Precision, Inc.)

Hamilton, Jim, Rte. 5, Box 278, Guthrie, OK 73044/405-282-3634

Hamilton, Keith, P.O. Box 871, Gridley, CA 95948/916-846-2316

Hammans, Charles E., P.O. Box 788, 2022 McCracken, Stuttgart, AR 72106/501-673-1388

Hammerli USA, 19296 Oak Grove Circle, Groveland, CA 95321/209-962-5311; FAX: 209-962-5931

Hammerli Ltd., Seonerstrasse 37, CH-5600 Lenzburg, SWITZERLAND/064-50 11 44; FAX: 064-51 38 27 (U.S. importer—Hammerli USA; Mandall Shooting Supplies, Inc.; Sigarms, Inc.)

Hammets VLD Bullets, P.O. Box 479, Rayville, LA 71269/318-728-2019

Hammond Custom Guns Ltd., 619 S. Pandora, Gilbert, AZ 85234/602-892-3437

Hammonds Rifles, RD 4, Box 504, Red Lion, PA 17356/717-244-7879

Handgun Press, P.O. Box 406, Glenview, IL 60025/847-657-6500; FAX: 847-724-8831

HandiCrafts Unltd. (See Clements' Custom Leathercraft, Chas)

Hands Engraving, Barry Lee, 26192 E. Shore Route, Bigfork, MT 59911/406-837-0035

Hank's Gun Shop, Box 370, 50 West 100 South, Monroe, UT 84754/801-527-4456

Hanned Line, The, P.O. Box 2387, Cupertino, CA 95015-2387

Hanned Precision (See Hanned Line, The)

Hansen & Co. (See Hansen Cartridge Co.)

Hansen Cartridge Co., 244-246 Old Post Rd., Southport, CT 06490/203-259-6222, 203-259-7337; FAX: 203-254-3832

Hanson's Gun Center, Dick, 233 Everett Dr., Colorado Springs, CO 80911

Hanus Birdguns, Bill, P.O. Box 533, Newport, OR 97365/541-265-7433; FAX: 541-265-7400

Hanusin, John, 3306 Commercial, Northbrook, IL 60062/708-564-2706

Hardin Specialty Dist., P.O. Box 338, Radcliff, KY 40159-0338/502-351-6649

Hardwood, Jack O., 1191 Pendlebury Ln., Blackfoot ID 83221/208-785-5368

Harold's Custom Gun Shop, Inc., Broughton Rifle Barrels, Rt. 1, Box 447, Big Spring, TX 79720/915-394-4430

Harper's Custom Stocks, 928 Lombrano St., San Antonio, TX 78207/210-732-5780

Harrell's Precision, 5756 Hickory Dr., Salem, VA 24133/703-380-2683

Harrington & Richardson (See H&R 1871, Inc.)

Harrington Cutlery, Inc., Russell, Subs. of Hyde Mfg. Co., 44 River St., Southbridge, MA 01550/617-765-0201

Harris Engineering, Inc., 999 Broadway, Barlow, KY 42024/502-334-3633; FAX: 502-334-3000

Harris Enterprises, P.O. Box 105, Bly, OR 97622/503-353-2625

Harris Hand Engraving, Paul A., 113 Rusty Lane, Boerne, TX 78006-5746/512-391-5121

Harris Gunworks, 12001 N. cave Creek Rd., Phoenix, AZ 85020-4733/602-997-5370; FAX: 602-997-5335

Harris Publications, 1115 Broadway, New York, NY 10010/212-807-7100; FAX: 212-627-4678

Harrison Bullets, 6437 E. Hobart St., Mesa, AZ 85205

Hart & Son, Inc., Robert W., 401 Montgomery St., Nescopeck, PA 18635/717-752-3655, 800-368-3656; FAX: 717-752-1088

Hart Rifle Barrels, Inc., P.O. Box 182, 1690 Apulia Rd., Lafayette, NY 13084/315-677-9841; FAX: 315-677-9610

Hartford (See U.S. importer— EMF Co., Inc.)

Hartmann & Weiss GmbH, Rahlstedter Bahnhofstr. 47, 22143 Hamburg, GERMANY/(40) 677 55 85; FAX: (40) 677 55 92

Harvey, Frank, 218 Nightfall, Terrace, NV 89015/702-558-6998

Harwood, Jack O., 1191 S. Pendlebury Lane, Blackfoot, ID 83221/208-785-5368

Haselbauer Products, Jerry, P.O. Box 27629, Tucson, AZ 85726/602-792-1075

Hastings Barrels, 320 Court St., Clay Center, KS 67432/913-632-3169; FAX: 913-632-6554

Hawk, Inc., 849 Hawks Bridge Rd., Salem, NJ 08079/609-299-2700; FAX: 609-299-2800

Hawk Laboratories, Inc. (See Hawk, Inc.)

Hawken Shop, The (See Dayton Traister)

Haydel's Game Calls, Inc., 5018 Hazel Jones Rd., Bossier City, LA 71111/318-746-3586, 800-HAYDELS; FAX: 318-746-3711

Haydon Shooters' Supply, Russ, 15018 Goodrich Dr. NW, Gig Harbor, WA 98329-9738/253-857-7557; FAX: 253-857-7884

Heatbath Corp., P.O. Box 2978, Springfield, MA 01101/413-543-3381

Hebard Guns, Gil, 125-129 Public Square, Knoxville, IL 61448

HEBB Resources, P.O. Box 999, Mead, WA 99021-09996/509-466-1292

Hecht, Hubert J., Waffen-Hecht, P.O. Box 2635, Fair Oaks, CA 95628/916-966-1020

Heckler & Koch GmbH, P.O. Box 1329, 78722 Oberndorf, Neckar, GERMANY/49-7423179-0; FAX: 49-7423179-2406 (U.S. importer—Heckler & Koch, Inc.)

Heckler & Koch, Inc., 21480 Pacific Blvd., Sterling, VA 20166-8903/703-450-1900; FAX: 703-450-8160

Hege Jagd-u. Sporthandels, GmbH, P.O. Box 101461, W-7770 Ueberlingen a. Bodensee, GERMANY

Heidenstrom Bullets, Urds GT 1 Heroya, 3900 Porsgrunn, NORWAY

Heilmann, Stephen, P.O. Box 657, Grass Valley, CA 95945/916-272-8758

Heinie Specialty Products, 301 Oak St., Quincy, IL 62301-2500/309-543-4535; FAX: 309-543-2521

Heintz, David, 800 N. Hwy. 17, Moffat, CO 81143/719-256-4194

Hellweg Ltd., 40356 Oak Park Way, Suite H, Oakhurst, CA 93644/209-683-3030; FAX: 209-683-3422

Helwan (See U.S. importer—Interarms)

Henckels Zwillingswerk, J.A., Inc., 9 Skyline Dr., Hawthorne, NY 10532/914-592-7370

Hendricks, Frank E., Inc., Master Engravers, HC03, Box 434, Dripping Springs, TX 78620/512-858-7828

Henigson & Associates, Steve, P.O. Box 2726, Culver City, CA 90231/310-305-8288; FAX: 310-305-1905

Henriksen Tool Co., Inc., 8515 Wagner Creek Rd., Talent, OR 97540/541-535-2309

Henry Repeating Arms Co., 110 8th St., Brooklyn, NY 11215/718-499-5600

Hensler, Jerry, 6614 Country Field, San Antonio, TX 78240/210-690-7491

Hensley & Gibbs, Box 10, Murphy, OR 97533/541-862-2341

Hensley, Gunmaker, Darwin, P.O. Box 329, Brightwood, OR 97011/503-622-5411

Heppler, Keith M., Keith's Custom Gunstocks, 540 Banyan Circle, Walnut Creek, CA 94598/510-934-3509; FAX: 510-934-3143

Heppler's Machining, 2240 Calle Del Mundo, Santa Clara, CA 95054/408-748-9166; FAX: 408-988-7711

Hercules, Inc. (See Alliant Techsystems, Smokeless Powder Group)

Heritage Firearms (See Heritage Manufacturing, Inc.)

Heritage Manufacturing, Inc., 4600 NW 135th St., Opa Locka, FL 33054/305-685-5966; FAX: 305-687-6721

Heritage/VSP Gun Books, P.O. Box 887, McCall, ID 83638/208-634-4104; FAX: 208-634-3101

Heritage Wildlife Carvings, 2145 Wagner Hollow Rd., Fort Plain, NY 13339/518-993-3983

Herrett's Stocks, Inc., P.O. Box 741, Twin Falls, ID 83303/208-733-1498

Hertel & Reuss, Werk f¸r Optik und Feinmechanik GmbH, Quellhofstrasse, 67/34 127 Kassel, GERMANY 0561-83006; FAX: 0561-893308

Herter's Manufacturing, Inc., 111 E. Burnett St., P.O. Box 518, Beaver Dam, WI 53916/414-887-1765; FAX: 414-887-8444

Hesco-Meprolight, 2139 Greenville Rd., LaGrange, GA 30241/706-884-7967; FAX: 706-882-4683

Heydenberk, Warren R., 1059 W. Sawmill Rd., Quakertown, PA 18951/215-538-2682

Hickman, Jaclyn, Box 1900, Glenrock, WY 82637

Hidalgo, Tony, 12701 SW 9th Pl., Davie, FL 33325/954-476-7645

High Bridge Arms, Inc., 3185 Mission St., San Francisco, CA 94110/415-282-8358

High North Products, Inc., P.O. Box 2, Antigo, WI 54409/715-627-2331

High Performance International, 5734 W. Florist Ave., Milwaukee, WI 53218/414-466-9040

High Standard Mfg. Co., Inc., 4601 S. Pinemont, Suite 144, Houston, TX 77041/713-462-4200; FAX: 713-462-6437

High Tech Specialties, Inc., P.O. Box 387R, Adamstown, PA 19501/215-484-0405, 800-231-9385

Highline Machine Co.,Randall Thompson, 654 Lela Place, Grand Junction, CO 81504/970-434-4971

Hill, Loring F., 304 Cedar Rd., Elkins Park, PA 19117

Hill Speed Leather, Ernie, 4507 N. 195th Ave., Litchfield Park, AZ 85340/602-853-9222; FAX: 602-853-9235

Hillmer Custom Gunstocks, Paul D., 7251 Hudson Heights, Hudson, IA 50643/319-988-3941

Hines, S.C., P.O. Box 423, Tijeras, NM 87059/505-281-3783

Hinman Outfitters, Bob, 1217 W. Glen, Peoria, IL 61614/309-691-8132

Hi-Grade Imports, 8655 Monterey Rd., Gilroy, CA 95021/408-842-9301; FAX: 408-842-2374

Hi-Point Firearms, 5990 Philadelphia Dr., Dayton, OH 45415/513-275-4991; FAX: 513-522-8330

Hi-Performance Ammunition Company, 484 State Route 366, Apollo, PA 15613/412-327-8100

Hiptmayer, Armurier, RR 112 750, P.O. Box 136, Eastman, Quebec J0E 1P0, CANADA/514-297-2492

Hiptmayer, Heidemarie, RR 112 750, P.O. Box 136, Eastman, Quebec J0E 1P0, CANADA/514-297-2492

Hiptmayer, Klaus, RR 112 750, P.O. Box 136, Eastman, Quebec J0E 1P0, CANADA/514-297-2492

Hirtenberger Aktiengesellschaft, Leobersdorferstrasse 31, A-2552 Hirtenberg, AUSTRIA/43(0)2256 81184; FAX: 43(0)2256 81807

HiTek International, 484 El Camino Real, Redwood City, CA 94063/415-363-1404, 800-54-NIGHT; FAX: 415-363-1408

Hiti-Schuch, Atelier Wilma, A-8863 Predlitz, Pirming Y1 AUSTRIA/0353418278

HJS Arms, Inc., P.O. Box 3711, Brownsville, TX 78523-3711/800-453-2767, 210-542-2767

H.K.S. Products, 7841 Founion Dr., Florence, KY 41042/606-342-7841, 800-354-9814; FAX: 606-342-5865

Hoag, James W., 8523 Canoga Ave., Suite C, Canoga Park, CA 91304/818-998-1510

Hobbie Gunsmithing, Duane A., 2412 Pattie Ave., Wichita, KS 67216/316-264-8266

Hobson Precision Mfg. Co., Rt. 1, Box 220-C, Brent, AL 35034/205-926-4662

Hoch Custom Bullet Moulds (See Colorado Shooter's Supply)

Hodgdon Powder Co., 6231 Robinson, Shawnee Mission, KS 66202/913-362-9455; FAX: 913-362-1307; WEB: http://www.hodgdon.com

Hodgman, Inc., 1750 Orchard Rd., Montgomery, IL 60538/708-897-7555; FAX: 708-897-7558

Hodgson, Richard, 9081 Tahoe Lane, Boulder, CO 80301

Hoehn Sales, Inc., 2045 Kohn Road, Wright City, MO 63390/314-745-8144; FAX: 314-745-8144

Hoelscher, Virgil, 11047 Pope Ave., Lynwood, CA 90262/310-631-8545

Hoenig & Rodman, 6521 Morton Dr., Boise, ID 83704/208-375-1116

Hofer Jagdwaffen, P., Buchsenmachermeister, Kirchgasse 24, A-9170 Ferlach, AUSTRIA/04227-3683

Hoffman New Ideas, 821 Northmoor Rd., Lake Forest, IL 60045/312-234-4075

Hogue Grips, P.O. Box 1138, Paso Robles, CA 93447/800-438-4747, 805-239-1440; FAX: 805-239-2553

Holland & Holland Ltd., 33 Bruton St., London, ENGLAND 1W1/44-171-499-4411; FAX: 44-171-408-7962

Holland, Dick, 422 NE 6th St., Newport, OR 97365/503-256-7556

Holland's Gunsmithing, P.O. Box 69, Powers, OR 97466/541-439-5155; FAX: 541-439-5155

Hollis Gun Shop, 917 Rex St., Carlsbad, NM 88220/505-885-3782

Hollywood Engineering, 10642 Arminta St., Sun Valley, CA 91352/818-842-8376

Holster Shop, The, 720 N. Flagler Dr., Ft. Lauderdale, FL 33304/305-463-7910; FAX: 305-761-1483

Homak, 5151 W. 73rd St., Chicago, IL 60638-6613/312-523-3100, FAX: 312-523-9455

Home Shop Machinist, The, Village Press Publications, P.O. Box 1810, Traverse City, MI 49685/800-447-7367; FAX: 616-946-3289

Hondo Ind., 510 S. 52nd St.,I04, Tempe, AZ 85281

Hoover, Harvey, 5750 Pearl Dr., Paradise, CA 95969-4829

Hoppe's Div., Penguin Industries, Inc., Airport Industrial Mall, Coatesville, PA 19320/610-384-6000

Horizons Unlimited, P.O. Box 426, Warm Springs, GA 31830/706-655-3603; FAX: 706-655-3603

Hornady Mfg. Co., P.O. Box 1848, Grand Island, NE 68802/800-338-3220, 308-382-1390; FAX: 308-382-5761

Horseshoe Leather Products, Andy Arratoonian, The Cottage Sharow, Ripon HG4 5BP ENGLAND/44-1765-605858

Horton Dist. Co., Inc., Lew, 15 Walkup Dr., Westboro, MA 01581/508-366-7400; FAX: 508-366-5332

House of Muskets, Inc., The, P.O. Box 4640, Pagosa Springs, CO 81157/970-731-2295

Houtz & Barwick, P.O. Box 435, W. Church St., Elizabeth City, NC 27909/800-775-0337, 919-335-4191; FAX: 919-335-1152

Howa Machinery, Ltd., Sukaguchi, Shinkawa-cho, Nishikasugai-gun, Aichi 452, JAPAN (U.S. importer—Interarms)

Howell Machine, 815 1/2 D St., Lewiston, ID 83501/208-743-7418

Hoyt Holster Co., Inc., P.O. Box 69, Coupeville, WA 98239-0069/360-678-6640; FAX: 360-678-6549

H-S Precision, Inc., 1301 Turbine Dr., Rapid City, SD 57703/605-341-3006; FAX: 605-342-8964

HT Bullets, 244 Belleville Rd., New Bedford, MA 02745/508-999-3338

Hubertus Schneidwarenfabrik, P.O. Box 180 106, D-42626 Solingen, GERMANY/01149-212-59-19-94: FAX: 01149-212-59-19-92

Huebner, Corey O., P.O. Box 2074, Missoula, MT 59806-2074/406-721-7168

Huey Gun Cases, P.O. Box 22456, Kansas City, MO 64113/816-444-1637; FAX: 816-444-1637

Hugger Hooks Co., 3900 Easley Way, Golden, CO 80403/303-279-0600

Hughes, Steven Dodd, P.O. Box 545, Livingston, MT 59047/406-222-9377; FAX: 406-222-9377

Hume, Don, P.O. Box 351, Miami, OK 74355/918-542-6604; FAX: 918-542-4340

Hungry Horse Books, 4605 Hwy. 93 South, Whitefish, MT 59937/406-862-7997

Hunkeler, A. (See Buckskin Machine Works)

Hunter Co., Inc., 3300 W. 71st Ave., Westminster, CO 80030/303-427-4626; FAX: 303-428-3980

Hunters Supply, Rt. 1, P.O. Box 313, Tioga, TX 76271/800-868-6612; FAX: 817-437-2228

Hunter's Specialties, Inc., 6000 Huntington Ct. NE, Cedar Rapids, IA 52402-1268/319-395-0321; FAX: 319-395-0326

Hunterjohn, P.O. Box 771457, St. Louis, MO 63177/314-531-7250

Hunting Classics Ltd., P.O. Box 2089, Gastonia, NC 28053/704-867-1307; FAX: 704-867-0491

Huntington Die Specialties, 601 Oro Dam Blvd., Oroville, CA 95965/916-534-1210; FAX: 916-534-1212

Hutton Rifle Ranch, P.O. Box 45236, Boise, ID 83711/208-345-8781

Hydrosorbent Products, P.O. Box 437, Ashley Falls, MA 01222/413-229-2967; FAX: 413-229-8743

Hyper-Single, Inc., 520 E. Beaver, Jenks, OK 74037/918-299-2391

I

I.A.B. (See U.S. importer—Taylor's & Co., Inc.)

IAI (See A.M.T.)

IAR, Inc., 33171 Camino Capistrano, San Juan Capistrano, CA 92675/714-443-3642; FAX: 714-443-3647

Ibberson (Sheffield) Ltd., George, 25-31 Allen St., Sheffield, S3 7AW ENGLAND/0114-2766123; FAX: 0114-2738465

ICI-America, P.O. Box 751, Wilmington, DE 19897/302-575-3000

I.D.S.A. Books, 1324 Stratford Drive, Piqua, OH 45356/937-773-4203; FAX: 937-778-1922.

IGA (See U.S. importer—Stoeger Industries)

Illinois Lead Shop, 7742 W. 61st Place, Summit, IL 60501

Image Ind. Inc., 864 Lively, Wood Dale, IL 60191/630-616-1340; FAX: 630-616-1341

Image Ind. Inc., 382 Balm Court, Wood Dale, IL 60191/630-766-2402; FAX: 630-766-7373

IMI, P.O. Box 1044, Ramat Hasharon 47100, ISRAEL/972-3-5485617;FAX: 972-3-5406908

IMI Services USA, Inc., 2 Wisconsin Circle, Suite 420, Chevy Chase, MD 20815/301-215-4800; FAX: 301-657-1446

Impact Case Co., P.O. Box 9912, Spokane, WA 99209-0912/800-262-3322, 509-467-3303; FAX: 509-326-5436

Imperial (See E-Z-Way Systems)

Imperial Magnum Corp., P.O. Box 249, Oroville, WA 98844/604-495-3131; FAX: 604-495-2816

Imperial Russian Armory, 10547 S. Post Oak, Houston, TX 77035/1-800-MINIATURE

Imperial Schrade Corp., 7 Schrade Ct., Box 7000, Ellenville, NY 12428/914-647-7601; FAX: 914-647-8701

Import Sports Inc., 1750 Brielle Ave., Unit B1, Wanamassa, NJ 07712/908-493-0302; FAX: 908-493-0301

IMR Powder Co., 1080 Military Turnpike, Suite 2, Plattsburgh, NY 12901/518-563-2253; FAX: 518-563-6916

I.N.C., Inc. (See Kick Eez)

Independent Machine & Gun Shop, 1416 N. Hayes, Pocatello, ID 83201

Info-Arm, P.O. Box 1262, Champlain, NY 12919/514-955-0355; FAX: 514-955-0357

Ingle, Engraver, Ralph W., 112 Manchester Ct., Centerville, GA 31028/912-953-5824

Innovative Weaponry, Inc., 337 Eubank NE, Albuquerque, NM 87123/800-334-3573, 505-296-4645; FAX: 505-271-2633

Innovision Enterprises, 728 Skinner Dr., Kalamazoo, MI 49001/616-382-1681; FAX: 616-382-1830

INTEC International, Inc., P.O. Box 5708, Scottsdale, AZ 85261/602-483-1708

Inter Ordnance of America LP, 3904-B Sardis Church Rd., Monroe, NC 28110/704-821-8337; FAX: 704-821-8523

Interarms, 10 Prince St., Alexandria, VA 22314/703-548-1400; FAX: 703-549-7826

Intercontinental Munitions Distributors, Ltd., P.O. Box 815, Beulah, ND 58523/701-948-2260; FAX: 701-948-2282

International Shooters Service (See I.S.S.)

Intratec, 12405 SW 130th St., Miami, FL 33186-6224/305-232-1821; FAX: 305-253-7207

Ion Industries, Inc., 3508 E. Allerton Ave., Cudahy, WI 53110/414-486-2007; FAX: 414-486-2017

Iosso Products, 1485 Lively Blvd., Elk Grove Village, IL 60007/847-437-8400; FAX: 847-437-8478

Iron Bench, 12619 Bailey Rd., Redding, CA 96003/916-241-4623

Ironside International Publishers, Inc., P.O. Box 55, 800 Slaters Lane, Alexandria, VA 22313/703-684-6111; FAX: 703-683-5486

Ironsighter Co., P.O. Box 85070, Westland, MI 48185/313-326-8731; FAX: 313-326-3378

Irwin, Campbell H., 140 Hartland Blvd., East Hartland, CT 06027/203-653-3901

Island Pond Gun Shop, P.O. Box 428, Cross St., Island Pond, VT 05846/802-723-4546

Israel Arms International, Inc., 5709 Hartsdale, Houston, TX 77036/713-789-0745; FAX: 713-789-7513

Israel Military Industries Ltd. (See IMI)

I.S.S., P.O. Box 185234, Ft. Worth, TX 76181/817-595-2090

I.S.W., 106 E. Cairo Dr., Tempe, AZ 85282

Ithaca Gun Co., LLC, 891 Route 34-B, King Ferry, NY 13081/315-364-7171, 888-9ITHACA; FAX: 315-364-5134

Ivanoff, Thomas G. (See Tom's Gun Repair)

J

J-4, Inc., 1700 Via Burton, Anaheim, CA 92806/714-254-8315; FAX: 714-956-4421

J&D Components, 75 East 350 North, Orem, UT 84057-4719/801-225-7007

J&J Products, Inc., 9240 Whitmore, El Monte, CA 91731/818-571-5228, 800-927-8361; FAX: 818-571-8704

J&J Sales, 1501 21st Ave. S., Great Falls, MT 59405/406-453-7549

J&L Superior Bullets (See Huntington Die Specialties)

J&R Engineering, P.O. Box 77, 200 Lyons Hill Rd., Athol, MA 01331/508-249-9241

J&R Enterprises, 4550 Scotts Valley Rd., Lakeport, CA 95453

J&S Heat Treat, 803 S. 16th St., Blue Springs, MO 64015/816-229-2149; FAX: 816-228-1135

J.A. Blades, Inc. (See Christopher Firearms Co., Inc., E.)

Jackalope Gun Shop, 1048 S. 5th St., Douglas, WY 82633/307-358-3441

Jaeger, Inc./Dunn's, Paul, P.O. Box 449, 1 Madison Ave., Grand Junction, TN 38039/901-764-6909; FAX: 901-764-6503

J‰gerSport, Ltd., One Wholesale Way, Cranston, RI 02920/800-962-4867, 401-944-9682; FAX: 401-946-2587

Jamison's Forge Works, 4527 Rd. 6.5 NE, Moses Lake, WA 98837/509-762-2659

Jantz Supply, P.O. Box 584-GD, Davis, OK 73030-0584/405-369-2316; FAX: 405-369-3082; WEB: http//www.jantzsupply.com; E-MAIL: jantz@brightok.net

Jarrett Rifles, Inc., 383 Brown Rd., Jackson, SC 29831/803-471-3616

Jarvis, Inc., 1123 Cherry Orchard Lane, Hamilton, MT 59840/406-961-4392

JAS, Inc., P.O. Box 0, Rosemount, MN 55068/612-890-7631

Javelina Lube Products, P.O. Box 337, San Bernardino, CA 92402/714-882-5847; FAX: 714-434-6937

J/B Adventures & Safaris, Inc., 2275 E. Arapahoe Rd. Ste. 109, Littleton, CO 80122-1521/303-771-0977

JB Custom, P.O. Box 6912, Leawood, KS 66206/913-381-2329

Jedediah Starr Trading Co., P.O. Box 2007, Farmington Hill, MI 48333-2007

Jeffredo Gunsight, P.O. Box 669, San Marcos, CA 92079/619-728-2695

Jenco Sales, Inc., P.O. Box 1000, Manchaca, TX 78652/800-531-5301; FAX: 800-266-2373

Jenkins Recoil Pads, Inc., 5438 E. Frontage Ln., Olney, IL 62450/618-395-3416

Jensen Bullets, 86 North, 400 West, Blackfoot, ID 83221/208-785-5590

Jensen's Custom Ammunition, 5146 E. Pima, Tucson, AZ 85712/602-325-3346; FAX: 602-322-5704

Jensen's Firearms Academy, 1280 W. Prince, Tucson, AZ 85705/602-293-8516

Jericho Tool & Die Co. Inc., RD 3 Box 70, Route 7, Bainbridge, NY 13733-9494/607-563-8222; FAX: 607-563-8560

Jester Bullets, Rt. 1 Box 27, Orienta, OK 73737

Jewell Triggers, Inc., 3620 Hwy. 123, San Marcos, TX 78666/512-353-2999

J-Gar Co., 183 Turnpike Rd., Dept. 3, Petersham, MA 01366-9604

JGS Precision Tool Mfg., 1141 S. Summer Rd., Coos Bay, OR 97420/541-267-4331; FAX:541-267-5996

Jim's Gun Shop (See Spradlin's)

Jim's Precision, Jim Ketchum, 1725 Moclips Dr., Petaluma, CA 94952/707-762-3014

J.I.T., Ltd., P.O. Box 230, Freedom, WY 83120/708-494-0937

JLK Bullets, 414 Turner Rd., Dover, AR 72837/501-331-4194

Johanssons Vapentillbehor, Bert, S-430 20 Veddige, SWEDEN

John's Custom Leather, 523 S. Liberty St., Blairsville, PA 15717/412-459-6802

Johns Master Engraver, Bill, 7927 Ranch Roach 965, Fredericksburg, TX 78624-9545/210-997-6795

Johnson's Gunsmithing, Inc., Neal, 208 W. Buchanan St., Suite B, Colorado Springs, CO 80907/800-284-8671 (orders), 719-632-3795; FAX: 719-632-3493

Johnson Wood Products, 34968 Crystal Road, Strawberry Point, IA 52076/319-933-4930

Johnston Bros. (See C&T Corp. TA Johnson Brothers)

Johnston, James (See North Fork Custom Gunsmithing)

Jonad Corp., 2091 Lakeland Ave., Lakewood, OH 44107/216-226-3161

Jonas Appraisals & Taxidermy, Jack, 1675 S. Birch, Suite 506, Denver, CO 80222/303-757-7347: FAX: 303-639-9655

Jones Co., Dale, 680 Hoffman Draw, Kila, MT 59920/406-755-4684

Jones Custom Products, Neil A., 17217 Brookhouser Road, Saegertown, PA 16433/814-763-2769; FAX: 814-763-4228

Jones Moulds, Paul, 4901 Telegraph Rd., Los Angeles, CA 90022/213-262-1510

Jones, J.D. (See SSK Industries)

J.P. Enterprises, Inc., P.O. Box 26324, Shoreview, MN 55126/612-486-9064; FAX: 612-482-0970

J.P. Gunstocks, Inc., 4508 San Miguel Ave., North Las Vegas, NV 89030/702-645-0718

JP Sales, Box 307, Anderson, TX 77830

J.R. Distributing, 2976 E. Los Angeles Ave., Simi Valley, CA 93065/805-527-1090; FAX: 805-529-2368

JRP Custom Bullets, RR2 2233 Carlton Rd., Whitehall, NY 12887/518-282-0084 (a.m.), 802-438-5548 (p.m.)

JRW, 2425 Taffy Ct., Nampa, ID 83687

JS Worldwide DBA (See Coonan Arms)

JSL Ltd. (See U.S. importer—Specialty Shooters Supply, Inc.)

Juenke, Vern, 25 Bitterbush Rd., Reno, NV 89523/702-345-0225

Jumbo Sports Products (See Bucheimer, J.M.)

Jungkind, Reeves C., 5001 Buckskin Pass, Austin, TX 78745-2841/512-442-1094

Jurras, L.E., P.O. Box 680, Washington, IN 47501/812-254-7698

K

K&M Industries, Inc., Box 66, 510 S. Main, Troy, ID 83871/208-835-2281; FAX: 208-835-5211

K&M Services, 5430 Salmon Run Rd., Dover, PA 17315/717-292-3175; FAX: 717-292-3175

K&T Co., Div. of T&S Industries, Inc., 1027 Skyview Dr., W. Carrollton, OH 45449/513-859-8414

KA-BAR Knives, 1116 E. State St., Olean, NY 14760/800-282-0130; FAX: 716-373-6245

Kabar Arms, Inc., P.O. Box 718, Tualatin, OR 97062/503-256-0144; FAX: 503-253-7810

Ka Pu Kapili, P.O. Box 745, Honokaa, HI 96727/808-776-1644; FAX: 808-776-1731

Kahles, A Swarovski Company, 1 Wholesale Way, Cranston, RI 02920-5540/800-426-3089: FAX: 401-946-2587

Kahr Arms, P.O. Box 220, 630 Route 303, Blauvelt, NY 10913/914-353-5996; FAX: 914-353-7833

Kalispel Case Line, P.O. Box 267, Cusick, WA 99119/509-445-1121

Kamik Outdoor Footwear, 554 Montee de Liesse, Montreal, Quebec, H4T 1P1 CANADA/514-341-3950; FAX: 514-341-1861

Kamyk Engraving Co., Steve, 9 Grandview Dr., Westfield, MA 01085-1810/413-568-0457

Kane, Edward, P.O. Box 385, Ukiah, CA 95482/707-462-2937

Kane Products, Inc., 5572 Brecksville Rd., Cleveland, OH 44131/216-524-9962

Kapro Mfg. Co., Inc. (See R.E.I.)

Kasenit Co., Inc., 13 Park Ave., Highland Mills, NY 10930/914-928-9595; FAX: 914-928-7292

Kasmarsik Bullets, 4016 7th Ave. SW, Puyallup, WA 98373

Kaswer Custom, Inc., 13 Surrey Drive, Brookfield, CT 06804/203-775-0564; FAX: 203-775-6872

K.B.I., Inc., P.O. Box 6625, Harrisburg, PA 17112/717-540-8518; FAX: 717-540-8567

K-D, Inc., Box 459, 585 N. Hwy. 155, Cleveland, UT 84518/801-653-2530

KDF, Inc., 2485 Hwy. 46 N., Seguin, TX 78155/210-379-8141; FAX: 210-379-5420

KeeCo Impressions, Inc., 346 Wood Ave., North Brunswick, NJ 08902/800-468-0546

Keeler, R.H., 817 "N" St., Port Angeles, WA 98362/206-457-4702

Kehr, Roger, 2131 Agate Ct. SE, Lacy, WA 98503/360-456-0831

Keith's Bullets, 942 Twisted Oak, Algonquin, IL 60102/708-658-3520

Keith's Custom Gunstocks (See Heppler, Keith M.)

Kelbly's, Inc., 7222 Dalton Fox Lake Rd., North Lawrence, OH 44666/216-683-4674; FAX: 216-683-7349

Keller Co., The, 4215 McEwen Rd., Dallas, TX 75244/214-770-8585

Kelley's, P.O. Box 125, Woburn, MA 01801/617-935-3389

Kellogg's Professional Products, 325 Pearl St., Sandusky, OH 44870/419-625-6551; FAX: 419-625-6167

Kelly, Lance, 1723 Willow Oak Dr., Edgewater, FL 32132/904-423-4933

Kel-Tec CNC Industries, Inc., P.O. Box 3427, Cocoa, FL 32924/407-631-0068; FAX: 407-631-1169

Kemen America, 2550 Hwy. 23, Wrenshall, MN 55797

Ken's Kustom Kartridges, 331 Jacobs Rd., Hubbard, OH 44425/216-534-4595

Ken's Gun Specialties, Rt. 1, Box 147, Lakeview, AR 72642/501-431-5606

Ken's Rifle Blanks, Ken McCullough, Rt. 2, P.O. Box 85B, Weston, OR 97886/503-566-3879

Keng's Firearms Specialty, Inc., 875 Wharton Dr., P.O. Box 44405, Atlanta, GA 30336-1405/404-691-7611: FAX: 404-505-8445

Kennebec Journal, 274 Western Ave., Augusta, ME 04330/207-622-6288

Kennedy Firearms, 10 N. Market St., Muncy, PA 17756/717-546-6695

KenPatable Ent., Inc., P.O. Box 19422, Louisville, KY 40259/502-239-5447

Kent Cartridge Mfg. Co. Ltd., Unit 16, Branbridges Industrial Estate, East, Peckham/Tonbridge, Kent, TN12 5HF ENGLAND 622-872255; FAX: 622-872645

Keowee Game Calls, 608 Hwy. 25 North, Travelers Rest, SC 29690/864-834-7204; FAX: 864-834-7831

Kershaw Knives, 25300 SW Parkway Ave., Wilsonville, OR 97070/503-682-1966, 800-325-2891; FAX: 503-682-7168

Kesselring Gun Shop, 400 Hwy. 99 North, Burlington, WA 98233/206-724-3113; FAX: 206-724-7003

Ketchum, Jim (See Jim's Precision)

Kick Eez, P.O. Box 12767, Wichita, KS 67277/316-721-9570; FAX: 316-721-5260

Kilham & Co., Main St., P.O. Box 37, Lyme, NH 03768/603-795-4112

Kimar (See U.S. importer—IAR, Inc.)

Kimball, Gary, 1526 N. Circle Dr., Colorado Springs, CO 80909/719-634-1274

Kimber of America, Inc., 1 Lawton St., Yonkers, NY 10705/800-880-2418, 914-964-0771; FAX: 914-964-9340; WEB: www.kimberamerica.com

King & Co., P.O. Box 1242, Bloomington, IL 61702/FAX: 309-473-2161

King's Gun Works, 1837 W. Glenoaks Blvd., Glendale, CA 91201/818-956-6010; FAX: 818-548-8606

Kingyon, Paul L. (See Custom Calls)

Kirkpatrick Leather Co., P.O. Box 677, Laredo, TX 78040/956-723-6631; FAX: 956-725-0672

KJM Fabritek, Inc., P.O. Box 162, Marietta, GA 30061/770-426-8251; FAX: 770-426-8252

KK Air International (See Impact Case Co.)

K.K. Arms Co., Star Route Box 671, Kerrville, TX 78028/210-257-4718; FAX: 210-257-4891

Kleen-Bore, Inc., 16 Industrial Pkwy., Easthampton, MA 01027/413-527-0300; FAX: 413-527-2522

Klein Custom Guns, Don, 433 Murray Park Dr., Ripon, WI 54971/414-748-2931

Kleinendorst, K.W., RR 1, Box 1500, Hop Bottom, PA 18824/717-289-4687

Klinger Woodcarving, P.O. Box 141, Thistle Hill, Cabot, VT 05647/802-426-3811

Kmount, P.O. Box 19422, Louisville, KY 40259/502-239-5447

Kneiper, James, P.O. Box 1516, Basalt, CO 81621-1516/303-963-9880

Knife Importers, Inc., P.O. Box 1000, Manchaca, TX 78652/512-282-6860

Knight & Hale Game Calls, Box 468 Industrial Park, Cadiz, KY 42211/502-924-1755; FAX: 502-924-1763

Knight Rifles (See Modern MuzzleLoading, Inc.)

Knight's Mfg. Co., 7750 9th St. SW, Vero Beach, FL 32968/561-562-5697; FAX: 561-569-2955

Knippel, Richard, 1455 Jubal Ct., Oakdale, CA 95361-9669/209-869-1469

Knock on Wood Antiques, 355 Post Rd., Darien, CT 06820/203-655-9031

Knoell, Doug, 9737 McCardle Way, Santee, CA 92071

Koevenig's Engraving Service, Box 55 Rabbit Gulch, Hill City, SD 57745

KOGOT, 410 College, Trinidad, CO 81082/719-846-9406

Kokolus, Michael M. (See Custom Riflestocks, Inc.)

Kolpin Mfg., Inc., P.O. Box 107, 205 Depot St., Fox Lake, WI 53933/414-928-3118; FAX: 414-928-3687

Kongsberg America L.L.C., P.O. Box 252, Fairfield, CT 06430/203-259-0938: FAX: 203-259-2566

Kopec Enterprises, John (See Peacemaker Specialists)

Kopp Professional Gunsmithing, Terry K., Route 1, Box 224F, Lexington, MO 64067/816-259-2636

Korth, Robert-Bosch-Str. 4, P.O. Box 1320, 23909 Ratzeburg, GERMANY/451-4991497; FAX: 451-4993230 (U.S. importer—Interarms; Mandall Shooting Supplies, Inc.)

Korzinek Riflesmith, J., RD 2, Box 73D, Canton, PA 17724/717-673-8512

Koval Knives, 5819 Zarley St., Suite A, New Albany, OH 43054/614-855-0777; FAX: 614-855-0945

Kowa Optimed, Inc., 20001 S. Vermont Ave., Torrance, CA 90502/310-327-1913; FAX: 310-327-4177

Kramer Designs, P.O. Box 129, Clancy, MT 59634/406-933-8658; FAX: 406-933-8658; WEB: www.snipepod.com

Kramer Handgun Leather, P.O. Box 112154, Tacoma, WA 98411/206-564-6652; FAX: 206-564-1214

Krause Publications, Inc., 700 E. State St., Iola, WI 54990/715-445-2214; FAX: 715-445-4087; Consumer orders only 800-258-0929

Krico Jagd-und Sportwaffen GmbH, Nurnbergerstrasse 6, D-90602 Pyrbaum GERMANY/09180-2780; FAX: 09180-2661 (U.S. importer—Mandall Shooting Supplies, Inc.)

Krieger Barrels, Inc., N114 W18697 Clinton Dr., Germantown, WI 53022/414-255-9593; FAX: 414-255-9586

Krieghoff Gun Co., H., Boschstrasse 22, D-89079 Ulm, GERMANY/731-401820; FAX: 731-4018270 (U.S. importer—Krieghoff International, Inc.)

Krieghoff International, Inc., 7528 Easton Rd., Ottsville, PA 18942/610-847-5173; FAX: 610-847-8691

Kris Mounts, 108 Lehigh St., Johnstown, PA 15905/814-539-9751

KSN Industries, Ltd. (See U.S. importer—Israel Arms International, Inc.)

Kudlas, John M., 622 14th St. SE, Rochester, MN 55904/507-288-5579

Kulis Freeze Dry Taxidermy, 725 Broadway Ave., Bedford, OH 44146/216-232-8352; FAX: 216-232-7305; WEB: http://www.kastaway.com; E-Mail: jkulis@kastaway.com
KVH Industries, Inc., 110 Enterprise Center, Middletown, RI 02842/401-847-3327; FAX: 401-849-0045
Kwik Mount Corp., P.O. Box 19422, Louisville, KY 40259/502-239-5447
Kwik-Site Co., 5555 Treadwell, Wayne, MI 48184/313-326-1500; FAX: 313-326-4120

L

L&R Lock Co., 1137 Pocalla Rd., Sumter, SC 29150/803-775-6127; FAX: 803-775-5171
L&S Technologies, Inc. (See Aimtech Mount Systems)
La Clinique du .45, 1432 Rougemont, Chambly, Quebec, J3L 2L8 CANADA/514-658-1144
Labanu, Inc., 2201-F Fifth Ave., Ronkonkoma, NY 11779/516-467-6197; FAX: 516-981-4112
LaBounty Precision Reboring, P.O. Box 186, 7968 Silver Lk. Rd., Maple Falls, WA 98266/360-599-2047
LaCrosse Footwear, Inc., P.O. Box 1328, La Crosse, WI 54602/608-782-3020, 800-323-2668; FAX: 800-658-9444
LaFrance Specialties, P.O. Box 178211, San Diego, CA 92177-8211/619-293-3373
Lage Uniwad, P.O. Box 2302, Davenport, IA 52809/319-388-LAGE; FAX: 319-388-LAGE
Lair, Sam, 520 E. Beaver, Jenks, OK 74037/918-299-2391
Lake Center, P.O. Box 38, St. Charles, MO 63302/314-946-7500
Lakefield Arms Ltd. (See Savage Arms, Inc.)
Lakelander USA, Inc., Bldg. 9313, Suite 103, Stennis Space Center, MS 39529/800-894-8464; FAX 601-255-7595
Lakewood Products, LLC, 275 June St., Berlin, WI 54923/800-US-BUILT; FAX: 414-361-7719
Lampert, Ron, Rt. 1, Box 177, Guthrie, MN 56461/218-854-7345
Lamson & Goodnow Mfg. Co., 45 Conway St., Shelburne Falls, MA 03170/413-625-6331; FAX: 413-625-9816
Lanber Armas, S.A., Zubiaurre 5, Zaldibar, SPAIN 48250/34-4-6827702; FAX: 34-4-6827999
Langenberg Hat Co., P.O. Box 1860, Washington, MO 63090/800-428-1860; FAX: 314-239-3151
Lanphert, Paul, P.O. Box 1985, Wenatchee, WA 98807
Lapua Ltd., P.O. Box 5, Lapua, FINLAND SF-62101/6-310111; FAX: 6-4388991 (U.S. importer—Keng's Firearms Specialty, Inc.
L.A.R. Mfg., Inc., 4133 W. Farm Rd., West Jordan, UT 84088/801-280-3505; FAX: 801-280-1972
LaRocca Gun Works, Inc., 51 Union Place, Worcester, MA 01608/508-754-2887; FAX: 508-754-2887
Laseraim Technologies, Inc., P.O. Box 3548, Little Rock, AR 72203/501-375-2227; FAX: 501-372-1445
Laser Devices, Inc., 2 Harris Ct. A-4, Monterey, CA 93940/408-373-0701; FAX: 408-373-0903
Laserlyte, 3015 Main St., #300, Santa Monica, CA 90405/800-255-9133; FAX: 310-392-1754
LaserMax, Inc., 3495 Winton Place, Bldg. B, Rochester, NY 14623-2807/716-272-5420; FAX: 716-272-5427
Lassen Community College, Gunsmithing Dept., P.O. Box 3000, Hwy. 139, Susanville, CA 96130/916-251-8800; FAX: 916-251-8838
Lathrop's, Inc., 5146 E. Pima, Tucson, AZ 85712/520-881-0266, 800-875-4867; FAX: 520-322-5704
Laughridge, William R. (See Cylinder & Slide, Inc.)
Laurel Mountain Forge, P.O. Box 224C, Romeo, MI 48065/810-749-5742
Laurona Armas Eibar, S.A.L., Avenida de Otaola 25, P.O. Box 260, 20600 Eibar, SPAIN/34-43-700600; FAX: 34-43-700616 (U.S. importer—Galaxy Imports Ltd., Inc.)
Law Concealment Systems, Inc., P.O. Box 3952, Wilmington, NC 28406/919-791-6656, 800-373-0116 orders; FAX: 910-791-8388
Lawrence Brand Shot (See Precision Reloading, Inc.)
Lawrence Leather Co., P.O. Box 1479, Lillington, NC 27546/910-893-2071; FAX: 910-893-4742
Lawson Co., Harry, 3328 N. Richey Blvd., Tucson, AZ 85716/520-326-1117
Lawson, John G. (See Sight Shop, The)
Lazzeroni Arms Co., P.O. Box 26696, Tucson, AZ 85726/888-492-7247; FAX: 520-624-4250
LBT, HCR 62, Box 145, Moyie Springs, ID 83845/208-267-3588
Le Clear Industries (See E-Z-Way Systems)
Lea Mfg. Co., 237 E. Aurora St., Waterbury, CT 06720/203-753-5116
Lead Bullets Technology (See LBT)

Leapers, Inc., 7675 Five Mile Rd., Northville, MI 48167/810-486-1231; FAX: 810-486-1430
Leather Arsenal, 27549 Middleton Rd., Middleton, ID 83644/208-585-6212
Leatherman Tool Group, Inc., 12106 NE Ainsworth Cir., P.O. Box 20595, Portland, OR 97294/503-253-7826; FAX: 503-253-7830
Lebeau-Courally, Rue St. Gilles, 386, 4000 Liege, BELGIUM/042-52-48-43; FAX: 32-042-52-20-08 (U.S. importer—New England Arms Co.)
Leckie Professional Gunsmithing, 546 Quarry Rd., Ottsville, PA 18942/215-847-8594
Lectro Science, Inc., 6410 W. Ridge Rd., Erie, PA 16506/814-833-6487; FAX: 814-833-0447
Ledbetter Airguns, Riley, 1804 E. Sprague St., Winston Salem, NC 27107-3521/919-784-0676
Lee Precision, Inc., 4275 Hwy. U, Hartford, WI 53027/414-673-3075; FAX: 414-673-9273; Web: www.leeprecision.co
Lee Supplies, Mark, 9901 France Ct., Lakeville, MN 55044/612-461-2114
Lee's Red Ramps, 4 Kristine Ln., Silver City, NM 88061/505-538-8529
Lee Co., T.K., 1282 Branchwater Lane, Birmingham, AL 35216/205-913-5222
LeFever Arms Co., Inc., 6234 Stokes, Lee Center Rd., Lee Center, NY 13363/315-337-6722; FAX: 315-337-1543
Legend Products Corp., 21218 Saint Andrews Blvd., Boca Raton, FL 33433-2435
Leibowitz, Leonard, 1205 Murrayhill Ave., Pittsburgh, PA 15217/412-361-5455
Leica USA, Inc., 156 Ludlow Ave., Northvale, NJ 07647/201-767-7500; FAX: 201-767-8666
LEM Gun Specialties, Inc., The Lewis Lead Remover, P.O. Box 2855, Peachtree City, GA 30269-2024
Lestrom Laboratories, Inc., P.O. Box 628, Mexico, NY 13114-0628/315-343-3076; FAX: 315-592-3370
Lethal Force Institute (See Police Bookshelf)
Lett Custom Grips, 672 Currier Rd., Hopkinton, NH 03229-2652
Leupold & Stevens, Inc., P.O. Box 688, Beaverton, OR 97075/503-646-9171; FAX: 503-526-1455
Lever Arms Service Ltd., 2131 Burrard St., Vancouver, B.C. V6J 3H7 CANADA/604-736-0004; FAX: 604-738-3503
Lewis Lead Remover, The (See LEM Gun Specialties, Inc.)
Liberty Antique Gunworks, 19 Key St., P.O. Box 183, Eastport, ME 04631/207-853-4116
Liberty Metals, 2233 East 16th St., Los Angeles, CA 90021/213-581-9171; FAX: 213-581-9351
Liberty Safe, 1060 N. Spring Creek Pl., Springville, UT 84663/800-247-5625; FAX: 801-489-6409
Liberty Shooting Supplies, P.O. Box 357, Hillsboro, OR 97123/503-640-5518; FAX 503-640-5518
Liberty Trouser Co., 3500 6 Ave S., Birmingham, AL 35222-2406/205-251-9143
Light Optronics (See TacStar Industries, Inc.)
Lightfield Ammunition Corp. (See Slug Group, Inc.)
Lightforce U.S.A. Inc., 19226 66th Ave. So., L-103, Kent, WA 98032/206-656-1577; FAX:206-656-1578
Lightning Performance Innovations, Inc., RD1 Box 555, Mohawk, NY 13407/315-866-8819, 800-242-5873; FAX: 315-866-8819
Lilja Precision Rifle Barrels, P.O. Box 372, Plains, MT 59859/406-826-3084; FAX: 406-826-3083
Lincoln, Dean, Box 1886, Farmington, NM 87401
Lind Custom Guns, Al, 7821 76th Ave. SW, Tacoma, WA 98498/253-584-6361
Linder Solingen Knives, 4401 Sentry Dr., Tucker, GA 30084/770-939-6915; FAX: 770-939-6738
Lindsay, Steve, RR 2 Cedar Hills, Kearney, NE 68847/308-236-7885
Lindsley Arms Cartridge Co., P.O. Box 757, 20 College Hill Rd., Henniker, NH 03242/603-428-3127
Linebaugh Custom Sixguns, Route 2, Box 100, Maryville, MO 64468/816-562-3031
Lion Country Supply, P.O. Box 480, Port Matilda, PA 16870
List Precision Engineering, Unit 1, Ingley Works, 13 River Road, Barking, Essex 1G11 0HE ENGLAND/011-081-594-1686
Lithi Bee Bullet Lube, 1728 Carr Rd., Muskegon, MI 49442/616-788-4479
"Little John's" Antique Arms, 1740 W. Laveta, Orange, CA 92668
Little Trees Ramble (See Scott Pilkington, Little Trees Ramble)
Littler Sales Co., 20815 W. Chicago, Detroit, MI 48228/313-273-6888; FAX: 313-273-1099
Littleton, J.F., 275 Pinedale Ave., Oroville, CA 95966/916-533-6084

Ljutic Industries, Inc., 732 N. 16th Ave., Suite 22, Yakima, WA 98902/509-248-0476; FAX: 509-576-8233

Llama Gabilondo Y Cia, Apartado 290, E-01080, Victoria, SPAIN (U.S. importer—Import Sports, Inc.)

L.L. Bean, Inc., Freeport, ME 04032, 207-865-4761; FAX: 207-552-2802

Loch Leven Industries/Convert-a-pell, P.O. Box 2751, Santa Rosa, CA 95405/707-573-8735; FAX: 707-573-0369

Lock's Philadelphia Gun Exchange, 6700 Rowland Ave., Philadelphia, PA 19149/215-332-6225; FAX: 215-332-4800

Lodewick, Walter H., 2816 NE Halsey St., Portland, OR 97232/503-284-2554

Log Cabin Sport Shop, 8010 Lafayette Rd., Lodi, OH 44254/330-948-1082; FAX: 330-948-4307

Logan, Harry M., Box 745, Honokaa, HI 96727/808-776-1644

Lohman Mfg. Co., Inc., 4500 Doniphan Dr., P.O. Box 220, Neosho, MO 64850/417-451-4438; FAX: 417-451-2576

Lomont Precision Bullets, RR 1, Box 34, Salmon, ID 83467/208-756-6819; FAX: 208-756-6824

London Guns Ltd., Box 3750, Santa Barbara, CA 93130/805-683-4141; FAX: 805-683-1712

Lone Star Gunleather, 1301 Brushy Bend Dr., Round Rock, TX 78681/512-255-1805

Lone Star Rifle Company, 11231 Rose Road, Conroe, Texas 77303/409-856-3363

Long, George F., 1500 Rogue River Hwy., Ste. F, Grants Pass, OR 97527/541-476-7552

Lorcin Engineering Co., Inc., 10427 San Sevaine Way, Ste. A, Mira Loma, CA 91752

Lortone, Inc., 2856 NW Market St., Seattle, WA 98107/206-789-3100

Lothar Walther Precision Tool, Inc., 3425 Hutchinson Rd., Cumming, GA 30040/770-889-9998; Fax: 770-889-4918

Lovestrand, Erik, 206 Bent Oak Circle, Harvest, AL 35749-9334

Loweth (Firearms), Richard H.R., 29 Hedgegrow Lane, Kirby Muxloe, Leics. LE9 2BN ENGLAND/(0)116 238 6295

L.P.A. Snc, Via Alfieri 26, Gardone V.T., Brescia, ITALY 25063/30-891-14-81; FAX: 30-891-09-51

LPS Laboratories, Inc., 4647 Hugh Howell Rd., P.O. Box 3050, Tucker, GA 30084/404-934-7800

Lucas, Edward E., 32 Garfield Ave., East Brunswick, NJ 08816/201-251-5526

Lucas, Mike, 1631 Jessamine Rd., Lexington, SC 29073/803-356-0282

Luch Metal Merchants, Barbara, 48861 West Rd., Wixon, MI 48393/800-876-5337

Lutz Engraving, Ron, E. 1998 Smokey Valley Rd., Scandinavia, WI 54977/715-467-2674

Lyman Instant Targets, Inc. (See Lyman Products Corp.)

Lyman Products Corp., 475 Smith Street, Middletown, CT 06457-1541/860-632-2020, 800-22-LYMAN; FAX: 860-632-1699

Lynn's Custom Gunstocks, RR 1, Brandon, IA 52210/319-474-2453

Lyons Gunworks, Larry, 110 Hamilton St., Dowagiac, MI 49047/616-782-9478

Lyte Optronics (See TracStar Industries, Inc.,)

M

M&D Munitions Ltd., 127 Verdi St., Farmingdale, NY 11735/800-878-2788, 516-752-1038; FAX: 516-752-1905

M&M Engineering (See Hollywood Engineering)

M&N Bullet Lube, P.O. Box 495, 151 NE Jefferson St., Madras, OR 97741/503-255-3750

MA Systems, P.O. Box 1143, Chouteau, OK 74337/918-479-6378

Mac-1 Airgun Distributors, 13974 Van Ness Ave., Gardena, CA 90249/310-327-3581; FAX: 310-327-0238

Mac's .45 Shop, P.O. Box 2028, Seal Beach, CA 90740/310-438-5046

Macbean, Stan, 754 North 1200 West, Orem, UT 84057/801-224-6446

Madis Books, 2453 West Five Mile Pkwy., Dallas, TX 75233/214-330-7168

Madis, George, P.O. Box 545, Brownsboro, TX 75756/903-852-6480

MAG Instrument, Inc., 1635 S. Sacramento Ave., Ontario, CA 91761/909-947-1006; FAX: 909-947-3116

Mag-Na-Port International, Inc., 41302 Executive Dr., Harrison Twp., MI 48045-1306/810-469-6727; FAX: 810-469-0425

Mag-Pack Corp., P.O. Box 846, Chesterland, OH 44026

Magma Engineering Co., P.O. Box 161, 20955 E. Ocotillo Rd., Queen Creek, AZ 85242/602-987-9008; FAX: 602-987-0148

Magnolia Sports, Inc., 211 W. Main, Magnolia, AR 71753/501-234-8410, 800-530-7816; FAX: 501-234-8117

Magnum Grips, Box 801G, Payson, AZ 85547

Magnum Power Products, Inc., P.O. Box 17768, Fountain Hills, AZ 85268

Magnum Research, Inc., 7110 University Ave. NE, Minneapolis, MN 55432/800-772-6168, 612-574-1868; FAX: 612-574-0109; WEB:http://www.magnumresearch.com

Magnus Bullets, P.O. Box 239, Toney, AL 35773/256-420-8359; FAX: 256-420-8360; Email: magnusinc@juno.com

MagSafe Ammo Co., 2725 Friendly Grove Rd NE, Olympia, WA 98506/360-357-6383; FAX: 360-705-4715

MagTech Recreational Products, Inc., 5030 Paradise Rd., Suite A104, Las Vegas, NV 89119/702-736-2043; FAX: 702-736-2140

Mahony, Philip Bruce, 67 White Hollow Rd., Lime Rock, CT 06039-2418/203-435-9341

Mahovsky's Metalife, R.D. 1, Box 149a Eureka Road, Grand Valley, PA 16420/814-436-7747

Maine Custom Bullets, RFD 1, Box 1755, Brooks, ME 04921

Maionchi-L.M.I., Via Di Coselli-Zona Industriale Di Guamo, Lucca, ITALY 55060/011 39-583 94291

Makinson, Nicholas, RR 3, Komoka, Ont. N0L 1R0 CANADA/519-471-5462

Malcolm Enterprises, 1023 E. Prien Lake Rd., Lake Charles, LA 70601

Mallardtone Game Calls, 2901 16th St., Moline, IL 61265/309-762-8089

M.A.M. Products, Inc., 153 B Cross Slope Court, Englishtown, NJ 07726/908-536-3604; FAX:908-972-1004

Mandell Shooting Supplies, Inc., 3616 N. Scottsdale Rd., Scottsdale, AZ 85252/602-945-2553; FAX: 602-949-0734

Manufacture D'Armes Des Pyrenees Francaises (See Unique/M.A.P.F.)

Mar Knives, Inc., Al, 5755 SW Jean Rd., Suite 101, Lake Oswego, OR 97035/503-635-9229; FAX: 503-223-0467

Marathon Rubber Prods. Co., Inc., 510 Sherman St., Wausau, WI 54401/715-845-6255

Marble Arms (See CRR, Inc.,/Marble's Inc.)

Marchmon Bullets, 8191 Woodland Shore Dr., Brighton, MI 48116

Marent, Rudolf, 9711 Tiltree St., Houston, TX 77075/713-946-7028

Markell, Inc., 422 Larkfield Center 235, Santa Rosa, CA 95403/707-573-0792; FAX: 707-573-9867

Markesbery Muzzle Loaders, Inc., 7785 Foundation Dr., Ste. 6, Florence, KY 41042/606-342-5553; 606-342-2380

Marksman Products, 5482 Argosy Dr., Huntington Beach, CA 92649/714-898-7535, 800-822-8005; FAX: 714-891-0782

Marlin Firearms Co., 100 Kenna Dr., North Haven, CT 06473/203-239-5621; FAX: 203-234-7991

MarMik, Inc., 2116 S. Woodland Ave., Michigan City, IN 46360/219-872-7231; FAX: 219-872-7231

Marocchi F.lli S.p.A, Via Galileo Galilei 8, I-25068 Zanano di Sarezzo, ITALY/ (U.S. importers—Precision Sales International, Inc.)

Marple & Associates, Dick, 21 Dartmouth St., Hooksett, NH 03106/603-627-1837; FAX: 603-627-1837

Marquart Precision Co., P.O. Box 1740, Prescott, AZ 86302/520-445-5646

Marsh, Johnny, 1007 Drummond Dr., Nashville, TN 37211/615-833-3259

Marsh, Mike, Croft Cottage, Main St., Elton, Derbyshire DE4 2BY, ENGLAND/01629 650 669

Marshall Enterprises, 792 Canyon Rd., Redwood City, CA 94062

Martin Bookseller, J., P.O. Drawer AP, Beckley, WV 25802/304-255-4073; FAX: 304-255-4077

Martin's Gun Shop, 937 S. Sheridan Blvd., Lakewood, CO 80226/303-922-2184

Martz, John V., 8060 Lakeview Lane, Lincoln, CA 95648/FAX:916-645-3815

Marvel, Alan, 3922 Madonna Rd., Jarretsville, MD 21084/301-557-6545

Marx, Harry (U.S. importer for FERLIB)

Maryland Paintball Supply, 8507 Harford Rd., Parkville, MD 21234/410-882-5607

Masen Co., Inc., John, 1305 Jelmak, Grand Prairie, TX 75050/817-430-8732; FAX: 817-430-1715

MAST Technology, 4350 S. Arville, Suite 3, Las Vegas, NV 89103/702-362-5043; FAX: 702-362-9554

Master Engravers, Inc. (See Hendricks, Frank E.)

Master Lock Co., 2600 N. 32nd St., Milwaukee, WI 53245/414-444-2800

Master Products, Inc. (See Gun-Alert/Master Products, Inc.)

Match Prep—Doyle Gracey, P.O. Box 155, Tehachapi, CA 93581/805-822-5383

Matco, Inc., 1003-2nd St., N. Manchester, IN 46962/219-982-8282

Mathews & Son, George E., Inc., 10224 S. Paramount Blvd., Downey, CA 90241/562-862-6719; FAX: 562-862-6719

Matthews Cutlery, 4401 Sentry Dr., Tucker, GA 30084/770-939-6915

Mauser Werke Oberndorf Waffensysteme GmbH, Postfach 1349, 78722 Oberndorf/N. GERMANY/ (U.S. importer—GSI, Inc.)

Maverick Arms, Inc., 7 Grasso Ave., P.O. Box 497, North Haven, CT 06473/203-230-5300; FAX: 203-230-5420

Maxi-Mount, P.O. Box 291, Willoughby Hills, OH 44094-0291/216-944-9456; FAX: 216-944-9456

Maximum Security Corp., 32841 Calle Perfecto, San Juan Capistrano, CA 92675/714-493-3684; FAX: 714-496-7733

Mayville Engineering Co. (See MEC, Inc.)

Mazur Restoration, Pete, 13083 Drummer Way, Grass Valley, CA 95949/530-268-2412

MCA Sports, P.O. Box 8868, Palm Springs, CA 92263/619-770-2005

McBros Rifle Co., P.O. Box 86549, Phoenix, AZ 85080/602-582-3713; FAX: 602-581-3825

McCament, Jay, 1730-134th St. Ct. S., Tacoma, WA 98444/206-531-8832

McCann Industries, P.O. Box 641, Spanaway, WA 98387/253-537-6919; FAX: 253-537-6919

McCann's Muzzle-Gun Works, 14 Walton Dr., New Hope, PA 18938/215-862-2728

McCluskey Precision Rifles, 10502 14th Ave. NW, Seattle, WA 98177/206-781-2776

McCombs, Leo, 1862 White Cemetery Rd., Patriot, OH 45658/614-256-1714

McCormick Corp., Chip, 1825 Fortview Rd., Ste. 115, Austin, TX 78704/800-328-CHIP, 512-462-0004; FAX: 512-462-0009

McCullough, Ken (See Ken's Rifle Blanks)

McDonald, Dennis, 8359 Brady St., Peosta, IA 52068/319-556-7940

McFarland, Stan, 2221 Idella Ct., Grand Junction, CO 81505/970-243-4704

McGowen Rifle Barrels, 5961 Spruce Lane, St. Anne, IL 60964/815-937-9816; FAX: 815-937-4024

McGuire, Bill, 1600 N. Eastmont Ave., East Wenatchee, WA 98802/509-884-6021

McKee Publications, 121 Eatons Neck Rd., Northport, NY 11768/516-575-8850

McKenzie, Lynton, 6940 N. Alvernon Way, Tucson, AZ 85718/520-299-5090

McKillen & Heyer, Inc., 35535 Euclid Ave. Suite 11, Willoughby, OH 44094/216-942-2044

McKinney, R.P. (See Schuetzen Gun Co.)

McMillan Fiberglass Stocks, Inc., 21421 N. 14th Ave., Suite B, Phoenix, AZ 85027/602-582-9635; FAX: 602-581-3825

McMillan Optical Gunsight Co., 28638 N. 42nd St., Cave Creek, AZ 85331/602-585-7868; FAX: 602-585-7872

McMillan Rifle Barrels, P.O. Box 3427, Bryan, TX 77805/409-690-3456; FAX: 409-690-0156

McMurdo, Lynn (See Specialty Gunsmithing)

MCRW Associates Shooting Supplies, R.R. 1 Box 1425, Sweet Valley, PA 18656/717-864-3967; FAX: 717-864-2669

MCS, Inc., 34 Delmar Dr., Brookfield, CT 06804/203-775-1013; FAX: 203-775-9462

McWelco Products, 6730 Santa Fe Ave., Hesperia, CA 92345/619-244-8876; FAX: 619-244-9398

McWhorter Custom Rifles, 4460 SW 35th Terrace, Suite 310, Gainesville, FL 32608/352-373-9057; FAX: 352-377-3816

MDS, P.O. Box 1441, Brandon, FL 33509-1441/813-653-1180; FAX: 813-684-5953

Meadow Industries, 24 Club Lane, Palmyra, VA 22963/804-589-7672; FAX: 804-589-7672

Measurement Group, Inc., Box 27777, Raleigh, NC 27611

MEC, Inc., 715 South St., Mayville, WI 53050/414-387-4500; FAX: 414-387-5802

MEC-Gar S.r.l., Via Madonnina 64, Gardone V.T., Brescia, ITALY 25063/39-30-8912687; FAX: 39-30-8910065 (U.S. importer— MEC-Gar U.S.A., Inc.)

MEC-Gar U.S.A., Inc., Box 112, 500B Monroe Turnpike, Monroe, CT 06468/203-635-8662; FAX: 203-635-8662

Mech-Tech Systems Inc., 1602 Foothill Rd., Kalispell, MT 59901/406-755-8055

Meister Bullets (See Gander Mountain)

Mele, Frank, 201 S. Wellow Ave., Cookeville, TN 38501/615-526-4860

Melton Shirt Co., Inc., 56 Harvester Ave., Batavia, NY 14020/716-343-8750; FAX: 716-343-6887

Men-Metallwerk Elisenhuette, GmbH, P.O. Box 1263, D-56372 Nassau/Lahn, GERMANY/2604-7819

Menck, Gunsmith Inc., T.W., 5703 S. 77th St., Ralston, NE 68127

Mendez, John A., P.O. Box 620984, Orlando, FL 32862/407-344-2791

Meprolight (See Hesco-Meprolight)

Mercer Custom Stocks, R.M., 216 S. Whitewater Ave., Jefferson, WI 53549/414-674-5130

Merit Corp., Box 9044, Schenectady, NY 12309/518-346-1420

Merkel Freres, Strasse 7 October, 10, Suhl, GERMANY/ (U.S. importer—GSI, Inc.)

Merkuria Ltd., Argentinska 38, 17005 Praha 7, CZECH REPUBLIC/422-875117; FAX: 422-809152

Metal Merchants, 48861 West Rd., Wixom, MI 48393

Metal Products Co. (See MPC)

Metalife Industries (See Mahovsky's Metalife)

Metaloy Inc., Rt. 5, Box 595, Berryville, AR 72616/501-545-3611

Metals Hand Engraver/European Hand Engraving, Ste. 216, 12 South First St., San Jose, CA 95113/408-293-6559

Michael's Antiques, Box 591, Waldoboro, ME 04572

Michaels of Oregon Co., P.O. Box 1690, Portland, OR 97045/503-557-0536; FAX: 503-655-7546

Micro Sight Co., 242 Harbor Blvd., Belmont, CA 94002/415-591-0769; FAX: 415-591-7531

Microfusion Alfa S.A., Paseo San Andres N8, P.O. Box 271, Eibar, SPAIN 20600/34-43-11-89-16; FAX: 34-43-11-40-38

Mid-America Guns and Ammo, 1205 W. Jefferson, Suite E, Effingham, IL 62401/800-820-5177

Mid-America Recreation, Inc., 1328 5th Ave., Moline, IL 61265/309-764-5089; FAX: 309-764-2722

Middlebrooks Custom Shop, 7366 Colonial Trail East, Surry, VA 23883/757-357-0881; FAX: 757-365-0442

Midway Arms, Inc., 5875 W. Van Horn Tavern Rd., Columbia, MO 65203/800-243-3220, 573-445-6363; FAX: 573-446-1018

Midwest Gun Sport, 1108 Herbert Dr., Zebulon, NC 27597/919-269-5570

Midwest Sport Distributors, Box 129, Fayette, MO 65248

Military Armament Corp., P.O. Box 120, Mt. Zion Rd., Lingleville, TX 76461/817-965-3253

Miller Arms, Inc., P.O. Box 260 Purl St., St. Onge, SD 57779/605-642-5160; FAX: 605-642-5160

Miller Custom, 210 E. Julia, Clinton, IL 61727/217-935-9362

Miller Co., David, 3131 E. Greenlee Rd., Tucson, AZ 85716-1267/520-326-3117

Miller Single Trigger Mfg. Co., Rt. 209 Box 1275, Millersburg, PA 17061/717-692-3704

Millett Sights, 7275 Murdy Circle, Adm. Office, Huntington Beach, CA 92647/714-842-5575, 800-645-5388; FAX: 714-843-5707

Mills Jr., Hugh B., 3615 Canterbury Rd., New Bern, NC 28560/919-637-4631

Milstor Corp., 80-975 Indio Blvd. C-7, Indio, CA 92201/760-775-9998; FAX: 760-772-4990

Miltex, Inc., 2225 Pinefield Station, Waldorf, MD 20601/888-642-9123

Miniature Machine Co. (See MMC)

Minute Man High Tech Industries, 10611 Canyon Rd. E., Suite 151, Puyallup, WA 98373/800-233-2734

Mirador Optical Corp., P.O. Box 11614, Marina Del Rey, CA 90295-7614/310-821-5587; FAX: 310-305-0386

Miroku, B.C./Daly, Charles (See U.S. importer—Bell's Legendary Country Wear; K.B.I., Inc.; U.S. distributor—Outdoor Sports Headquarters, Inc.)

Mitchell Bullets, R.F., 430 Walnut St., Westernport, MD 21562

Mitchell Optics Inc., 2072 CR 1100 N, Sidney, IL 61877/217-688-2219, 217-621-3018; FAX: 217-688-2505

Mitchell's Accuracy Shop, 68 Greenridge Dr., Stafford, VA 22554/703-659-0165

MI-TE Bullets, 1396 Ave. K, Ellsworth, KS 67439/785-472-4575; FAX: 785-472-5579

Mittermeier, Inc., Frank, P.O. Box 2G, 3577 E. Tremont Ave., Bronx, NY 10465/718-828-3843

MJK Gunsmithing, Inc., 417 N. Huber Ct., E. Wenatchee, WA 98802/509-884-7683

MJM Mfg., 3283 Rocky Water Ln. Suite B, San Jose, CA 95148/408-270-4207

MKS Supply, Inc. (See Hi-Point Firearms)

MMC, 2513 East Loop 820 North, Ft. Worth, TX 76118/817-595-0404; FAX: 817-595-3074

MMP, Rt. 6, Box 384, Harrison, AR 72601/501-741-5019; FAX: 501-741-3104

M.O.A. Corp., 2451 Old Camden Pike, Eaton, OH 45320/513-456-3669

Modern Gun Repair School, P.O. Box 92577, Southlake, TX 76092/800-493-4114; FAX: 800-556-5112

Modern MuzzleLoading, Inc., 234 Airport Rd., P.O. Box 130, Centerville, IA 52544/515-856-2626; FAX: 515-856-2628
Moeller, Steve, 1213 4th St., Fulton, IL 61252/815-589-2300
Molin Industries, Tru-Nord Division, P.O. Box 365, 204 North 9th St., Brainerd, MN 56401/218-829-2870
Mo's Competitor Supplies (See MCS, Inc.)
MoLoc Bullets, P.O. Box 2810, Turlock, CA 95381-2810/209-632-1644
Monell Custom Guns, 228 Red Mills Rd., Pine Bush, NY 12566/914-744-3021
Moneymaker Guncraft Corp., 1420 Military Ave., Omaha, NE 68131/402-556-0226
Montana Armory, Inc. (See C. Sharps Arms Co. Inc.)
Montana Outfitters, Lewis E. Yearout, 308 Riverview Dr. E., Great Falls, MT 59404/406-761-0859
Montana Precision Swaging, P.O. Box 4746, Butte, MT 59702/406-782-7502
Montana Vintage Arms, 2354 Bear Canyon Rd., Bozeman, MT 59715
Montgomery Community College, P.O. Box 787-GD, Troy, NC 27371/910-576-6222, 800-839-6222; FAX: 910-576-2176
Moore & Co., Wm. Larkin, 8727 E. Via de Commencio, Suite A, Scottsdale, AZ 85258/602-951-8913; FAX: 602-951-8913
Morini (See U.S. importers—Mandall Shooting Supplies, Inc.; Nygord Precision Products)
Morrison Custom Rifles, J.W., 4015 W. Sharon, Phoenix, AZ 85029/602-978-3754
Morrow, Bud, 11 Hillside Lane, Sheridan, WY 82801-9729/307-674-8360
Morton Booth Co., P.O. Box 123, Joplin, MO 64802/417-673-1962; FAX: 417-673-3642
Moss Double Tone, Inc., P.O. Box 1112, 2101 S. Kentucky, Sedalia, MO 65301/816-827-0827
Mossberg & Sons, Inc., O.F., 7 Grasso Ave., North Haven, CT 06473/203-230-5300; FAX: 203-230-5420
Mountain Hollow Game Calls, Box 121, Cascade, MD 21719/301-241-3282
Mountain Plains, Inc., 244 Glass Hollow Rd., Alton, VA 22920/800-687-3000
Mountain Rifles Inc., P.O. Box 2789, Palmer, AK 99645/907-373-4194; FAX: 907-373-4195
Mountain South, P.O. Box 381, Barnwell, SC 29812/FAX: 803-259-3227
Mountain State Muzzleloading Supplies, Inc., Box 154-1, Rt. 2, Williamstown, WV 26187/304-375-7842; FAX: 304-375-3737
Mountain States Engraving, Kenneth W. Warren, P.O. Box 2842, Wenatchee, WA 98802/509-663-6123
Mountain View Sports, Inc., Box 188, Troy, NH 03465/603-357-9690; FAX: 603-357-9691
Mowrey Gun Works, P.O. Box 246, Waldron, IN 46182/317-525-6181; FAX: 317-525-9595
Mowrey's Guns & Gunsmithing, 119 Fredericks St., Canajoharie, NY 13317/518-673-3483
MPC, P.O. Box 450, McMinnville, TN 37110-0450/615-473-5513; FAX: 615-473-5516
MPI Stocks, P.O. Box 83266, Portland, OR 97283/503-226-1215; FAX: 503-226-2661
MSC Industrial Supply Co., 151 Sunnyside Blvd., Plainview, NY 11803-9915/516-349-0330
MSR Targets, P.O. Box 1042, West Covina, CA 91793/818-331-7840
Mt. Alto Outdoor Products, Rt. 735, Howardsville, VA 24562
Mt. Baldy Bullet Co., 12981 Old Hill City Rd., Keystone, SD 57751-6623/605-666-4725
M.Thys (See U.S. importer—Champlin Firearms, Inc.)
MTM Molded Products Co., Inc., 3370 Obco Ct., Dayton, OH 45414/513-890-7461; FAX: 513-890-1747
Milberry House Publishing, P.O. Box 575, Corydon, IN 47112/888-738-1567; FAX: 888-738-1567
Mulhern, Rick, Rt. 5, Box 152, Rayville, LA 71269/318-728-2688
Mullins Ammunition, Rt. 2, Box 304K, Clintwood, VA 24228/540-926-6772; FAX: 540-926-6092
Mullis Guncraft, 3523 Lawyers Road E., Monroe, NC 28110/704-283-6683
Multi-Caliber Adapters (See MCA Sports)
Multiplex International, 26 S. Main St., Concord, NH 03301/FAX: 603-796-2223
Multipropulseurs, La Bertrandiere, 42580 L'Etrat, FRANCE/77 74 01 30; FAX: 77 93 19 34
Multi-Scale Charge Ltd., 3269 Niagara Falls Blvd., N. Tonawanda, NY 14120/905-566-1255; FAX: 905-276-6295

Mundy, Thomas A., 69 Robbins Road, Somerville, NJ 08876/201-722-2199
Munsch Gunsmithing, Tommy, Rt. 2, P.O. Box 248, Little Falls, MN 56345/612-632-6695
Murmur Corp., 2823 N. Westmoreland Ave., Dallas, TX 75222/214-630-5400
Murphy Co., Inc., R., 13 Groton-Harvard Rd., P.O. Box 376, Ayer, MA 01432/617-772-3481
Murray State College, 1 Murray Campus St., Tishomingo, OK 73460/580-371-2371 ext. 238
Muscle Products Corp., 112 Fennell Dr., Butler, PA 16001/800-227-7049, 412-283-0567; FAX: 412-283-8310
Museum of Historical Arms Inc., 2750 Coral Way, Suite 204, Miami, FL 33145/305-444-9199
Mushroom Express Bullet Co., 601 W. 6th St., Greenfield, IN 46140-1728/317-462-6332
Muzzleload Magnum Products (See MMP)
Muzzleloaders Etcetera, Inc., 9901 Lyndale Ave. S., Bloomington, MN 55420/612-884-1161
MWG Co., P.O. Box 971202, Miami, FL 33197/800-428-9394, 305-253-8393; FAX: 305-232-1247

N

N&J Sales, Lime Kiln Rd., Northford, CT 06472/203-484-0247
Nagel's Custom Bullets, 100 Scott St., Baytown, TX 77520-2849
Nalpak, 1937-C Friendship Drive, El Cajon, CA 92020/619-258-1200
Napoleon Bonaparte, Inc. (See Metals Hand Engraver)
Nastoff's 45 Shop, Inc., Steve, 12288 Mahoning Ave., P.O. Box 446, North Jackson, OH 44451/330-538-2977
National Bullet Co., 1585 E. 361 St., Eastlake, OH 44095/216-951-1854; FAX: 216-951-7761
National Security Safe Co., Inc., P.O. Box 39, 620 S. 380 E., American Fork, UT 84003/801-756-7706, 800-544-3829; FAX: 801-756-8043
National Target Co., 4690 Wyaconda Rd., Rockville, MD 20852/800-827-7060, 301-770-7060; FAX: 301-770-7892
Nationwide Airgun Repairs (See Airgun Repair Centre)
Nationwide Sports Distributors, Inc., 70 James Way, Southampton, PA 18966/215-322-2050, 800-355-3006; FAX: 702-358-2093
Naval Ordnance Works, Rt. 2, Box 919, Sheperdstown, WV 25443/304-876-0998
Navy Arms Co., 689 Bergen Blvd., Ridgefield, NJ 07657/201-945-2500; FAX: 201-945-6859
N.B.B., Inc., 24 Elliot Rd., Sterling, MA 01564/508-422-7538, 800-942-9444
N.C. Ordnance Co., P.O. Box 3254, Wilson, NC 27895/919-237-2440; FAX: 919-243-9845
NCP Products, Inc., 3500 12th St. N.W., Canton, OH 44708/330-456-5130; FAX: 330-456-5234
Necessary Concepts, Inc., P.O. Box 571, Deer Park, NY 11729/516-667-8509; FAX 516-667-8588
NECO, 1316-67th St., Emeryville, CA 94608/510-450-0420
Necromancer Industries, Inc., 14 Communications Way, West Newton, PA 15089/412-872-8722
NEI Handtools, Inc., 51583 Columbia River Hwy., Scappoose, OR 97056/503-543-6776; FAX: 503-543-6799; E-MAIL: neiht@mcimail.com
Nelson, Gary K., 975 Terrace Dr., Oakdale, CA 95361/209-847-4590
Nelson, Stephen, 7365 NW Spring Creek Dr., Corvallis, OR 97330/541-745-5232
Nelson/Weather-Rite, Inc., 14760 Santa Fe Trail Dr., Lenexa, KS 66215/913-492-3200; FAX: 913-492-8749
Nesci Enterprises, Inc., P.O. Box 119, Summit St., East Hampton, CT 06424/203-267-2588
Nesika Bay Precision, 22239 Big Valley Rd., Poulsbo, WA 98370/206-697-3830
Nettestad Gun Works, RR 1, Box 160, Pelican Rapids, MN 56572/218-863-4301
Neumann GmbH, Am Galgenberg 6, 90575 Langenzenn, GERMANY/09101/8258; FAX: 09101/6356
Nevada Pistol Academy Inc., 4610 Blue Diamond Rd., Las Vegas, NV 89139/702-897-1100
New England Ammunition Co., 1771 Post Rd. East, Suite 223, Westport, CT 06880/203-254-8048
New England Arms Co., Box 278, Lawrence Lane, Kittery Point, ME 03905/207-439-0593; FAX: 207-439-6726
New England Custom Gun Service, 438 Willow Brook Rd., RR2, Box 122W, W. Lebanon, NH 03784/603-469-3450; FAX: 603-469-3471
New England Firearms, 60 Industrial Rowe, Gardner, MA 01440/508-632-9393; FAX: 508-632-2300

New Orleans Jewelers Supply Co., 206 Charters St., New Orleans, LA 70130/504-523-3839; FAX: 504-523-3836

New SKB Arms Co., C.P.O. Box 1401, Tokyo, JAPAN/81-3-3943-9550; FAX: 81-3-3943-0695

New Win Publishing, Inc., 186 Center St., Clinton, NJ 08809/908-735-9701; FAX: 908-735-9703

Newark Electronics, 4801 N. Ravenswood Ave., Chicago, IL 60640

Newell, Robert H., 55 Coyote, Los Alamos, NM 87544/505-662-7135

Newman Gunshop, 119 Miller Rd., Agency, IA 52530/515-937-5775

NgraveR Co., The, 67 Wawecus Hill Rd., Bozrah, CT 06334/860-823-1533

Nicholson Custom, 17285 Thornlay Road, Hughesville, MO 65334/816-826-8746

Nickels, Paul R., 4789 Summerhill Rd., Las Vegas, NV 89121-5638/702-435-5318

Nicklas, Ted, 5504 Hegel Rd., Goodrich, MI 48438/810-797-4493

Nic Max, Inc., 535 Midland Ave., Garfield, NJ 07026/201-546-7191; FAX: 201-546-7419

Niemi Engineering, W.B., Box 126 Center Road, Greensboro, VT 05841/802-533-7180 days, 802-533-7141 evenings

Nightforce (See Lightforce U.S.A. Inc.)

Nikon, Inc., 1300 Walt Whitman Rd., Melville, NY 11747/516-547-8623; FAX: 516-547-0309

Nitex, Inc., P.O. Box 1706, Uvalde, TX 78801/210-278-8843

Noble Co., Jim, 1305 Columbia St., Vancouver, WA 98660/360-695-1309; FAX: 360-695-6835

Noreen, Peter H., 5075 Buena Vista Dr., Belgrade, MT 59714/406-586-7383

Norica, Avnda Otaola, 16, Apartado 68, 20600 Eibar, SPAIN

Norin, Dave, Schrank's Smoke & Gun, 2010 Washington St., Waukegan, IL 60085/708-662-4034

Norinco, 7A, Yun Tan N Beijing, CHINA/ (U.S. importers—Century International Arms, Inc.; Interarms)

Norincoptics (See BEC, Inc.)

Norma Precision AB (See U.S. importers—Dynamit Nobel-RWS Inc.; Paul Co. Inc., The)

Norman Custom Gunstocks, Jim, 14281 Cane Rd., Valley Center, CA 92082/619-749-6252

Normark Corp., 10395 Yellow Circle Dr., Minnetonka, MN 55343-9101/612-933-7060; FAX: 612-933-0046

Norrell Arms, John, 2608 Grist Mill Rd., Little Rock, AR 72207/501-225-7864

North American Arms, Inc., 2150 South 950 East, Provo, UT 84606-6285/800-821-5783, 801-374-9990; FAX: 801-374-9998

North American Correspondence Schools, The Gun Pro School, Oak & Pawney St., Scranton, PA 18515/717-342-7701

North American Munitions, P.O. Box 815, Beulah, ND 58523/701-948-2260; FAX: 701-948-2282

North American Shooting Systems, P.O. Box 306, Osoyoos, B.C. V0H 1V0 CANADA/604-495-3131; FAX: 604-495-2816

North Devon Firearms Services, 3 North St., Braunton, EX33 1AJ ENGLAND/01271 813624; FAX: 01271 813624

North Fork Custom Gunsmithing, James Johnston, 428 Del Rio Rd., Roseburg, OR 97470/503-673-4467

North Mountain Pine Training Center (See Executive Protection Institute)

North Pass, 425 South Bowen St., Ste. 6, Longmount, CO 80501/303-682-4315/ FAX: 303-678-7109

North Specialty Products, 2664-B Saturn St., Brea, CA 92621/714-524-1665

North Star West, P.O. Box 488, Glencoe, CA 95232/209-293-7010

North Wind Decoy Co., 1005 N. Tower Rd., Fergus Falls, MN 56537/218-736-4378; FAX: 218-736-7060

Northern Precision Custom Swaged Bullets, 329 S. James St., Carthage, NY 13619/315-493-1711

Northlake Outdoor Footwear, P.O. Box 10, Franklin, TN 37065-0010/615-794-1556; FAX: 615-790-8005

Northside Gun Shop, 2725 NW 109th, Oklahoma City, OK 73120/405-840-2353

No-Sho Mfg. Co., 10727 Glenfield Ct., Houston, TX 77096/713-723-5332

Nosler, Inc., P.O. Box 671, Bend, OR 97709/800-285-3701, 541-382-3921; FAX: 541-388-4667

Novak's, Inc., 12061/2 30th St., P.O. Box 4045, Parkersburg, WV 26101/304-485-9295; FAX: 304-428-6722

Now Products, Inc., P.O. Box 27608, Tempe, AZ 85285/800-662-6063; FAX: 602-966-0890

Nowlin Mfg. Co., Rt. 1, Box 308, Claremore, OK 74017/918-342-0689; FAX: 918-342-0624

NRI Gunsmith School, 4401 Connecticut Ave. NW, Washington, D.C. 20008

Nu-Line Guns, Inc., 1053 Caulks Hill Rd., Harvester, MO 63304/314-441-4500, 314-447-4501; FAX: 314-447-5018

Null Holsters Ltd., K.L., 161 School St. NW, Hill City Station, Resaca, GA 30735/706-625-5643; FAX: 706-625-9392

Numrich Arms Corp., 203 Broadway, W. Hurley, NY 12491

Nu-Teck, 30 Industrial Park Rd., Box 37, Centerbrook, CT 06409/203-767-3573; FAX: 203-767-9137

NW Sinker and Tackle, 380 Valley Dr., Myrtle Creek, OR 97457-9717

Nygord Precision Products, P.O. Box 12578, Prescott, AZ 86304/520-717-2315; FAX: 520-717-2198

O

Oakland Custom Arms, Inc., 4690 W. Walton Blvd., Waterford, MI 48329/810-674-8261

Oakman Turkey Calls, RD 1, Box 825, Harrisonville, PA 17228/717-485-4620

Oakshore Electronic Sights, Inc., P.O. Box 4470, Ocala, FL 32678-4470/904-629-7112; FAX: 904-629-1433

Obermeyer Rifled Barrels, 23122 60th St., Bristol, WI 53104/414-843-3537; FAX: 414-843-2129

October Country Muzzleloading, P.O. Box 969, Dept. GD, Hayden, ID 83835/208-772-2068; FAX: 208-772-9230

Oehler Research, Inc., P.O. Box 9135, Austin, TX 78766/512-327-6900

Oglesby & Oglesby Gunmakers, Inc., RR 5, Springfield, IL 62707/217-487-7100

Oil Rod and Gun Shop, 69 Oak St., East Douglas, MA 01516/508-476-3687

Ojala Holsters, Arvo, P.O. Box 98, N. Hollywood, CA 91603/503-669-1404

Oker's Engraving, 365 Bell Rd., P.O. Box 126, Shawnee, CO 80475/303-838-6042

Oklahoma Ammunition Co., 3701A S. Harvard Ave., No. 367, Tulsa, OK 74135-2265/918-396-3187; FAX: 918-396-4270

Oklahoma Leather Products, Inc., 500 26th NW, Miami, OK 74354/918-542-6651; FAX: 918-542-6653

OK Weber, Inc., P.O. Box 7485, Eugene, OR 97401/541-747-0458; FAX: 541-747-5927

Old Wagon Bullets, 32 Old Wagon Rd., Wilton, CT 06897

Old West Bullet Moulds, P.O. Box 519, Flora Vista, NM 87415/505-334-6970

Old West Reproductions, Inc., R.M. Bachman, 446 Florence S. Loop, Florence, MT 59833/406-273-2615; FAX: 406-273-2615

Old Western Scrounger, Inc., 12924 Hwy. A-l2, Montague, CA 96064/916-459-5445; FAX: 916-459-3944

Old World Gunsmithing, 2901 SE 122nd St., Portland, OR 97236/503-760-7681

Old World Oil Products, 3827 Queen Ave. N., Minneapolis, MN 55412/612-522-5037

Ole Frontier Gunsmith Shop, 2617 Hwy. 29 S., Cantonment, FL 32533/904-477-8074

Olson, Myron, 989 W. Kemp, Watertown, SD 57201/605-886-9787

Olson, Vic, 5002 Countryside Dr., Imperial, MO 63052/314-296-8086

Olt Co., Philip S., P.O. Box 550, 12662 Fifth St., Pekin, IL 61554/309-348-3633; FAX: 309-348-3300

Olympic Optical Co., P.O. Box 752377, Memphis, TN 38175-2377/901-794-3890, 800-238-7120; FAX: 901-794-0676, 800-748-1669

Omark Industries, Div. of Blount, Inc., 2299 Snake River Ave., P.O. Box 856, Lewiston, ID 83501/800-627-3640, 208-746-2351

Omega Sales, P.O. Box 1066, Mt. Clemens, MI 48043/810-469-7323; FAX: 810-469-0425

One Of A Kind, 15610 Purple Sage, San Antonio, TX 78255/512-695-3364

Op-Tec, P.O. Box L632, Langhorn, PA 19047/215-757-5037

Optical Services Co., P.O. Box 1174, Santa Teresa, NM 88008-1174/505-589-3833

Orchard Park Enterprise, P.O. Box 563, Orchard Park, NY 14227/616-656-0356

Ordnance Works, The, 2969 Pidgeon Point Road, Eureka, CA 95501/707-443-3252

Oregon Arms, Inc. (See Rogue Rifle Co., Inc.)

Oregon Trail Bullet Company, P.O. Box 529, Dept. P, Baker City, OR 97814/800-811-0548; FAX: 514-523-1803

Original Box, Inc., 700 Linden Ave., York, PA 17404/717-854-2897; FAX: 717-845-4276

Original Mink Oil, Inc., 10652 NE Holman, Portland, OR 97220/503-255-2814, 800-547-5895; FAX: 503-255-2487

Orion Rifle Barrel Co., RR2, 137 Cobler Village, Kalispell, MT 59901/406-257-5649

Or-Un, Tahtakale Menekse Han 18, Istanbul, TURKEY 34460/90212-522-5912; FAX: 90212-522-7973

Orvis Co., The, Rt. 7, Manchester, VT 05254/802-362-3622 ext. 283; FAX: 802-362-3525

Ottmar, Maurice, Box 657, 113 E. Fir, Coulee City, WA 99115/509-632-5717

Outa-Site Gun Carriers, 219 Market St., Laredo, TX 78040/956-722-4678, 800-880-9715; FAX: 956-726-4858

Outdoor Connection, Inc., The, 201 Cotton Dr., P.O. Box 7751, Waco, TX 76714-7751/800-533-6076; 817-772-5575; FAX: 817-776-3553

Outdoor Edge Cutlery Corp., 2888 Bluff St., Suite 130, Boulder, CO 80301/303-652-8212; FAX: 303-652-8238

Outdoor Enthusiast, 3784 W. Woodland, Springfield, MO 65807/417-883-9841

Outdoor Sports Headquarters, Inc., 967 Watertower Ln., West Carrollton, OH 45449/513-865-5855; FAX: 513-865-5962

Outdoorsman's Bookstore, The, Llangorse, Brecon, Powys LD3 7UE, U.K./44-1874-658-660; FAX: 44-1874-658-650

Outers Laboratories, Div. of Blount, Inc., Sporting Equipment Div., Route 2,, P.O. Box 39/Onalaska, WI 54650 608-781-5800; FAX: 608-781-0368

Ox-Yoke Originals, Inc., 34 Main St., Milo, ME 04463/800-231-8313, 207-943-7351; FAX: 207-943-2416

Ozark Gun Works, 11830 Cemetery Rd., Rogers, AR 72756/501-631-6944; FAX: 501-631-6944

P

P&M Sales and Service, 5724 Gainsborough Pl., Oak Forest, IL 60452/708-687-7149

P&S Gun Service, 2138 Old Shepardsville Rd., Louisville, KY 40218/502-456-9346

Pac-Nor Barreling, 99299 Overlook Rd., P.O. Box 6188, Brookings, OR 97415/503-469-7330; FAX: 503-469-7331

Pace Marketing, Inc., P.O. Box 2039, Stuart, FL 34995/561-871-9682; FAX: 561-871-6552

Pachmayr Div. Lyman Products, 1875 S. Mountain Ave., Monrovia, CA 91016/626-357-7771

Pacific Cartridge, Inc., 2425 Salashan Loop Road, Ferndale, WA 98248/360-366-4444; FAX: 360-366-4445

Rimrock Rifle Stocks, P.O. Box 589, Vashon Island, WA 98070/206-463-5551; FAX: 206-463-2526

Pacific Research Laboratories, Inc. (See Rimrock Rifle Stocks)

Pacific Rifle Co., P.O. Box 11, Newberg, OR 97132/503-538-7437

Paco's (See Small Custom Mould & Bullet Co.)

P.A.C.T., Inc., P.O. Box 531525, Grand Prairie, TX 75053/214-641-0049

Page Custom Bullets, P.O. Box 25, Port Moresby Papua, NEW GUINEA

Pagel Gun Works, Inc., 1407 4th St. NW, Grand Rapids, MN 55744/218-326-3003

Paintball Games International Magazine (Aceville Publications), Castle House, 97 High St./Colchester, Essex, CO1 1TH ENGLAND 011-44-206-564840

Palmer Manufacturing Co., Inc., C., P.O. Box 220, West Newton, PA 15089/412-872-8200; FAX: 412-872-8302

Palmer Security Products, 2930 N. Campbell Ave., Chicago, IL 60618/800-788-7725; FAX: 773-267-8080

Palsa Outdoor Products, P.O. Box 81336, Lincoln, NE 68501/402-488-5288; FAX: 402-488-2321

PanaVise Products, Inc., 7540 Colbert Drive, Sparks, NV 89431/702-850-2900; FAX: 702-850-2929

Para-Ordnance Mfg., Inc., 980 Tapscott Rd., Scarborough, Ont. M1X 1E7, CANADA/416-297-7855; FAX: 416-297-1289 (U.S. importer—Para-Ordnance, Inc.)

Para-Ordnance, Inc., 1919 NE 45th St., Ft. Lauderdale, FL 33308

Paragon Sales & Services, Inc., P.O. Box 2022, Joliet, IL 60434/815-725-9212; FAX: 815-725-8974

Pardini Armi Srl, Via Italica 154, 55043 Lido Di Camaiore Lu, ITALY/584-90121; FAX: 584-90122 (U.S. importers—Nygord Precision Products;MCS, Inc.)

Paris, Frank J., 17417 Pershing St., Livonia, MI 48152-3822

Park Rifle Co., Ltd., The, Unit 6a, Dartford Trade Park, Power Mill Lane, Dartford, Kent, ENGLAND DA7 7NX/011-0322-222512

Parker & Sons Shooters Supply, 9337 Smoky Row Rd., Straw Plains, TN 97871-1257;

Parker Div. Reageant Chemical (See Parker Reproductions)

Parker Gun Finishes, 9337 Smokey Row Rd., Strawberry Plains, TN 37871/423-933-3286

Parker Reproductions, 124 River Rd., Middlesex, NJ 08846/908-469-0100; FAX: 908-469-9692

Parsons Optical Mfg. Co., P.O. Box 192, Ross, OH 45061/513-867-0820; FAX: 513-867-8380

Parts & Surplus, P.O. Box 22074, Memphis, TN 38122/901-683-4007

Partridge Sales Ltd., John, Trent Meadows, Rugeley, Staffordshire, WS15 2HS ENGLAND/0889-584438

Pasadena Gun Center, 206 E. Shaw, Pasadena, TX 77506/713-472-0417; FAX: 713-472-1322

Paser Pal, 200 W. Pleasantview, Hurst, TX 76054/817-285-9888, 800-501-1603; FAX: 817-285-8769

Passive Bullet Traps, Inc. (See Savage Range Systems, Inc.)

PAST Sporting Goods, Inc., P.O. Box 1035, Columbia, MO 65205/314-445-9200; FAX: 314-446-6606

Paterson Gunsmithing, 438 Main St., Paterson, NJ 07502/201-345-4100

Pathfinder Sports Leather, 2920 E. Chambers St., Phoenix, AZ 85040/602-276-0016

Patrick Bullets, P.O. Box 172, Warwick QSLD 4370 AUSTRALIA

Paul Co., The, 27385 Pressonville Rd., Wellsville, KS 66092/785-883-4444; FAX: 785-883-2525

Paulsen Gunstocks, Rt. 71, Box 11, Chinook, MT 59523/406-357-3403

Payne Photography, Robert, P.O. Box 141471, Austin, TX 78714/512-272-4554

PC Bullet, 52700 NE First, Scappoose, OR 97056-3212/503-543-5088; FAX: 503-543-5990

PC Co., 5942 Secor Rd., Toledo, OH 43623/419-472-6222

PCE, Ltd., Little Tree Ramble,P.O. Box 97, Monteagle, TN 37356/931-924-3475; FAX: 931-924-3489

Peacemaker Specialists, P.O. Box 157, Whitmore, CA 96096/916-472-3438

Pearce Grip, Inc., P.O. Box 187, Bothell, WA 98041-0187/206-485-5488; FAX:206-488-9497

Pease Accuracy, Bob, P.O. Box 310787, New Braunfels, TX 78131/210-625-1342

Pease International, 53 Durham St., Portsmouth, NH 03801/603-431-1331; FAX: 603-431-1221

PECAR Herbert Schwarz, GmbH, Kreuzbergstrasse 6, 10965 Berlin, GERMANY/004930-785-7383; FAX: 004930-785-1934

Pecatonica River Longrifle, 5205 Nottingham Dr., Rockford, IL 61111/815-968-1995; FAX: 815-968-1996

Pedersen, C.R., 2717 S. Pere Marquette Hwy., Ludington, MI 49431/616-843-2061

Pedersen, Rex C., 2717 S. Pere Marquette Hwy., Ludington, MI 49431/616-843-2061

Pedersoli and Co., Davide, Via Artigiani 57, Gardone V.T., Brescia, ITALY 25063/030-8912402; FAX: 030-8911019 (U.S. importers—Beauchamp & Son, Inc.; Cabela's; Cape Outfitters; Cimarron Arms; Dixie Gun Works; EMF Co., Inc.; Navy Arms Co.; Track of the Wolf, Inc.)

Peerless Alloy, Inc., 1445 Osage St., Denver, CO 80204-2439/303-825-6394, 800-253-1278

Peet Shoe Dryer, Inc., 130 S. 5th St., P.O. Box 618, St. Maries, ID 83861/208-245-2095, 800-222-PEET; FAX: 208-245-5441

Peifer Rifle Co., P.O. Box 192, Nokomis, IL 62075-0192/217-563-7050; FAX: 217-563-7060

Pejsa Ballistics, 2120 Kenwood Pkwy., Minneapolis, MN 55405/612-374-3337; FAX: 612-374-5383

Pelaire Products, 5346 Bonky Ct., W. Palm Beach, FL 33415/561-439-0691; FAX: 561-967-0052

Pell, John T. (See KOGOT)

Peltor, Inc. (See Aero Peltor)

PEM's Mfg. Co., 5063 Waterloo Rd., Atwater, OH 44201/216-947-3721

Pence Precision Barrels, 7567 E. 900 S., S. Whitley, IN 46787/219-839-4745

Pendleton Royal, c/o Swingler Buckland Ltd., 4/7 Highgate St., Birmingham, ENGLAND B12 0XS/44 121 440 3060, 44 121 446 5898; FAX: 44 121 446 4165

Pendleton Woolen Mills, P.O. Box 3030, 220 N.W. Broadway, Portland, OR 97208/503-226-4801

Penguin Industries, Inc., Airport Industrial Mall, Coatesville, PA 19320/610-384-6000; FAX: 610-857-5980

Penn Bullets, P.O. Box 756, Indianola, PA 15051

Penna Gunsmith School, 812 Ohio River Blvd., Pittsburgh, PA 15202-2699

Penna Gun Parts, 1701 Mud Run Rd., York Springs, PA 17372-8826/717-259-8010; FAX: 717-259-0057

Penn's Woods Products, Inc., 19 W. Pittsburgh St., Delmont, PA 15626/412-468-8311; FAX: 412-468-8975

Pennsylvania Gun Parts, 1701 Mud Run Rd., York Springs, PA 17372/717-259-8010; FAX: 717-259-0057

Pennsylvania Gunsmith School, 812 Ohio River Blvd., Avalon, Pittsburgh, PA 15202/412-766-1812

Penrod Precision, 312 College Ave., P.O. Box 307, N. Manchester, IN 46962/219-982-8385

Pentax Corp., 35 Inverness Dr. E., Englewood, CO 80112/800-709-2020; FAX: 303-643-0393

Pentheny de Pentheny, 2352 Baggett Ct., Santa Rosa, CA 95401/707-573-1390; FAX: 707-573-1390

Perazone-Gunsmith, Brian, Cold Spring Rd., Roxbury, NY 12474/607-326-4088; FAX: 607-326-3140

Perazzi m.a.p. S.p.A. (See Armi Perazzi S.p.A.)

Perazzi USA, Inc., 1207 S. Shamrock Ave., Monrovia, CA 91016/818-303-0068; FAX: 818-303-2081

Performance Specialists, 308 Eanes School Rd., Austin, TX 78746/512-327-0119

Peripheral Data Systems (See Arms Software)

Perugini Visini & Co. S.r.l., Via Camprelle, 126, 25080 Nuvolera (Bs.), ITALY

Peters Stahl GmbH, Stettiner Strasse 42, D-33106 Paderborn, GERMANY/05251-750025; FAX: 05251-75611 (U.S. importer—Franzen International, Inc.)

Petersen Publishing Co., 6420 Wilshire Blvd., Los Angeles, CA 90048/213-782-2000; FAX: 213-782-2867

Peterson Gun Shop, Inc., A.W., 4255 W. Old U.S. 441, Mt. Dora, FL 32757-3299/352-383-4258; FAX: 352-735-1001

Petro-Explo, Inc., 7650 U.S. Hwy. 287, Suite 100, Arlington, TX 76017/817-478-8888

Pettinger Books, Gerald, Rt. 2, Box 125, Russell, IA 50238/515-535-2239

Pflumm Mfg. Co., 10662 Widmer Rd., Lenexa, KS 66215/800-888-4867; FAX: 913-451-7857

PFRB Co., P.O. Box 1242, Bloomington, IL 61702/309-473-3964; FAX: 309-473-2161

Phil-Chem, Inc. (See George & Roy's)

Phillippi Custom Bullets, Justin, P.O. Box 773, Ligonier, PA 15658/412-238-9671

Phillips, Jerry, P.O. Box L632, Langhorne, PA 19047/215-757-5037

Phillips & Rodgers, Inc., 100 Hilbig, Suite C, Conroe, TX 77301/409-756-1001, 800-682-2247; FAX: 409-756-0976

Phoenix Arms, 1420 S. Archibald Ave., Ontario, CA 91761/909-947-4843; FAX: 909-947-6798

Photronic Systems Engineering Company, 6731 Via De La Reina, Bonsall, CA 92003/619-758-8000

Piedmont Community College, P.O. Box 1197, Roxboro, NC 27573/910-599-1181

Pierce Pistols, 55 Sorrellwood Lane, Sharpsburg, GA 30277-9523/404-253-8192

Pietta (See U.S. importers—Navy Arms Co.; Taylor's & Co., Inc.)

Pilgrim Pewter, Inc. (See Bell Originals Inc., Sid)

Pine Technical College, 1100 4th St., Pine City, MN 55063/800-521-7463; FAX: 612-629-6766

Pinetree Bullets, 133 Skeena St., Kitimat BC, CANADA V8C 1Z1/604-632-3768; FAX: 604-632-3768

Pioneer Arms Co., 355 Lawrence Rd., Broomall, PA 19008/215-356-5203

Pioneer Research, Inc., 216 Haddon Ave., Suite 102, Westmont, NJ 08108/800-257-7742; FAX: 609-858-8695

Piotti (See U.S. importer—Moore & Co., Wm. Larkin)

Piquette, Paul R., 80 Bradford Dr., Feeding Hills, MA 01030/413-781-8300, Ext. 682

Plaxco, J. Michael, Rt. 1, P.O. Box 203, Roland, AR 72135/501-868-9787

Plaza Cutlery, Inc., 3333 Bristol, 161, South Coast Plaza, Costa Mesa, CA 92626/714-549-3932

Plum City Ballistic Range, N2162 80th St., Plum City, WI 54761-8622/715-647-2539

PlumFire Press, Inc., 30-A Grove Ave., Patchogue, NY 11772-4112/800-695-7246; FAX:516-758-4071

PMC/Eldorado Cartridge Corp., P.O. Box 62508, 12801 U.S. Hwy. 95 S., Boulder City, NV 89005/702-294-0025; FAX: 702-294-0121

P.M. Enterprises, Inc., 146 Curtis Hill Rd., Chehalis, WA 98532/360-748-3743; FAX: 360-748-1802

Poburka, Philip (See Bison Studios)

Pohl, Henry A. (See Great American Gun Co.)

Pointing Dog Journal, Village Press Publications, P.O. Box 968, Dept. PGD, Traverse City, MI 49685/800-272-3246; FAX: 616-946-3289

Police Bookshelf, P.O. Box 122, Concord, NH 03301/603-224-6814; FAX: 603-226-3554

Polywad, Inc., P.O. Box 7916, Macon, GA 31209/912-477-0669

Pomeroy, Robert, RR1, Box 50, E. Corinth, ME 04427/207-285-7721

Ponsness/Warren, P.O. Box 8, Rathdrum, ID 83858-0008/208-687-2231; FAX: 208-687-2233

Pony Express Reloaders, 608 E. Co. Rd. D, Suite 3, St. Paul, MN 55117/612-483-9406; FAX: 612-483-9884

Pony Express Sport Shop, Inc., 16606 Schoenborn St., North Hills, CA 91343/818-895-1231

Potts, Wayne E., 912 Poplar St., Denver, CO 80220/303-355-5462

Powder Horn Antiques, P.O. Box 4196, Ft. Lauderdale, FL 33338/305-565-6060

Powder Horn, Inc., The, P.O. Box 114 Patty Drive, Cusseta, GA 31805/404-989-3257

Powell & Son (Gunmakers) Ltd., William, 35-37 Carrs Lane, Birmingham B4 7SX ENGLAND/121-643-0689; FAX: 121-631-3504 (U.S. importer—The William Powell Agency)

Powell Agency, William, The, 22 Circle Dr., Bellmore, NY 11710/516-679-1158

Power Custom, Inc., 29739 Hwy. J, Gravois Mills, MO 65037/513-372-5684; FAX: 573-372-5799

Powley Computer (See Hutton Rifle Ranch)

Practical Tools, Inc., Div. Behlert Precision, 7067 Easton Rd., P.O. Box 133, Pipersville, PA 18947/215-766-7301; FAX: 215-766-8681

Pragotrade, 307 Humberline Dr., Rexdale, Ontario, CANADA M9W 5V1/416-675-1322

Prairie River Arms, 1220 N. Sixth St., Princeton, IL 61356/815-875-1616, 800-445-1541; FAX: 815-875-1402

Pranger, Ed G., 1414 7th St., Anacortes, WA 98221/206-293-3488

Precise International, 15 Corporate Dr., Orangeburg, NY 10962/914-365-3500; FAX: 914-425-4700

Precise Metalsmithing Enterprises, 146 Curtis Hill Rd., Chehalis, WA 98532/206-748-3743; FAX: 206-748-8102

Precision Airgun Sales, Inc., 5139 Warrensville Center Rd., Maple Hts., OH 44137-1906/216-587-5005

Precision Cartridge, 176 Eastside Rd., Deer Lodge, MT 59722/800-397-3901, 406-846-3900

Precision Cast Bullets, 101 Mud Creek Lane, Ronan, MT 59864/406-676-5135

Precision Castings & Equipment, Inc., P.O. Box 326, Jasper, IN 47547-0135/812-634-9167

Precision Components, 3177 Sunrise Lake, Milford, PA 18337/717-686-4414

Precision Components and Guns, Rt. 55, P.O. Box 337, Pawling, NY 12564/914-855-3040

Precision Delta Corp., P.O. Box 128, Ruleville, MS 38771/601-756-2810; FAX: 601-756-2590

Precision Metal Finishing, John Westrom, P.O. Box 3186, Des Moines, IA 50316/515-288-8680; FAX: 515-244-3925

Precision Munitions, Inc., P.O. Box 326, Jasper, IN 47547

Precision Reloading, Inc., P.O. Box 122, Stafford Springs, CT 06076/860-684-7979; FAX: 860-684-6788

Precision Sales International, Inc., P.O. Box 1776, Westfield, MA 01086/413-562-5055; FAX: 413-562-5056

Precision Shooting, Inc., 222 McKee St., Manchester, CT 06040/860-645-8776; FAX: 860-643-8215

Precision Specialties, 131 Hendom Dr., Feeding Hills, MA 01030/413-786-3365; FAX: 413-786-3365

Precision Sport Optics, 15571 Producer Lane, Unit G, Huntington Beach, CA 92649/714-891-1309; FAX: 714-892-6920

Premier Reticles, 920 Breckinridge Lane, Winchester, VA 22601-6707/540-722-0601; FAX: 540-722-3522

Prescott Projectile Co., 1808 Meadowbrook Road, Prescott, AZ 86303

Preslik's Gunstocks, 4245 Keith Ln., Chico, CA 95926/916-891-8236

Pre-Winchester 92-90-62 Parts Co., P.O. Box 8125, W. Palm Beach, FL 33407

Price Bullets, Patrick W., 16520 Worthley Drive, San Lorenzo, CA 94580/510-278-1547

Prime Reloading, 30 Chiswick End, Meldreth, Royston SG8 6LZ UK/0763-260636

Primos, Inc., P.O. Box 12785, Jackson, MS 39236-2785/601-366-1288; FAX: 601-362-3274

PRL Bullets, c/o Blackburn Enterprises, 114 Stuart Rd., Ste. 110, Cleveland, TN 37312/423-559-0340

Pro Load Ammunition, Inc., 5180 E. Seltice Way, Post Falls, ID 83854/208-773-9444; FAX: 208-773-9441

Pro-Mark, Div. of Wells Lamont, 6640 W. Touhy, Chicago, IL 60648/312-647-8200

Pro-Port Ltd., 41302 Executive Dr., Harrison Twp., MI 48045-1306/810-469-7323; FAX: 810-469-0425

Pro-Shot Products, Inc., P.O. Box 763, Taylorville, IL 62568/217-824-9133; FAX: 217-824-8861
Professional Firearms Record Book Co. (See PFRB Co.)
Professional Gunsmiths of America, Inc., Route 1, Box 224F, Lexington, MO 64067/816-259-2636
Professional Hunter Supplies (See Star Custom Bullets)
Professional Ordnance, Inc., 1215 E. Airport Dr., Box 182, Ontario, CA 91761/909-923-5559; FAX: 909-923-0899
ProlixÆ Lubricants, P.O. Box 1348, Victorville, CA 92393/800-248-LUBE, 760-243-3129; FAX: 760-241-0148
Proofmark Corp., PO Box 610, Burgess, VA 22432-0610
Protecto Plastics, Div. of Penguin Ind., Airport Industrial Mall, Coatesville, PA 19320/215-384-6000
Protector Mfg. Co., Inc., The, 443 Ashwood Place, Boca Raton, FL 33431/407-394-6011
Protektor Model, 1-11 Bridge St., Galeton, PA 16922/814-435-2442
Prototech Industries, Inc., Rt. 1, Box 81, Delia, KS 66418/913-771-3571; FAX: 913-771-2531
P.S.M.G. Gun Co., 10 Park Ave., Arlington, MA 02174/617-646-8845; FAX: 617-646-2133
PWL Gunleather, P.O. Box 450432, Atlanta, GA 31145/770-822-1640; FAX: 770-822-1704
Pyramid, Inc., 3292 S. Highway 97, Redmond, OR 97756/503-548-1041; FAX: 503-923-1004

Q

Quack Decoy & Sporting Clays, 4 Ann & Hope Way, P.O. Box 98, Cumberland, RI 02864/401-723-8202; FAX: 401-722-5910
Quaker Boy, Inc., 5455 Webster Rd., Orchard Parks, NY 14127/716-662-3979; FAX: 716-662-9426
Quality Arms, Inc., Box 19477, Dept. GD, Houston, TX 77224/713-870-8377; FAX: 713-870-8524
Quality Firearms of Idaho, Inc., 659 Harmon Way, Middleton, ID 83644-3065/208-466-1631
Quality Parts Co./Bushmaster Firearms, 999 Roosevelt Trail, Bldg. 3, Windham, ME 04062/800-998-7928, 207-892-2005; FAX: 207-892-8068
Quarton USA, Ltd. Co., 7042 Alamo Downs Pkwy., Suite 370, San Antonio, TX 78238-4518/800-520-8435, 210-520-8430; FAX: 210-520-8433
Que Industries, Inc., P.O. Box 2471, Everett, WA 98203/800-769-6930, 206-347-9843; FAX: 206-514-3266
Queen Cutlery Co., P.O. Box 500, Franklinville, NY 14737/800-222-5233; FAX: 716-676-5535
Quigley's Personal Protection Strategies, Paxton, 9903 Santa Monica Blvd.,, 300/Beverly Hills, CA 90212/310-281-1762

R

R&C Knives & Such, P.O. Box 1047, Manteca, CA 95336/209-239-3722; FAX: 209-825-6947
R&J Gun Shop, 133 W. Main St., John Day, OR 97845/503-575-2130
R&S Industries Corp., 8255 Brentwood Industrial Dr., St. Louis, MO 63144/314-781-5400
Rabeno, Martin, 92 Spook Hole Rd., Ellenville, NY 12428/914-647-4567; FAX: 914-647-2129
Radack Photography, Lauren, 21140 Jib Court L-12, Aventura, FL 33180/305-931-3110
Radiator Specialty Co., 1900 Wilkinson Blvd., P.O. Box 34689, Charlotte, NC 28234/800-438-6947; FAX: 800-421-9525
Radical Concepts, P.O. Box 1473, Lake Grove, OR 97035/503-538-7437
Rainier Ballistics Corp., 4500 15th St. East, Tacoma, WA 98424/800-638-8722, 206-922-7589; FAX: 206-922-7854
Ram-Line Blount, Inc., P.O. Box 39, Onalaska, WI 54650-0039
Rampart International, 2781 W. MacArthur Blvd., #B-283, Santa Ana, CA 92704/800-976-7240, 714-557-6405
Ranch Products, P.O. Box 145, Malinta, OH 43535/313-277-3118; FAX: 313-565-8536
Randall-Made Knives, P.O. Box 1988, Orlando, FL 32802/407-855-8075
Randco UK, 286 Gipsy Rd., Welling, Kent DA16 1JJ, ENGLAND/44 81 303 4118
Randolph Engineering, Inc., 26 Thomas Patten Dr., Randolph, MA 02368/800-541-1405; FAX: 800-875-4200
Range Brass Products Company, P.O. Box 218, Rockport, TX 78381
Ranger Mfg. Co., Inc., 1536 Crescent Dr., P.O. Box 14069, Augusta, GA 30919-0069/706-738-2023; FAX: 404-738-3608
Ranger Products, 2623 Grand Blvd., Suite 209, Holiday, FL 34609/813-942-4652, 800-407-7007; FAX: 813-942-6221

Ranger Shooting Glasses, 26 Thomas Patten Dr., Randolph, MA 02368/800-541-1405; FAX: 617-986-0337
Ranging, Inc., Routes 5 & 20, East Bloomfield, NY 14443/716-657-6161; FAX: 716-657-5405
Ransom International Corp., P.O. Box 3845, 1040-A Sandretto Dr., Prescott, AZ 86302/520-778-7899; FAX: 520-778-7993; E-MAIL: ransom@primenet.com; WEB: http://www.primenet.com/òransom
Rapine Bullet Mould Mfg. Co., 9503 Landis Lane, East Greenville, PA 18041/215-679-5413; FAX: 215-679-9795
Raptor Arms Co., Inc., 115 S. Union St., Suite 308, Alexandria, VA 22314/703-683-0018; FAX: 703-683-5592
Rattlers Brand, P.O. Box 311, 115 E. Main St., Thomaston, GA 30286/706-647-7131, 800-825-7131; FAX: 706-646-5090
Ravell Ltd., 289 Diputacion St., 08009, Barcelona SPAIN/34(3) 4874486; FAX: 34(3) 4881394
Ray's Gunsmith Shop, 3199 Elm Ave., Grand Junction, CO 81504/970-434-6162; FAX: 970-434-6162
Raytech, Div. of Lyman Products Corp., 475 Smith Street, Middletown, CT 06457-1541/860-632-2020; FAX: 860-632-1699
RCBS, Div. of Blount, Inc., Sporting Equipment Div., 605 Oro Dam Blvd., Oroville, CA 95965/800-533-5000, 916-533-5191; FAX: 916-533-1647
Reagent Chemical & Research, Inc. (See Calico Hardwoods, Inc.)
Reardon Products, P.O. Box 126, Morrison, IL 61270/815-772-3155
Recoilless Technologies, Inc., 3432 W. Wilshire Dr., Suite 11, Phoenix, AZ 85009/602-278-8903; FAX: 602-272-5946
Red Ball, 100 Factory St., Nashua, NH 03060/603-881-4420
Red Cedar Precision Mfg., W. 485 Spruce Dr., Brodhead, WI 53520/608-897-8416
Red Diamond Dist. Co., 1304 Snowdon Dr., Knoxville, TN 37912
Redding Reloading Equipment, 1089 Starr Rd., Cortland, NY 13045/607-753-3331; FAX: 607-756-8445
Redfield, Inc., 5800 E. Jewell Ave., Denver, CO 80224/303-757-6411; FAX: 303-756-2338
Redman's Rifling & Reboring, 189 Nichols Rd., Omak, WA 98841/509-826-5512
Redwood Bullet Works, 3559 Bay Rd., Redwood City, CA 94063/415-367-6741
Reed, Dave, Rt. 1, Box 374, Minnesota City, MN 55959/507-689-2944
Refrigiwear, Inc., 71 Inip Dr., Inwood, Long Island, NY 11696
R.E.I., P.O. Box 88, Tallevast, FL 34270/813-755-0085
Reiswig, Wallace E. (See Claro Walnut Gunstock Co.)
Reloaders Equipment Co., 4680 High St., Ecorse, MI 48229
Reloading Specialties, Inc., Box 1130, Pine Island, MN 55463/507-356-8500; FAX: 507-356-8800
Remington Arms Co., Inc., 870 Remington Drive, P.O. Box 700, Madison, NC 27025-0700/800-243-9700; 910-548-8700
Remington Double Shotguns, 7885 Cyd Dr., Denver, CO 80221/303-429-6947
Renegade, P.O. Box 31546, Phoenix, AZ 85046/602-482-6777; FAX: 602-482-1952
Renfrew Guns & Supplies, R.R. 4, Renfrew, Ontario K7V 3Z7 CANADA/613-432-7080
Reno, Wayne, 2808 Stagestop Rd., Jefferson, CO 80456/719-836-3452
Republic Arms, Inc., 15167 Sierra Bonita Lane, Chino, CA 91710/909-597-3873; FAX:909-393-9771
R.E.T. Enterprises, 2608 S. Chestnut, Broken Arrow, OK 74012/918-251-GUNS; FAX: 918-251-0587
Retting, Inc., Martin B., 11029 Washington, Culver City, CA 90232/213-837-2412
R.F.D. Rifles, 8230 Wilson Dr., Ralston, NE 68127/402-331-9529
R.G.-G., Inc., P.O. Box 1261, Conifer, CO 80433-1261/303-697-4154; FAX: 303-697-4154
Rhino, P.O. Box 787, Locust, NC 28097/704-753-2198
Rhodeside, Inc., 1704 Commerce Dr., Piqua, OH 45356/513-773-5781
Rice, Keith (See White Rock Tool & Die)
Richards, John, Richards Classic Oil Finish, Rt. 2, Box 325, Bedford, KY 40006/502-255-7222
Richards Micro-Fit Stocks, 8331 N. San Fernando Ave., Sun Valley, CA 91352/818-767-6097; FAX: 818-767-7121
Rickard, Inc., Pete, RD 1, Box 292, Cobleskill, NY 12043/800-282-5663; FAX: 518-234-2454
Ridgetop Sporting Goods, P.O. Box 306, 42907 Hilligoss Ln. East, Eatonville, WA 98328/360-832-6422; FAX: 360-832-6422
Riebe Co., W.J., 3434 Tucker Rd., Boise, ID 83703
Ries, Chuck, 415 Ridgecrest Dr., Grants Pass, OR 97527/503-476-5623
Rifle Works & Armory, 707 12th St., Cody, WY 82414/307-587-4919

Rifles Inc., 873 W. 5400 N., Cedar City, UT 84720/801-586-5996; FAX: 801-586-5996

RIG Products, 87 Coney Island Dr., Sparks, NV 89431-6334/702-331-5666; FAX: 702-331-5669

Rigby & Co., John, 66 Great Suffolk St., London SE1 0BU, ENGLAND/0171-620-0690; FAX: 0171-928-9205

Riggs, Jim, 206 Azalea, Boerne, TX 78006/210-249-8567

Riling Arms Books Co., Ray, 6844 Gorsten St., P.O. Box 18925, Philadelphia, PA 19119/215-438-2456; FAX: 215-438-5395

Rim Pac Sports, Inc., 1034 N. Soldano Ave., Azusa, CA 91702-2135

Ringler Custom Leather Co., 31 Shining Mtn. Rd., Powell, WY 82435/307-645-3255

Ripley Rifles, 42 Fletcher Street, Ripley, Derbyshire, DE5 3LP ENGLAND/011-0773-748353

R.I.S. Co., Inc., 718 Timberlake Circle, Richardson, TX 75080/214-235-0933

River Road Sporting Clays, Bruce Barsotti, P.O. Box 3016, Gonzales, CA 93926/408-675-2473

Rizzini, Battista, Via 2 Giugno, 7/7Bis-25060 Marcheno (Brescia), ITALY/ (U.S. importers—Wm. Larkin Moore & Co.; New England Arms Co.)

Rizzini F.lli (See U.S. importers—Moore & CEngland Arms Co.)

RLCM Enterprises, 110 Hill Crest Drive, Burleson, TX 76028\

R.M. Precision, Inc., Attn. Greg F. Smith Marketing, P.O. Box 210, LaVerkin, UT 84745/801-635-4656; FAX: 801-635-4430

RMS Custom Gunsmithing, 4120 N. Bitterwell, Prescott Valley, AZ 86314/520-772-7626

Robar Co.'s, Inc., The, 21438 N. 7th Ave., Suite B, Phoenix, AZ 85027/602-581-2648; FAX: 602-582-0059

Roberts/Engraver, J.J., 7808 Lake Dr., Manassas, VA 22111/703-330-0448

Roberts Products, 25328 SE Iss. Beaver Lk. Rd., Issaquah, WA 98029/206-392-8172

Robinett, R.G., P.O. Box 72, Madrid, IA 50156/515-795-2906

Robinson, Don, Pennsylvania Hse., 36 Fairfax Crescent, Southowram, Halifax, W. Yorkshire HX3 9SQ, ENGLAND/0422-364458

Robinson Firearms Mfg. Ltd., 1699 Blondeaux Crescent, Kelowna, B.C. CANADA V1Y 4J8/604-868-9596

Robinson H.V. Bullets, 3145 Church St., Zachary, LA 70791/504-654-4029

Rochester Lead Works, 76 Anderson Ave., Rochester, NY 14607/716-442-8500; FAX: 716-442-4712

Rockwood Corp., Speedwell Division, 136 Lincoln Blvd., Middlesex, NJ 08846/908-560-7171, 800-243-8274; FAX: 980-560-7475

Rocky Mountain Arms, Inc., 1813 Sunset Place, Unit D, Longmont, CO 80501/800-375-0846; FAX: 303-678-8766

Rocky Mountain High Sports Glasses, 8121 N. Central Park Ave., Skokie, IL 60076/847-679-1012, 800-323-1418; FAX: 847-679-0184

Rocky Mountain Rifle Works Ltd., 1707 14th St., Boulder, CO 80302/303-443-9189

Rocky Mountain Target Co., 3 Aloe Way, Leesburg, FL 34788/352-365-9598

Rocky Mountain Wildlife Products, P.O. Box 999, La Porte, CO 80535/970-484-2768; FAX: 970-484-0807

Rocky Shoes & Boots, 294 Harper St., Nelsonville, OH 45764/800-848-9452, 614-753-1951; FAX: 614-753-4024

Rodgers & Sons Ltd., Joseph (See George Ibberson (Sheffield) Ltd.)

Rogers Gunsmithing, Bob, P.O. Box 305, 344 S. Walnut St., Franklin Grove, IL 61031/815-456-2685; FAX: 815-288-7142

Rogue Rifle Co., Inc., P.O. Box 20, Prospect, OR 97536/541-560-4040; FAX: 541-560-4041

Rogue River Rifleworks, 1317 Spring St., Paso Robles, CA 93446/805-227-4706; FAX: 805-227-4723

Rohner, Hans, 1148 Twin Sisters Ranch Rd., Nederland, CO 80466-9600

Rohner, John, 710 Sunshine Canyon, Boulder, CO 80302/303-444-3841

Rolston, Fred W., Inc., 210 E. Cummins St., Tecumseh, MI 49286/517-423-6002, 800-314-9061 (orders only); FAX: 517-423-6002

Romain's Custom Guns, Inc., RD 1, Whetstone Rd., Brockport, PA 15823/814-265-1948

Rooster Laboratories, P.O. Box 412514, Kansas City, MO 64141/816-474-1622; FAX: 816-474-1307

Rorschach Precision Products, P.O. Box 151613, Irving, TX 75015/214-790-3487

Rosenberg & Sons, Jack A., 12229 Cox Ln., Dallas, TX 75234/214-241-6302

Rosenthal, Brad and Sallie, 19303 Ossenfort Ct., St. Louis, MO 63038/314-273-5159; FAX: 314-273-5149

Ross & Webb (See Ross, Don)

Ross, Don, 12813 West 83 Terrace, Lenexa, KS 66215/913-492-6982

Rosser, Bob, 1824 29th Ave., Suite 214, Birmingham, AL 35209/205-870-4422; FAX: 205-870-4421

Rossi S.A., Amadeo, Rua: Amadeo Rossi, 143, Sao Leopoldo, RS, BRAZIL 93030-220/051-592-5566 (U.S. importer—Interarms)

Roto Carve, 2754 Garden Ave., Janesville, IA 50647

Round Edge, Inc., P.O. Box 723, Lansdale, PA 19446/215-361-0859

Rowe Engineering, Inc. (See R.E.I.)

Royal Arms Gunstocks, 919 8th Ave. NW, Great Falls, MT 59404/406-453-1149

Roy's Custom Grips, Rt. 3, Box 174-E, Lynchburg, VA 24504/804-993-3470

RPM, 15481 N. Twin Lakes Dr., Tucson, AZ 85739/520-825-1233; FAX: 520-825-3333

Rubright Bullets, 1008 S. Quince Rd., Walnutport, PA 18088/215-767-1339

Rucker Dist. Inc., P.O. Box 479, Terrell, TX 75160/214-563-2094

Rudnicky, Susan, 9 Water St., Arcade, NY 14009/716-492-2450

Ruger (See Sturm, Ruger & Co., Inc.)

Rundell's Gun Shop, 6198 Frances Rd., Clio, MI 48420/313-687-0559

Robert P. Runge, 94 Grove St., Ilion, NY 13357/315-894-3036

Rumanya, Inc., 4994-D Hwy. 6N, Ste. 101, Houston, TX 77084/281-345-2077; FAX: 281-345-2005

Rupert's Gun Shop, 2202 Dick Rd., Suite B, Fenwick, MI 48834/517-248-3252

Russ Trading Post, 23 William St., Addison, NY 14801-1326/607-359-3896

Russell Knives, Inc., A.G., 1705 Hwy. 71B North, Springdale, AR 72764/501-751-7341

Rusteprufe Laboratories, 1319 Jefferson Ave., Sparta, WI 54656/608-269-4144

Rusty Duck Premium Gun Care Products, 7785 Foundation Dr., Suite 6, Florence, KY 41042/606-342-5553; FAX: 606-342-5556

Rutgers Book Center, 127 Raritan Ave., Highland Park, NJ 08904/908-545-4344; FAX: 908-545-6686

Rutten (See U.S. importer—Labanu, Inc.)

Ruvel & Co., Inc., 4128-30 W. Belmont Ave., Chicago, IL 60641/773-286-9494; FAX: 773-286-9323

RWS (See U.S. importer—Dynamit Nobel-RWS, Inc.)

Ryan, Chad L., RR 3, Box 72, Cresco, IA 52136/319-547-4384

Rybka Custom Leather Equipment, Thad, 134 Havilah Hill, Odenville, AL 35120

S

S&B Industries, 11238 McKinley Rd., Montrose, MI 48457/810-639-5491

S&K Mfg. Co., P.O. Box 247, Pittsfield, PA 16340/814-563-7808; FAX: 814-563-4067

S&S Firearms, 74-11 Myrtle Ave., Glendale, NY 11385/718-497-1100; FAX: 718-497-1105

Sabatti S.r.l., via Alessandro Volta 90, 25063 Gardone V.T., Brescia, ITALY/030-8912207-831312; FAX: 030-8912059 (U.S. importer—E.A.A. Corp.)

SAECO (See Redding Reloading Equipment)

Saf-T-Lok, 5713 Corporate Way, Suite 100, W. Palm Beach, FL 33407

Safari Outfitters Ltd., 71 Ethan Allan Hwy., Ridgefield, CT 06877/203-544-9505

Safari Press, Inc., 15621 Chemical Lane B, Huntington Beach, CA 92649/714-894-9080; FAX: 714-894-4949

Safariland Ltd., Inc., 3120 E. Mission Blvd., P.O. Box 51478, Ontario, CA 91761/909-923-7300; FAX: 909-923-7400

SAFE, P.O. Box 864, Post Falls, ID 83854/208-773-3624

Safeguard Ordnance Systems Inc., P.O. Box 2028, Eaton Park, FL 33840/941-682-2829; FAX: 941-682-2829

Safety Speed Holster, Inc., 910 S. Vail Ave., Montebello, CA 90640/213-723-4140; FAX: 213-726-6973

Sako Ltd. (See U.S. importer—Stoeger Industries)

Salter Calls, Inc., Eddie, Hwy. 31 South-Brewton Industrial Park, Brewton, AL 36426/205-867-2584; FAX: 206-867-9005

Samco Global Arms, Inc., 6995 NW 43rd St., Miami, FL 33166/305-593-9782

Sampson, Roger, 2316 Mahogany St., Mora, MN 55051/320-679-4868

San Francisco Gun Exchange, 124 Second St., San Francisco, CA 94105/415-982-6097

San Marco (See U.S. importers—Cape Outfitters; EMF Co., Inc.)
Sanders Custom Gun Service, 2358 Tyler Lane, Louisville, KY 40205/502-454-3338; FAX: 502-451-8857
Sanders Gun and Machine Shop, 145 Delhi Road, Manchester, IA 52057
Sandia Die & Cartridge Co., 37 Atancacio Rd. NE, Albuquerque, NM 87123/505-298-5729
Sarco, Inc., 323 Union St., Stirling, NJ, Stirling, NJ 07980/908-647-3800; FAX: 908-647-9413
S.A.R.L. G. Granger, 66 cours Fauriel, 42100 Saint Etienne, FRANCE/04 77 25 14 73; FAX: 04 77 38 66 99
Sauer (See U.S. importers—Paul Co., The; Sigarms, Inc.)
Saunders Gun & Machine Shop, R.R. 2, Delhi Road, Manchester, IA 52057
Savage Arms, Inc., 100 Springdale Rd., Westfield, MA 01085/413-568-7001; FAX: 413-562-7764
Savage Arms (Canada), Inc., 248 Water St., P.O. Box 1240, Lakefield, Ont. K0L 2H0, CANADA/705-652-8000; FAX: 705-652-8431
Savage Range Systems, Inc., 100 Springdale RD., Westfield, MA 01085/413-568-7001; FAX: 413-562-1152
Saville Iron Co. (See Greenwood Precision)
Savino, Barbara J., P.O. Box 1104, Hardwick, VT 05843-1104
Scanco Environmental Systems, 5000 Highlands Parkway, Suite 180, Atlanta, GA 30082/770-431-0025; FAX: 770-431-0028
Scansport, Inc., P.O. Box 700, Enfield, NH 03748/603-632-7654
Scattergun Technologies, 620 8th Ave. S., Nashville, TN 37203/615-254-1441; FAX: 615-254-1449
Sceery Game Calls, P.O. Box 6520, Sante Fe, NM 87502/505-471-9110; FAX: 505-471-3476
Schaefer Shooting Sports, P.O. Box 1515, Melville, NY 11747-0515/516-379-4900; FAX: 516-379-6701
Scharch Mfg., Inc., 10325 CR 120, Salida, CO 81201/719-539-7242, 800-836-4683; FAX: 719-539-3021
Scherer, Box 250, Ewing, VA 24240/615-733-2615; FAX: 615-733-2073
Schiffman, Curt, 3017 Kevin Cr., Idaho Falls, ID 83402/208-524-4684
Schiffman, Mike, 8233 S. Crystal Springs, McCammon, ID 83250/208-254-9114
Schiffman, Norman, 3017 Kevin Cr., Idaho Falls, ID 83402/208-524-4684
Schmidtke Group, 17050 W. Salentine Dr., New Berlin, WI 53151-7349
Schmidt & Bender, Inc., Brook Rd., P.O. Box 134, Meriden, NH 03770/603-469-3565, 800-468-3450; FAX: 603-469-3471
Schmidtman Custom Ammunition, 6 Gilbert Court, Cotati, CA 94931
Schneider Bullets, 3655 West 214th St., Fairview Park, OH 44126
Schneider Rifle Barrels, Inc., Gary, 12202 N. 62nd Pl., Scottsdale, AZ 85254/602-948-2525
School of Gunsmithing, The, 6065 Roswell Rd., Atlanta, GA 30328/800-223-4542
Schrimsher's Custom Knifemaker's Supply, Bob, P.O. Box 308, Emory, TX 75440/903-473-3330; FAX: 903-473-2235
Schroeder Bullets, 1421 Thermal Ave., San Diego, CA 92154/619-423-3523; FAX: 619-423-8124
Schuetzen Pistol Works, 620-626 Old Pacific Hwy. SE, Olympia, WA 98513/360-459-3471; FAX: 360-491-3447
Schulz Industries, 16247 Minnesota Ave., Paramount, CA 90723/213-439-5903
Schumakers Gun Shop, 512 Prouty Corner Lp. A, Colville, WA 99114/509-684-4848
Schwartz Custom Guns, David W., 2505 Waller St., Eau Claire, WI 54703/715-832-1735
Schwartz Custom Guns, Wayne E., 970 E. Britton Rd., Morrice, MI 48857/517-625-4079
Scobey Duck & Goose Calls, Glynn, Rt. 3, Box 37, Newbern, TN 38059/901-643-6241
Scope Control, Inc., 5775 Co. Rd. 23 SE, Alexandria, MN 56308/612-762-7295
ScopLevel, 151 Lindbergh Ave., Suite C, Livermore, CA 94550/925-449-5052; FAX: 925-373-0861
Score High Gunsmithing, 9812-A, Cochiti SE, Albuquerque, NM 87123/800-326-5632, 505-292-5532; FAX: 505-292-2592; E-MAIL: scorehi@rt66.com; WEB: http://www.rt66.com/òscorehi/home.htm
Scot Powder, Rt.1 Box 167, McEwen, TN 37101/800-416-3006; FAX: 615-729-4211
Scot Powder Co. of Ohio, Inc., Box GD96, Only, TN 37140/615-729-4207, 800-416-3006; FAX: 615-729-4217
Scott Fine Guns, Inc., Thad, P.O. Box 412, Indianola, MS 38751/601-887-5929

Scott, McDougall & Associates, 7950 Redwood Dr., Cotati, CA 94931/707-546-2264; FAX: 707-795-1911
Scott, Dwight, 23089 Englehardt St., Clair Shores, MI 48080/313-779-4735
S.C.R.C., P.O. Box 660, Katy, TX 77492-0660/FAX: 713-578-2124
Scruggs' Game Calls, Stanley, Rt. 1, Hwy. 661, Cullen, VA 23934/804-542-4241, 800-323-4828
Second Chance Body Armor, P.O. Box 578, Central Lake, MI 49622/616-544-5721; FAX: 616-544-9824
Security Awareness & Firearms Education (See SAFE)
Seebeck Assoc., R.E., P.O. Box 59752, Dallas, TX 75229
Seecamp Co., Inc., L.W., P.O. Box 255, New Haven, CT 06502/203-877-3429
Segway Industries, P.O. Box 783, Suffern, NY 10901-0783/914-357-5510
Seligman Shooting Products, Box 133, Seligman, AZ 86337/602-422-3607
Selsi Co., Inc., P.O. Box 10, Midland Park, NJ 07432-0010/201-935-0388; FAX: 201-935-5851
Semmer, Charles (See Remington Double Shotguns)
Sentinel Arms, P.O. Box 57, Detroit, MI 48231/313-331-1951; FAX: 313-331-1456
Serva Arms Co., Inc., RD 1, Box 483A, Greene, NY 13778/607-656-4764
Service Armament, 689 Bergen Blvd., Ridgefield, NJ 07657
Servus Footwear Co., 1136 2nd St., Rock Island, IL 61204-3610/309-786-7741; FAX: 309-786-9808
S.G.S. Sporting Guns Srl., Via Della Resistenza, 37, 20090 Buccinasco (MI) ITALY/2-45702446; FAX: 2-45702464
Shanghai Airguns, Ltd. (U.S. importer—Sportsman Airguns, Inc.)
Shappy Bullets, 76 Milldale Ave., Plantsville, CT 06479/203-621-3704
Shaw, Inc., E.R. (See Small Arms Mfg. Co.)
Sharp Shooter Supply, 4970 Lehman Road, Delphos, OH 45833/419-695-3179
C. Sharps Arms Co. Inc., 100 Centennial, Box 885, Big Timber, MT 59011/406-932-4353
Shay's Gunsmithing, 931 Marvin Ave., Lebanon, PA 17042
Sheffield Knifemakers Supply, Inc., P.O. Box 741107, Orange City, FL 32774-1107/904-775-6453; FAX: 904-774-5754
Shell Shack, 113 E. Main, Laurel, MT 59044/406-628-8986
Shepherd & Turpin Distributing Co., P.O. Box 40, Washington, UT 84780/801-635-2001
Shepherd Scope Ltd., Box 189, Waterloo, NE 68069/402-779-2424; FAX: 402-779-4010
Sheridan USA, Inc., Austin, P.O. Box 577, 36 Haddam Quarter Rd., Durham, CT 06422/203-349-1772; FAX: 203-349-1771
Sherwood, George, 46 N. River Dr., Roseburg, OR 97470/541-672-3159
Shilen, Inc., 205 Metro Park Blvd., Ennis, TX 75119/972-875-5318; FAX: 972-875-5402
Shiloh Creek, Box 357, Cottleville, MO 63338/314-925-1842; FAX: 314-925-1842
Shiloh Rifle Mfg., 201 Centennial Dr., Big Timber, MT 59011/406-932-4454; FAX: 406-932-5627
Shockley, Harold H., 204 E. Farmington Rd., Hanna City, IL 61536/309-565-4524
Shoemaker & Sons, Inc., Tex, 714 W. Cienega Ave., San Dimas, CA 91773/909-592-2071; FAX: 909-592-2378
Shooten' Haus, The, 102 W. 13th, Kearney, NE 68847/308-236-7929
Shooter's Choice, 16770 Hilltop Park Place, Chagrin Falls, OH 44023/216-543-8808; FAX: 216-543-8811
Shooter's Edge, Inc., P.O.Box 769, Trinidad, CO 81082
Shooter's World, 3828 N. 28th Ave., Phoenix, AZ 85017/602-266-0170
Shooters Supply, 1120 Tieton Dr., Yakima, WA 98902/509-452-1181
Shootin' Accessories, Ltd., P.O. Box 6810, Auburn, CA 95604/916-889-2220
Shootin' Shack, Inc., 1065 Silver Beach Rd., Riviera Beach, FL 33403/561-842-0990
Shooting Chrony, Inc., 3269 Niagara Falls Blvd., N. Tonawanda, NY 14120/905-276-6292; FAX: 416-276-6295
Shooting Gallery, The, 8070 Southern Blvd., Boardman, OH 44512/216-726-7788
Shooting Specialties (See Titus, Daniel)
Shooting Star, 1825 Fortview Rd., Ste. 115, Austin, TX 78747/512-462-0009
Shoot-N-C Targets (See Birchwood Casey)
Shotguns Unlimited, 2307 Fon Du Lac Rd., Richmond, VA 23229/804-752-7115

ShurKatch Corporation, 50 Elm St., Richfield Springs, NY 13439/315-858-1470; FAX: 315-858-2969

S.I.A.C.E. (See U.S. importer—IAR, Inc.)

Siegrist Gun Shop, 8754 Turtle Road, Whittemore, MI 48770

Sierra Bullets, 1400 W. Henry St., Sedalia, MO 65301/816-827-6300; FAX: 816-827-6300; WEB: http://www.sierrabullets.com

Sierra Specialty Prod. Co., 1344 Oakhurst Ave., Los Altos, CA 94024/FAX: 415-965-1536

SIG, CH-8212 Neuhausen, SWITZERLAND/ (U.S. importer—Mandall Shooting Supplies, Inc.)

Sigarms, Inc., Corporate Park, Exeter, NH 03833/603-772-2302; FAX: 603-772-9082

SIG-Sauer (See U.S. importer—Sigarms, Inc.)

Sight Shop, The, John G. Lawson, 1802 E. Columbia Ave., Tacoma, WA 98404/206-474-5465

Sightron, Inc., 1672B Hwy. 96, Franklinton, NC 27525/919-528-8783; FAX: 919-528-0995

Signet Metal Corp., 551 Stewart Ave., Brooklyn, NY 11222/718-384-5400; FAX: 718-388-7488

Sile Distributors, Inc., 7 Centre Market Pl., New York, NY 10013/212-925-4111; FAX: 212-925-3149

Silencio/Safety Direct, 56 Coney Island Dr., Sparks, NV 89431/800-648-1812, 702-354-4451; FAX: 702-359-1074

Silent Hunter, 1100 Newton Ave., W. Collingswood, NJ 08107/609-854-3276

Silhouette Leathers, P.O. Box 1161, Gunnison, CO 81230/303-641-6639

Silver Eagle Machining, 18007 N. 69th Ave., Glendale, AZ 85308

Silver Ridge Gun Shop (See Goodwin, Fred)

Simmons, Jerry, 715 Middlebury St., Goshen, IN 46526/219-533-8546

Simmons Enterprises, Ernie, 709 East Elizabethtown Rd., Manheim, PA 17545/717-664-4040

Simmons Gun Repair, Inc., 700 S. Rogers Rd., Olathe, KS 66062/913-782-3131; FAX: 913-782-4189

Simmons Outdoor Corp., 201 Plantation Oak Parkway, Thomasville, GA 31792/912-227-9053; FAX: 912-227-9054

Sinclair International, Inc., 2330 Wayne Haven St., Fort Wayne, IN 46803/219-493-1858; FAX: 219-493-2530

Singletary, Kent, 2915 W. Ross, Phoenix, AZ 85027/602-582-4900

Sipes Gun Shop, 7415 Asher Ave., Little Rock, AR 72204/501-565-8480

Siskiyou Gun Works (See Donnelly, C.P.)

Six Enterprises, 320-D Turtle Creek Ct., San Jose, CA 95125/408-999-0201; FAX: 408-999-0216

SKAN A.R., 4 St. Catherines Road, Long Melford, Suffolk, CO10 9JU ENGLAND/011-0787-312942

SKB Arms Co. (See New SKB Arms Co.)

SKB Shotguns, 4325 S. 120th St., P.O. Box 37669, Omaha, NE 68137/800-752-2767; FAX: 402-330-8029

Skeoch Gunmaker, Brian R., P.O. Box 279, Glenrock, WY 82637/307-436-9655

Skip's Machine, 364 29 Road, Grand Junction, CO 81501/303-245-5417

Sklany's Machine Shop, 566 Birch Grove Dr., Kalispell, MT 59901/406-755-4257

S.L.A.P. Industries, P.O. Box 1121, Parklands 2121, SOUTH AFRICA/27-11-788-0030; FAX: 27-11-788-0030

Slezak, Jerome F., 1290 Marlowe, Lakewood (Cleveland), OH 44107/216-221-1668

Slings 'N Things, Inc., 8909 Bedford Circle, Suite 11, Omaha, NE 68134/402-571-6954; FAX: 402-571-7082

Slug Group, Inc., P.O. Box 376, New Paris, PA 15554/814-839-4517; FAX: 814-839-2601

Slug Site, Ozark Wilds, 21300 Hwy 5, Versailles, MO 65084/573-378-6430

Small Arms Mfg. Co., 5312 Thoms Run Rd., Bridgeville, PA 15017/412-221-4343; FAX: 412-221-4303

Small Arms Review, 223 Sugar Hill Rd., Harmony, ME 04942

Small Arms Specialties, 29 Bernice Ave., Leominster, MA 01453/800-635-9290

Small Custom Mould & Bullet Co., Box 17211, Tucson, AZ 85731

Smart Parts, 1203 Spring St., Latrobe, PA 15650/412-539-2660; FAX: 412-539-2298

Smires, C.L., 5222 Windmill Lane, Columbia, MD 21044-1328

Smith & Wesson, 2100 Roosevelt Ave., Springfield, MA 01102/413-781-8300; FAX: 413-731-8980

Smith, Art, 230 Main St. S., Hector, MN 55342/320-848-2760; FAX: 320-848-2760

Smith, Mark A., P.O. Box 182, Sinclair, WY 82334/307-324-7929

Smith, Michael, 620 Nye Circle, Chattanooga, TN 37405/615-267-8341

Smith, Ron, 5869 Straley, Ft. Worth, TX 76114/817-732-6768

Smith, Sharmon, 4545 Speas Rd., Fruitland, ID 83619/208-452-6329

Smith Abrasives, Inc., 1700 Sleepy Valley Rd., P.O. Box 5095, Hot Springs, AR 71902-5095/501-321-2244; FAX: 501-321-9232

Smith Saddlery, Jesse W., 16909 E. Jackson Road, Elk, WA 99009-9600/509-325-0622

Smokey Valley Rifles (See Lutz Engraving, Ron E.)

Snapp's Gunshop, 6911 E. Washington Rd., Clare, MI 48617/517-386-9226

Sno-Seal (See Atsko/Sno-Seal)

Societa Armi Bresciane Srl. (See U.S. importer—Cape Outfitters; Gamba, USA)

Soque River Knives, P.O. Box 880, Clarkesville, GA 30523/706-754-8500; FAX: 706-754-7263

SOS Products Co. (See Buck Stix—SOS Products Co.)

Sotheby's, 1334 York Ave. at 72nd St., New York, NY 10021/212-606-7260

Sound Technology, Box 391, Pelham, AL 35124/205-664-5860; Summer phone: 907-486-2825

South Bend Replicas, Inc., 61650 Oak Rd., South Bend, IN 46614/219-289-4500

Southeastern Community College, 1015 S. Gear Ave., West Burlington, IA 52655/319-752-2731

Southern Ammunition Co., Inc., 4232 Meadow St., Loris, SC 29569-3124/803-756-3262; FAX: 803-756-3583

Southern Armory, The, 25 Millstone Road, Woodlawn, VA 24381/703-238-1343; FAX: 703-238-1453

Southern Bloomer Mfg. Co., P.O. Box 1621, Bristol, TN 37620/615-878-6660; FAX: 615-878-8761

Southern Security, 1700 Oak Hills Dr., Kingston, TN 37763/800-251-9992

Southwind Sanctions, P.O. Box 445, Aledo, TX 76008/817-441-8917

Sparks, Milt, 605 E. 44th St. No. 2, Boise, ID 83714-4800

Spartan-Realtree Products, Inc., 1390 Box Circle, Columbus, GA 31907/706-569-9101; FAX: 706-569-0042

Specialty Gunsmithing, Lynn McMurdo, P.O. Box 404, Afton, WY 83110/307-886-5535

Specialty Shooters Supply, Inc., 3325 Griffin Rd., Suite 9mm, Fort Lauderdale, FL 33317

Speer Products, Div. of Blount, Inc., Sporting Equipment Div., P.O. Box 856, Lewiston, ID 83501/208-746-2351; FAX: 208-746-2915

Spegel, Craig, P.O. Box 3108, Bay City, OR 97107/503-377-2697

Speiser, Fred D., 2229 Dearborn, Missoula, MT 59801/406-549-8133

Spence, George W., 115 Locust St., Steele, MO 63877/314-695-4926

Spencer Reblue Service, 1820 Tupelo Trail, Holt, MI 48842/517-694-7474

Spencer's Custom Guns, Rt. 1, Box 546, Scottsville, VA 24590/804-293-6836

Spezial Waffen (See U.S. importer—American Bullets)

SPG, Inc., P.O. Box 1625, Cody, WY 82414/307-587-7621; FAX: 307-587-7695

Sphinx Engineering SA, Ch. des Grandes-Vies 2, CH-2900 Porrentruy, SWITZERLAND/41 66 66 73 81; FAX: 41 66 66 30 90 (U.S. importer—Sphinx USA Inc.)

Sphinx USA Inc., 998 N. Colony, Meriden, CT 06450/203-238-1399; FAX: 203-238-1375

Spokhandguns, Inc., 1206 Fig St., Benton City, WA 99320/509-588-5255

Sport Flite Manufacturing Co., P.O. Box 1082, Bloomfield Hills, MI 48303-1082/248-647-3747

Sporting Arms Mfg., Inc., 801 Hall Ave., Littlefield, TX 79339/806-385-5665; FAX: 806-385-3394

Sports Innovations, Inc., P.O. Box 5181, 8505 Jacksboro Hwy., Wichita Falls, TX 76307/817-723-6015

Sportsman Safe Mfg. Co., 6309-6311 Paramount Blvd., Long Beach, CA 90805/800-266-7150, 310-984-5445

Sportsman Supply Co., 714 East Eastwood, P.O. Box 650, Marshall, MO 65340/816-886-9393

Sportsman's Communicators, 588 Radcliffe Ave., Pacific Palisades, CA 90272/800-538-3752

Sportsmatch U.K. Ltd., 16 Summer St., Leighton Buzzard, Bedfordshire, LU7 8HT ENGLAND/01525-381638; FAX: 01525-851236

Sportsmen's Exchange & Western Gun Traders, Inc., 560 S. "C" St., Oxnard, CA 93030/805-483-1917

Spradlin's, 113 Arthur St., Pueblo, CO 81004/719-543-9462; FAX: 719-543-9465

Springfield, Inc., 420 W. Main St., Geneseo, IL 61254/309-944-5631; FAX: 309-944-3676

Springfield Sporters, Inc., RD 1, Penn Run, PA 15765/412-254-2626; FAX: 412-254-9173

Spyderco, Inc., 4565 N. Hwy. 93, P.O. Box 800, Golden, CO 80403/303-279-8383, 800-525-7770; FAX: 303-278-2229

SSK Industries, 590 Woodvue Lane, Wintersville, OH 43953/740-264-0176; FAX: 740-264-2257

Stackpole Books, 5067 Ritter Rd., Mechanicsburg, PA 17055-6921/717-796-0411; FAX: 717-796-0412

Stalker, Inc., P.O. Box 21, Fishermans Wharf Rd., Malakoff, TX 75148/903-489-1010

Stalwart Corporation, 76 Imperial, Unit A, Evanston, WY 82930/307-789-7687; FAX: 307-789-7688

Stanley Bullets, 2085 Heatheridge Ln., Reno, NV 89509

Star Ammunition, Inc., 5520 Rock Hampton Ct., Indianapolis, IN 46268/317-872-5840, 800-221-5927; FAX: 317-872-5847

Star Bonifacio Echeverria S.A., Torrekva 3, Eibar, SPAIN 20600/43-107340; FAX: 43-101524 (U.S. importer—E.A.A. Corp.; Interarms; P.S.M.G. Gun Co.)

Star Custom Bullets, P.O. Box 608, 468 Main St., Ferndale, CA 95536/707-786-9140; FAX: 707-786-9117

Star Machine Works, 418 10th Ave., San Diego, CA 92101/619-232-3216

Star Master-Match Bullets (See Star Ammunition, Inc.)

Star Reloading Co., Inc. (See Star Ammunition, Inc.)

Starke Bullet Company, P.O. Box 400, 605 6th St. NW, Cooperstown, ND 58425/888-797-3431

Starkey Labs, 6700 Washington Ave. S., Eden Prairie, MN 55344

Starkey's Gun Shop, 9430 McCombs, El Paso, TX 79924/915-751-3030

Stark's Bullet Mfg., 2580 Monroe St., Eugene, OR 97405

Starline, 1300 W. Henry St., Sedalia, MO 65301/816-827-6640; FAX: 816-827-6650

Starlight Training Center, Inc., Rt. 1, P.O. Box 88, Bronaugh, MO 64728/417-843-3555

Starnes Gunmaker, Ken, 32900 SW Laurelview Rd., Hillsboro, OR 97123/503-628-0705; FAX: 503-628-6005

Starr Trading Co., Jedediah, P.O. Box 2007, Farmington Hills, MI 48333/810-683-4343; FAX: 810-683-3282

Starrett Co., L.S., 121 Crescent St., Athol, MA 01331/617-249-3551

State Arms Gun Co., 815 S. Division St., Waunakee, WI 53597/608-849-5800

Steelman's Gun Shop, 10465 Beers Rd., Swartz Creek, MI 48473/810-735-4884

Steiner (See Pioneer Research, Inc.)

Steffens, Ron, 18396 Mariposa Creek Rd., Willits, CA 95490/707-485-0873

Stegall, James B., 26 Forest Rd., Wallkill, NY 12589

Steger, James R., 1131 Dorsey Pl., Plainfield, NJ 07062

Steves House of Guns, Rt. 1, Minnesota City, MN 55959/507-689-2573

Stewart Game Calls, Inc., Johnny, P.O. Box 7954, 5100 Fort Ave., Waco, TX 76714/817-772-3261; FAX: 817-772-3670

Stewart's Gunsmithing, P.O. Box 5854, Pietersburg North 0750, Transvaal, SOUTH AFRICA/01521-89401

Steyr Mannlicher AG & CO KG, Mannlicherstrasse 1, A-4400 Steyr, AUSTRIA /0043-7252-78621; FAX: 0043-7252-68621 (U.S. importer—GSI, Inc.; Nygord Precision Products)

STI International, 114 Halmar Cove, Georgetown, TX 78628/800-959-8201; FAX: 512-819-0465

Stiles Custom Guns, RD3, Box 1605, Homer City, PA 15748/724-479-9945

Stillwell, Robert, 421 Judith Ann Dr., Schertz, TX 78154

Stoeger Industries, 5 Mansard Ct., Wayne, NJ 07470/201-872-9500, 800-631-0722; FAX: 201-872-2230

Stoeger Publishing Co. (See Stoeger Industries)

Stone Enterprises Ltd., Rt. 609, P.O. Box 335, Wicomico Church, VA 22579/804-580-5114; FAX: 804-580-8421

Stone Mountain Arms, 5988 Peachtree Corners E., Norcross, GA 30071/800-251-9412

Stoney Baroque Shooters Supply, John Richards, Rt. 2, Box 325, Bedford, KY 40006/502-255-7222

Stoney Point Products, Inc., P.O. Box 234, 1815 North Spring Street, New Ulm, MN 56073-0234/507-354-3360; FAX: 507-354-7236

Storage Tech, 1254 Morris Ave., N. Huntingdon, PA 15642/800-437-9393

Storey, Dale A. (See DGS, Inc.)

Storm, Gary, P.O. Box 5211, Richardson, TX 75083/214-385-0862

Stott's Creek Armory, Inc., 2526 S. 475W, Morgantown, IN 46160/317-878-5489; FAX: 317-878-9489

Stott's Creek Printers, 2526 S. 475W, Morgantown, IN 46160/317-878-5489

Stratco, Inc., P.O. Box 2270, Kalispell, MT 59901/406-755-1221; FAX: 406-755-1226

Strawbridge, Victor W., 6 Pineview Dr., Dover, NH 03820/603-742-0013

Streamlight, Inc., 1030 W. Germantown Pike, Norristown, PA 19403/215-631-0600; FAX: 610-631-0712

Strong Holster Co., 39 Grove St., Gloucester, MA 01930/508-281-3300; FAX: 508-281-6321

Strutz Rifle Barrels, Inc., W.C., P.O. Box 611, Eagle River, WI 54521/715-479-4766

Stuart, V. Pat, Rt.1, Box 447-S, Greenville, VA 24440/804-556-3845

Sturgeon Valley Sporters, K. Ide, P.O. Box 283, Vanderbilt, MI 49795/517-983-4338

Sturm, Ruger & Co., Inc., 200 Ruger Rd., Prescott, AZ 86301/520-541-8820; FAX: 520-541-8850

"Su-Press-On," Inc., P.O. Box 09161, Detroit, MI 48209/313-842-4222 7:30-11p.m. Mon-Thurs.

Sullivan, David S. (See Westwind Rifles, Inc.)

Summit Specialties, Inc., P.O. Box 786, Decatur, AL 35602/205-353-0634; FAX: 205-353-9818

Sundance Industries, Inc., 25163 W. Avenue Stanford, Valencia, CA 91355/805-257-4807

Sunny Hill Enterprizes, Inc., W1790 Cty. HHH, Malone, WI 53049/414-795-4822

Sun Welding Safe Co., 290 Easy St. No.3, Simi Valley, CA 93065/805-584-6678, 800-729-SAFE; FAX: 805-584-6169

Surecase Co., The, 233 Wilshire Blvd., Ste. 900, Santa Monica, CA 90401/800-92ARMLOC

Sure-Shot Game Calls, Inc., P.O. Box 816, 6835 Capitol, Groves, TX 77619/409-962-1636; FAX: 409-962-5465

Survival Arms, Inc., P.O. Box 965, Orange, CT 06477/203-924-6533; FAX: 203-924-2581

Svon Corp., 280 Eliot St., Ashland, MA 01721/508-881-8852

Swampfire Shop, The (See Peterson Gun Shop, Inc., A.W.)

Swann, D.J., 5 Orsova Close, Eltham North, Vic. 3095, AUSTRALIA/03-431-0323

Swanndri New Zealand, 152 Elm Ave., Burlingame, CA 94010/415-347-6158

SwaroSports, Inc. (See J‰gerSport, Ltd.)

Swarovski Optik North America Ltd., One Wholesale Way, Cranston, RI 02920/401-946-2220, 800-426-3089; FAX: 401-946-2587

Sweet Home, Inc., P.O. Box 900, Orrville, OH 44667-0900

Swenson's 45 Shop, A.D., P.O. Box 606, Fallbrook, CA 92028

Swift Bullet Co., P.O. Box 27, 201 Main St., Quinter, KS 67752/913-754-3959; FAX: 913-754-2359

Swift Instruments, Inc., 952 Dorchester Ave., Boston, MA 02125/617-436-2960; FAX: 617-436-3232

Swift River Gunworks, 450 State St., Belchertown, MA 01007/413-323-4052

Swiss Army Knives, Inc., 151 Long Hill Crossroads, 37 Canal St., Shelton, CT 06484/800-243-4032

Swivel Machine Works, Inc., 11 Monitor Hill Rd., Newtown, CT 06470/203-270-6343

Szweda, Robert (See RMS Custom Gunsmithing)

T

Tabler Marketing, 2554 Lincoln Blvd., Suite 555, Marina Del Rey, CA 90291/818-755-4565; FAX: 818-755-0972

TacStar Industries, Inc., 218 Justin Drive, P.O. Box 70, Cottonwood, AZ 86326/602-639-0072; FAX: 602-634-8781

TacTell, Inc., P.O. Box 5654, Maryville, TN 37802/615-982-7855; FAX: 615-558-8294

Taconic Firearms Ltd., Perry Lane, PO Box 553, Cambridge, NY 12816/518-677-2704; FAX: 518-677-5974

Tactical Defense Institute, 574 Miami Bluff Ct., Loveland, OH 45140/513-677-8229

Talbot QD Mounts, 2210 E. Grand Blanc Rd., Grand Blanc, MI 48439-8113/810-695-2497

Talley, Dave, P.O. Box 821, Glenrock, WY 82637/307-436-8724, 307-436-9315

Talmage, William G., 10208 N. County Rd. 425 W., Brazil, IN 47834/812-442-0804

Talon Mfg. Co., Inc., 621 W. King St., Martinsburg, WV 25401/304-264-9714; FAX: 304-264-9725

Tamarack Products, Inc., P.O. Box 625, Wauconda, IL 60084/708-526-9333; FAX: 708-526-9353

Tanfoglio Fratelli S.r.l., via Valtrompia 39, 41, 25068 Gardone V.T., Brescia, ITALY/30-8910361; FAX: 30-8910183 (U.S. importer—E.A.A. Corp.)

Tanglefree Industries, 1261 Heavenly Dr., Martinez, CA 94553/800-982-4868; FAX: 510-825-3874

Tank's Rifle Shop, P.O. Box 474, Fremont, NE 68026-0474/402-727-1317; FAX: 402-721-2573

Tanner (See U.S. importer—Mandall Shooting Supplies, Inc.)

Taracorp Industries, Inc., 1200 Sixteenth St., Granite City, IL 62040/618-451-4400

Tar-Hunt Custom Rifles, Inc., RR3, P.O. Box 572, Bloomsburg, PA 17815-9351/717-784-6368; FAX: 717-784-6368

Tarnhelm Supply Co., Inc., 431 High St., Boscawen, NH 03303/603-796-2551; FAX: 603-796-2918

Tasco Sales, Inc., 7600 NW 26th St., Miami, FL 33122-1494/305-591-3670; FAX: 305-592-5895

Taurus Firearms, Inc., 16175 NW 49th Ave., Miami, FL 33014/305-624-1115; FAX: 305-623-7506

Taurus International Firearms (See U.S. importer—Taurus Firearms, Inc.)

Taurus S.A., Forjas, Avenida Do Forte 511, Porto Alegre, RS BRAZIL 91360/55-51-347-4050; FAX: 55-51-347-3065

Taylor & Robbins, P.O. Box 164, Rixford, PA 16745/814-966-3233

Taylor's & Co., Inc., 304 Lenoir Dr., Winchester, VA 22603/540-722-2017; FAX: 540-722-2018

TCCI, P.O. Box 302, Phoenix, AZ 85001/602-237-3823; FAX: 602-237-3858

TCSR, 3998 Hoffman Rd., White Bear Lake, MN 55110-4626/800-328-5323; FAX: 612-429-0526

TDP Industries, Inc., 606 Airport Blvd., Doylestown, PA 18901/215-345-8687; FAX: 215-345-6057

Techni-Mec (See F.A.I.R. Techni-Mec s.n.c. di Isidoro Rizzini & C.)

Techno Arms (See U.S. importer—Auto-Ordnance Corp.)

Tecnolegno S.p.A., Via A. Locatelli, 6, 10, 24019 Zogno, ITALY/0345-55111; FAX: 0345-55155

Tele-Optics, 630 E. Rockland Rd., P.O. Box 6313, Libertyville, IL 60048/847-362-7757

Ten-Ring Precision, Inc., Alex B. Hamilton, 1449 Blue Crest Lane, San Antonio, TX 78232/210-494-3063; FAX: 210-494-3066

10-X Products Group, 2915 Lyndon B. Johnson Freeway, Suite 133, Dallas, TX 75234/972-243-4016, 800-433-2225; FAX: 972-243-4112

Tennessee Valley Mfg., P.O. Box 1175, Corinth, MS 38834/601-286-5014

Tepeco, P.O. Box 342, Friendswood, TX 77546/713-482-2702

Testing Systems, Inc., 220 Pegasus Ave., Northvale, NJ 07647

Teton Arms, Inc., P.O. Box 411, Wilson, WY 83014/307-733-3395

Tetra Gun Lubricants (See FTI, Inc.)

Texas Armory (See Bond Arms, Inc.)

Texas Longhorn Arms, Inc., 5959 W. Loop South, Suite 424, Bellaire, TX 77401/713-660-6323; FAX: 713-660-0493

Texas Platers Supply Co., 2453 W. Five Mile Parkway, Dallas, TX 75233/214-330-7168

T.F.C. S.p.A., Via G. Marconi 118, B, Villa Carcina, Brescia 25069, ITALY/030-881271; FAX: 030-881826

Theis, Terry, HC 63 Box 213, Harper, TX 78631/830-864-4438

Theoben Engineering, Stephenson Road, St. Ives, Huntingdon, Cambs., PE17 4WJ ENGLAND/011-0480-461718

Thiewes, George W., 14329 W. Parada Dr., Sun City West, AZ 85375

Things Unlimited, 235 N. Kimbau, Casper, WY 82601/307-234-5277

Thirion Gun Engraving, Denise, P.O. Box 408, Graton, CA 95444/707-829-1876

Thomas, Charles C., 2600 S. First St., Springfield, IL 62794/217-789-8980; FAX: 217-789-9130

Thompson, Norm, 18905 NW Thurman St., Portland, OR 97209

Thompson, Randall (See Highline Machine Co.)

Thompson Bullet Lube Co., P.O. Box 472343, Garland, TX 75047-2343/972-271-8063; FAX: 972-840-6743

Thompson/Center Arms, P.O. Box 5002, Rochester, NH 03866/603-332-2394; FAX: 603-332-5133

Thompson Precision, 110 Mary St., P.O. Box 251, Warren, IL 61087/815-745-3625

Thompson Target Technology, 618 Roslyn Ave., SW, Canton, OH 44710/216-453-7707; FAX: 216-478-4723

Thompson Tool Mount (See TTM)

3-D Ammunition & Bullets, 112 W. Plum St., P.O. Box J, Doniphan, NE 68832/402-845-2285, 800-255-6712; FAX: 402-845-6546

300 Below Services (See Cryo-Accurizing)

300 Gunsmith Service, Inc., at Cherry Creek State Park Shooting Center, 12500 E. Belleview Ave./Englewood, CO 80111 303-690-3300

3-Ten Corp., P.O. Box 269, Feeding Hills, MA 01030/413-789-2086; FAX: 413-789-1549

T.H.U. Enterprises, Inc., P.O. Box 418, Lederach, PA 19450/215-256-1665; FAX: 215-256-9718

Thunden Ranch, HCR1, Box 53, Mt. Home, TX 78058/830-640-3138

Thunder Mountain Arms, P.O. Box 593, Oak Harbor, WA 98277/206-679-4657; FAX: 206-675-1114

Thunderbird Cartridge Co., Inc. (See TCCI)

Thurston Sports, Inc., RD 3 Donovan Rd., Auburn, NY 13021/315-253-0966

Tiger-Hunt Gunstocks, Box 379, Beaverdale, PA 15921/814-472-5161

Tikka (See U.S. importer—Stoeger Industries)

Timber Heirloom Products, 618 Roslyn Ave. SW, Canton, OH 44710/216-453-7707; FAX: 216-478-4723

Time Precision, Inc., 640 Federal Rd., Brookfield, CT 06804/203-775-8343

Timney Mfg., Inc., 3065 W. Fairmont Ave., Phoenix, AZ 85017/602-274-2999; FAX: 602-241-0361

Tink's Safariland Hunting Corp., P.O. Box 244, 1140 Monticello Rd., Madison, GA 30650/706-342-4915; FAX: 706-342-7568

Tinks & Ben Lee Hunting Products (See Wellington Outdoors)

Tioga Engineering Co., Inc., P.O. Box 913, 13 Cone St., Wellsboro, PA 16901/717-724-3533, 717-662-3347

Tippman Pneumatics, Inc., 3518 Adams Center Rd., Fort Wayne, IN 46806/219-749-6022; FAX: 219-749-6619

Tirelli, Snc Di Tirelli Primo E.C., Via Matteotti No. 359, Gardone V.T., Brescia, ITALY 25063/030-8912819; FAX: 030-832240

Titus, Daniel, Shooting Specialties, 119 Morlyn Ave., Bryn Mawr, PA 19010-3737/215-525-8829

TMI Products (See Haselbauer Products, Jerry)

TM Stockworks, 6355 Maplecrest Rd., Fort Wayne, IN 46835/219-485-5389

Tom's Gun Repair, Thomas G. Ivanoff, 76-6 Rt. Southfork Rd., Cody, WY 82414/307-587-6949

Tom's Gunshop, 3601 Central Ave., Hot Springs, AR 71913/501-624-3856

Tombstone Smoke`n'Deals, 3218 East Bell Road, Phoenix, AZ 85032/602-905-7013; Fax: 602-443-1998

Tonoloway Tack Drives, HCR 81, Box 100, Needmore, PA 17238

Tooley Custom Rifles, 516 Creek Meadow Dr., Gastonia, NC 28054/704-864-7525

Top-Line USA, Inc., 7920-28 Hamilton Ave., Cincinnati, OH 45231/513-522-2992, 800-346-6699; FAX: 513-522-0916

Torel, Inc., 1708 N. South St., P.O. Box 592, Yoakum, TX 77995/512-293-2341; FAX: 512-293-3413

Totally Dependable Products (See TDP Industries, Inc.)

TOZ (See U.S. importer—Nygord Precision Products)

TR Metals Corp., 1 Pavilion Ave., Riverside, NJ 08075/609-461-9000; FAX: 609-764-6340

Track of the Wolf, Inc., P.O. Box 6, Osseo, MN 55369-0006/612-424-2500; FAX: 612-424-9860

TracStar Industries, Inc., 218 Justin Dr., Cottonwood, AZ 86326/520-639-0072; FAX: 520-634-8781

Tradewinds, Inc., P.O. Box 1191, 2339-41 Tacoma Ave. S., Tacoma, WA 98401/206-272-4887

Traditions, Inc., P.O. Box 776, 1375 Boston Post Rd., Old Saybrook, CT 06475/860-388-4656; FAX: 860-388-4657

Trafalgar Square, P.O. Box 257, N. Pomfret, VT 05053/802-457-1911

Traft Gunshop, P.O. Box 1078, Buena Vista, CO 81211

TrailTimer Co., 1992-A Suburban Ave., P.O. Box 19722, St. Paul, MN 55119/612-738-0925

Trail Visions, 5800 N. Ames Terrace, Glendale, WI 53209/414-228-1328

Trammco, 839 Gold Run Rd., Boulder, CO 80302

Trappers Trading, P.O. Box 26946, Austin, TX 78755/800-788-9334

Trax America, Inc., P.O. Box 898, 1150 Eldridge, Forrest City, AR 72335/501-633-0410, 800-232-2327; FAX: 501-633-4788

Treadlok Gun Safe, Inc., 1764 Granby St. NE, Roanoke, VA 24012/800-729-8732, 703-982-6881; FAX: 703-982-1059

Treemaster, P.O. Box 247, Guntersville, AL 35976/205-878-3597

Treso, Inc., P.O. Box 4640, Pagosa Springs, CO 81157/303-731-2295

Trevallion Gunstocks, 9 Old Mountain Rd., Cape Neddick, ME 03902/207-361-1130

de Treville & Co., Stan, 4129 Normal St., San Diego, CA 92103/619-298-3393

Trico Plastics, 590 S. Vincent Ave., Azusa, CA 91702

Trigger Lock Division/Central Specialties Ltd., 1122 Silver Lake Road, Cary, IL 60013/847-639-3900; FAX: 847-639-3972

Trijicon, Inc., 49385 Shafer Ave., P.O. Box 930059, Wixom, MI 48393-0059/810-960-7700; FAX: 810-960-7725

Trilux Inc., P.O. Box 24608, Winston-Salem, NC 27114/910-659-9438; FAX: 910-768-7720

Trinidad State Junior College, Gunsmithing Dept., 600 Prospect St., Trinidad, CO 81082/719-846-5631; FAX: 719-846-5667

Triple-K Mfg. Co., Inc., 2222 Commercial St., San Diego, CA 92113/619-232-2066; FAX: 619-232-7675

Tristar Sporting Arms, Ltd., 1814-16 Linn St., P.O. Box 7496, N. Kansas City, MO 64116/816-421-1400; FAX: 816-421-4182

Trius Products, Inc., P.O. Box 25, 221 S. Miami Ave., Cleves, OH 45002/513-941-5682; FAX: 513-941-7970

Trooper Walsh, 2393 N. Edgewood St., Arlington, VA 22207

Trophy Bonded Bullets, Inc., 900 S. Loop W., Suite 190, Houston, TX 77054/713-645-4499, 888-308-3006; FAX: 713-741-6393

Trotman, Ken, 135 Ditton Walk, Unit 11, Cambridge CB5 8PY, ENGLAND/01223-211030; FAX: 01223-212317

Tru-Balance Knife Co., P.O. Box 140555, Grand Rapids, MI 49514/616-453-3679

Tru-Square Metal Prods., Inc., 640 First St. SW, P.O. Box 585, Auburn, WA 98071/206-833-2310; FAX: 206-833-2349

True Flight Bullet Co., 5581 Roosevelt St., Whitehall, PA 18052/610-262-7630; FAX: 610-262-7806

Trulock Tool, Broad St., Whigham, GA 31797/912-762-4678

TTM, 1550 Solomon Rd., Santa Maria, CA 93455/805-934-1281

Tucker, James C., P.O. Box 575, Raymond, NH 03077

Tucson Mold, Inc., 930 S. Plumer Ave., Tucson, AZ 85719/520-792-1075; FAX: 520-792-1075

Turkish Firearms Corp., 522 W. Maple St., Allentown, PA 18101/610-821-8660; FAX: 610-821-9049

Turnbull Restoration, Doug, 6426 County Rd. 30, P.O. Box 471, Bloomfield, NY 14469/716-657-6338; WEB: http://gunshop.com/dougt.htm

Tuttle, Dale, 4046 Russell Rd., Muskegon, MI 49445/616-766-2250

Twin Pine Armory, P.O. Box 58, Hwy. 6, Adna, WA 98522/360-748-4590; FAX: 360-748-1802

Tyler Manufacturing & Distributing, 3804 S. Eastern, Oklahoma City, OK 73129/405-677-1487, 800-654-8415

U

Uberti USA, Inc., P.O. Box 469, Lakeville, CT 06039/860-435-8068; FAX: 860-435-8146

Uberti, Aldo, Casella Postale 43, I-25063 Gardone V.T., ITALY/ (U.S. importers—American Arms, Inc.; Cabela's; Cimarron Arms; Dixie Gun Works; EMF Co., Inc.; Forgett Jr., Valmore J.; IAR, Inc.; Navy Arms Co; Taylor's & Co., Inc.; Uberti USA, Inc.)

UFA, Inc., 6927 E. Grandview Dr., Scottsdale, AZ 85254/800-616-2776

Ugartechea S.A., Ignacio, Chonta 26, Eibar, SPAIN 20600/43-121257; FAX: 43-121669 (U.S. importer—Aspen Outfitting Co.; The Gun Shop; Bill Hanus Birdguns; Lion Country Supply)

Ultimate Accuracy, 121 John Shelton Rd., Jacksonville, AR 72076/501-985-2530

Ultra Dot Distribution, 2316 N.E. 8th Rd., Ocala, FL 34470

Ultra Light Arms, Inc., P.O. Box 1270, 214 Price St., Granville, WV 26505/304-599-5687; FAX: 304-599-5687

Ultralux (See U.S. importer—Keng's Firearms Specialty, Inc.)

UltraSport Arms, Inc., 1955 Norwood Ct., Racine, WI 53403/414-554-3237; FAX: 414-554-9731

Uncle Bud's, HCR 81, Box 100, Needmore, PA 17238/717-294-6000; FAX: 717-294-6005

Uncle Mike's (See Michaels of Oregon Co.)

Unertl Optical Co., Inc., John, 308 Clay Ave., P.O. Box 818, Mars, PA 16046-0818/412-625-3810

Unique/M.A.P.F., 10, Les Allees, 64700 Hendaye, FRANCE 64700/33-59 20 71 93 (U.S. importer—Nygord Precision Products)

UniTec, 1250 Bedford SW, Canton, OH 44710/216-452-4017

United Binocular Co., 9043 S. Western Ave., Chicago, IL 60620

United Cutlery Corp., 1425 United Blvd., Sevierville, TN 37876-1549/423-428-2532, 800-548-0835; FAX: 423-428-2267

United States Ammunition Co. (See USAC)

United States Optics Technologies, Inc., 5900 Dale St., Buena Park, CA 90621/714-994-4901; FAX: 714-994-4904

United States Products Co., 518 Melwood Ave., Pittsburgh, PA 15213-1136/412-621-2130; FAX: 412-621-8740

Unmussig Bullets, D.L., 7862 Brentford Drive, Richmond, VA 23225/804-320-1165

Upper Missouri Trading Co., 304 Harold St., Crofton, NE 68730/402-388-4844

USAC, 4500-15th St. East, Tacoma, WA 98424/206-922-7589

U.S.A. Magazines, Inc., P.O. Box 39115, Downey, CA 90241/800-872-2577

USA Sporting Inc., 1330 N. Glassell, Unit M, Orange, CA 92667/714-538-3109, 800-538-3109; FAX: 714-538-1334

U.S. Patent Fire Arms, No. 25-55 Van Dyke Ave., Hartford, CT 06106/800-877-2832; FAX: 800-644-7265

U.S. Repeating Arms Co., Inc., 275 Winchester Ave., Morgan, UT 84050-9333/801-876-3440; FAX: 801-876-3737

Utica Cutlery Co., 820 Noyes St., Utica, NY 13503/315-733-4663; FAX: 315-733-6602

Uvalde Machine & Tool, P.O. Box 1604, Uvalde, TX 78802

V

Valade Engraving, Robert, 931 3rd Ave., Seaside, OR 97138/503-738-7672

Valmet (See Tikka/U.S. importer—Stoeger Industries)

Valor Corp., 5555 NW 36th Ave., Miami, FL 33142/305-633-0127; FAX: 305-634-4536

Valtro USA Inc., 1281 Andersen Dr., San Rafael, CA 94901/415-256-2575; FAX: 415-256-2576

Van Epps, Milton (See Van's Gunsmith Service)

Van's Gunsmith Service, 224 Route 69-A, Parish, NY 13131/315-625-7251

Van Gorden & Son, Inc., C.S., 1815 Main St., Bloomer, WI 54724/715-568-2612

Van Horn, Gil, P.O. Box 207, Llano, CA 93544

Van Patten, J.W., P.O. Box 145, Foster Hill, Milford, PA 18337/717-296-7069

Vancini, Carl (See Bestload, Inc.)

Vann Custom Bullets, 330 Grandview Ave., Novato, CA 94947

Varner's Service, 102 Shaffer Rd., Antwerp, OH 45813/419-258-8631

Vega Tool Co., c/o T.R. Ross, 4865 Tanglewood Ct., Boulder, CO 80301/303-530-0174

Venco Industries, Inc. (See Shooter's Choice)

Venus Industries, P.O. Box 246, Sialkot-1, PAKISTAN/FAX: 92 432 85579

Verney-Carron, B.P. 72, 54 Boulevard Thiers, 42002 St. Etienne Cedex 1, FRANCE/33-477791500; FAX: 33-477790702; E-MAIL: Verney-Carron@mail.com

Versa-Pod (See Keng's Firearms Specialty, Inc.

Vest, John, P.O. Box 1552, Susanville, CA 96130/916-257-7228

VibraShine, Inc., P.O. Box 577, Taylorsville, MS 39168/601-785-9854; FAX: 601-785-9874

Vibra-Tek Co., 1844 Arroya Rd., Colorado Springs, CO 80906/719-634-8611; FAX: 719-634-6886

Vic's Gun Refinishing, 6 Pineview Dr., Dover, NH 03820-6422/603-742-0013

Victory USA, P.O. Box 1021, Pine Bush, NY 12566/914-744-2060; FAX: 914-744-5181

Vihtavuori Oy, FIN-41330 Vihtavuori, FINLAND/358-41-3779211; FAX: 358-41-3771643

Vihtavuori Oy/Kaltron-Pettibone, 1241 Ellis St., Bensenville, IL 60106/708-350-1116; FAX: 708-350-1606

Viking Leathercraft, Inc., 1579A Jayken Way, Chula Vista, CA 91911/800-262-6666; FAX: 619-429-8268

Viking Video Productions, P.O. Box 251, Roseburg, OR 97470

Vincent's Shop, 210 Antoinette, Fairbanks, AK 99701

Vintage Arms, Inc., 6003 Saddle Horse, Fairfax, VA 22030/703-968-0779; FAX: 703-968-0780

Vintage Industries, Inc., 781 Big Tree Dr., Longwood, FL 32750/407-831-8949; FAX: 407-831-5346

Viper Bullet and Brass Works, 11 Brock St., Box 582, Norwich, Ontario, CANADA N0J 1P0

Viramontez, Ray, 601 Springfield Dr., Albany, GA 31707/912-432-9683

Visible Impact Targets, Rts. 5 & 20, E. Bloomfield, NY 14443/716-657-6161; FAX: 716-657-5405

Vitt/Boos, 2178 Nichols Ave., Stratford, CT 06497/203-375-6859

Voere-KGH m.b.H., P.O. Box 416, A-6333 Kufstein, Tirol, AUSTRIA/0043-5372-62547; FAX: 0043-5372-65752 (U.S. importers—J‰agerSport, Ltd.)

Volquartsen Custom Ltd., 24276 240th Street, P.O. Box 271, Carroll, IA 51401/712-792-4238; FAX: 712-792-2542

Vom Hoffe (See Old Western Scrounger, Inc., The)

Von Minden Gunsmithing Services, 2403 SW 39 Terrace, Cape Coral, FL 33914/813-542-8946

Vorhes, David, 3042 Beecham St., Napa, CA 94558/707-226-9116

Vortek Products, Inc., P.O. Box 871181, Canton, MI 48187-6181/313-397-5656; FAX:313-397-5656

VSP Publishers (See Heritage/VSP Gun Books)

Vulpes Ventures, Inc., Fox Cartridge Division, P.O. Box 1363, Bolingbrook, IL 60440-7363/708-759-1229

W

W. Square Enterprises, 9826 Sagedale, Houston, TX 77089/713-484-0935; FAX: 281-484-0935

Wagoner, Vernon G., 2325 E. Encanto, Mesa, AZ 85213/602-835-1307

Wakina by Pic, 24813 Alderbrook Dr., Santa Clarita, CA 91321/800-295-8194

Waldron, Herman, Box 475, 80 N. 17th St., Pomeroy, WA 99347/509-843-1404

Walker Arms Co., Inc., 499 County Rd. 820, Selma, AL 36701/334-872-6231; FAX: 334-872-6262

Walker Mfg., Inc., 8296 S. Channel, Harsen's Island, MI 48028

Walker Co., B.B., P.O. Box 1167, 414 E. Dixie Dr., Asheboro, NC 27203/910-625-1380; FAX: 910-625-8125

Wallace, Terry, 385 San Marino, Vallejo, CA 94589/707-642-7041

Waller & Son, Inc., W., 2221 Stoney Brook Road, Grantham, NH 03753-7706/603-863-4177

Walls Industries, Inc., P.O. Box 98, 1905 N. Main, Cleburne, TX 76031/817-645-4366; FAX: 817-645-7946

Walnut Factory, The, 235 West Rd. No. 1, Portsmouth, NH 03801/603-436-2225; FAX: 603-433-7003

Walt's Custom Leather, Walt Whinnery, 1947 Meadow Creek Dr., Louisville, KY 40218/502-458-4361

Walters Industries, 6226 Park Lane, Dallas, TX 75225/214-691-6973

Walters, John, 500 N. Avery Dr., Moore, OK 73160/405-799-0376

Walther GmbH, Carl, B.P. 4325, D-89033 Ulm, GERMANY/ (U.S. importer—Champion's Choice; Interarms; P.S.M.G. Gun Co.)

WAMCO, Inc., Mingo Loop, P.O. Box 337, Oquossoc, ME 04964-0337/207-864-3344

WAMCO—New Mexico, P.O. Box 205, Peralta, NM 87042-0205/505-869-0826

Ward & Van Valkenburg, 114 32nd Ave. N., Fargo, ND 58102/701-232-2351

Ward Machine, 5620 Lexington Rd., Corpus Christi, TX 78412/512-992-1221

Wardell Precision Handguns Ltd., 48851 N. Fig Springs Rd., New River, AZ 85027-8513/602-465-7995

Warenski, Julie, 590 E. 500 N., Richfield, UT 84701/801-896-5319; FAX: 801-896-5319

Warne Manufacturing Co., 9039 SE Jannsen Rd., Clackamas, OR 97015/503-657-5590; FAX: 503-657-5695

Warren & Sweat Mfg. Co., P.O. Box 350440, Grand Island, FL 32784/904-669-3166; FAX: 904-669-7272

Warren Muzzleloading Co., Inc., Hwy. 21 North, P.O. Box 100, Ozone, AR 72854/501-292-3268

Warren, Kenneth W. (See Mountain States Engraving)

Washita Mountain Whetstone Co., P.O. Box 378, Lake Hamilton, AR 71951/501-525-3914

Wasmundt's Gun Shop, 680 Main St., Fossil, OR 97830-0551/541-763-3041

WASP Shooting Systems, Rt. 1, Box 147, Lakeview, AR 72642/501-431-5606

Waterfield Sports, Inc., 13611 Country Lane, Burnsville, MN 55337/612-435-8339

Watson Bros., 39 Redcross Way, London Bridge, London, United Kingdom, SE1 1HG/FAX: 44-171-403-3367

Watson Trophy Match Bullets, 2404 Wade Hampton Blvd., Greenville, SC 29615/864-244-7948; 941-635-7948 (Florida)

Wayne Firearms for Collectors and Investors, James, 2608 N. Laurent, Victoria, TX 77901/512-578-1258; FAX: 512-578-3559

Wayne Specialty Services, 260 Waterford Drive, Florissant, MO 63033/413-831-7083

WD-40 Co., 1061 Cudahy Pl., San Diego, CA 92110/619-275-1400; FAX: 619-275-5823

Weatherby, Inc., 3100 El Camino Real, Atascadero, CA 93422/805-466-1767; FAX: 805-466-2527

Weaver Arms Corp. Gun Shop, RR 3, P.O. Box 266, Bloomfield, MO 63825-9528

Weaver Products, P.O. Box 39, Onalaska, WI 54650/800-648-9624, 608-781-5800; FAX: 608-781-0368

Weaver Scope Repair Service, 1121 Larry Mahan Dr., Suite B, El Paso, TX 79925/915-593-1005

Webb, Bill, 6504 North Bellefontaine, Kansas City, MO 64119/816-453-7431

Weber & Markin Custom Gunsmiths, 4-1691 Powick Rd., Kelowna, B.C. CANADA V1X 4L1/250-762-7575; FAX: 250-861-3655

Weber Jr., Rudolf, P.O. Box 160106, D-5650 Solingen, GERMANY/0212-592136

Webley and Scott Ltd., Frankley Industrial Park, Tay Rd., Rubery, Rednal, Birmingham B45 0PA, ENGLAND/011-021-453-1864; FAX: 021-457-7846 (U.S. importer—Beeman Precision Airguns; Groenewold, John)

Webster Scale Mfg. Co., P.O. Box 188, Sebring, FL 33870/813-385-6362

Weems, Cecil, P.O. Box 657, Mineral Wells, TX 76067/817-325-1462

Weigand Combat Handguns, Inc., 685 South Main Rd., Mountain Top, PA 18707/717-868-8358; FAX: 717-868-5218

Weihrauch KG, Hermann, Industriestrasse 11, 8744 Mellrichstadt, GERMANY/ 09776-497-498 (U.S. importers—Beeman Precision Airguns; E.A.A. Corp.)

Weisz Parts, P.O. Box 20038, Columbus, OH 43220-0038/614-45-70-500; FAX: 614-846-8585

Welch, Sam, CVSR 2110, Moab, UT 84532/801-259-8131

Wellington Outdoors, P.O. Box 244, 1140 Monticello Rd., Madison, GA 30650/706-342-4915; FAX: 706-342-7568

Wells Creek Knife & Gun Works, 32956 State Hwy. 38, Scottsburg, OR 97473/541-587-4202; FAX: 541-587-4223

Wells Custom Gunsmith, R.A., 3452 1st Ave., Racine, WI 53402/414-639-5223

Wells, Fred F., Wells Sport Store, 110 N. Summit St., Prescott, AZ 86301/520-445-3655

Wells, Rachel, 110 N. Summit St., Prescott, AZ 86301/520-445-3655

Welsh, Bud, 80 New Road, E. Amherst, NY 14051/716-688-6344

Wenig Custom Gunstocks, Inc., 103 N. Market St., P.O. Box 249, Lincoln, MO 65338/816-547-3334; FAX: 816-547-2881

Werner, Carl, P.O. Box 492, Littleton, CO 80160

Werth, T.W., 1203 Woodlawn Rd., Lincoln, IL 62656/217-732-1300

Wescombe, Bill (See North Star West)

Wessinger Custom Guns & Engraving, 268 Limestone Rd., Chapin, SC 29036/803-345-5677

Wesson Firearms, Dan, 119 Kemper Lane, Norwich, NY 13815/607-336-1174; FAX: 607-336-2730

West, Jack L., 1220 W. Fifth, P.O. Box 427, Arlington, OR 97812

Western Cutlery (See Camillus Cutlery Co.)

Western Design (See Alpha Gunsmith Division)

Western Gunstock Mfg. Co., 550 Valencia School Rd., Aptos, CA 95003/408-688-5884

Western Missouri Shooters Alliance, P.O. Box 11144, Kansas City, MO 64119/816-597-3950; FAX: 816-229-7350

Western Munitions (See North American Munitions)

Western Nevada West Coast Bullets, 2307 W. Washington St., Carson City, NV 89703/702-246-3941; FAX: 702-246-0836

Westley Richards Agency USA (U.S. importer for Westley Richards & Co.)

Westley Richards & Co., 40 Grange Rd., Birmingham, ENGLAND B29 6AR/010-214722953 (U.S. importer—Westley Richards Agency USA)

Westrom, John (See Precision Metal Finishing)

Westwind Rifles, Inc., David S. Sullivan, P.O. Box 261, 640 Briggs St., Erie, CO 80516/303-828-3823

Weyer International, 2740 Nebraska Ave., Toledo, OH 43607/419-534-2020; FAX: 419-534-2697

Whildin & Sons Ltd., E.H., RR2, Box 119, Tamaqua, PA 18252/717-668-6743; FAX: 717-668-6745

Whinnery, Walt (See Walt's Custom Leather)

Whiscombe (See U.S. importer—Pelaire Products)

White Flyer Targets, 124 River Road, Middlesex, NJ 08846/908-469-0100, 602-972-7528 (Export); FAX: 908-469-9692, 602-530-3360 (Export)

White Laboratory, Inc., H.P., 3114 Scarboro Rd., Street, MD 21154/410-838-6550; FAX: 410-838-2802

White Owl Enterprises, 2583 Flag Rd., Abilene, KS 67410/913-263-2613; FAX: 913-263-2613

White Pine Photographic Services, Hwy. 60, General Delivery, Wilno, Ontario K0J 2N0 CANADA/613-756-3452

White Rock Tool & Die, 6400 N. Brighton Ave., Kansas City, MO 64119/816-454-0478

White Muzzleloading Systems, 25 E. Hwy. 40, Suite 330-12, Roosevelt, UT 84066/801-722-5996; FAX: 801-722-5909

White Shooting Systems (See White Muzzleloading Systems)

Whitestone Lumber Corp., 148-02 14th Ave., Whitestone, NY 11357/718-746-4400; FAX: 718-767-1748

Whitetail Design & Engineering Ltd., 9421 E. Mannsiding Rd., Clare, MI 48617/517-386-3932

Wichita Arms, Inc., 923 E. Gilbert, P.O. Box 11371, Wichita, KS 67211/316-265-0661; FAX: 316-265-0760

Wick, David E., 1504 Michigan Ave., Columbus, IN 47201/812-376-6960

Widener's Reloading & Shooting Supply, Inc., P.O. Box 3009 CRS, Johnson City, TN 37602/615-282-6786; FAX: 615-282-6651
Wideview Scope Mount Corp., 13535 S. Hwy. 16, Rapid City, SD 57702/605-341-3220; FAX: 605-341-9142
Wiebe, Duane, 33604 Palm Dr., Burlington, WI 53105-9260
Wiest, M.C., 10737 Dutchtown Rd., Knoxville, TN 37932/423-966-4545
Wilcox All-Pro Tools & Supply, 4880 147th St., Montezuma, IA 50171/515-623-3138; FAX: 515-623-3104
Wild Bill's Originals, P.O. Box 13037, Burton, WA 98013/206-463-5738; FAX: 206-465-5925
Wild West Guns, 7521 Old Seward Hwy, Unit A, Anchorage, AK 99518/800-992-4570, 907-344-4500; FAX: 907-344-4005
Wilderness Sound Products Ltd., 4015 Main St. A, Springfield, OR 97478/503-741-0263, 800-437-0006; FAX: 503-741-7648
Wildey, Inc., P.O. Box 475, Brookfield, CT 06804/203-355-9000; FAX: 203-354-7759
Wildlife Research Center, Inc., 1050 McKinley St., Anoka, MN 55303/612-427-3350, 800-USE-LURE; FAX: 612-427-8354
Wilkinson Arms, 26884 Pearl Rd., Parma, ID 83660/208-722-6771; FAX: 208-722-5197
Will-Burt Co., 169 S. Main, Orrville, OH 44667
William's Gun Shop, Ben, 1151 S. Cedar Ridge, Duncanville, TX 75137/214-780-1807
Williams Bullet Co., J.R., 2008 Tucker Rd., Perry, GA 31069/912-987-0274
Williams Gun Sight Co., 7389 Lapeer Rd., Box 329, Davison, MI 48423/810-653-2131, 800-530-9028; FAX: 810-658-2140
Williams Mfg. of Oregon, 110 East B St., Drain, OR 97435/503-836-7461; FAX: 503-836-7245
Williams Shootin' Iron Service, The Lynx-Line, 8857 Bennett Hill Rd., Central Lake, MI 49622/616-544-6615
Williamson Precision Gunsmithing, 117 W. Pipeline, Hurst, TX 76053/817-285-0064; FAX: 817-280-0044
Willow Bend, P.O. Box 203, Chelmsford, MA 01824/508-256-8508; FAX: 508-256-8508
Willson Safety Prods. Div., P.O. Box 622, Reading, PA 19603-0622/610-376-6161; FAX: 610-371-7725
Wilson Arms Co., The, 63 Leetes Island Rd., Branford, CT 06405/203-488-7297; FAX: 203-488-0135
Wilson Case, Inc., P.O. Box 1106, Hastings, NE 68902-1106/800-322-5493; FAX: 402-463-5276
Wilson, Inc., L.E., Box 324, 404 Pioneer Ave., Cashmere, WA 98815/509-782-1328; FAX: 509-782-7200
Wilson's Gun Shop, Box 578, Rt. 3, Berryville, AR 72616/870-545-3618; FAX: 870-545-3310
Winchester (See U.S. Repeating Arms Co., Inc.)
Winchester Div., Olin Corp., 427 N. Shamrock, E. Alton, IL 62024/618-258-3566; FAX: 618-258-3599
Winchester Press (See New Win Publishing, Inc.)
Winchester Sutler, Inc., The, 270 Shadow Brook Lane, Winchester, VA 22603/540-888-3595; FAX: 540-888-4632
Windish, Jim, 2510 Dawn Dr., Alexandria, VA 22306/703-765-1994
Windjammer Tournament Wads, Inc., 750 W. Hampden Ave. Suite 170, Englewood, CO 80110/303-781-6329
Wingshooting Adventures, 0-1845 W. Leonard, Grand Rapids, MI 49544/616-677-1980; FAX: 616-677-1986
Winkle Bullets, R.R. 1 Box 316, Heyworth, IL 61745
Winter, Robert M., P.O. Box 484, 42975-287th St., Menno, SD 57045/605-387-5322
Wise Guns, Dale, 333 W. Olmos Dr., San Antonio, TX 78212/210-828-3388
Wiseman and Co., Bill, P.O. Box 3427, Bryan, TX 77805/409-690-3456; FAX: 409-690-0156
Wolf's Western Traders, 40 E. Works, No. 3F, Sheridan, WY 82801/307-674-5352
Wolfe Publishing Co., 6471 Airpark Dr., Prescott, AZ 86301/520-445-7810, 800-899-7810; FAX: 520-778-5124
W.C. Wolff Co., P.O. Box 458, Newtown Square, PA 19073/610-359-9600, 800-545-0077; FAX: 610-359-9496; WEB: www.gunsprings.com
Wolverine Footwear Group, 9341 Courtland Dr. NE, Rockford, MI 49351/616-866-5500; FAX: 616-866-5658
Wood, Frank (See Classic Guns, Inc.)
Wood, Mel, P.O. Box 1255, Sierra Vista, AZ 85636/602-455-5541
Woodleigh (See Huntington Die Specialties)
Woods Wise Products, P.O. Box 681552, 2200 Bowman Rd., Franklin, TN 37068/800-735-8182; FAX: 615-726-2637
Woodstream, P.O. Box 327, Lititz, PA 17543/717-626-2125; FAX: 717-626-1912
Woodworker's Supply, 1108 North Glenn Rd., Casper, WY 82601/307-237-5354

Woolrich Inc., Mill St., Woolrich, PA 17701/800-995-1299; FAX: 717-769-6234/6259
Working Guns, 250 NW Country Club Lane, Albany, OR 97321/541-928-4391
World of Targets (See Birchwood Casey)
World Class Airguns, 2736 Morningstar Dr., Indianapolis, IN 46229/317-897-5548
World Trek, Inc., 7170 Turkey Creek Rd., Pueblo, CO 81007-1046/719-546-2121; FAX: 719-543-6886
Worthy Products, Inc., RR 1, P.O. Box 213, Martville, NY 13111/315-324-5298
Wosenitz VHP, Inc., Box 741, Dania, FL 33004/305-923-3748; FAX: 305-925-2217
Wostenholm (See Ibberson [Sheffield] Ltd., George)
Wright's Hardwood Gunstock Blanks, 8540 SE Kane Rd., Gresham, OR 97080/503-666-1705
W. Square Enterprises (See Load From A Disk)
WTA Manufacturing, Bill Wood, P.O. Box 164, Kit Carson, CO 80825/800-700-3054, 719-962-3570
Wyant Bullets, Gen. Del., Swan Lake, MT 59911
Wyant's Outdoor Products, Inc., P.O. Box B, Broadway, VA 22815
Wyoming Bonded Bullets, Box 91, Sheridan, WY 82801/307-674-8091
Wyoming Custom Bullets, 1626 21st St., Cody, WY 82414
Wyoming Knife Corp., 101 Commerce Dr., Ft. Collins, CO 80524/303-224-3454

X, Y

X-Spand Target Systems, 26-10th St. SE, Medicine Hat, AB T1A 1P7 CANADA/ 403-526-7997; FAX: 403-528-2362
Yankee Gunsmith, 2901 Deer Flat Dr., Copperas Cove, TX 76522/817-547-8433
Yavapai College, 1100 E. Sheldon St., Prescott, AZ 86301/602-776-2359; FAX: 602-776-2193
Yavapai Firearms Academy Ltd., P.O. Box 27290, Prescott Valley, AZ 86312/520-772-8262
Yearout, Lewis E. (See Montana Outfitters)
Yee, Mike, 29927 56 Pl. S., Auburn, WA 98001/206-839-3991
Yellowstone Wilderness Supply, P.O. Box 129, W. Yellowstone, MT 59758/406-646-7613
Yesteryear Armory & Supply, P.O. Box 408, Carthage, TN 37030
York M-1 Conversions, 803 Mill Creek Run, Plantersville, TX 77363/800-527-2881, 713-477-8442
Young, Paul A., RR 1 Box 694, Blowing Rock, NC 28605-9746
Young Country Arms, P.O. Box 3615, Simi Valley, CA 93093
Yukon Arms Classic Ammunition, 1916 Brooks, P.O. Box 223, Missoula, MT 59801/406-543-9614

Z

Z's Metal Targets & Frames, P.O. Box 78, South Newbury, NH 03255/603-938-2826
Zabala Hermanos S.A., P.O. Box 97, Eibar, SPAIN 20600/43-768085, 43-768076; FAX: 34-43-768201 (U.S. importer—American Arms, Inc.)
Zander's Sporting Goods, 7525 Hwy 154 West, Baldwin, IL 62217-9706/800-851-4373 ext. 200; FAX: 618-785-2320
Zanoletti, Pietro, Via Monte Gugielpo, 4, I-25063 Gardone V.T., ITALY/ (U.S. importer—Mandall Shooting Supplies, Inc.)
Zanotti Armor, Inc., 123 W. Lone Tree Rd., Cedar Falls, IA 50613/319-232-9650
Z-Coat Industrial Coatings, Inc., 3375 U.S. Hwy. 98 S. No. A, Lakeland, FL 33803-8365/813-665-1734
ZDF Import Export Inc., 2975 South 300 West, Salt Lake City, UT 84115/801-485-1012; FAX: 801-484-4363
Zeeryp, Russ, 1601 Foard Dr., Lynn Ross Manor, Morristown, TN 37814/615-586-2357
Zeiss Optical, Carl, 1015 Commerce St., Petersburg, VA 23803/800-388-2984; FAX: 804-733-4024
Zero Ammunition Co., Inc., 1601 22nd St. SE, P.O. Box 1188, Cullman, AL 35056-1188/800-545-9376; FAX: 205-739-4683
Ziegel Engineering, 2108 Lomina Ave., Long Beach, CA 90815/562-596-9481; FAX: 562-598-4734; Email: ZIEGEL@aol.com
Zim's Inc., 4370 S. 3rd West, Salt Lake City, UT 84107/801-268-2505
Z-M Weapons, 203 South St., Bernardston, MA 01337
Zoli, Antonio, Via Zanardelli 39, Casier Postal 21, I-25063 Gardone V.T., ITALY
Zriny's Metal Targets (See Z's Metal Targets & Frames)
Zufall, Joseph F., P.O. Box 304, Golden, CO 80402-0304

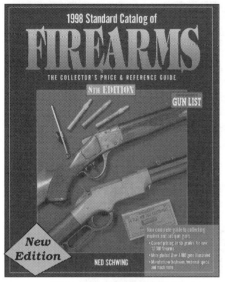

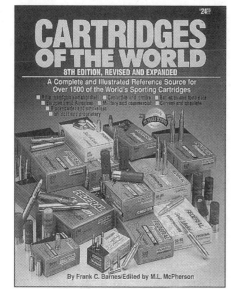

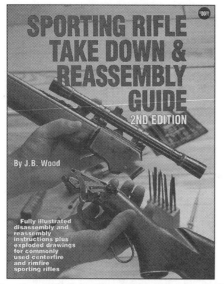
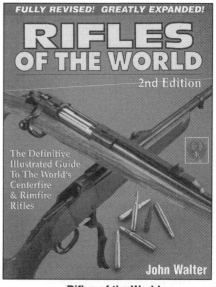